THE BLACK MIND
A History of African Literature

THE BLACK MIND
A History of
African Literature

O. R. DATHORNE

UNIVERSITY OF MINNESOTA PRESS, MINNEAPOLIS

Library of Congress Catalog Card Number: 74-76744

ISBN 0-8166-0719-2

*To my wife Hilde
and my children Shade Cecily
and Alexander Franz Keith.
And to Janheinz Jahn,
a true pioneer
in African literature.*

Preface

To understand ourselves, we ought to take a hard look at our place of origin—Africa. But the consequences of history have resulted in our displacement and the nature of this also becomes important if we are to see ourselves as we are. In *The Black Mind* I have focused on the oral and written literatures of Africa and the question throughout the book is—what do we say about ourselves? There are different answers and the artists at times admit to a confusion. But this is no handicap; in the search for legacy, in putting our minds together, in acquainting those who live near us with the nature of our heritage, there can be only one aim—trying to understand. I hope that *The Black Mind* is a beginning in this direction of understanding ourselves and helping others to understand us.

Acknowledgments

I am indebted to many people who helped me during the ten years it took me to research and write this book. I am particularly grateful to my students in Nigeria, Sierra Leone, Uganda as well as the United States.

Equally I must express gratitude to the Guyana government and the College of the Virgin Islands for their kind invitations to visit. Thanks are also due to the University of Wisconsin and The Ohio State University for small grants that aided me in compiling this work. In this connection I would like to thank the School of Humanities of The Ohio State University for personal encouragement as well as Jan Austin and Eleanor Sapp for being extremely patient with the typing.

For help with specific sections I wish to thank Rajak Solaja (Yoruba), Iya Abubukar (Hausa), B. Okonkwo (Ibo), Timothy Bazzarabusa (Runyoro/Rutooro and Luganda), Solomon Mutswairo (Shona and Ndebele), Veronica Matabese (Sotho, Xhosa, and Zulu), and others too numerous to mention who kindly helped with sections on Twi, Fanti, Ewe, Rwandan, Nyanja, Bemba, and Kamba.

For general help, I am grateful to Veronica Manokian and Edward Blyshen of the BBC and to Ulli Beier, Janheinz Jahn, and W. Feuser.

Contents

PART I TRADITION

Chapter 1

The Traditional Artist

The artist in traditional African society is a difficult figure to understand, for his function corresponds to nothing comparable in present-day western society. He is at once inheritor and donor of the literature, its custodian and its liberator. He is a spokesman for the society in which he lives, sharing its prejudices and directing its dislikes (in a limited form of satire) against what is discountenanced. He is not recognized as an individual, for he has no personal voice, but he is a highly respected member of the community. He can be a professional or an amateur, but this is not a qualitative judgment, since he has to be ingenious in expressing whatever he chooses to express.

Traditionally the artist was the link that bound art to the life of the people, or rather he was the continuous expression of a living art. As T. Adeoye Lambo once said:

[W]hile Western art has become largely just a by-product without immediate function in daily life, African tribal art is integrated into the community with specific functions. African traditional art was not, as is the art of more contemporary societies, a luxury or a pastime. It was the expression of a crude but intensely earnest religion and arose partly out of a social necessity to express and communicate through and partly out of a natural instinct for adornment.

The profound and intensely emotional links which exist between magic, religion, social organisation and creative motivity can be observed among a number of African peoples. The daily life of the tribal African shows the interaction of *mores,* economic demands and religious ceremonials with artistic expression.[1]

3

The significance of the priest and narrator cannot be overlooked; they participated in all aspects of group life and joined with their audience in all activities associated with existence.

Although the functional expressions of both the spoken and the sung or chanted art are occasioned by similar references—to the experiences of life—various forms of artistic expression did have their own specialized artists, from original composer on the one hand to what might be termed bard, rhapsodist, improviser, or reciter on the other. The extent to which the artist could "convert" his material depended on the nature of the material itself and the role that he was required to play. There is no doubt that among certain societies, memory was the artist's most important attribute; for instance, Deborah Lifchitz has commented that in Upper Volta and Chad "the people who recite the myths and the tales do not form a special class among the Dogon. Every man and above all every old man can tell a story. But there exists in the community a certain number of people whose memory, superior to that of the others, allows them to tell tales and myths better than anybody else. These men do not have a special position but they are given special respect and they are often asked to tell one tale or another." But no artistic display was simply a test of memory. Although the traditional artist obviously associated his work with a body of material, in many cases it was unformed and only partly helped him to create. Nketia makes this point when discussing the Akan dirge singers in Ghanaian society: "In dealing with the dirge, then, we are dealing in the main with traditional expression stored up in the minds of individuals and re-created by them in appropriate contexts, traditional expressions cast in forms which individuals learnt to handle because society expects them to use them in the situation of the funeral."[2] The fact that the oral tradition was a reservoir from which the artist drew meant that he was restricted; this was the formal limitation imposed on him.

The audience was also responsible to this unformed ideal of art that was present in everyone's memory. The artist did not so much perform for them as act as a mask for them, impersonating in turn each member of his audience. Alta Jablow describes the accomplished virtuosity of the narrator as follows: "In West Africa, as in other parts of the continent, story telling is an art form, as much theater as narrative. A good story teller knows how to spin a yarn to capture the interest and stimulate the participation of the audience. He is an accomplished mime as well, changing his voice, his posture and his mannerisms; acting out the parts, embellishing the fictional characters and situations. He shifts from role to role with fluidity and grace." The roles, ostensibly the characters

4

in the folktale, were transpositions of the personalities of the audience, changes that might well have been taking place under the catalytic effect of the narration. The link between audience and narrator was their direct involvement in, and their utter responsibility to, the absoluteness of this experience. H. L. M. Butcher comments that "the various actions described are imitated, and onomatopoeic sounds are freely used. Any misfortune to the characters of the story, particularly if caused by the 'villain,' draws forth roars of laughter, and any magical or mysterious happening elicits a chorus of grunts and exclamations of surprise."[3]

The artist in oral traditional literature came to mean everyone who participated in this creative ordering; the idea of alienation of the artist from his audience is therefore incongruous and irrelevant. In a "full" society no such cultural atomism is apparent; art like life is whole. Both artist and audience were interested not only in the transposition of the experience from the absolute to the representative, but also in the complete restructuring of that experience. The artist refashioned it topically, he recast it locally; in all cases it was dictated by social necessity, never by individual option. As W. E. Abraham remarked, "It was open to the raconteur to change the images handed down to him in a composition, and even surround salient details in his account with more local and topical allusions. A raconteur revealed his verbal virtuosity in the way in which he adorned the bare substance of his recitative. The account as presented and publicly received was therefore already affected by purely literary creativity, even if it was not an individual creation."[4] The alteration, then, was of enormous significance, for the image was resurveyed, the means of apprehension completely reorganized. The members of the audience were judges of this: even though they knew the ending, they could evaluate the literary process by which the conclusion emerged.

Because artists in traditional society inhabited this curious limbo between fleshlessness and corporality, they could not exist by name. Each one was the means by which the accrescent nature of the literature altered. Naturally there were individual composers of songs, as Hugh Tracey has noted, but because they were tribally contained, they were restricted by the sheer nature of their effort. The Senegalese *griots* are a case in point. "The *griots* formed a low caste—superior only to the liberated slaves and slaves—in traditional Wolof society, before the arrival of Islam. They are the minstrels of Senegal, and they were often attached to free-born families with the duty to sing their praises, genealogy and history. They were story-tellers, actors, acrobats and buffoons, privileged to mock and criticise their superiors." F. Brigaud notes that they were also musicians. But it is wrong to imply, as André Sauvaut does, that "all his [the *griot*'s] poor life passes in his song," for his song was not about himself but about the people to whom he was attached.[5] In a poem as if to his own family *griot,* Mbaye Dyob, Senghor writes:

Dyob! You cannot trace back your ancestry and bring order into black history, your forefathers are not sung by the voice of the *tama*

You have never killed a rabbit, who went to ground under the bombs of the great vultures

Dyob! you are not captain or airman or trooper, not even in the baggage train

But a second class private in the Fourth Regiment of the Senegal Rifles

Dyob! I will celebrate your white honour.[6]

It is this inarticulate historical role that the *griot* has played which makes him a passive actor and gives Senghor occasion for celebration.

The function of the *griots* therefore is to retell history. Again the same kinds of conditions apply: the audience, here the family, already knows what is going to be recounted. Thus, the *griot* is not the retainer of history, but its interpreter. A similar function is played by the Ruandan *aèdes* who sang the praises of their chiefs. Hampaté Ba is credited with having said that "every old man that dies is a library that burns down" and he was possibly thinking of the traditional methods of retention and bequeathal. The way experience, then, is stored in the memory of the tribe and the method by which it is manipulated in the creative process is through "form," which, according to K. R. Srinivasa Iyengar, "is not an extraneous something superimposed by the artist on matter. Form is really inherent in matter, and is but helped to fulfil itself by the artist."[7]

Obviously the extent to which the artist is able to alter the nature of this inheritance depends on the degree to which the *word itself* constitutes the experience. This is clearly the case with formulas relating regularized parts of narratives or songs, or with religious incantations and charms. The *babalawo* who recite the Ifa oracle of the Yoruba would at first sight seem to be an example of the type of traditional artist who must depend on the letter rather than on the idea. Beier writes that

the ritual poetry of Ifa is divided into 16 principal sections called *ODU*. Each of these is subdivided into sixteen further sections, and these are divided again: the total number of the poems is said to be 4696. The oracle priest or *babalawo* (that is the father of secrets), must know all the poems

6

by heart. In order to arrive at a particular poem that is relevant to the case of his client he goes through a set ritual with palm nuts. He has a carved wooden board covered with white flour, and sixteen nuts. He throws the nuts in the air with one hand and tries to catch as many as he can. If an even number remains in his hand he draws one line on to the board. If an uneven number remains he draws two lines. Repeating this two times he arrives at a sacred figure which is named after one of the *Odu*. The *babalawo* then recites the poem and interprets it to his client.[8]

But here as well the question of interpretation—of the idea—comes in, and it would seem that even in the memorizing of the *Odu* some measure of art is essential in the selectivity. E. Bolaji Idowu points out that "this is an intricate art which is painfully and laboriously learnt before it can be mastered to any appreciable degree. To master it completely is a counsel of perfection. One has to learn the two hundred and fifty-six *Odu* with the endless stories connected with them, the practical applications of the stories, and the pharmacopoeia which is part of the system, all by heart."[9] In addition to interpreting, the *babalawo* is allowed the power of invention. His own personal stories are incorporated into the *Odu* corpus, which accounts in part for the disparity between Beier's figure and Idowu's. Even here, where artistic expression is firmly yoked to ritual, the nature of the oral tradition is still one of accretion. So Wande Abimbola has collected an *Odu* which describes the good luck of a *babalawo* (who had himself followed the advice of other *babalawo*) who had journeyed to Benin at a time when the king died and when, according to custom, a great portion of the dead king's wealth had to be given to the fortunate newcomer. As the *babalawo* himself chants:

I arrive in good time
I travelled in good time
I am the only man who travels in time of fortune
When valuable objects of wealth are being deposited, I entered
    unannounced like the heir to wealth.
I am not the heir to wealth
I am only good at travelling in time of fortune.
These people divined for the fat stranger
Who would enter unannounced
On the day the property of the dead king of Benin was
    being shared.[10]

By now it should be evident that the traditional artist, though functioning in society and responsible to it, was never a mere instrument of society. Although an anonymous intermediary, he was expected to reorder the group experience, not merely because there was a "need to create an 'atmosphere,'" but because he was ultimately responsible to that absolute ideal of art present in the collective memory of the tribe. In this way he was no different from the craftsmen who seemingly functioned in a more utilitarian fashion. Ekwensi stressed the need to consider "our musicians and ballad singers, our dramatists and carvers"[11] as identical exponents of a common culture. Above everything else the versatility of the African artist demonstrates the plural role he played in a society relatively free from overfine distinctions.

Chapter 2

African Script

According to Gelb, a phonetic script evolves out of the need "to express words and sounds which could not be adequately indicated by pictures or combinations of pictures . . . Its principle consists in associating words which are difficult to express in writing with signs which resemble these words in sound and are easy to draw." Writing in Africa did not undergo this kind of process. Side by side with the "ancient" pictographs and the "prehistoric" rock engravings, forms of writing were properly developed. In addition to Swahili writing in the Arabic script, which has been going on for at least three hundred years, and Hausa writing, also in the Arabic script, which is about two and a half centuries old, there are several indigenous forms of writing. Among them are Vai, which was "discovered" in Liberia in 1849, and other scripts possibly allied to Vai—Mende syllabic writing in Sierra Leone, Basa writing in Liberia, Kapelle or Kpelle north of Basa, the Toma syllabary in Guinea and Liberia, and Gerse writing in Guinea.[1] There is also Bamum writing in Cameroon and at least two Nigerian scripts.

Köelle mentions that Lieutenant F. E. Forbes, the man who first directed the attention of the European world to Vai, was told that "four men had once brought this art from the interior of Africa." One does not know how much credence should be given to this, but certainly the influence and knowledge of Swahili writing must have spread. Stanley noted, in 1887, that many people in Uganda knew the Arabic script and that they wrote and sent messages to one another on thin slabs of cotton wool. It is possible, however, that these messages in the Arabic script had been penetrating into Africa for two centuries before Stanley made his observation. It is known that penetration caused specific scripts to be developed in Africa, and it is not unlikely that this contact could have stimulated the development of more indigenous scripts. For instance, the T'ifinagh script among the Tuareg was "not evolved in Africa but came from without, probably from the east or north-east, into the continent where it developed independently," yet it was not really "a literary script at all, but an alphabet of consonantal symbol used for inscribing monuments of stone." Palmer argues further that its origin was possibly Ethiopian or even, ultimately, Greek.[2] Because the Tuareg were a nomadic people, their alphabet was in fact not used for much else than inscriptions on rocks, weapons, musical instruments, and clothes. In this way they could have exported the idea of writing far beyond their own frontier.

Recently two scripts were invented in Somaliland; both are written from left to right but the older, invented about 1929 by Isman Yuusuf Kana, owed little to Arabic. The other, created in the 1930s by Sheikh 'Abdurahmaan Skeikh Nuur, was known to, and employed only by, a small number of people, mostly the Sheikh's associates.[3] But a consideration of Vai shows not only the indigenous growth and development of a script, but also that it enjoyed great currency at some time.

Vai

It was on January 18, 1849, that Lieutenant F. E. Forbes excitedly wrote to his commanding officer, "It has fallen to my lot to make a discovery of such importance to the civilisation of Africa, that I am anxious my own profession should bear the honour that it may deserve. The discovery consists of a written language of the Phonetic order." He was later to add in a lecture given to the Royal Geographical Society "that the characters [of the language] are not symbolical and, according to my teacher, it was invented ten or twenty years ago . . . by eight men." But it was Köelle, a German missionary stationed in Sierra Leone, who went more thoroughly into the matter. He spent five months in Liberia and recorded his conversation with the supposed inventor of the language—Doalu Bukele. Köelle says that Bukele died of sleeping sickness at forty, that he was assisted in his invention by five other people, and that he saw the possibilities of developing the language in a dream in which a white man explained to him the advantages of writing. Köelle added that the Vai wrote "with pens of reed"

10

and made their ink from a special type of leaf. The script, made up of 215 different syllables, was dependent on neither Arabic nor Latin and was written from left to right. Köelle also remarked that the script was "independent, original, syllabic and phonetic."[4] He pointed out that there were prototypal signs which originated in picture writing; for example, there were signs for "to die" and "to kill," which were illustrated by a withered tree and branches, and there were signs representing diacritical marks. For instance, the sign for "mother" was the familiar encircled dot, which Köelle felt depicted the child in the womb.

If only because Köelle noted that this "development" from pictographic to syllabic script occurred within such a short time, some doubt should be cast on Bukele's claim to having invented the script. During Köelle's several visits, one of his informants, tiring of the pertinacity of his white visitor, complained that "a black man is not able to sit down a whole day in one place and do nothing but book-palaver."[5] If this is any indication of the vigorous environment in which Bukele and his contemporaries lived, it would seem unlikely that they set about inventing the script after a dream. What seems far more feasible is that the writing itself developed from a previous semasiological system to a pictographic system and then (perhaps with some initiative from Bukele) into a syllabic system. What Momolu Massaquoi has said could be put even more strongly: "Great credit is ascribed to Duala Bukelle [sic] and his literary party; but even prior to his dream there were a few rude signs used by the Vais which did not express, but merely suggested ideas. These signs were in the form of hieroglyphics and Duala seems to have improved upon and utilised them thoroughly in his new compositions." It is improbable that within the period of a few years Bukele could have developed his "few rude signs" to such an extent that manuscripts were actually produced. Lieutenant Forbes showed Köelle such a manuscript, and Bukele showed him another describing the birth of his first son and the death of his father. Köelle also refers to one Kāri Bára Nkóre as the author of a manuscript. Norris, writing in 1849, added, "Within a few years of its first promulgation, we find it written and read by large numbers of all ages, in as great a proportion perhaps as readers and writers are found in most countries of Europe . . . Even now, in Bāndakoro the chief Vai town all the grown up people of the male sex are more or less able to read and write. And this, be it observed, was wholly uninfluenced by European teaching." Norris also mentioned that he possessed three manuscripts. One can readily conclude from this that the language had been written for many years, perhaps centuries, and that it developed from the kind of pictographic representations discussed above. As for Bukele's "dream," one can concur with H. H. Johnson that "Doalu Bokere's [sic] mind especially was so entirely wrapped up in his ardent desire to be able to read and write that it occupied his thoughts night and day, and this formed the natural basis of his curious dream, which seems to have been the reflex of his waking thoughts."[6]

The actual age of the writing is not subject to a great deal of dispute. Delafosse argues quite plausibly that the Vai used the script before the Islamic invasion; if not they would most certainly have adopted the Arabic script. He maintains that the probable date could be as early as the beginning of the sixteenth century, and there is some support for this. For although F. W. Migeood thinks the Vai settled in Liberia in 1700, there is evidence to support A. P. Kup's contention that there was a movement of the Vai from Sierra Leone after the defeat of the troops of the Songhai empire in 1590 by the Sultan of Morocco. It is not surprising, therefore, that P. E. Hair, analyzing an early seventeenth-century vocabulary of Vai, mentioned that "a vocabulary of Vai had been collected and printed two centuries earlier under another name." It is more than possible that these efforts by Europeans to reduce Vai to a written form might have stimulated indigenous interest in attempting the same. This was not, as Johnson has claimed, "clumsy adaptations of Roman letters or of conventional signs employed by Europeans," but rather, as Klingenheben has suggested, a development from the "ancient and imperfect mode of indicating conceptual contents by pictures into the phonetically perfect system of syllabic writing."[7] Vai was a developed form of writing which was widely used and which could express a literature.

Bamum

A form of writing known in Cameroon had its roots in Vai, but also showed signs of outside influence. Actually there were two types of writing, one used in the area of Bagam and the other, the more elaborate, near Bamum. The Bagam script, which is the written form of the Eyap language, has been summarily dismissed by L. W. G. Malcolm as "imitations or perversions of Roman capitals or else of the trade marks stencilled on the goods of European traders." But Bamum writing is given more respectability—it is said that it was invented by a Cameroonian chief, Njoya. During his father's reign, Hausa traders introduced Njoya to books in Arabic which interested him, and he decided to experiment with some form of writing. Dugast and Jeffreys note that when Njoya was thirty (in approximately 1895 or 1896), he produced his first alphabet, which was pictographic and had over 500 signs. He continued to improve this alphabet and by 1900 he had shortened it to 437 signs. His third attempt was partly syllabic and had 300 signs. He was encouraged in his efforts (to what extent is not known) by the Basel missionary Gohring and in 1910 he produced his sixth alphabet which was fully syllabic. He had by then reduced his signs to eighty and had added ten numerals; all resemblance to pictographic writing had completely disappeared. His final alphabet, his seventh, was phonetic. Dugast and Jeffreys give facsimiles of the various stages of the script and analyze the final alphabet.[8]

Another version of this story relates that Njoya, when he became chief, called a number of warriors together as a result of a dream. He gave one the task of inventing a sign for every monosyllable in the language and a series of signs for polysyllables. He then selected some of these signs, bought slates from the missionaries, gave them out to his subjects, and started to instruct them. It is said that he wrote letters to his pupils, kept his accounts, and recorded important events. Dugast and Jeffreys state that several of these manuscripts survive—one on the history and customs of the Bamum, another on religion, a third on medicine, and a fourth in the form of a map of the country. Whatever may be the truth concerning Njoya's actual contribution, it seems apparent that he merely improved on a well-known form of writing which had been extant for a long time. Gelb adds that the syllabary now consists of seventy signs which are "showing certain tendencies towards alphabetization."[9] Bamum, like Vai, seems to have been indigenous and to have been developed to a certain extent by the ingeniousness of an individual.

Nsibidi

In Nigeria there are a number of scripts worthy of attention, but it is not known how correct it would be to regard them, with the exception of the most important, as "indigenous." One such exception is Nsibidi, a form of writing perfected by the Ekpe Secret Society and probably dating from the seventeenth century, which is used in the Calabar area of eastern Nigeria. The extent to which several other such scripts might have survived in Africa can only be guessed at; for instance, quite by chance at a court trial in 1931 the fact emerged that there was a developed form of writing in another part of eastern Nigeria. This script had thirty-two symbols. When it was first used, people wrote on sand, leaves, and trees; only after the coming of the missionaries did they write on paper. Similarly there exists a booklet which has an alphabet of thirty-two large and small letters.[10] Although this script was used for the commandments of the church, Roman letters were employed for the rest of the book, which contained extracts from Genesis and Exodus.

The signs making up the Nsibidi script are fairly conventional, consisting mainly of bent or straight lines in a number of combinations. Originally these were cut or painted on slit palm leaf stalks. J. K. McGregor has indicated that this writing was used to record such events as court cases: "I have in my possession a copy of the record of a court case from a town on the Enion Creek taken down in it, and every detail, except the evidence, is most graphically described—the parties in the case, the witnesses, the dilemma of the chief who tried it, his sending out messengers to call other chiefs to help him, the finding of the court and the joy of the successful litigants and of their friends are all told by the use of a few strokes." From the Nsibidi "sketch" McGregor carefully works out the precise details of meaning. But he seems to be emphasizing that Nsibidi could only be communicated in a spasmodic kind of way—in parts rather than as a whole. Elphinstone Daryell, however, argues that "many of the signs reproduced are connected with one another and form short stories."[11] He gives several examples of how this is done and one folktale in particular is worthy of mention—the story of the miracle child, born from his mother's knee, who is disowned by his father. In this version the child kills his father with a spear and disappears up a long rope into the sky. This is all skillfully narrated by the clever assembling of four geometrically patterned symbols, each one representing a section of the story.

By now it should be apparent that it is quite wrong to say that writing, or for that matter a written literature, did not exist in Africa. As has been shown, writing existed—writing that was not unrelated to literature and that was pictographic. Side by side with this existed highly developed forms of writing which were in some cases applied to literature. What has been considered here, however, is by no means exhaustive; it is merely a pointer to possibilities, for so much is still so little known in Africa. But it has been shown that prehistoric representations, pictographs, and developed alphabets existed alongside one another, and are an indication of the imaginative ability of the African to rise above the temporal imposition of the word. His art is a unity of time.

Chapter 3

Spoken Art

The study of oral literature is the consideration of folklore or "the traditional beliefs, legends, and customs, current among the common people." In the European context the problem is complicated: "It is a moot question whether traditional tales should be considered folklore. In practice it is extremely difficult to separate oral from written traditions."[1] As has been shown, although there was a written tradition in Africa, it was not always applied to literature. Therefore at this moment in African history it is not too difficult to make the distinction between oral and written literature, since the oral is still being passed down from one generation to another. But if it is to be preserved, it has to be collected and written down; and if it is collected and written down, the spontaneity of the oral flavor is once and forever lost. No longer will one be able to claim that each oral performance is unique, for literary artists might themselves come to depend on the written text.

In a study of various forms of the folktale Stith Thompson said of the *Märchen* that it was "a tale of some length evolving a succession of motifs or episodes. It moves in an unreal world without locality or definite characters and is filled with the marvellous. In the never-never land humble heroes kill adversaries, succeed to kingdoms, and marry princesses." Since the world of the African tale is essentially a real one, concerned with down-to-earth issues, it is probably true to say that there are no real *Märchen* in the African tradition. But certainly there is myth, that is, "all tales having to do with an imaginary world existing

15

before the present order was created," and legend, or "unauthenticated narrative, folk-embroidered from historical material, sometimes popularly deemed historical." It is in myths that the repetitive formulas occur, but it must not be felt that they have any greater claim on our attention because of this. If there is little of the fantastic in African folktales, and consequently little of the true *Märchen*, then those tales that are found should be classified as belonging to the "novella" where "action occurs in a real world with definite time and place and though marvels do appear, they are such as apparently call for the hearer's belief in a way that the *Märchen* does not."[2]

What one does find a great deal of are "hero tales," which recount the adventures of a single person as he attempts to overcome various tasks and quests, etiological tales, which attempt to explain natural phenomena, and fables, which are animal stories with a moral purpose. People have tended to imagine that African oral literature is simply made up of fables because Black folklore has been widely disseminated throughout Africa, North and South America, and the West Indies, and "the attitudes of the masters towards song and dances and folktale varied throughout the New World from hostility and suspicion through indifference to actual encouragement. Such a trivial matter as the extent to which recreational forms tended to interfere with the master's personal convenience was important; such irrelevant features as the amount of noise made in dancing or while singing tended to influence white attitudes. The quiet with which tales are told, plus their appeal to the whites as stories for children, made the retention of this element of African culture as ubiquitous as it is in the New World." Consequently the view popularly held was that children's stories were in fact all that existed in African folklore literature. Frobenius's attempts to "popularize" his discoveries of African oral literature were partly an effort to redress the balance. ". . . I regretted that I alone could only enjoy the treasures of this beautiful art and that later on I should bury them from the world in the archives of scholarship."[3] Frobenius's work is above all an attempt to show the deeper significance of African oral literature and, in particular, the spoken art.

Any literary study such as this calls for a complete reorientation of thought. One must be wary of conclusions like that of the Chadwicks: "The memorisation of exact verbal tradition is seldom widespread or long-lived, and though the composition of extempore poetry is very general, the quality is not such as demands great artistic powers from the reciter or composer." As will be shown later, this is quite untrue. Equally untrue is the assertion that the tales are about animals, since

16

the animals usually represent human beings and the tales concern the intermingling of animal, tree, and object—the harnessing of the animate to the inanimate. Some would deny that there is true myth in African oral art, yet there are various types of myths present. Not least among them is the etiological kind, in which God lives in the world before he creates it, and the cosmogonic, which describe the origin of man. Folk literature no longer should be considered as something tangential to social anthropology, but as the imaginative expression of a culture. Malinowski may be right in the assertion that folktales are concerned not with fault, ritual, or human destiny but with the everyday considerations of human conduct; nevertheless our concern would still be with the literary significance of that human intercourse. For there is no doubt that there is always a social reference, as Nketia rightly agrees: "Oral literature has tended to give prominence to persons, inter-personal relationships and attitudes and values derived from our conception of the universe. We do not spend time on the daffodils or the nightingale or on reflections on abstract beauty, the night sky and so on as things in themselves, but only in relation to social experience." What Nketia means is that the literature is extremely earthbound and is linked to social functions. He does not deny the aesthetic element, without which there can be no appraisal, or the blend of thought and vision, without which there can be no discovery. As Bernard Dadié, the Ivory Coast novelist, once said: "To little children the tale is merely a fantastic story; to women spinning cotton or persons who husk maize or decorticate groundnuts, it is a pleasant pastime; but to the old people, the thinkers and the sages, sensitive to subtleties and differences, it is nothing less than a revelation."[4]

Any literary assessment of the tale must take into consideration all its aspects—the ways in which it expresses fantasy, aestheticism, and thought.

Myth: Men as Gods

Myths are essentially a poetic interpretation of the world, and in the world of African mythology men, gods, and animals intermingle. If anyone is to be singled out as hero it must be the chameleon who is the messenger from God to man. In several creation myths his role is a minor one, but in many of the African creation myths he does play a very important part. For example, in the Nigerian Ibo version of the creation, an egg is cast into the water and is then hatched by an eagle sent by Chi. In this way the water becomes covered and the chameleon is dispatched to see if the land is firm. According to Amadou Hampaté Ba, the role of the chameleon in a Mande creation myth from Mali is more directly concerned with *human* creation. After Massa Dambali had gone through the whole process of creating, he

descended by the heavenly bridge, the Rainbow. He came to plant in the midst of the islet a miraculous tree. He called it "Bolanza."

This tree is not like all those which will be created afterwards. In fact the rains which revive other plants dry up the leaves of the Bolanza, and the great heats which dry up other vegetable growths revive the Bolanza.

Bolanza grew. It thrust four branches towards the sun. It became loaded with golden yellow flowers.

Nonsi, the chameleon, stole the secret of colours from the Rainbow. He coloured the four branches of Bolanza; the Eastern one yellow, the Northern one white, the Western one red and finally the Southern one black.

Thus a dualism was established between North and South, East and West.[5]

It is from this tree that human beings were created, and, incidentally, discord.

Often the conflict that occasionally takes place in myths is between the chameleon and some other form of life. In other cases, as in the Nigerian Bini creation myth, the chameleon's task is fulfilled at the very end of creation when he performs the last labor to establish the world. In this myth, the male god Osanobuwa and the female god Ede-Day give birth to a palm tree, at the base of which is some earth, to sky, and then to a number of other children. On the advice of a bird, the youngest child takes a shell containing some dry earth, a hen, and a chameleon with him in a canoe; as they travel along, the child opens the shell and land appears. The hen scatters the earth and the chameleon goes out to ensure that the earth is firm.

Hans Abrahanson has shown that the most common African myth about death is centered on the message that failed. Stories about this message are similarly developed and usually include three stages. First God sends a reptile to man to promise him immortality; then another intercepts the message (in some cases God sends two conflicting messages); and finally the wrong message is delivered and man becomes subject to the laws of mortality. Baumann has demonstrated in a carefully prepared table that in 80 percent of the stories the chameleon is the original bearer of the message of immortality. Indeed, according to Stayt, among the Venda there are two chameleons—one bearing the message of mortality, the other carrying the news about immortality.[6] In African mythology, therefore, the chameleon plays its sacred roles

18

as an arbitrator in the creation of life and as a grim messenger in the fortuitous occurrence of death.

African creation myths often deny man the status of first created beings. Among the Yao of Tanzania, God exists with animals on the earth before man is created, and the chameleon catches man in its first trap. Frobenius gives two examples of how the tortoise was superior to man; among the Nupe the tortoise is created before man, and among the Yoruba it exploits women's love for dance and lures them into the men's village, thus bringing about sexual intercourse.[7]

Although man is not necessarily the first created form of life, he still stands very solidly at the core of most myths. Baumann writes that "at the centre of African myths stands a creative principle which in most cases is identified with the Highgod and the first man created, formed and called forth by this creative force. The greatest part of African mythology deals with the way this man came into the world, the way he lived and what he experienced. They make the myths of the origin of Heaven and Earth, the stars and the supernatural beings, which on other continents make up a large share of the cosmogony, almost appear insignificant." As has been shown, the view of man often is not particularly flattering, but he does play an important role in the cosmic drama. Among the Nyoro the first human couple sent down from heaven have tails and they give birth to the chameleon and the moon;[8] the fact that they are thought of as having given birth to the chameleon endows them with a symbolic grandeur. In the Bini creation myth, Igan and Obura appear from nowhere and become man and wife; among the Ibos the first human being, Odede, gives birth to the gods of farming and hunting, the goddesses of the sea, and the god of idols. Humans are therefore assigned a role of gigantic importance; not only are they ultimately responsible for the gods, but they also bring about life itself.

What is even more significant is that the gods (like the animals in the tales) are frequently humanized or, rather more than that, they are not thought of as being any different from human beings. Even the sun once lived on earth, according to a "Bushman" myth, but the Great Mother instructed her children to lift it up into the sky to give light to the "Bushmen." Bleek and Lloyd have retained something of the original nature of this drama:

The children were those who approached gently to lift up the Sunarmpit, while the Sunarmpit lay sleeping.

The children felt that their mother was the one who spoke; therefore the children went to the Sun; while the Sun shone, at the place where the Sun lay, sleeping lay.

Another old woman was the one who talked to the other about it; therefore the other one spoke to the other one's children. The other old woman said to the other that, the other one's children should approach gently to lift up the Sunarmpit, that they should throw up the Sunarmpit, that the Bushman rice might become dry for them, that the Sun might make bright the whole place.[9]

In an Efik-Ibibio myth the sun is forced into the sky because of a hasty invitation it extends to the water to pay a visit.

When the water arrived, he called out to the sun and asked him whether it would be safe for him to enter, and the sun answered, "Yes, come in, my friends."

The water then began to flow in, accompanied by the fish and all the water animals.

Very soon the water was knee-deep, so he asked the sun if it was still safe, and the sun again said, "yes" so more water came in.

When the water was level with the top of a man's head, the water said to the sun, "Do you want more of my people to come?"

The sun and the moon both answered, "Yes," not knowing any better, so the water flowed in, until the sun and moon had to perch themselves on the top of the roof.

Again the water addressed the sun, but, receiving the same answer, and more of his people rushing in, the water soon overflowed the top of the roof, and the sun and moon were forced up into the sky, where they have remained ever since.[10]

The water's politeness and the grim obstinacy of the sun are apparent here, as is the myth's general meaning that the truest and fullest life is closely bound to the earth; it is folly that forced the sun into the sky.

One literary theme which achieves and reestablishes the earth-sky connection concerns the spider weaving his web. The Mbundu of Angola relate a story of a man who aspires to the daughter of the Sun and the Moon. He wants someone to take a message to the sky, and at last the frog manages to ascend by hiding himself in a water vessel. He does all the wooing for the man and at last brings him his intended wife by getting the spider to weave a large web on which she climbs down.[11]

Although the spider web might suggest only a tenuous relationship between sky and earth, nothing could be further from the truth and indeed in some myths it is a chain that is used to establish the link. So Oduduwa, among the Yoruba, descends to earth on a chain, and among the Ndorobo God himself climbs down to earth on a rope with the first men.[12]

20

The divine role of human beings is emphasized repeatedly in African myths; humans are even considered responsible for the origin of natural phenomena. Among the Baganda, "most of the rivers were thought to have originated from a human being. Thus for example the river May-anja was said to have taken its rise from the spot where a princess gave birth to a child, and to have been caused by the birth-flood." Two other myths depict man as the originator of rivers. In a Poto myth from the Congo, Libanza fights with his brother and when his brother dies all the warriors weep, and in a Sotho myth Hare pricks the belly of a woman who has swallowed water.[13] Human beings are also responsible for the making of mountains.

Frobenius wrote of the role of human beings in myths and said that they lived at a time far back in the past when "they themselves took part in cosmic events." In addition, the myths that describe the early life of the first ancestors vividly portray the bizarre quality of the African imagination. In Dahomey eyeless creatures rolled on the ground, and the Kirri-Dakka tell the story of how some small people with large scrotums left marks whenever they sat on rocks.[14]

In African prehistorical times there is no hint of sin or of displeasing the gods; indeed the gods themselves were often anything but virtuous. There is no weight of guilt or any later divine forgiveness. In fact one wonders whether the myths concerning the great flood, the caving in of the firmament, and the big fire may have been influenced by Islam and Christianity. The flood occurs for no important reason; among the Gogo, it was simply because they never had any rain and the frogs started croaking.[15] In an Ekoi (Nigeria and the Cameroon) myth, it is the human element which again explains the flood. This time sky and earth allow their offspring to marry each other, but Obassi Nsi mistreats the sky maiden Ara, and she climbs up a rope to return to her father, Obassi Osaw. In revenge Osaw dispatches his son-in-law back to earth, after cutting off his ears:

Osaw took the ears and made a great juju, and by reason of this a strong wind arose and drove the boy earthward. On its wings it bore all the sufferings of Ara and the tears which she had shed through the cruelty of Obassi Nsi. The boy stumbled along, half blinded by the rain, and as he went he thought, "Obassi Osaw may do to me what he chooses. He has never done any unkind thing before. It is only in return for my father's cruelty that I must suffer all this."

So his tears mixed with those of Ara and fell earthward as rain.

Until that time there had been no rain on the earth. It fell for the first time when Obassi Osaw made the great wind and drove forth the son of this enemy.[16]

The flood caused by the tears brings about the final separation between men and God.

It is to be noted that the discovery of sexual intercourse is not associated with sin in African mythology. Most myths describe the time when the sexes lived separately; the women have to be lured away. A Nupe myth depicts how the women were lured by honey and sugarcane to the village of the men and how they learned about sex. Among the Shambala in East Africa the ancestors of the ruling house visit the land of the women and by the aid of a gift of honey enlighten the queen and the women about sex. Often sex is associated with pain; among the Saramo a man with an ax climbs a tree to fetch honey. The ax drops and wounds the man between his legs. The Kulwe in Rhodesia tell the story of how a woman thought her vulva was a wound and asked a man to wash it, and among the Loango a man tries to sew up the wound with his penis after God had failed to do so.[17] The view of sex arises from an uncomplicated oneness with the world, a world that man dominates in every possible way.

African myth compensates to some extent for oral literature's general lack of concern with description. For example, some of the richest poetry is found in African myths describing the moon and stars. Among the Isubu in Cameroon, it is said that the moon "comes at night like a sheep on earth and eats around the huts the banana skins which have been thrown aside." A Kikuyu myth tells of how the sun and moon were always fighting and how the sun bit off a piece of the moon, reducing it to nothing. In order to grow again the moon has to hide, whereupon a battle between the two ensues.[18] A Sandaw myth similarly expresses faith in the presence of the dead moon:

An old man saw a dead body lying in the moonlight. He called a number of animals together and said to them: "Which of you, my friends, will undertake to carry the dead man or the moon across to the other side of the river?"

Two tortoises came forward: the first, which had long paws, took the moon and arrived with her safe and sound on the opposite shore. The other, who had small paws, took away the dead man, and was drowned.

That is why the dead moon reappears always, but the dead man never comes back.[19]

Myths, however, also operate on a more personal level. Laurens van der Post maintains that "the myth is the tremendous activity that goes on in humanity all the time, without which society has no hope or direction, and no personal life has meaning." In attempting to explain race, myths deal with the African's deepest conflicts and arise from "the way in which he quickly responds to a new experience, and weaves a tale to explain it." The African's "new experience" often involved his contact with the white man and in Angola racial difference is thus explained as follows: "The first men who dwelt in the middle of the Earth were black. From there they went out to discover the world. All started at the same time, but some fell behind and when they arrived at a river where they were to take baths to cleanse themselves, they found that the water was low. Their companions had travelled far ahead; they had bathed when the sacred river had been high, and they had emerged white from its waters."[20] The West African version relates that the man who came late delayed on the way because he ate and had a bath and the man who arrived first was selfish and only left enough water for the second to scoop up in his hands and wet his soles—thereby explaining why the palms and soles of Africans are not black.

As was mentioned before, there is a Mali myth that describes the origin of the various races in terms of a dualism present from the very beginning of time. Indeed many African myths are solely concerned with expressing this principle of the innate contradictions in life—whether they be between mortality and immortality, man and animal, man and woman, or destruction and life. If a myth is, in Robert Graves's term, a "verbal iconograph" by which abstracts are more easily apprehended, then it is also the imaginative link between apparent contraries. In the world of African myths, nothing is assumed; neither death nor evil is seen as just one thing or the other. The Basumbwa in East Africa have a story in which Death appears to a man and shows him two sides—an ugly and a beautiful,[21] and the Yoruba tell the tale of Eshu and his hat with three colors which set three farmers arguing. These myths express the existence of the contradictions and the dissimilar views of the same life.

Although myths are considered here under the heading of "the spoken art," their appeal bypasses the logic of everyday prose. New collectors have managed to capture the austere, precise, dedicated language of the myth, and perhaps the truest myths are not those which are painstakingly written down, but those which are re-creations. Examples of such re-creations are the "myths" of Laduma Madela, a Zulu born about 1906, who "incorporates traditional stories, adds entirely new features, and combines all into a magnificent whole." His descrip-

23

tion of the creation is as vivid and powerful as any traditional myth. The Creator is "one who created everything except the world which created him," the Creator's wife is said to have merged with him "in the manner of mushrooms," and the story of the creation reaches a high point when Madela exclaims, "At the Ocean's brink the Creator struck the surface of the water with his *kirrie*; the water receded and was gathered up to form the headring of the world." He has managed to retain the essential quality of the myth—its song and its drama. The same can be said of the telling of a certain Mwetsi myth: "From the way the priest recited it, it could easily be realised that it was originally a legend sung melodramatically and secondly that it was accompanied by action. Also it was a ritual song." Robert Graves found similar characteristics in Greek myths and noted that they were "the reduction to shorthand of ritual mime performed on public festivals."[22] It is the myth's song and drama that one might miss in the printed texts, but myths nevertheless remain as eloquent survivals from the childhood of the human race.

Legend: Men as Heroes

Maria Leach has said that "when the hero is man rather than a god, myth becomes legend,"[23] but as has been seen, in African mythology God *is* man. What happens in African legend is that man aspires to be God and succeeds. However, because legends are local, they do not have the wide associations that myths have. In some cases their artistic scope is limited simply to explaining certain geographical features and to describing the heroes of the race and the reasons for popular prejudices.

For instance the Ijaw's dislike of eating snails is explained in the story of the man who wrongly kills his wife when he thinks she is hissing at him like a snail during a quarrel. A story from northern Ghana similarly illustrates how Kambongona, escaping from Arab slave dealers, gets a swollen leg and cannot proceed. A squirrel helps to heal his wound and since then his descendants do not eat squirrel meat.[24]

Often the dislike might be simple prejudice against "strangers"; for example, in southern Iboland the Ngwa explain their separation from the Ohuhu in the following way. The two groups were once seeking out their present abode and when they stopped to eat, the Ngwa cooked and ate their yams faster than did the Ohuhu who insisted on roasting theirs. As a result the Ngwa (the fast ones) were able to cross a certain river and so became separated from the Ohuhu (the roasters). This legend might well refer to the Imo River which separates the Ngwa from the Mbaise.

Because the function of legend is often so blatantly etiological in its most restrictive sense, it is only in the legends of hunters, warriors, and the relatives of gods that the hero comes into his own. The legends of hunters and warriors do not simply illustrate how mortals perform marvels; they also depict how mortals overcome their limitations. Heroes perform impossible and often unrewarding tasks; a tale from Togoland tells how Kwaku searches for the tale of the Queen of the Elephants to fulfill a promise to his dead mother. Always the legends portray the triumph of the human spirit, and although there are many legends which, unlike the myth and the *Märchen*, describe contests with the animal world, there are others too in which the heroes succeed because they are closely linked with the animals. A Bini hero, Eneka, after defeating Igbadaken in a wrestling match, is condemned to death but his animal friends tell him of herbs that enable him to save the life of the princess as well as his own.[25]

Often the tasks imposed seem to ridicule human values. In a Meru story from Kenya the warrior Kamankura wishes to marry a beautiful girl, Ciari; he returns from a hunting expedition to find that his cattle have been stolen. Kamankura wants to discover which ones were stolen, but Ciari refuses to cooperate because she had been prevented from pummeling a dog. Then follows a succession of conditions which all have to be fulfilled; the dog will agree to be pummeled only if it can have an afterbirth, the cow will provide an afterbirth only if it can have pasture, the hawk will help "out the sky so that rain may fall" only if it can have a baby rat, the baby rat wants millet, the harvester refuses to supply millet unless he gets a little knife, and finally the smith agrees to supply the knife if he can have charcoal. The smith is given his charcoal and each one in turn is then satisfied. Finally Kamankura goes after the cattle and returns and marries Ciari.[26]

Despite the absurdity of the various tasks, this legend is no different from, say, that of Kintu, who has to undergo all sorts of tasks demanded by the King of Heaven in order to win Nambi. The winning of the woman is merely the completion of an achievement, and the adventure illustrates that "the standard path of the mythological adventure of the hero is the magnification of the formula represented in the role of passage; separation—initiation—return; which might be named the nuclear unit of the monomyth."[27]

A typical hero-quest legend is the history of Magoda, an orphan who sets out from his village with an ox. On the way his ox fights a bull

25

and wins. During their ride, the ox produces food out of its right horn whenever Magoda is hungry; when Magoda is full, the food goes into the ox's left horn. Although later the ox dies in a fight, the horns are still useful and with them Magoda is able to feed a hungry village. Finally the horns are stolen but are recovered and then Magoda buys new clothes and wins a beautiful wife.[28] The story is divided into carefully defined sections which center on the three categories of separation, initiation, and return. First, the departure from his village places on Magoda a double burden to succeed, for he is both an alien and an orphan. His ox is his link with the natural world and with the gods; its defeat of the bull is the first task that *he* successfully overcomes. During the journey, the hero is usually given various forms of supernatural aid; in this case it is the horns, which later become the boon that Magoda is able to retain because he has been triumphant.

The story of Magoda is but one example of the many legends which employed the quest as a motif and followed the familiar pattern of separation, initiation, and return—all of which proves that legends are in fact a studied art. As is typical in African oral literature, the tasks depicted in legends can be slight, almost ludicrous; for instance in a Mende legend two strangers are welcomed into a village on condition that they do not snore.[29] This admixture of the startlingly droll and the arrestingly profound make for a healthy profanity.

Frequently the task not only is impossible, but also presupposes a certain amount of irrationality on the part of the main participators. In the Nyanja legend, for instance, a hunter in the bush kills five deer. A lion confronts the hunter and demands that he feed the deer to some dogs and then eat the dogs himself; finally the lion would devour him. A way out of this impasse is found when a rabbit comes along and tricks the lion.[30]

The triumphs at the end of some legends are not always obvious; in a story from the Bosso-Sorokoi people in Niger, a sorceress named Pa-sini-Jobu resurrects a ram and then fights three water spirits to help her friend Queen Namanj. But she is defeated in the end, ironically by the slave of the water spirits.[31] In the tale the sorceress is depicted as strong, defiant, and proud. Her greatest attribute is her ability to accept gracefully her defeat. She too has performed her task and fulfilled her role, changing from a minor spectator to a major participator in the pattern of events. Her part in the story expresses this; at first dominant and forceful, she is ultimately a mere silent witness to her own defeat.

One important event in the hero monomyth is the symbolic initiation. Joseph Campbell associates this with the theme of separation, but

26

it seems far more relevant if it is regarded as part of the initiation process. There are many instances of symbolic initiation in legends; perhaps the most classical is found in the Zulu story of the mother and two children who are swallowed by an elephant in whose insides are "large forests and great rivers, and many high lands; on one side there were many rocks; and there were many people who had built their village there; and many dogs and many cattle . . . ." In another version the woman is swallowed with her cookingpot and knife and in the elephant's stomach she feeds her children and others. When the elephant dies, she hacks her way out and frees the others.[32]

In these tales the elephant is rightly regarded as a monster because he is guilty of locking off the life-flow. The hero achieves stature because he releases it, and existence is thus no longer thwarted. By entering the womb, the hero goes through a process of initiation as does the hero who is caught in a bag. Often the point is made that as a result of the experience the novice has matured into an initiate. For instance there is the Fingo and Pongo legend of a little girl who is caught and kept in a bag by a *zimu* (spirit); when she is released, she is an adult. This theme is even clearer in the Duala version that describes how a father finds his missing daughter who has been taken away in a bag by a man when she is bathing by the river. When the father and his companions meet the man, "they bound the man who had stolen the girl, and took the child from the bag. Then they killed the man. But when they took the girl out, they were astonished at her appearance; because when the girl was stolen she had no breasts yet; she was still a child. But when her father took her out of the bag, the breasts were developed. The child had become a woman."[33]

At the end of such accounts the boon might well be a material gift; more often than not it is an egg. In these legends the heroes of African folk-imagination express their fullest significance. They are of course culture heroes, but they are not bound in by the culture. From them emanate the prototypal characteristics of all humans, qualities which enable them to surmount obstacles and to emerge victorious at the end. This is their strongest claim to our attention.

Tales: Animals as Humans and Gods

The study of African myth, legend, and tale must take into account hieratic, parochial, and demotic differences. Any such consideration inverts the landmarks of normally recognized values—in myths there is no clear demarcation between men and gods, in legends men assume the proportion of gods, and in tales animals are men and gods, and only seldom animals. This inverted view of the world is quite intentional, for through it every anonymous folk-artist perceives a new conviction—the superimposition of an absolute reality.

Jack Berry has differentiated between "serious explanatory and moralising tales, humorous trickster tales, and tales developed wholly or essentially in human society." Many of these tales involve animals and the importance of the animals is usually established quite early in them. The Nigerian critic Adeboye Babalola has written, "It is a small minority of [Yoruba] folk-tales that concern human beings only. The great majority of the tales feature human beings, animals behaving like human beings and often also superhuman beings; demons, ogres, deities."[34]

This is true of folktales throughout Africa. In West Africa the Ashanti say that the spider tales once belonged to someone else: "Kwaku Ananse, the Spider, once went to Nyankonpon, the Sky-god, in order to buy the Sky-god's stories. The Sky-god said, 'Will you be able to buy them?' The Spider said, 'Rather I shall be able.'" After a trial the Spider gets the stories, and the Sky-god says, "No more we shall call them the stories of the Sky-god, but we shall call them Spider-stories." Not only does this establish a right to the stories sanctioned by divinity, but it also sets up Ananse as a hero; other such heroes are Tortoise and Hare. There is no overlapping of heroes and, with few exceptions, there never is more than one hero in the same story. With reference to the tales in Sierra Leone it has been noted that "certain definite qualities and characteristics are ascribed to particular animals, and to these they hold consistently through all the stories. The Deer is always stupid and helpless; the Elephant enormously strong but lacking in mental acuteness; the Cunning Rabbit intelligent and lovable; and the Spider shrewd, designing, selfish and sometimes vindictive and cruel."[35]

This consistency of characterization enables the audience to know at the beginning of the tale what the character intends for them at the end. This is not as inhibiting as it seems, since inventiveness does figure into the telling, and in any case the tales do not really describe animals at all but personify certain qualities, attitudes, and ideas. Indeed it has been asserted by Rattray that "the names of the animals, and even that of the Skygod himself, were substituted for the names of real individuals, whom it would have been very impolitic to mention." This is clearly exemplified not only in what they do and say, but also in how closely they resemble ordinary people. For in traditional life there was no such thing as the rounded self-contained individual. Cardinall has suggested that Ananse was probably a name of convenience given to typify an average man.[36]

Ananse's actions are sometimes representative of what man dares—how he aspires to dominate the minds of others, to master life. A Ga story describes how Ananse wanted to monopolize all thoughts. He puts them in a bottle and decides to throw it away. As he journeys he comes to a tree trunk in the middle of the road and is uncertain what to do. His son says to him, "O father you are too stupid! Could you not put down the bottle of thoughts that you might cross the tree and then take it up again?" And Ananse replies, "O my child, I meant to bring away all the thoughts; it seems I have left some behind." The rebuke from son to *father* is far more pointed than any other could have been. But more often than not Ananse succeeds and proves man's ability to survive. In a Krachi (Ghana) story, he helps to establish the separation of God from man and to satisfy Wulbari's (God's) wish for something, he fetches the sun and the moon.[37] In another encounter with Wulbari, Ananse outsmarts him; in Togoland a tale relates how Ananse leaves the sky with a corncob and promises to bring back a hundred slaves. By a ruse, he exchanges the corncob for a basket of corn, this in turn for a fowl, then a sheep, a corpse, and finally the corpse for a hundred men. Ananse symbolizes man's ability to surmount physical obstacles and to defy even destiny itself; he represents the triumph of the human will.

Frequently the Ananse tales are told in the form of task and reward. For instance the Sierra Leonean Krio version describes how Ananse manages to win the daughter of a reluctant mother after satisfying her many demands. The tale, appropriately told in semi-Krio, begins: "One woman get girl pickin. Dis girl done do fo' married, but no man de wey able fo' married um, because de mammy no' gree. Well, Spider come, he say go married de girl." The mother then sets the various tasks which, as the entire audience knows, Ananse will accomplish. It should be noted that in Sierra Leone Ananse was a "returned" hero—he had emigrated to the New World and then had come back. What survived of him in Sierra Leone is what remained of him from the West Indies and America. No longer is he the hero of a quest-story or a companion to God, but only a clever trickster, speaking "in a new language, shaped to his own needs."[38]

The Ananse tales that survive in the New World are those which could amuse. A typical story of this nature describes how Ananse goes to steal and is trapped by becoming stuck to a rubberman. This, however, is more the exception than the general pattern of Ananse's adventures. In one story he is the typical hero of legend; his son, Kweku Tsin, in a time of famine enters a hole in the ground and reaches a town of absolute silence. He performs various tasks and is given a magic drum. Ananse then decides to try his luck but disobeys the instructions of an old woman who had helped his son. He returns with a drum which, when beaten, inflicts punishment on him.[39] The story's setting is the familiar one of famine, and the parallel action of son and father is another device frequently employed—a certain deed is rewarded with fortunate results, while another brings about suffering. Often no moral judgment is made; the consequences are only the result of the nature of circumstances. The audience knows the pattern and the trend that the tale will take.

Tales about Ananse sometimes grow into myth; his encounters with gods and the ways in which he becomes the reason for natural phenomena have a mythical flavor. In one such tale, Ananse changes into the moon, his son becomes the sun, and their companions stars.[40] The cycle of Ananse's adventures illustrates that he is at once half-god and half-clown.

Tortoise, on the other hand, does not rise above the level of being a mere trickster. The story about how Ananse collects the wisdom of the world is also told about Tortoise. But Tortoise's disillusionment is not tragic like Ananse's. Tortoise boasts to Calabash, "I have collected all the wisdom of this world and have it right inside me. I can race even faster than a deer. Let's see if you can beat that." Here there is no attempt to give the story depth or to lend some dignity to Tortoise. It is just funny. A further indication of Tortoise's role is that he is frequently used as a mere device in etiological tales. A well-known tale simply illustrates how the tortoise got a cracked shell. The Yoruba say that at a time of famine Tortoise met Cock pounding yam, and wanting to discover where he got the yam, Tortoise hides in Cock's bag. When they arrive at the farm, Tortoise disregards Cock's advice and is beaten, thus getting his shell smashed. Another Yoruba version tells how Tortoise, in a time of drought, helps other animals to find water, but as they go to the place, they do not notice Tortoise. They walk over him, crack his shell, and leave their footprints on his back. In a Calabar tale, Tortoise commits a dreadful crime and at his own request is left in a tree without food and water until he drops to the ground and smashes his shell to pieces. In yet another account Tortoise fights with Dog, gets his shell broken, and has it fixed by a passing traveler. In all these stories Tortoise does not demonstrate through action his known attributes, but instead is merely used as a foil for the action. During the course of action, his ability to outwit, his selfishness, and his ingratitude might emerge, but they are only incidental to the process of explaining.[41]

Although Tortoise's character is fixed, this need not inhibit either the tale or the teller. Certainly it has not prevented the adaptation of Tortoise, and indeed among modern folktales "are those tales in which Tortoise attends adult literary classes and aspires to becoming a clerk in the civil service or in a commercial house."[42] Yet even these modern tales are traditional, for they describe a time that may not be the present but is nevertheless curiously relevant and contemporary. It is the presentation of Tortoise's psychology which gives the tales this particular attribute.

The actions of Tortoise demonstrate certain aspects of the tale. For instance, his ability to outwit illustrates an important device—the manner in which impossible demands are met by attaching equally impossible conditions to them. In an Ibo tale Tortoise is asked by the King of Animals to build a very tall house in one day. He agrees to do this on condition that the king climb a kite-string to inspect the house. Another Ibo tale describes how Tortoise, when requested to weave a mat from a grain of rice, asks his father-in-law for a pattern. Frequently, however, Tortoise is outwitted; a cat with a stronger juju outsmarts him in a wrestling match in a Yoruba tale, and in another Yoruba tale he roasts his friend Pig, but is outsmarted by Dog who gets the meat from Tortoise's wife. But he can outwit even the gods and he does this to the Yoruba God of Thunder (Shango) and Iron (Ogun). In a Dahomeyan tale he is the diviner and links the earth to Mawu (God).[43]

Tortoise features in another kind of tale in which cumulative incidents add up to a significant whole. In a Calabar tale he borrows money from the worm, cock, wildcat, leopard, and hunter. When they come to collect, he sets cock on worm, wildcat on cock, leopard on wildcat, and hunter on leopard; in the last encounter both are killed. The end of the tale demonstrates his cruelty—all he does is laugh. In a "Bushman" tale the humor is even more grim; Tortoise gets foolish people, including the "Bushman" hero, the Mantis, to rub his head. Then he pulls it in, holding on to his helper's hands until they decay.[44]

In other tales, Tortoise challenges the heroes of East and southern Africa—Hare and Mantis. The Matebele tell a tale in which Tortoise beats Hare in a race. In a Swahili tale from Zanzibar, Tortoise and Hare are caught stealing honey in a tree by a lion. In the subsequent battle of wits, both escape—Hare tells the lion to get hold of his tail and wheel him around, and Tortoise tells the lion to rub him in the mud until his shell comes off. In a Sierra Leonean story Hare discovers a way of getting food by taking blows from a tree. Ananse or Spider cannot endure as well and it is only Hare who gets the food. But generally in these encounters where two heroes meet, it is understood that neither will win.[45]

Hare is the protagonist in various types of tales. In a particular Yao story incidents again combine into a meaningful whole. In exchange for a stick for weaving, Hare gives wild fruit to a man who is eating earth. The stick he exchanges for hoes, then for arrows, poultry-feed, and red ocher, which he finally gives to some frogs. But unlike the pattern of the tales examined before, this last action does not lead him back to his first, and the tale concludes, "The hare just went away. He said, 'The frogs have gone into the water.' "[46] Perhaps something is missing here or perhaps this is an example of how the teller can surprise his listeners. Instead of triumph, there is bathos.

Hare has been described as "Senegal's counterpart to the Spider in the legends of Ghana and the Ivory Coast." Indeed Hare, since he is known in West, East, Central, and southern Africa, is a far more continental hero than either Ananse or Tortoise. Unlike Tortoise, he not only exhibits his cleverness, but at times makes serious moral decisions. In a well-known plot Hare induces Hyena and Ostrich to tie up their mothers and beat them. If the mothers do not succeed in breaking the ropes, they have to be sold into slavery. Hyena and Ostrich sell their mothers, while Hare only pretends to observe the agreement regarding his own mother. At the end of the story Hare manages to cheat them both of their ill-gotten wealth and escapes free. In another version of the tale Hare kills Tortoise because Tortoise told Lion of Hare's hidden mother. In still another, Hare hides his own mother while the leopard, rat, and wildcat drown their mothers as a joke. Later Hare gets the leopard to eat the rat and the wildcat, and then he kills the leopard. In all these tales Hare comes out firmly on the side of order and respect for the group ethic.[47]

In most of the Hare tales that tell about the threat to kill his mother, famine is the setting and the reason for the action. This helps to emphasize Hare's moral values and to strip the tale of everything but his moral actions. Indeed in many of the tales the animal heroes are concerned with overcoming the impositions of their environment and the extent to which they fail or succeed determines their stature. The importance of famine and of the quest for sustenance reduces necessity to its barest minimum, and the symbol of all need. Just as human beings are dissected and their psychological attributes isolated in the characters of

Ananse, Tortoise, and Hare, in the same way background is reduced to its barest minimum. It is through this process of atomization that the folk-artist works, and it is against this bare outline of character and setting that plot develops.

The concern of the tales is therefore not character (which is fixed), or setting (which is either bush or famine), or even incident (which is after all a result of character operating through setting), but the philosophical analysis of conduct. Usually there is no moral problem of choice and the dilemma involves no more than, as in a Bakongo (Congo) tale, the trivial fact that Frog's two wives have both made his favorite dish of *ndibs* pudding and he is in a quandary over which one he should visit. Sometimes the dilemma does not seem like one at all; a Mbaka (Angola) story relates how two hunters quarrel over an elephant—one has stalked and shot it, the other has followed the first hunter. The solution betrays an indifferent attitude toward right and wrong, but one closest to the logic of the heart—the first hunter is given the meat since he stayed up all night crying for the elephant. Some dilemma tales, however, do pose intellectual problems, as for example the tale of the three men each of whom has some magic property which is instrumental in bringing a dead girl back to life.[48] The problem is—to whom does she owe her life and whom should she marry?

Since no clear distinctions exist one way or another, the tales should be considered amoral. Even those which frequently make a "moral" point do so for reasons that are not properly the issue of morality. For instance, a Lamba tale relates how Kawunda is expelled from the sky and slays his stepfather, Chipimpi. At the end of the story he dies a natural death and is not punished in any way. In a Venda tale about the tree and the forbidden fruit, the people eat the fruit in spite of the chief's warning. Although they die, the chief returns and brings them back to life.[49]

As has been shown, in the world of the tale man is at peace with animal. Nevertheless, something of the nature of a dilemma is present in the tales that describe the conflict between man and monster. A Yoruba tale, for example, tells the story of a head that acquires the properties of a man and proposes to a squeamish woman. In another Yoruba version of the same tale, the man is a spirit "who had only a head. All the other parts of the body were borrowed from some other different spirits." The Fanti version turns the man into a snake and has a hunter rescue the woman, and in the Duala tale a whale wants to marry the woman. A Ngoni (Malawi) version relates that "a person (a girl) refused (all) men; there came a baboon; he took off the skin from his body and was turned into a man. The Angoni woman marries the baboon, and he hoed the crops and his companions came from the Bush and ate the crops of his mother-in-law's garden, and (so) he went (with them) into the Bush."[50] These tales all clearly make the point that the head, spirit, snake, whale, and baboon are the same. Man is not at ease in this environment, but he is not defeated and often seeks a compromise with the monster.

The wonder-child, half-man, half-monster, is such a compromise attempting to wreak an illogical vengeance of its own making. More often than not he kills his father. This Yoruba version of the story illustrates his unnatural origins, his precociousness, and his macabre actions:

> Once a childless woman went to the Deity to beg a child of him. He said that he had none left, for they had all gone on errands, except one who would be wiser than any father, and who was very disobedient. The woman said she would have him, and the Deity told her to go home. On the way she stumbled and her big toe became swollen, and when she entered the house, again she stumbled, and out of the swelling of her toe came a tiny child. He walked and talked almost as soon as he was born, and the next morning told his father that he wanted to go to the farm and work with him.
>
> He soon came up to his father at the farm, who was surprised to see his little son. The child told him he had found the way through his wisdom, and then he told his father that they must play a game. His father was at the top of a palm tree cutting a bunch of ripe palm nuts, and he wanted to know what the game was. Child-Wiser-Than-His-Father then covered himself with a basket and stood at the foot of the palm and asked his father to throw down one bunch on him and see what would happen. His father, thinking this a rather dangerous game, did not want to do it at first, but Mogbonjuba persuaded him, and he threw down a heavy bunch on to the basket. But while he was preparing to throw it, Mogbonjuba had slipped out of the basket, so that when the bunch came down and crushed the basket, he was not under it; but then, rolling the bunch aside, he pretended that he had been, and told his father that he was unhurt. He then said it was his father's turn to stay under the basket, and when he had climbed the palm tree, he threw down a big bunch on the basket, and the poor father was crushed to death . . .[51]

The wonder-child is representative of absolute freedom and this accounts for the manner of his birth. Among the Zulu, Uthlakanyana speaks in the womb, cuts his own umbilical cord, and eats as soon as he is born. In a Lamba tale a woman gives birth to a blue snake and out of it comes a child who speaks immediately.[52] These children are a link between human and monster; their actions are intentionally "irresponsible," for they symbolize the tensions in all life, the tension between impetuosity and rationality.

A similar motif depicting the link between man and monster is found in the tales that describe transformation, usually from thing or animal to human, and then reversion to the original state. This type of tale does not assume that there is any connection between the human and the nonhuman world, as so many other tales do. Rather, by emphasizing the apparent link and then the final unavoidable separation, these tales seem to be striving to break down this relationship. A Hausa tale describes how a man married an antelope woman who, when her husband reveals her secret, returns to the forest with her children. In a Venda tale the blue monkeys come to claim their kin who was changed into a beautiful wife for the chief at a time of famine. Always the reversion takes place, usually because the secret of transformation has been revealed. In most tales the initial transformation seems to augur well, as in this Venda tale about a man who wanted a wife: "Since his loneliness was great, one day he carved a veranda-pole, (and) made it like a beautiful girl, even put on it a beautiful top patch of hair, (and) stood it up at the doorway of that house of his . . . One day when he had gone out to the cattle, that veranda-pole was left behind (and) fell, changed (and) became a beautiful girl."[53] Here again the pattern of the story is known—man and object cannot live together—and the listeners wait to hear the process of the disillusionment. But the theme of separation is the exception rather than the rule and, as has been shown, the world of the folktale is one in which the animate and the inanimate blend into, and partake of, the living.

There is no difference between animal and man and, thus by inference, between animal and gods. The people and the animals of the tales have similar adventures which by way of summary may be classified into three types. First there are those tales which establish a model and then abandon it. In these stories a certain fortunate pattern of events follows a certain action, and later another person fails to carry out the precise instructions, suffering as a result. The second type of tale establishes a link in a particular order and then inverts that order; this inversion usually depends on the satisfaction of certain conditions which reintroduce the order. The third type attaches impossible conditions to impossible requests; the denouement occurs when the impossibility of the conditions is recognized by the person who imposed the requests. Most tales describe a challenge—for example, a contest between two animals trying to outsmart one another or an attempt to overcome the environment—but always the challenge is met by the intellect. What René Basset has called "the triumph of cunning over brutal force"[54] insists that the mind is dominant; nevertheless it is severely anchored to earth. Certainly there is fantasy, but it is always expressed in terms of a familiar existence. The purpose of the tales is to deepen the awareness of this existence.

Proverbs as Equation

Although proverbs and riddles are frequently categorized together, it is wrong to do this, for they are vastly different not only in form and purpose, but in the different attitudes of mind they express. For whereas the world view of proverbs is a rational one in which events are fitted into their proper place, riddles express irrationality and doubt. "The riddle presents a mental problem. The proverb is a criticism of life. Both are products of the popular mind and therefore both reflect prevalent attitudes. But while the riddle is hardly more than a form of entertainment, the proverb is more serious and has a didactic intent. Hence riddling is associated mainly with the younger people, while the propounding and expounding of proverbs is associated with the older people, especially the men."[55] They therefore provide useful counterparts to each other—the riddle questioning, the proverb answering. This gives them an invaluable place in any study of oral literature.

In tracing the source of proverbs, C. L. S. Nyembezi surmised that some originated from myths and tales, but he wondered whether the proverb was responsible for the tale or vice versa. He also added that some proverbs referred to history but that the bulk "are the result of the observations of the people, of human behaviour, of animal behaviour, and the observations of things in general in their environment." It is this observation that will be emphasized. For although proverbs (like all other forms of oral literature) have their didactic function, which is to help people to "cope with a situation as it arises by regarding it in the light of something that has occurred before,"[56] what must be stressed here is that the proverb is in fact literature.

Indeed it was seen in just this context by traditional society. The Yorubas say that "a proverb is the horse of words; if a word is lost we search for it with proverbs," and the Ibos describe it as "the palm-oil with which words are eaten." In fact this is so throughout Africa, and O. F. Raum's remarks that "we have four big possessions: land, cattle, water and proverbs"[57] is true of the entire continent.

Fortunately a great deal of the worth of proverbs comes over in translation. Naturally there are difficulties with social or historical allusions, but many proverbs describe universal situations, and what the Ashanti say is very true, "When a fool is told a proverb, the meaning of it has to be explained to him." In this way proverbs differ from tongue twisters which, because of their essential appeal in the primary language, must remain closed to us in an investigation of this nature. In the main, then, concern here will be with "the 'metaphorical proverb,' which because of the metaphorical use of simple event or statement has wide applicability."[58]

Proverbs that have the most significant meanings are those which express universal human fears. A note of pathos is struck in the Baganda one which affirms that "death is like a wild animal," as well as in the Ga proverb that states cryptically "the dry leaf falls and the green leaf falls."[59] The form of these two should be noted. Both express a certain kind of uncertainty about life but the first does it through simile by means of apt comparison, and the second through statement which intimates a conclusion. Both operate through the medium of imagery.

Frequently the device is to make use of some reference to nature, to generalize on the basis of that reference but again to omit the conclusion. So for instance the Taveta (Kenya) declare that "if one bird ceases singing the dawn will not stop."[60] Here also the proverb works through a familiar image and withholds a conclusion. Some African proverbs, in other words, express the first part of a syllogistic argument.

This form is to a large extent apparent in translated proverbs, although at times their poetic quality is lost. About Gweabo (Liberia) proverbs Edward Sapir felt that "the form . . . is fixed. Many of them have a poetic structure, and not a few of them use words of constructions that are not found in ordinary prose." These in the main are archaic words and illustrate another function of the proverb—the preservation of the language. Nketia goes a little further and claims that "the use of proverbs is not confined to the poem; they are quoted in many situations—in the home, at work, at the court. They are considered a mark of eloquence and wit, and anyone who is able to quote or to use proverbs habitually may be regarded as a poet of a sort."[61] Indeed the poetic appeal is not only in the language but in the vigor with which the images are worked.

A Kanuri proverb has something of this tough underlayer of imagery in it—"at the bottom of patience there is heaven." A new note has been introduced this time—an obvious didactic appeal. Some make the point even more obviously; a Kikuyu proverb warns that "one's body is not a banana leaf which should be rent." Here the appeal is still

37

through image but there is no withholding device: the statement is severely and openly corrective. Proverbs do not always advise in this solemn manner, however, and humor is sometimes employed to instruct—"if your neighbour's beard catches fire quench it for him," or "God is sharp surpassing a razor," or even more explosive, "arguing stopped the chicken's teeth from growing."[62]

Often the note is ironical as if the proverb's reflective nature might best be voiced in this way. A Rimi (Tanzania) proverb states, "O Dry Season, give me a garden, the rainy season will reveal those who went to work." This erupts into cynicism, especially about human relationships. A Nyika (Uganda) proverb suggests that "a stranger is like rain, he strikes you as he passes by," a message which is described in a more straightforward manner (which helps emphasize the despair) in the Ibo proverb "If someone I know wrongs me, I don't know him any more." Often this view of the world can be quite bitter, and is in sharp contrast with the views expressed in other forms of oral literature. Spiritual disillusionment also is depicted; for example, an Ibo proverb declares that "the crying of the world does not reach the spirits," and a Lamba proverb laments with no embellishment that "the righteous also dies."[63]

Proverbs that owe their origin to myth, legend, and tale cannot be explained without reference to them. Moreover, it has been said about Gweabo proverbs that "some of them refer by implication to a myth or tale which is current, and the applicability of the proverb to ordinary life can sometimes be appreciated only if the legendary background is clear to the hearer." An example of such a proverb is the Lango "Gladness killed Atile." This makes little sense to someone outside the culture unless he knows that Atile was the first person to discover how to make beer. The chief drank too much and died, and his followers, suspecting Atile of poisoning their chief, killed him. A similar example is the Kikuyu proverb "I gave you the beauty of the guinea fowl and you gave me the beauty of a francolin," which Barra explains as follows: "The proverb originates in the following fable. Once upon a time the guinea fowl wanting to go to dance, called upon the francolin to have its feathers dressed. The francolin, hoping to have the same favour returned by the guinea fowl, assented. But the latter taking as an excuse of its laziness that the dance was about to begin, left the other bird in the lurch. This is why the guinea fowl has now got much finer plumage than the francolin."[64]

Often the proverb is a summary of the tale, as can be seen in the Ibo proverb "The rat which goes hunting in the rain with the lizard must know that his skin will get wet." But the link between the proverb and the tale is not simply a way of emphasizing the "moral" point; it is often a direct reference to the psychological fiber of the culture. It is only by this process that the Kanuri proverb "I arose early but the dawning day overtook me on the way" could mean "I married a wife in early youth but had no children by her," or that the Kikuyu proverb "The wind is most violent in the trees" could mean "The price is raised for those who can pay."[65]

Little can be said about the rhythmical structure of proverbs in the original because not enough work has been done on this. Nyembezi, however, noted "definite metrical forms" in Zulu proverbs and suggested that there were twenty-one types in various combinations. Obviously since proverbs are basically a form of the spoken art, they rely heavily on a rhythmical appeal and on the devices of parallelism and elision. In the original language, part of the effect of proverbs results from their being couched in archaic terms, but what survives in translation and what is noticeable on the whole continent is the rich imagery on which most depend. This helps to transform what Robert Marett has called the "peculiar wit and wisdom"[66] of a tribe into the intricate poetic statement of a continent.

Riddles as Inversion

If proverbs can be said to affirm the order of the world, then riddles deny that such an order exists. This function is inherent in their form, for whereas proverbs juxtapose similar images, riddles emphasize their point by placing unlike images side by side. As Jack Berry has said, "The enigma is developed generally, though not universally, through the opposition of two apparently inconsistent declarative sentences." The riddle may consist of a question to which a short answer is required or a statement where certain allusions have to be identified.[67] There can be no dispute over the answer, since riddles depend solely on a logic of their own, and from this viewpoint, at least, they offer the traditional artist practically no opportunity to alter his material. By their very nature they are a form of social satire, which, as will be seen later, is also true of allusions in praise songs and in masquerade verse, but which is generally absent in African oral literature.

The Herskovitses point out that in Dahomey riddles there was "reference to the grotesque, the seemingly incongruous and the forbidden," and their style was either in couplet form or in the language of everyday speech. Arnott, writing about Fulani riddles, mentions that "the 'question' consists of a brief description of some phenomenon and its

39

situation, character and behaviour, and the 'answer' is another common object resembling the first, the resemblance being hinted at in the description given." Bascom, in an excellent analysis of the Yoruba riddle, adds that it is "an enigma presented by two statements which appear to be mutually contradictory, incongruous or impossible." Berry notes that a fairly widespread device is to give a proper name to what is being guessed at; that "acoustic" riddles exist which depend on sound rather than on the eye for effect. He also identifies not only a type in which numerous questions are asked and answers are given in the order of the questions, but the "erotic tone" riddles in which "the listener attempts to provide an answer which has one-to-one correspondence tonally with the question posed." In all cases riddles are asked during the evenings and are a pastime of children, and obviously they require "some form of dialogue."[68]

All over the continent there are riddling contests that have formalized beginnings and in some cases endings. The Venda (South Africa) precede each riddle by the word *Thai*, which means riddle, and oppose two teams rather than two individuals. Before each riddle the Kaniramba (South Africa) make the propounder say "Lalilali" to which the response is "Lali." Among the Ronga (South Africa), "*teka, teka, teka* [is uttered] at the beginning of the game of riddle-asking. It may be omitted however, even before the first riddle is asked. This formula is usually used between riddles, when the person who is questioning is temporarily stuck and wants to gain time." Most of these words merely mean "riddle," have no meaning, or are thought to have no meaning because they are obsolete. Among the Giryana, "before propounding a riddle one says, 'Chondoni!' and the challenge is answered with 'Dekeha!' (both obsolete words). Then comes the riddle . . . If the one challenged 'gives it up', he is told 'P'a mudsi—give me a town!'— and then has to name some place, as, 'Haya enda Kisiwani! Go to Mombasa!' He is then told the answer. The riddle is usually in an obsolete dialect."[69]

Riddles, therefore, both in their formalized introductions and in the manner in which they are asked, are like proverbs and assist in the preservation of language.

There are certain types of riddles that are worth further explanation. One of these is the "bird riddle," which is found in southern Africa. According to A. C. Jordan, "The essence of the bird riddle is to display one's knowledge of the ways and habits and/or colour markings of birds." An example, given by Jordan, describes the white-necked raven as a missionary "because he wears a white collar and a black cassock and is always looking for bodies to bury." Another type of riddle is fairly uninhibited and makes references to parts of the body, natural functions, sex, and so on; examples are the Venda riddle which describes excrement as "I went with it but left it there behind me" and two Tlokwa (South Africa) riddles which describe fire as "my grand-father's testicles which cannot be touched by a fly" or "my grand-mother's excrements on which no fly can sit." Then there are problem riddles, such as the Ila (Lamba) riddle in which a leopard, a rat, a goat, and a basket of corn have to be ferried one at a time across a river. If the leopard is taken the rat will eat the corn, if the rat is taken the leopard will eat the goat, and so on. The Ila solution is that nobody should be ferried. In Ghana the characters are a peasant, a fox, a hen, and a basket of corn. The solution is different: "The peasant first takes the hen across leaving the fox and the corn together. He then returns alone and ferries across the corn, leaving the fox on the other side of the river. But as he cannot leave the corn with the hen he returns with the hen and, leaving it on the side of the river from which they started, he ferries the fox across. Finally leaving the fox with the corn he collects the hen." Ingenious though this answer appears to be, it is not expected to be thought out—it is learned. And it must be assumed that there is a "right" answer in Zambia and another in Ghana. But indeed all riddles are "problems"; in the example just given the problem is intellectual rather than purely visual. Beidelmann asserts that some riddles teach no moral lesson and are intended "solely to amuse,"[70] but it seems of little use to place these in a special category, since to some extent the function of all riddles is to amuse.

Many riddles refer to religion and to Christianity; for example, an Efik (Nigeria) riddle asks, "What is it that God our Father made but which we cannot sit on?" The answer is "a palm fruit with thorns." If one is to judge from some of the Efik riddles collected by Donald Simmons, it would seem that it is almost in the nature of a stylistic device to allude to "our father God." This is very much like the references to "my grandmother" and "my grandfather" which have been observed. The intention is the same—the flippant reference shocks the listener into a new awareness. Part of this shock is sometimes caused simply by the way the world is turned upside down; a Yoruba riddle states that "two brothers slept in the same bed. Before daybreak they had both eaten each other." The answer, which is two logs in the fire burning up one another, scarcely matters; the shock is already elicited by the perverted view of human relationships. Among the Kamba the leaves of the *taro* palm are said to do "a dance which has no conductor." Others

41

show an acute poetic observation of the world, like the Nyanja riddle which alludes to rain as "the animal which dies in the dry season and whose scent is smelt here" and the Kxatla (Bechuanaland) riddle in which the sun is "the bull in the east which gives birth to calves and eats them." In some the poetic view is grim, as can be seen in the Lamba one which describes a grave as "the house in which one does not turn round."[71] But more often than not they are purely descriptive and pregnant with the most enormous nuances—for the Yoruba, the tongue is "a lonely god in the midst of an ocean" and rain is "the thin reed that reaches from the earth to heavens."

In riddles, as in other forms of oral literature, the African accommodates himself to new experiences, and his traditional literature illustrates the manner of this alteration. A match among the Lamba becomes "a little thing that swallows its mother,"[72] and among the Yoruba, something of the joy of unsophisticated discovery is expressed in "he talks, he sings, he laughs but never waits for an answer," which is the enigmatic reference to a radio.

By way of conclusion, it should be emphasized that riddles constitute an important element in the oral literature. Bascom estimated that there were as many as twenty-nine formulas in the fifty-five riddles he examined, varying from the simplest "Who is X that a" (Who is it that drinks maize beer with the king? The fly.) to the more complex Ya, X; YaX, Xb; Zax, Xb. ("Ancient well of my father, ancient well of my father; if a child gets into it, it reaches his neck; if an elder gets into it, it reaches his neck. A shirt.") In addition, riddles also conform to rigid rhythmical devices. Endelmann has found that among the Sotho "the person who asks the riddles puts his question in a rhythm whose strong tones are expressed in a strophe, and the person who replies answers in a strophe whose rhythm corresponds to the question." One must be a little suspicious of such a statement, if only because of the convenience of its classical terminology, but it would nevertheless seem to indicate an attempt at a certain rhythmical control. Therefore both in their buildup of sense patterns and in their sound riddles have a definite structure, which suggests that even though they might be regarded as a trivial pastime, they nevertheless constitute an important art form. It has been noted elsewhere that some Venda riddles are used for special ritual purposes,[73] and certainly all riddles seem to demonstrate the flexibility of language, for expressing both the trivial and the profound.

Chapter 4

Sung or Chanted Art

A consideration of African oral poetry or the sung or chanted art must take into account all nonspoken forms, including at the one end songs and at the other end everything which is declaimed. Perhaps the Chadwicks put it best when they defined oral poetry as "speech which is sung." Frobenius has added that "with people who work everything into experience there can be no exuberance in story-telling, for life itself is poetry, poetry of the highest degree, but non-communicable poetry. Life itself is the poetry of these people." On the other hand, the Chadwicks felt that "the memorisation of exact verbal tradition is seldom widespread or long-lived, and though the composition of extempore poetry is very general, the quality is not such as demands great artistic powers." The Chadwicks' assertion arose out of ignorance, for not only was there a large body of verse which was recited, but it also was of a high quality. As A. C. Jordan claimed about Zulu oral verse, "In the indigenous language of Southern Africa, including Zulu, there is a wealth of traditional poetry covering, in its subject matter, the whole range of human experience and emotion . . . These emotional experiences are expressed communally in song, speech and action."[1]

African oral poetry, however, is not used merely as a vehicle of emotion, for often a more complicated and significant meaning has to be expressed. The poetry therefore is used for working out ideas, which explains "why song has so prominent a place in primitive life. While it makes sense of daily pursuits and relaxation and enhances interest in

43

them, it is even more useful in dealing with problems which trouble man and call for a solution acceptable to his ways of thought."[2]

Only by realizing that the sung or chanted art is an expression of the *wholeness* of life can the significance and meaning of the poetry be appreciated. In other words, because it is closely geared to ritual, ceremony, and occupation, it can be called a complete activity.

The Song in the Tale

The songs that are part of the tale are perhaps the most obvious separate category in oral poetry. They make sense only in the context of the tale and, since they are intended to be sung by a group, they make use of repetition. A few examples will suffice. There is a song (supplied by a Yoruba informant) that occurs in the Yoruba tale of how Alabawum (Tortoise) drinks his wife's medicine, which was to cure her barrenness, and rushes back to the doctor singing:

> Doctor I come back to ask for your forgiveness,
>   *alugbinrin.*
> The medicine you gave me some time ago,
>   *alugbinrin.*
> And you warned me never to take,
>   *alugbinrin.*
> I fell down on my way home,
>   *alugbinrin.*
> And mistakenly put my fingers to my lips,
>   *alugbinrin.*
> I looked and found my stomach protruding,
>   *alugbinrin.*
> Please doctor I am back to ask for your forgiveness,
>   *alugbinrin.*

In a Bantu tale a young king is murdered and changes into a bird. He follows his murderer singing:

> Let the big drum roll, let the big drum roll
> It flaps the wings,
> The little bird that has come out from a deep river
> From the great river of God.   Let the big drum roll.[3]

Among the Venda, children sing the following song in a tale to warn their father of the coming of a python:

> *Homio swielele*

They are coming, there they are, they are coming
Homio swielele[4]

As has been observed, these songs have no relevance outside the tale, but within it their artistic importance serves to bring audience and narrator together and to help the audience to participate in the telling.

Chants: The Semipersonal Element

A type which may be unsatisfactorily classified as "chants" seems to have survived from the tales and legends. Long after the tales had ceased being told, the chants were still sung, although quite frequently people did not know what they meant. One from Bayeke (Congo) expresses a woman's fears that she has failed in her obligations toward her husband:

> I have not milled the maize,
> My husband went to sleep hungry,
> O yes, this is very sad, O mother!
> My husband criticised me,
> My husband went to bed hungry.[5]

Some chants are in the form of a duet; for example, in the Ibo oral literature the *egleŋkwa* consist "of alternate lines of solo and chorus" and are sung on big market days, at festivals, and at the time of a baby's birth.[6] A similar duet form is found among the Temne (Sierra Leone); in one song a man says (almost prosaically), "Don't go to Mange" and the woman replies:

> To Mange I must go!
> Ah me alas! Today—those dancing girls at Mange!
> Lolo—kalula—lula—lo!
>
> Ah yes to Mange, to Mange I must go!
> Can you hear from afar the drums beating at Mange, oh![7]

Others simply are the songs of individuals, as for instance this Vandau (Mozambique) chant in which a woman cries,

> I spoil everything!
> They all laugh at me!
> I go to the lake—I draw muddy water,
> I go to the gardens—I gather grass,
> I make porridge—it is all watery,
> I brew beer—it is all lumpy.
> They all laugh at me!
> I spoil everything.[8]

45

The song, voicing the good wishes of an individual, reaches its finest expression in new year greetings, of which an Akan example follows:

> The year has come round,
> I have come to greet you,
> To shower blessings on you,
> Live long, live long, live long,
> Live to a good old age,
> The drummer of the talking drums says,
> He showers his blessings on you,
> Live long, live long, live long.
> Live to a good old age.
> The God of old says,
> He showers his blessings on you.
> Live to a good old age, chief,
> The Earth Amponyinamoa says,
> She showers her blessings on you,
> Live to a good old age.
> Live long, live long, live long.
> Live to a good old age.
> May years be added to your years.[9]

This semipersonal type of song, which has been inadequately termed a chant, seems worth isolating, if only because it possesses a personal element and, with the exception of the Akan example (which is more a praise song), seems geared to no social function. But it constitutes a minority—the major part of oral African song is praise poetry.

Praise Poems: The Verse of Kings and Cattle

The praise poem is a genre found all over Africa. Its laudatory verse is addressed to kings, chiefs, and even ordinary persons, including children. In a way the term *praise poem* is a misnomer since such poems contain elements of satire, and at times whole passages can be abusive. According to A. C. Jordan, "The subject of the praise-poem may be a nation, a tribe, a clan, a person, an animal or lifeless object. The poem may be partly narrative, or partly or wholly descriptive."[10] When the praise poem is in the form of a narrative, it glorifies the deeds of individuals and gives details of successful battles waged; when it is descriptive, usually some attribute of the person addressed is singled out for extended treatment.

In a Kanuri (Nigeria) praise song, for instance, someone is commended because "his eye-lashes are as arrows."[11] As a matter of interest, a great deal of Kanuri praise singing is descriptive in the most "romantic" of conventions; the singer stands apart from his subject and

46

praises him for his protection and his beauty. Such "romanticism" is not generally the case, however; there is praise but very rarely adoration. So a Yoruba praise singer, reciting the *ege* (supplied by a Yoruba informant) at a funeral, would say to the dead:

> Partake fully of heavenly food,
> Thatches are not good for roofs.
> Build no corridor with palm-leaves.

Not only is the praise singer on equal terms with the person being extolled, but he even advises the dead man with the lofty superiority of one who is still alive. This is very unlike the Kanuri praise song to the Sultan of Bornu, part of which has been translated: "To see you is to see the world filled with light / And to attain one's desire."[12]

Yoruba praise singing can be notoriously repetitive although it frequently does introduce the singer into the praises. Among Yorubas there is no such tradition of self-praise as will be examined with reference to the Bahima, but praise is often made the occasion for solicitation. For instance in a praise song to Obatala, the god of creation, the Yorubas proclaim:

> He is patient, he is not angry.
> He sits in silence to pass judgment.
> He sees you even when he is not looking.
> He stays in a far place—but his eyes are on the town.
>
> The granary of heaven can never be full.
> The old man full of life force.
>
> He kills the novice.
> And awakens him to let him hear his words.
> We leave the world to the owner of the world.
> Death acts playfully till he carries away the child.
> He rides on the hunchback.
> He stretches out his right hand.
> He stretches out his left hand.
>
> He stands by his children and lets them succeed.
> He causes them to laugh—and they laugh.
> Ohoho—the father of laughter.
> His eye is full of joy.
> He rests in the sky like a swarm of bees.
>
> We dance to our sixteen drums that sound jingin, jingin.
> To eight of the drums we dance bending down,
> To eight of the drums we dance erect.
> We shake our shoulders, we shake our hips,
> Munusi, munusi, munusi,
> We dance to your sixteen drums.

Those who are rich owe their property to him.
Those who are poor owe their property to him.
He takes from the rich and gives to the poor.
Whenever you take from the rich—come and give it to me.

Obatala—who turns blood into children.
I have only one cloth to dye with blue indigo,
I have only one headtie to dye with red camwood,
But I knew that you keep twenty or thirty children for me
Whom I shall bear.[13]

This song is within the African praise song tradition since it specifies that the object of praise has to reward the singer in some fashion and it uses the literary device of mentioning both the poet and the hope for reward.

The pattern that emerges in this type of praise song moves from the abstract to the concrete and ends with a direct appeal for some form of help. An Akan poem, which Nketia calls a "maiden song," for it is sung by women, is really a praise song dedicated to an outstanding man in the community. It follows the same pattern. In the first stanza Agyei is said to be "treading along on camel blanket in triumph" and is praised for his courage and conquests. The second stanza introduces the appeal for help:

Let the Nobleman leave me a farm.
Obonsafe Anin Agyei,
Please leave me a farm.[14]

As in the previous song, this one ends with a reference to children. In the Yoruba song Obatala's generosity was praised because he could give children to the barren; in this poem the mother mourns the loss of a child, but is satisfied that she will have others.

Disrespectful references are another common feature of African praise songs. Irreverent remarks are intended to relieve the tedium of accumulated praises. An example can be found in a eulogy to the bald-headed King Kyabagu:

The head of the bald man is bored like a tree
    turned to powder by insects
Now he no longer seems to be a prince
The head is bored.[15]

The personal plea can also be introduced in a derogatory way. So, when referring to policemen, whose cummerbunds make them look like mothers carrying their children on their backs, the Yoruba praise singer says:

48

Akanji, you confused all those
Who tie cloth round their waists, without carrying a child.
I beg you in the name of God, the great king, confuse me not.[16]

Such flippant disrespect reaches its climax in more modern poems where the satiric element is uppermost. For instance, a Yoruba song (supplied by a Yoruba informant) sarcastically praises a glutton:

His trousers are in patches,
His mouth, in the same way, is torn like an oil can.
The glutton, whose stool is poison to dogs.
He carries the corpse to Oyo for a plate of *amala*
And matchets his mother's nose for the leftovers of
    last night's pounded yam.

Praise singer and subject become one in Bahima (Uganda) verse. H. F. Morris states that there is a type of praise song, the *ebyevugo*, which "deals with exploits in battle and records not only the composer's heroism but also that of his companions."[17] The effect of the poems is achieved by the repetition of praise with a magnificent emphasis on egocentricity. There is little progress; the poem is fixed and static, being solely concerned with self-glorification:

I Who Am Praised thus held out in battle among foreigners
    along with the Overthrower;
I Who Ravish Spear in Each Hand stood out resplendent
    in my cotton cloth;
I Who Am Quick was drawn from afar by lust for the fight
    and with me was the Repulser of Warriors;
I Who Encircle The Foe, with Bitembe, brought back the
    beasts from Bihanga;
With Bwakwakwa, I fought at Kaanyabareega,
Where Bantura started a song that we might overcome them.[18]

What was before a personal reference has become the subject of the entire poem. But this is unusual in the tradition under discussion and does not seem to be found even in neighboring Rwanda.

It must not be thought that all praise poems center themselves on men; this would be very unlikely within the conventions of oral literature that have been mentioned thus far. A great many poems are devoted to natural life and even to landscape. Mungo Park published a song addressed to him which began "the winds roared and the rains fell."[19] This is worth noting since natural descriptions are infrequent in oral literature—nature is either personified or nonexistent. But in praise poems there are direct references to the natural world. However, the personification usually found in tales sometimes also appears in praise poems. For example, in a Basutoland *lithoko* to corn, corn is described as

> The daughter-in-law of every house
> The brown one which with its many grains rejoices the hearts
> Rejoices even those who are always sulking.[20]

Often the reference can be mildly funny; in Northern Sotho *dirêtô* the snake is the "zigzagger which hides itself" and the baboon is "Mr. Handsome-fellow of the precipice." But often the description arises out of minute observation; the hawk in Lesotho verse is "there where the road dips down / Tearing to pieces the remains of a dove."[21] And in a Swahili poem a detailed, prosaic account is given of the uses of the coconut tree:

> Give me the minstrel's seat that I may sit and tell
> you of the praises of the coco-palm.
> This tree when it begins to sprout its leaves spread
> outwards widely.
> Then it thrusts forth its bole and puts forth its
> leaf-sheath and its spreading roots
> Lastly it brings forth its fruits and its fruits are
> known as coco-nuts.
> They are plucked down and stripped of their husks and
> cooked with boiled rice and sauces.
> From the empty shell they carve a ladle and the
> handmaiden Saada cooks with it.
> Its grated nut, squeezed free of juice, is scattered
> on the midden and the cook scratches for it there.
> Its fibre they plait into cord for the rigging of
> clippers and dhows.
> With its fronds they thatch a house and ward off the
> winds and the wind-swept sand,
> Of its trunk they make a door to resist the enemy and
> the robber.[22]

This poetry in praise of nature reaches its perfection in the Bahima *ekirahiro*, which Morris calls a poem "in praise of a man's cattle. The members of a herd are introduced one by one and their beauty extolled."[23] In an example which he gives, composed by a herdsman in 1918, the suffering of the cattle from rinderpest is pathetically described. Both pride and admiration come over in these lines:

> She Whose Horns Out Above the Herd gave birth
> and so did She Who Has Straightened Her Horns
> She Who Prevents Others' Approaching became friendly
> With The One Whose Horns Are As Straight As Planks.[24]

The same devices noted before are used here as well: the spinning out of detailed, excessive description to the most ingenious length and the juxtaposing of praise phrases. A Hurutsche (South Africa) poem illustrates the same detached adoration for cattle that was observed in the Kanuri tribute. Here, quite naturally, since this is the art of a pastoral people, the cow is equated with the divine:

> Very powerfully built one of arms,
> Cooker of waiting food,
> God with the moist nose.[25]

There is a certain absence of movement in these lines and in this way the praise poem is like a piece of sculpture. There is an arrest of movement so that detailed analysis can take place.

In Batutsi (Rwanda) poems the praises of the king can be expressed in the imagery of cattle, and Cyilima I Rugwe (1345–78) is described in this way in a poem composed about 1820:

> Right from thine accession, thou allowest thyself
>   to be milked without protest;
> Thou hast supplied us with milk as abundant as rain.[26]

This particular praise poem traces the king's lineage, invokes the assembly of dead kings, praises his mother, describes the exploits of past kings, offers a prayer by the poet, and concludes with commendation to the greatness of the new king who is a "bull of boldness."[27] Running through the poem is the imagery of cattle-farming people who express in this way their satisfaction with the new king.

Kings were of course the great patrons of oral poetry, and praise songs are in the main addressed to them. The finest examples of this type of verse occur in Zulu *izi6ongo*. Both B. W. Vilakazi and C. L. S. Nyembezi have emphasized that though praises are meted out to kings, women, and natural objects, it is in the poems to kings that the language is at its best, the feeling most intense: "I give stealthy looks at Nda6a, and satisfy myself / Tears rain down my eyes."[28] In a Swazi poem to Ngwane, familiar elements of the praise poem are present:

> Ngwane amongst the waters I may liken to a great black
>   pool with spirits;
> Ngwane amongst the paths I may liken to a path which
>   stretches across the horizon;
> Ngwane amongst the trees I may liken to a Nyamati tree;
> Ngwane amongst the goats I may liken to a young he-goat;
> Ngwane amongst the cattle I may liken to a polled cow.[29]

51

The love for the chief is proclaimed by repetition. The praise singer makes use of relevant and familiar natural sights in the environment and concludes with the most superb praise of all—the comparison with cattle.

Praise singing, whether to God, man, or cattle, is important because it constitutes a large bulk of the sung art and because it tells of the nature of the cultural experiences of African man. Both the praised and the praiser belong to a tradition in which they are involved in the functional nature of the culture. This is a tradition that did not survive among Blacks in the New World, since there was no functional need for it. But it is no accident that the first Black writers in Latin, English, and French were group spokesmen and directed their praise toward objects and people within the new cultures in which they found themselves. The ancient African heroes might have been forgotten but the manner of addressing them seems to have been part of the ancestral memories.

Sacred Songs: Poetry for the Divine

When the object of admiration is a god rather than a man the praise poem becomes a sacred song. The attitudes of the singer, however, are the same—withdrawal and solicitation. There are few derogatory asides, which were noticed as a feature of the praise poem, but there is the same aggregation of repetitive phrases which suggest that these verses were probably intended for many voices. The Hottentot hymn to Tsui-Xgoa, the supreme god of creation, is as follows:

> You, O Tsui-Xgoa
> you, all-father
> you, our father!
> Let stream to earth the thundercloud,
> give life to us.
> I am so stricken with weakness,
> I thirst and I hunger.
> Allow that I gather and eat the field fruits,
> for are you not our first one?
> the father of fathers,
> you, Tsui-Xgoa—
> that we may sing to you in praise
> that we may measure to you in return,
> you, all-father
> you, our maker
> you, O Tsui-Xgoa.[30]

First the generosity of Tsui-Xgoa is proclaimed, after which he is offered the supreme praise for being responsible for all life. The personal theme of destitution is delicately introduced, this time in the middle of the poem, and is then dropped. Nevertheless, the god must satisfy this need to merit completely the praise showered on him. This point, however, is not stressed, only suggested. The poem concludes as it began with an evocation. This rigidity of structure will again be observed in other sacred songs.

Often the poem takes the form of solo and chorus, as can be seen in this example from the Massai in Kenya:

Solo   O God of thunder and lightning . . .
Chorus (After each line) That thy seed may commingle with
      God's whose
dwellings are in the springs,
    I will pray night and day.

O listen to my constant plea.
O hear that which my companions deserve:
Their heads should be covered with hair,
They should rest while donkeys move on errands,
They deserve to move always in the coolness of the shade.
O God, pay this debt,
This debt which our cattle cannot pay . . .
This debt which cannot be paid by the labour of our hands
O God, regard us only in ways that are proper,
That you may give to women the gift of children,
That you may give children to all forgetting none . . .
That you may beget children,
That your children may be strong,
That they may live to make a great clan,
That through them the house of Massai may receive strength,
That God may give you his blessing,
That he may guard you always,
That he may strengthen your backs,
That he may put seed into your wombs,
That he may give you faces of joy,
That he may enable you to come victorious over all trouble.[31]

Here the central theme is fertility, "the gift of children." The poem makes its impression by hypnotic repetition and by references to familiar objects which help to anchor it in the real world. This is what saves African oral sacred verse from being mystical; the god is always close to his people and his participation in their lives is assumed.

The scope of sacred songs encompasses even the most diverse elements, for the universe in which the religion operates and to which the myths and tales belong is but one complete whole. According to Germaine Dieterlen, "No real place is reserved for what we call the profane. . . . The African who practises a traditional religion does not only believe in a creator and an almighty God aided by a certain number of supernatural forces who are the intermediaries between Him, nature and man. He does not only believe in the power of God and of dispensation over man and the universe. He lives his belief in the most complete sense of the term."[32] Consequently the occasions for these sacred poems are not only the deaths of priests, chiefs, and kings, but the everyday life of the people; the songs are sung at social events like birth, initiation, marriage, and death, at times of grave incidents, new year festivities, and divination, and while working, fishing, and hunting. At times the mundane and the divine exist side by side, but there is no discord. At the Odwira ceremony, which honors dead Ashanti kings, the participants say:

> The edges of the years have met, we have come
>   to celebrate the *Odwira*
> Come and receive the food and eat.[33]

One of the ways in which the sacred verse still functions most satisfactorily is in divination. The *Odu* corpus in Nigeria is the best example of this kind of verse. It has a definite structure, divided into five sections—"a pithy saying which is conveyed in verse," a story which is "the kernel of the recital from the point of view of divination," a liturgy which is the "means of communication with the object of worship," songs, and proverbs. These are all linked as "facets of one central doctrine." Ulli Beier has explained the manner of divination:

The Ifa system of divination could be called "divination by poetry." The priests must know a vast stock of Odu (ritual poems) by heart. Each of these Odu has a name and a number. Whenever the oracle priest is consulted by a client he prepares a round wooden board called *Opan Ifa* on which he spreads some cassava flour. He then takes sixteen palm nuts in his hand, throws them up and catches as many as he can. If the number in his hand is an even number, he draws one little line on the cassava flour. If it is an odd number, he draws two little lines. This is repeated eight times and as a result there will be a pattern of lines on the board.

Each of these patterns corresponds to an Odu; and from this Odu the priest selects the verse which appears to him to fit his client's case. He recites this and interprets it. Thus the Ifa system combines in a strange way the element of chance with the wisdom and psychological insight of the priest.[34]

The poetry is cryptic and meanings frequently have to be explained. A great deal of it is still uncollected, but what has been collected reveals

54

a wealth of prophetic visions closely related to life. Not only is it relevant to divination but it has larger ramifications. The universal scope is seen in the manner in which statements are made; often the tone is strictly pious: "God of The Igbo, I stretch out my hand, / Give the reins of the world to me."[35] This couplet ends the verse of an *Odu* which tells the seeker to worship Obatala. Sometimes the sound can be that of a prose poem:

> Ogbe was hunting in the bush
> He was told to sacrifice lest he should meet disaster there.
> When he went hunting again, rain began to beat him hard,
> He ran for shelter into a big hole.[36]

On extremely few occasions sacred songs can be mildly satirical:

> The Moslems are still lying.
> They say: we are fasting for God every year.
> One day Eshu went to them and said:
> Why do you fast for God?
> Do you believe God is dead?[37]

But a great deal seems to be strictly functional and, quite naturally, to have no meaning beyond the immediate occasion.

Since there is a "wholeness" to African group life, sacred songs belong to life itself. For they speak of man's relationship with his gods, his environment, and his fellow living creatures. Unlike praise songs, they frequently can help man to know his future, but like praise songs they tell him of his past and his relationship with the deity. Within certain specific cultures it would be a moot point to establish differences between "praise" and "sacred" songs since, in large measure, they both assume the attention of the object of praise.

Dirges: The Germination of Sorrow

According to Nketia, funeral dirges are concerned with expressing reflections and messages as well as the themes of "the ancestor," "the deceased," and "the place of domicile." "In arranging the themes, a conventional pattern may be followed in which the references are made in the order of the themes given above, or they may be mixed up in a free style. In this respect, at least four types of dirges may be distinguished."[38] This is the pattern that Nketia sees in Akan dirges, but it is not always the case. The allusion at times can be all the more poignant. There is a Ugandan funeral dirge which simply states:

55

> Oh separator!
> Oh Sematimba!
> They tied goats
> They tied goats for him in vain.[39]

The opening evocation and the repetition in the last lines illustrate the meaning of the dirge—death is inevitable. Sometimes the dirge is addressed to the corpse and simply states that he is dead. Such is true in the following Ibo dirge:

> Ojea, noble Ojea, look round before you depart,
> Ojea, see, the fight is over;
> Fire has consumed the square and then the home,
> Ojea, see, the fight is over.[40]

Despite the sad strain that runs through these songs, the dead are considered to be reduced living energies and therefore are only temporarily out of sight. Their presence is still in everything:

> He is dead,
> He becomes a goat that feeds on leaves.
> He is dead,
> He becomes a sheep that feeds on palm-leaves.
> He is dead,
> He becomes a lizard that feeds on the walls.[41]

Consequently funeral dirges frequently are directed at the living. Among the Adangme (Ghana) there is a funeral dirge which refers to the mourners at the wake:

> Let the day break
> And we shall know our friends.
> A brother in the darkness is not known.
> We shall know our friends.[42]

Here it is shown that death is a way of helping the living understand one another better.

Funeral dirges also at times dramatize the plight of the living. A favorite device is to have a mother, a child, or in some cases a widow sing the funeral hymn. Many dirges describe the anguish of a child mourning for a parent, as in this Urhobo (Nigeria) song (supplied by an Urhobo informant) which the child sings to himself:

> If I had known
> My father would die
> I ought to have prepared for his burial.

In a similar Efik (Nigeria) song (supplied by an Efik informant) the child addresses his mother:

56

Nne, my mother, wake up, wake up!
The best of mothers, wake up!
He who travels out cannot see his house,
He doesn't know that the house has become a market.

In many of these dirges the orphan theme is prominent; the child has
lost both parents—it is never explained how—but the situation is of
course sufficiently emotional so that even if the theme is merely stated,
an appropriate response is guaranteed by the listeners. For instance
there is the Ngoni (Malawi) song which simply states:

> My father is dead
> and I was not told.
> My mother is dead
> and I was not told.
> My heart in pain
> cries:
> to
> toto
> totototo.[43]

The poem tails off to the plaintive sounds at the end. An Ashanti song
similarly takes its inception from the situation:

> I am an orphan and when I recall the death of my
> father, water from my eyes falls upon me.
> When I recall the death of my mother, water from
> my eyes falls on me.[44]

Frequently the form of the dirge is itself dramatic when it uses the
traditional device of a chorus. For instance in the poem above, the
orphan's predicament is dramatized by a chorus. Some dirges utilize
three voices, as is illustrated in the following Sotho dirge, which has a
chorus of women, a woman, and the widow herself. The chorus states
the predicament, the woman expresses a religious hope, and the widow
utters her fears:

> *Chorus of women*: Now we are left out,
> Alone we sit and cry,
> Left with nothing but sorrow
> Empty and dull with pain,
> It has bruised our hearts.
> *Woman*: Ah, let God make a place for me in the sky!
> And keep me a fire and a cooking pot.
> As I am I would journey up there—
> If I grew the wings of a bird
> I would fly to him there.

57

The Widow: Dull and faint is my heart.
When the first dark brings the night
I go out under the eaves,
Alone I stand there and listen
I am quiet and try to hear
I think that he is coming.[45]

What dramatic element there is in these poems does not always take an obvious external form. Many times the dramatic effect is accomplished by a monologue. There is an Akan funeral dirge in which the mother pretends to be addressing a sleeping child, who does not answer. Only in the last stanza is it revealed that someone has taken away the child.[46]

Often the misery seems to be nurtured entirely for its own sake. A Zulu poem begins: "Come let us sing of fallen leaves and spears / Of the bad omens of black crows . . ."[47] The best example of this type of poem, which is also a faithful expression of sorrow, is a Ngoni (Malawi) dirge:

> The earth does not ever grow fat,
> it swallows the head-plumed fighters—
> and we shall die too on this earth, alas!
> The earth does not ever grow fat,
> it swallows up the swift-acting heroes—
> and shall we die then, we too?
>
> > Listen, Earth! Do you wish to make us mourn?
> > Listen, Earth! Shall all of us perish, alas?
>
> The earth does not ever grow fat,
> it makes an end of the kings—
> and shall we die too on this earth?
> The earth does not ever grow fat,
> it makes an end to the royal women—
> and shall we die then, we too?
>
> The earth does not ever grow fat,
> it finishes off the common herd—
> and we shall die too on this earth, alas!
> The earth does not ever grow fat,
> it swallows as well all the hearts—
> and shall we die then, we too?
>
> > Listen, O you who sleep, close wrapped in the grave,
> > Shall we all go down in the ground?
> > Listen, O World! for the sun is setting now, we all
> > shall enter the earth.[48]

The central idea of the insatiable earth is really the imaginative expansion of a proverb—"The earth does not ever grow fat." Greater rapport between the dead object and the living voices which express death emerges from their both being subject to death—everyone will die. The dirge achieves its effect by repetition and by the same enumeration observed in other examples of oral verse. The method of the following Yoruba song is comparable to that of the Ngoni song, although there is a closer identification between the singer and his subject in the latter. The Yoruba dirge (supplied by a Yoruba informant) says of death:

> Iku kills the head of the camwood powder makers,
> Iku kills Lekeleke, the head of the chalk makers,
> Iku kills Aloko, he kills the head of the singers,
> Iku kills Babalawo, as if he is not well learnt in oracles.
> Iku kills Onisegun, as if he does not know any charm,
> Iku kills a Moslem, as if he is not well learnt in the Koran,
> Iku kills a Christian, as if he does not have God as his king.

An element of cynicism, absent from the Ngoni poem, is apparent here. Nevertheless cynicism is not usually a feature of dirges—they are long, heartfelt cries of agony, sometimes dramatized, but almost always stated directly. In all cases dirges lament the dead but concern themselves with the living.

Wedding Songs: Loss and Joy

As has been mentioned, several of the genres found in oral literature overlap. It is rarely easy to distinguish between a "praise song" and a "sacred song," and masquerade verse frequently employs the attitude of one or the other. The wedding songs are no different, for they are often sad, bemoaning the loss of virginity or the departure of a member of the household. If a generalization can be made about them, it is that they are usually centered on the woman. Often the song is sung by the bride, but at times she is sung to by a chorus of women.

The Ndienyi clan in Akwa (eastern Nigeria) perform certain ceremonies at weddings. It is customary for a group of women to gather round the bride when she is about to depart for her husband's house; the eldest daughter of the household places her palms on the ground, then on the breasts of the bride, and sings:

> Our sister
> Go in peace to your husband's house.
> Be a pillar that holds his household:
> Be a mother of many children!
> Live long to see your children's children!
> May our great ancestor protect you all your days!

Unlike this joyous song (supplied by an Ibo informant), most of the songs dramatize the bride's conflict of loyalties. In one South African wedding song, the bride asks plaintively:

O father! O mother!
Why marry me off so young?
Think of her who is not my mother,
How is she likely to handle me?[49]

An Edo (Nigeria) song (supplied by an Edo informant) is equally full of pathos:

Father when I was a child, you promised me
We never would be separated.
Mother when I was a child, you promised me
We never would be separated.
But what of today?
Have you not broken your word?
Am I not leaving now?

This strain of melancholy, which was also observed in the dirges—the expression of sadness for its own sake—emerges time and time again in the marriage songs.

Dramatization also characterizes some wedding songs, such as the following Chopi (Mozambique) song in which a certain young man, Nyagumbe, tries to win his bride by refusing to eat at her parents' house.

Bride	Nyagumbe! Nyagumbe! Why do you refuse?
Bridegroom	I am refusing. In my heart is the love of refusing.
Bride	I will go To the *banza* of the men. Father! Father! Nyagumbe refuses.
Father	Why does he refuse?
Bride	He is refusing. In his heart is the love of refusing. I will go to the hearth. Mamane! Mamane!

Mother	Why does he refuse?
Bride	He is refusing.
	In his heart
	is the love
	of refusing.[50]

This song is really a kind of play; it dramatizes the conflict that is present in any relationship between a man and a woman. Like most of the examples of oral literature that have been discussed, there is an arrest of movement; the song ends on the same impasse on which it began. Use is also made of the familiar device of repetition, and once more the habitual cataloguing is apparent; here the bride approaches the bridegroom, her father, and then her mother. But the song is obviously the bride's, for she has the major role to play. She summons the various soloists and explains the predicament to them, and it is she who restates the problems. In most songs the bride expresses the wedding themes— the loss of innocence, the new duties to the husband, and the wish for children; in a Yoruba song she wants "sixty seven times two hundred children."[51]

African wedding songs therefore deal with the loss of the bride and the joy of her being married. The form can vary from a monologue to a chant, sung by people at the wedding, and even to a dramatic re-enactment of courtship. The Creoles in Sierra Leone have a particularly interesting "gaging" (engagement) ceremony where the mother of the intended bride is praised. Later on a staged ceremony enacts the "refusal" of the bride; for when the relatives of her suitor seek her, her own relatives pretend she is not there. Virginity is to be prized and only surrendered when a suitor has observed all the mores of the society. Then the African woman's role as farm-help and market-seller places her high up on the economic structure of her family's welfare. Her ability to bear children confirms her status.

Rhythm in Oral Verse: Line and Meter

It seems worthwhile adding a note about the rhythm of these poems, if only because it does not survive in translation. In an introduction to a dictionary, written in 1857, J. L. Döhne put forth an odd contention: "Some have expected to find poetry among the Zulu-Kaffirs, but there is in fact none. Poetical language is extremely rare, and we meet only with a few pieces of prose . . . But nothing like poetry or song exists—no meter, no rhyme, nothing that interests or soothes the feelings or arrests the passions."[52] One now recognizes the absurdity of this statement, but if Döhne was basing his observation on the fact that no apparent formal meter existed in the verse, then there is some truth in what he said. For the verse belongs to an occasion and it takes its rhythm and form from that occasion.

It is wrong to seek to impose "classical" meters on African oral verse; it is equally wrong to see the poetry as free verse. Ulli Beier has maintained that "one cannot in fact speak of Yoruba metre. There is neither an important difference in the length of vowels nor a marked difference between stressed and unstressed syllables on which metre could be based. In writing down the poetry it is even difficult to decide what constitutes a line as there are in fact no regular lines."[53] What Beier failed to comprehend was that there was a rhythm to which the trained African audience could respond, a rhythm that they and the poet had inherited. This rhythm is not as elusive as it has been made to sound, but depends on what Vilakazi has called a "breath-group of words." Writing about Zulu poetry, Vilakazi concluded:

From the oral recitation of the poet I discovered that a unit of poetry of verse in Zulu is a breath-group of words. Allow the poet to recite slowly, and he will always breathe at certain intervals, and inhale before starting on another verse. But if you allow the poet to be carried away with ecstasy, he may take two verses in one breath. Further if you notice very intently you will detect in the middle of the verse a very short break, which I would mark with a caesura. Then the verse is composed of two rhythmic parts, each of which may have one or more stressed sounds, accompanied by unstressed ones. Each of the component parts of a verse or breath-group, I prefer to call a poetic bar. Then a Zulu poem is a series of poetic bars occurring in pairs in a verse.[54]

A salient feature of this argument is that it establishes the presence of an inherent rhythm which is noticeable to the native speaker of the language. Adeoye Babalola, who has done research on ijala chants, confirms this view and adds an interesting comment on Beier's remarks:

The point that Beier misses is that it is not difficult for an ijala-chanter's audience to distinguish the successive breath-groups (that is, stretches of utterances in between the breath pauses) which make up the ijala chants. As they have grown up within the indigenous Yoruba culture, and the language of the ijala chant is their mother tongue as well as that of the chanter, they can easily recognise the breath pauses made by the chanter and can feel as units the utterances delimited by these pauses. Even when the ijala chanter, carried away, as he often is, by ecstasy or the desire to show dexterity, chants two or more normal breath-groups in one breath, the audience is not at a loss to know what the different utterances are and what they mean. Moreover, the chanter himself can, if requested, give a slow rendering of a chant that he usually performs fast and in this way the normal breath-groups of words can be ascertained.[55]

It is no accident that Babalola's findings in Yoruba substantiate those made by Vilakazi almost thirty years earlier. For it can be seen that in this poetry there are commonly regular speech units which are marked out by breath-pauses and which together constitute a line.

As has been observed, the rhythmical pattern of Yoruba and Zulu poetry could be altered and was frequently changed by the artist; this again illustrates the independence of the traditional artist and his ability to modify his material to suit his audience and his theme. Analyzing an Ibo women's song, Green noted that "it is when the theme alters that the pattern changes," and it was of course up to the artist to ensure that these rhythmical changes took place smoothly. In some songs the rhythm not only was related to the function of the poem but was closely geared to it. As was seen in Barundi verse, it is difficult to separate poetry, music, and dance; indeed they cannot be said to exist separately. This applies to all African oral verse and in the same way that poetry is connected to other artistic functions, it is also linked to work. Alice Warner has remarked that "in canoe songs and the like, time is marked by the beat of the paddles, the rise and fall of the women's pestles; at a dance it is given by the drums." Not only does the drum accompany the poetry, marking out the rise and fall in tone, but it can frequently take the place of the poem and sound "the tones of the poem while the hearers interpret them into words in their own minds."[56] Flutes, bells, handclapping, and so on can be substituted for the drum, for they all help to emphasize the rhythm of the poetry.

Because African languages frequently depend on tones in order to be most effective, African poetry, especially children's verse, has developed the use of rhythm. The poetry draws heavily on this aspect of the language, and although one is perhaps not aware of rhythm in translation, it is from this rhythmic structure that the poems are created. Speaking of the Bantu group of languages, Lestrade remarked, "Moreover, the existence, in Southern Bantu language especially, of a system of intonation also gives to these languages a musical quality not possessed by less markedly and even intoned language." Applying this to the use of rhythm in Zambia, A. M. Jones has added that the artist "in the complex interweaving of contrasting rhythmic patterns . . . finds the greatest aesthetic satisfaction."[57] The tonal patterns of the words are therefore brought together in a variety of rhythmical combinations;

the archetypal pattern that is present in the mind of the artist and the audience is the standard by which they judge the finished work.

Rhythm is aided by the use of modern words and archaic terms, which are included for their special artistic effect. Archaic words are very expressive, and also help to jolt the listener into a new awareness.[58] Their intended effect is rhythmical and they act as *les mots justes* in the fine balance that is required for the organization of breath-groups. But it must not be thought that these were rigid rules which had to be implicitly obeyed. The poet and the audience inherited the structure and they were free to do what they wanted, within certain limitations. For example, a Mende (Sierra Leone) singer tells of the Yomeh (praise poem) in his song:

> I know the Yomeh as a woman-lover knows the night.
> I know the Yomeh as an alligator knows the river,
> I know the Yomeh as a guinea-fowl knows the bush.
> There are some who say that there are no riches or
> civilisation in the bush,
> But witness these things:
> An ant-hill has a helmet that shelters it from the bush.[59]

It is this culture of the bush that the oral poet expressed and he was intrinsically conscious of its rhythmical possibilities. His greatest contribution, which cannot be fully judged here, was his ability to manipulate the original language, to distort it and play with its nuances of meaning, and to expose the rich imaginative fabric of the language and its rhythmical texture. His repertoire was composed of archetypes that suited a variety of situations and experiences; he codified them and related them to the ephemeral. This explains why worldliness characterized gods, kings, and the dead in the oral literature of Africa.

PART II HERITAGE

Chapter 5

African Literature in Latin

O f the Africans who wrote in Latin two were not creative writers and another two were poets. Anton Wilhelm Amo, born in 1703 near Axim, Ghana, was brought to Amsterdam as a slave when he was only four. He was presented to Duke Anton Ulrich von Braunschweig-Wolfenbüttel who gave him to his son Wilhelm—hence his two names. He was educated at the University of Halle and secured a junior post in jurisprudence in 1729. The following year he began his doctorate at Wittenberg and in 1735 he completed his degree. He afterwards went to Halle as a professor.

Four of Amo's Latin works on philosophy and law have survived, but there is also a poem, addressed to a friend of his, a Jewish student of medicine, which was written in German in standard Alexandrines. In translation it reads as follows:

> To the vivacious spirit in clever meditation.
> And unwearied in the matters of thorough study.
> High noble person, you show that in the order of the scholars
> You are accepted as a star, a brilliant star of the first dimension.
>
> Which becomes brighter and brighter in the halo of new comers,
> Such a big reward Wisdom gives her sons.
> That's enough! From Heaven, pleasure, which is enormous,
> Must crown you and yours in the fullness of blessing.[1]

The other writer, Jacobus Eliza Capitein (1717–47), was taken as a boy-slave to Zeeland and brought to Elmina Castle in Ghana; in 1726 he returned with a new master to Holland where he was educated. He was baptized in 1735 and attended the University of Leyden where in 1742 he delivered an oration in Latin proving that slavery was not contrary to the laws of God. In the same year he was ordained and went back to Ghana as a missionary. He made a success of teaching, translating the Lord's Prayer, the Twelve Articles of Belief, and the Ten Commandments into Fanti. He also published his oration and some sermons. He married a Dutch girl in 1745. J. W. Schulte Nordholt mentions that Capitein introduced a new element into the Ten Commandments, namely, "I am Jan Company who brought you out of Egypt."[2] He had obviously been well schooled.

Two Black poets, Juan Latino and Francis Williams, wrote their verse in Latin, for this ensured them a larger audience. Juan Latino was born in West Africa in 1516 and died about 1594. According to Ambrosio de Salazar, he was brought to Spain from "Ethiopia" with his mother at the age of twelve. They became slaves of the Duke of Sesa's household, and here Latino grew up and was educated with the duke's young grandson. At the Cathedral School in Granada he translated Horace and first started composing in Latin. Called "avis rara" by his tutor, he went on to the University of Granada where he studied poetry, music, and some medicine. He is said to have become a professor at the university in 1556, but Marin Ocete, one of his biographers, notes that the records do not support this. In approximately 1549 he married Dona Ana Carlobal, the daughter of a Spanish nobleman and a former pupil of his. In one of his plays, *La dama boba*, Lope de Vega has a character speak of Latino's courtship: "He taught her to conjugate / When they came to 'amo' 'amas.'" Bermúdes de Pedraza, in a history of Granada, remarks that Latino became blind in later life.[3]

The minor details of Latino's life are not known but five of his works survive. These include his *Epigrammatum Liber*, written to celebrate the birth of Prince Ferdinand in 1571, an elegy to Pius V in four parts, and the two-part *Austriad*, which narrates the victory of Don Juan of Austria at the Battle of Lepanto. In the British Museum's copy of these works they are bound in one volume and the publication date is given as 1573. In 1574 (according to Spratlin), Juan Latino published *Translatione,* in praise of Philip II's filial devotion, and much later, in 1585, a short poem dedicated to his former master and companion, the Duke of Sesa, who had died in 1579.

Although most of the poems take the form of panegyrics, it would be underestimating Latino to call him a mere eulogist. For in addition to a rigid stylistic device, he makes use of heightened narrative techniques and dramatic moments to intensify his poetry.

Latino's preoccupation with panegyrics might in some measure have been the result of his African origin. This is quite a plausible view, for in Africa the praise singer is still the most popular vernacular artist. It is more than possible that both Latino and Francis Williams transferred the model of the African praise poem to a European setting. The objects of Latino's laudatory effusions became less anonymous than those of his African counterpart (the oral praise singer), and his was the first *individual* African poetic voice to address the pope and royalty.

In *Epigrammatum Liber*, the preface is made up of various praises to Latino by contemporary poets. Latino's poem then begins with a formal request asking for Philip II's permission to sing his brother's praises: "The conqueror is unique, he seeks a unique poet / A new deed means that the kings should have a new poet" (p. 9).[4] And Latino adds, with characteristic boldness: "For if our black face, O King, displeases / Your ministers, a white face does not please the men of Ethiopia" (p. 9). This is followed by lines that establish the link between "Ethiopians" and Spaniards through Christianity: "When Philip met the Ethiopian he taught him about Christ verbally / Christ sent a disciple to an Ethiopian" (p. 10). Before Latino comes to the central theme—the victory of Don Juan of Austria over the Turks (also the subject of the *Austriad*)—he devotes a number of short pieces to Philip himself and to Queen Anna, his wife and the mother of the new prince. About Philip he says:

> O Holy Philip, although you rule over the whole earth
> Let your royal mind for a little while escape its cares
> It is joy for us to write these epigrams for the prince
>   that is born.
> They will bring pleasure, and as king and father you
>   will read them. (p. 12)

Perhaps the finest poetry of the *Epigrammatum* is achieved when he breaks off the repetitive monologue of praises to royalty and has the city of Granada address Queen Anna:

> Fate has now vouchsafed to our ancestral realm a prince.
> Behold, Queen Anna, how he lightens the burden of your
>   childbearing.
> Though grievous was the pain she suffered in her travail
> The birth of a son into the world dispels the recollections
>   of her pain.
> Mother of your prince and wife of Philip
> Long may you live to bring blessings upon Spain.
> Royal mother may you present to your king a fair progeny

Bringing blessings to your children's children.
May you see them lords of the world enthroned in power
So that in your marriage, Anna, the king may prosper. (p. 13)

Apart from this stanza, which is in the form of a dialogue, the other poems consist of short pieces with a hexameter/pentameter metrical pattern. On the whole they are unambitious, for Latino really did not come into his own until he published the *Austriad*. Nevertheless, his *Elegy to Pius V* is a moving piece because it expresses his intense religious feelings about the Catholic church. In the first of four parts, Pius V speaks to Philip and encourages him to fight a naval battle against the Turks, in the second he advises Philip from his deathbed, and in the third the death of the pope and its effect on the people are described. The poem concludes with an elegy on Pius's death. Marin Ocete has commented that the entire work dedicated to the pope is the most interesting of all Latino's compositions.[5]

The *Elegy* demonstrates a certain kind of dramatic progression. The language with which the pope first addresses Philip is not particularly interesting and is merely Latino's own pious effusions:

> In Heaven we have Christ as our patron
> Who is wont to plead our cause with the Father.
> We take refuge with you, you alone.
> We pour forth our prayers that you might be a
>   Conqueror.
> Your renown, which vies with the valour of
>   your father
> Inspires your mind, son Philip.
> It is an inborn trait of the kings of Spain to
>   recognize Christ
> Whom He rules with His piety. (p. 26)

But the words spoken by the dying pope display a different type of vision, quite appropriate in the context:

> As you fight on the golden age will come to us
> And at the same time to the Romans and the
>   Venetians under Philip's leadership.
> The barbarous people will be converted both in
>   body and mind and will obey Christ.
> The world will fear the conquering standards. (p. 33)

The strength of faith implied in these lines contrasts with the frailty of the dying pope.

The first two parts of the poem are in the form of a dialogue between Pius and Philip, but, as in the *Epigrammatum Liber*, Latino realized that his approach had to vary. The third section is therefore in narrative form, and Latino reaches levels of pathos when he describes the dignity of the dying pope and the anxiety of the crowd who wait to learn of the pope's condition. At one time it even seems that the pope will not die. The depiction of the pope's illness, with its savage directness, is truly pathetic:

> Finally consumed with a disease, his years advancing
> He was unable for a whole month to drive away the illness.
> A raging disorder reached his holy body . . . (p. 36)

Finally he dies and in the epitaph which forms the fourth part of the poem the poet himself comes forward to describe the effect on the peoples of the world:

> Cities shed tears, the palaces of Rome weep.
> The Spaniards pour forth the sign of their pious feelings.
> Now men's faces appear in mourning,
> Men show forth in their words the sorrow in their hearts.
> The temples of the saints are mourning,
> The priest and the choir sing songs of mourning,
> The singers chant sad dirges with their tongues
> Every organ is silent; no flutes play.
> The crowds, in black garments, make their way
>   through the street,
> The aged ruler and the royal company of princes.
> And through the streets of Rome the raucous
>   trumpet is mourning.
> And thus Libitina carries on her funeral ceremony. (p. 38)

The quietness and dignity of the last part of this poem strikingly contrast with the mood of the *Austriad* which can be called an epic poem, although, as Spratlin has remarked, it is really made up of a number of rather banal eulogies relieved by occasional passages of grandeur. In fact, the description of the Battle of Lepanto at which Don Juan defeats the Turks is the high point of the poem; Latino relates it as if he were actually present. He begins the poem with an invocation to Apollo—a standard convention in classical epic poetry. Then the historical background of the Turkish-Spanish conflict is sketched in, depicting the expulsion of the Moors from Spain and the reasons for the war with Turkey. This is followed by a description of the preparation for battle and finally the battle itself—the two fleets and the thoughts of the chief contestants, Bassam the Turk and Don Juan, are portrayed in detail. Latino also compares the contemporary battle scene with the classical one of the Greeks against the Trojans; this is no fortuitous

71

association. There is of course the geographical proximity of the two battles; in addition, the Trojans, like the Turks, were the oriental enemy. The Latin hexameters are in the classical epic tradition of Homer and help to heighten the effect of the slow, deliberative tragedy that is being enacted: the microcosmic panorama of a collision of worlds.

A particularly moving passage is the one in which Latino evokes Bassam's fears:

> From here Bassam looks upon the sea and upon his ships
> And contemplating their sacking, he fears the powers
> of the deep
> And the changed attitude of the gods.
> With downcast eyes, pitying the unequal fortune
> of the Turks,
> And that the leaders must endure great anguish,
> And at last must fight in combat with the brother
> of Philip. (p. 17)

In these lines Bassam's thoughts are described in reported speech, which has the effect of bringing the reader closer to what is taking place in his mind. The passage also builds up suspense and, finally, one has no doubt that Don Juan deserves to win. Even in the first book Don Juan addresses his troops in Caesar's words ("Alea iacta est" were Don Juan's actual words), and in his soliloquy what does emerge, above everything else, is that he is a Catholic and therefore invincible. Moreover, Christ leads the Spaniards in battle; Bassam does not stand much of a chance and rightly feels, "If God is fighting here, who could fight against Him?" Latino's description of the battle in which Bassam is shamelessly defeated further conveys the truth of Bassam's sense of futility; even in translation the urgency and immediacy of the conflict are apparent:

> Men fought with men and foot closes with foot
> And thus clinging to them they struck the Turks at close
> range with swords.
> When Don Juan saw this his heart blazed with war
> But his bold enterprise was obstructed by the guards.
> Three times our men burst through the enemy lines,
> wounded in the process.
> Three times the Parthians, putting themselves forward,
> Turned the enemy and scattered them with slaughter.
> At the fourth onslaught the Spaniards reached the very ship.
> The Turks are shattered by a sudden fear of death.
> On the decks and among the oars they are stricken with terror.
> They abandon their leader Bassam and all the royal company
> And their leaders, the captains, in the sea.
> They left the royal ship, its ensigns and its arms

And they could see young men like the great body of dolphins
Looking for safety in the waves in panic.
Here it is said Bassam fell and died by the sword
And that a humble soldier left his body headless. (pp. 21–22)

Latino's poetry reveals that he was on the side of "right"—Catholicism
and Spanish conquest. He was conscious that he was an outsider and
this made him all the more aggressively patriotic, but it did not impair
his dramatic ability. Not only is Latino capable of capturing the pathos
of Pope Pius as he speaks to Philip from his deathbed, but he is equally
able in the second book of the *Austriad* to express the Turkish leader's
consternation as he confronts the massive array of Don Juan. Latino's
success lies in his ability to switch roles and to depict effectively the
full scope of the human predicament.

The dramatic technique of the *Austriad* and the elegy to Pope Pius V
makes them the most successful of Latino's poems. His poetic epigrams,
written to celebrate the birth of the young prince, do not have the com-
pactness of these longer pieces and lack total development. After one
has read the first few, their excessive praises begin to pall. Furthermore,
the Latin of some of these earlier pieces is stilted and at times startlingly
ungrammatical. The poet relies too heavily on an Ovidian pattern and
his handling of the elegiac couplet is far from satisfactory. In one passage, however, use is made of onomatopoeic sounds which have a grand
cumulative effect. Here one sees something of Latino's technical ability
which was to reach its heights in the battle scenes of the *Austriad* and
in the poem to Pius where Virgilian echoes help to muffle the sounds
of death.

Although Juan Latino was an African, judging from his writing one
could almost think that he was a Spaniard. In a play by Diego Jiméne
de Enciso entitled *The Famous Drama of Juan Latino*,[6] Latino tells the
duke who brought him up:

> Your excellency reared me with such love
> That if my mother were not black, I'd think
> My father him who holds me as his slave. (p. 109)

In this way Latino is similar to the West Indian Francis Williams, who
two centuries later also wrote panegyrics in Latin and who, according
to a contemporary, thought of himself as "a white man acting under
black skin."[7]

The youngest son of two freed slaves, Francis Williams was born in
Jamaica about 1700; he lived to the age of seventy. In the great humanitarian era of the eighteenth century, there was a great deal of Christian

speculation about whether Blacks were human or not. In an attempt to prove that Blacks could be educated, the Duke of Montagu instituted an experiment whereby Williams was sent to England to attend grammar school and the University of Cambridge where he read mathematics. Williams returned to Jamaica and set up a school in Spanish Town, where he taught reading, writing, Latin, and mathematics.[8]

It is said that during his stay in England he composed a ballad, but it was not until his return to Jamaica that he wrote a great deal of Latin poetry, mostly to successive governors. He was obviously known, but suspect; according to David Hume, "In Jamaica, indeed, they talk of one negroe as a man of parts and learning but 'tis likely he is admired for very slender accomplishments, like a parrot who speaks a few words plainly." Only one of Williams's poems survives; it is an ode to George Haldane, a governor of Jamaica. Edward Long has preserved it in his *History of Jamaica* even though he felt it was much too derivative to deserve serious attention. However, the Abbé Grégoire, who wrote in 1808, disagreed.[9] Nevertheless, Long's opinion is partly true, although the poem does manage to operate successfully within the framework of an ode and it expresses a refreshing pastoralism, a certain amount of religious exhortation, something of the dirge, and an affinity with what Williams called "a land where the sun scatters his fiery rays." The opening lines of the poem show some of these qualities:

> Finally as destiny rolls round the year that is to come
> All things are to be seen rejoicing the livelong day
> Driving away their cares the happy folk attend
> And beneath the bright image the earth grows green.
> Under your leadership acts committed with ill intent
> Are annulled, and will not return beneath your gaze.
> Therefore the entire people, even the humble folk, will see
> That you have removed the yoke which could have clung about
>   their neck.
> And the evils, which in the dread tortures of former days
> The innocent island suffered; they would have bewailed
>   their burden
> Had not your hand, already made famous in war and victory,
> Been willing of your own free will, to come to rescue us from our
>   desperate position.
> You are the best of servants to serve a British king,
> Since Scotland rejoices in your genius.
> The best of heroes to repair the ruin of the people.
> Whilst the island survives, you will survive.
> Guadeloupe will recognise you as conqueror
> And will look down on the camp of her leaders,
>   justly destroyed

74

The golden Iris will weep, her standards scattered,
And along with her people, the conquered will bewail the
   conquered town.
Believe me, it is not my task to sing the praises of war . . .[10]

Like Juan Latino, Francis Williams knew that, despite his fierce identification with the conqueror, he was an outsider, that, in his words, "Minerva denies to an Ethiopian to sing of the wars of chieftains." But they both felt compelled to write because at the basis of all art is tension, and their lives were ones of tension; for although they shared the piety, the glories, and the failures of their ages, they were never dominated by these since they were aliens. But glimpses of their inner vision enable one to view them today as worthy pioneers of African literature.

Chapter 6

Three Eighteenth-Century African Writers in English

Francis Williams had only gone to England to study, but in the eighteenth century Blacks who were permanently settled there were not unusual; indeed there were so many of them who had come up from West Africa by way of the West Indies that they were given the name of "St. Giles blackbirds," since they congregated around St. Giles Circus in London.[1] Most of them were simply chattels employed in the households of prominent people; three managed to overcome this status and wrote and published during their lifetimes.

K. Little in his *Negroes in Britain* quotes a letter that the Duchess of Devonshire sent to her mother in which she referred to her new servant as "a Cheap Servant" whom she would make into "a Christian . . . and a good boy." This attitude, partly a mixture of ideological paternalism and domestic necessity, was the basis of what was called humanitarianism. As N. V. McCullough has remarked, "In turning to the eighteenth century we discover that one of the broader aspects of the thought of this period was that of humanitarianism. In a sense it was merely one of the aspects of the romanticism of the period; and its over-all aim was to make the best of all possible worlds in which to live."[2] This accounts in large measure for the eighteenth-century view of Africans as being partly savage and partly noble. The Blacks who will be considered here saw themselves in precisely the same way.

Among the better known servants who lived during this period were Soubise and Francis Barber. Soubise had a high opinion of his charms and "fancying he was admired by the ladies, he boasted much of his amours and his epistolary correspondence." Soubise's employer intended to send him to a university but the youth apparently proved to be too arrogant, and his master changed his mind. Soubise then went to India to teach fencing and there he died. He was a correspondent of one of the eighteenth-century writers, as will be shown further on. Francis Barber came to England in 1750 and was Samuel Johnson's servant. Dr. Johnson sent him to school and taught him Latin; in a letter dated September 25, 1770, he wrote to Francis: "I am very well satisfied with your progress, if you can really perform the exercises which you are set . . . Let me know what English books you read for your entertainment. You can never be wise unless you love reading."[3]

The more liberal at the time would have liked to believe that the Black man, if given the chance, could become a cultured man. There were a few who believed that he was even capable of writing; some, however, doubted this and around Francis Williams, as has been observed, a lively controversy developed. It is against this eighteenth-century background that the literary contributions of Ignatius Sancho, Ottobah Cugoano, and Ouladah Equiano can best be understood. They were all West Africans who had been enslaved and shipped to the West Indies; only as servants did they manage to get to England. That they survived is a testament to their fortitude. That they could write at all demonstrated considerable ability and, as Vernon Coggins has said, they "proved [themselves to] their sponsors."[4]

Sancho (1729–80) was the first Black to publish a work in England in the eighteenth century. His *Letters*, edited by Joseph Jekyll, was published in London in 1782, two years after Sancho had died there.[5] The letters were collected by a Miss Crewe, whose introduction to the published volume gives some information about Sancho's life. He was born on a slave ship going to the Spanish West Indies; his mother died and his father committed suicide on the journey. He was baptized at Cartagena and given the name Ignatius, Sancho being added when he became an adult. At the age of two he was taken to England where he became a servant of two sisters. The Duke of Montagu liked him and used to give him books; when the duke died, Sancho was employed as a butler in the duchess's household where he remained until her death. She left him an annuity and for some time he lived an extravagant life. When the annuity was gone, Sancho returned to Montagu House and worked for the chaplain until illness forced him to retire in 1773. He then married and started a small grocery store in Westminster. After his death one of his six children carried on the business and edited the fifth edition of his letters in 1803.

Sancho was well known in polite and literary circles, and, as can be seen from his correspondence, he was an acquaintance of Garrick's; he also wrote to, and admired, Sterne. From his letters one can glimpse the personality of the man—his sense of humor, his love for his wife, his concern with the predicament of his fellow Africans. One sees too something of his raw love of life and his conceit.

The "advertisement" for the *Letters* mentioned that the reasons for publishing the work were "the desire of showing that an untutored African may possess abilities equal to a European; and the still superior motive of wishing to serve his worthy family" (p. iii). The highmindedness of these reflections, however, is not followed up, for the editor displays the typical ambiguity toward Blacks when he explains Sancho's life of dissipation after receiving the duchess's annuity by saying, "Freedom, riches and leisure naturally led a disposition of African texture into indulgence" (p. viii). Such a statement exemplifies the vacillating attitude prevalent toward Blacks in the eighteenth century.

From February 14, 1768, until December 7, 1780, just seven days before his death, Sancho wrote 157 private letters as well as five to the press.[6] Though he knew of the intended publication of his letters, he was quite modest about it; writing to a Mr. E, he remarks, "As to the letters in question, you know Sir, they are not mine but the property of the parties they are addressed to—if you have had their permission and think that the simple effusions of a poor Negro's heart are worth mixing with better things, you have my free consent to do as you please with them" (p. 225). The Miss C who is mentioned in several letters is probably Miss Crewe, for in one of his letters he sends "respectful compliments to the good Mrs. C— and Miss C— (what a C—!)" (p. 171). Sancho was addicted to making obvious puns and "crew" would make sense in the context.

His correspondents were many and varied; among them were three different people referred to as Mr. S. From his letters it can be deduced that one was probably Soubise, another, a young man who went to India, was a relative of the Duke and Duchess of Queensberry, and the third was in all likelihood the publisher William Stevenson. Fifteen letters were written to Stevenson, who inherited Sancho's portrait from his daughter after his death.[7] Letters are also addressed to J. M., Jonathan Matchett, Stevenson's partner in his publishing firm, to Sterne, to a Miss L, who was his son's godmother, and to J. S., probably John Scott, a member of the Society of Friends and an acquaintance of the Montagus.

In spite of Sancho's apparent modesty, his letters do show signs of ability. Thomas Jefferson felt, however, that "upon the whole, though we admit him to the first place among those of his own colour who have presented themselves to the public judgment, yet when we compare him with the writers of the race among whom he lived and particularly with the epistolary class in which he has taken his own stand, we are compelled to enroll him at the bottom of the column."[8] Although Sancho was not an outstanding letter writer of his time, he was a good one. When one considers his humble origins, the way he managed to educate himself, and the difficulties he must have experienced in rearing a large family and running a grocery store, it is praiseworthy that he found time for his art.

Some of his love for learning is expressed in his letters; he sends books to his correspondents, advising them to read. In a letter to Miss L, a lady who lived in Tunbridge (his child was named Lydia after her), he mentions that he was reading Bossuet's *Universal History* (p. 31). In another letter he enclosed Pope Ganganellius's *Letters* to a Mr. I asking him to read it and pointing out that he had underlined particular passages (p. 175). The editor of his letters notes that a certain letter was written after Sancho had read Voltaire (p. 99). Several of the letters are prefixed by quotations—from Shakespeare, Dryden, Sterne, Pope, and Addison—but he is cautious not to parade his learning and "strut like the fabled bird in his borrowed plumage" (p. 39).

Just as Sancho informed people about what to read, so he offered them moral counsel as well; his letters abound with moral exhortations. A Mr. J. W. is advised to "read your Bible—as day follows night, God's blessing follows virtue" (p. 187). And to Soubise he says, "The more you study the word of God, your peace and happiness will increase more with it" (p. 220). He did not feel, however, that Christianity had rescued him from barbarism; he adopted one of the more palatable eighteenth-century views about the noble savage and in a letter to a young man who was disappointed in India and the Indians he wrote, "In some of your letters, which I do not recollect, you speak (with honest indignation) of the treachery and chicanery of the natives—My good friend, you should remember from whom they learnt those vices; the first Christian visitors found them a simple harmless people" (p. 188). At times he could be strongly censorious of the English "pagans" among whom he had found himself, and he complained about the ways in which the Sabbath was spent: the trader went on excursions, the poorer people got drunk, the upper classes drank whisky and gambled, and their servants indulged in debauchery (pp. 338–39).

Not all the letters strike these public postures. Some are simply personal accounts of his family life—his wife's pregnancies, illness in the family—while others express thanks for gifts received. It is in these letters that his sense of humor sometimes emerges, even in spite of his obvious worry. For instance when he contracted gout, he wrote, "I assure you that of my pair of feet—two are at this instant in pain" (p. 72), and when his daughter Lydia was ill, he wrote somewhat cynically that he was glad they were a poor family, for "had he been rich, the doctors would have had the honour of killing her a twelve month ago" (p. 77). Nor was he so pious, as some of the letters might make one believe, that he was always solemn about religion; in one letter he describes a young, flashy parson who preached so well that he "has many converts among the ladies" (p. 32).

Sancho's care with language is evident in many of his letters. He abhored what he called "a see-saw of dialogue" (p. 178), and he could achieve the right tone in any letter—condolence, joy, mischievous teasing. He was simultaneously always very much himself and the conscious craftsman; he once commented, "My pen, like a drunkard, sucks up more liquor than it can carry, and so disgorges it at random—I will that ye observe the above simile to be a good one" (p. 249). Some of his "wit" is forced but at times his writing displays a tenderness which makes up for the occasional bursts of showmanship. For example, in one letter he laments, "I am as melancholy as a tea-kettle when it sings (as the maidens call it) over a dead fire" (p. 141).

He was as passionate a royalist as he was a Christian; in a letter to Miss L he remarks, "I am pleased with the Tunbridgians for their respectful loyalty on his Royal Highness' birthday; it is too much the fashion to treat the royal family with disrespect" (p. 64). His political predispositions sprung from his genuine concern for his adopted country. At times his fierce identification with the English cause is amusing: "We fought like Englishmen" (p. 269), he writes in one letter and in another he describes a battle the English won "with little or no loss on our side" (p. 304). But on the whole he manages to identify himself without appearing too zealous. Some of his last letters vividly depict the Gordon Riots of June 1780.

In spite of his Englishness, Sancho never forgot that he was a Black man; he refers several times to the slave trade and to the plight of Africans. A letter to Sterne asked him to support the antislavery campaign for "that subject, handled in your striking manner would ease the yoke (perhaps) of many" (p. 90). Writing to Miss Crewe he expressed the hope that "this cursed carnage of the human species may end" (p. 149), and he condemned the "most diabolical usage of my brother Negroes" (p. 125). But never does Sancho allow such feelings to dominate his letters, and often he was very detached and off-handed about color, as can be seen in a letter of recommendation he wrote for a fellow Black: He is "a merry, chirping, white-toothed, clean, tight and light, little fellow! with a wooly pate—and face as dark as your humble; Guiney-born, and French bred—the sulky gloom of Africa dispelled by Gallic vivacity" (p. 65). He adds that "I like the rogue's looks, or a similarity of colour should not have induced me to recommend him" (p. 66).

Certain letters consciously imitate Sterne, who seemed to have had considerable influence on Sancho: "Zooks! why do you forget to say your prayers—to take your physick—to wash your—Pray how does Mrs. H? . . . And when saw you Nancy?—Has the cat kittened?—I suppose you have heard the news:—great news!—a glorious affair! (and is two ff's necessary?)—O! Lord, Sir!—" (p. 292). Such an attempt to imitate does not succeed in the previous example, or in the one that follows: "Zounds alive—what ails you? if dead—why did you not send me word?—Where's my Tristram?—What are all the bucks alike?—all promise and no—but I won't put myself in a passion" (p. 100). A reviewer in the *Monthly Review* of December 1783 criticized this aspect of his style, saying that "it bears in general some resemblance to that of his admired Sterne—with its breaks—and dashes—which, by the way, are in this wild indiscriminate use of them, an abomination to all accurate writers . . ."[9]

Despite Sancho's inability to copy Sterne, it can be concluded that when he wrote about his family and what was closest to him, when he was most completely himself, his letters "breathe the purest effusions of friendship and general philanthropy."[10] Long after the events about which he wrote have ceased to matter, his letters still remain interesting for their simplicity and quiet charm.

Besides his letters, Sancho also wrote verse, music, and two pieces for the theater; some of his poetry was published in 1803.[11] But little of this survives, although Sancho does mention his verse in his letters. It is possible that his letters were the best of his compositions.

Ottobah Cugoano (b. 1748) was less an artist but a greater propagandist than Sancho. His *Thoughts and Sentiments on the Evil and Wicked Traffic of the Slavery and Commerce of the Human Species, Humbly Submitted to the Inhabitants of Great Britain* was published in London in 1787. The book, part autobiography and part propaganda, recounts the story of how he was captured and sold into slavery and how he made his way to England. However, the work is mainly an attack on the slave trade, with Cugoano attempting to demonstrate from biblical passages that slavery is incompatible with religious laws.

In his autobiographical account, Cugoano describes how he and some other children were captured by several men when they were out playing. After being imprisoned for three days, they are sent to the slave ship. On the ship a plot is hatched to blow it up, but it is discovered and thus the slaves have to subject themselves to the terrors of the journey. Cugoano says he would not give any details regarding the "middle passage," because he feels that "the familiar cases of thousands which suffer by this informal traffic are well known" (p. 10).[12] However, he does mention that "I saw many of my miserable countrymen chained two and two, some hand-cuffed, and some with their hands tied behind" (p. 9). (One wonders, though, to what extent he was dependent on other sources for such information, for he was only two years old when he was taken into slavery.) But Cugoano was more fortunate than his fellow slaves; he became the personal servant of an Englishman who took him to England where he applied himself "to learn reading and writing, which soon became my recreation, pleasure and delight" (p. 12). With this Cugoano ends his personal account and begins his attack on slavery, which concludes with a suggestion of how Britain and Africa could be united in friendship.

Although Cugoano's attack on slavery is not as interesting or as convincing as his life story, its salient points should at least be mentioned. Cugoano anticipates some of the arguments that he was going to take up by interrupting his personal account to compare the treatment of slaves in Africa with that of those captured by the English. He tries to counter the contention that the Africans themselves sold their families into slavery by saying that "nothing would be more opposite to everything they hold dear and valuable" (p. 27).

This argument is taken up again in the second part, which begins with the assertion that since all the races of the earth originate from God, there can be no inferior race. The mark of Cain and the belief that Africans were the progeny of Cain are discussed in great detail; and Cugoano refutes this belief by maintaining that all Cain's descendants were destroyed in the flood. He adds that even though slavery was an ancient custom, this does not necessarily make it right. He also mentions that Christianity advocated certain duties toward fellow-humans, but he is quick to enunciate that this same religion was used to dupe innocent natives.

Cugoano then attempts to analyze the disadvantages of slavery for Great Britain. He points out that the national debt is a direct consequence of slavery and offers three suggestions for improving Britain's economy—religious dedication, the abolition of the slave trade, and a fleet of ships to enforce it. These proposals, Cugoano feels, would effectuate a fruitful alliance between Africa and Britain—Britain could help Africa improve its land and in return Africa could give manpower for industries and defense. They would also lead the way toward a rebuilding of Britain.

As has been mentioned, Cugoano's method of denouncing the slave trade frequently bears the heavy sententiousness of biblical exhortations. For example, he writes, "It is surely to the great shame and scandal of Christianity among all the Heathen nations that those robbers, plunderers, destroyers and enslavers of men should call themselves Christians, and exercise their power under any Christian government and authority. I would have my countrymen understand that the destroyers and enslavers of men can be no Christians; for Christianity is the system of benignity and love, and all its votaries are devoted to honesty, justice, humanity, meekness, peace and goodness to all men" (p. 84). This style of writing often causes him to attitudinize and in his description of his misery at being captured he combines a personal predicament and the agony associated with the captured slave in the literature of his day: "All my help was cries and tears and these could not avail; nor suffered long till one succeeding woe and dread swallowed up another. Brought from a state of innocence and freedom, and in a barbarous and cruel manner, conveyed to a state of horror and slavery. This abandoned situation may be easier conceived than described" (p. 101).

Sancho had written about the "horrid cruelty and treachery of the petty kings" (p. 3), and Cugoano makes the same point when he says, "Though the common people are free, they often suffer by the villainy of their different chieftains and by the wars and feuds which happen among them" (p. 28). But, unlike Sancho, Cugoano seems to strike an anti-European pose; this may be a result of his tendency to attitudinize. For example, he advances this theory about the origins of the English: "Many of the Canaanites who fled away in the time of Joshua, became mingled with the different nations, and some historians think some of them came to England as far back as that time" (p. 35). Occasionally, however, Cugoano does achieve something of the private warmth of Sancho, as in his description of his capture while out hunting birds and of the confusion that followed. The language here, though biblical in tone, succeeds in expressing the bewilderment of a child: "Next morning there came three other men, whose language differed from ours, and spoke to some of those who watched us all the night, but he that pretended to be our friend with the great man, and some others, were gone away" (p. 7).

Cugoano's style throughout varies so drastically between his "experienced accounts" and his exhortations against the slave trade that one can maintain that the simpler, more convincing accounts are probably his, while the diatribes against slavery are probably the work of some well-intentioned hack. If the second part of the book is his own, then one should conclude that it is heavily dependent on secondary material. Cugoano does mention Ramsay's "Essay on the Treatment and Conversion of the African Slaves in the British Sugar Colonies," Clarkson's "Essay on the Slavery and Commerce of Human Species," and *The Historical Account of Guinea*.[13] Moreover, Cugoano frequently refers to and quotes from the Bible, and much of his imagery owes its origin to the Bible. In fact Cugoano himself admits that his account is only partly drawn from his own direct experiences: "What I intend to advance against the evil, criminal and wicked traffic of enslaving men are only some thoughts and sentiments which occur to me, as being obvious from the scriptures of divine truth, or such arguments as are chiefly deduced from thence, with other such observations as I have been able to collect" (p. 3).[14]

Equiano (b. 1745), on the other hand, draws more from his own recollected experiences. This was in itself an achievement, for most of the antislavery, as well as the proslavery, propaganda of the period was written by Englishmen, as was the imaginative literature of the antislavery campaign. Thomas Day's "Dying Negro" is a good example of this; the dying Negro passionately proclaims:

> And thou, whose impious avarice and pride
> Thy God's blest symbol to my brows deny'd,
> Forbad me or the rights or man to claim
> Or share with thee a Christian's hallowed name,
> Thou, too, farewell! for not beyond the grave,
> Thy power extends, nor is my dust thy slave.[15]

As has been seen, Cugoano's writing also sentimentalized the Black man's predicament; Equiano was the greater craftsman who sought to get away from this and still retain popularity.

Equiano's *Interesting Narrative of the Life of Ouladah Equiano or Gustavus Vassa, the African*, published in 1789 in London, was a very popular book though Equiano too tended to romanticize the Black man. At least two editions were printed in England in 1787; a third edition appeared four years later, and by 1794 it had run through eight English editions and one American. It was reprinted in 1814 and as late as

1969.[16] The reasons for its popularity were twofold: it made an important contribution to the campaign against slavery, and it had significance both as a documentation of factual experiences and as a worthwhile literary endeavor. Its literary quality still makes it readable today, even though the conditions which it opposed have long ceased to exist.

In *The Narrative*, Equiano traces his life back to the peaceful days of his childhood. He says he was born in "a charming fruitful vale named Essaka" (p. 5),[17] where his father was a chief. Probably of Nigerian origin, he was kidnapped and sold into slavery when he was only twelve, after which he was taken to the West Indies and later to America. He worked for a sea captain from whom he bought his freedom in 1766, but he continued working on merchant ships for the next eleven years. He led quite an adventurous life, and on an expedition to find a Northeast passage to India, he was stranded in the Arctic circle. At another time he narrowly escaped death in the Bahamas. But he eventually settled down in London, where, according to the *Gentleman's Magazine* of April 1792, he married a Miss Cullen, an Englishwoman. He remarks that he even contemplated becoming a minister of the Church of England and returning to West Africa, but the Bishop of London refused, in Equiano's half-whimsical words, "from certain scruples of delicacy" (p. 222). In 1787 he was appointed by the government as a "commissary of Provisions and Stores for the Black Poor Going to Sierra Leone"—a testimony to his worth as a citizen.

Equiano's experience as a slave made him acutely aware of human suffering. Thinking back on how he became separated from his sister during their captivity he comments, "Yes thou partner of all childish sports, Thou sharer of my joys and sorrows, Happy should I have ever esteemed myself to encounter every misery for you, and to procure your freedom by the sacrifice of my own" (p. 61). But his was an unselfish, a-racial compassion. When he recalls the horrors of the "middle passage," he remembers not only the agony of the slaves, but also the death of a white sailor who "was flogged so unmercifully with a large rope near the foremast, that he died in consequence of it; and they tossed him over the side as they would have done a brute" (p. 75). It is this very compassion that enables him, in spite of his later becoming a Christian, to look back on the Africa of his childhood with relish and longing. With assurance he tells his readers, "Let the polished and haughty European recollect that his ancestors were once, like the Africans, uncivilized and even barbarous" (p. 43).

Equiano's account of his boyhood in Africa possesses the liberating imaginativeness of creative literature as well as the crispness of an authentic document. He writes objectively about his own language, religion, social customs, and legends, but his descriptions are enlivened with wit, pathos, and an easy charm. For instance, when on the slave ship he first sees white people, he is perplexed. His realistic telling of this perplexity is followed by a humorous observation: "I was now persuaded that I had gotten into a world of bad spirits, and that they were going to kill me. Their complexions, too, differing so much from ours, their long hair and the language they spoke (which was different from any I had ever heard) united to confirm me in this belief . . . I asked them [his slave companions] if we were not to be eaten by those white men with horrible looks, red faces and long hair. They told me I was not" (pp. 70–71). Equiano's sense of humor was occasionally directed even at himself; in his master's house in Virginia he sees a watch for the first time and makes fun of his own gullibility: "I was quite surprised at the noise it made and was afraid it would tell the gentleman anything I might do amiss" (p. 92).

But his humor is not pervasive; frequently there are also flashes of pathos, as seen when he relates the story of how he was lost in a forest when trying to escape from his captors: "I heard frequent rustlings among the leaves; and being pretty sure they were snakes, I expected every instant to be stung by them—This increased my anguish and the horror of the situation became now quite unsupportable. I at length quitted the thicket, very faint and hungry, for I had not eaten or drunk anything all the day; and crept to my master's kitchen from whence I set out at first and laid myself down in the ashes with an anxious wish for death to relieve me from all my pains" (pp. 56–57). Here the language conveys the stark realistic terror of his predicament and also that extra dimension of personal feeling inherent in all successful art.

Equiano certainly suffered from no false modesty. Frequently he can be irritatingly patronizing. For instance, he describes the Turks as "well looking and strong made" (vol. 2, p. 89), much as one might describe a favorite mastiff. On a visit to the Isle of Wight he graciously referred to the inhabitants as "very civil" (p. 152). He had no small opinion of his appearance and commented on how well he looked in his "Georgia superfine blue clothes" (vol. 2, p. 19) after he had bought his freedom. When his ship was almost wrecked near the Bahamas, he complained that many of the white sailors did nothing to assist and therefore the responsibility of saving the crew fell to him. He adds, "I could not help but look on myself as the principal instrument in effecting our deliverance" (vol. 2, p. 47). Indeed he knew full well that he rather fancied himself and after relating how he had successfully sailed a ship from

Georgia to Antigua when the captain died, he asserts that everybody addressed him as Captain and admits, "This elated me not a little, and it was quite flattering to my vanity to be thus styled" (vol. 2, p. 35).

Despite such egotism, Equiano was above all else a devoted African who loved and venerated his origins. Though an emancipationist, he praised the Ibos (his own tribe) for their "hardiness, intelligence, integrity and zeal" (p. 21). He also boasted that among his people deformity was almost unknown, and he maintained that West Indian planters preferred the Ibos as slaves over the other African groups. He blamed the European traders for many of the intertribal wars and pulls no punches when he directs his satire at the harsh brutality of eighteenth-century Europe; he says that by fifteen he had seen so much terror that he was "in that respect at least, almost an Englishman" (p. 132).

Equiano's *Narrative*, written with ease and dignity, displays a touching and humane tenderness. His religion never obtrudes, although he was in all probability a true believer. Perhaps it was his essential Christian kindliness that endeared him to John Wesley, who, on his deathbed, asked two friends to read aloud to him from Equiano's book.[18]

The account of Equiano's life must have been as widely read as Sancho's; it draws not only from the Bible, but also from historical books, travel books, antislavery literature, Christian commentaries, as well as from the popular Day's "Dying Negro." He was obviously so much a part of his century that he was capable of seeing himself as his contemporaries saw him—that is, in some way connected with the myth of the noble savage. But he was able to detach himself from this myth and expand into a mature individual, whose mind was emancipated and whose work became a public confession of his private tensions; this is its truest artistic relevance for us today.

To be properly understood, Equiano must not only be considered within the framework of humanitarianism and the myth of the noble savage—both essential to an understanding of the Black man in the eighteenth century—but also be compared with the two other West Africans who wrote and published in English in the eighteenth century. When Equiano is compared with them, it is realized that whereas Sancho had grace and charm, Cugoano vigor and didacticism, Equiano combined all those qualities. His book is more in keeping with what today would be regarded as imaginative writing. This is not to say that he was unrealistic or sought to transfer lived experiences into fiction; what is meant is that he possessed an abundance of human sympathy and his varied life offered him a broad canvas on which to portray his experiences. This prevented him from descending to the sententious moralizing of Cugoano and in large measure from being as unconcerned as Sancho was at times. Although Equiano had undergone a colonizing experience, he still remained conscious of the importance of his African origin and its significance for him as a man. It was this that enabled him to recollect the innocence of his childhood years, and it was this too that made him aware of what was worthwhile in his childhood. From this vantage point he was able to be part of his century, secure in his roots and his traditions, knowing that he had had the best of two possible worlds and had triumphed in both of them.

All three of these writers were to a great extent absorbed in eighteenth-century English society. This, paradoxically, helped to make them more completely themselves, for it was a century concerned with the great humanitarian fervor for emancipation. But because their society encouraged them to extend themselves in this public way—to proclaim their most private tensions—one must ask just how genuine their responses were to the matters of slavery and freedom, which, though close to them, nevertheless required certain kinds of stock responses. One must be wary of ascribing too much to their individual authorship; any knowing hack could have attempted to imitate them or indeed to recast or simply write whole passages. Therefore, one should be dubious of the authorship of Joseph Jekyll's edition of Sancho's letters two years after his death, the long antislavery diatribes in Cugoano's work, and some of the more overdone effusions of Equiano and Cugoano. But their heavy reliance on the Bible, their weighty sermonizing, and their care with the language indicate that their writing was in the main their own composition. They were expressing the contemporary liberal thoughts and attitudes of the Englishmen whom they had partly become. Therefore they managed to create an interesting genre which not only gave an embryo life of the artist, but also explored the writer's significance within a foreign culture. Because they were, in a very special way, privileged insiders who shared all the license but none of the prejudices of outsiders, their work is a valid commentary on the entire cycle of eighteenth-century inquiry and resolution.

Chapter 7

Written
Indigenous Literatures

The literature in the written vernacular languages of Africa provides an imaginative and essential link between unwritten indigenous literature and writing in European languages. It is true only in part that vernacular written literature is closely related to literary oral forms, for apart from translations the written vernacular literature has drawn from standard European writing as well as from the more "popular" European models like the "love" story and the "detective" story. But in a way this literature indicates the adaptability of the oral tradition in that through the written vernacular literature the oral tradition expresses its versatility and diversity.

In considering this literature, one must also mention the struggle that was going on (and, in some cases, is still going on) to establish standard orthographies. The difficulty facing writers cannot be overestimated; they were in the main transforming a category of experience which in oral literature was a *whole* to one which depended solely on visual elements (although to some extent they did exploit aural qualities). Therefore these writers not only had to acquire an education; they needed to dismantle the apparatus of reception—to reorganize their entire sensibility.

Most vernacular literature has been written by South Africans (and here one might include writing in Afrikaans) and in general by Africans who once lived in English-speaking areas. Little appears that is worthwhile in former French territories and still less in Portuguese territories. The reason for this is not far to seek; it is linked with the meaning of the colonizing process and what it sought to achieve. Although a vernacular literature was not particularly encouraged in former British territories (with the exception of South Africa where it was encouraged as an expression of *apartheid*), in French and Portuguese territories it was actively discouraged; competence in vernacular languages had little to do with one becoming an *évolué* or an *assimilado*.

There are approximately seven hundred African languages but only forty-nine have been used for written literary expression, and of these eighteen are southern African languages.[1] An examination of what has been written in Africa shows that 818 works by 481 authors can be classified as vernacular literature.

Christian Influence

Besides the oral sources, the Bible and Bunyan's *Pilgrim's Progress*, which were usually the earliest books translated into the vernacular languages and thus provided examples of writing, had the greatest influence on indigenous literature. According to one missionary secretary in Bechuanaland, Rhodesia, and Zambia between 1930 and 1931, "The books that are in greatest demand are Bibles, hymn-books and catechisms. They are regarded by the people as so clearly a part of the necessary apparatus of a Christian that they purchase them without demur. *The Pilgrim's Progress* enjoys a steady sale in almost every African vernacular into which it has been translated, and in some renderings it is a most entertaining book."[2]

It might now be considered unfortunate that Africans were introduced to written European literature through Christian propaganda, but it is a historical fact, and if it had not taken place vernacular literature would have taken far longer to emerge.

Religious leaflets, ethnographical accounts, history and geography books, written translations of the oral literature (suitably expurgated) intended for schools and in some cases the general public were the main publications of these missionary bodies. It would be unrealistic to castigate the missionary presses because their "literature" was closely geared to their evangelizing. Their efforts tended to channelize the literature into a single outlook but it could not be otherwise; one should at least be grateful that because of this many people either were encouraged to write within these limitations or managed to go beyond them.

The earliest mission presses on the continent were established in southern Africa. One begun in 1823 at a mission station in Lovedale published in Xhosa; the Marianhill Mission Press printed books in Zulu;

and the Sesuto Book Depot in Morija, Basutoland, was concerned with publications in Sotho. Within the last twenty years literary bureaus have been formed in East and Central Africa; in addition to publishing the type of educational and religious books already mentioned, they have introduced a whole host of "popular" literature. As early as the nineteenth century, some of these indigenous publishing houses published newspapers,[3] and there have been translations of Shakespeare.

When discussing vernacular literature it is necessary to see it in the context of its origin and of its function as a utilitarian message calculated to advance the Christian cause. But this was only in the beginning; the literature did not remain embedded in this single purpose. David Nicol has commented that the first literatures in Mende, Twi, and Yoruba had "heavy Biblical overtones (because of their missionary script origin) but some [became] increasingly modernized for journalistic and Adult Education purposes."[4] This process of change is noticeable throughout Africa; beginning as didactic sermonizing in which (as in oral literature) the individual is inarticulate, the literature developed to such an extent that many vernacular works can stand qualitatively side by side with any of the writings in European languages. It is the emergence of the individual voice that is noticed, if only because it required a certain amount of individuality to opt out of the norms of the tribe, to indulge in the superstitions of the Christian strangers. A survey of the literature of West, Central, East, and southern Africa will reveal these qualities that have been mentioned.

Western Africa

The examination of the vernacular literature in western Africa must attempt to reconstruct the adventure of history. This history is closely linked to slavery, Christianity, the setting up of schools and presses. Freetown had been established in 1787 as a place for resettling slaves captured on the high seas. Schools were built and from there the missionary interest in education spread to Gambia (1826), Ghana (1841), and Nigeria (about 1842). The missionary societies had been founded toward the end of the eighteenth century in response to the spate of protest literature throughout the century highlighting the plight of the Black man.[5]

In western Africa 111 authors have written approximately 166 works. There has been no central publishing agency as in eastern and southern Africa and subsequently the literature for the most part has been privately published. The major languages represented in the literature are

91

Twi, Yoruba, Hausa, Ewe, and Ga. Following is a brief survey of the highlights of this literature.

Yoruba Literature: Prostitutes and Hunters

The first translations into Yoruba were undertaken soon after the arrival of the missionaries. By 1850 the Bible, prayer books, a hymn book, and church liturgy had been rendered into Yoruba. By 1859 the first Yoruba newspaper had been started in Abeokuba, but seventy years elapsed before the appearance of the first extended attempt at imaginative writing—"The Autobiography of Segilola: The Lady with the Delicate Eye-Balls," which was serialized in *Akede-Eko* (Lagos Herald) between July 1929 and March 1930.[6] The work can probably be attributed to the editor of the newspaper, Isaac Thomas, who hoped that his readers would learn much from the prostitute's life story. It was written in an epistolary style—in all, thirty letters to the editor. Segilola's autobiography also offers some information about Lagos in the twenties; from it we learn that the popular music was "gumbe" and "pandero" and the leading drummer was Adelakun (p. 12). Frequently she relates some of the songs of the day to herself:

> When a woman goes stale
> She suffers alone

That was a popular tune to which we used to dance in Lagos with thousands of men; now I am left alone to it (p. 8).

Thomas's use of true information about Lagos and his device of pretending that Segilola was an actual person help to bring over the realism of the account. By the fifteenth letter people had begun to send in donations which the editor promised to deliver personally to Segilola.

The story of Segilola, in spite of its apparent ribaldry, was within two traditions—the gloomy moralism of missionary exhortations and the ethical emancipation of the tales. To some extent this accounts for the blend of solemn didacticism and hilarious comedy. The fantasy that was to dominate Yoruba writing is absent here; Segilola is an intentional foil to Tortoise, because she exhibits the certainty of retribution. It took another generation before Ekwenski could create in Jagua Nana a prostitute who was responsible to no code of convention outside herself.

D. O. Fagunwa, the next great Yoruba writer, sought a return to the hero-quest stories. He borrowed freely from Yoruba tales, translating and altering them, but he also invented much that was original. As Beier has pointed out, the evangelizing intention is uppermost in Fagunwa's works; he is a Christian writer who "loses no opportunity to moralise and improve his reader."[7] His first novel, published in 1938, was *Ogboju ode ninu igbo irunmale* (The Brave Hunter in the Forest of the Four Hundred Gods). Akara-Ogun, the son of a witch and a well-known hunter, encounters a number of adventures, including a frightening meeting with Agbako who beats him in wrestling, as he journeys through a forbidden jungle. He finally makes his way to a town where he kills a one-eyed leopard which has been destroying people and where he warns the chief that some of his subjects are planning to kill him. In another adventure Akara-Ogun sets out with companions to discover peace and prosperity. With his few brave followers he kills a monster, fights a ghost, and defeats Wereorun, a madman from the land of dead people. At the end of the novel they spend seven days with the chief who tells them a story each night to illustrate the theme of peace and prosperity.[8] Fagunwa wrote two other novels as sequels to *Ogboju*, but the first of these was not published until 1949.

Thus in *Igbo Olodumare* (The Forests of Olodumare), Olowo-Aiye, the father of the hero of the previous novel, also travels in forbidden forests. First he overcomes a spirit, marries a witch, and kills the gatekeeper at the entrance to the forests. In the forest he is feasted by the king and is about to leave with his new bride when, missing his way, he once more embarks on another series of adventures which last three years. Finally, he manages to escape. *Irinkerindo nimu Igbo Elégbèje* (Adventures in the Forest of Elégbèje), a novel in eleven parts, is also narrated by a hunter, Irinkerindo, who describes his adventures while traveling in a forest. The beginning of the journey takes him to the Mountain of Thought; from there he goes to a town where the "twice-foolish" is king and where the "thrice-foolish" succeeds to the throne. In the forest he meets the familiar spirits, including Elegbara who sets the forest on fire. But again the hunter escapes, this time by crossing a stream.

These novels cover the realm from fantasy to realism, from wooden-faced sermonizing to hearty humor, and this is also true of *Ìrèké Oníbùdó* although in no other way is it similar to any of the three adventure stories. In this novel Ireke Onibudo wants to be a trader but is kidnapped by a ghost. He is taken to a town where the chief's daughter Ifepade has to be sacrificed to a snake which is molesting the inhabitants. He kills the snake and wins Ifepade. But the chief's jealous wives falsely accuse Ireke Onibudo of visiting them at night and thus he is banished from the town. At first Ifepade believes the story but later she finds out the truth and goes in search of Ireke. In a touching climax they are united and receive her father's good wishes.

In this novel, Fagunwa deals less with the fanciful and more with real people and situations. This tendency is further apparent in *Igbo Olodumare*. For example, the manner in which the witch is portrayed is an accurate and perceptive description of human nature in a particular situation. The son who tells the story explains that as the hunter (his father) journeyed through the forest he was "surprised to find such sophisticated women in such a remote forest, and he turned back in wonder to look at them. At exactly the same moment, the smaller woman was also looking back, and when they saw each other, they laughed. But they continued on their separate ways. When my father looked back a second time, his eyes met again with those of the woman. But he forced himself to continue on his way—even though he had no wife at the time. But when my father looked back the third time, the woman was again looking at him, and she was laughing and her teeth were shining like a whitewashed wall. Then Olowo Aiye turned round; he turned his back on the Forest of the Almighty and he walked towards the women."[9]

Fagunwa's attempts at realistic portrayal served as a model for Chief Isaac Delano (as well as Amos Tutuola), and because of this Delano was more objective, more detached, and less a novelist than Fagunwa. In his *Aiye d' aiye oyinbo* (The World Belongs to the Europeans), Delano contrasts the traditional African way of life with that which replaced it after the coming of the Europeans. Polygamy, the system of pawning individuals, slavery, and local government are all treated sociologically. The novel, written in 1955, points to the possible development of creative writing in Yoruba. Despite Fagunwa's excursions into fantasy, it must not be forgotten that he was, above all else, attempting to present a religious view of the world. His son, writing about him soon after his death in 1963, remarked, "His rationale was simple. Firstly a recognition of the profundity of the universe and thence on to the conclusion that 'He must be.' But there he stopped his questions. Queries concerning how God came to be, or how He came about His powers . . . were to be left in abeyance for they were beyond human comprehension."[10] Some of this emerges in Fagunwa's fifth and last book, *Àdììtu Olódùmarè* (Olodumare's Secret), which is an extended parable. In it the hero has spiritual experiences as distinct from the merely fantastic; he dreams of heaven being a mixture of the ridiculous and the materialistic. Since Olodumare has risen from humble beginnings to become the richest man in town, Fagunwa makes him question the very nature of his existence.

There is no similar interrogation in the poetry of Adeboye Babalola,

94

but rather an acceptance of the world as it is. None of his verse in the original has appeared in book form, but translations of his poems have been broadcast by the British Broadcasting Corporation (BBC) and published in an anthology of West African verse edited by Olumbe Bassir. The poems were written in the forties and in Babalola's own words are based on "the oral poetry that I used to hear recited by farmers . . . they are in the same cycle of oral poetry called *ijala* in Yoruba and deal with certain aspects of country life of farmers and hunters."[11] To some extent therefore his work is so close to oral traditional poetry that it can be considered almost identical to it; nevertheless, unlike oral verse, Babalola's poetry is more the expression of an individual. For although a great deal of his verse is derived from the oral tradition, it also represents Babalola's own experiments. In a poem, "When I First Heard of Forest Farms," he says,

> I wish I could depart at once for such
> A virgin forest-land, where I may have
> Big game to kill whene'er my fancy bids.
> I'm sick of all the farms I have near home.[12]

It is the familiar rustic yearning, but here it is effete and does not ring quite true. Such pastoralism obviously originates from the poetry of Yoruba hunters, but other characteristics of Babalola's poetry do not derive from this tradition. For instance, the device of isolating a character and making fun of him is more in keeping with masquerade verse:

> Ojo is his name, Ojo the Trouble-Lover.
> He loudly calls to trouble when it's passing by,
> Inviting him to come into his home and spend some time.[13]

Even more characteristic of Babalola's writing are his gentle, cautionary verses about good manners—"beauty's essence,"[14] as he calls it in one poem. In another:

> When you go into a house, you must first
> Call on the master of the place, a man
> Whose wives may total sevenscore and ten.
> To every hunter, great or small, I give
> Due honour and respect, impartially.
> Before I cross the threshold of a house,
> I shout, "All inmates here, please welcome me."
> And from the dog standing as a sentinel
> I crave excuse before I enter in.
> A man who goes into a town without
> Appearing to the porters at the rampart gate,
> Is but behaving like a dog; and hence,

When once some aged men did dare to pass
Into a town without first showing themselves
To those on duty at the gate, the king
Decreed their penalty. So, they were tied
Like goats to stakes within the market place.[15]

In translation the poem is rather stilted, but its sonorous sententiousness is in keeping with some of the oral verse, which, while not so flagrantly didactic, was nevertheless firmly affixed to ceremony.

Babalola's verse displays the moral rectitude of "Segilola," the humor and fantasy of Fagunwa, and some of Delano's realism. In addition there is a sober quality of thought very much his own. Consequently, although he calls his verses "my English versions of extracts from the oral poetry,"[16] they possess enough of the individual voice to set them apart. They are not mere reproductions but re-creations in the manner of Fagunwa.

Hausa Literature: Islam and Quest

In the latter part of the eighth century, Arab ideas and culture began to penetrate into Africa, following the trade routes from the Mediterranean across the Sahara. By the twelfth century Arabic was stabilized as a language and was actually written in West Africa; not until the second half of the fourteenth century, however, was it established in Hausaland. Although learned works on government and religion were soon being written in Arabic, creative literature in the Arabic script by Hausas did not appear until the seventeenth century. One of the first poems written in this period was an ode by Dan Marina of Katsina (d. c. 1655), commemorating the victory of Mai Ali, a ruler of Bornu, over the Jukuns. In the eighteenth century Muhammad b Muhammad (d. 1741) composed, besides learned works, a poem on logic, and Tahir b Ibrahim wrote satirical verse on the Kanuri.[17] The poetry of Shehu Usman Dan Fodio spearheaded the Jihad, a religious reform movement in the nineteenth century. His verse (some of which is in Hausa) exhibits the religious devotion and humility which were to characterize later Hausa verse:

I am pleased to thank Allah
For giving me the opportunity to praise His generosity.
I am introducing myself to our Prophet.
You should know that I know many of his qualities;
I will surely mention them in thanking Allah
For Muslims to know them in the East and West.[18]

96

In like manner, an anonymous Moslem who wrote toward the end of the nineteenth century composed a long poem in praise of Allah, overtly didactic and varying in tone between resolution and penitence. There is an alarming note of the obituary in some of the lines:

> Were it for this world, which is coming to an end, I would not pray.
> Why should we feel glad at a long continuance (in this world?)
> I have no object to desire here.
> You my brethren, abandon the business of this world,
> Whoever follows after the business of this world serves not Allah . . .
> Look carefully, behold this earth, it is deceitful,
> It will not continue for ever.
> It is a house in which there is no relaxation or rest;
> There is no health in it, nothing but sickness.[19]

The idea expressed here is somewhat foreign to the African tradition; the denial of the everyday world is obviously a concept more in keeping with Islam and the Arabian world than with sub-Saharan Africa. It shows that the Arabic influence was still very pronounced even though people began to compose in Hausa in the later nineteenth and early twentieth centuries.

In modern Hausa poetry one finds the popularizing of secular themes which are nearer to African oral literature. Aliyu Mangi has written eight books of verse which derive certain qualities from the praise poem; Saadu Zungur has contributed to the literature a poem about the Burma war and another about what form of government northern Nigeria ought to have; Mu'azu Hadeja's "Wakar Karuwa" is a witty, moral song about a prostitute; even boxing has been mentioned in Hausa verse: Salihu Kwantagora composed an ode to Hoggan Bassey when he won the world featherweight title.[20]

Many Hausa prose texts, such as the Kano and Katsina chronicles and the more recent Abuja Chronicle (now translated into English),[21] unfortunately must be omitted in an examination of this nature. Although, strictly speaking, they are not history, their purpose is nevertheless historical, for they link ancient legend to what people remember. A similar chronicle, though more personal, is *Baba of Karo*, the life story of a Hausa woman.[22] But the book is not a novel; the story vacillates between accounts of social issues like wars, taxes, and slavery and descriptions of domestic upheavals like the jealousy of husbands (she was married four times), family quarrels, and so on.

Hausa creative prose developed more slowly than poetry. The reason is not difficult to comprehend since poetry was linked to the praise of Allah and prose was reserved for biography and chronicles. By 1936 only five books of imaginative writing had been produced.[23] Among them were *Gandoki* (1934) by Muhammadu Bello and *Rowan Bagaja* by Abubakar Bello. Muhammadu Bello's book shows affinities with the marvels of the tales as well as with the assurances of Islam:

On this journey [to Yola] the English saw signs and wonders, magic and strange happenings, in the Sarkin Soudan. If they locked him into an iron-roofed house, they would presently see him outside saying his prayers, though the door was still bolted, and the sentries and police were at their posts . . .
To the Sarkin Soudan God granted prosperity and victory from his youth up. Though all men were afraid, he feared not. Though everyone fled, he would go on. His kindness and patience were wide as the earth, his prowess in battle equalled that of Antaru. Never have we seen a ruler as humble as he. Son of Aarba, Miraculous Fetish, the Old Hyena who seizes his prey lying down.[24]

The praise song was also transferred into prose along with the tale. Abubakar Bello's novel similarly describes a quest and the adventures of a hero, but East felt that it lacked continuity and had an abrupt ending.[25]

Abubakar Imam Kagara's mammoth *Magana jari ce* (Ability to Tell Stories Is an Excellent Possession), published in 1940,[26] deserves mention even though it is only a collection of eighty folktales from all over the world retold by a parrot. But the author has not just simply translated; he gives Hausa names to the characters and the places and all the stories an African setting. In "Kalala da Kalatu" (Kalala and Kalatu), for instance, Kalala's overabundance of hospitality is humorously portrayed.

Abubakar Imam has also written novels, of which perhaps the best is *Tafiya mabudin ilmi* (Traveling Is the Key to Knowledge).[27] In it an amusing and irreconcilable attitude is sometimes adopted toward western institutions; on a sea voyage to England, for instance, the hero, tiring of knife and fork, takes to eating in his cabin and afterwards smearing the cutlery with the remains of his food.

Other contemporary Hausa writers who deserve mention are Ahmadu Ingawa and Abubakar Tafawa Balewa, the first prime minister of Nigeria. Ahmadu Ingawa's *Iliya, dam-mai-karfi* (Iliya, Son of a Brave Man), re-creates the legend in written prose and Abubaker Tafawa Balewa in *Shaihu Umar*,[28] published in 1955, portrays life in Africa before the coming of the Europeans. The hero is captured by a professional kidnapper and sold to an Arab slave dealer who takes him to Egypt. Forced to stay there he acquires knowledge and becomes learned in Islamic studies.

He then returns home. It is the hero-quest story given a religious motif and a pedagogical garb.

Ibo Literature: The Black Man's Burden

Bishop Crowther wrote in his journal that by 1865 many Ibo school-children could read portions of the New Testament,[29] but there was no complete translation of the Bible until the twentieth century. The late development of Ibo vernacular literature can be attributed to this and to the fact that after an orthography had been devised in 1929 by a committee from the School of Oriental and African Studies, the Protestants refused to adopt it. What has been published is therefore sparse and spasmodic, and is confined mainly to school readers, books of religious instruction, and the writing down of tales.

The first important Ibo writer was Pita Nwana whose short novelette *Omenuko* won first prize in a competition organized by the International Institute of African Languages and Culture in 1933 and was first published two years later.[30] It relates the story of how Omenuko, a trader, loses all his possessions on his way to market when a bridge collapses. He is in the company of carriers, apprentices, and a close relative, all of whom he sells into slavery upon reaching his destination. When he arrives back home, he realizes that his crime is too great to suppress so he decides to kill the elders of the town as well as the parents of the children he has sold. But members of his family advise him to run away and he, his three wives, his mother, his brothers, and their families move to another town. There the chief treats him well, and even though he has a son, he grooms Omenuko to succeed him. When the son grows up, a tense situation develops, for Omenuko is already the chief; plans are devised to oust him but he returns to his own town. With the money he has made he is able to repurchase the slaves and after many sacrifices he finally manages to expiate his guilt.

Nwana's short novel is more than a hero-quest story; it is an examination of conflicting loyalties and the psychology of crime and retribution. The writer does not disguise the didactic intent of what he claims to be a true story: "I have set on record some of the events and incidents in the life of Maze Omenuko so that readers may learn something from such a life . . . From his childhood Omenuko was blessed with riches; but when he came to manhood all his money vanished, anguish and disillusionment drove him to contemplate death as the only restful end, while peace and fraternal love counselled him not to hasten what was to come at its chosen time" (pp. 1–2).[31] The melancholy which entered Africa with the coming of Christianity is uppermost in this book.

Throughout the novel Omenuko is dogged by a continuous trail of misfortunes and at one stage he prays to the gods to help him out of the state of living death in which he has found himself. The author is not in sympathy with his hero's beliefs and when Omenuko offers a sacrifice and looks upon the coming of the vultures as a sign that it was acceptable to the gods. Nwana comments: "It is true that he rang the bell and the vultures came, but you should know that even the most stupid of domestic animals soon begin to answer to the name you apply to it very often. The vultures had learnt that whenever he rang the bell he was calling them together" (p. 65).

The author is obviously impatient with the society he describes. Nevertheless the novel attempts to canvas something of historical proportions—of "what happened in our town in ancient times" (p. 88), that is, in the first few years of the twentieth century. In all probability this was one of the models that Chinua Achebe was to use when he attempted a historical novel of Ibo life in English.

Just as Nwana's work resembles *Pilgrim's Progress*, so L. B. Gam's novel, *Ije Odumodu Jere* (Odumodu's Travels),[32] has much in common with *Robinson Crusoe* and *Gulliver's Travels*. Odumodu is the son of poor parents who cannot afford to send him to school. After working as a carpenter's apprentice, he decides to go to sea as a ship's cook. He is shipwrecked and marooned on a desert island in the kingdom of Finda. There he encounters a race of small white men to whom he brings civilization and learning. He starts a large farm and establishes a school where he teaches the local people agricultural techniques, carpentry, and boat-building. Later, after having won the king's daughter, he returns home a rich man. The year is 1886.

The story has obvious allegorical implications. Odumodu enlists on a vessel called *The World* and is evidently embarking on an archetypal adventure to reform both himself and the world. His early life had prepared him for his later role—he learned farming and cattle-rearing on his father's farm and carpentry in Lagos. Of particular interest is Gam's intention of demonstrating that the Black man has certain attributes to give to the white man; for example, the reader learns that on the island "the ruler was astounded to see a man of my size and above all to see that I had a black skin" (p. 13). Above all, the novel celebrates the church and the farm; Odumodu stresses that "we must give thanks to those who spread the word all over the world" (p. 45), and earlier on he argues that "farming is the chief of all occupations" (p. 27). Of his two sons one becomes a priest and the other a farmer.

In some ways Gam's work resembles Nwana's; both heroes are involved in a controversy regarding the succession to the throne. Both novels describe a departure and a return and have a historical setting; these similar themes indicate that Gam and Nwana not only were consciously, or unconsciously, using the form of the tale and adding Christian didacticism, but they were attempting to create character as well.

A more obvious parable than Gam's is D. N. Achara's *Ala Bingo* (The Land of Bingo),[33] which has much in common with the tale. It is about a king who journeys to the sky for six months and spends the other six on earth. His movements result in the seasons; it rains when he lives in the sky and it is dry when he is on earth. In many ways, however, *Ala Bingo* is more than an allegory, for the king is given warm human attributes. In the sky one day he sees a human footprint near the river where he bathes; the footprint is that of a beautiful princess whom he eventually marries. His two sons both become his prodigies and to decide which one should succeed him he sets them the task of answering riddles. The elder finds the correct solutions and this is why, Achara adds in a most unsatisfactory ending, the eldest always succeeds.

In a way the novel concerns human pride and the search for humility. At the beginning of the book we learn that the king was so important that there was "only one man [the king himself] and his slaves in a whole town" (p. 2). Finally the moral point is made when the king is forced to accept the advice of his slaves and to return to earth—"hunger makes one accept what he refused before" (p. 38). He undergoes all types of humiliations, including having to visit a leper and also a sick servant in "the house of sickness." He has to wait several days before the Chief of the East gives him an audience.

The theme of love, which will be noticed time and again in vernacular literature, is very much present here. It has little to do with the African creative tradition, and this description, for instance, of the king's feelings after his first encounter with the princess has no parallel in oral literature and few in written literature:

One day the king met her suddenly while she was eating what was being laid out for her. On earth she is unrivalled in beauty. Her face is like the moon. Her hair is like English wool. Her skin is as smooth as a well smoothened piece of wood. Her teeth were glistening like saliva. Her smile looks like the early morning sun in the dry season. She is a perfect piece of creation. Her beauty upset the mind of the King. Every word that comes from him is about the princess. All his dreams are centered in her. He no longer feels hungry. The satisfaction that he gets from seeing her is as good as food. (p. 25)

Although the passage is emotional, the comparisons are farfetched and absurd; what is said about the king contrasts strangely with the later description of his giving up the insubstantiality of the sky for the security of the earth.

In recent years official attempts have been made to encourage Ibo literature. In 1960 the African Literature Bureau in eastern Nigeria awarded prizes for three winning short stories, and more recently the Society for Promoting Ibo Language and Culture has published prize-winning short stories. One can only hope that now that the difficulties of orthography have been overcome writers will begin to experiment with verse.

Tiv and Efik Literature: Group Pride

Akiga's Story, the autobiography of a Tiv published in English in 1939, has been called "a first hand account of a fading society."[34] The translator, Rupert East, comments in the introduction that Akiga "writes as freely as he would talk, in his own natural style, untrammelled by any literary conventions or inhibitions" (p. 4). In his story Akiga deals with the Tiv's origin and their organizations; his diverse account treats marriage, various local matters, magic, and chieftaincy. But it is not a novel, nor is it mere biography or sociology: it is uncomfortably a mixture of all three, although the flashes of occasional humor, as when he discusses tribal markings, make it more a personal account. Perhaps what is recognizable as being within the African oral tradition are the occasional public posturings; Akiga says about his work that it "fulfils a father's duty to all Tivs who have a care for that which concerns their own tribe. You then, my Tiv brothers of the new generation that can read, read it and tell others, who cannot, of the things of our ancestors; so that, whether we have learnt to read or not, we all may still know something of our fathers who have gone before us. And do you, however great your knowledge may be, remember that you are a Tiv, remain a Tiv, and know the things of Tiv; for therein lies your pride" (p. 4).

Such identification with certain attitudes and with a specific way of life is an inheritance from the tales. In written literature, as will be seen, the association was first with the group and then with the nation and the continent (as in négritude). Time and again in African literature this note of complete and unquestioning identification with the group experience will emerge.

The Efiks have produced little that could be called literature. After the Bible had been translated, the extent of Efik literature has been the "Ama Hu" series of textbooks for primary schools and an epic written by

102

Nkana entitled *Nmmtand a Oyam Namondo*. It concerns the good King Mutanda's search for his son, Namondo, who had been seized by a god who lives in "the sky, the sea and under the earth." Mutanda has to make various sacrifices to placate God. Nkana describes the whole community's involvement in the loss of the prince—"the hen quarrelled with the maize and the goat separated from the yams"—which again forms an obvious link with the world of folklore in which all living things participated and communed.

GHANA

Twi, Ewe, and Fanti Literature: Public Poetry

The Bible was introduced in Ghana at quite an early stage; Elisa Johannes Capetein, himself an African, reduced Fanti to writing and from approximately 1742 to 1746 he translated the Lord's Prayer, parts of the catechism, and the Ten Commandments into Fanti. Not until a century later, however, did Christaller translate the four gospels into Twi. He completed the Bible in 1871 and wrote twenty-eight books in Twi between 1857 and 1890. Since then a great deal has been written in Twi, most of it within the last twenty years. Much, however, is of an ephemeral nature. From the publication of J. J. Adaye's *Bere adu!* (Now Is the Time!) in 1913 to the present-day verse of Nketia, Twi literature has been very much within the oral tradition, borrowing heavily from the public nature of spoken and sung art.[35]

The tradition of "public" utterance became to some extent perverted in the poetry of the thirties. It will be observed, when consideration is given to African verse in English at this period, that the poetry was largely devoted to nonpersonal issues—country and God are but two examples of this. Ephraim Amu (an Ewe who wrote in Twi) published *Twenty-Five African Songs in the Twi Language*[36] in 1932 and divided them into "sacred" and "patriotic." This was the poetry of moral exhortation and the tone seldom varied:

> This is our own land
> It is to us a priceless heritage
> Our fathers shed their blood
> To win it for us.[37]

It was very much the poetry of national identification and many of the Twi plays of the period echo this same sentiment. Indeed whether they were moral stories, outright reproductions of traditional tales, or biographies like the one on Aggrey,[38] the emphasis was twofold: the expression of evils—social and spiritual—and the urge for reformation.

103

The poetry of Nketia marks an intentional return to the oral tradition. He had himself translated a good deal of Akan verse but his volume of Twi poems, *Anwonsem*, is slim, barely forty pages.[39] Published in 1952, it contains poems written between 1949 and 1952 when he was at work on Akan funeral dirges.

Nketia's poetry, however, canvasses nothing of the proportions of R. Gaddiel Acquaah's epic poem *Oguaa Aban*, written in Fanti and published in 1939.[40] It describes the wanderings of the Fanti, their contacts with earlier tribes, their kings, the Ashanti war, and the coming of the missionaries. The reason for their wanderings is expressed in heroic verse and is in keeping with the quasi-religious flavor that has been noted in Ewe poetry:

> 'Twas their refusal to accept Islam
> That made the forbears of both Fanti and other Gold Coast tribes
> Start their wanderings to this country.
> They fought bloody battles.[41]

But Acquaah's epic seems to lack true feeling. It reads like an exercise in patriotism and shows few examples of poetic insight. The Fantis and their migrations are stolidly followed; every detail is given even if it lends nothing to the heroic nature of the work. For instance, a long passage is devoted to describing how the Fantis built their first city; like the previous extract quoted it does not quite succeed because it is labored and clumsily prosaic.

Like Amu's verse in Twi, Acquaah's poetry has the same annoying didacticism, which will also emerge later in the pioneer poets in English:

> In nakedness and in prosperity,
> In cold season and hot season,
> For the future's sake be not discouraged,
> Think and look ahead.
> Life is like a farmer's seed
> Which grows into the future.
> Goodness yields good crop,
> Think and look ahead![42]

In Fanti the poem has an obvious end-rhyme in "a," but one wonders whether in the original this does not simply emphasize the labored effect.

On the other hand, the Fanti verse of Joseph Ghartey, a contemporary of Acquaah's, has a certain proximity to the oral literature which redeems it. As has been mentioned, new year greetings play an active part in the oral poetry; one such poem (see p. 46) expresses "greetings to the chief of an Akan state on the occasion of the new year" (p. 6) by communicating the joy that everything within the universe feels at the beginning of a new year. Ghartey's poem "Nde ye ehurusi da" (This is the Day of Rejoicing)[43] is of the same genre:

> The year has gone round full circle
> And brought us the blessings of the harvest,
> The festal day is here,
> It has brought all joys,
> All labour is at an end,
> It is with gratitude
> That all people today
> Lift up their voices
> In exultation.
> This is the day of rejoicing
> Let's all rejoice.
> The fields have yielded their harvest
> Let's all rejoice.
> The seas are yielding their harvest too.
> Let's all rejoice,
> Let us sing songs of exultation
> For our labours have not been in vain.
> We have gathered home plenty,
> This is the day of rejoicing
> Let's all rejoice.
> The year has yielded its harvest
> Let's all rejoice.

The poem echoes the mood of the new year greetings poem given on page 46, but there have been certain alterations. For example, the personal element is more assertive here than in the oral poem. Biblical terms and catchphrases of popular hymns have been introduced—"the blessings of harvest," "lift up their voices," "day of rejoicing," and so on. Furthermore the landscape is different: in the oral poem it is *personalized* (or, rather, it quite naturally functions as a person); in Ghartey's poem it is *personified*. An artificial element has entered the verse; nature is no longer assumed but looked at through western eyes. This will also be noted in the creative writers of the period who wrote in English. Indeed many of Ghartey's poems are preoccupied with effusions to "Adzekyee" (Morning) when "The sun kindly / Is climbing / The Eastern horizon" and to "Nwimbir" (Evening) when "Evening calm is scattering / Over town and country." These statements are no doubt as effete in the vernacular as in the English. Ghartey's verse also represents the beginning of romantic longing in African poetry. In "Na Me Wo Do" (Give Me Thy Love) he exclaims, not very convincingly, "Give me thy voice that I may learn of thy love / Sweet contentment thy rich voice breathes," and in "Nda" (Sleep), he expresses the melancholic introspection which entered African literature with the coming of the missionaries:

> I am pressed on all sides
> By the world and its cares,
> The sea is raging
> The clouds are gathering,
> O comforter!
> Come and drive away my cares,
> Come and wipe away my tears,
> Come and comfort me.

Since in fact the Christian God had been provided as a comforter, it was only necessary to simulate the quietude. A similar cause of artificial uneasiness is in Kwasi Fiawoo's play *The Fifth Landing Stage* (1937) which deals with slavery.

Ewe verse, however, always expressed a kind of insatiable longing. There is a "pervasive sadness"[44] about much of it, and not surprisingly this quality seems uppermost in poets who write both in the vernacular and in English; obvious examples are Kofu Hoh and George Awoonor-Williams (now Kofi Awoonor), who writes in the vernacular and then translates his work into English. The sadness germinates a yearning which is exemplified in Hoh's poem "Dzifo le fie" (The Sky):

> The sky at night is like a big city
> Where beasts and men abound
> But never once has anyone
> Killed a fowl or a goat,
> And no bear has ever caught a prey.
> There are no accidents; there are no losses.
> Everything knows its way.[45]

Sadness also results in rejection of and disillusionment with, the universe; the world, according to Hoh, is so small that

> When you rise too high
> You might break your neck against the clouds;
> When you spread yourself too far,
> You might dash your arms against its sides;
> And when you tread too heavily,
> The earth might break under you,
> And make you sink into the ground.[46]

But the rejection is not total; Hoh does not discard the prejudices of the tribe and the following poem of identification (which might be considered satirical) is a praise poem with its built-in element of abuse:

> A baby is a European,
> *He does not eat our food*;
> He drinks from his own water pot.

A baby is a European,
He does not speak our tongue;
He is cross when the mother understands him not.

A baby is a European,
He cares very little for others;
He forces his will upon his parents.

A baby is a European,
He is always very sensitive;
The slightest scratch on his skin results in an ulcer.[47]

It is a clever poem because it subtly ridicules the overfine constraints of the European abroad. Hoh's verse is within the tradition of the public nature of some oral poetry, as has been noticed, but here the tone is modulated, more individualistic, and less assertive.

On the whole one sees a movement in this local literature which is above all else moral in tone. The morality is at times borrowed from a Christian ethic, sometimes from the group beliefs. These writers create for small audiences, often schoolchildren, and their work is conservative and identifies with group issues. In western Africa the group concerns are also with Islam as well as with family life and the European presence. These writers began an important tradition of restrained tension in their writing, a tradition which later writers in English took up and redefined as the theme of the individual divided between two cultures.

Central Africa

Some of the generalizations concerning the literature of western Africa are applicable to that of Central Africa. No longer is it possible to speak only of missionary influence and the translation of the Bible, for the flag invariably followed the cross and one finds that the missionaries were spokesmen not only for the Christian religion but for the unspoken wishes of the colonizing power as well. It is no accident that only two works were written in former Belgian territories, one in a former French territory, and none in Portuguese—except for an Angolan grammar compiled in 1697 by Pedro Dias, a Jesuit priest. Most Central African writing is in Nyanja (Malawi) and Bemba (Zambia), and these works are in the main intended for school use.[48]

Unabated curiosity of explorers preceding the economic penetration of European powers more or less forms the historical pattern of the area. Livingstone's name is associated both with Zambia and with Malawi; in 1855 he "discovered" Victoria Falls and in 1859 Lake Nyasa. Since 1874 there has been intense missionary activity in Malawi and, indeed,

107

there was Portuguese contact with Zambia as early as the end of the eighteenth century. But the history is one of penetration not only from the West but from the East as well; Swahili, first a trading language, found its way into the written literature. However, its influence can be more properly seen in East Africa.

Congo Kinshasa is associated with another explorer, Stanley, who managed to interest Leopold II of Belgium in the possibilities of bringing "civilization" to the area. The result was the formation in 1876 of an International African Association dedicated to the monopolization of the wealth of the area; it existed until 1908 when the Belgian government took over the administration. The last quarter of the nineteenth century also brought the French into contact with Congo Brazzaville which in 1887 was extended to include the Central African Republic.

Patterns of development evident on the western coast do not seem operative here. The missionary influence is considerably less; all effort is geared toward economic penetration and political mastery. Hand in hand with this went the immigration of settlers and as part of the whole complex puzzle of this history must be seen the perverted aspirations of the African to become Europeanized. Not until the beginning of the twentieth century was any attempt made to encourage writing in the vernacular languages.

Such encouragement first came through educational programs; later the Northern Rhodesia and Nyasaland Publications Bureau, in conjunction with such firms as Longmans, Oxford University Press, Heinemann, University of London Press, and Macmillan, was to publish vernacular books, but many of them are translations of standard English authors, while others are written solely for the school market. It is the few exceptions which will be considered here.

RUANDA LITERATURE: FAMINE AND GOD

Of the publications in French-speaking Africa, one, *Masapo ma Bangala* (Stories of the Bangala) by André Roumain Bokwango, is a collection of folktales published in 1955. The main contribution in the vernacular, however, has been made not by Bokwango, but by a priest from Ruanda and before him Kayonga, half traditional artist, half modern poet. During the reign of King Mutara III a publishing house was founded to provide educational books for adults. Among the books published was *Icara nkumare irungu* (Sit Down So I Can Take Your Boredom Away), a collection of mock heroic verses published in 1946 dealing with famine and its ultimate defeat in Ruanda.[49] With the possible exception of Kayonga's verse, these poems would appear to be the works of traditional artists. Kayonga contributed two poems to this volume; one, divided into seven songs, personifies the famine as a wild beast, which had to be fought as one would wage a military campaign. The other exalts the hoe as an efficacious weapon which triumphs over the terrible invader (the famine).

Although these poems are obviously similar to the traditional war songs and praise poems, Kayonga has succeeded in blending the traditional with the contemporary. The place names and the praise epithets are in keeping with the oral tradition, but the way in which the famine is described, the narrative movement of the poem, is a definite innovation:

> The attacker which does not fear the rich.
> The famine attacks the fields,
> Offspring of Gakondwe, and an enemy of young children,
> Having overthrown the country of the Bagina
> It made a journey of four hours
> And reached the unlucky sub-district of Mushuru.
> It watched people leading the Ndushabandi army of cattle
>   to the drinking places.
> They were made to drink till night fell.
> There one speaks of riches only in terms of cattle . . . (p. 6)

The last line of course gives the poet away. No longer is he the local spokesman, secure in tribal mask, for it is necessary for him to explain to an outside audience the significance of cattle-farming in Ruanda. The individual voice, soon to become a dominant aspect of African literature, is apparent here but is still not distinct. Since the famine is seen as an offspring of an older famine and therefore called Gakondwe and is praised in the first three lines, the poem has obvious links with oral verse. Nevertheless, because it is overtly a piece of propaganda for more extensive farming, certain lines have nothing to do with this tradition: "the winnowing-baskets were used to purify the flour. According to the orders of Monsieur Feltz" (p. 8). M. Feltz, presumably a Belgian official, is mentioned again in the poem when Kayonga describes the way the famine invaded his own province of Mutara. Here the personal and descriptive elements (both foreign to oral tradition) are more apparent:

> It was routed with blows of corn,
> Of melons and sweet pumpkins,
> By fields of cassava which had grown like forests,
> And by beans overflowing in giant baskets,
> In a word the people here have taken first place
>   in agriculture;
> I even believe that this was noted down by M. Feltz. (pp. 11–12)

In the second poem the pictorial device is even more evident, individual-
izing the poem and liberating it from traditional convention:

> It was only a thief thirsting for pillage,
> But from now on it is obsessed by the nightmare of potatoes.
> From now on we have only to harvest.
> Famine fled without looking backwards,
> It went away on lonely paths.
> Was it carried away by the whirlwind?
> Or perhaps was it drowned in the mud of the rain?
> Nobody remembers its ravages. (pp. 12–13)

Kagamé's own work is a continuation of the novelty of individual self-
assertion. His best known work, *Umulirimbyi wa nyili-ibiremwa* (The
Song of the Mother of Creation), was published in 1952. He has translated it into French under the title *La divine pastorale*. In the introduction Kagamé states that the poem is " 'Divine' because it has as its
subject and object, God, His essence and His work, 'Pastoral' because
the work is an adaptation of the 'pastoral' poetry of Ruanda." The poem,
an interpretation of the history of man told in Christian terms, attempts
to set forth "the whole of the teaching of the Christian religion from the
very beginning—the fall of the bad angels and the six days of creation—
until the church of today and the last day."[50] In tracing the entire cycle
of Christian myth, it deals with the concepts of hell, purgatory, heaven,
and the end of the world. In general the tone is that of the praise poems
which Kagamé had himself collected. About God Kagamé says:

> He is the meeting place of all that is good.
> The man who perceives this does not hesitate anymore:
> He contains everything that one has ever seen;
> He surpasses in beauty any object of our desires.
>
> He turns our glance away from earthly belongings,
> And towards Him our eyes are directed.
> I would not know how to relate in detail his perfections:
> Our God defies the *aèdes* who describe him. (p. 31)

The praise poem to the Ruandan kings is here addressed to God and God
is eulogized in the familiar praise epithets of a cattle-farming tribe.

As was seen in the Latin poetry, Christian devotion was eventually
incorporated into the praise poem. It is not really surprising that one
of the most common genres in modern African verse—praise poetry—
should originate in sacred and laudatory poetry, since praise poetry
abounds in oral literature. In Kagamé what is preserved is the form—a
reviewer in *Zaïre* felt that he had "scrupulously observed the laws of
rhapsody in Ruanda." What is also preserved are the words of praise,

although the absolute adoration is foreign to the oral tradition. In *La divine pastorale* there are no heretical asides "because, in fact, his form is complete" (p. 31). And it is this that spoils the poem; the praises are too intense, too exaggerated, too unrelieved. The traditional poet was the better craftsman, for he knew the virtue of contrast.

MALAWI

Cewa and Nyanja Literature: Reformation

In Malawi the beginning of local writing is connected with the missionaries and the formation in 1906 of a newspaper in English. The newspaper, however, immediately failed, but was replaced by *Makani* (Report), which lasted only two years. Not until 1928 did Africans in Malawi start writing in any numbers and in *Vyaro na vyara* (Countries and Countries) about 80 percent of the contributors were Africans.[51] Most of the publications in Nyanja belong to the late fifties and sixties. In general they are biographical accounts of chiefs and many of them have a pointed moral ending. In the main they are not novels but novelettes and would seem to possess only an ephemeral interest. There are, however, a few exceptions.

S. A. Paliani published a play in 1952 and has recently written *1930 kunadza mchape* (In 1930 There Came a Witchdoctor), a story about the triumph of superstition. It describes the process by which a local magician gains power over his unsuspecting villagers. Paliani stresses the point that will be noticed in some early South African vernacular writings—"superstitions" are wrong, Christianity must be cherished.[52] Within the tradition of this and other stories already discussed is Samuel Ntara's *Headman's Enterprise* (1949), a rather romanticized biography of Msyamboza, a village chief, written in Cewa.[53] The moral element observed before is uppermost in this work. The climax of the book is Msyamboza's conversion to Christianity: "I have fired this gun today as a sign that from now onwards I shall follow Jesus. You my wives! all of you! I put away for Jesus' sake and I do not wish to leave out even one of you since it is my life and your lives that are concerned. I know that you will have anxiety and sorrow but I cannot give up honouring Christ who is Master of Life" (p. 178). Somehow such moralizing does not quite succeed. The posturings of Msyamboza become identified with the author's attitudes which are easy to understand but are not convincing in the novel. Jailos Chingotu has attempted autobiographical writing in Nyanja, but a condensed version of the original reveals little more than the painstaking documenting of what, a half century later, looks very much like trivia. The events described up to 1915 offer fascinating glimpses of the world that David Livingstone did not see, but the work does it in a most plodding, unimaginative way.[54]

The majority of books in Nyanja explore human situations; Jacob Zulu's *Zomfula mkazi wacimaso-maso* (The Girl Who Was Never Satisfied) is a moral story about a girl who fails to remain virtuous; his other work, *Cibwana ndi ukwati* (A Teenage Marriage), is a love story set in the Copperbelt.[55] All the stories touch on moral issues, but nothing more significant than malicious gossips who are punished, thieves who become penitent, or chiefs who try out various reforms. They do not deal with subtleties in character or plot, preferring instead to offer only black and white interpretations of life.[56]

ZAMBIA

Bemba, Tonga, and Lozi Literature: Robbers and Farmers

Most productive of the writers in Bemba is Stephen Andrea Mpashi who has written five short novels as well as poetry. His novels frequently reveal a sense of humor and *Cekesoni aingila ubusoja* (Jackson Becomes a Soldier) published in 1950 is a comedy of army life. One of his novelettes is in the form of a detective story set in the Copperbelt, and a sequel to it is in the form of a love story. He was the earliest writer to be published: after his first book appeared in 1950, many other writers became occupied with the "popular" themes he had explored. Urban Chishimba's *Bamusha ulweko* (Caught Unawares) is also humorous; it relates the adventures of two thieves, one of whom is arrested as he is about to be married.[57]

In Bemba literature, one finds the customary children's stories, the stories of which seek to make a moral point in the usual uncompromising manner. But M. K. Chifwaila has published a historical novelette concerning the slave trade, and Albert Kacuka has written an account of Ushifwayo, who becomes a trustworthy person and helps to teach his fellow villagers how to live well;[58] both seem to be little different from the standard works with strong didactic appeal.

Besides Mpashi's verse, I Braim Nkonde, better known as a playwright, has published "This Is the Land," which celebrates the virtues of the soil.[59] This long poem steers a deliberate middle course between an agricutlural pamphlet, in the manner of Kayonga, and a political manifesto advocating patriotism and love of the land. As Nkonde says:

To the aged there came thoughts: When I was youth or maid
Had they held back the days, I would have lent a helping hand,

112

But thus it could not be; and so still on ahead we go.
This is the land; how happy he of its hardness shall have learnt. (pp. 275–76)

This poem was published in 1947 and despite its stiff moralizing it is much better than the prose of the period. Not only is it an organized piece of writing but it is within the tradition of oral literature, being part dirge and part praise poem. Bemba prose, on the other hand, has in the main borrowed from bad European models and seems unable to free itself from this morass.

Only two novels have been written in Tonga; one is a love story about two friends who are rivals for the same girl, and the other concerns a boy who causes some confusion over the Tonga matrilineal law of inheritance. In Lozi little poetry exists but there are seven imaginative prose writers. Their themes do not vary much—detective stories, adaptations of legends and tales, moral stories about young men who go wrong or others in search of an education, and so on. With regard to the literature in Tonga and Lozi (as well as in Bemba and Nyanja) it must be added in all fairness that it is directed at a popular market. The books sell for at most a quarter or so and are clearly intended for either schools or adult literary classes. Perhaps in the final analysis these writers should be regarded as pioneers; they have shown that it is possible to write. It will remain for others to exploit the potentiality of the languages.

Eastern Africa

In 1947 the East African Literature Bureau was formed. Its purpose was "to meet and indeed foster the ever-increasing demand among the literate Africans for books of all kinds, and to encourage African authorship—needs which cannot adequately be met by the ordinary publishing trade." Although such a bureau was essential in Kamba, Luganda, Runyoro/Rutooro, and elsewhere, East Africa differs radically from the rest of sub-Saharan Africa in that a literature written in Swahili already existed for two centuries. It is probably correct to call Swahili a "trade language," since the need for it arose out of contacts with the Arabs, contacts which began in the fourteenth century.[60] The language had had a great deal of time to entrench itself, for European "ownership" of the area did not come about until the latter part of the nineteenth century.

It is not surprising to find that the majority of what has been written has been composed in Swahili and has not been translated.[61] Some of the best of this literature is still in manuscript form, although the language has declined in importance in Uganda and Kenya. Here more recently other vernacular languages are being developed and authors are attempting to free themselves from the rigors of a missionary press. Apart from South Africa, which already has a sizable and important body of literature in the vernacular languages, East Africa seems the most likely region on the continent to develop its indigenous literatures.

SWAHILI LITERATURE: RELIGIOUS ASSENT

One of the greatest contemporary Swahili poets, Shaaban Robert, once said that "Swahili poems and epics are composed to be sung."[62] Although this is indeed their main link with the oral tradition, they represent the personification of that tradition and so are strictly speaking neither "oral" nor "written." Because ideas about religion and modes of courtship, as well as other customs, were imported from the Arabic world, it is only partly true to say that the poetry retained the flavor of African oral verse. Perhaps the *mashairi* verse composed for public occasions can be considered closest to the oral tradition, for the *tendi* (or *tenzi*) and the *hadithi*, those forms most similar to the *mashairi*, introduced a narrative element into the verse. Furthermore Swahili poetry made use of rhyme, a feature that scarcely appears anywhere else in the written literature of the continent. There is, however, little creative prose.

When speaking of Swahili, we must therefore take into account two traditions—a distinctly Arabic one and an indistinct, indigenous African one. It is extremely difficult to separate these traditions; nevertheless, such a separation is desirable since we are dealing here not with anonymous oral expression but with a literature of individuals which has changed and has undergone certain definitive alterations in the process.

A large portion of Swahili poetry was contained within the tradition of Islamic religion. A nineteenth-century poet, Muyaka bin Haji of Mombasa, who, according to Harries, "brought poetry out of the mosque into the market-place,"[63] incidentally established the element of individualism in the poetry. But this is not to say that the moral quality was lacking. As he wrote:

> Thy friend, (thy) friend.
> If thou wouldst know him
> Go thou with him in a caravan on a journey
> And journey together a far journey
> Or leave him in (thy) house
> And go abroad and delay (returning).
> If he prove not to be a kite
> This is thy friend.[64]

Muyaka bin Haji may have been writing within a tradition completely alien to Africa. To some extent this was also true of Mwana Kupona, who was born in Pate and died about 1860. In a poem addressed to her daughter, she discusses the position of Swahili women, rules for good conduct, and the duties owed to God, Mohammed, father, mother, and husband. She then advises her daughter on how to conduct her household, describes the bliss of a successful marriage, and ends the poem with a firm confession of religious belief. Very often the autobiographical basis becomes apparent:

> I was wed to your father
> With happiness and laughter
> She who composed the poem
> Is one lonely and sorrowful.[65]

It is through such personal statements that she manages to say something with larger ramifications.

Because Swahili was "ill equipped to express any modern concepts, and [had] none of the advantages of being able to appeal to sentiment and national pride," its development is said to have been inhibited. But as late as 1913 a poem was written to Liongo Fumo, a legendary Swahili hero who was himself a poet and to whom Steere has attributed a poem which probably dates from the fourteenth century.[66]

Some of the more famous *tendi,* like the "Utendi Wa Ayubu" or the story of Job, as well as a great deal of Swahili verse, seem to stand on the border line between oral literature that has been written down and written literature that has been composed by individuals. Our difficulty in a study of this nature is that it is not clear in most cases to which tradition such poetry belongs. Furthermore, its dependence on Arabic forms and ideas and the fact that it was written in the Arabic script help to complicate the issue. But above all what is interesting is that the individual voice emerges in Swahili literature as a delicate blend of African and Arab elements, the impersonal and the oral, the personal and the written. In a brief survey of this nature little more need be said.

KENYA AND UGANDA

Kamba, Runyoro/Rutooro and Luganda Literature: Detective Story and Legend

A great deal of the work in both Kikuyu and Kamba is translations of standard English authors or reproductions of tales. T. M. Ngotho has reworked a number of tales, but perhaps the most original and conscious vernacular writer is John Mbiti, whose adventure story *Mũtũnga na ngewa yake* (Mutunga and His Story) appeared in 1954.[67]

Possibly the most interesting literature has been done in Uganda. Michael Nsimbi has written a nonfictional work in the Ganda language on the origin of names and more recently he has attempted a short novel. Edward K. N. Kawere has published poems. By 1912 the Bible had been translated into Runyoro/Rutooro and after the usual spate of missionary writing and translations from oral literature, an interesting body of writing has emerged.

The most important writer in Runyoro/Rutooro is Timothy Bazzarabusa, whose novels show the same tendency that was observed in Malawian and Zambian literature—the use of the love story and the detective story to make a moral statement. His first novel, *Ha munwa gw'ekituuro* (At the Point of Death), concerns the attempted murder of a man and how he manages to escape twice. In the end his would-be assailant is arrested. *Kalyaki na Marunga* (Kalyaki and Marunga)[68] utilizes a similar "popular" plot; in this case the hero is a well-educated man, Kalyaki, who steals a car. Realizing he has done wrong, he decides to return it but is ambushed by the police and runs away. He finds himself in the house of Marunga, the girl he wishes to marry, who persuades him to give himself up. This he does and after serving two years in prison he marries her.

In Bazzarabusa's later work, he attempts to avoid his preoccupation with moral issues and to develop a form that is more closely related to the tale. His last volume, *Obu ndikura tindifa* (I Will Never Die),[69] demonstrates a growing interest in a philosophical analysis of the truth of existence. The form of this book, a blend of narrative and poetry, is more in keeping with traditional literature. In the story after which the collection is named, Karutuba is told by doctors that he does not have long to live; the main plot centers on his preparations for death and how he must reorganize his entire life. At first the news is shattering: "When the doctors had told me this chilling and sorrowful news, I broke into pieces, felt all energy go out of me and became like chaff. It took a long time to admit that I too was destined to die, and not only that, but to die in a short while. All the time I credited death to others, old ladies and old men. I counted myself as one who would remain here for ever and ever. I think that is how we all think when we are young or before we become sick; but after just one week I accepted my lot and knew that I had to die. Death is universal; some die soon, others linger on but in the end all go and will go" (p. 78). Despite such intense introspective concern, Bazzarabusa has attempted in this work to accommodate idiomatic expressions and references to the folk past. Moreover, a new development—a sense of humor—in Bazzarabusa as well as in vernacular literature becomes evident. In Bazzarabusa's poem "Kakonko nya-mugona" (Kakonko, the Snorer), the theme of marriage is lightheartedly treated: because of "the trumpets of her darling," Majege has to flee the marital home and seek consolation with her father—she cannot sleep, for her husband is always "making music with his nose." The touch is different but equally successful in another poem, "Whose Love Answers Mine," where Bazzarabusa writes:

> And I touched her hand, like a forked stick
> On water lilies on the lake of Ntuntu
> Which automatically draw towards you as you pull a little.

Bazzarabusa's work expresses the individual voice in all its various moods, but it is still very close to the source of its strength, the tradition of oral literature.

In the early part of the twentieth century, Sir Apolo Kagwa had already given an example of the potentiality of the Baganda tongue when he produced his studies of the Baganda dynastic institutions on his hand press at Mengo. His monumental work *Ekotabo kye bika Baganda* (The Customs of the Baganda People) was published in 1905, and since then people have tended to write about anthropology rather than to compose creatively. Among such persons was J. T. K. Ggomotoka (d. 1942), a recognized authority on the history and language of Baganda, who in 1932 summoned a conference to stabilize Luganda orthography.[70] More recently, in 1950, the life story of Duhaga II, the Nukama of Bunyoro-Kitara from 1902 to 1924, has been published. In all these works, fact is blended with fancy (the imaginative element), and, certainly, in Sir Apolo's writing a great deal of creativity is reflected in the poems he reproduced.

Y. B. Lubambula is the best known of the first generation of poets writing in Luganda. His *Ennyimba ezimu* (Some Songs) appeared in 1953, and in the main it shows that he has succeeded in incorporating narratives of the tales into his verse. This has resulted (in translation at least) in a certain prosaic quality. For instance, his poem "Kintu"[71] follows a well-known version of a legend about Kintu; how he catches in turn a spider, an ant, an ant-bear, and a snake, and how he makes a pact with them. He even traps his wife, Nambi, who stays with him for a time and then disappears. With Spider (the familiar agent in the tales) he climbs the "doorless house" to heaven to find his wife. He is then set the usual tasks: he must eat a large quantity of food, which the ant-bear helps him to bury, and he has to carry some heavy rocks, which the ant nibbles at and the snake carries. So, with the help of the agents of the natural world, he regains Nambi. But she insists on turning back (against her father's warning) to retrieve her millet and Death follows them into the world. The poem, however, ends on a note of hope:

> Kintu and Nambi gave it up in despair
> And comforted themselves saying, Let Mr. Death be,
> The children of Kintu will never be entirely destroyed. (p. 48)

What Lubambula did was to poetize the tale; before him the tradition of narrative, as has been shown, was foreign to "verse." His experiment (and it is an experiment) also employed elements of the praise poem; Kintu, for instance, is called "a trapper of animals / A man who learnt to trap very skilfully" (p. 45). The stanza form is loose and obviously well adapted to the tale. Lubambula's achievement in Baganda must be placed side by side with Bazzarabusa's in Runyoro/Rutooro. Both drew from and altered the oral tradition. Their achievement lies in the extent of that alteration.

Southern Africa

Southern Africa—Rhodesia, Bechuanaland, Lesotho, and South Africa proper—is an area where the sphere of European influence has been most pronounced. However, there is a "vernacular" literature in Afrikaans—little over a century old, it is true, but nevertheless extant—which must be noted in a complete consideration of this subject. In Rhodesia the pattern has been much the same as that in other southern African countries: exploration (David Livingstone discovered Victoria Falls in 1855), missionary expeditions, and the establishment of European "colonies." But this took place toward the end of the nineteenth century. South Africa, on the other hand, had its early conflicts in the mid-seventeenth century, and the confrontation of Black with white, as well as the multiracial trilemma and the origins of the modern state, dates back to this period.[72]

Southern Africa has produced the greatest amount of vernacular texts in all of Africa and they go back the furthest in time. The two exceptions are Shona and Ndebele (Rhodesia) which is only about nine years old and in which only twenty-seven works have been written. The first Sotho novel, however, was published in 1907. The majority of the works in this area derive from southern Sotho (Basutoland) and number about 111.[73]

The heavy concentration of vernacular literature in southern Africa is undoubtedly the result of the implied, if not legalized, process of separate development. This has meant that little has been written in English (and most of it is recent) and that Black southern African writers have had to express their attitudes toward themselves, their own past, Christianity, and the encroaching European presence in towns in the vernacular languages. The consequences of this are the most complete vernacular record on the continent, a record which can serve as an indication of the capabilities and failings of the literature in other parts of Africa.

ZIMBABWE (RHODESIA)

Shona and Ndebele Literature: The Big City

A system of Shona orthography was adopted by the Rhodesian government as early as 1931, but certain departments, including the press, continued to use an earlier orthography based on Biehler's dictionary of Shona. The usual orthographical war was waged, the Bible being published in 1947 in the revised orthography. Matters came to a climax in 1955 when the Shona Orthography Committee met. Five years later a dictionary was published incorporating its new recommendations.[74] From 1955 the Southern Rhodesia Literary Bureau has published Shona books in the new modified orthography and a series of school readers have been edited by Fr. Hannan.

There is only a limited amount of poetry in Shona; in 1959 *Madetembedzo* (Ritual Praise Songs Old and New) was published and contained poems by two of the oldest and most outstanding Shona poets—Solomon Mutswairo and Wilson Chivaura.[75] Of the two Chivaura is the more prolific; his poetry is highly regarded and in 1958 he won first prize in a Shona poetry competition.

Ten of Chivaura's poems are included in the 1959 anthology, and one of them in particular provides a good insight into the nature of his poetry.

> Come the month of October
> The sap runs strongly in the trees;
> We see the paths in the hills covered over,
> With new trees springing up,
> We hear the singing of the cicadas.[76]

As has been observed there is little of this overt reference to, and romanticizing of, nature in either oral traditional or written vernacular verse; it comes as no surprise to learn then that Chivaura is an agricultural inspector. Fr. Fortune, commenting on the range of themes present in his poetry, lists them as follows: "pieces on a storm, the month of October, creatures in nature that pass away, the months of the year, the kaffirboom

119

flower and the death of a hunter."[77] Chivaura is obviously a novelty in vernacular literature—the poet of the great out-of-doors.

Mutswairo is better known for his novels, but in addition to the poems published in the 1959 anthology he has also written several for the daily press. He has translated widely, from his Shona version of "Grave of an Unknown Soldier" to "Taima, taima nyenyedzi yedenga" (Twinkle, Twinkle Little Star). His importance, as well as that of Chivaura, is that he has shown the adaptability of the Shona language to verse. It has been claimed that "one cannot say as yet that they have discovered a form suitable to their language, nor are they conscious of the features which should be carried over, in perhaps a modified form, from the oral to the written language."[78] But Mutswairo has asserted that this is untrue. In a personal interview he commented that by utilizing the oral tradition they were frequently able to appeal to local African readers on a level that non-Africans could not comprehend.

Others have tended to imitate these two poets: among them is Edison Zzobgowho, "a skilful user of metaphor, finding inspiration from his own life, country and institutions." He has written poems to the moon, a bat, and a whirlwind but a new note enters with his poetry—racial consciousness. For instance, one poem, addressed to Ghana, describes it as the eldest son of Mother Africa.[79] This new search for identification has led a more recent poet, Gibson Mandishona, to re-create in poetry the history of his people. His "Vatsunga" is an epic poem of the wanderings of his clan, his "Kusakura" portrays the life of a family working on farms, and what has been called "his most polished work"—"Muunda wangu wegova" (My Garden of Red Soil)—is a descriptive poem utilizing Shona idiom.

Shona novels are an equally interesting contribution to the literature. The earliest novel written by Solomon Mutswairo and entitled *Feso* depicts life in the Mazoe Valley before the coming of the Europeans and offers a great wealth of ethnographical information about the manner of administration, the marriage customs, and the wars during this period. His second novel, *Murambiwa Goredema* (1959), has a familiar plot first used by South African writers in Sotho and Xhosa. His hero, Murambiwa, leaves his village for the town and after a series of adventures he is involved in dealing in illicit gold. He hopes that a charm he has will protect him, but when it fails to do so, he returns to his village a disappointed man. A similar moral note is stuck in Paul Chidyausiku's *Nhoroondo dzukuwanana* (Getting Married).[80] Here the heroine is meant to illustrate how a good life brings about fortunate results. After qualifying as a nurse, she marries and creates a happy home with her husband. Indeed, Chidyausiku's three novels express the same theme: in one a faithful wife avoids her husband's attempts to have her killed because of her faith in God; in the other an old man gives advice on marriage, agriculture, and health. But though the moral lesson is uppermost, Chidyausiku's works do have other levels of meaning; for instance, Fr. Fortune has commented that in the marriage scene in his first novel "past and present are blended. His intention is to show that new customs should blend with the old shapely and valuable customs in which marriage is symbolically celebrated. He shows for example what a great contribution the kin, both of the bride and the bridegroom, have to make towards the happiness and stability of the individual couple."

One would rather have expected that moral issues would have figured predominantly in the work of Patrick Chakaipa, a Roman Catholic priest. But this is not so. His first novel, *Karikoga gumiremiseve* (Karikoga and His Ten Arrows),[81] resurrects the ancient hero of legend. Set at the time of the raids by the Matabele, the novel describes the feats of Karikoga, how he battles with a lion and goes into Matabeleland to rescue his wife. In the second novel, with a similar historical setting, the hero has a special spear. His two most recent novels are love stories, but they both make a moral point; in one the heroine is an embodiment of strong Christian faith, and in the other the heroine is presented as a woman of incredible love and mercy.

Shona novels are a literature of morality, as can also be seen in the works of Bernard Chidzero and J. W. Marangwanda, who use the evil city as the setting and depict the gradual disintegration of the hero when he is exposed to it. Despite Fr. Fortune's assertion that Shona novels succeed in presenting character, it seems that little is accomplished beyond the portrayal of heroes too good to be credible or too evil to be recognizable. The novels, unlike the poetry, are too obsessed with the "message," and the significance of that message seems to be mainly concerned with Christian salvation. The only novels that seem to redeem themselves are those which attempt to give some historical depth to the characters and the story.

In Ndebele literature much the same pattern is revealed; the familiar plot of the young man who leaves home for the big city is found in David Ndoda's *Uvusezindala* (In Days Gone By), except that the hero's reason for going is to earn money for the bride-price. When he returns he finds that his intended bride has married someone else. A similar theme of tragic love is related in the two novels of Isaac Mpofu. But Lassie Ndondo's only novel is not about love at all, which is a little surprising since she is one of the few women writing in the vernacular. Instead, and perhaps more naturally, *Qaphela ingane* (Take Care of the Boy) concerns the upbringing of two children with different personalities. In Ndebele what can be considered the most successful novel is Ndabaningi Sithole's *Amande6ele kaMzilikazi* (The Matabele of Mzilikazi);[82] the primary reason for its success is that it deals with a historical theme— the Matabele rebellion, its causes, the subsequent fighting, and the disappearance of Lobengula.

There is little verse in Ndebele, although Ndabezinhle Sigogo has written about twenty-five poems and has broadcast some of them. A small anthology of verse has also been published, containing traditional praise poems and some modern verse. Perhaps the reason for the apparent paucity of writing in Ndebele is that as yet the language has not been introduced into the secondary schools; as late as January 1965 the Ndebele Language Committee drafted proposals to have Zulu replaced by Ndebele in schools. A comparison of the number of entries in the bureau's literary competitions shows that in 1962 there were twenty-six entries in Shona and only four in Ndebele; in 1963 there were 103 Shona entries to seventeen Ndebele. Obviously the future seems to lie with Shona, but the writers, especially the novelists, will have to free themselves from the desire to document and from their propensity for moral upliftment if they are ever to make any statement beyond the dogmatic exhortations of a parish priest.

LESOTHO

Sotho Literature: The Rejection of Nature

About sixty-five works have been published in Sotho, the largest single group of languages in the vernacular literature of the entire continent. Sotho, like the other southern African vernacular languages, was influenced by the Christian missionaries. The Bible and *Pilgrim's Progress* were translated into Sotho, the latter in 1857; a mission station was established at Morija in 1853 and began publishing in 1862. According to Jahn, "The mission was both help and hindrance: needing teachers and text-books, it educated, encouraged and supported the gifted; but they grew away from it and chafed at the pettiness of that simple pious world."[83]

As has been seen, this pattern was repeated throughout Central and eastern Africa, and it would be churlish to blame the missionaries too much for the conflict that developed. The missionaries were no different from the collectors of the oral literature who had had specific functions in mind—sociological, social, anthropological, and linguistic. Neverthe-

122

less, that the missionaries were as inhibiting as they seemed to have been is unfortunate; nowhere are the restrictions they imposed as prohibitive as in South Africa, nor indeed as important, since they were to affect the entire southern and western parts of the continent.

E. L. Segoete (b. 1858) and Z. D. Mangoela (b. 1883) were the ancestors of Sotho writing. They both drew heavily on folk literature and on Christian moral ideas, and their intention, in Mangoela's words, was "to preserve for the nation some of our stories, to make a Mosotho love what is his own, and to arouse a love for books and for reading in our nation." Mangoela laid the foundations of a literature in Sotho; he edited the "Paliso" series of school readers, collected *lithoko* (praise songs), and wrote fifty-four short stories about the adventures of hunters and travelers which were published in his *Har'a libatana le linyamat'sane* (Among the Beasts and Animals). This was more than an ethnological accumulation of legend, however; written in rhetorical style, it was an intentional attempt at conjuring up a romantic past: "And now that these times have passed and are gone forever, who will take the trouble to live again in them, to remember them if he knows anything about them? Who will take pains that we should picture to our children of today, and to those who are yet to be born, the times of the beasts and the wild animals?"[84] Mangoela himself undertook this responsibility and told the adventurous stories of how Hoko fought a leopard and tired it, how Ralitau overpowered a lion, and how Lesenya's friends rescued him from an ant-bear. Mangoela does not describe the world of the tale, but a system that has become disoriented (owing to the advent of Christianity?). No longer is there the oneness with nature; rather, there is the quest of man for dominion—all his heroes seek mastery over nature.

Segoete met Mangoela in 1907, and though he was some twenty-five years older, his classical contribution to Sotho literature did not appear until 1910. Segoete also had published a collection of tales, and his *Raphepheng* (1915) was inspired by motives similar to Mangoela's. As he himself said, he wanted "to collect some of the things about the Basotho, about birds, about grasshoppers and about riddles."[85] The narrator, Raphepheng, tells the stories with the same nostalgia that is noticeable in Mangoela. Raphepheng is more critical of his contemporaries than of his ancestors and describes a time when the "beauty of the body was not hidden by these sacks of clothes. Today men and women creep into bags . . ." (p. 7). Nevertheless, the stories are not all wooden-faced venerations of the past or serious denunciations of the present, and it is laughable when Raphepheng, whose "teeth had been worn down to the gums," criticizes the people of modern times because sugar "robs people of their teeth" (p. 21). Through Raphepheng the whole world of traditional Sotho belief is presented and when, at times, his ability seems to pall, Segoete invents certain situations, such as a meeting of locusts and grasshoppers to choose their king, so that he could describe them. The last section of the book deals with the communal customs of the Basotho.

Raphepheng cannot be truly classified as creative literature, and indeed Segoete's importance is that he wrote a Sotho classic in 1910—*Monono ke moholi ke mouoane* (Riches Are a Haze, a Mist).[86] Although it contains the pattern of many stories that were to follow in Sotho literature, of the wicked hero being converted from his pagan practices, Segoete's novel was based on personal experience. In the account Khitsane tells Tim, a neighbor of his who is rich but godless, the story of his life. It is a life of tribulations; four times he loses all his possessions. When he leaves his tribal lands, the laws of the whites confuse him. His wicked companion, Malebaleba, encourages him to attack a policeman. He falls into the hands of murderers and robbers, becomes a fugitive, and has to hide in towns and forests. But later on he again meets Malebaleba who is now an evangelist and Malebaleba converts him. Khitsane returns home—a cripple with wooden legs but happy in this newfound joy. To add to the melodrama and the stories of sudden conversions, the end of the novel tells how Khitsane is summoned to the City of Life, crosses a stream by four stepping-stones, Hope, Peace, Gladness, and Longing, and disappears beyond the clouds. His friend Tim is so moved that he too becomes converted.

It is easy from this distance of time to criticize the overt religiosity of Mangoela and Segoete, to attack them for being mere colporteurs of the Christian message, but it must be realized that within their own context they were revolutionary. Both products of the Mountain School at Morija, they intentionally turned their backs on their own tradition and used the myths and images of the new superstition. At best they can be considered as apologists for the Christian life and western values; at worst they were merely harsh detractors of their own past.

To some extent this is what Edward Motsamai was; born in 1870 he comes midway in time between Segoete and Mangoela, but differs from them in the important respect that he saw the past as harsh and brutal. All these writers, however, imply that the present was better simply by virtue of the Christian message. Motsamai's *Mehla ea malimo* (The Times of the Cannibals) is a collection of eighteen stories.[87] Most of the stories follow a similar pattern: the hero falls into the hands of cannibals and finally escapes by some form of guile. For instance, Ramalitse begins to sing and dance and, as the cannibals watch, he flees to safety. In a way Motsamai's world is like that of his two predecessors; man is in conflict with what is around him, and, perhaps even more bitter and pertinent, man is in conflict with man.

Thomas Mofolo (1877–1948), the greatest writer of the period, was seven years Motsamai's junior. He too was a product of Morija and even worked for the missionaries at one time. Perhaps Mofolo's work, more than that of any of his contemporaries, shows what Jahn has called "the synthesis of Sotho tradition and Christianity." In 1868, the New Testament was rendered into southern Sotho, a southern Sotho-English dictionary was produced at Morija in 1876, and an anonymous collection of folklore was published at Platberg in 1850. It is therefore not surprising that in 1907 Mofolo published *Moeti oa bochabela* (The Traveler to the East).[88] In the story Fekisi, disgusted with the life around him, begins to ask certain questions about the source of cloud and rain, the origin of the sun, the nature of God. He finds that the world of nature is, in contrast to his own, happy and more pleasant. An old man, Ntsoanatsati, tells him that men formerly originated from the place where the sun rises every morning, and in a vision he sees a man rising out of a pool, brighter than the sun. It is this he decides to seek.

Mofolo's form is the familiar hero-quest story found in the tale. But the impetus for the hero's departure in the tale is never the disgust that Fekisi feels; this alienation is a direct result of the Christian presence which had driven a wedge through tribal society and had divided kinsmen on the question of ideology. To seek the Christian ideal Fekisi has to leave the familiar haunts of his tribe and his gods and to travel far away across open fields and deserted lands. It is as if the thoughtful, honest Mofolo were telling the reader that Christianity was far removed from the African plane of realism and was an elusive, insubstantial phantom which had to be sought. But his hero, until he leaves, remains very much a Mosotho; appropriately he sings a praise song to his father's cattle before he finally departs.

The first stages of his journey are disappointing; the people he encounters are no better than those he has left behind. It is with relief that he leaves all human company and treks across the desert. When he reaches the sea, he faints and then he meets three white elephant hunters who convert him and return to him some of the happiness he had lost. Mofolo adds that his hero "accepted all they told him, he believed them" (p. 111). On the occasion of receiving the first sacrament he sees Christ at the altar and rushes forward. There Fekisi is found dead.

Mofolo alters the hero-quest tale in an important way; not only is there little link with nature but, as has been shown, there is an abomination of man. In addition the whole allegorical interpetation is centered on the protagonist; it is *his* search, for *his* needs, for *his* boon. Nothing like this had existed in traditional oral literature, and perhaps Mofolo is really visualizing this as the only possibility for the new emerging individual consciousness; it should bear the consequences of egocentricity. The burden of the responsibility of the tribe could be carried by one man in the oral tales, because behind him and ahead of him there was the *wholeness* of the tribe. He had come from the tribe and to the tribe he would return. His adventures only made him more loyal, more readily able to appreciate what he had left behind; they confirmed the superiority of the tribe. But Mofolo's hero is alienated because he has lost the ability to connect with the consciousness of the tribe, which is itself disintegrating. His death confirms his pointless vacillations and the illogicality of alienation.

By contrast Mofolo's *Pitseng* (1910) is a disappointment. All his life Mofolo had to choose between the amiable offerings of Christian camaraderie and the set diet of an uncompromising art. The difficulties of the situation were made even more emphatic, especially since he was an employee of Morija. Only by taking this into consideration can one accept the second novel at all; it was an attempt to pacify his teachers, employers, and publishers. The world had to wait until 1925 for his third novel, *Chaka*, because it was rejected by the missionaries.[89] Another, *Masaroa*, still remains unpublished.

The second novel is named after the village of Pitseng in which it is set. Mr. Katse has brought Christianity to the village and soon has a very large following, including Alfred Phakoe and Aria Sebaka. Katse, rather arbitrarily, dispenses the benefits of the good life and decides that Alfred and Aria should in time marry. Alfred goes off to a training school and Aria becomes an assistant at the village school. Alfred withstands all temptations and returns to marry Aria.[90] These are the bare bones of this highly moral story, and it seems scarcely possible that the author of *Moeti oa bochabela* was capable of seeing the world in such unequivocal and obvious terms.

What, however, seems to deserve some mention is the relationship that the hero of *Pitseng* has with nature. It is a relationship that is to become more evident in *Chaka*. The rejection of nature in Mofolo's first novel, as well as in the works of Mangoela, Segoete, and Motsamai, was part of the rejection of their tradition. In the oral literature there is rapport between man and nature, and therefore nature is never rhapsodized

126

or objectified. It is intrinsic, whole, and consummative. After Mofolo's initial rejection, he returns to nature because it has been rediscovered through European influence; it is now seen through European eyes. For instance, as Alfred journeys to Aria's home, "the finches again flew up in a swarm and passed by quite close to them, but a little distance away they wheeled and rushed past them and settled in the reeds. It was as though they were trying to greet him in this manner" (p. 24). The hesitation "as though" is important; in the world of oral literature they would have greeted him. Mofolo vacillates because, like the hero of his first novel, he has journeyed away from his people's ethos on a voyage of repudiation.

This is the key to an understanding of *Chaka*. It is no simple debunking of legend, but in Noni Jabavu's words "it becomes the apocalyptic vision of a monstrous beast, consumed by an all-destroying blood-lust."[91] The historical Chaka is only the impetus for Mofolo's psychological study of the nature of repudiation. Mofolo reverts to the theme of the first novel, a theme which becomes his testament—the individual cannot survive alone. Both Christian and pagan need the props of tribal security. It is no accident that both Fekisi, who saw Christ, and Chaka, who conspired with the devil, have to die.

Chaka is forced into individuality; he is the illegitimate son of Senzangakoma, chief of the Ifenilenja tribe, and Nandi. Hated by his jealous brothers he is forced to flee from home. He grows up quite alone, but brave. His mother wants to ensure that he inherits the chieftainship, so she has him anointed by the great serpent of the deep and he is put in the care of the evil Isanusi. His brothers continue to harass him and finally his own father orders that he be killed. This marks the turning point in Chaka's alienation:

> When Chaka left his home in flight he left it as Chaka, a man like other men with the weaknesses of his kind. But now he was returning entirely changed. It was his body only that returned, his outward appearance; his inner nature he left in the place from which he had come. He returned with a different spirit and a different soul. Even before Chaka had been a man of extraordinary endurance. He persevered, however difficult his heart's desire: nothing could stop him from carrying out his intentions. But he was still only a man, he was not quarrelsome, and did not know what it was to be the aggressor. But after seeing his own father's sons trying to kill him without a cause and his father himself taking their part, he had fled away, and when he was in the desert his inner nature died, and this was the spirit with which he now returned: "I will kill without a cause him whom I wish to kill, be he guilty or be he innocent, for this is the law upon earth. I will hearken to the entreaties of none. (p. 57)

When Chaka's father dies King Dingiswayo, who has befriended Chaka, makes him chief on the condition that he marry Noliwe, the dead king's favorite sister. It is she whom Isanusi demands as a sacrifice if Chaka wants to dominate the world. Chaka consents and kills her. After this, murder follows upon murder; he kills his child, his soldiers, and finally his own mother. By then Chaka is completely insane and is killed at the end by his half-brother Dingana.

Chaka has suffered from being regarded too much as historical reconstruction and too little as a great novel which, apart from the melodrama, it is. A *Times Literary Supplement* review of July 30, 1931, thought it was a partly accurate and partly imaginary account. Mphahlele sees Chaka as a king given the moral problem of choice.[92] But *Chaka* is neither pure history nor ethics; it is part of the tradition of the praise poem and the hero monomyth, although both have undergone a startling blend and a unique transformation. The catalytic effect of the missionaries caused a radical change in concepts; a new melancholy has entered the African soul and no longer can the natural world, gods, and man be accepted in toto, without question. To say that Mofolo's two great novels belong to the genre of *Pitseng* and are mere exercises in the complacency of missionary teaching is to misunderstand them and Mofolo. They are above all the quests of befuddled individuals, catapulted from the security of tribal consciousness into the personal uncertainty of metaphysical speculation. What should concern the reader of today is not the individual inquiry but the tragic necessity for it.

Mofolo dominates the literary scene in the early years of the century. He attempts to work within the framework imposed on him and his contemporaries by Morija and to write missionary literature capable of a larger interpretation. But the poetry written during this period denies the artistic activity of the individual emphasized by Mofolo and is merely reproductive. There are two exceptions: D. T. Bereng's rewritten versions of the praise poems of Moshoeshoe and others in 1931 and Z. D. Mangoela's reproductions of eighty-two praise poems on the Basuto chiefs published in 1921. Bereng attempted to re-create the praises in a modern style and idiom, illustrating something of the same melancholy that has been discussed before—the cultivated morbidity of *l'homme moyen sensuel*. For instance, he reflects at the tomb of Moshoeshoe:

> And if the years pass,
> If they go and we no longer see them,
> How is it that your name, Moshesh,
> Your name, son of Mokhachane,
> Could pass away and we could live?

128

> But what are these thoughts?
> Why sing these reflections?
> What is my mind searching for there?
> Why speak of these subtle matters?[93]

The praise singer has been caught off guard. Bereng realizes that the nature of this introspection does not belong to the praise song. Rather, his questions express the bewilderment of Chaka and Fekisi.

Mangoela's praise poems were also re-creations but were more within the heroic tradition, as can be seen in his portrayal of a triumphant warrior:

> As the fire caught with red-flamed tongues
> Nkau, fiery blooded, who eats the meat hot,
> the swooping eagle, son of my lord,
> like a hunting dog he came, fire in his eyes
> and fangs bared.[94]

Neither the detailed description nor the histrionic fury is within the tradition of the *lithoko*. It is therefore these qualities that Mangoela added to the praise poem.

With Mofolo Sotho literature saw both its ascendancy and its demise; in the late twenties one solitary figure deserves mention—Azariele Sekese (b. 1849). In 1910 Sekese wrote a satire on the tyranny of the chiefs.[95] The individual, whose manifestation Mofolo had articulated, had begun to castigate society. In Sekese's story (he was himself secretary to a chief) the birds at a meeting protest against the tyranny of Phakoe, the hawk. Lenong, the vulture, is chief and judge. From the hawk's defense it becomes apparent that he is guilty but he is set free. The way in which the leader of the birds complains is both pathetic and funny. He says to the judge: "Even though I am withered I am kept busy all day running away from him, dodging midst hedges. I do not know how he will ever masticate me seeing I am so old."[96] One would have hoped that Segese's satire could have set a trend, but it proved abortive.

In the forties the literature in Sotho seemed to imitate the worst aspects of the works of the pioneers. E. K. K. Matlala's *Tšhukudu* is nothing more than a northern Sotho version of the Samson and Delilah story. Other northern Sotho novels like Madiba's *Tsiri* and Phalane's *Motangtang* are really only guides for raising children, while Sehlodimela's *Moêlêlwa* is about a lazy wife. The recurring theme of the country boy who fares badly in the town is present in Serote's *Molato*. This, unfortunately, is the kind of literature which has influenced vernacular writing in Rhodesia, Zambia, and East Africa. The more recent writers, incapable of depicting the heroic grandeur of *Chaka*, prefer instead the tame, flat, uninvolved world of *Pitseng*. In southern Sotho the situation is the same. Khaketla's *Meokho ea thabo* (Tears of Joy) is a love story in which the hero, refusing his uncle's choice of a bride, goes to Durban and falls in love—only to discover that this was the girl his uncle had originally intended for him. There is something of Mofolo's supernatural vision in Moikangoa's short stories; for example, in one of them his heroine visits the world of the dead. But Nqheku's *Lilahloane* brings us back to the world of straightforward conflicts; this time Lilahloane refuses to marry and disregards her father's wishes—all in defense of Catholicism. Another writer, Machobane, attempts nothing new, choosing instead to depict only Motsamai's world of cannibals. In the fifties M. L. Maile wrote on the nature of marriage and the need to be acquainted with the husband's family background.[97] The trends set in motion by Segoete, Mangoela, and Mofolo have by now completely petered out. This is not unconnected with the fact that writers have increasingly turned to English as a popular literary medium.

SOUTH AFRICA

Xhosa Literature: The Origins of Protest

In 1821, John Bennie of the Glasgow Missionary Society brought a printing press to South Africa and within three years he had translated the commandments and the Lord's Prayer into Xhosa. By 1864 the translation of the Bible was completed. Lovedale, the missionary center for Xhosa, was founded in 1824 and the Scottish missionaries living nearby initiated a Xhosa-English magazine, *Ikwezi* (Morning Star), in 1841, which was replaced by *Indaba* (The News) in 1862. Tiyo Soga, an African who at one time was a pupil at Lovedale, translated a part of *Pilgrim's Progress* in 1866, and his son the second part in 1929.[98] Therefore, well before the last quarter of the nineteenth century important work had been done in Xhosa and the foundation had been laid for the beginnings of creative writing.

There is some evidence of oral creation in the vernacular. Prince Ntsikana, one of the first converts, could neither read nor write but he formed a breakaway church and composed a number of hymns. His only surviving hymn, which was written down, indicates that he was no narrow evangelist but a poet of merit. Three translations[99] still exist and parts of them demonstrate what Ntsikana was attempting. Certainly he was drawing on the form and imagery of the *izi6ongo* (praise poem) with its use of repetition, laudatory phrases, and imagery associated with cattle:

130

The horn soundeth aloud, calling us
To thee, great Hunter, Hunter of souls
Who maketh one herd of friend and foe
All covered and sheltered under thy cloak.[100]

An earlier translation by John Brownlee stresses Ntsikana's use of imagery from war songs to communicate the omnipotence of God: "He alone is a trusty shield / He alone is our bush of refuge."[101] Ntsikana intentionally domesticated the concept of the meek lamb and conveyed the Christian idea of God in more masculine terms. The translation by D. J. Darlow best expresses the succinctness of the nature of God; again the statement is in the manner of the praise poem:

Great 'I am' of truth the Buckler,
Great 'I am' of truth the Stronghold.
Great 'I am' of whom truth shelters.[102]

The more militant aspects of the living God were also proclaimed.

Although Sotho writing was firmly stabilized and developed in the first decade of the twentieth century, not until the twenties did a similar development take place in Xhosa. Before the publication of an anthology in 1906, the published literature "consist[ed] mainly of history, biography, ethnology, didactic verse and religion." The two important writers of the period before 1906 are Tiyo Soga (1831–71) and William Gqoba (1840–88). They wrote short stories, essays, and verse as offshoots of their religious publications. When W. B. Rubusana compiled his anthology in 1906, he collected prose and poetry principally from *I6wi labantu* (The Voice of the People). But Rubusana's work was made up mainly of a hundred proverbs with explanations of some of them in Xhosa, an entry on customs and history, a large number of praise poems, and only a limited amount of verse by individuals.[103]

The work of H. M. Ndawo opens the post-1906 period, though the books for which he is best known were not published until the thirties. His *U-Hambo luka Gqoboka* (The Progress of a Traveler) was published in 1909. Like Mangoela's stories which were to appear three years later, it describes the adventures of a man battling against nature, illustrating his progress from "heathenism" to Christianity. S. E. K. Mqhayi (1875–1945) is the most important writer of this period. His *Ityala lama wele* (The Case of the Twins) is considered by D. D. T. Jabavu to be "an original effort to give a picture of Xhosa court life before the advent of the Europeans."[104] The story is a kind of extended riddle—who is the elder of the two twins who are claiming the right of chieftainship? The whole trial, which adheres to a strict routine, is dramatized. The first twin complains that his brother, They-are-Two, is usurping his place. His brother replies to these charges, and then the midwives have to be called in. Finally the court is cleared so a decision can be made.

Although from the onset Mqhayi tried to get away from mission-school writing, he did not involve himself with recreating the oral literature. Instead he worked fairly closely with oral sources (in addition to indigenous idioms, his work is full of the precision of one directed but not hamstrung by a tradition) and his story emerges as another exercise in the attempt to establish individuality. Mqhayi makes the "case" even more difficult by presenting the contestants as twins. Who could claim to be different? His story, ostensibly about the right to rule, concerns the dubious assertion of individuality. The mere fact that they are twins not only heightens their similarity, but makes their case for separate recognition futile and ridiculous. The author asserts the predominance of the tribe, since it is an old tribal member who finally helps the court to decide.

Mqhayi, who did not publish his book until 1914, remarked that "the manuscript had been lying around in my house for a long time." This might have been the result of missionary censorship, for Mqhayi was considered a "difficult" person. Indeed his name has been expunged from the official record of the history of Lovedale, written by Shepherd. Mqhayi relates in his biography that he was in conflict with the missionaries and after a spell at Lovedale he was forced to leave.[105]

What Mqhayi did was to establish the artist's independence from the patronage of religious bodies. This does not mean that he was ahead of his time, for as late as 1942 when he published *I-nzuzo* (Gain), a collection of verse, the sections into which he divided the poems were along fairly conventional lines. For instance, the selection includes poems on "truth," "hope," and "love," on the "passing of years," on death, and perhaps, nearest to the tradition, poems of praise for Africans who had gone overseas. He imitated English rhyme as well as the sonnet and heroic couplet. But his poetic gifts were not entirely dissipated in producing conventional laudations. He expressed the new individual consciousness through satire and in the manner of the Sotho writer Azariel Sekese he even attacked royalty. One of his most successful pieces is his "praise song" to the then Prince of Wales, composed in 1925:

> Ah Britain! Great Britain!
> Great Britain of the endless sunshine!
> She hath conquered the oceans and laid them low;
> She hath drained the little rivers and lapped them dry;
> She hath swept the little nations and wiped them away;

And now she is making for the open skies.
She sent us the preacher, she sent us the bottle,
She sent us the Bible, and barrels of brandy;
She sent us the breechloader, she sent us cannon;
O, Roaring Britain! Which must we embrace?
You sent us the truth, denied us the truth;
You sent us the life, deprived us of life;
You sent us the light, we sit in the dark,
Shivering, benighted in the bright noonday sun.[106]

The last line is too obvious and does not accord with the unspoken suggestions in the rest of the stanza. The poem is remarkable in many ways: written in a European sonnet form it makes use of various devices of the African praise song—an important technical development. It also initiated a literature of protest in Xhosa.

These Xhosa writers are especially to be admired for their versatility and for their ability to work within the impositions of missionary censorship and still produce works of merit. Although L. Kakaza, a woman, published the novel *U-Zandiwe wakwa-Gcaleka* (Zandiwe of Gcaleka) in 1914, the next major novelist is Enoch S. Guma. His *U-Nomalizo*, named after the heroine, initiated a series of moral stories centered on girls. Nomalizo withstands all manner of temptations and tribulations before she and her fiance, Rangela, are able to marry. Guma's point is that the heroine triumphed "because of the deep faith which she had, and because of putting her trust in God."[107] The novel's moral lesson explains why it was translated into English ten years after it was first published. But *U-Nomalizo* has a greater significance: it bears no trace of the contest with nature. The assumption is made that Christianity, westernization, and urban life had won. There is no backward look, no mention of tribal organization. The individual has become the center of the cosmos.

The work of G. B. Sinxo and James J. R. Jolobe (b. 1902) belongs to the twenties, as does that of D. D. T. Jabavu, who, though not a creative writer, was most active during this period. His numerous travel books based on personal visits to America, Jerusalem, and India helped to promote the possibilities of Xhosa as a literary language. Sinxo, a prolific writer, published three novels, two books of short stories, as well as pieces for the theater. According to John Riordan, his second novel was "ruined by sentimentality." His short stories, however, are better. Three of them were published in one volume as late as 1956.[108] The main story, "Isakhono somfazi" (A Woman's Dexterity), pursues the theme of the good woman, in this case a boy's widowed mother who, with his sister, works as a domestic servant in Johannesburg to provide her son with a higher education. But the story's pattern is not original; the inevitable happens—the boy goes to Johannesburg, gets involved with a prostitute, and has to be rescued by the virtuous girl from home. The theme of the second story is almost the same; again the setting is Johannesburg and the chief character, new to the city, is kidnapped by robbers who plan to kill him. But at the last moment he is recognized by the leader as the son of a man who had once been kind to him.

Jolobe dominates the twenties as a novelist, a poet, and a writer of straight prose. Writing for schools and an adult reading public, he was equally versatile in English and Xhosa. In a foreword to his first novel, published in 1923, J. K. Mather singles him out as the most important of the Xhosa triumvirate including Guma and Sinxo.[109] But Jolobe's real contribution to Xhosa literature was in the field of poetry. His *UmYezo* (An Orchard), published in 1936, was the second volume in a series of books intended for schools and he himself translated some of the poems in 1946. The style and content of the poems varied according to the audiences for which they were intended; those intended for children deal with nature, but mainly they are descriptive pieces. In addition, the poems for children concern diligence, respect, trustworthiness, and truth and offer advice on such things as hygiene and even crossing a street. This verse also is humorous, as for instance his "Umkhosi weencukuthu neentakumba" (The Army of Bed Bugs and Fleas), which is written in a mock-heroic fashion. "Amafu" (Clouds) is a detailed observation of nature:

> They are the robe of the skies
> Even though they might look rugged,
> In a beautiful white-like milk-curd
> And more seasoned when getting dark.
> They are terrifying when they are really sullen and dark.
> With lightning flashing from a distance,
> Roaring in great thunderous sounds
> Like a man threatening in anger.
> They are also the forebearers of the storm
> And call for everything to be silenced.
> Another of their family is the snows,
> The snows that fall in flaky drizzles.
> Even the dews are traced back to them
> The dews that look like beautiful beads along the wearer's neck.
> They are a protection against the sun.[110]

The tradition of oral literature is completely absent in this poem, which is in the convention of European romanticism and has no relation to any of the forms of traditional oral poetry.

It was Jolobe who introduced protest into Xhosa poetry. For him Christianity did not have the coercive effect that it had on many of his colleagues. According to Jolobe, it was through Christianity that Africans could gain a new revolutionary awareness of themselves. "Therefore all those who would sing our National Anthem, 'God Bless Africa' with sincerity, must strive to prepare the ground for the outpouring of those blessings by gathering His lambs unto the fold through the Sunday School."[111] Jolobe used Christianity as a means of national awakening. And it is in Christian terms again that he realizes that Africans as

> Heroic defenders of the tree of life and hope
> Shall never cease to conquer all,
> Like a victorious warrior on crusade.[112]

Here he celebrates the return to the tribe, to the wholeness of being which had existed in pre-Christian times, and he praises, above all, men who cherish patriotism: "When mountains are no more, forever thus / Will they remain, for love outlives all change."[113] But because Jolobe worked within the tradition of missionary literature, he had to steer a righteous middle course between their gods and his. His poem "Thuthala" is not as successful as some of his others, though it does bring to life Ntsikana, not so much as a hymn-singing *gravitas*, but as an overwhelming figure of inspiring legend.

A poem from *UmYezo,* unfortunately not translated by Jolobe into English, is his most obvious attempt at protest. The poem is entitled "The Making of a Slave," and it describes in allegorical terms "how a slave was made of a young yoke ox." The end of the poem expresses Jolobe's protest against the economic enslavement of Africans.

> I saw it ascend steep mountainous roads
> Loaded with burdens, earning a living,
> Wet with much sweat enriching its lord.
> The sweetness of labour is share in the harvest,
> For I beheld how a slave was made
> Of a young yoke ox.
>
> I saw it in want under this rule,
> The eye with a tear, the spirit oppressed.
> It no longer knew even how to resist.
> Hope lies in efforts sweet freedom to gain,
> For I beheld how a slave was made
> Of a young yoke ox.[114]

The identification with race was a new tribal assertion which was to manifest itself in various forms in African literature. Since the breakup of the tribal organization with the coming of Christianity, there was a latent desire for the individual to return to the solidarity of tribe. But how could this be accomplished without the rejection of Christianity? The new consciousness of race was the way back to an old concept. Jolobe led the individual back into the tribal organization; he did this within the confines of a poetry that reached into the past for origins, into a past that had been shattered and regarded as worthless, and in the process Jolobe combined what Jabavu has called his "delicately cultured mind with true poetic poise."[115]

These writers not only performed a sociological function by walking the tightrope between Christian (and western) values on the one hand and indigenous norms on the other, but also consciously strove to modify the dictates of mission-school literature. At the same time they attempted to inject a hint of protest, of dissatisfaction, which might pass unnoticed. This called for a certain stylistic aptitude; the girl of mission-school literature had to be reformed (or punished) at the end to be thought of as good. But in the meantime, much could be done to illustrate her revolt, her independence from the parish.

Ndawo, who has been mentioned before and whose best work belongs to the thirties, created such a person in Nolishwa. This is ostensibly the story of a young girl who suffers because she refuses to toe the line. The missionaries twice refuse to confirm her, on the second occasion because she had assaulted a teacher. Finally she becomes pregnant and deserts her newborn son; she meets him in later life and is about to marry him when the truth is told her. She then drowns herself. But what is not apparent in a summary of this nature is her love of life, her irrepressible zest. When, for instance, she refuses to get off the path for a preacher from the village and he threatens to report her, she roundly abuses him: "Go straight back to the minister. I can see that you don't get enough to eat up at that place. I know you very well. Go and get yourself some bread and tea and all the coffee that you can get and then you can start pouring out your news to him."[116] Her protest is on behalf of everyone. In the tradition of mission-school literature it was necessary for her to come to a bad end, but reader, writer, and heroine enjoy themselves in the process at the expense of the missionaries.

This kind of writing is best expressed in A. C. Jordan's *Ingqumbo yeminyanya* (The Wrath of the Ancestors), published in 1940. The clash between "those who advocate progress and those who cling to the past," a conflict which until now had been only suggested, is uppermost in this novel.[117] To some extent King Zwelinzima represents westernization and Dingindawo, his rival, the traditional way of life. But there are complications, which result in westernization being associated with tradition, for Zwelinzima is a new king who, against the wishes of his people, wants to marry Thembeka. She is neither of royal blood nor a member of the tribe and her sole claim to Zwelinzima is that she is "educated." She regards the tribal norms as ridiculous, and feelings come to a climax when, to protect her child, she kills a sacred snake, Majola. In the end Zwelinzima has to take his own life.

In the story the snake symbolizes the integrity of the tribe. Like Zwelinzima, Thembeka was educated at Lovedale and in a way she represents the modern brashness, the corrosiveness of Christianity, which assumes that everything "heathen" is worthless. In Jordan's novel the group succeeds in thwarting Thembeka's attempt to destroy it, and when "the royal family are claimed by the ominous river" the tribe reasserts its superiority. What Jordan is trying to illustrate is not the "internal disintegration in persons torn between two forces,"[118] but the necessary breakup of the individual (Christian or otherwise) who challenges the sovereignty of tribe.

Because "the forces of evil, of paganism and reaction win," there were pressures on Jordan to give the book "a different and a more happy ending."[119] That he resisted this and that the book was nevertheless published by a missionary press testify to his artistic fortitude and to a certain liberal emancipation by the missionaries. Jordan's book was part of a tradition, but it exposed that tradition as being a mere literature of bondage. However, he could not have written what he did unless Mqhayi, Guma, and Jolobe had demonstrated that it was possible to work within the missionary framework and yet assert the omnipotence of the tribe. With Zulu literature one encounters the full development of this protest in the writing of B. W. Vilakazi.

Zulu Literature: The Reassertion of the Group

Zulu literature developed later than any other South African vernacular literature, and indeed D. D. T. Jabavu has noted that as late as 1921 the only writings in Zulu were grammars, vocabularies, and translations of the scriptures. The New Testament had been translated in 1865, but not until 1883 was the Bible completely translated. The two centers for Zulu writing have been the Marianhill Mission Press in Natal and the publishing house of Shuter and Shooter at Pietermaritzburg. The Stewart Zulu readers for schools, published by Lovedale, did not begin appearing until 1939. However, in 1868 Callaway had started publishing his folklore in Zulu, an English-Zulu dictionary had appeared in 1880, and a translation of Bunyan followed in 1895. The first work by a Zulu writer—a history—was not published until 1922. This encouraged a series of publications in Zulu.[120]

Because Zulu was the last of the South African groups to develop a written literature, it did not go through the long process of publishing ethology, folklore, history, and translations from the Bible; rather the process was compressed into a few years. This was not a disadvantage, however, for almost from the beginning Zulu attained the radical position reached by Xhosa literature much later in its development, and J. L. Dube's *Isitha esikhulu somuntu emnyama nguya ugobo iwa khe* (The Greatest Enemy of the Black Man Is He Himself) was a trenchant piece of self-criticism. After R. R. R. Dhlomo had served his apprenticeship beginning in 1928 by publishing two school readers and three biographies, he attempted fiction. Both Dube and Dhlomo wrote about Chaka and faced the same problem of working within the tradition of mission-school literature. Their contemporary, Vilakazi, spoke for them and for himself when he said of Dhlomo, "I wish Dhlomo was not working in water-tight compartments in adapting the book and style of his language to the classroom." Dhlomo does attempt to overcome this problem in his two later novels; *Indlela yabibi* (The Way of the Wicked) "gives a rather lurid picture of the seamy side of Zulu life in Johannesburg," and *UNomalanga kaNdengezi* (Nomalanga, the Daughter of Ndengezi) has been called a "character study of the life of the Zulu in Natal."[121]

The Zulu writer who deserves the greatest attention and is perhaps one of the finest African authors is B. W. Vilakazi (1906–47). Like Dube and Dhlomo, Vilakazi was interested in the historical novel, a result of which is his *UDiNgiswayo kaJobe* (Dingiswayo, Son of Jobe), published in 1939. But his first novel, *Noma nini* (For Ever and Ever) is in the mission-school tradition. Its familiar plot tells of a young man who leaves home to work in nearby Durban, in this case to save up for the bride-price. In the meantime his betrothed works in a missionary household and becomes a Christian. She is about to marry someone chosen for her by the missionaries when, after having the usual adventures involving robbers, the hero comes home to claim her. In his third novel Vilakazi deals once more with history and describes the Bambatha uprising of 1906.[122]

It is in his poetry that Vikalazi develops the Xhosa tradition of protest. His first book of verse, a collection of twenty-one poems entitled *Inkondlo kaZulu* (Zulu Poems), deal with a number of topics. The consciousness of race, so apparent in Vilakazi's second volume of poems, is hinted at in this earlier book. *Inkondlo kaZulu* does have one flaw, however; the poems rigidly adhere to rhyme and stanza arrangements foreign to the spirit of the poetry Vilakazi was attempting to write. J. Dexter Taylor, while admiring the way he sought "to make Zulu experience dance to the music of his words," deplored the "limited success" of his rhymes. Nevertheless one of his great poems, "Impophoma ye Victoria" (Hymn to Victoria Falls), is in this volume.[123] The author expressed pride in Victoria Falls not because he was attempting a mere exercise in rustic poetizing, but because he was seriously concerned with Africa's heritage. As he was to ask:

> Who then shall dare arise in mood audacious
> With pipings shrill of grasshopper and cricket
> From out the dust the milliped inhabitants
> To vie with thee, Dumase, Smoke that thunders?[124]

The object of praise had become too great to be praised.

Protest and national pride come together in Vilakazi's best work, *Amal'ezulu* (Zulu Horizons), which was published in 1945. Perhaps the poem most typical of his work of this period is "Tell Me," which is an outspoken cry of protest. In it the poet asks the white overlord for an explanation of the Black man's plight; at one point he bursts out into rhetorical interrogatives: "Say to me son of a white man Who am I, what am I, why am I?" The end is bitter:

> I take a look at the whole damn show
> And believe me now I'm convinced,
> That I'm lost whatever the way I choose . . .[125]

Such pessimism is a new note and represents the culmination of Zulu writing. "On the Gold Mines" is equally cynical; the machines personify the means by which the Black man is humiliated, and the only escape is death, which will bring about

> Long sleep from where there's no waking
> Folded around in my people's arms
> Under the green hills of the sky.[126]

The melancholic tone is no longer a quaint device; it is a genuine cry of the agony of the individual who is completely alone, alienated from the familiar.

Although the literary record in Zulu is mainly confined to the achievements of Dhlomo and Vilakazi (in verse), it marks the pinnacle of Black South African vernacular literature. It was a literature which had evolved from the religious commitment of the nineteenth century to become an intense dedication to race, a dedication best represented by Vilakazi. Without the background, without the foundation, writers could not have been free enough in English to enlarge on Vilakazi's protests or bold enough to make, what protest literature is, a reassertion of the dominance of the group. A survey of Sotho, Xhosa, and Zulu literatures shows the gradual emergence of the individual, his rejection of his past, and finally, associated with the national quest, his desire for racial awareness. This explains his resurrection of the past, his defection from urban values, and his enlistment with village norms. It is from here that Black South African writers in English take their stance; to a large extent they have inherited the virtues and failings of the vernacular writers, but their legacy has enabled them to disregard missionary issues of a generation ago and to strike out into new and more pertinent directions. In the literature in European languages the individual consciousness, having been alienated, is seeking a way back into the tribal enclosure.

PART III
THE PRESENCE
OF EUROPE

Chapter 8

Beginnings in English

In Africa the novel is the only literary art form that has been totally imported and imposed over and above development from an indigenous pattern. Drama and poetry, on the other hand, were an integral part of the African heritage; they functioned within the oral tradition, contributing to ceremonial and festival occasions. In a preliterate society no such function existed for the novel—there was no need for it to *perform*. It is not surprising, therefore, that with the advent of literacy, the novel has most interested the new writers. The novel, by its nature, establishes a terrain of private communication and response, and it does this partly by a visual process. In Africa it completed the artistic view of the world, and in a larger and more important sense it incorporated into this view the aesthetic of an oral tradition to which it never truly belonged. A European conception, articulated by an indigenous African exposition, has resulted in what is today regarded as the African novel; its development has been a process from flat, bald statement to elaborate experiment.

The statement first expressed in the novel centered on an idyllic world—Africans without Europeans, innocence of village life, detailed descriptions of group ceremonies. Such a work might well be termed "anthropological," for the writer was interested not in characterization, but in the detailed examination of culture. Those characters that did exist were stereotypes, and the importance of the narration was in the telling. This might well be a hangover from the folktale. However, these generalizations apply mostly to West Africa; in East and South Africa one immediately finds the fiction of revolt. But for the origin of fiction in English one must look toward West Africa.

Pioneers in West African Fiction

The beginnings of West African fiction are to be found in two works by Ghanaians. R. E. Obeng's *Eighteenpence* (1943) distinguishes itself historically by being the first West African novel in English. But before this E. Casely-Hayford had written a prose narrative—*Ethiopia Unbound*—in 1911. Both are interesting, though dissimilar, ancestors of the West African novel in English.

Ethiopia Unbound, a work which takes the reader to London, West Africa, and even the underworld, is a literary expression of a wide variety of ideas. Kwamankra, the main character, is first seen in London conversing with Whiteley, a divinity student, on Christianity, a subject which is taken up time and again throughout the book. Kwamankra believes in a Black God and feels that Christ was "born of an Ethiopian woman" (p. 10). He is next seen in West Africa where he is helping to establish a national university. Casely-Hayford devotes many pages to discussing the implications of such a university, arguing that "no people could despise its own language, customs and institutions and hope to avoid national death" (p. 17). Kwamankra is then sent back to London to help translate books for the proposed university; he also becomes a law student and makes friends with another West African called "the Professor."

Education and Christianity, however, are not the only focal points of the book. Love also plays its part: one character, Tandor-Kuma, cannot marry the woman he loves because she is a maid; Kwamankra is more fortunate. After not having seen Mansa, his former girl friend, for many years, he finally meets her again. They marry and have a son, but Mansa dies when giving birth to their second child. Her death returns the author to the theme of Christianity; Kwamankra feels that through his love for Mansa "he had touched the depths of human happiness and the depths of human sorrow, and had come to know that the way to God led from one to the other" (p. 43).

He visits her in the underworld, where she is a goddess. The style alters as the author smoothly blends a biblical prose with the rhythm of classical verse in his description of the underworld: "A number of peaceful avenues, wearing a beautiful green; like unto mass, which met in one grand broadway. Each avenue was edged with luxuriant shrubs and plants whose leaves showed the most delicate tints of the rainbow in beautiful blend" (p. 54). Kwamankra's uncertainty about religious matters and his gesture toward Heaven are symbolized in a new structure which Mansa shows him and in which there is "unevenness in place where [there] should be uniformity" (p. 56). His wife gives him advice on how he should live, and the visit concludes with a promise: "Say unto the mighty that the cry of the afflicted and the distressed among the sons of Ethiopia has come up to us, and we will visit the earth. . . . Lo! Nyiakrapon will establish in Ethiopia a kingdom which is different therein, and an angel of light, with a two-edged sword, shall guard the gate thereof" (p. 63).

When Kwamankra returns to the Gold Coast, he comes to the conclusion that he must restore the practice of indigenous religion to his people, instead of following "emasculated sentimentalities which men shamelessly and slanderously identify with the Holy one of God, His Son, Jesus Christ" (p. 72).

Abruptly scene and character again switch; Kwamankra's old acquaintance Whiteley has decided to go to the Gold Coast as a missionary. In his mission work, he proves to be an ideal imperialist; he quarrels with his Black assistant chaplain and has him dismissed over the question of segregated cemeteries.

An attempt is now made to reintroduce Kwamankra into the story; Bilcox, a Gold Coaster, Whiteley, and Kwamankra meet at a party given by the chief magistrate. During the affair, Kwamankra describes his plan for segregating by ability, rather than by race: "If you took mankind in the aggregate, irrespective of race and shook them up together, as you would the slips of paper in a jury panel box, you would find after the exercise that the cultured would shake themselves free and come together, and so would the uncouth, the vulgar, and the ignorant; but, of course, you would ignore the law of nature, and, with a wave of the hand, confine the races in separate airtight compartments" (p. 105). Kwamankra seems to be concerned solely with his own position, that of the privileged in an underprivileged community.

After a melodramatic meeting between Kwamankra and his son, Ekru Kwow, a meeting that has nothing to do with the development of the book, the Professor and Tandor unexpectedly re-enter the story. An amusing description is given of a train journey they take with Kwamankra iń the Gold Coast. The Professor refuses to surrender his ticket, saying firmly to the ticket-collector, "I have made it a rule never to give up my ticket on this line till I have landed safely at my destination, do you understand?" (p. 123). The bewildered ticket-collector does not know what to make of his passengers.

Another character is then introduced and dropped: Tony Palmer is of a Sierra Leonean family and with him Kwamankra talks about marriage, asserting that any woman who is worthy of his love is worthy to be his wife. Although no more is heard of Tony Palmer, this scene is juxtaposed with another, in which Tandor-Kuma, now married and ill, is nursed back to health by the mother of his child and the woman he had deserted.

Toward the end of the book, a meeting of the nations of the world on Mount Atlas is described. In this section the writer states his own opposition to colonialism and Christianity. Kwamankra is mentioned only tangentially, as giving a lecture at the African National University in America, where he puts forth his views on Edward Blyden, a pioneer African Pan-Africanist. Kwamankra is again dropped, and the author discusses the possibilities of the cultural unity of Africa, America, and the Caribbean. Kwamankra reappears as a delegate to the Pan-African Congress of 1905 where he again expounds Blyden's ideas for a unity of all Blacks. He criticizes "the African who comes to his brethren with red-hot civilisation straight from Regent Circus or the Boulevards of Paris" (p. 184), and identifies himself with those who "walked the banks of the Nile in the days of yore" (p. 185). At the end of the book, the author reinforces this idea of the equality of Africans and discusses Fanti belief and custom.

As has been seen, *Ethiopia Unbound* is a means by which Casely-Hayford attempted to express a hotchpotch of ideas. As far as action is concerned little happens, and the book vacillates between fantasy and detailed documentation. Kwamankra is allowed to disappear from the story for long periods, and either his place is taken by other characters or the author develops the ideas himself. Many of the ideas, however, lack clarity and consistency. For instance, Kwamankra goes to Britain to translate important books into his own language for the founding of the national university. Furthermore, when the author is not attacking the evils of westernization, he is advocating the study of the classics or giving his story a classical setting, as with Kwamankra's visit to the underworld and the meeting of the nations of the world on Mount Atlas.

The same vacillation is observed in his attitude toward class and Christianity. One character learns the lesson of social snobbery when he is nursed back to health by a woman he despises, but at the magistrate's party Kwamankra advocates a meritocracy. There is, however, cohesion between Kwamankra's ideas and the author's; although it is not satisfactory art when they interchange roles, it is nevertheless worth pointing out, in a book with so many deficiencies, that their ideological world is a mutual one.

If *Ethiopia Unbound* were intended as a novel, the conversations also seem unreal. Often they are stilted and in attempting to be always profound, they lack the ease which is associated with normal conversation. Pidgin English is only used once—in the train episode. This succeeds in maintaining balance, for so much of the book is serious and there are few light moments of relief.

Kwamankra has little private life. His thoughts are all concerned with the public issues of his day. One learns little about him as a person but a great deal about his attitude toward various matters. For example, in an unsuccessful scene he discusses colonialism and the "yellow peril" with his son. According to the author, "he had a call to duty, and that in the service of his race" (p. 25). But his race is identified with any that seems convenient at the moment—Egyptians, Greeks, Ethiopians, Chinese, Japanese, and West Indians. After a while Kwamankra's soul-searching inquiries about Christianity and his self-consciousness about race become a bore.

As the summary has indicated, the book abounds in sudden inexplicable shifts in time. But there seems to be no accompanying development in the characters. Kwamankra meets Whiteley at the beginning of the novel and then three years later, yet one is not aware of any change in Kwamankra. The marriage to Mansa is not treated in detail; it is as if Casely-Hayford feels that his book is one of ideas and that he must reserve the greater part for the expression of these ideas.

Archaisms predominate—"twain," "the wind blowing where it listeth," "he wot not the full meaning of what he had done"—although they are only appropriate in the description of the visit to the underworld. When Casely-Hayford aspires to a back-to-nature romanticism, the writing becomes absurd and trite.[1] He has Mansa tell her husband: "When we arrived in England the life of the people seemed to me artificial . . . Chance took me to Germany—there in the Black Forest, I got into direct touch with Nature; the song of the birds, the bleating of the lambs, the fragrance of the fields, all seemed so natural, and I said to myself; Here is my proper place; here the atmosphere wherein my nature may expand" (p. 36). These seem strange sentiments coming from Kwamankra's wife, who, in the next breath, preaches world government by "Ethiopians."

Ethiopia Unbound is really a record of the author's own uncertainties and those of his generation. They were *évolués* who cherished their position, at the same time paying lip service to indigenous African beliefs. When Casely-Hayford therefore writes of a Fanti god, Nyiakrapon, he takes pains to show that he is like the Christian God. Without knowing it, Casely-Hayford was the earliest representative of a conflict—the man with irreconcilable cultural loyalties.

Obeng-Akrofi, the main character of Obeng's *Eighteenpence*, is more certain of his world.[2] And although *Eighteenpence* is incontestably a novel, it is in some ways similar to *Ethiopia Unbound*—particularly in its moral awareness, expressed at times in the language of the Bible, and in its concern with documentation, in this case the legal system of the then Gold Coast.

Eighteenpence is really extended allegory. Akrofi, to pay for a cutlass he has bought for eighteenpence to begin farming, agrees to work free for his creditor, the farmer Owusu. When Konaduwa, Owusu's wife, falsely accuses him of attempting to rape her, there begins a series of trials. Konaduwa is first tried for failing to report the rape and for abusing certain aristocrats. Refusing to be tried in the native courts, she leaves to report her case to the district commissioner. On her way a ferryman, who later marries her, falls in love with her, and as she is about to leave the ferry her suitcase is knocked into the river. In annoyance, she insults a policeman and is once more brought to court.

She had previously accused her husband of employing slave labor, and he is now tried for this. Then Akrofi's trial for attempted rape takes place, and also the trial of a girl who had insulted a sword-bearer. They are all let off quite leniently; the author seems interested mainly in detailing the formalities of court procedure. The rest of the novel is almost a new story dealing with Akrofi's marriage and his success at farming by using European methods. Akrofi finds treasure on his land and is arrested for not reporting it. In the inevitable trial that follows, he proves through documentation that the farm is his own property, despite the chief's covetousness toward his land. Later on, however, an uncle arrives and destroys all his good work. Akrofi had built a school in the village and was happily married, but because of his uncle's offensive ways his wife leaves him. Finally, even he cannot stand his uncle and, after making three separate speeches of farewell to his daughters Violet, Lily, and Rose, he leaves the village. When the uncle dies, Akrofi is asked by the village people to return. He finds more treasure and is reunited with his family.

Akrofi is not a real person but a representative of commendable virtues. At times he is in danger of becoming a pious bore, especially when he lectures guests at a function to celebrate his son's government post, when he chastizes a teacher for using corporal punishment at his school, and when he bids farewell to his daughters. A more likable and significant person is Konaduwa, a rebellious woman opposed to every type of authority. When she refuses to be tried in the native courts and the white district commissioner tries to dodge her by claiming that he is busy, she roundly upbraids him: "If you have no time why do you say you will settle cases? You are not cultivating or trading for the Government, but you receive a good salary each month. Perhaps your pay is much higher than your father's is in your own country. You have nothing to do but sit in your office, come to Court and ask one or two questions, and go back to eat and sleep, yet you get your pay" (pp. 48–49). But she is not anti-white, as Kwamankra tended to be; she is simply an angry individual. When it suits her purpose, however, she feigns contrition and is let off scot-free.

As in *Ethiopia Unbound*, the language of *Eighteenpence* is at times heavy; one finds expressions like "poverty knows no alternative" (p. 17), "comprehensive insult" (which appears twice in the novel, pp. 33 and 80), "horticultural advice" (p. 161), and "transient impulse" (p. 103). At times there are stock uses of the language: "Akrofi's heart thudded with joy" or "in a tremulous voice Akrofi ejaculated" (p. 20). In other passages, Obeng's linguistic quaintness is directly influenced by the Bible, as was Casely-Hayford's; for example, even though Akrofi is a pagan, one learns that "he knew that it [Sunday] was a universal Sabbath Day on which he must not labour" (p. 19). At another point, Konaduwa is labeled "the woman taken in adultery." Nevertheless, such biblical language is not out of place in a story purporting to be didactic, and the novel, which attempts to show what can be achieved by industry, is a didactic work.

Unlike *Ethiopia Unbound*, *Eighteenpence* does show signs of humor, though frequently it is unintentional. For instance, when Konaduwa is asked to pay for her ferry crossing, she parts her lips in a smile, displaying a gap in her teeth. This wins over the ferryman: "'What exceptionally fine teeth this woman has!' the ferryman explained. 'Keep your sixpence,' he added, 'and I will pay it for you'" (p. 37). However, at times the humor is evidently more intentional. For example, Akrofi plays a gramophone given him as a present: "The labourers had never heard one before, and when it began to play some ran away from the house. . . . In the morning the other labourers asked their master not to use the machine again; otherwise they would have to give notice" (p. 110). And Konaduwa is herself very funny when, refusing to plead guilty or not guilty in court, she argues quite plausibly: "When a case has not been tried, how can one say whether one is guilty or not? Even if the case has been tried, how can you expect one to pronounce judgment against oneself? Tell the Commissioner that I cannot possibly

149

answer that question" (p. 41). It is a type of humor of which Casely-Hayford was incapable, since his work was much too serious. Obeng, with less rigid intentions, has his moments of relaxation.

Both writers, however, are interested in displaying their culture. Large sections of *Ethiopia Unbound* deal with Fanti religion, law, and customs, and the greater part of *Eighteenpence* is concerned with courtroom etiquette. Comparisons are made between contemporary and former methods of punishment and much attention is paid to the formalities of court assembly—the manner and order in which the various participators enter and leave, the ritual involved in conducting a case, and so on. The ferryman's courtship and marriage to Konaduwa is also described at great length, with some of Obeng's sense of fun creeping in. So the conditions of marriage begin: "Should Amoake marry another woman or take a concubine, and his first wife commit suicide, he would not be held responsible. He would only have to provide the ordinary material for a wife's funeral, viz. a coffin, a pillow, cloths, waist-beads, a fathom of silk, a mat, a sheep and refreshments and gunpowder for firing at the funeral" (p. 86). And later, when Akrofi makes a success of farming, Obeng gives details on agricultural methods.

There is a certain diffuseness in the novel; it is first centered on Obeng, then on Owusu and his family quarrel. Before Konaduwa and her own trials are depicted, the episode of the girl who insulted the sword-bearer is introduced. The story returns to Owusu, switches to Akrofi and his son Sam, and then abruptly and irrelevantly to Akrofi's uncle. The various lawsuits after a while become a strain on the reader, since each trial is treated as a major event in the story.

Besides the frequent character changes, there are other unsatisfactory elements in this novel. One wonders why Konaduwa is still interested in Owusu's case after her divorce, for the story could well have ended with her marriage. Akrofi's attempt to become a successful farmer is an anticlimax and makes the theme and action unnecessarily diffuse.

J. B. Danquah has commented that *Eighteenpence* "is the first long novel in English ever published by a Gold Coast man. Casely-Hayford's *Ethiopia Unbound*, which in a way, was an imaginative story, was political in motive. *Eighteenpence* is a true novel. . . ."[3] Though differing in artistic intention, both works are important attempts in imaginative writing. It is true that Obeng's artistic purpose is more evident than Casely-Hayford's, but both pioneered the way for a significant development in West African fiction.

Imaginative Biography

The second generation of West African novelists in English includes Chinua Achebe, T. M. Aluko, Cyprian Ekwensi, Onuora Nzekwu, Gabriel Okara, and Amos Tutuola. Although Tutuola's *Palm-Wine Drinkard* (1952) was the first novel of any of these authors to be published, the real descendants of *Ethiopia Unbound* and *Eighteenpence* are the nonfictional, semibiographical works that appeared in the 1960s.

Robert Wellesley Cole's *Kossoh Town Boy* (1960) is the true story of his childhood in Sierra Leone. The father of the three boys and two girls in the family is portrayed as a patriarchal figure, the mother as devoted but strict. Cole also depicts the broader extension of an African family as well as the numerous visitors to his home. All in all, Cole's canvas is wide, but he keeps his immediate family very much the center of attraction. Their everyday life—childhood punishment, dosings of castor oil, and family service—is the book's primary focus.

A reviewer in *Ibadan* considered *Kossoh Town Boy* "an unsophisticated narrative of the day-to-day happenings in the life of a boy," but the assessment of the Nigerian novelist Onuora Nzekwu, who described it as "exciting and pleasing to read,"[4] is probably closer to the truth. In fact the book correlates style and subject matter. Describing his life from birth to the age of seventeen, the author has sought to use appropriate language to relate the relevant events and selected experiences of his childhood. But at any given moment he employs a shift in time which establishes ease and fluidity, as can be seen in his portrayal of a fight between him and the class bully:

> Suddenly, as we came outside the gates, without warning, Horace aimed a violent kick at me. What is more, he connected. It hurt. Immediately we grabbed hold of each other and wrestled. Stung by the kick, I soon had him on the ground, and according to the unwritten rules I had won, and honour was served. I got up, and started to dust my clothes, worried about what father would say, when a shout made me turn round. Horace had an open clasp knife in his hand and was coming after me!
>
> I was frightened, I hated the sight of blood, or the thought of being cut. Even today I cannot watch a boxing in the flesh, although I enjoy it on the television or cinematograph screen.
>
> That day, however, I was in a quandary. To run away was unthinkable. In any case at the moment I was the adjudged victor. But I was frightened; and dreadfully tensed. I dared not take my eyes off the deadly weapon in his hand. My one compulsive thought was to snatch it from him and use it on him, before he could hurt me. The instinct of self-preservation turned me from a coward into a potential killer.

Fortunately the bigger boys promptly intervened and kicked the thing from his hand, and threatened to thrash him unless he behaved himself. We were never friends again. (pp. 101–2)

As an autobiography, *Kossoh Town Boy* manages to maintain the reader's interest both in the boy's development and in the exact picture that is given of Freetown in the early part of this century.

William Conton's *African*, published in the same year as Cole's work, is different. The hero is not the author, although Conton bases much of the account on his own experiences as a boy in Sierra Leone and as a student in the United Kingdom. Because the setting is the imaginary Songhai, the childhood of the main character can be that of any boy in West Africa. Conton, unlike Cole, writes with a definite aim in mind: he wants to show the shattering effect of Europe on a boy who has grown up apart from European influence. The opening of the book illustrates the innocence of village life and the naïveté of the children toward things modern, in this case a lorry:

> We grew to tell quite a long way ahead, from the note of the engine, whether or not the driver was looking for somewhere to stop; and we would race out to inspect with solemn awe the wheezing machines we believed to be possessed of some mighty spirit, the conjuring up of which had been done in a distant land called Britain. The supercilious drivers who looked so knowingly under bonnets and chassis during the halt we thought of as a type of high priest, ministering to this spirit; and we would hand them a leaking kerosene tin of muddy well-water with almost as much reverence as a server passing the bishop the holy water. The dust-covered passenger, however, we somehow despised rather than envied; for they seemed so helpless and unhappy, whether they were in the first-class compartment beside the driver, or in the second-class behind.[5]

It is an innocence that is later to be shattered when the hero, Kisimi Kamara, goes to Europe.

Although the two books chart the same course (both authors are Sierra Leoneans) and deal with youth in a West African background, the humor that frequently emerges in Conton's work is absent in Cole's. Also, although at times they are both heavyhanded in their use of English, Conton has a lighter touch and can write with far more ease. His book has an obvious political ax to grind, whereas Cole's has none. This in fact is what spoils *The African*. Conton's hero goes to England where he meets Greta, a white South African, who is killed by her jilted lover. The dedicated Kamara returns to Songhai and becomes prime minister, but he gives up everything and enters South Africa to avenge Greta's death.

Like Kwamankra in Casely-Hayford's *Ethiopia Unbound*, Kamara has far too many public posturings to be convincing as a real person. One learns very little about his private agonies, and his zest for a united Africa and his love for Greta seem all part of the same thing—a noble gesture toward African unity. Too much happens in *The African*, and not only is it an incredulous book but it contrasts strangely with *Kossoh Town Boy* which develops logically from the boy's childhood to his academic success.

Ezekiel Mphahlele criticized Conton because he was "all the time advertising the African way of life to the foreign reader with an air of discovery";[6] the same can also be said of the earlier *I Was a Savage* (1958) by Prince Modupe, supposedly a Guinean. But *The African Child* (1955) by Modupe's fellow Guinean Camara Laye displays more conscious craftsmanship. Like Conton, Modupe has a message: the idyllic peace of his youth and village is destroyed by European influence, and, because he is unable to live amidst the ruins of a civilization he had cherished, he leaves Africa for the United States in 1922 and never returns. Laye, on the other hand, follows Cole's method, faithfully recounting a story of boyhood. But his account is not devoid of imagination. To the growing boy there was magic in the way that his father, a goldsmith by occupation, fashioned a woman's ornament, and there was wonder in the initiation ceremony with Konden Diara. In describing this ceremony, Laye also delves into the mind and imagination of the boy facing the ordeal:

> Now that we are on our knees with our foreheads on the ground and our hands pressed over our eyes, Kondén Diara's roaring suddenly bursts out.
> We were expecting to hear this hoarse roar, we were not expecting any other sound, but it takes us by surprise, and shatters us, freezes our hearts with its unexpectedness. And it is not only a lion, it is not only Kondén Diara roaring: there are ten, twenty, perhaps thirty lions that take their lead from him. . . .[7]

There are no real lions, only the older boys testing the younger ones, preparing them to face the dangers of the world. Whereas Laye's ceremony is related for its magical effect, Modupe's merely describes physical prowess. Judith Gleason has commented that "what is unique about Camara Laye's book in comparison with other novels, with ostensibly the same theme is . . . that Laye simply evokes the music and symbolism of daily life with more sensitivity and power than anyone else."[8] Most of the other writers simply chronicle events, hoping that the exotic setting will maintain the reader's interest. Laye's method is poetic; he recollects with feeling and awe.

More recently three other books have appeared which imitate Modupe's method of dramatizing the conflict of cultures, while emphasizing African traditions. Both J. W. Abruquah's *Catechist* (1965) and Francis Selormey's *Narrow Path* (1966) take place in Ghana. The life story of Afram in *The Catechist* is related by his son. Though the son of a fisherman, Afram is ambitious and is determined to learn English and to read and write. He decides to go to school in one of the big cities; before leaving his village, he muses that he may never hear again the noises of the night to which he had grown accustomed. He takes what few possessions he has, and is given five shillings by his mother and uncles. He manages to obtain his education and much of the book follows him from one parish to another. Although he is never able to achieve his goal of speaking English like an Englishman, one of his children does achieve this. He dies a happy man who had succeeded in raising himself by his own efforts.

Although the account is well conceived, it does have its flaws; for example, the son tells the story in the first person, attempting to establish his father's separate identity and yet writing the account himself. This has meant that Abruquah has fallen between two stools—he tends to describe Afram's values with reference to his own and, for instance, he has the catechist explain his attitude toward witchcraft. A reviewer in *West Africa* has argued that "a man born into a society which takes witchcraft for granted, would not gratuitously explain why he believed in witchcraft: it would not occur to him that it needed explaining. An author could only *contrive* an explanation through circumstances—confronting him with a sceptic or in some similar fashion."[9] Abruquah fails to do this and the catechist remains a curious figure, only partly alive in his own world, because his biographer insists on imposing his own values on his subject.

The Narrow Path is straight autobiography: the author recounts the story of his boyhood in a village, his school days, his parents, his grandfather, and the talk of the fisherfolk who live in the village. Certain common themes emerge here—the kind, long-suffering mother, the patriarchal male (the grandfather), Christianity, and education. But instead of emphasizing in the usual manner the head-on clash between Europe and Africa, Selormey makes it more personal, in the way that modern African plays do. The child's increasing alienation from the father is no longer viewed as a conflict of values, for the father was himself an educated man and a schoolteacher; it stands for much more—the inevitable discord that takes place before two generations can sever.

This cultural clash, which will be noticed repeatedly in the novels, has been documented by Dilin Okafor-Omali in his *Nigerian Villager in Two Worlds* (1965). As in Abruquah's book, a son relates the life story of his father. But here no first-person device is manufactured—the son writes as a member of a different generation from that of his father, Nweke. Like the catechist, Nweke educates himself through primary school and then spends the rest of his life working for the post office and in business. But neither *The Catechist* nor *A Nigerian Villager in Two Worlds* is content simply with describing the life of one person. Both also describe the society around them breaking up under the impact of new ways. Because Okafor-Omali lacked Laye's poetic insight, his approach seems cruder, more obvious, but his meaning is the same—Africa had undergone a serious change. It was a transformation with which the novelists proper, who will now be discussed, were obsessed. The biographical accounts of fathers and of societies in turmoil help one to understand the reasons for the preoccupations of contemporary African novelists.

Chapter 9

West African Novelists
in English

A primary reason for examining the cultural environment of the African writer is to provide a basis for understanding the consciousness of the present-day artist. His culture is an absorptive one, demonstrating a clear capacity for inheritance and the assimilation of new values. The resulting dualism has created a dynamic disorder which in turn has engendered a great deal of present-day art. In the synthesis of the art form the material is resolved into a new whole—part past, part present. In some of the writers who will be considered here, one will find cultural accommodation; in others, a refusal to come to terms with what at least seemingly *is*. No matter how these writers approach their environments and transpose them into an imaginative reality, they are dedicated to the same purpose—the construction of a myth of being.

Since the novelist in West Africa exists as a cultural hybrid, he accumulates all he can from his past in order to invest in the future. The chief characters are men whose umbilical ties to the past seem never to have been severed, and collectively they generate the attitude of their group. They possess almost legendary reserves of physical and intellectual abilities which they use to coerce society into believing that the past was indeed wonderful. Their alienation from the present and their recollections of fragmented disintegration help these "spokesmen" in the novels enter new realms of possibilities.

Chinua Achebe: Ancestor Worshipper

Chinua Achebe has called himself an "ancestor worshipper" and this, together with this recent statement on his work, should illustrate his interests: "I would be quite satisfied if my novels (especially the ones set in the past) did no more than teach their readers that their past— with all its imperfections—was not one long night of savagery."[1] His novels, three of which pose the problems of the man divided between past and present, between Africa and Europe, venerate the African past and attempt to reconcile the conflicting forces in the present. By implication they are addressed to the African reader.

Things Fall Apart (1958), Chinua Achebe's first effort to deal with the problem of conflict, centers on Okonkwo, a man proud of his strength. Because his father had been a failure, Okonkwo is determined to become a successful farmer. Early in the story the reader is told that "although Okonkwo was still young, he was already one of the greatest men of his time" (p. 6). The greatness that the novel emphasizes is his physical prowess, a virtue that belongs to a dying age.

Although Okonkwo becomes a success, the driving force behind his success is the fear of failure—his father's failure. Out of fear he seems at times to be irrational and even cruel. During the Week of Peace he beats one of his wives, and on another occasion he shoots at his second wife and almost kills her. And because of the fear of being thought weak, he kills a small boy who had been entrusted to his care.

As a result he is banished almost penniless among his mother's people. In time he recovers some of his wealth, but his existence is one of despair. As Achebe puts it, "His life had been ruled by a great passion—to become one of the lords of the clan. That had been his life-spring. And he had all but achieved it. Then everything had been broken. He had been cast out of his clan like a fish on to a dry, sandy beach, panting" (p. 117). To add to his despair, Okonkwo learns of what is happening in Umoufia, the village from which he had been exiled. He hears of the advent of the missionaries and the inroads they are beginning to make in traditional society, of how his own son Nwoye has joined them.

When he finally goes home, he returns to a different village where Christianity has made an enormous impact. The aristocrats as well as the outcasts have joined up with the white strangers. Christianity has

157

become associated with the government and its commercial business, as well as with education. It is against this that Okonkwo pits himself, and he determines to fight the white missionaries and drive them away. Being practical by nature, he leads a group of people to demolish the church; the church retaliates by marshaling the forces of the state against Okonkwo. When he beheads one of the insolent messengers from the government, he expects his clansmen to support him but they refuse to do so. Okonkwo hangs himself before the hands of foreign justice can reach him.

Things Fall Apart is the epic story of a hero who tries to defy the forces of change. It has become fashionable to see such a hero as an upholder of the group, but as the novel demonstrates he himself has broken tribal law on a number of occasions. Perhaps what Okonkwo really represents is the individual asserting himself against tribal norms and the encroachment of Christianity. Because the theme is a definite one, the story remains fixed on Okonkwo, who lacks the subtleties that one would wish from a character witnessing and participating in the psychological processes of change. He is always the strong man: his weak moments are the result of his overriding desire to prove himself and to avoid failure. Because he has no dimensions other than his purely physical ambitions, because there is no reflective side to his nature, he is incapable of standing up to the centrality which the novel imposes on him.

Okonkwo's story is not, however, like the semibiographical or straight biographical accounts examined in the preceding chapter. Achebe does succeed in creating a hero of fiction, a convincing man with strange, old-world qualities. Because Achebe imaginatively brings his world to life, one can believe in Okonkwo's values, and because these values matter the message of the novel becomes important, relevant, and convincing.

To aid the conviction, Achebe resorts to a number of devices. For example, he closely documents the social background. One learns about the importance and position of first wives, the significance of oracles, the dispensation of justice, wrestling, festivals, religious attitudes, superstitious beliefs and funeral ceremonies. Achebe accurately records sociological data—the fact that the early converts to Christianity were tribal outcasts, that slaves and the unfit were first offered as hostages to the new education, that church and state banded together in an unholy alliance.

Folktales and proverbs, which help to give a flavor of authenticity to the writing and the conversations, do not simply exist as anthropological curiosities but are well integrated into the novel. Folktales aid in underscoring the action; for instance, when Okonkwo discusses the fate of a village which had killed a white man, someone recollects a tale that has relevant implications in the novel. It is the story of a young kite which goes out foraging for food and comes back on one occasion with a duckling. When the older kite asks what the duckling's mother had said and is told that she had done nothing, the duckling is returned. But when the young kite brings back a chicken, whose mother had raved, the two kites eat it. The point is that one should be wary of silent people, as the villagers had to be wary of the silent strangers among them.

Proverbs are liberally interspersed through the novel, and although at times they are authentic and appropriate, in that they illustrate real situations and are put into the mouths of the old, they do become boring. But some do succeed; for instance, Okonkwo's house is burned, his animals killed, and his barns destroyed before he is forced to flee his village because "if one brought oil it soiled the others" (p. 112). The proverb helps justify the action of the elders. But some proverbs seem merely tautologous; for instance, "there must be a reason for it. A toad does not run in the daytime for nothing" (p. 17). The reader has been prepared for the proverbs, however, for quite early in the novel Achebe writes that to the Ibos "proverbs are the palm oil with which words are eaten."

Ben Obumselu, reviewing this book in *Ibadan*, argues that Achebe's "generation did not know the life he is out to present," and it should be recalled that much the same criticism was leveled at *The Catechist* and *A Nigerian Villager in Two Worlds*. It is extremely difficult to straddle two centuries and the creative writer who seeks to do this not only must bring out "the harshness of some of the old usage along with the beauty and charm of the fading traditional way of life," but must be so deeply immersed in the traditional past that it appears contemporary and real to him.[2] The judgments of a later generation can have no validity when assessing this past.

However, the virtues of *Things Fall Apart* must be considered in relation to Okonkwo's character. As Gerald Moore has stated, "Achebe is essentially a heroic novelist, whose books are infused by the dominant presence of a man who expresses in his very flesh the tragedy of change."[3] This is true of Okonkwo, as it is true of his grandson, Obi, the hero of Achebe's next novel, *No Longer at Ease* (1960). Obi returns to Nigeria after university life in England, full of new ideas; he wants to see a new nation free from corruption. But not only is he a hero with the gargantuan values of Okonkwo—he is an ordinary man as well. And it is as an ordinary individual that he encounters troubles soon after his return. The Umuofia Progressive Union, which had sub-sidized him overseas, demands he repay his loan as quickly as possible. It requires him to live up to the standards of a senior government official and it feels it has the right to interfere in his private life. Clara, the girl with whom he is having an affair, is an *osu*, a descendant of cult-slaves, and the members of the union consider it unthinkable that Obi should have anything to do with her, much less marry her.

Obi attempts to assert his rights as an individual: he will do what he pleases. But how free is he of centuries of tribal stricture? His very bid for freedom suggests a recognition of the tribal enclosures. He tries to be both the tribesman and the individual living in the big city, and this is his downfall. He quarrels with the union and finds himself more and more involved in debt; he is forced to encourage Clara to have an abortion when it seems that even his parents object to the marriage. He resorts to accepting bribes in order to redeem himself, and is soon found out. The book suggests the inevitability of Obi's position. For a flashback at the beginning of the novel reveals that Obi will be involved in disgrace and a trial.

Obi falls because he is placed in a position that demands too much of him, because the role he is compelled to play is that of a man precariously poised between commitment to tribal norms and involvement in a westernized society. Unlike Okonkwo, Obi is himself the man who straddles both worlds. The portrait therefore of his white departmental head is necessary from the viewpoint of the novel's theme, but it tends to be too obviously an accumulation of undesirable qualities rather than the creation of a real man.

Achebe attempts to portray white characters in all his books and the reason for their flatness is that they are never seen as people, but as symbolic forces against which his protagonists react. In *Things Fall Apart* there is precious little difference (except a degree of militancy) between the Rev. Brown and the Rev. Smith. In *No Longer at Ease* Obi's head, Mr. Green, is a pale evocation of the old colonial, and Mr. Winterbottom in *Arrow of God* (1964) is used as a foil against the wishes of an obstinate local priest. These characters have no life of their own—they are only important in that they deepen the conflict of issues. And in the latest novel, *A Man of the People* (1966), the American couple who worship all things African are again a creation out of a generalization. Perhaps it is part of Achebe's intention to make his white characters phantoms. Their very names suggest their anonymity and in this way, at least in the first three novels, Achebe seems to be hinting at their insignificant role in the history of his own people.

No Longer at Ease is not a dutiful delineation of society, as *Things Fall Apart* tends to be. Achebe had been interested in some of the controversial ideas in the novel ten years before it was published. In a short story entitled "The Old Order in Conflict with the New," a father similarly objects to his son's marriage to a Lagos girl, arguing that because she was urbanized she "knew very little about people in remote parts of the country." An untitled short story, published in January 1953,[4] relates the story of Michael Obi, an idealistic teacher at a mission school. When he closes the "ancestral footpath" because it passes through the school compound, the village high priest regards this as an act of defiance. Like Obi in the novel, both characters in the short stories lose in the end. They have to surrender their western idealism since the tribal pressures are much too insistent.

Although Achebe has never stated explicitly that his first two novels concern the conflicting pattern of cultures, he has admitted this much: "Surely it is unnatural to flit between two cultures so easily and so outrageously. And that is why observers have built up the myth of the man of two worlds suffering from intolerable internal stresses and liable to desert his education and civilization at a crisis. No doubt there are some Africans suffering from such stresses." But this cultural conflict is not nearly as distant as Achebe would have us believe. Certainly it is paramount in his own fiction and two other African writers have spoken of it. William Abraham in *The Mind of Africa* has written of the kind of person who well might be a hero from Achebe: "His is a cultural ambiguity, not cultural ambivalence, for it is characteristically accompanied by misgivings. These misgivings, this tension, this near neurosis, can be most tragic. The man of two worlds, uncomfortably striding both, is the real displaced man." Ezekiel Mphahlele, on the other hand, has expressed the consequences of such a preoccupation for the artist, or rather for his artistic creation. As he writes, "The artist must keep searching, searching for this African personality. He can't help doing so because, after all, it is really a search for his own personality, for the truth about himself. But if he thinks of the African Personality as a battlecry, it is bound to throw him into a stance, an attitude, and his art will suffer."[5] To some extent, this is Achebe's problem and accounts in part for the pattern of his first three novels.

Achebe's preoccupation with the "man of two worlds" has resulted in an unnecessary concern with documentation. His Black and white characters are portrayed as mere prototypes, and he has to some extent sacrificed the novel form in his effort to show the clash between Africa and westernization. Wole Soyinka's comment is appropriate here:

161

"Enactments of tribal peculiarities must emerge from characters in that society, not interfere with our recognition of basic humanity, not be just a concession to quaintness-mongers."[6] At times, Achebe's writing seems tailored for just this purpose, and one wonders how honest this description of Obi's difficulties can be: "His mind was troubled not only by what had happened but also by the discovery that there was nothing in him with which to challenge it honestly. All day he had striven to raise his anger and his conviction, but he was honest enough with himself to realize that the response he got, no matter how violent it sometimes appeared, was not genuine. It came from the periphery and not the centre" (p. 137).

In the second novel, despite Achebe's attempt at a larger canvas, despite his concern with the inner life of his characters, Clara, so important in illustrating Obi's disillusionment, simply disappears from the book after her abortion. Ben Mkapa has remarked that in *No Longer at Ease* Achebe's characters are "representational rather than real," and Todd Matshikiza has added that "a little more attention to his characters would score more for this book, than trying to sell the writer's endless fund and knowledgeability of Nigerian folklore."[7] The flaws in Achebe's characterizations are evidence of the truth of both these statements.

Arrow of God (1964) examines the problem of African tradition and new European modes through the relationship between a priest and his god. The novel is set in the 1920s in eastern Nigeria, and Ezeulu, the preserver of the old, has much in common with Captain Winterbottom, the upholder of the new. To both of them authority has brought loneliness and they recognize admirable qualities in one another. But though they respect each other, they are too far apart, each too sure of his own area of authority, to compromise. And it is no compromise when Ezeulu sends his son Odochi to the new mission school, for he wants him to learn about the secret of the strangers. This, Ezeulu hopes, will give the priest added power.

Meantime Winterbottom summons the old priest to inform him that he has been appointed warrant chief in the area. But the messengers, as in *Things Fall Apart*, are much too arrogant; Ezeulu insults one of them and does not heed the summons. He is further harassed by a deputy who detains him on Government Hill for five weeks for insulting the government. As a result Ezeulu, as priest of the protector-god of Umuaru, is unable to eat two of the sacred yams, a necessary prelude to the Feast of the New Yam. When he is released, he avenges the villagers for their lack of support. He delays the feast for two more

162

months to show the omnipotence of his god. Harvest cannot take place until Ezeulu has performed his rites and the people starve while the yams rot in the ground. Then disaster strikes: one of Ezeulu's sons dies while participating in a night-masquerade and in agony Ezeulu's mind snaps. He becomes another victim of the passing glories of the old ways.

Because of the psychological problems that Achebe poses through the relationship between Ezeulu, his god, his community, and the district officer, *Arrow of God* is his most ambitious novel. The author attempts to remain detached from the forces in conflict. He does not commit himself to a veneration of the old as in *Things Fall Apart* or to a vilification of the new as in *No Longer at Ease*. But there is a greater pitfall: Achebe seems unable to enter satisfactorily into either character. He is at times cynical toward Ezeulu, and Winterbottom is a conventional, sketchy European figure. However, the tragedy of Ezeulu, decisively articulated at the end of the book, is the tragedy of Okonkwo and Obi: "Their god had taken sides with them against this headstrong and ambitious priest and thus upheld the wisdom of their ancestors—that no man however great was greater than his people; that no man ever won judgment against his clan" (p. 287). Like Okonkwo and Obi, Ezeulu seeks to make himself greater than the collective wisdom of the clan, like them he dares to individuate his role as tribesman, and like them he fails.

There is the usual interest here in social documentation—in the festival of the New Pumpkin Leaves (a purification ceremony), in the ceremony to commemorate the first appearance of a new mask, in the marriage ceremony. Also Achebe deals with the trivia of everyday concourse—the women bantering scandals in the marketplace, the men sharing food and playfully insulting one another, and the courtesy of the people in their various activities. At times, and this is quite new in Achebe, there is a note of humor. But the anthropological detail is top-heavy and is not artistically worked into the story. When Adisa Williams comments on Achebe's "success in presenting traditional rural life from the inside," he is wrong in implying that this is a good quality in the novel. For not only is there a plethora of proverbs, but also the translation of a song, and the homegrown similes are at times absurd. For instance when one of Ezeulu's sons goes home to face his father's anger, he is said to be "looking like a fowl soaked in the rain." These plodding attempts at an obvious realism slow down the pace of the action; Achebe has tried it all before and, as I. N. C. Aniebo has stated, "after sometime the gimmick must become stale."[8]

Achebe's latest novel, *A Man of the People*, is different from his earlier efforts in that the man of two worlds is no longer the main character. Here Achebe returns to one of the themes of *No Longer at Ease*—corruption and greed in high places. Chief Nanga, the bête noire and a corrupt politician, invites Odili, the principal character, to visit him in Lagos. There Odili becomes involved in Chief Nanga's world. When Odili and Chief Nanga quarrel over Elsie, Odili's girl friend, Odili leaves the chief's home and goes to his old friend Maxwell's house. The rest of the novel is at times not very convincing: Odili helps Maxwell and his friends in the founding of a new party, dedicated to the overthrow of Chief Nanga and the corruption that he stands for.

When Odili decides to contest Chief Nanga's seat in Maxwell's party, he is first dismissed from his school and then encounters various difficulties during his campaign. Chief Nanga tries to bribe Odili, through Odili's own father, with the offer of a cash payment and a scholarship if Odili withdraws his candidacy.

At a public meeting Odili attempts to confront Nanga but is beaten up by him and ends up in the hospital. There he learns that through the artifice of his opponent, his nomination papers had not even been filed and it seems certain that Chief Nanga, as usual, will be victorious. But Maxwell is killed and when the hired thugs of both parties go beserk, the government has to enlist the support of the army.

Despite Achebe's attempt to portray Chief Nanga as an ogre, he actually seems to possess far more human warmth than Odili who, because he is out to rectify, hardly ever relaxes. Odili is always at a loss in his private war with Chief Nanga, who greets him breezily as "Odili my great enemy" (p. 129); their exchange on a public platform shows Chief Nanga as much the more superior person:

> "My people," said Nanga again. "This is the boy who is thrusting his finger into my eye. He came to my house in Bori, ate my food, drank my water and my wine and instead of saying thank you to me he set about plotting how to drive me out and take over my house." The crowd roared again. My panic had now left me entirely and in its place I found a rock-cold fearlessness that I had never before felt in my heart. I watched Nanga, microphone in one hand, reeling about the dais in drunken jubilation. I seemed to see him from a superior, impregnable position. (pp. 156–57)

But there is nothing that occurs before in the novel to give Odili this "superior, impregnable position." Whatever may be Achebe's intended moral point, Chief Nanga seems to deserve this victory, however temporary, over Odili.

The ending of *A Man of the People* is contrived and does not ring true. Although a reviewer has spoken of the novel's "magic air of conviction,"[9] Achebe seems to have sacrificed a convincing development of plot to the presentation of a theme. In pursuit of this theme—the corruption of politicians—Achebe has introduced too many characters who appear and disappear without making much impact. Odili's friend Andrew is simply used to sketch in Odili's background; then he is dropped. It is not easy to distinguish the women: the female lawyer who visits Chief Nanga and the lawyer who is Maxwell's girl friend are both clever and extremely beautiful. There is little difference between Edna, Chief Nanga's fiancée, and Elsie, Odili's girl friend; both are beautiful and spirited. Equally Edna's father and Odili's father are the stock figures of the patriarchal male of Achebe's books.

T. M. Aluko: Haranguing the Tradition

T. M. Aluko first published two novels—*One Man, One Wife* (1959) and *One Man, One Matchet* (1964)—which in the manner of the later plays of Wole Soyinka treat the debunking of the African tradition. In this he differs from Achebe, who is more concerned with upholding the values of a way of life. Aluko brings the sense of humor evident in Achebe's *Man of the People* to bear against the customs and traditions of his people.

Some of his preoccupations are manifested in his short stories. "The New Engineer" shows signs of humor but has little plot. It relates how a lazy roadgang, expecting a visit from a new engineer, feel cheated when their efforts to appear active prove futile since the engineer does not stop. Aluko comes more into his own with "The Vision of Brother Sandrach,"[10] a satirical portrayal of a small religious sect. When Sandrach collapses on the floor "in that most treasured experience of the Church—a trance," some members of the congregation doubt the truth of his trance, but Brother Jacob, the leader, exhorts them all to listen. Brother Sandrach reveals that the Second World War had spread to Lagos, and thus his church elevates him to the status of prophet. Soon after he goes mad.

As yet Aluko's writing has little control, though occasional descriptions are accurate and immensely funny. For instance, Aluko writes of a character that "when he spoke, he revealed what tremendous change time had affected in the corner of his mouth. Only one solitary tooth was left behind to tell the tale of comrades of the dental army that had fallen in the service of its master." To Aluko nothing is sacrosanct. "The Judgment of Heaven" is another story that makes fun of the village elders and especially Chief Lotun, who vows vengeance on the man who has seduced his wife. Aluko himself said he recognized that "the English sense of humour is vastly different from our West African idea of humour,"[11] but his novels and some of his short stories achieve a common level of comicality.

One Man, One Wife does not satisfactorily operate as a novel. Although it is made up of a number of episodes, many of which are amusing, they do not add up to a total statement. It concerns the struggle in a village between traditional religion and Christianity. The Reverends David and Royasin, two Christian ministers, are the novel's main characters. Among their first converts are Elder Jeremiah, Joshua, and his son Jacob. In the course of the book, Royasin is dismissed when Jacob's wife of four days is discovered to be pregnant, and Royasin is suspected of being the father.

On Royasin (who now changes his name to Royanson), a great deal of the humor of the novel is centered. Ulli Beier has remarked on the "humorous indulgence"[12] with which his character is drawn, and, though he eventually goes mad, his attempts to set himself up as public letter-writer and his delightful improvidence are truly laughable. The Reverend David is too solemn, too predictable in his actions. His zeal helps to break up the church and when trying to reunite it, he finds that one of the stalwarts, Joshua, has been killed by the Yoruba god Shango.

There is far too much action in the novel. Besides the activities of Royasin, the marriages and divorces, there is a tendency to kill off the characters. Jacob's wife dies in childbirth, Chief Asolo's favorite wife dies of smallpox as does Bada, the high priest of the god of smallpox, and Chief Asolo drinks poison to avoid arrest. Melodrama is also evident in some of Aluko's stories, but in the main the humor sees them through successfully. However, in the novel incredible incidents follow one after another and characters appear in swift succession. There is no centrality and the entire piece disintegrates into fragments at the end.

Nevertheless certain aspects of the work are worth discussing since they succeed superbly. Aluko captures Pastor David's hypocrisy as well as Royasin's rapacity and skepticism when the latter asks for an increase in salary and is told by Pastor David, " 'You and I, my dear Royasin, are workers together in the Lord's vineyard. Why must you and I seek after worldly returns when we know that returns a hundred-fold await us in Heaven? Isolo here looks difficult. Here men and women continue to worship trees, rivers and rocks. Here your labours are required. Required by the Lord Jesus in the service of your fellow men. Will you desert Him? Will you abandon this little oasis of the Church of Christ in this desert of heathenism—all because of another two shillings and six pence increase in salary?'" (p. 21)

In similar vein Aluko satirizes the village elders who assemble with equal aplomb in Asolo's parlor to drink palm-wine no matter what the occasion. And Aluko makes fun of illiterates and semiliterates like Royasin. After Royasin has set himself up as a public letter-writer ("friend of the illiterate, advocate of the oppressed" as his advertisement proclaims), he is consulted by Jacob. Royasin compliments him, saying, "Many clients come into this office and behave and conduct themselves in an ignorant and unintelligent and unintelligible manner. These uneducated illiterate masses constitute an impending impediment to the great work of the Friend of the Illiterate and Advocate of the Oppressed" (p. 130). These asides in the novel are self-contained; in isolation they are amusing, but they never make any large impact.

Aluko achieved something more in the manner of a total statement with his second book. In five years he had shown remarkable development as a novelist; whereas one Nigerian novelist, Onuora Nzekwu, criticized *One Man, One Wife* for being "dull . . . and badly written," another Nigerian writer said of the second that it presented "a vivid picture of the difficulties of the administration during the transfer of power from a colonial to an independent state."[13] If this were all the book accomplished, it would scarcely be a novel, but it also brings to life its characters and assembles them in a neat and coherent fashion, thereby delivering a clearer statement.

One Man, One Matchet is set among the villagers of Ipaja. A young agricultural officer, newly arrived from England, orders the destruction of diseased cocoa trees before they can infect the entire crop. The farmers, however, oppose the plan and feel that the government has teamed up with their traditional enemies, the Apenos. The new Nigerian district officer, Udo Akpan, sides with the agricultural officer, much to the consternation of the villagers. Their own leader is the inimitable Benja-Benja, a loudmouthed politician and journalist, whose gruff charm is reminiscent of Achebe's Chief Nanga. Benja-Benja and Udo Akpan's antagonism toward one another results in chaos and violence before eventual calm is restored.

Although the novel's meaning is clearer than that of *One Man, One Wife* in that there are fewer characters, fewer episodes, and the whole theme is centered on the disorder caused by the introduction of western norms, little of Aluko's humor is evident in the book. Apart from descriptions of Benja-Benja, who in any event is too much a caricature to be real, too grotesquely farcical to convince, the rest of the story is told in the jargon of a civil servant's memorandum. There is none of the ease of language and the relaxed style of the earlier work. This is apparent from the book's opening sentence regarding "cocoa disease—the new threat to the prosperity of the farmers and to the premier industry of the nation." Heavy sentences abound: "At cockcrow of the morning following the night on which Udo Akpan had had to drink and read himself to sleep, an unusual caller was received by His Highness the Oba of Ipaja . . ." (p. 73). Not only is there this preponderance in style, but there are certain ornate expressions as well as occasional dismal notes in the language: an "excellent view of the town" is also called a "vantage point," and Aluko writes that the news of a chief's death "shook the town to its ancient foundations." It is as if Aluko had made up his mind to compensate for his artistic detachment and to dedicate himself to a theme that has plagued many West African writers. From this standpoint, Udo Akpan and Benja-Benja become stereotypes of radical and conservative attitudes within the Nigerian social environment.

Aluko's *Kinsman and Foreman* (1966) describes a personal clash between a new engineer who returns to Nigeria and the Public Works Department foreman, a corrupt relation, who is a pillar of his society.

Chief the Honourable Minister (1970) is a satire of the national "democratic" government, the "Freedom for All Party," which is established at the end of British colonial rule. The story is set in an imaginary state called Afromacoland.

Throughout the novel, attention is directed not at the people of the state, but at the government officials. Hardly any mention is made of there even being people over which the officials rule. Each official is titled a minister in charge of a department, but it is never established what the function or purpose of each department is in regard to the people. The people of Afromacoland are not served by the government; they are only used by the government officials to support their selfish gains.

Aluko's failure to portray each minister in detail does not weaken the book's impact; rather it highlights the meaninglessness of the government and contributes to the general satirical nature of the novel. Actually, the ministers are not individuals; they are stereotyped as selfish, ridiculous, fat men. Their actions, judgments, and minds are all one. Their lengthy, meaningless titles are the only identity they possess; never do they identify with the country or people they control.

Aluko was always a social satirist, but his early novels were in a light vein. Now as an outsider, he is able to treat seriously the plight of the ordinary man, surrounded by self-seeking politicians. The laughter in the last two novels is not merely laughter for its own sake but laughter directed at reforming society. This was the function of masquerade verse in traditional Yoruba society, and, as has been seen, Aluko has moved strongly in this direction.

Cyprian Ekwensi: The Popular Novelist

Chinua Achebe stated that the 1964 sales figures for *Things Fall Apart* were "about 600 copies in Britain; 20,000 in Nigeria; and about 2500 in all other places." Although most of the sales in Nigeria can be attributed to the fact that the book is required reading for the West African School Certificate, the figures still suggest that cheaply priced books can ensure a mass audience for the West African writer. However, Ekwensi does not write primarily for his school audience: "Readers of Nigerian writing—Nigerian creative writing—must be those who are willing to read simply for pleasure and entertainment first, and for education and knowledge incidentally."[14] Whereas Achebe has tended to stress the role of the West African novelist as teacher, Ekwensi has emphasized his own role as entertainer. In part, this accounts for the difference between the two writers.

According to M. J. C. Echeruo, "Ekwensi began his writing career as a pamphleteer."[15] An early pamphlet by Ekwensi was *When Love Whispers* (1948), published locally in book form and intended for the popular Nigerian market. Similar locally produced works abound in Nigeria and Ghana, and at this point it would be relevant to digress briefly and consider them, since Ekwensi does in fact attempt to reach the same market.

Most of these "pamphlets" are published in and around Onitsha, a town in eastern Nigeria, although Aboso in Ghana has also produced works by Benibengor Blay. The books, priced between twenty and twenty-five cents, are usually poorly printed on cheap paper, and in some cases author, printer, publisher, and bookseller are one and the same person. According to Ulli Beier, there are as many as a hundred titles, but recent estimates put the total closer to two hundred and fifty.[16]

Ogali's *Veronica My Daughter* (1956)[17] is typical of the literature. The heroine is being forced to marry a man of means who is a rigid traditionalist. Veronica's illiterate father can understand neither her objections nor her preference for Mike. Whereas she speaks a restrained type of English, Mike is full of bombast (to leave no doubt that he is "educated"), and the father talks in pidgin. Almost from the beginning

169

he is made to look the fool: "What kind trouble be dis. My dauther get strong ear too much. I floggam tire, no change. Dis boy Mikere go killi my daughter. . . . I tell Veronica leave Mikere, Veronica say no. I tell Mikere leave Veronica, Mikere say no. Wetten you say make I do?" (p. 6.) The father loses at the end because Ogali, like most of the other writers in this vein, is on the side of "enlightenment."

Other pamphlets will illustrate something of their range. Okenwa Olisa's *Lumumba's Last Days*[18] is recounted partly in an epistolary style, partly in narrative, and partly as a play. It is a straightforward account of Lumumba's fall, and the style varies from Mrs. Lumumba writing fearfully, "My dear husband I am dreaming much nowadays, and I am afraid and restless in mind" (p. 4), to the author's own version of how "the wicked and ungodly Belgian officer shot Mr. Lumumba to death with his rifle" (p. 6).

Speedy Eric's *Mabel the Sweet Honey* (1963) and Miller Albert's *Rosemary and the Taxi Driver* (1963) are close to pornography, although the writers still persist in their moral preoccupations. Mabel's story is that of a young girl who goes to work in a bar; she has a succession of affairs, her marriage fails, and finally she turns to prostitution. She dies when trying to abort a child. In the other book, Rosemary falls in love with a taxi driver and also comes to a bad end. The writers seem to suggest that women are intrinsically bad, unless they follow the approved road of marriage and childbearing. In *Rosemary and the Taxi Driver* Albert becomes carried away by the sheer poetry of words as he describes Rosemary: "She was in her maiden form and had remained untampered since her generate days. Even to meddle with her zestful glamour of beauty, nobody had succeeded. The grim enthusiasm of her ardent lust was bubbling on her romantic face . . ." (p. 8). He is far less outspoken than Eric, who, under the guise of advising the young, gives page after page of uninhibited sexual descriptions.

It is in this tradition that Ekwensi began writing. Moralism and its demonstration in the characters' lives were its criteria, a popular, ready-made language its medium. His book *When Love Whispers* has these ingredients. Like Veronica, Rosemary, and Mabel, Ekwensi's heroine, Ashoka, is an educated girl. Like Veronica, she is forbidden by her father to associate with John Ike, a young man who is soon to go to England to study. Because she is independent and can earn her own living, she becomes the butt of envious men. She falls into the hands of a carefree bachelor who almost sells her to a dealer. Her fiancé learns of her disappearance and attempts to find her, but he has to leave for England. However, she does escape from being shipped to

Dahomey, and receives a letter from John asking her to remain faithful to him.

Ashoka then decides to go home to her village. There the predictable happens: her father wants her to marry an old, illiterate chief, but she refuses. What is worse, she soon discovers that she is pregnant by Olu Tayo, who has been holidaying in the village. He will not marry her so she procures an abortion from a herbalist, nearly dying in the process. Finally John returns, but Ashoka is married to someone else and has two children. They both decide that they have to accept their present position.

It will be noticed that the ingredients of this story are the qualities of the popular Onitsha fiction mentioned. Ekwensi's added dimension is the unfulfilled relationship between the lovers—there is no Onitsha recipe for the happy ending. It was a theme that he was to return to later in his writing career; in *Jagua Nana* (1961) Ashoka is Jagua, and John is Freddie. But by then he was not content with the stock figures of popular Nigerian literature. The story is much more significant and the issues more real.

Before writing *Jagua Nana*, Ekwensi passed through a period of apprenticeship, writing short stories. He published five in 1947 as well as *Ikolo the Wrestler*, a small collection of folktales. The stories and folktales were preparation for his first novel, *People of the City* (1954). Indeed, according to Leslie Murby, by November 1947 Ekwensi had written about fifty short stories in the course of four years. Ekwensi has continued to draw from the world of popular entertainment and even as early as 1947 the stories "betray his influences; the cinema with its Humphrey Bogart types and its flick change scenes, reading, as a boy, of the Wild West type . . ."[19] Thirteen years later, after Ekwensi had written four novels, the same influences can be seen in his work: "When he tells us that Jagua Nana was famous for her "stunning fashions" we know where we are, in the world of *Schoolgirl's Own* (though *True Detective* and the *News of the World* also display their sinister charms)."[20] It is exported European "pop" culture that has always affected Ekwensi's work, and from this viewpoint he stands in striking contrast to Achebe and Tutuola, steeped in the ritual of their Ibo and Yoruba cultures.

Ekwensi's world is evident from his first publication, *Ikolo the Wrestler*. In the title story, Ikolo wrestles against a number of spirits. In all cases he is victorious, but then he wrestles with his own *chi* (personal spirit) and loses. Finally a friend helps him to escape from the spirit world. The story is a compromise; it retells a folktale but emphasizes

171

Ekwensi's own preoccupations: the strength of the wrestler, the power of his antagonists, and his final victory over them all. The idea of a man wrestling with his soul, however, is the supreme irony; the moral is that no man can fight himself and survive.

In two other stories, "Ritual Murder" and "Law of the Grazing Fields,"[21] Ekwensi describes men who are prepared to defy tradition, one through evil, the other through chivalry. And even if social anthropologists were to suggest that such situations are unreal, the stories are exciting. Ekwensi, by intentional distorting, succeeds in popularizing the West African customs of succession and courtship. Nevertheless, the stories have their faults; one can criticize them not so much because the characters cannot operate in a genuine West African setting, but because, in borrowing an approach, Ekwensi also inherits many of the prejudices that go with it. In "Law of the Grazing Fields" he speaks of "gruesome rites" and "ancient evil," and he overemphasizes the theme of lust for blood. This is particularly apparent in the violent chase scene when Yalla is shot with a poisoned arrow and "more arrows twanged past even as the distance between them and their pursuers narrowed" (p. 161). By portraying such gruesomeness, Ekwensi alienates the sympathy of the serious reader.

"Law of the Grazing Fields" and an earlier short story, "Sharro,"[22] in which Rikku undergoes a traditional ordeal to win Amina's love, both concern the Fulani of northern Nigera. "Sharro" does not emphasize the lovers' relationship but Rikku's excruciating torture. Yet these two short stories provided the valuable groundwork for Burning Grass (1962), a full-length novel set among the Fulanis.

From the point of view of plot and development, Ekwensi's first novel, People of the City (1954), is perhaps his weakest work. It centers on Sango, a crime reporter and dance-band leader, and the three women in his life, Aina, Beatrice, and Beatrice the Second. Sango eventually marries Beatrice the Second and, after losing his job on the newspaper, he leaves with her for Ghana where they are to start a new life together.

What merit there is in the book is its criticism of city life: the prostitution, the bad housing conditions, the unscrupulous landlords. The delightful confusion of events and characters contributes to the slick effect of the chaos of big-city life.

Ekwensi's language is reminiscent of that of the Onitsha pamphleteers, as can be seen in this description of Beatrice's first appearance in the nightclub where Sango works:

As the hours grew smaller they poured in from the cinemas, from the other clubs with early-closing licences. A very short man was trotting beside a girl who might have come from the pages of a South Sea travel book. Yet Sango knew she was a West African. Everything about her was petite, delicate. Her almost transparent dress was cleverly gathered at the waist. Her ear-rings and smile shone.

"Who is she?" said Sango, his heart beating faster. His eyes followed her to her seat.

"I don't know," said the first sax.

"My, my!"

"Who is she?"

Faces lifted from music scores. Heads shook.

"Don't know her. . . . Must be new! . . . Yes, sir!" (pp. 75–76)

The account is indicative of the mood of the book. No serious attempt is made to grapple with anything more than the superficial aspects of human relationships. The humor is as obvious as some of the descriptions of the characters' activities, and the comments from the bandsmen seem a little ridiculous. But it is not the purpose of the popular novelist to plumb the depths of human relationships. His achievement lies in making the phantom characters act and behave as if they have an inner life, all the time stressing their outward gestures; hence the involvement with plot. But *People of the City* fails as a popular work; it has no story and one has to be content with the occasional successful descriptions and Sango's three affairs.

In Ekwensi's next novel, *Jagua Nana* (1961), many of these faults are corrected. B. I. Chukwukere argues that *Jagua Nana* is a better work than any of Achebe's fiction because "the conflict is multiple, for the physical is not excluded."[23] The "physical" is very much present in Jagua, an aging Lagos prostitute, who has an affair with Freddie, a young teacher. He is quite infatuated with her, and she promises to send him to England. The relationship continues with its normal ups and downs, but ends in disaster. Jagua loses both her lover and a rival in death. In a contrived, happy anticlimax, she leaves Lagos and when she returns she wins a fortune of fifty thousand pounds.

Some of the sensuousness apparent in earlier pieces, such as *Mabel the Sweet Honey* comes to the forefront here. Ekwensi delights in Jagua's nakedness—the book opens with her combing her hair, semi-nude, having just come from the bath. He gives teasing descriptions of "the dark naked hair under her armpits" (p. 5) and of "her breasts hanging down pendulously" (p. 31). Jagua's irresistible attraction is demonstrated by the succession of men who fall in love with her: a trinket dealer who feels she is "killing him off with temptation" as she

173

stands before him in her chemise, Uncle Taiwo who makes love to her brutally with "rough lips close on the nipple," and Chief Ofubara, who is carried away by ecstasy and proposes marriage to her, later changing his mind and casually giving her wads of hundred-pound notes.

Jagua herself comes over as a loudmouthed, brawling woman, who is prepared to fight for what she wants. Her pidgin English emphasizes her earthiness: it is in pidgin that she abuses her rival Nancy when she discovers her with Freddie in his room, and it is with a fierce, raw anger that she assaults Nancy and bites her, with Freddie feebly pleading to Nancy, "Bite her back! You got no teeth? Nancy, bite am back good and proper" (p. 56). Freddie is no weakling, but he is captive to her love, and whatever she does he has to remain with her. At one point he hints that perhaps she had given him a love potion, for when he discovers her soliciting after their quarrel, he is hurt and, Ekwensi adds, "for once she actually felt unclean and he was to her a god with the power to pass judgment" (p. 63).

Jagua Nana is both a book with a popular theme and a study of conflict in a woman's mind. In an interview conducted by the Transcription Centre in London, Ekwensi remarked that he was a "writer for the masses" and "not a literary stylist," and certainly this emerges in *Jagua Nana*. As in *People of the City*, there are some ill-matched expressions—"dancing hips" and "lips, soft, aggressively kissable"—but the pathetic picture of Uncle Taiwo lying out in the rain is a truly poetic evocation. In this novel Ekwensi was concerned with the outer manner of action, but he was also involved in the psychological nature of disaster.

Although Ekwensi said he was no "stylist," he has been able to adapt his subject matter and language to suit various tastes; for example, *The Drummer Boy* (1960), *The Passport of Mallam Ilia* (1960), and *An African Night's Entertainment* (1962) were written for young readers. Because Ekwensi's world is not one of depth, because his characters exist on a superficial level of action, and because, in large measure, the curve of plot dictates their lives, he is a superb writer of children's stories. Since these stories are intended for a young audience, there is more restraint about sexual matters. Love in *An African Night's Entertainment* is an excursion into the pseudo-Arabian world of courtship and ceremony. Shehu's position in this book differs greatly from Freddie's in *Jagua Nana*; in the same way Zainobe is unlike the heroines in his adult fiction who defy tradition. To her it is sacrosanct.

Ekwensi's settings offer a vivid contrast between the physical pressures of town life and the idyllic retreat of rustic pastures. It is the world of "Sharro," "Law of the Grazing Fields," and *An African Night's Entertainment* (the culture of northern Nigeria) that Ekwensi uses for the setting of *Burning Grass* (1962). More accurately the tribe in this novel is the Fulani and the story traces the fortunes of the family of a "cow-Fulani" (Fulani who are cattle-raisers). Mai Sunsaye saves a beautiful slave-girl, Fatimeh, from her master and buys her himself. Indirectly Sunsaye's act of generosity brings about the breakup of his family. Hodio, one of his sons, elopes with her, thereby breaking a tradition that slaves and freeborn must not marry. The father himself falls victim to the magic of a rival and becomes afflicted with the wandering sickness, *sokugo*. He leaves his home and wanders aimlessly; when he is away, his cattle are stolen and his property burned.

As he wanders from place to place he meets each of his sons. At the end Sunsaye is attacked by a lion tamed by Fatimeh. She rescues him and cures him of his affliction. However, just when his family is about to be reunited, he dies. Sunsaye's search is in the manner of a folktale. He leaves everything behind and attempts to discover what is good in himself. He proves himself on his journey, since he is still very much a father, but he has no values of which he can be sure. It is ironic that a slave-girl should have inadvertently brought about his misfortune and his release, and that he should die at the moment of reunion with his family.

It is not Ekwensi's purpose merely to document life among the cow-Fulani; he is not simply writing a diary. Because Ekwensi's world is the popular one of western fiction, his work is intended to belong to the common property of all popular art. He begins with this assumption, but by conforming he still reveals his differences.

Lagos, perhaps Ekwensi's favorite setting, is the scene of another novel. Though he is at home in Fulani pastures, the end of *Burning Grass* indicates that he was becoming more favorably inclined toward the town. Rikku, the main character, is helped by Kantuma to adjust to life in the city. After only a couple of days, he already feels separated from the world of cattle and desert which he had just left.

Ekwensi himself returns in another novel to the big city of his first work. In *Beautiful Feathers* (1963) he introduces politics into the confusion of big-city life. Wilson Iyari is a Lagos pharmacist, the father of three children, and the leader of the Nigerian Movement for African and Malagasy Solidarity. But though he is a success in his public life, at home all is not well. He is completely disregarded by his wife, who has a lover. As his success with the movement increases, so conditions at home deteriorate. When the members of the movement demonstrate to make their views known to the prime minister, Wilson's wife runs off to Benin. The leaders of the movement are arrested, including Wilson, though he is later released on bail. After leading a delegation to a Conference of African Unity in Dakar, where he is involved in a shooting incident, he returns to Nigeria to find that his movement is breaking up. He decides to dissolve it himself although an attempt is later made on his life. His wife, now reconciled with Wilson, is stabbed instead, but eventually recovers. The family is finally united.

Beautiful Feathers is free from the harsh brutality of some of Ekwensi's other works, although it is not stripped of sensationalism. All the characters are at the mercy of the plot, with the exception of Wilson who is an honest idealist. Ekwensi shows a delicate ability in the handling of his theme, for the point he intends to make is apparent throughout the story: Wilson cannot really be considered a success if his homelife is a failure. Ekwensi suggests that although Wilson publicly failed in the end, he was much happier, and indeed had really achieved something within the private framework of his family.

Ekwensi's interest in the two different settings, country and city, has continued in his more recent fiction—in *Yaba Roundabout Murder* (1962) and *Lokotown and Other Stories* (1966) he emphasizes crime in a large city, whereas in *Rainmaker and Other Stories* (1965) he returns to a rural setting and gives to his main story a touch of superstition. Perhaps Ekwensi has to learn to link his two settings, or at least to avoid the divorce in attitudes which separation of them brings about. For *Beautiful Feathers* fails because, lacking the descriptions of bustling town life, it is simply an imaginative gesture toward African solidarity. True enough the conflict is present, between Wilson's public and private lives, but there is little else besides. Finally Ekwensi's recourse to melodrama flaws the novel, and this criticism can be applied to *Burning Grass* as well. His two best works remain his first, *People of the City* for its authentic view of city life, and *Jagua Nana*, for its touching, yet eminently credible, portrayal. In a novelist who seeks to transform his Nigerian characters into the cowboys and Indians, cops and robbers of conventional western entertainment, credibility is surely the least that should be required.

Ekwensi's next novel, published in 1966, was a political version of *Jagua Nana*. In it he attempts to show something of the chaos ("Africhaos" as he calls it elsewhere) which came about with the Nigerian Civil War. The importance of the work is not in its documentation but in Ekwensi's tender treatment of the unhappiness brought into a young girl's life.

Iska (1966; a Hausa word for wind) tells the story of Filia, a young girl from Kaduna, and her rude awakening to the realities of life. Brought up in the security of a convent, she is in the beginning naive about life going on around her. But at the time of her marriage to Dan Kaybi, a man not of her tribe, Kaduna like other large cities was beset by unrest fomented by different political groups. Dan Kaybi is killed in a tavern brawl for sticking up for what he believes in. When Filia hears the news, she is bitter and confused, and remains so throughout the book.

To start a new life away from the people and things she knows, Filia goes to Lagos (like many an Ekwensi heroine), a large politically oriented city, full of many temptations. She shares an apartment with a girl she does not at first realize is a prostitute and is introduced to the life of the typical street girl. Not wanting to end up like her roommate, she searches frantically for a job and eventually succeeds in obtaining employment with a modeling agency.

As a model, she has occasion to meet many people in government circles; as a result she is flung into the center of political party embroilment. One night at a party given by her employer where important artists, writers, and political figures are present, Filia meets Dapo Ladele, a young journalist who is disliked by the country's leaders because of his degrading articles about them.

Dapo and Filia fall in love; he becomes the editor of the *Reformer*, a party newspaper run by Nafotim, a man whom Filia's parents wanted her to marry. Forced to write what the party wants, Dapo lies about how the party will make the country prosper, and at the same time he downgrades the other parties. Filia's fate and his are closely bound together, for after her rape and death, Dapo realizes that he has to face up to the truth.

Iska tells us something important about Ekwensi. He is extremely interested in handling female characters and can treat them with deep sensitivity. Iska is not the brawling Jagua nor is the Lagos here that of his earlier *People of the City*. No longer does Ekwensi seem primarily interested in the surface attraction of success in the political world or the superficial beauty of a woman. Instead he writes of the good, pure life of Filia; her friend, Remi, was to confess afterwards that she had tried to "tempt" Filia—unsuccessfully. Filia's death, when she is still pregnant, makes Dapo wonder about the future. These were dark days, for the book appeared on the eve of the Nigeria-Biafra Civil War. The novel shows a firmer commitment on Ekwensi's part to the inner worth of humanity.

Onuora Nzekwu: The Church and the Shrine

The three novels of Onuora Nzekwu take us back to the world of Achebe. *Wand of Noble Wood* (1961), his first work, is in many ways similar to *No Longer at Ease*. Both heroes are Ibos, both live in Lagos, and both are, to a greater or lesser extent, involved in the traditional life of their community. Pete Obiesie, however, is more a part of his community than Obi Okonkwo had been, and consequently Nzekwu's attempt to imitate the theme of the divided man does not succeed.

Wand of Noble Wood is concerned with tribal marriage customs and ceremonies. Thirty-year-old Pete Obiesie, the main character, has saved the bride-price, but custom requires that he cannot take a wife until his two elder brothers have done so. When his brothers finally marry, Pete begins to search earnestly for a wife. His cousin introduces him to a number of girls, all of whom are related to him, and therefore he cannot marry any of them since custom forbids marriage between two persons even distantly related. At last he meets Nneka, who is no relation and of whom his family approves. Nneka accepts Pete's proposal but her father reveals that she is under a curse, so Pete takes part in a ceremony to free her. However, on the morning of the wedding, she is found dead. A letter from her intimates that she was forced to take her own life to save his. Pete returns disillusioned to Lagos, and there he discovers that a rival for Nneka's affections had tampered with the ceremony to revoke the curse.

In outline, the plot suggests a combination of the manner of Ekwensi and the content of Achebe, but Nzekwu is even more the documentarian than Achebe is. In the novel the hero is rigidly bound in tradition; there is little hint of rebellion in his nature, although early in the novel he agrees with a West Indian friend that traditional marriage is outmoded. Nzekwu goes further than Achebe in describing traditional customs—the Ibo custom of courtship and marriage (perhaps justified by the action), the significance of the kola-nut, the "ozo" society, the various gods, the chief's role in the community—which on the whole the action does not demand. Such descriptions, together with the proverbs interspersed throughout the work, give the impression that the book is more a study of Ibo society than a novel.

Wand of Noble Wood has been called a "powerful tragedy"[24] but the action does not convince one of this. For instance when the author interrupts his narrative to describe in detail the significance of the kola-nut, the action is delayed and the reader's interest is interfered with. Nzekwu writes:

Among us kola-nut is a highly valued and indispensable product. It commands our respect in a way no other product has done. Though it is one of the commonest vegetable products seen in Nigeria, it represents, in our society, a vital social and religious element. Kola-nut is a symbol of friendship, the proper offering at meetings and religious occasions. Its presentation to a guest surpasses any other sign of hospitality which any host among us can show even though in some places it costs only a penny. (p. 79)

Though some may consider the work a "powerful tragedy," the conclusions of a reviewer in *West Africa* seem nearer the mark: "Many West African novelists use novels as political tracts. Mr. Nzekwu uses his well-written story almost as a manual of popular anthropology. . . . Some of the conversation is artificial, particularly when it is used to argue problems of polygamy, interracial marriage, and the like."[25] Nzekwu uses Pete as a medium to express his views on various issues, and neither he nor the other characters succeed in being genuine or plausible.

Nzekwu's next work, *Blade among the Boys* (1962), is also not without flaws, but it is far more convincing as a novel and as a propaganda piece. Nzekwu isolates and treats an aspect of the theme of conflicting cultures—Christianity and paganism. Patrick Ikenga, the main character, receives his education from European teachers and enters a seminary, intending to become a Roman Catholic priest. This decision horrifies his family; they well understood his serving at the altar to achieve his secondary education but, as his mother points out, celibacy is a curse. Patrick vacillates between conforming and not conforming to her views. At the end he has to give up the priesthood to marry, for Nkiru's love potion makes him succumb to her and she becomes pregnant.

Although the hero is better developed in this novel than in *Wand of Noble Wood*, he too is used as a device for the author to communicate his ideas. When to this are added Nzekwu's plodding narration in the manner of a village storyteller, his recurrent use of Ibo proverbs, his interlarded descriptions of masquerades, and the transcriptions of prayers and charms, one is forced to agree with Donatus Nwoga that "*Blade Among the Boys* also suffers from the defect that is found in much realistic writing, the defect which gives rise to the impression that the novelist went out with a notebook, jotting down various things as he saw them, and then transcribed them, at no stage of the operation calling his imagination into activity."[26] This results in the obsessive authority of Nzekwu's works; he informs rather than creates.

Reviewing the novel, the *Times Literary Supplement* referred to its "plain straightforward English,"[27] but this is not accurate. Certainly a language different from that in his previous novel is used. A number of Americanisms appear which seem very unusual in the context. Words like "baby" and "right data" and the slapdash approach to language make the writing crude in places. This is dissimilar to the method of Nzekwu's first novel, where, for instance, the joy of Pete's homecoming is captured in simple, direct, and austere English:

> Children had heard the taxi stop. They first peeped from the doors of their homes to see who it had brought. Then, as recognition dawned on them, they started running towards me.
> "Teacher is home, Teacher is home!" they chanted, as they ran. Some embraced me and others shook hands with me. By the time I reached the house more than fifteen boys and girls were trailing me. Bessie ran out when she heard their shouts. She embraced me and took charge of the portmanteau I was carrying. A couple of boys and girls were despatched to the taxi to collect the rest of my things. When we entered our house everyone came forward to welcome me. The women embraced me, but the men simply shook hands. All around me there was laughter. (p. 128)

In part the crudity of language in *Blade among the Boys* is intended to be a harsh criticism of Catholicism and some of its more pernicious effects. But in addition to marring the style of the book, it alienates sympathy.

Similarly the language fails in *Highlife for Lizards* (1966). At times there is an old-fashioned quaintness about it—"Is his cloth the bone of contention?" "How can you remain adamant to our pleas?"—as well as the usual heavy factual descriptions:

> Land in Onitsha was communal property broken up among the nine villages that made up the town. Ojele's share was built up a long time before and there was no parcel of land which was not occupied by one family or the other. There was certainly no free land anywhere (except perhaps on the arable land across the village stream; but then people did not build permanent homes on arable land) which could be allocated to Ogbuli. The council was faced with only two alternatives: to restrict him to what remained of his father's property or secure an unbuilt land from one of the families. But the latter was going to be most difficult if ever possible. Land was becoming a male child, very precious, and not at all easily parted with. (p. 65)

The conversations are sometimes flat and do not hold the reader's interest, as can be seen when Udezue's two wives attempt to settle their domestic difficulties:

> The next morning when they arrived at the cassava plot Agom said to Nwadi: "Any time you are in difficulty don't just wander off to Udezue. Come to me and if I can't help you, at least I'd have some sound advice to give you."

They were now digging up cassava roots from the previous year's crop and cutting off their stems. They put the roots together in one heap and the stems made another heap.

"Have you any cassava fermenting at home?" Agom asked.

"No! the little left over after your term of cooking I sieved and cooked on my first day." Agom paused in the process of digging up a root. "So you bought all the cassava you used in the last three days?" she asked, her voice crammed with disbelief.

Nwadi nodded. (p. 65)

This conversation is indicative of some of the issues in the novel, which is less serious than the earlier two. Udezue has been married for five years to Agom who still has not borne him a child. After a quarrel with her, he takes a second wife, Nwadi, and plays one wife off against the other. But soon Agom bears her husband a son, and the rival, caught in adultery, is evicted. From then on Agom performs a more important role in family matters. Agom, a symbol of Onitsha maidenhood, comes to be the most significant character in the book, and in her Nzekwu succeeds in portraying a real person, giving her representative qualities as well.

Highlife for Lizards, although hindered by unimaginative language and little plot, is the most ambitious of Nzekwu's works. In the novel, he has attempted to come to terms with the ritualistic significance of Ibo life, not in the way that it would concern the anthropologist, which he was in his first two novels, but insofar as it affects the individual. Agom, the bride, later the wife, and still later the head of the household, is something larger than a mere person. In his effort to get away from the too realistic, Nzekwu has created a poetic character with mythological ramifications.

Gabriel Okara: Ijaw Syntax and English Words

The style of Gabriel Okara's prose, like that of his poetry, straddles two generations. His novel, *The Voice* (1964), is an experiment in the manner of Wole Soyinka's *Interpreters*, and his hero is a modern dissenter engaged on a search. But Okara is of the same generation as Achebe, Ekwensi, and Tutola. His story is thinly disguised allegory: Okolo, the protagonist, is the searcher after "it." Not only does he question himself and his society, but he awakens in others the need to explore their most basic assumptions.

After an education abroad, Okolo begins his search in his own village, Amatu. His first opponent is Chief Izongo who, representing the

181

conservative tradition with its rigid, inexorable values, orders his deportation. His former friend Abadi deserts him and it is significant that only a cripple and a witch, themselves outcasts of his society, decide to help him. Okolo voluntarily exiles himself to Sologa, a nearby town. On the way there, he is accused of attempting to seduce a girl, and though both deny the charge, he is only absolved after taking an oath. In Sologa, the Big One is in charge: the police, the informers on the street, and the white man who runs the lunatic asylum are all his servants. The Big One is the travesty which has resulted from the perverted ideals of democracy. Exposed to these pernicious influences, Okolo soon finds himself in the lunatic asylum. He is rescued by the family of the girl whom he had been accused of seducing. In spite of a witch's advice, he goes back to Amatu where he comes face to face with Chief Izongo celebrating his victory over Okolo. But some of Okolo's values have begun to take root, and he witnesses Abadi openly opposing Chief Izongo. However, Okolo is in no position to defy Chief Izongo and survive, and he and the witch are bundled into a canoe and set adrift. Okara suggests that though Okolo dies, his values still remain.

Yet nowhere in the novel is it clear what these values are. Since Okolo's search never becomes identified with any definite values, "it" is at first simply elusive and finally boring. One's sympathies become alienated from Okolo and, although this is foreign to the author's intention, one begins to agree with the people who have become hostile to him because of his strangeness. On his search, there is no imaginative justification for the sequence of events or for the characters' actions. Why does Okolo leave his village at all, except to give the author an opportunity to introduce different characters? Why does the witch befriend him, except to allow Okara to prove that Okolo was as much an "outsider" as she was? Okolo's search can only be understood in relation to the monomyth, but this does not justify it in terms of a novel.

Okara's view is grim and pessimistic. He seems to feel that the only recipe for existence in a corrupt world is the negation of all values. So a carver in the story claims that it is right to "believe in everything or believe in nothing," a group at an eating-house feels that "the people who have the sweetest insides are the think-nothing people," and the white administrator cautions Okolo to "learn to shut your eyes at certain things." This frightening image of the achievement of nothingness dominates the book; it is what Okolo fights against, since he himself realizes that "the insides of the low and the insides of the high are filled with nothing but yam." Okolo's search is for anything that can be substituted for a vast, yawning vacuity. The emptiness that Okolo sees is, in Sunday Anozie's words, really "between what is and what ought to be."[28]

As a corollary to this theme of the omnipresence of nothingness, images of light and darkness are deftly deployed. Light is used to suggest the penetrating significance of Okolo's search: he is last seen standing under a lamp in the darkness of the witch's hut, where they try to light a fire together. In patterns of light and darkness Okara also contrasts Okolo's youth with his adulthood: "Seeing only darkness in front like the wall, Okolo looked back at his early days when he was a small boy, a small boy going down to the farm with his mother in a canoe and making earth heaps to receive the yam seedlings. How sweet his inside used to be when at the day's finishing time with the sun going down, they paddled home singing . . ." (p. 125). The sunset foreshadowed the darkness of his own future. It tolled the death of a world which he knew and was the harbinger of the nothingness that he now faced.

Okara attempts to render a different English by using Ijaw syntax. In some cases it is effective but at times it seems contrived and does not work. For example, there are expressions like "do not anything fear," "his inside is sweeter than sweetness," and when Okolo returns to Amatu he clumsily asks himself, "Is his meaning in life to plant it in people's insides by asking if they've got *it*?" The language isolates the characters from the reader, since the author's pyrotechnic display dims both action and characters. In addition, everything seems to be sacrificed to Okara's own "vision." The book therefore remains only an idea; within the framework of a novel there is little motivation for the search and what little incident there is, is insignificant in itself and rigidly yoked to symbolism.

Amos Tutuola: The Folktale in Literature

Okara's attempt in *The Voice* to set the legend of the folktale hero and his quest into a larger and more significant framework is not altogether successful because the novel is flawed by too much abstract thought. Tutuola, on the other hand, tells his story almost in the manner of a folktale narrator, but the allegorical implications are implicit rather than explicit. This is the real achievement of *The Palm-Wine Drinkard* (1952), about which Wole Soyinka has commented, "Of all his novels, *The Palm-Wine Drinkard* remains his best and the least impeachable. This book, apart from the work of D. O. Fagunwa, who writes in Yoruba, is the earliest instance of the new Nigerian writer gathering multifarious experience under, if you like, the two cultures, and exploiting them in one extravagant, confident whole."[29] Tutuola has therefore succeeded in presenting attitudes on a level higher than that attained by Achebe, and in taking the quest out of the genre used by Okara.

Because of this, Tutuola stands at the forefront of western African literature and, by inference, African writing in English. He not only was among the first Black African writers to be published and to win a measure of international recognition, but he was also the first writer to see the possibilities of the imaginative translation of mythology into English. But it must be pointed out that he was misunderstood for these very reasons: Dylan Thomas, writing a review in *The Observer*, called *The Palm-Wine Drinkard* a "brief, thronged, grisly and bewitching story" and added that "nothing is too prodigious or too trivial to put down in this tall, devilish story." In the British National Bibliography it is classified not under "Modern Fiction in English," but under "English Miscellany."[30]

Tutuola was well received in England and in Europe (where *The Palm-Wine Drinkard* was translated into French, German, Dutch, and Italian), but for the wrong reasons; in West Africa he was, and still is, not accepted for reasons equally mistaken. In an article on "Nigerian Literature," Ulli Beier commented on possible causes for Tutuola's non-acceptance in West Africa: "Nigerian readers complained . . . that Tutuola wrote 'wrong' English, that his books were a mere 'rehash' of grandmother tales they had all heard before. They alleged that Europeans were mainly attracted by the quaint exotic qualities of the book and that they did not judge the work on literary merits." A young Ghanaian, writing in 1963, asked the question "Has Tutuola anything besides a good imagination and bad grammar?"[31]

Somewhere between these two extremes—Tutuola the "natural" teller of the fantastic and Tutuola the syllogist, the infringer on the copyright of folklore—lies his true significance. And his significance is that he is a literary paradox: he is completely part of the folkloric traditions of the Yorubas and yet he is able to modernize these traditions in an imaginative way. It is on this level that his books can best be approached. His characters are not *on* the threshold of a cultural dilemma as are Chinua Achebe's and Onuora Nzekwu's—they are involved *in* it. They have no rationale like Okolo's, for their spiritual dichotomy is expressed in the vacillatory manner in which they move between bush and town, between the rigors of the inner demands of a superstition they cherish and the necessities of an external materialism to which they must conform. This is how in *The Palm-Wine Drinkard* myth grows into man.

Tutuola's first novel is the story of how a man, much addicted to drinking palm-wine, goes in search of his dead palm-wine tapper. He has a number of adventures, including one in which he captures Death, another in which he overcomes the Skull and brings back a lady whom the Skull had held captive. The protagonist subsequently marries this woman. His victories prove that he is the "Father of gods" and therefore he is worthy of discovering the whereabouts of his tapper. Later the couple have a child who plays all kinds of harmful pranks so they attempt to kill him; out of the ashes a "half-bodied" baby emerges. They are forced to carry him with them on their journey but dispose of him when they meet Drum, Song, and Dance. Being by now penniless, the protagonist changes himself into a canoe, and his wife operates a ferry. Eventually they have enough money to continue their travels and they manage to escape from the long white creatures and the field creatures. They experience kindness from the creatures of "Wraith-Island," find the horses of the inhabitants of the "Greedy Bush" too much for them, narrowly avoid capture by the Spirit of Prey, and, after being tortured, escape from unreturnable "Heavenly Town." They are then looked after by the "Faithful Mother in the White Tree." Before they leave her, they have to sell their death but retain their fear. Later they meet the Red People in the Red Town, enter a "Wrong Town" by mistake, and finally come to the "Deads Town" where the dead palm-wine tapper is. Though he cannot return with them, he gives them an "egg." On the way back they are pursued by dead babies, seized by a man, and put in a sack. After their escape, they find themselves in the "Hungry Creature's" stomach and meet the "Mountain Creatures." But the protagonist arrives back in time to help save his town from famine with the aid of his magic egg.

Tutuola deserves to be considered seriously because his work represents an intentional attempt to fuse folklore with modern life. In this way he is unique, not only in Africa, where the sophisticated African writer is incapable of this tenuous and yet controlled connection, but in Europe as well, where this kind of writing is impossible. J. P. Sartre, contrasting poetry in French by Frenchmen and Africans, asserted that "it is almost impossible for our poets to realign themselves with popular tradition. Ten centuries of erudite poetry separate them from it. And, further, the folkloric inspiration is dried up; at most we could merely contrive a sterile facsimile."[32] The more westernized African faces the same problem. When he does introduce folklore into his writing, it is more in the nature of a gloss; in Tutuola it is intrinsic.

The raison d'être for Tutuola's hero is as beguiling in its simplicity as it is suggestive of larger interpretation. Setting out to find his dead palm-wine tapper in the Deads Town, he wants to perpetuate the transient, to give to the sensual, qualities of spiritual longevity. The language which expresses the hero's decision to undertake his journey has just this combination of the legendary and the more immediately material, the impulsively supernatural and the compulsively natural: "When I saw that there was no palm-wine for me again, and nobody could tap it for me, then I thought within myself that old people were saying that the whole people who had died in this world, did not go to heaven directly, but they were living in one place somewhere in this world. So that I said that I would find out where my palm-wine tapster who had died was" (p. 9).

In choosing to put the tapper in a town in the world, Tutuola is not blindly incorporating mythology. He intentionally perverts the Yoruba belief about death, or rather he merges and reinterprets two beliefs on the subject. In *Olódùmarè: God in Yoruba Belief* (1962), the author has this to say of afterlife: "Generally one may say that there are slightly varying opinions on the matter. There are those who believe that to die is only to change places on this earth. The deceased continues in existence in another country or region far away from his former home. He settles down in his new environment by beginning life all over again . . . *until he either dies again or moves because his whereabouts have been discovered by people who knew him in his former life*" (my italics). Tutuola purposely suppresses this last point since he wants his palm-wine tapper to be found by the drinkard, and if the tapper disappears as soon as he is discovered (as he ought to) then there would be no reason whatever for the journey. Furthermore, as Idowu once said, "A slightly modified form of this belief is that *only the wicked and those whose days on earth are not yet fulfilled,* and, therefore, cannot be received back into heaven continue like that in some part of the earth" (my italics).[33] Tutuola's hero is in search of his tapper, the symbol of physical and spiritual purity. Therefore what he stands for is almost an inversion of the legend.

As the protagonist progresses on his journey, his adventures become significant for two main reasons. First, they help him to grow spiritually, so that after his meeting with Death and his experience of dying (by entering into the village of the palm-wine tapper), his eventual apotheosis (his egg gives him the power of life and death over mankind) comes as no surprise to the reader. Secondly, his adventures, which are all closely integrated into the pattern of the narrative, give Tutuola the opportunity to incorporate folklore and myth into his novel. Tutuola's ability to weave these elements into the texture and pattern of the writing exemplifies his mature craftsmanship. Nevertheless, Tutuola does not hesitate to distort, expand, or summarize, as can be seen when the protagonist acquires, quite early in the novel, the sine qua non of the myth-hero—what Gerald Moore calls "the ever-faithful and helpful female companion (Dante's Beatrice, Theseus's Adriadne, Jason's Medea)."[34] First the protagonist rescues her from the Skull, who is disguised as a "complete gentleman," and later she bears him a child.

Unlike the account of the tale which was published in 1929 in a collection of Yoruba legends,[35] Tutuola's book does not emphasize the superhuman abilities of the Skull to take on human form, since this is largely irrelevant to the narrative. Instead Tutuola poetizes on the dichotomy between appearance and reality and so immediately establishes a sympathetic relationship between his hero and the woman he is to marry. Tutuola revitalizes the Yoruba legend, reinvigorating it through imagery of the modern experience (thus making it more directly relevant), introduces the tragedy of unrealizable ideals (which is not in the legend), and shortens the mere mechanics of the Skull's transformation (which is the core of the legend). In short, Tutuola has made of the legend what he wanted, omitting elements irrelevant to him. For the same reasons he omits the moral lesson which is stressed at the end of another version of the legend.

It is perhaps pertinent to add that Tutuola changes "Head" and "Spirit" to "Skull," since he wishes to emphasize the utter emptiness of mere appearances. Also it is interesting to note that the transfer of folklore into modern imaginative literature involves a certain necessary acceptance of Christianity. This fusion of pagan myth and Christian belief occurs naturally and easily in Tutuola and is part of his much wider and more universal literary cosmos. In him the paradoxes of culture are balanced.

In another instance, Tutuola only lightly touches on a particular legend—the Legend of Child-Wiser-Than-His-Father, which is found in *Folk Tales and Fables* (1953) collected by Phebean Itayemi and P. Gurrey. In Tutuola's story the child is also born in an unusual manner and is just as wise as the child in the legend, but Tutuola relates the child's birth to his theme: he is born when his mother's swollen thumb touches a palm-tree thorn and he drinks vast quantities of palm-wine. In addition his exploits are infused with all the rich vigor of Tutuola's humor and exaggeration, and his death is not the end of an interlude but a further step toward the protagonist's apotheosis.

Although Tutuola borrows from legend, he is no mere plagiarist. His writing, a dramatic reliving of the folktale, "preserves at least two essential qualities of the native folktale: its dramatic spirit and its identity as lived experience integrated into the whole of life as seen and felt by the writer." But Ramsaran adds that "all these are only effective in Tutuola's writing in so far as they are subordinated to the working out of the drama in the context of the lives of the chief protagonists in his stories."[36]

Part of Tutuola's success at this imaginative modernizing of folklore is due to his use of language. Those who argue that he writes "wrong" English do not take two factors into consideration. The story, written in the first person, concerns a palm-wine drinker and palm-wine in West Africa is to a large extent the drink of the poor working classes. If the narrator were to speak standard English, anyone acquainted with the realities of West African speech would find the results ludicrous. Secondly, Tutuola's English is a sensible compromise between raw pidgin (which would not be intelligible to European readers) and standard English.

The effect of this compromise is to enliven the story, to project it beyond the level of sociological documentation. Tutuola is therefore neither "quaint" nor "semiliterate," neither a "natural" nor a "sophisticate." He is a conscious craftsman, who knows where his talents lie. In a recent interview he expressed a desire to collect world folklore and incorporate it into his novels,[37] and he told me recently of his wish to travel through Nigeria gathering folklore for use in his work. Indeed in an age when Africa is to a large extent in the process of cultural evolution, it is more important than ever to ensure that written literature should carry over from the past some aspects of the oral tradition. About Tutuola, Jacob Drachler has said, "He undoubtedly adds something to the old themes by his extraordinarily graphic style, which is helped and not hindered by his limited education. We can only speculate about the forms that this traditional material will take in the work of the more sophisticated literary artists in the future; but Tutuola's success is a sign that very old themes and motifs of African oral literature will not be completely cast aside."[38]

After *The Palm-Wine Drinkard*, there is a falling off in Tutuola's work, although *My Life in the Bush of Ghosts* (1954) and *Simbi and the Satyr of the Dark Jungle* (1955) are not written on the "fairy-tale" level of *The Brave African Huntress* (1958) and *Feather Woman of the Jungle* (1962). *My Life in the Bush of Ghosts* and *Simbi and the Satyr of the Dark Jungle* both pose problems of ethics. The boy of the former novel undergoes various experiences to discover the meaning of "good," and in the latter a spoiled rich girl passes through a number of grueling tests to discover the meaning of poverty.

However, Tutuola fails to connect the protagonist's disorganized adventures with the ethical significance of the novels. In *My Life in the Bush of Ghosts*, the young hero is the victim of jealousies among his father's wives. At the age of seven, he has to run away from his town when raiders come looking for slaves, and he stumbles into the Bush of Ghosts where his adventures begin. Tutuola relates the boy's various experiences, how he is changed into various objects and animals, how he marries twice, first a ghostess and then a Super Lady. After twenty-four years in the Bush of Ghosts, he is given the chance to escape by the Television-Handed Ghostess, a weird creation, half-mythological, half-ordinary. He encounters other misfortunes before he finally returns to his village.

Women play the central role in two of Tutuola's novels, one of which is *Simbi and the Satyr of the Dark Jungle*. Simbi is a more active character than the protagonist of *My Life in the Bush of Ghosts*, for her adventures do not just simply happen—she wills them upon herself. As she is later to remind the satyr, she is the most beautiful girl in her village, the daughter of the wealthiest woman, and her voice could wake "deads." An Ifa priest suggests a way for her to embark on her adventures, and, following his advice, she makes a sacrifice at the crossroads. From there Dogo carries her off on the Path of Death. She experiences great tribulations before she meets two of her friends who had been similarly kidnapped. They wander on for some time, barely escaping from various threats to their lives, and finally Simbi and one of her friends reach home. Her travels have brought her into contact with sinners, tigers, birds, a snake, a Siamese twin who changes into a cock, and the satyr himself. She escapes from him by changing into a fly and flying up his nostril.

The protagonists' adventures in these two novels illustrate the process of growing up. Both of them return as adults to their villages, and Tutuola's fantasy is of the mind where the phantoms of childhood battle in a last desperate effort with the concrete materialities of the adult world. On another level, they represent a transition—from the innocence of a traditional way of life to the turbulence of another. But these interpretations must be read into the novels; they never obtrude as they do in *The Voice*. However, although both novels make use of the folk-

189

tale and the personae of mythology and legend, they lack the force of *The Palm-Wine Drinkard*. It is true that *My Life in the Bush of Ghosts* and *Simbi* are about "the initiation of a child" and "initiation into the trouble and adventure of living," as Anne Tibble argues,[39] but they are only ephemerally so. Unlike *The Palm-Wine Drinkard* they do not demonstrate these stated themes in action.

Tutuola's next two books are solely concerned with the more sensational side of adventure. It is as if one were suddenly exiled from Achebe's closed villages to Ekwensi's open towns. In *The Brave African Huntress*, a girl masters the hunting skill of her father and rescues her brothers from the Jungle of the Pygmies. The novel's fantasy is paramount, even though *The Feather Woman of the Jungle* has a male spokesman, an old chief who tells stories for ten nights to his people. In actual fact both works are simply short stories weakly linked together by a central narrator. Tutuola attempts to capture the atmosphere of an African storyteller, but the works fail as coherent pieces of writing.

In these last two books the style has altered; instead of the semi-pidgin and the solecisms that contributed to the success of *The Palm-Wine Drinkard*, biblical language is used and is sometimes equally as effective:

> It was the "Day of Confusion" Wednesday, that I entered this Jungle of the Pygmies, at about eleven o'clock in the morning. After I travelled in this jungle for a few minutes—the great fears, wonders, and uncountable of undescriptive strange things, which I was seeing here and there were stopped me by force. When I was unable to travel further because of these things then I thought within myself to climb a tree to the top so that I might see these things to my satisfaction. And at the same time I climbed a tall tree to the top. I sat on one of its branches and as it was a leafy tree therefore these leaves were covered me and I peeped out very seriously as when an offender peeped out from the small window of his cell. Then I was looking at these handiworks of God with great wonder. (p. 55)

This quotation also illustrates that an element of nature description has entered the work and, incidentally, the West African novel as well. Prudence Smith has commented that Tutuola's language is "constantly invented, constantly unexpected,"[40] a virtue which pervades all his novels. The extract above is dissimilar to the following episode in *The Palm-Wine Drinkard*:

> When the debit-collector asked for the £1 which he (borrower) had borrowed from his friend since a year, the debitor (borrower) replied that he never paid any of his debits since he was born, then the debit-collector said that he never failed to collect debits from any debitor since he had begun the work. The collector said further-more that to collect debits about

was his profession and he was living on it. But after the debitor heard so from the collector, he also said that his profession was to owe debits and he was living only on debits. In conclusion, both of them started to fight but, as they were fighting fiercely, a man who was passing that way at that time saw them and he came nearer; he stood behind them looking at them, because he was very interested in this fight and he did not part them. But when these two fellows had fought fiercely for one hour, the debitor who owed the £1 pulled out a jack-knife from pocket and stabbed himself at the belly, so he fell down and died there. But when the debit-collector saw that the debitor died, he thought within himself that he had never failed to collect any debit from any debitor in this world since he had started the work and he (collector) said that if he could not collect the £1 from him (debitor) in this world, he (collector) would collect it in heaven. So he (collector) also pulled out a jack-knife from his pocket and stabbed himself as well, and he fell down and died there.

As the man who stood by and looking at them was very, very interested in that fight, he said that he wanted to see the end of the fight, so he jumped up and fell down at the same spot and died there as well so as to witness the end of the fight in heaven. So when the above statement was given in the court, I was asked to point out who was guilty, either the debit-collector, debitor, the man who stood by looking at them when fighting, or the lender? (pp. 111–12).

The reason for the difference in language lies in the nature of the experience. In the first instance, Tutuola is describing a moment of awareness, whereas in the second he is intentionally abstruse, since the incident he recounts is the extension of a riddle.

Tutuola's disharmonious symbols unite the paradoxes of his world. No matter if he relates his heroes' success in attaining mythical grandeur and fulfillment or leaves them in a muddle, his task is above all the ennobling of man. His characters seek fulfillment within the traditional format of the myth. Therefore, since he is himself a Christian, it comes as no surprise to discover that one man's search is for the keys of the kingdom. This is the thesis of his latest work, *Ajaiyi and His Inherited Poverty* (1967), a moral tale told through the medium of the imagination and the fantastic. Ajaiyi and his family are poor, and the harder they work, the poorer they become. His mother and father die leaving Ajaiyi and his sister, Aina, nothing but an inheritance of poverty. In an effort to alleviate their destitution, Ajaiyi sets out with two poverty-stricken friends, Ojo and Alabi, to search for the Creator, who they hope will give them money. After a hazardous journey (reminiscent of *The Palm-Wine Drinkard*), they reach the Creator's town, but being such wretched sinners they are forbidden to visit him personally. They make their requests for money known to a Holy Man who in turn discusses their problems with the Creator. After seven days, he returns to tell them that the only way they can get money is to go to the Devil.

After many more adventures, one in which they acquire three talking lumps of iron which imprison them, the three friends meet the Devil. He is willing to give them as much wealth as they want on certain conditions: the Devil can take the life of a sister of each of them; the three must take on their burdens of the lumps of iron after death; they must become the Devil's servants and do his will; and they must allow their lives to be shortened from sixty-six to six years. Oyo and Alabi agree to the conditions, but Ajaiyi does not. (His refusal to betray his kin, his sister, is borrowed from a folktale.) In a few months, Oyo and Alabi receive bags of money which almost crowd them out of their houses. But shortly afterward, their sisters die and they begin to regret the vows they made to the Devil.

After another unsuccessful search for money, Ajaiyi decides to return to his village, but on the way home he stops to visit his sister. Her husband takes Ajaiyi to the Iron-worshipper of the village, who removes the spirit from Ajaiyi's lump of iron. Since Ajaiyi has no money to pay the Iron-worshipper, he is forced to pawn himself. When a few years later Ajaiyi wishes to marry, he has to pawn himself again for the price of the dowry. In destitution he goes to see the local village doctor, who tells him that he will become rich if he makes certain sacrifices on his father's grave. Ajaiyi discovers that the local doctor is tricking him and threatens to kill him. In exchange for his life, the doctor gives Ajaiyi and his wife all his wealth. Even though Ajaiyi had been searching for money his entire life, he does not spend it at first because he remembers his encounter with the Creator and the lesson that "money was the father of sins and insincerities." Therefore, he decides to build churches with the money in order to put it to use for God's work instead of the Devil's. He builds churches in four towns, and with the knowledge he has gained from the Creator he converts people to Christianity. The novel's ending is unsatisfactory, but Tutuola again has successfully used the folktale for his own purposes—to recount the historical contact of his people with Christianity.

New West African Novelists

Within the last few years, several new novelists have appeared on the West African literary scene who are worthy of our consideration here. Some have continued the tradition of documenting village life, others have tended to express the sensational, a few have elaborated on the theme of the divided man, and a number can truly be called experimental.

Clement Agunwa's novel *More Than Once* (1967) is a partly serious, partly funny account of Nweke Nwakor, a businessman from eastern Nigeria on the make, whose demise is caused by his lack of education. Beginning the story with Akowe's tirade on Nwakor's deficiency in education, as evidenced by his reading his newspaper upside down in the marketplace, Agunwa then takes the reader back to Nwakor's childhood to explain how he arrived at his present condition.

Nwakor fails to obtain an education because as a child he feared he would miss the traditional aspects of village life if he were to attend a Christian school. Nweke was also very much afraid of teachers. When some schoolboys give Nweke lumps of sugar to entice him to attend school, he goes only to find the teacher "caning" the boys. Even though Nweke is not caned and is given more lumps of sugar, the experience thoroughly turns him against remaining in school.

Regardless of Nwakor's village ways and lack of education, he becomes a highly respected trader. He buys honorable titles for his father and gifts for his mother. He even builds a sumptuous house and marries. But there is a flaw in the whole scheme of things. With no education Nwakor has to rely on others to keep his accounts, to write his letters, and to read for him. Through overspending and chance events, he loses most of his money. The circular pattern of the novel shows him in this depressed condition at both the beginning and the end of the book.

At the very end of the novel Nwakor, while lamenting his circumstances, meets Henry Obi, who as a boy used to write letters for Nwakor. As Nwakor and Obi talk, Nwakor learns that he has not lost respect for traditional ways even though he has become a teacher. Nwakor, happy to see that teachers have changed and still convinced that the root of his troubles is his lack of schooling, decides to attempt once more to acquire an education.

More Than Once is a novel that reads as if one has read it before. The search for education, the description of tribal life, the rise and fall of Nwakor all belong to the lore of novelists from eastern Nigeria. Agunwa's humorous touches, however, save the novel from becoming another sermon on the insubstantiality of wealth.

Some of Ekwensi's interests and style are apparent in Elechi Amadi's *Concubine* (1966), the story of a young woman destined for unhappiness. Ihuoma's unhappiness is predictable and the reader knows that the various men with whom she comes into contact are all doomed, for she is guarded by the reincarnation of a water-spirit. Therefore the novel follows an obvious development, since nothing can be done with the characters. However, this flaw is mitigated somewhat by Amadi's concern with form. He also intimately describes spiritual experiences and analyzes such characters as Ihuoma and Ekwueme through the use of dreams. But the characters' depths are never plumbed; instead they are only labeled—Ekwueme is "childish" (p. 136) and "boyish" (p. 169) and Ihuoma is "loyal" (p. 39)—as if the writer intended to create cardboard figures to prove the fatalistic insignificance of man.

Occasionally the novel is redeemed by passages of grandeur; for example there are expressions like "evening of the brother of tomorrow" (p. 81), and in speaking of Ihuoma's headache Amadi writes, "Her head contained a drummer relentlessly beating a monotonous tattoo" (p. 46). There are at times fine descriptions, of the weather, of nature (ears of corn "caressing passers-by"), and of a dance in Emenike's honor. And, unusual for a West African novelist, Amadi offers close objective observations on the nonhuman world: Ihuoma watches lizards playing on the walls of her house, a goat withdraws upon seeing the unhappy Ihuoma, and a hen feeds her chickens when Ekwueme returns after his disappearance. Although such observations point to the author's fine eye for detail and contribute to the total effect of the novel, they do nothing to dismiss the feeling of bathos at the end.

Amadi's *Great Ponds* (1969), a story of tribal conflict and law set in the early twentieth century, is considerably better. A full-scale war between two clans develops out of a crisis over the right to fish in Wangaba Pond. When men are killed and other clans become involved, the chiefs call a meeting to bring about a settlement. It is agreed that the gods will decide who is the rightful owner. The villagers of Chiolu choose Olumba, a tough warrior, to execute their right to the pond. If Olumba dies in six months, the Aliakoro can claim the pond; if he lives the Chiolu can. Olumba has many trials; Wago disguises himself as a leopard and attacks Olumba in an effort to claim the pond once and for all. But Wago's trick is discovered and Olumba's allies attack him; as a result he drowns himself in Wangaba Pond. Since it is against tribal law to fish in a pond where a suicide has been committed, the pond is therefore of no use to either group. This end is a development, unlike *The Concubine*, which grinds its way to an obvious conclusion. Amadi has used the form of a folktale to point to the necessity for cooperation and to highlight the evil of greed. The element of surprise at the end accounts for the success of this novel.

Ayi Kwei Armah's *Beautyful Ones Are Not Yet Born* (1968) is a great milestone in that it represents best the coming-of-age of African literature. It is individualized in style and language, radical in thought, and frightening in its frank and fearless realism.

The novel's main plot centers on an honest man of unshakable integrity (nameless and simply called The Man) who works as a minor civil service functionary in a railway station in Ghana. One of the beautiful people, he is considered foolish because he refuses to participate in the bribery, cheating, and corruption which are all around him.

Moreover, he is despised by his wife and her family because he has failed to use his education and his position to get ahead. They ridicule him because he is not like Koomson, his former classmate who had joined a political party as an opportunist and is now a minister in the government.

Eventually a coup occurs and Koomson's party is ousted. When his corrupted colleagues are hunted and jailed, he runs to The Man for help. With the police rapidly approaching, The Man and Koomson are forced to escape through a latrine hole where they have to wade through excreta. Before that, while eating at The Man's house, Koomson is gripped with fear and starts to give off a horrible stench from his corpulent body. When The Man's wife smells this, she finally understands her husband and says to him, "I am glad you never became like him."

The novel shows Armah as an independent individual. No longer does he feel that he has to prop up tribal mores; he is free to attack the group. Throughout the book, Armah intentionally nauseates us to force us to see the corruption and filth around us; references to smells, especially excreta, are frequent, and we learn that we might very well be like the chichidodo, a bird that hates excreta but eats maggots. Apart from the personal hope in the wife's confession to The Man, Armah offers us little cause for optimism; on his way home, The Man sees the soliders of the new regime taking a bribe.

The Man is not an activist but he is no outsider either. Although he is not tainted by corruption, he manages to survive within a corrupt society. Ironically, we are told at the end that only the wicked survive. The Man is good and his goodness is emphasized throughout. He is unlike Teacher who is an outsider, who reads, listens to the radio, and admits he is not free. Teacher has left the "loved ones" (his family, his ancestors) and he realizes he is nothing without them. At least The Man has his family and is able to survive in an era of crass materialism.

The theme of materialism is taken up in *Fragments* (1970). Baako, a re-creation of The Man, is a young Ghanaian writer who returns home after having spent five years in America. He is idealistic and is saddened to find that his beliefs are not echoed by his countrymen who desire to become westernized and materialistic. Symbolism helps to emphasize Baako's position as seen by society; for example, a mad dog is killed at the beginning of the book. Soon Baako himself has a breakdown and is considered insane by those around him.

Although there is some satire and nostalgia in *Fragments*, Armah again is very realistic in his treatment. For instance, Baako cannot obtain employment with the television station because a junior official wants to be bribed. The directors of the station are more interested in pandering to the head of state then in making educational films. And Baako's relatives cannot understand why he is not rich. So in many ways, his insanity is a result of his alienation from his people. In *Why Are We So Blest* (1970), Armah's sentiments are still with the people. Set in Algiers, the novel deals with freedom fighters; but the people are again betrayed for, as Armah points out, a chasm always exists between the rhetoric of the revolution and its evolution in reality.

Rebel (1969) by Bediako Asare portrays the reaction of an isolated African society to the coming of independence. The author determines to make hard and fast distinctions between the "civilized" and the "uncivilized" by contrasting the traditional ways of Mzee Matata, the local priest who is greedy and autocratic, with the modern ways of Shabani who brings "civilization" to the people of Pachanga.

Also pitted against Mzee Matata is Nguromo whose life is threatened when he challenges the priest's authority. Asare's meaning here is clear: the forces of tradition, backed up by traditional tribal authority, seek to keep people in bondage. Nguromo revolts against this, and proclaims his stance as an individual.

After Mzee Matata's unsuccessful attempt to kill Nguromo, he is forced to leave with his wife. The importance of this act is emphasized: "In all of the oral tradition and history of the people there had been no mention of anyone deserting the tribe." When Mzee Matata discovers where they are, he tells his people that they are suffering because the gods have been disobeyed and as a result they are angry. They will only be appeased by human sacrifice and twelve men are dispatched to retrieve Nguromo and Seitu. They are captured but are saved just as they are about to be sacrificed. Part one of the novel closes with the shooting of Mzee Matata.

The second part of *Rebel* depicts the coming of "civilization" to Pachanga. Shabani, the harbinger of the new way, arrives in the village equipped with all the paraphernalia of the western world. His gun, haversack, khaki clothes, hat, glasses, boots, binoculars, camera, and bicycle are described in minute detail as if being viewed for the first time. Hence, his glasses "on the bridge of his nose and linked to the ears were two transparent oval pieces through which he blinked." Of course one tends to laugh at Shabani even though this is not the author's intention. He becomes a bit of a bore as he indoctrinates the people to the wonders of the world beyond the mountains. He introduces potatoes; he lectures the people on purifying water, on democracy, on motorcars and airplanes. Then he summarily orders them to elect a leader. Naturally, Nguromo, the representative of democracy, is elected over Fundi, the advocate of traditional ways.

That the novel presents a one-sided view cannot be disputed. Shabani's utter disregard for tradition is, to say the least, ridiculous. His sudden arrival and his rejection of tribal ethics would hardly have been accepted, since no one man is the repository of custom. Asare's novel simplifies an issue: tradition does not die with the death of a ruler. Also the description of Pachanga is absurd, for no nation could exist in such complete isolation. No people could possibly be as docile and unquestioning as Asare suggests, or could switch loyalties as easily and as unaccountably as they do. Finally, Asare's insistence on the superiority of western values and his total disregard for African traditions make this book an unpalatable piece of propaganda.

Kofi Awoonor's only novel, *This Earth My Brother* (1971), describes the plight of Amamu, a Ghanaian lawyer who returns home from England only to find that the Africa he once knew has drastically changed. He takes refuge in nostalgia and finally he drowns himself. Awoonor intends this tale to have symbolical ramifications for all Africa and to some extent he does succeed. Certain poetical devices—references to the sea for instance—are used and work beautifully. The book is a poet's novel and at times Awoonor's language is the language of poetry gone sour, not the language of prose. Nevertheless, reinforced by rich imagery, the novel does succeed in showing that Amamu's breakdown represents the obvious collapse of a legacy of colonialism and the corrupt influences in the present. In his study of African culture, *The Breast of the Earth*, Awoonor speaks of "the nightmare for the African caught in between the anvil and the hammer." His work expresses this tension, but leaves it unresolved.

Mbella Sonne Dipoko is extremely different from any of the novelists so far considered in this section, for his concern is not with tradition or group loyalty. Instead he belongs more to the world of the French outsiders who laugh at the antics of the group. In a way his

197

background explains this, for he is bilingual, speaking both French and English. Having lived in both Cameroon and Nigeria he has had wide exposure to two types of colonial regimes. At present Dipoko lives in Paris.

He has had poetry published in Nigeria, in *Présence Africaine*, and in other journals. His first novel, *A Few Nights and Days* (1966), comments on European sexual morality and on the nature of interracial love. Doumbe, a young Cameroonian living in Paris, indulges in a wild extravaganza of sexual promiscuity. He constantly judges the standards of his partners in relationship to African values. At one point when Doumbe is making love to Thérèse, a young girl who commits suicide because of him, he abuses her in his own tongue and she unsuspectingly says, "I like your language." The book succeeds because it is a very readable account of young lovers.

Because of Women (1969) returns to the rivers of Dipoko's native Cameroon. Again the story centers on a man who brings tragedy to a woman. Ngoso, a womanizer, wants to have a large family, but the woman who is carrying his child dies of a miscarriage after he has beaten her. Ngoso, too, dies a tormented man. In the author's words, the novel "ends tragically—to feel beauty you must have tragedy." This applies equally well to *A Few Nights and Days.*

Both novels are overly concerned with the relationship between a man and a woman, and Dipoko at times fails to place his accounts in the realm of probability. In the second novel, however, the narrator looks back on events and this helps the reader to see all aspects of Ngoso's personality. No moral judgments are passed in these books—perhaps that is their greatest appeal. Dipoko delights in describing a full life where men and women meet, mate, and sometimes love. His world has been criticized as a distorted one; perhaps it is more accurate to see it as selective.

Amu Djoleto's contribution to West African fiction includes his novel, *The Strange Man* (1967), and a short story, "The Lone Horse," which was published in Henry Swanzy's *Voices of Ghana.*

A lively account, *The Strange Man* relates the story of Old Mensa's struggles through life, as seen against the somber background of his brother's funeral. It begins leisurely, giving detailed descriptions of Mensa's boyhood—his adventures in school, his pranks—but the time sequence quickens toward the end and suddenly Mensa is old and sickly. There is some rich comedy in the story, especially in the author's dialogues, which he delights in, and in his constant attacks on church-schools and corporal punishment. The "message" (if he intends one) is not clear, for he suggests that Mensa, despite his liberal views, will die a disappointed man. As a "one-man" story, it does not attempt to make anybody live except Mensa who comes over as sprightly and bold when young, and cunning and ambitious when old. Always Mensa, like Djoleto, is enjoyable.

The Gab Boys by Cameron Duodu is in part a fictional portrayal of Ghana as experienced by half-educated but intelligent youth, called "gab boys" because they wear gabardine trousers. Most of them spend their time in idling, and the political events of their country only touch them insofar as they use these events to express their own frustrations. But the hero does find a job on the lower rung of the civil service where he witnesses rigged elections and the machinations of politicians. He finds he is soon in a position—and this is Duodu's "moral" point—to pass judgment. He can look down on his so-called superiors, for he realizes that they are greedy, hypocritical, and crude. However, all he can do is speak out; he is still a nobody and too weak to oppose them.

Pleasantly written, The Gab Boys documents an important era in Ghana's history, just before Nkrumah's demise. It is tempting to read (with the sagacity of hindsight) a warning parable in what it says. But Duodu's style, varying from a superficial use of language to heavy sententious observations, makes for lack of balance in the book. The reader comes away feeling that perhaps he has missed the allegory.

One laughs with the gab boys—with their scorn of authority, their airs, their quickness to detect solecisms. At times the humor is one derived from his own society but the writer points out the meaning (not always with enough care for the niceties of style) to his (western) reader. Humorous flashbacks enliven certain scenes and the excellent use of pidgin helps to create amusing characters. But the explanations tucked in to interpret the secret language of the gab boys are clumsy.

The gab boys represent an interesting side of West African city youth. They are tough and resistant to authority (especially policemen) and they fight like and identify with Hollywood movie heroes. But there is an underlying emptiness: "we had nothing to live for." They have turned their backs on the farm and look now toward the promises of their "education." But colonial culture and the new independence have failed them. Their resentment is the basis of the novel.

With Obi Egbuna's Wind versus Polygamy (1964), one quite definitely encounters a thoroughly bad novel. Although its verbal infelicities place it in the Onitsha tradition, the attitudinizing of the characters prevents it from being as refreshingly naive as other books in that tradition. The story is about Elima, "an African girl of tantalizing beauty"

(p. 7), and her many love affairs, which end with her marriage to Jerome, the chief's son.

The novel fails in its serious moments, for Egbuna is at times unintentionally funny. Chief Ozoumba, whom the author seriously wants his readers to see as a champion of the old order, fails hopelessly: his monologue to the court, supposedly spoken by an illiterate chief, is quite ridiculous. Furthermore, the Onitsha-type descriptions add to the absurdity of the book—the hunter who "walked with a limp, an indication that he had weathered many storms" (p. 21), and the chief's "intelligent laughing eyes" (p. 35). The dialogue is stilted, and the satire on the overindulgence of politicians falls flat. Councillor Ogidi, who dismisses a driver because he winks at him with his left eye, is simply set up for the author to demolish. In addition, some of Ogidi's jokes and his general conversation are definitely out of context: Egbuna does not know him or his other characters very well. For instance, Ogidi says of Elima, "She is the cutest thing I ever saw. I will make our wedding the talk of the continent. I will bathe her in champagne thrice daily all through our honeymoon. And clean her teeth with gold-paste. We will spend a kinky week-end at Port Harcourt" (p. 19). One sees here that the standard obsessions of another geographical locality have become confused with those of Africa. The *New Statesman* reviewer of the novel thought that even though Egbuna might be too polished and off-beat for the marketplace, he seems " 'quaint' in London."[41] *Wind versus Polygamy* is an utter failure because Egbuna has written neither a tract nor an Onitsha pamphlet.

Chukwuemeka Ike's *Toads for Supper* (1965) is different, for it is a far more successful novel. A comedy about university life, it is reminiscent of the first part of Achebe's *Man of the People*. Amobi, a first year Ibo student at the University of Southern Nigeria, gets entangled with three women. The story covers three years of his undergraduate life—its moments of splendor and its disappointments.

The novel has a fair sprinkling of Ibo language and customs with some Yoruba lore added, rather arbitrarily. At times the proverbs do succeed. When Amobi's father speaks to him, proverbs are a natural, easy part of his conversation, but they seem slightly forced in the author's own descriptions. Union elections take up too much space in the book, and the social "musts" of Amobi's first homecoming are too greatly detailed. But it can be argued that the author has deliberately given so much attention to Amobi's first homecoming in order to emphasize the difference between it and his homecoming after his expulsion from the university.

Perhaps the book's most redeeming quality is that it has no ax to grind. Just a look at life, it has no obtrusive message. Such matters as the riskiness of intertribal marriages are only touched on. The white administrator and his Black successor (Amobi's friend) are satirized *en passant* in delightful asides, as are Christianity and the oft-repeated polygamy of the chiefs. Ike is at his best when he is humorous, and in a short anecdote he relates the story of a girl called "Natural" who was taken out of school by the chief who had an eye for "all things bright and beautiful" (p. 66).

In *Toads for Supper* the satire does succeed. Education, politicians, and religion, as well as the *nouveau riche* and Amobi's friend Chima, who as an assistant district officer feels he must behave like an Englishman, are all satirical targets. Ike's sense of fun rarely misses its mark. He writes, for instance, of how the mission fund was known as "the bag that was open at both ends" (p. 59), since one always paid in. There is nothing vindictive in his attitudes, nor do his characters strike the postures of Egbuna's.

There are, however, two elements that seem out of place in the novel. The melodramatic aspect, for example, does not blend smoothly with the comic approach. Aduke goes mad at the end of the story and at one point Amobi thinks of drowning himself in the River Niger. The evangelical flavor also is out of keeping with the general tone of the book; Ike is always directly trumpeting the virtues of Christianity. Characters call on God for help, Aduke is tied up with the Student Christian Movement, and Amobi considers his work on a fund-raising scheme as "an hour spent in His service" (p. 138).

Like *Toads for Supper*, *The Naked Gods* (1970) is a comedy of university life, but it is more humorous though more committed. British and American educators wage a bitter battle over the type of education suitable for Songhai University. The selfish aims of nearly everyone and every institution involved in the controversy are skillfully portrayed, but the climax comes as a disappointment because the battle ends in a compromise.

Ike is an excellent satirist when not extolling Christianity. He looks at what he knows best—university life—and through this microcosm examines the foibles and failings of the African world at large. His people are painted brightly, excessively so, because he wishes to emphasize stupidities. In a way his are the novels without "heroes" for he cannot side with anyone for long. Amobi barely survives in *Toads for Supper* and Professor Ikin fails to inherit the mantle of power in *The Naked Gods*.

201

Samuel Asare Konadu, the owner of Anowuo Educational Publishers, which he established in 1965, is the author of seven works. An early novel, *Come Back Dora* (1966), was to be brought out abroad as *Ordained by the Oracle* in 1968. *Shadow of Wealth* (1966) and *Nightwatchers of Korlebu* (1968), both published in Ghana, mark Konadu as an important popular writer in Ghana (like Blay). Akan customs figure prominently in his novels: *Come Back Dora* richly describes Akan funeral ceremonies and *Nightwatchers of Korlebu* deals with the world of dead spirits and how they interact with the living.

Like other popular West African writers, Konadu is also concerned with urban situations. *Shadow of Wealth* exposes a familiar aspect of city life—corruption—but the author makes no moral point as the Onitsha writers do.

Nightwatchers of Korlebu, with a more traditional setting, offers good insights into traditional ritual as it affects the life of a young man of royal lineage. The book also juxtaposes African and European mores, a technique which is at the core of many of Konadu's novels. *A Woman in Her Prime* (1967), for example, asks the question of whether or not a woman who is childless and will soon be unable to bear children should observe the rites of the priest, attend the shrine of Tano, and divorce her third husband or make what she can of life without children. Finally Pokuwaa does conceive but she insists that the "Tano has nothing to do with it." Instead she credits it to Nyankopon Twedeampong, the Great Benevolent One. The novel ends on a tender note as the couple choose a name for their child.

There is little story in *Ordained by the Oracle* (1969), but, as has been mentioned, it poignantly depicts funeral rites and rituals and strongly conveys the idea that the dead live on after death.

Konadu is a novelist with a public in mind. When he writes for a "home" audience, he emphasizes the familiar but for his "overseas" audience he tends not to reproduce his Hollywood-type settings or his neat comparisons of corruption and good. In fact most of his books spare his reader any moralizing. *Ordained by the Oracle* points in the direction that his future works will probably go—the celebration of ritual. It makes for slow action in the novel as the West knows the genre, but it offers an interesting insight into the traditions of Africa.

There is a definite trend developing then among some of these new writers, a trend evidenced by the work of Dipoko, Duodu, and Ike. And if one affirms that these writers seem to be outside group identification, one must acknowledge that they seem conscious of an alien group. In other words the tribe is being substituted with the English-speaking public. When a novelist like Konadu (and the poet Benibengor Blay, along with the numerous writers of Onitsha "ferry" literature) expressly appeals to an English-speaking group *within* Africa, the issue is further complicated. Such writers belong to the tradition of Aluko and Ekwensi; the next author to be considered, however, belongs more to the tradition of Achebe.

Munonye's *Only Son* (1966) portrays the separation of a mother from her son, Naana, because of their religious differences. Posing the familiar problem of the contact of cultures, Munonye sees it strictly from the viewpoint of education. There is little humor to save the book from its dry barrenness. In short, *The Only Son* is Laye's *African Child* told with limited ability and a lack of poetic insight.

Munonye's *Obi* (1969), a far more successful novel than *Only Son*, centers on Joe and Anna and their experiences in a changing society. Both of them are Christians living in a world torn between Christianity and tribal religion. Joe represents the man divided between two cultures, frequently basing his decisions on both aspects of his experience, attempting to encompass them both. This duality is shown in his decision to return to his father's village. Although he intends to rebuild and continue his father's homestead, he also wants to avoid military service (there is a war going on) and to start a rubber plantation which he hopes will make him wealthy.

Anna, like Joe, is apparently more modern than traditional, but she is not a strong person. All we learn is that her only concern is Joe and she cares little about tradition or anything else except the church. Although she is the focal point of all the turmoil, Munonye does not provide us with any profound insights into her character. Joe, in contrast, is portrayed in great depth. He emerges as a strong, determined, brooding man, stubborn at times, and sometimes given to explosiveness.

The extended family and members of the church also stand as significant characters in the book. The family represents broad and diverse personalities, as well as different interests and values. In Willie, one sees the early political activist who from his education and experience is beginning to understand the oppressive forces of colonialism. Obieke, a moderate, even-tempered, thoughtful man, is the established leader of the family. It is evident from the admiration the others have for him that his judgment is highly respected. Uzondu, the fat one, is the object of constant humor. And the entire family collectively, including the daughters of Umdemzue, is a pillar of strength. From the welcoming scene at the beginning of the book to the death council at the end, the family is depicted as a strong, viable force.

While the principal characters are Joe and Anna, the principal theme is change and transition in African society, not only in ideas and values, but also in devices and methods. Although the novel is not sociological, it does suggest that the institution primarily involved in change is religion and the church. Munonye excellently elucidates the conflict between Christian and traditional religious worship, and its effects on people. Scenes such as the one in which Ijeomea asks about the butterfly, "Does he go to church too?" point out the acute and often unconscious awareness of this conflict at all levels of society. Equally as important, Munonye shows the fierce rivalry between Christian religions in a well-written passage which describes a fight among children from rival sects who taunt each other on their way to Sunday school.

The conflict between young and old is also presented. In Joe's church, the old members who joined under circumstances different from those of the next generation find themselves at odds with the younger people. Willie's frequent speeches of liberation differ greatly from the response he receives from his older brothers. The clash within the church is also one of individuals and personalities. And it is here that Munonye is at his best. He brings ideological institutional conflicts down from their high intellectual level and makes them personal. He depicts what happens when ideological forces interact with an individual's personality, and realistically illustrates what happens when an attempt is made to assimilate new values into an old society.

There are other forces at work in the novel, not of change and conflict, but of change and its incorporation into daily life. For example, British gin instead of palm-wine is drunk at the house-building ceremony and western oil men come to the village to establish a new occupation instead of traditional farming. All this is contrasted against a backdrop of strongly personal scenes, which illustrate that somehow people do manage to avoid the effects of outside forces. The dance scene is one of pure delight, as are Anna and Joe's talks together at night. The church's influence on Joe's belief in rebirth (which is an important part of the extended family concept), for instance, serves to remind us that the novel is a story about people, and that ideological and institutional forces have no meaning or validity at all except in the way they determine and affect the lives of people. Herein lies the author's craftsmanship.

Oil Man of Obange (1971) is centered on Jeremiah, who abandons the ways of his people to join the Christian church. In so doing, he also gives up disputed family land to his adversary and moves to another place to begin life anew. Most people feel he has made the right decision, except his irate sister, Onugo, who never ceases calling him a fool. Jeremiah enters the palm-oil business, and most of his profits are used to send his children to school, for he has an insatiable desire to give his children an education. But just as things appear to be going well, Marcellina, Jeremiah's wife, becomes ill and dies. He promises to keep all the children in school despite the hardships. Yet tragedy continues to plague him and finally his mind cracks. Jeremiah dies in his own house with his head resting on the arm of his sister.

Munonye uses simple but picturesque language in all his books. His characters are believable; Naana, Joe, and Jeremiah all emerge as men of high principles—a son, a husband, and a father with deep concerns for the welfare of their families. Jeremiah's end is probably indicative of them all—under the new circumstances, the old ways cannot stand. Unfortunately, nearly always Munonye equates the new way of life with God and Christianity; as a result the platitudes and dogma sometimes make for heavy reading.

Although Nkem Nwankwo's *Danda* (1964) has a setting similar to that of Munonye's *Only Son*, it is a better novel. Danda, the eldest member of his family, flouts authority and breaks all the social codes in Aniocha. His father, Araba, induces Danda to marry and attempt to get him an Ozo title, but Danda cannot stand up to the ceremonial rigors of his position and runs away. Upon hearing of his father's death, he returns and exclaims, "Leave it to me. I have come to take possession of my *obi* and nothing will crumble." Although nothing in the novel suggests that this resolution will have the slightest effect on him, his return represents his determination to lead his life the way he wants to lead it. With his father's death, this is now possible.

Nwankwo emphasizes the comic side of Danda's life of irresponsibility, but Danda's character is one of paradox. It is difficult to accept a reformed Danda at the end of the novel, in terms of what has happened to him. Furthermore too many "characters" serve as choric commentators on the action, describing what Danda does. There are also intrusions by the author himself, commenting on Ibo music or dance.

In the novel the crisp dialogue is enlivened with proverbs and direct translations that occasion such poetic expressions as "scorch season" and "your word is bent" (p. 33). The narrative is conversational and easy and blends well with the subject matter. The rhythm of the writing is that of a dance—the kind of dance that Danda is always doing, which suggests his own special kind of responsibility to himself as an individual. Nwankwo's success lies in his ability to depict the uninhibited action of his characters and their world. The so-called clash of cultures is taken for granted, and Danda's leap to freedom when his father insists on his undergoing a ceremony of face-marking is well in character:

The *ogbu ici* first washed Danda's face with a soft cloth soaked in sweet-smelling ointment. Then he cut two almost parallel lines near the right eye and began to remove the pelt of skin between them.

There were some of the men around who were still squeamish about blood and involuntarily closed their eyes. But even those who were attentive could not be sure what really went wrong.

There were a few who hadn't time to get out of the way. They only felt a sensation of a body leaping over their heads. Some blood had dropped on the right hand of Nwafe Ugo. He rose and went to clean it on the body of an orange tree nearby. . . .

Araba walked firmly into his obi, sat down before Ikenga and began to murmur something. (p. 75)

Emmanuel Obiechina in reviewing *Danda* alluded to the "immense vivacity" of the hero and Francis Hope's article in the *Observer* praised the author's "comic touch."[42] These qualities mark the novel's success and are the ones that Flora Nwapa's *Efuru* so definitely lacks. Efuru, the main character, does not possess the distinctiveness of Danda, and hence the book fails where *Danda* succeeds. In her stock, ordinary way, Efuru resembles Amadi's heroine in *The Concubine*. Like Ihuoma, she is a select one of the gods and therefore she cannot marry or have children. Like Ihuoma's plight, Efuru's tragedy is expected: because she is irrevocably bound to the goddess of the deep, she is doomed to a life of tragic isolation.

Nwapa's style of writing is unimaginatively pedestrian. As a result the reader never becomes involved with Efuru and her problems. Moreover, detailed descriptions of everyday household activities spoil the effect of Efuru's magical existence. A good example is the following scene of Efuru and her first husband:

The young husband felt his work on the farm irksome now that he was married. It had not mattered before but now it was different. He had a lovely wife; so the least thing sent him home to her.

Efuru welcomed him.

"How are you?" she would ask him. "How is everything in the farm? What did you bring me from the farm?"

"I brought you some vegetables and fish. We caught plenty a week ago. I dried them for you. And here you are." He brought out the fish from his bag. They were very well dried on sticks.

"Thank you, my husband. Now go and have your bath while I prepare some food for you to eat."

The husband went off to have his bath in the stream. Efuru went to the

206

kitchen to cook. She used plenty of fish and cooked delicious nsala soup for her dear husband. When her husband came back from the stream she welcomed him and put the food before him. (pp. 5–6)

Such passages, which seem to be unnecessary exercises in recording trivia, contribute nothing to Efuru's development as a supernatural being or to the later turn of events.

Flora Nwapa, also the author of *Idu* (1970), is a celebrant; birth, marriage, and death play a ritual part in her works. However, almost inevitably the reader is disappointed by the results. Her heroines are good women but their very passivity contributes little to the action. And although her novels tell the reader a great deal about everyday life in Iboland, there is scant excitement. The novels grind their way to sudden (and sometimes obvious) conclusions—like Idu's death soon after her husband's.

Isidoro Okpewho's first novel, *The Victims* (1970), is one of the few books to explore the theory of the harmonious. Nevertheless, the book has been written before by more able novelists. Okpewho's use of proverbs and translations from the local language remind one of Achebe, but he is too solemn and too concerned with melodrama, which does not always succeed.

There is no clash in Efuru's world; she believes in river goddesses, and her society gives her no reason to feel that any contrary viewpoint could exist. In Lenrie Peter's *Second Round* (1965) there also is no violent collision of ideologies. His hero, Dr. Kawa, has everything that a person could desire in upper-crust Sierra Leonean society, but he is essentially a lonely man. His is a loneliness that nothing can cure; it is a *Weltschmerz* that can know neither spiritual nor physical satisfaction, and as such Dr. Kawa is a figure of tragedy.

Peter's humorous touches, however, counterbalance the tragic mood of the book. For example, when Dr. Kawa's mother goes with him to inspect his new house, she blesses it with "a symbolic shower of spit." It is the humor that makes the book eminently readable. For Dr. Kawa is essentially a poet and nothing is quite so boring as a poet as the central character in a novel, especially since his conversations are sprinkled with original verse or quotable lines from other poets.

Dr. Kawa's truest poetry is his intense ability to feel. When he meets Laura and they take the ferry, it is the poet who empathizes with the ferryman's songs: "His songs crystallized in Dr. Kawa's memory. He it was who had ferried the great Chief Zimba to the three-cornered island which lifts its head from the bottom of the lake at the moon-shifting hour of midnight, when the great fish of the ocean had sucked away

207

the water for the great cleansing of the Sea God" (p. 46). It is the poet who feels a sense of dedication, without complacency, but with some joy and much humor: "He mused over the quick substitution of his appetite for the burnt skeletons of the English autumn countryside, into his love of the ruthlessness and dynamism of the African bush, and the human pathos which underlay the calm flow of conviviality. His work was going well . . ." (p. 34). And it is as a poet that he is able to understand the sadness and the tragedy of Freddie's illness and death, and later Clara's.

One becomes irritated that the hero is constantly referred to as "Dr. Kawa"; he is never given a Christian name, neither by his mother nor by his mistress. One feels too that Dr. Kawa's tragedy of returning to a society he did not understand is insufficiently heightened at the end— too much is left to the impact of the narrative, and the poetry of his disillusionment and despair is not emphasized enough. But Lenrie Peters demonstrates in his first novel that his true forte is his ability to depict a balanced world of tragedy and joy. The way in which the characters exhibit "the human pathos which underlay the calm flow of conviviality" gives power and an extra dimension of meaning and significance to the novel.

Peters is primarily a poet and his verse will be considered later. His novel is the work of a poet, at times sentimental, but capable of poetizing on the tragedy of a man who returns to what he only half understands. *The Interpreters* (1965) is similarly the work of a poet, although the author, Wole Soyinka, is better known as a dramatist. There is little conventional plot in this book; instead it brings together a number of characters who act as spokesmen for various attitudes which the writer either praises or condemns.

In bars, offices, and on the university campus, Soyinka's characters meet and talk. There is Kola, who is painting a picture of Yoruba gods using his friends as models, and to some extent is the link in the novel. There is Sekoni, an engineer and an idealist, whose attempt to build an experimental power station is written off as unsafe. He goes insane and later dies in a car crash. Sagoe appears more frequently than any of the other characters: in trying to expose the unfair way in which Sekoni is treated, he comes up against the tyranny of the establishment. An angry young man, he is perhaps Soyinka's primary mouthpiece. Nevertheless, he can be quite funny, as when he reads to an illiterate messenger extracts from his "Book of Enlightenment" on his philosophy of Voidancy. There are also minor characters like Egbo, an aristocrat, who pays a visit to the village of his late mother and is seduced by Simi;

Monica, the rebellious English wife of a Nigerian academician; and Joe Golder, a homosexual Black American.

A reviewer in the *Times Literary Supplement* commented that "the characters merge like chameleons with their surroundings and often their individuality is secondary to something larger than themselves."[43] And this points to precisely what they lack—individuality. They are tribeless tribesmen caught up in the new society, and part of their predicament is brought out in the confrontation between Sagoe and Golder:

> His [Sagoe's] mind went to him now and it made him suddenly restless. He stood up.
> "Are you leaving?"
> "Yes."
> "So you don't find your skin beautiful?"
> "I have never given it any thought. I saw a white girl at a party the other night and I considered her beautiful. That is an aesthetic judgement. I cannot remember much about her colour. When you talk of this black vitality I can almost hear your salivating and since I happen to be black, neither fault nor credit to me—I find it all rather nauseating."
> "No, wait a minute . . ."
> "I am astonished that black men can bear to be slobbered over, even by black men." (p. 196)

Sagoe and his detribalized friends are, racially speaking, far more emancipated than Joe Golder. But their purposelessness shows that a new fear has entered their lives—the fear of not belonging.

Adaora Ulashi's intent in *Many Thing You Do Not Understand* (1970) is not as serious as Peter's in *The Interpreters*: it is to show in a humorous way the power of African magic and the limitations of British officialdom. Although the book is humorous and critics have said that Ulashi merely wishes to amuse, it can be considered a serious version of a "whodunit." Pidgin is used to heighten the reader's curiosity and to extend the mystery—"But make you no ask me how the news reach me. The thing be, the news reach me."

Many Thing Begin for Change (1972) is even more exaggerated. Again pidgin is used for comedy as well as to augment the effect of impenetrability:

> "About what time of night did you hear the noise?"
> "It no be for night-time, it be for early, early, this morning-time."
> "But you told Mr. Jenkins it was at night that you heard the noise," Hughes reminded him.
> "Yes, Sir," Eze agreed, and went on to explain, "It still be dark, but it be early morning. Sun no come yet, and bird no start for cry."
> Hughes nodded comprehendingly. "Oh, I see, towards dawn."

209

Both novels imitate Cyprian Ekwensi in that they are intended for light entertainment. But Adaora Ulashi also has a talent for the comic, the absurd, the farcical—a characteristic that few writers in English share. She exploits this in her excellently contrived dialogues and situations, which hold the reader's attention throughout.

On the whole these recent novels seem to point toward new possibilities. Most of them cannot be considered as mere extensions of the West African novel of a generation ago, for they have attempted to break fresh ground by dealing with the social problems of a new generation. By no means are these novels great fiction, but they have proved by concerning themselves with new issues that the West African novel is not static. These novelists have benefited from their predecessors' works in English, for they can assume that, because of these works, their European readers have a greater knowledge of local customs; this has afforded them greater laxity, less of a need to inform, and, as a result, a bolder attempt at creating. Through them the West African novel has given birth to a third generation of writers and the development of the novel is now in their hands. The groundwork had been laid by Casely-Hayford and Obeng; the first significant development was accomplished by Achebe, Ekwensi, and Tutuola. The new novelists are now able to utilize the achievement of their predecessors; with greater skill and control of language, knowledge and inventiveness, this new generation of novelists should bring about an important maturity to their work.

Chapter 10

East, Central, and South African Novelists in English

C onceivably writers in English living in East, Central, and South Africa can be seen as rebels against appearance. These sections of Africa saw not only the European administrator but the settler from Europe as well. On face value it seems that alien modes have taken hold here and the architecture of the cities certainly seems to testify to this. But the writers manipulate the cultural apparatus; they alert us to the fact that a true depth of artistic engagement can become a drama of consciousness. Therefore there are few "documents" in the manner of West African writing, for these are reports on a fixture in place and time. These writers are more concerned with the spirit within than with the world without; hence their interest in European paraphernalia which they scathingly condemn as one-upmanship. They advocate freedom in their art, which is particularly crucial in South Africa where censorship is rigorously exercised. And because their themes are directed against the environment (as opposed to West African writers who are not necessarily hostile to their world) they are more easily accessible to a reader from elsewhere who can detect uncomfortable parallels in the world situation.

Stylistically their verbal adornments are both a strength and a weakness. But because, relatively speaking, they are late to come to English, their nondenotative usage of words displays an opulence. In their very lives these authors have borne witness to the fact that the meaning of existence is a quest for the origins of change. They ask Why more often

211

than the writers from West Africa do, and their interrogatives help them to shed a century of miseducation and to give birth to a new turbulency of spirit. This is a complex, voluntary effort, an inner drama, which brings about both self-abandonment and recognition.

East and Central Africa

KHADAMBI ASALACHE: A NEW LEGEND

Khadambi Asalache's first novel, *A Calabash of Life* (1967), is the heroic story of Shiyuka, a young warrior, who is determined to repossess the chieftaincy of Vatirichi which has been stolen from his family by Dembla. Although Chief Dembla resolves to destroy him, at the climax of the novel Shiyuka kills all his enemies and succeeds in gaining his chieftaincy.

However, there is more to the novel than this simple plot summary indicates. Asalache's use of a multiplicity of characters makes for a realistic presentation of the extended family. The incidents in which they are engaged enhance the novel by heightening the theme of conflict and resolution. Both, for example, are excellently depicted in the relationship between Shiyuka and his bride, Ayako.

The legend of the warrior in *A Calabash of Life* is similar to a praise poem. Shiyuka is virtuous, brave, and noble. His enemies, on the other hand, lack these qualities and therefore are bound to suffer. Asalache translates this legacy into excellent writing and succeeds best when the "poetic" nature of a traditional encounter is implicit in the action.

LEGSON KAYIRA: SUPERSTITION

Legson Kayira has portrayed in his autobiography, *I Will Try* (1966), his years as a boy in Africa and his efforts to obtain an education—beginning with his birth in Mpale Village in the Karonga district of Malawi and ending with his entrance to the University of Washington in Seattle. The book grew out of letters addressed to organizations he could not visit and was later expanded into a paper at the University of Washington. It is highlighted by moving scenes of Kayira's early life—the death of his brothers and sisters, his poverty and dignity.

The Looming Shadow (1967), his first novel, concerns the conflict between traditional belief and modern standards. One of the characters, Musyani, is wrongly charged with practicing witchcraft, but the true hero of the novel is Yotamu Mwenimuzi, the village headman, for he has to balance the traditional method of punishing witches—by poisoning them—with the skeptical attitude of the western authorities. The true criminal is the white police officer who fails to understand Mwenimuzi's position. In contrast to these characters is the slightly ridiculous Simeon (whom we are expected to take seriously), a zealous worker for Christianity, complete with his *Watchtower*.

A second novel, *Jingala* (1969), deals with the relationship between Jingala, a widower, and his only son, Gregory. Although Jingala is respected by his peers in the village, Gregory regards him with scorn. Gregory's alienation from his father is a result of his Catholic education. He rejects the props of traditional society and does not want to marry; instead he desires to become a priest.

At the end Jingala dies—a disappointed man, broken by the new system which upturns his world. But the ending seems unsatisfactory. One wonders if traditions are as easily discarded as the author implies or if the stereotyped Jingala, customarily accorded respect in African society, should be so lightly dismissed by a convenient death.

Kayira's novels depict the conflict he himself experienced—between traditional modes and the new way of life. At times, he seems tóo critical of the traditionalists and dismisses many sacred beliefs as "superstition." His books frequently are uneven—in language and development—although he can tell a story and create character. Perhaps the most rewarding aspect of his work is his sad, truthful accounts of the victims of a fading past—Jingala's death and the imprisonment of the chief in *The Looming Shadow* who utilizes tribal law to settle the dispute.

LEONARD KIBERA: SHORT STORY TO NOVEL

Leonard Kibera first wrote short stories with his brother, which were collected in *Potent Ash* (1967); his radio play, based on the title story, has been broadcast. His first novel, *Voices in the Dark* (1970),[1] centers on Gerald Timundu, a playwright, and his girl friend Wilna. Disenchanted with university life, Gerald turns to writing "brilliantly unsuccessful" plays, which attack the society around him—the sad lot of the men who had fought for freedom in Kenya; the privileged few who had taken over from the whites. The book ends on a note of hope for the future.

The hope of the novel is reflected in Mama Njeri, an angry old woman who represents what the older generation would dare do if it tried. Her presence and that of the freedom fighters indicates that the struggle is not yet over. The bitterly morbid language suggests that this might well be so, but the symbols of hope remain. From the early part of the book where the land is portrayed as "naked, bare and spent" and "dreading the passionate rhythm of the sun," the reader realizes that he is in the country of those who endure silently.

Kibera's wit, so evident in some of his short stories, is present in *Voices in the Dark*. Life among the beggars is excellently depicted but even better are Gerald's descriptions of the failure of the politicians: "Gerald had taken a notebook along with him so that nothing might escape his notice but the Prime Minister had told the hungry and thirsty mob nothing new, beyond the fact that sooner or later it was bound to rain. The worthy electorate had sat basking in the sun while the police moved amongst them, smiling at the children and clubbing the big ones" (p. 27). The anger is severe but the art does not suffer.

Throughout the novel night and day, drought and rainfall, darkness and light are used as symbols of despair and hope. Kibera is a master of economic description which fills in just enough detail without becoming boring and he is always in control of his situations. And because he introduces few characters, he is able to develop them effectively; he manages to enter into their minds, thereby giving his readers a feeling of what they are really like.

An interesting book, *Voices in the Dark* integrates the episodic technique of the short story, the haunting lyricism of poetry, and the action of drama into a new type of novel. Its dark humor (occasionally lit up by jibes) blends with a pathetic (but never morose) concern to make this an account by a writer who honestly cares about the plight of Africans after independence.

Bonnie Lubega: The Outcast

Bonnie Lubega's *Outcasts* (1971)[2] is a descriptive novel set deep in the country. The Kraal—the cattle, the dung, the people—is the environment. The central figure, Karekyezi, is a husband and the father of many children, a believable and almost lovable man despite his antics and contrasting moods. Lubega uses spicy dialogue and good narrative techniques to move the story along. Though the plot is somewhat weak, it is tied together with pungent, rancid, stinking odors—cows urinating, wet dung burning in the early morning hours, human and animal waste mingling on the hillock; *mwenge* (a brew), strong tobacco, a loin cloth which has never been washed, and a lank man fresh from his chores with the cattle copulating with his oversized wife on the calfskin they had used on their wedding day.

Karekyezi, his family, and all his people were viewed by the villagers whose cattle they kept as filthy, uncivilized savages—outcasts. Karekyezi, however, outwits them by systematically stealing newborn calves and sending them into the interior where his relatives care for them. The story ends with the angry cattle owners dismissing him. Karekyezi seems sad but he and the cattle have a real understanding; he had explained to them that his was a practical undertaking to set his family free. When the impatient villagers leave him, he bursts into boisterous laughter. Tears roll down his face as he exclaims, "Outcasts! . . . Who ever heard of rich outcasts?" (p. 88.) A moving novel, *The Outcasts* sides with the peasantry against the rich who would seek to enslave them.

CHARLES MANGUA: THE LOSER

Mangua's *Son of Woman* (1970),[3] the story of an African graduate student and his social involvements, is a radical departure from most East African fiction in that it makes use of obscenities in an effort to integrate style and subject matter.

Dodge Kiunyu, the son of a whore, becomes involved with a young girl, Tonia, and is sent to Nyeri to attend a mission school. After losing two jobs, he winds up in prison where he becomes ill. In Kenyatta Hospital he meets his father for the first time. His father dies and the novel concludes with Dodge trying to convince Tonia to marry him.

Dodge's character is well created; unlike most African "heroes" he possesses individuality, and his amoral attitude toward life makes for pleasant reading. At one point he remarks, "I am a hungry jigger and I like to bite, I like to bite women—beautiful women. Women with tits that bounce . . ." (p. 7). And when pitted against the straight world he, like Nwankwo's Danda, emerges successful.

STEPHEN NGUBISH: FROM AFRICAN MYTHOLOGY TO CHRISTIAN MYTH

Stephen Ngubish's novel *A Curse from God* (1971)[4] is an attack on polygamy. Karuga, the main character, wishes to take a second wife and is violently opposed by his first wife. Ngubish uses flashbacks to show that Karuga's first marriage held much promise and that his desire to have another resulted in his break from the church. The author seems to suggest that monogamy was good because sanctioned by Christianity. The book has strong Christian overtones; even drought is caused by Satan and the Almighty wishes to put an end to it. In writing of God and Satan, Ngubish translates African mythology into Christian myth:

"They exchanged their murderous blows with incredible fury. The heavens splintered and cracked with the flash of their fiery blades. They chased one another about the heavens, their gigantic feet treading violently on the dark ceiling, with a deafening rumbling" (p. 35).

Ngubish makes the point that Christianity is superior to African belief by using the first wife as a symbol of goodness through suffering and by portraying the second as a selfish whore. Karuga himself is vile; he had run away from home when still young and had almost killed a brother. At the age of sixty-five, alone in a beerhall, he contemplates suicide: "I'll not be husband to anybody any more . . . My first duty in life now will be to myself."

This is a grim novel with nothing to relieve it. The author has a message, one that has a quietness about it, and he succeeds in delivering it. The book is saved from being a parable by Karuga's character and by vivid descriptions. Ngubish's style is for the most part good, but at the same time one must condemn his viewpoint and ask, What was good about traditional life? Was it all hard work and "sin"? The novel suggests that it was.

JAMES NGUGI: FOREST FIGHTERS AND FREEDOM

James Ngugi is the most important novelist from East Africa. In addition to his three novels *Weep Not Child* (1964), *The River Between* (1965), and *A Grain of Wheat* (1968), he has written a play, *The Black Hermit* (1967), which was originally produced as part of the Independence Celebrations at the Uganda National Theatre on November 16, 1962. His work illustrates a basic difference from that of his West African counterparts; it is closer to a "protest" tradition, closer to South Africa, for he is interested in, almost obsessed by, the struggle for freedom in Kenya and its destructive effects on the African way of life.

Ngugi's first novel, *Weep Not Child*, describes the breakup of a family during the Kenyan struggle for independence. At the center of the novel is land—perhaps the most important "character"—which Ngotho and Mr. Howlands, his employer, both consider theirs.

As in Ngugi's other novels, the virtues of formal education are stressed. Hence the young Njoroge must go to school, much to his mother's delight. At school he moves into closer contact with Mwihaki, the daughter of Jacobo, a rich landowner. It is on Jacobo's land that Ngotho has settled while working for Mr. Howlands. Ngotho had returned with hopes after the First World War; his eldest son, Boro, has recently come back from the Second World War embittered because he has lost a brother. With another brother, Kori, he works in Nairobi and becomes involved in the independence movement.

When the strike for better conditions ends in riot, Boro and Kori take to the forest with the freedom fighters. Slowly the young Njoroge realizes his own involvement and so moves from apathy to commitment. His father's house is under constant surveillance since Howlands (now a district officer) and Jacobo (a homeguard chief) see Ngotho as a potential threat. One of Ngotho's wives and his son Kori are arrested on a small pretext; Kori is sent to prison and since Boro is in hiding the burden of the family is now on Kaman.

When Boro brings about Jacobo's death, Ngotho and his two sons Njoroge and Kaman are arrested, beaten, and tortured. Ngotho confesses to the murder to save his sons. This is a noble act on the dying Ngotho's part, since he has witnessed the inevitable breakup of his family. Similarly Njoroge must now face reality and look after the family, for Boro kills Mr. Howlands and is caught. But this is more than Njoge can bear; he is unable to face life in Kenya and wants to run away. His mother saves him from a suicidal bid.

Ngugi's novel describes in full detail the Kenyan struggle for independence. The reader is aware of the suffering of ordinary people in their attempt to achieve realization. One is often impatient with Njoroge and his obsession with school, his unrealistic love for Jacobo's daughter. But this is part of Ngugi's intention. The disorientation from family and the forced emergence of the individual (whether as a brooding thinker like young Njoroge or as an active fighter like Boro) are the consequences of the physical clash of cultures. Ngugi does offer some hope, however, by leaving Njoroge alive at the end.

The River Between was written before *Weep Not Child*, but was not published until 1965. Ngugi relates the conflicts between two tribal groups, the Kameno and the Makuyu, which face one another across a valley. Their clashes symbolize the conflict between Kikuyu tradition and Christianity, with Kameno representing the former and Makuyu the latter.

Through the influence of Joshua Christianity becomes a viable force in Makuyu. When his daughter dies, he sees her death as a punishment for her sin of following tradition, and the mission school at Siriana decides that only those who renounce tribal ways can stay on.

Waiyaki, the descendant of a noble line and a leader of the Kameno, learns about the founders of his tribe and his ancestry, and is warned against Christianity. Because he is the last of an important line, he must

217

go to school at Siriana to discover the secrets of the white man. His role as leader emerges when he is forced to leave Siriana; he encourages the building of schools where non-Christians can acquire a formal western education, for he is convinced that his people can only be free if they know about the white man's ways.

Ngugi places Waiyaki in the interesting position of being, almost by divine right, the upholder of tradition. But Waiyaki is human and is caught up in the stream of changing circumstances—hence his brief flirtation with Christian school and church and, moreover, his love for the daughter of the deacon. Her love and commitment help him to realize that formal education alone cannot save his people. At this point he becomes their true leader, but it is too late. His old rival, Kabonyi, reveals the secret of his relationship with Nyambura, and they are both handed over to the Kiama for sentencing.

Ngugi offers little hope and no alternatives in this novel. Tribalism had divided the African people and the split was deepened by the introduction of Christianity. Those who sought to link two ways of life inevitably perished: hence Muthoni's death; hence Waiyaki's conversion and his ultimate destruction with Nyambura. The author seems to be saying that the extinction of man, of tribe, is the penalty for being unaware of the realities of history. Waiyaki is not so much divided as distorted by the forces with which he tries to grapple and for which neither shrine nor school has prepared him. His defeat (and one is left in doubt about what actually happens to him) suggests that the present confusion is a result of a past not fully understood nor yet realized.

A return to the struggle for independence is the immediate *raison d'être* for *A Grain of Wheat*, though the novel is also concerned with a larger question, Who is the hero in such a struggle? Through continuous flashbacks Ngugi introduces an assortment of interrelated characters and shows how their pasts have influenced each other and how their present is a mere masking of the past. The episodes in the novel, though seemingly singular, form an elaborate network of gateways which lead toward a central theme. Gikonyo and his wife, Mumbi, are important characters; their names are suggestive of Kikuyu gods and one would feel that their quarrel, her infidelity, his imprisonment are symbolic of all that happened to the Kikuyu people during this time. If Gikonyo and Mumbi are gods—humanized as they always are in the African tradition of myth—then Mugo and Karanja represent other facets of the human personality.

Whereas Gikonyo and Mumbi suffer while he is in prison for his political activities, Karanja and Mugo use the war of independence to gain power and prestige. Karanja, as a white man's lackey, is able to rise in the ranks, and Mugo, revered by the people of Thabai, is supposedly a hero of the Kenyan struggle for freedom. Actually he causes the betrayal and death of the freedom fighter Kihika. His feeling of guilt for his inability to participate in the historical crisis of his people and his jealousy of Kihika's capacity for action lead him to betray Kihika to John Thompson, the new district officer. Ironically people do not realize this; instead they only know of his spasmodic bid to rescue a pregnant girl from the homeguard and of his apparent defiance at Rira Camp (when in fact he was paying penance for having betrayed Kihika). Mugo, however, redeems himself by bravely confessing his part in Kihika's fate. The crowd's silence testifies to its shock at such news.

Mugo acts as a receptacle for everyone's guilt; his confession symbolically purges all of guilt. At the anniversary celebrations Gikonyo and Mumbi are free to love; Karanja is free to cherish memories and his just assessment of the future. Nevertheless, the white man's rule will undoubtedly continue after token freedom has been won. For John Thompson represents the idea that Africans cannot survive without the Europeans, and Karanja hopes too that the white influence will continue. Thompson's life has not been easy either; he came to Kenya full of missionary fervor, and as an agent of civilization his ardour turned to hatred and cruelty. Even though he leaves Kenya before independence, he and his wife, like Gikonyo and Mumbi, must plan for an uncertain future.

With *A Grain of Wheat*, Ngugi offers us a look at postindependence Africa. No longer is he necessarily committed to group loyalty: he boldly asserts that tribal distrust exists and that some now attain easy recompensations even though they did nothing to bring about freedom; he hints too at graft on the part of government ministers. However, Ngugi does suggest that with truth and effort the tribe can free itself.

Balancing interior monologues with overt action, *A Grain of Wheat* can be considered Ngugi's best artistic effort. Its characters move toward an inevitable recognition of disaster—the immediate past, far from being "noble," was in fact a mingling of the base and the good. The gods themselves, symbolized as humans in Gikonyo and Mumbi, were torn apart by the struggle. The "family" breakup of the first novel, the "tribal" rivalry of the second, represent a nationwide rift and an individual severance. By exploring the inner consciousness of his characters, Ngugi suggests that traditional order can be restored by a recognition of ancient values. Symbolically Gikonyo carves a stool for Mumbi upon which is a figure of a pregnant woman. The child is the Kenya of tomorrow.

OKELLO OCULI: ANOTHER OUTCAST

The chief character in Oculi's novel *Prostitute* (1968) is not given a name, for she is representative of all prostitutes. The author does not give a definite narrative pattern to the book; rather a total picture is painted as a series of incidents.

A flashback describes the circumstances under which the prostitute left her home for the city. In the city she is seen lying on her bed, which is plagued by bedbugs. They, like her clients, share her bed and always pursue her. Other episodes reveal different aspects of her life; one hears of how prostitutes force unwilling customers to part with money, one learns of their attitude toward abortion and Europeans, and one sees their relations with other women.

The prostitute desires to go home, but when she arrives in her high-heeled shoes and wig, she is ignored by her own mother. Symbolically, at that moment a hen eats its own egg "sucking the liquid of life that lay buried below there" (p. 51). The girl sadly returns to her squalid life in the city.

A reviewer has commented that the prostitute truly comes alive in the scenes with her lover Bisi, the son of a rich man who had lost his father's fortune. She is equally alive when she recalls Rebecca, her childhood friend who is now married and has children. Such is not the destiny of the prostitute.

Prostitute also succeeds stylistically. Verse is used in ways that remind one of the tale—as when the prostitute sings a lullaby or when she reflects on her lack of a university education. In addition, the use of proverbs and a direct literal translation into English help to flavor the novel with a delightful crispness.

GRACE OGOT: ROLE OF THE BLACK WOMAN

The Promised Land (1967), Grace Ogot's first novel, explores the theme of marriage and of a woman's duties to her husband. The book is an extension of a short story and is flawed by its slightness of plot. Nevertheless, it is saved from failure by the author's excellent portrayal of Nyapol, Ochola's wife and the main character.

Grace Ogot has also published a collection of short stories, *Land without Thunder* (1968). "Tekayo" is of particular interest for it is based on a folktale concerning an old cattleherder who unknowingly develops a taste for human liver. Finally, he has to kill children to satisfy his craving. Grace Ogot's works frequently stress the need for understanding; in "Karentina," for example, a starving Angolan refugee is a symbol of this lack of understanding. This theme is often reflected in relationships between men and women and is sustained by her use of myth. For instance, "The Rain Came" tells of a chief's daughter who has to sacrifice herself for the good of her people but is saved by her lover. Sometimes the man/woman relationship is depicted as being crude and cruel; in "Elizabeth," the heroine, pregnant by a rapist, kills herself.

On the whole Grace Ogot's work is concerned with the African woman. In *The Promised Land*, Nyapol is the saving grace, beautifully drawn as a sympathetic wife. Quick to blame herself instead of her husband for their problems, she leaves her village because she conceives this her wifely duty. Grace Ogot's women in the short stories also have a strong sense of duty—the chief's daughter to the family of the tribe and Elizabeth to a strict moral code.

DAVID RUBADIRI: INDIANS AND AFRICANS IN LOVE

David Rubadiri's *No Bride Price* (1967) is a novel of love and corruption. Lombe, the chief character, is a civil servant who lives with Miria, a Black girl. At the opening of the novel, she is pregnant and he is afraid of the consequences of their relationship since she is a mere village girl.

After a fight Lombe leaves Miria and eventually marries Sandra, the sister of his friend Chaundry and the daughter of the Indian high commissioner. He decides to take Chaundry and Sandra to his village, but is worried by their possible reaction since the people speak no English and are poor. He is not so much ashamed as bewildered; he idealizes the village and Sandra reminds him of his mother. But will the Indian couple understand? When they reach the village they find that they are in the midst of a celebration. Enthusiastically, Lombe dances and becomes aware of Miria dancing around him, but she soon disappears. She becomes to him more and more a symbol of the ideal of the village, and he increasingly feels guilty about having left her.

In the city he becomes involved in corruption; Minister Chozo accuses him of accepting bribes and of associating with enemies of the people. He is suspended and goes home to wait trial. At home he inquires about Miria and finally learns the truth about her—she is the child of his father and his father's sister. The villagers believe that Lombe's own incest and his troubles were the result of his father's wrongdoing. Rubadiri's portrayal of this scene is sheer melodrama. Lombe's ignorance of Miria's origins and of his father's incest seems improbable, for one is definitely given the social context of a closed tribal society. But even more incredible is Lombe's calm acceptance of his act.

The rest of the novel is rushed melodrama. Lombe returns to his apartment in the city and finds a sick Miria who is about to have his child. The next morning he learns that there has been a coup; Minister Chozo has been killed and the prime minister barely escaped with his life. Later he discusses the meaning of this with Chaundry and with Sammy, the leader of the coup. Miria dies in childbirth, and Sammy expresses the hope that someone like her would guide the new revolution.

On the whole, *No Bride Price* is a mediocre novel, marred by melodrama, a rushed ending, and a simplistic attempt to contrast the supposedly corrupt city with the innocent village. Lombe is not a "middleman" caught between two traditions; he is very much part of the new elite. One suspects that his only flaw was that he was not ruthless enough.

GABRIEL RUHIMBIKA: THE NEW ELITE

Gabriel Ruhimbika, a writer from Tanzania, has published a single novel, which is an important contribution to East African literature because it documents what must have poignantly faced him all his life— the problem of not belonging. As has been noted before, education meant alienation; in Ruhimbika's case he was twice-removed, since he studied in France.

Village in Uhuru (1969) dramatizes the conflict between young and old as traditional values are gradually broken down. Musilanga, the headman of Chamambo, has successfully guided his village under German and British rule. He is now old, but adaptable to change; his youngest son, Balinde, is sent to the white man's school. He passes examinations to attend the teachers' college, but is expelled.

At home in disgrace Balinde is advised to marry his childhood girl friend, Regina, and to take up farming. On the pretext of having been accepted by another school, he goes off to Dar with money from his father. As he journeys he becomes aware of how real and pressing the poverty of the people is. He realizes that "Uhuru" must mean a better life for people and in Dar he dedicates himself to this end. He joins the local party and devises a plan to overthrow British rule.

"Uhuru" finally arrives and Balinde becomes party chairman for a district of which Chamambo is part. The village is in the throes of change; democratic elections are held and Musilanga feels that his son is responsible for his being ousted from office. Balinde manages to assert something of his leadership when he averts scandal from his father's family. He succeeds in regaining his family's respect; only Musilanga remains aloof from him.

A further crisis develops when the government plans to move the people of the Chamambo to another place. Most of the older people, including Musilanga, oppose the move. Rumors spread that Balinde wishes to impress the officials from Dar and this will force his father to move. When Balinde visits the new village, he finds that the people are alienated from him because they consider him a government official. Finally at his father's old house his mother pleads with him to allow his father to stay; he tells her that he cannot for the laws of the government are inexorable. The novel ends on this note.

No easy solutions are offered in *Village in Uhuru*. The move away from tradition into the present is a painful and an inevitable shift in time. In the process much is discarded—old relationships, the sanctity of the elders. Even the good seems to happen for the wrong reasons; a particularly touching excerpt describes how a traditional ruler gives up his claims to an ambassadorship. His people send a delegation to him in Dar and the pathos of the situation is movingly captured when the delegation is met by two of his children who show no respect for the elders. Even the aide of *mtemi* cannot speak the people's language. The transition from past to present is bitter, the writer implies, and traditions are often discarded along the way. The conclusion of the novel is an enormous question mark.

Davis Sebukima: Uncommitment

Sebukima's first book, a novella called *A Son of Kabira* (1970), shows promise. Set in the village of Kabira, it relates the story of Lukuza, a conceited young man who returns from studying in England and cannot adjust to the village customs. Bored with life in the village, he decides to take the advice of his director of studies and begin a cooperative farm. However, he is not unlike his roguish father, the village chief; he squanders money that does not belong to him and ends up in prison.

The story is comically narrated; Lukuza meets his girl friend by the river impressively dressed in his school uniform. Lukuza's father is also made fun of because of his malpractices, as is the village pastor who describes a plane as "a flying village." No one escapes Sebukima's satire and he is particularly good at portraying his characters' attitudes and feelings. For example, a jealous co-wife asks Lukuza's mother, "When is he coming anyway, who is going to leave us destitute?" This novella is an important beginning of a literature of uncommitment to the beliefs of tribal life. The author seems to stand outside it all—unlike his oral counterpart—and laugh.

ENRIKO SERUMA: RACISM IN AMERICA

Enriko Seruma's *Experience* (1970) is concerned with a young Muganda schoolboy's rude awakening to the reality of racism. While still in Africa, Miti (a Swahili word for trees) is befriended by a young Englishman, much to his father's disapproval. It is not until he goes to school in New Hampshire that he experiences any racial prejudice. The first white girl with whom he has any relationship is a sexual pervert. While walking with another white girl, he is beaten by a gang of white men. He takes drugs with her and is later involved in an accident. The girl is sent home to her parents and he is deported.

Back in Uganda, Miti lies about the reasons for his return. Although unable to relate to his former white friends, he stays with the Englishman and eventually tells him of the prejudice he had experienced in America. The Englishman understands, but it is too late; while driving across a game reserve they have a puncture and are stranded. The novel ends with the roar of an approaching lion.

The main flaw of this novel is its overconcern with sexual matters and only secondary concern with race. But there is one redeeming quality: it attempts to define the history of Black-white relations. The boy who sets out is not the man who returns and the development from Negro to Black is the novel's justification.

ROBERT SERUMAGA: REVOLUTION AND THE CYNIC

Return to the Shadows (1969) by Robert Serumaga is an account of political upheaval and social wrong. Joseph Musizi, the principal character, is a lawyer-economist who has lived in England a long time and has absorbed two cultures. In London he feels that he and other dedicated men should try to rescue Adnagu, his country, from its history of coups. Therefore he returns home to carry out his plan.

Joe's indecisiveness makes it difficult for him to carry out his strategy, but he finds a routine for dealing with coups. Each time one occurs he leaves his town house for the country, returning just in time to defend the outgoing government.

Serumaga uses flashback as a major technique. The novel opens with Joe and his servant, Simon, walking along a dusty road to the village where Joe's mother lives. Joe's own device for coups has failed and master and servant for the first time see themselves as equals—as men in search of safety.

When another coup disrupts the city, Joe must remain in his home. He thinks he is safe until "Sergeant" Yacobo and "Corporal" Jeronimo, two brigands masquerading as soldiers, enter his house pretending to look for the minister of civilization. Soon they take over Joe's house; an announcement on the radio warning that there are hooligans at loose posing as soldiers gives them away and they flee, knocking Joe unconscious.

Up till now the humorous parts of the novel are credible. But when Yacobo and Jeronimo hide in the garden and later have to sneak into the bathroom to urinate, the humor is reduced to farce. There is another farcical scene in which Simon comes on Jeronimo in the garden just as he has removed his corporal's uniform. Simon thinks he is a prophet and he obliges with a long-winded utterance. As Simon kneels in prayer, Jeronimo escapes. Only when Simon is threatened by the "Sergeant" does he comprehend that he has been tricked.

Joe meantime is unconscious and has a fantasy (again humorous though partly macabre) of being brought before men who sit on lavatory seats and who take notes on toilet paper. When he holds his nose, he realizes he is not going to die. After gaining consciousness, he and Simon leave for his country house. On the way the car and all their belongings are seized. They are detained but eventually arrive at the village where they discover that Joe's mother has been raped as well as his cousins. Joe decides to engage in the fight and so returns to the city.

Return to the Shadows, besides its obvious political motif, is concerned with social ills. Yacobo and Jeronimo live in harsh surroundings and Yacobo, frequently out of work, vows to take vengeance on people like Joe. His only happiness is with his wife, Rozalia, but even this is taken from him. Rozalia had asked Yacobo time and again to buy some salt but he always forgot. Finally he buys it only to return home to learn that Rozalia had gone to the market to buy salt and that she had been shot by soldiers. Yacobo runs to her and takes her in his arms; she is dying and pathetically he shouts into her ear that he had bought the salt. Jeronimo's fate is just as depressing; he is mistaken for a soldier and is beaten to death by the crowd.

Joe, meantime, has forced his old friends Matthew and Stephen at gun point to go with him to Yacobo's. He expects that Yacobo will confess that Matthew and Stephen paid Jeronimo and him to raid Joe's house. Arriving at Yacobo's, they find the poor man frantically digging a hole into the wall of his hut. The mad Yacobo can be of no help; Joe has procrastinated too long.

Return to the Shadows is a good novel, even though the switches in time, the episodic treatment tend to be wearying. At its most dramatic point it is concerned with the function of the professional man in the changing political circumstances of Africa. At another level, it is a social commentary on inequality. Though humorous in many parts, it steers its way toward a pathetic and crushing conclusion.

GODWIN WACHIRA: REVOLUTION AND THE REVOLUTIONARY

Godwin Wachira's only novel, *Ordeal in the Forest* (1968), describes the psychological difficulties and the hardships endured by the freedom fighters during the Kenyan struggle for independence. The story centers on Nundo and his former schoolteacher Mrefu, who both grow to learn the meaning of this struggle for freedom. Nundo and his friends first become involved in the struggle for independence through a club to which they belong; later we see them actively engaged as freedom fighters in the forest.

As a novel *Ordeal in the Forest* fails. The language is over-anglicized and little attention is paid to the novel as a form. When the characters reflect upon their actions, they do so in the manner of a public posture. But as a tract *Ordeal in the Forest* is good for the insight it gives into life in the forest. However, the incidents in which Mrefu becomes involved are blown up out of proportion. The expatriate scenes at the Naro European Club, where Major Cook is chairman, are ridiculous, for the author fails to capture expatriate speech and attitudes. But he does document the people's fear during the struggle for independence, and he also manages to show how indigenous people work together— the frightened "boy" who serves in the club reports all that happens there to Nundu.

Wachira succeeds too in reporting objectively the events of the struggle for independence and the freedom fighters' role in those events. The scene describing the taking of the loyalty oath, in which the people must drink blood and make pledges, is carefully documented. After Nundu has taken his fifth oath, he begins to recruit freedom fighters, even on Major Cook's farm. His tactics to persuade others to join the fight are interesting; for example, he exaggerates all the news to cause panic. Nundu's dedication to the cause even compels him to reject his mother, "I am your son no longer." When the struggle is over and

Mrefu is back among his own people, he recalls and sees all that the fight for independence has brought about.

A disjointed novel with too many characters, little plot, an exaggerated emphasis on torture, and slight regard for artistic direction, *Ordeal in the Forest* is important for its account of the suffering and triumph of the freedom fighters. Though Mrefu and Nundu are excellently portrayed, the other characters are glossed over; Major Cook is not real nor are the other Europeans. Despite these flaws (and others, even in grammar) the novel is written with a great deal of intense feeling.

These are new writers; they have, for the most part, been less indoctrinated with western mores than their West African counterparts. When they began writing, they had already read Achebe and Tutuola and had got rid of any necessity to document local custom and practice. This, as well as their contact with white settlers, has enabled them to write less as group spokesmen and more as individuals. Furthermore, they are younger and while they know of the colonial past, they seem more conscious of the neo-colonial present. Their themes—freedom from white domination and disenchantment with Black domination—place them securely in the seventies. They are interpreting the "nowness" of Africa with precision, honesty, and vigor.

South Africa

Peter Abrahams: The Conflict of Races

Peter Abrahams is the most prolific author in Africa. It may be argued that writing in indigenous languages, although creditable in itself, had to a large extent retarded the growth and development in South Africa of a literature in English. Abrahams's first novel did not appear until 1942, long after novels in local languages had entrenched themselves. Not unnaturally he was influenced by them. One finds at first the theme of the corrupt city in his work but he moves away from this to deal in Vilakazi's terms with the evils of oppression.

Two of his works are autobiographical in scope. *Tell Freedom* (1954) offers retrospective insights into a despicable social system. Abrahams describes the perplexities of his youth and how he finally loses hope and leaves South Africa. It is also very much the story of the growing artist and it is within this context that he speaks of "desperate and overwhelming longings."

Tell Freedom portrays as well the politics of rejection. At home during a holiday from college, Abrahams reflects on the psychological implications of "Reserved for Europeans Only"; the simple indulgences he craved were forbidden, and the innumerable slights and humiliations he endured in Johannesburg were inflicted by white supremacy. Because of the implications of *apartheid*, he was condemned to a life of squalor and was forced to deny himself the love of a white girl. His contacts with whites reinforced his feeling of loss and all he could do was hope.

Abrahams notes in *Tell Freedom* that at one time he believed western education, which had been denied most Blacks and coloreds, could ameliorate the difficulties and eventually reconcile the races. But his failure to get a newspaper job makes him realize that education not only has alienated him from his own environment but has done nothing to assure him a place in white society.

One learns about formative influences—Shakespeare, Keats and poetry in general—that helped to temper the harshness of daily life in South Africa. Exposure to Black American writers awakened curiosity and pride in Abrahams. Art and *apartheid* finally conflicted. At college he had "first discovered the independent life possessed by a work of art and the strange loyalty art demands of those who would serve it" (p. 244). However, neither the consolation of books nor a love affair can rectify a situation rotten at base; he has to leave South Africa.

At first he is attracted to America for there he thought at least the Black man was free to proclaim his lack of freedom. England, however, exerted a different pull—strangely enough he felt attached to it culturally. In long, poetically evocative passages, Abrahams speaks of his love for South Africa, of the beauty of the land he had known, of his love for his family whom he must leave behind. But the artist has to be free of the crush of dehumanization in order to function so Abrahams is compelled to leave his native country.

Dark Testament (1942) and *Song of the City* (1945) show the preoccupations of Abrahams which would appear time and again in his later works. *Dark Testament* includes fourteen sketches and four short stories describing life in contemporary South Africa. The tone is protest; the scene, the notorious District Six. Also seen is Abrahams's concern with style—how "the stories became people." In "The Homecoming" Boy Davidson, a former murderer, learns to control his fits of temper, and Rosie in "The Virgin" is a prostitute who remains emotionally pure. The accounts in *Dark Testament* not only illustrate the author's social preoccupations, but document the problems of race in South Africa. Jane in "From an Unfinished Novel" is deserted by an English lover and in "Colour" John is laughed at for not acting like a white man. But in "Thanksgiving" the white girl Margaret helps Annie, a Black girl. The treatment in *Dark Testament* is episodic and telegraphic, but pointed.

Mine Boy (1946), the story of Xuma who comes from the country to the town, centers on one of the main themes found in much of the missionary literature published by the South African vernacular presses. Like the chief characters in these books, Xuma is alone, estranged from the people among whom he finds himself, a vagabond of the tribe. The harsh world of the city is made clear to him when he arrives—it makes one a stranger to one's own people, it is a violent place where one must fend for oneself. Only money matters, for it can buy the law.

Xuma goes to work in the mines. At Malay Camp, the sameness of the houses, the shoddiness of the people's lives as they gamble, pimp, and whore are what the boy first sees. But beneath the surface of moral and physical squalor there is "a warm, thick, dark blanket of life." Despite this he is very much a loner.

His job is frustrating because the mines involve hard work for little reward. At first, one hopes and therefore fears. But when all hope is gone, Xuma realizes that not even fear remains. Eventually he gains some confidence in his job, for the whites come to depend on him as the "boss boy."

Mine Boy is really about growth—from "boss boy" to Black man. This theme is especially developed in an interesting dialogue between Paddy, who is Xuma's boss, and Xuma. Paddy is convinced that he understands Xuma's problems and can help, once Xuma himself recognizes them. Xuma is equally convinced that Paddy is wrong, for as a white man Paddy cannot possibly conceive the degradation of daily life in South Africa. Paddy pleads with him to stop thinking merely in terms of black and white; only thus can he free himself and his people. For the white world, Paddy argues, is also caught up in this false kind of identification. After reflecting on this, Xuma understands that "there are no white people. Only people."

His conversion is important for what Abrahams means to portray. Since *Mine Boy* moves between subjective hankerings after truth and objective reportage, it is important that the inner quality of Xuma's conviction should be externalized in action. The occasion is a mine accident the day after his talk with Paddy. Xuma refuses to go down into the mine and does not allow his men to go either. He asserts that they are men not cattle, and in the context Abrahams is giving his views of the human condition. Xuma has grown to understand the nature of man and has acted upon this understanding; the dignity of this recognition is the somewhat idealized ending of the novel.

Song of the City (1945) had anticipated *Mine Boy* and, like its successor, it is the familiar story of the boy who leaves the village for the city (here Johannesburg). Dick goes to work for a liberal white professor who, along with an African, is planning the segregation of races in South Africa. He is then drawn into the political world by a more radical professor. He gets himself arrested and after his release he is beaten by some white men during a riot. Dick eventually returns to his village but still yearns for the city.

Path of Thunder (1948) is more concerned with the "colored" man in South Africa. Lanny Swartz, the central character, is seen as the archetype of a new South Africa, where divisions merge. His home in Stallwold is "the birthplace of a new people" who were neither Black nor white, and who might even be considered "a new nation."

Lanny leaves Cape Town to go and help his own people in the country. When he returns, he is overcome by the omnipresent signs of poverty and deprivation—a poverty that is within. He hears confirmations of the colored version of *apartheid*: "coloreds" are better than "Blacks." Later on Mako, a Black man, tells him that the "coloreds" seek to maintain their apartness because they lack tradition and they desire "white power." This, Mako asserts, is the psychology of a slave and he says that as a Black man he must hate those who hate him until he is politically free. Lanny in turn argues that the "coloreds" are only cruel toward Blacks because they themselves have suffered humiliation. Whites have denied them, just as they have the Blacks, the chance to be human.

These long, artificial social asides, however well intentioned and accurate, distort the narrative flow. For *Path of Thunder* is primarily concerned with the giant stride toward freedom; but because Lanny is not an exceptional person, he cannot possibly become the forger of a chain in the evolution of humanity—his "coloredness" is not enough and his character is only sketched in. Although it is true that he is vocal enough to put forth a view of "coloredness" to Mako and he rejects the preacher's facile argument that education brings material rewards, he is putty in the hands of Abrahams. He comes home on a mission to help his people and is merely used by the author to introduce the subject of interracial love. Sadie, the Afrikaaner girl, comes to a conclusion remote from the action—a naive and ridiculous conclusion—when she confesses that Lanny's sister, who works for her family, is "a colored person" but Lanny is "just a person." Her easy reflections seem far removed from Xuma's tortuous quest for truth in *Mine Boy*.

Abrahams overstates his case and makes Lanny seem a simpleton when he rambles on that he and Sadie "were just born. Nobody asked them. And so they would live and love without asking anybody." Lanny and Sadie's love is supposedly man's attempt to overcome obstacles, and through this love, Abrahams wishes to say, there is hope for all "coloreds." The novel ends, however, with their murder. This time the prescriptive model of interracial love and the laws of hate have not worked; they have not been molded into a novel but make up only a sketchy story with a melodramatic ending and long, semiphilosophical utterances.

Abrahams has come from a motley world—of Black Africans, white people of Dutch and English extraction, people of mixed blood, and Indians. The diversity of this world is depicted in his novels to emphasize the varied texture of human experience; in each novel, one particular aspect of Abraham's world dominates over the others. *A Night of Their Own* (1965), for instance, is about the liberation movement among Indians in South Africa. This novel does not seek to chart history but to dramatize the presence of uneasy conflict. Perhaps its overriding theme is that the social order must be altered by definite political action if justice is ever to be a reality.

As in his other novels, characters are used in *A Night of Their Own* to illustrate, almost graphically, the problems Abrahams poses. Thus we are introduced to Sammy Naidoo, an Indian committed to activism; Nkosi, a Black freedom fighter who falls in love with Dee, an upper-class Indian woman; Mildred, a colored schoolteacher; and Karl van As, a white official. The ingredients of South Africa's cosmopolitan existence are all present and Abrahams works them into art.

Quite early in the novel Sammy Naidoo expresses the need for social commitment, which is particularly necessary for the Indian in Black South Africa. Therefore, it is necessary within the social meaning of the novel to have Nkosi, a Black activist, fall in love with Dee, an Indian pacifist. Dee is crippled and their love affair is heightened considerably by the fact that Nkosi is sought by the police, for he has come to South Africa to deliver money to aid the Indians in their struggle for freedom. When he speaks to Dee, he emphasizes the value of human worth over the trappings of external conformity. Sammy echoes this belief when he laments that in the quick jump into adulthood people lose their childhood and their capacity for compassion.

Nkosi admits to the futility of changing the world but insists on the need to try. Thus emphasis is placed on activity, not ethics. Dr. Nunkhoo asserts that the nice distinctions between means and ends are irrelevant and academic, for the particular stresses of the present blur the

231

distinctions between good and evil. What Abrahams is saying is that only when South Africa and the world are freed from racism can the human spirit triumph. Until then many must die, as the novel indicates, and movements must fail—as the Indian liberation movement does. But within the country, a solid core of believers will continue to strive toward the better life.

Apart from the recent *This Island Now* (1966), which is about Jamaica, Abrahams's novels are set in Africa, all in South Africa with the exception of *A Wreath for Udomo* (1956), in which the action partly takes place in "Pan Africa" (West Africa?). The central character, Michael Udomo, leaves Europe for Pan Africa where he hopes to work for the freedom of his people. Udomo's motives are laudable, and Abrahams's devotion to his homeland comes over in the subtle use he makes of the praise song to Mother Africa which Udomo recites before his return.

For African exiles in Europe, Africa is "a little like a heart." Africa becomes the life of Black men everywhere (Udomo's home country is *Pan-Africa*) and symbolizes the unity they seek to achieve. One of Udomo's friends, Lanwood, frequently argues that there must be a physical confrontation if Africa is to be free, and at a political rally he comments on the desirability of freedom in and for itself and adds that imperialists and colonists have to remain at loggerheads until political freedom is accomplished. Udomo also expresses the need for freedom: "it is freedom we want, not easiness."

The emphasis on freedom is structurally essential to the novel for it anticipates the climax when Udomo is destroyed because he has failed to allow his countrymen the very freedom he has fought for and won. Abrahams's craftsmanship is supreme throughout, and end and beginning fit neatly together. The traditions which Udomo had invoked in the praise song at the beginning of the novel destroy him at the end with the sound of their drum. The climax is tightened when Udomo's name is exploited for its full onomatopoeic qualities. As he awaits his end, the drums keep up the refrain, at once calculating, cruel, and just, "Die Udomo die."

Before Udomo's downfall, one sees his earnestness at work. He recognizes three enemies in his struggle—tribalism, poverty, and the white expatriate. After his victory over the white overlord, he has to contend with tribalism and poverty. He accepts the white's help in his fight against poverty: schools and hospitals are built and young people leave to study abroad. He also hopes to utilize their energies against tribal superstitions because individuals cannot function if tied to superstition.

He recognizes too that only by developing strong nation states can Africa become free.

Udomo's attitude toward tribalism and his refusal to relinquish colonial assistance bring about his demise. Two of his closest colleagues resent his attack on the traditional past. Everything, he claims, must be sacrificed for the common good and he himself gives up all claim to possessing personal feelings. Hence, he does not hesitate to betray Mhendi, a close friend. After Udomo's assassination Mabi, his colleague, writes to Lois, Udomo's former lover in Europe. He blames Udomo's death on those who would seek to restore tribal glory in the name of progress and adds that Udomo's death did not destroy all hope for the progress he envisaged, for even his death could not turn the tide of events.

A beautifully written novel, well conceived, contrived with ability, and executed with concern and compassion, its only flaw is its tendency to rely too overtly on the gruesome spectacle of tribal orgy that haunts the European mind. Abrahams probably inherited this attitude from the prejudiced literature of the South African vernacular presses and from Thomas Mofolols's *Chaka* which portrays the warrior as bloodthirsty. But with its reconciliation of myth and reality, idea and fact, *A Wreath for Udomo* neatly links tradition with the present. Udomo's death was beyond his control, but Abrahams leaves us with a message of hope. The dream of Africa had come true for a startling moment and even with Udomo's death all was not lost.

Wild Conquest (1950), representing a historical and ethnical shift, focuses on the trek of the Boers northward between 1934 and 1935. The novel's two parts relate how both the Boers and the Matabele fail as humans and as a whole it graphically depicts the dehumanizing effects of war.

Early in the novel Abrahams writes of the British's abolition of slavery in Africa. Some of the hardships of the "free" are documented for they are strangers to this new freedom; they are without land and everywhere they are disdained. Thus the Boers decide to move north and take over their land. Abrahams deals with the Boers' aims and problems. Scornful of the "Kaffirs," they recruit both God and the young to their worthy cause of hatred. In the lust for land, moral depravity is at its lowest ebb. The young boy Stefan learns to hate and distrust all "Kaffirs"; a young man, Paul, is told that life in wartime means the banishment of pity. Paul learns this lesson well, for later on he tells his wife that murder means nothing to him. Nevertheless, he expresses fears for his future and that of his people.

The Matabele too crave power. They are overwhelmed by internal strife and are as bloodthirsty as the Boers. At the end, no one side triumphs—only bestiality wins. The Matabele cannot resist the force of guns and have to surrender; the wild conquest is complete.

The shift in emphasis in *Wild Conquest* makes the book slightly different from Abrahams's other novels. True, race—indeed racial warfare—is touched on, but what is more explicitly stressed is the psychological effects of war. No rigid demarcation of good and bad is drawn along color lines. All wars corrupt, and the people involved in them are accomplices in a deadly vendetta of self-destruction. The novel suggests that in wars the real enemy is contempt for human values.

From the beginning of his career as a writer until the most recent *This Island Now*, Abrahams's concern has been the social predicament of Black people. In *Return to Goli* (1953) he writes that "the burning anger in [his] heart and mind" never let him rest; the work before and after demonstrates this anger. Even when he moves away from South Africa as he does in *This Island Now*, this dimension of passion is present for the issues are still color, economics, and political struggle. Set in the Caribbean, the novel describes the hardships and poverty of the Black masses ruled by a tyrant. When he dies, Josiah, the main character, believes that his dream of reviving his people's dignity will come true. However, the whites and the coloreds, the big businesses and the press are all against him. Josiah ends up annihilating his own dream, for he is quick to follow in the footsteps of the dead tyrant. Though his enemies are different—white expatriates, "coloreds," the press—the laws remain the same and so does the plight of his people. Josiah is an everyman Udomo, stripped of color. Abrahams implies in *This Island Now* that the ruler will inevitably destroy the ruled; such is the nature of human psychology.

Abrahams's many novels demonstrate that he is solidly on the side of idealism and the ordinary man, and he speaks for both. His style, developing from the self-consciousness of the earlier pieces to a greater ease, is still concerned with documenting man's cruelty to man. He does not pretend to know the answers, but he poses the fundamental questions confronting every ruler in the world, be he king, chief, president, or prime minister: How does one steer a middle course between ideals and disaster?

ALEX LA GUMA: VIOLENCE AND PROTEST

Peter Abrahams's intentions are serious but his work often gives the impression of hostility recollected and removed from its sources. Exiled from his native South Africa for several years, he now lives in Jamaica. Alex la Guma is younger than Abrahams; though an exile, he, unlike Abrahams, was forced out of his country. His works thus express sincere earnestness and passion. There is no pretense that the writer is removed; he is *there*, in the slums, among the people, involved with their loves, their hatreds, and their defeats.

Set in District Six, *A Walk in the Night* (1962) is a violent and moving novel, evoking the world of stale smells, grease, and dirt. This world is seen at its worst in Michael Adonis's tenement—filthy, broken-down, with dustbins lining the street. Over everything is a pervasive mood of depression, brutality, and hopelessness, which inevitably affects the people who live there. They too are depressed, brutal, and hopeless. Basically the story describes how such an environment perverts even the normal course of justice. Michael Adonis is dismissed from his job and returns home drunk. He meets Doughty, an alcoholic, a relic of the past (he was once an Irish actor), drinks with him and accidentally kills him with a wine bottle. Willieboy, Adonis's friend and an ex-prisoner, happens on the body and is shot by a white policeman who mistakes him for the murderer.

A Walk in the Night concerns the problem of violence and crime and the nature of punishment. Through long, intense monologues, La Guma speaks of the shame of daily life within *apartheid*; Adonis not only loses his job but is searched by two white policemen. His attack on Doughty is a reaction against the society that dwarfs him. After his initial fear, he feels pride in what he has done, and La Guma further stresses the purpose of the novel in the unjust shooting of Willieboy. The cruel elements of society, whether clad in the uniform of law and order or the rags of Adonis, predominate. Willieboy's dying reflections on his father's brutality enforce the point.

Adonis, Willieboy, and Doughty were all lonely men and as lonely men they die. *And a Threefold Cord* (1964) moves from the cruelties of isolation in a world devoid of tribe to one in which a shantytown outside Cape Town becomes the brutal enclave. Charlie Pauls, the chief character, realizes that "people can't stand up to the world alone, they got to be together." He himself undergoes many hardships. His home is almost destroyed by a rainstorm and only when the family stays together do they manage to defy the elements. He suffers at the hands of the police when they accuse his girl friend Freda of being a prostitute. His family seems to be collapsing around him; his brother Ronald knifes his own girl friend Suzy. By the end of the novel, Charlie's father is dead, his brother in prison, the children of his lover dead in a fire. He resolves that only through a common togetherness can the tragedy which is life be endured. Charlie Pauls's resolution has political ramifications; South Africa must be united if it is to be strong.

Characters in *And a Threefold Cord* are painted in the same twilight world as those in the previous novel. Many of the people who exist in the shantytown have virtually been denied life because they cannot legally establish their claims to be. Their predicament is reflected in their environment—poverty-stricken dwellings crowded along the dirty road and near the railroad track, the effluvia of unpleasant odors, and a rubbish dump. Only a lonely carnation growing in the dump remains in the novel as La Guma's symbol of hope.

La Guma's next novel, *The Stone Country* (1967), describes some of his experiences in prison. Indeed, all his works draw on his own direct experiences, of *apartheid* life, of violence, of hatred and love. George Adams in *The Stone Country* is imprisoned for his fight against discrimination in South Africa. The barren inhumanity of prison life is dramatically evoked, and the inmates' sufferings and frustrations emerge partly through the graffiti on the walls. Frequently the prisoners are seen as nonhumans; Butcherboy Williams is like a jackal, a hyena, an ape; Solly is the "duplicate of a man." Both guards and prisoners are incarcerated by the system which is not unlike the outside world of *apartheid*, for even here nice distinctions among races are maintained and the identification card is regarded as a pass, a privilege. The prison is a microcosm of the larger prison without. The La Guma technique is by now apparent; the harsh world of objective reality (street, shantytown, and prison) blends with the equally vicious reality of human insubstantiality. Inevitably the cruel environment annihilates humane endeavor.

Social concerns also find themselves expressed in La Guma's short stories, some of which have been published in *Quartet* (1965). "Out of Darkness" and "A Glass of Wine" center on the theme of interracial love and the *apartheid* law that prohibits interracial marriage. A variation on this theme is played in "Slipper Satin," the story of a prostitute who is imprisoned for loving a white man. The interracial tone is absent in "Nocturne," although the reader finds himself once more in the world of criminals. Perhaps the least successful of La Guma's short stories, it is concerned with some criminals who plan to rob a café. A young girl is playing a piano across the street and one of the criminals is so moved that he goes to hear her play. When the time for the robbery arrives, he is, however, seen again with the other criminals. La Guma seems to imply that no aesthetic experience can avert the bloody future that awaits South Africa. Out of the grim squalor of the stunted lives poignantly depicted in his novels and short stories, a strange brooding disaster awaits everyone—victim and agent alike.

ANDEREYA MASIYE: LOVE AND WAR

Andereya Masiye has published *The Lonely Village* (1951), a small collection of short stories, as well as a book of short stories in Nyanja, a Zambian language. His *Before Dawn*, published in English in 1971, describes life in a village in the Chiparamba Valley during the 1930s and 1940s. Masiye documents the customs of the people, but centers his story on one character. Kavumba is left an orphan when his mother, caught in the "clash that was taking place between our traditional way of life and the new European medicine" (p. 43), dies of a septic ulcer. The young boy goes to work for the Bwalo or village council, and for the menial tasks he performs he is rewarded only with leftovers because of the scarcity of food. The story plods on with little form, merely filling out details of Kavumba's life.

Parts of the novel, however, do come to life. For instance, the whites introduce a tax system and the Africans make up a song of mockery which the Europeans cannot understand. Masiye's description of the white man's entrance into the village on bicycle preceded by "two running carriers" whose job was "to relieve their master of the machine when the occasion arose" (p. 60) is hilarious.

Before Dawn has occasional passages of documentary interest but because the writer is at times unsure of his role as novelist, he tries to pack too much into his one hundred and thirty-six pages. It would have been enough to have concentrated on any one aspect of this transition period, but to have bundled them all together means that the reader ends up with a bad love story, a sloppy war account (Kavumba goes to fight the Japanese), a halfhearted treatment of the African/European confrontation, and a superficial portrayal of local life and customs.

EZEKIEL MPHAHLELE: SEARCH FOR HOME

A South African, Ezekiel Mphahlele did not attend school until he was thirteen. He completed high school and later taught English and Afrikaans, but was dismissed when he openly opposed the Bantu Education Act. He became the fiction editor of *Drum* magazine and earned B.A. and M.A. degrees from the University of London while in South Africa. After working as an extramural tutor at the University of Ibadan in Nigeria, he went to Paris as head of the African Department of the

Congress for Cultural Freedom. Meantime, he was one of the advisers for *Black Orpheus*; later he returned to Africa as head of Chemchemi Centre, Nairobi. He then taught at the University of Zambia before going to the University of Denver to obtain his Ph.D. He now teaches English and Black literature there. Mention of his life is appropriate because his work is an account of his life.

Mphahlele published a collection of short stories in 1947, but his first major work, *Down Second Avenue*, did not appear until 1959. Largely autobiographical in scope and written with an obvious flair for language, it describes the author's years as a child in South Africa and bears witness to the terrifying conditions of life under *apartheid*. The book ends when he has to leave South Africa.

In an anthology which Mphahlele edited with Ellis Ayitey Komey in 1964, he spoke of how in South Africa "the socio-political life presents the kind of challenge that produces writers." Mphahlele has taken up this challenge in his work as can be seen in his *Living and the Dead* (1961) and *In Corner b* (1967), two books of short stories that display the problems of the entire continent. Mphahlele writes savagely and well, sometimes with humor, often with pathos, never without good craftsmanship. He has a good ear for pidgin English and a good eye for comedy. In "The Master of Doornvlei," he gently pokes fun at the preacher; "The Barber of Bariga" demonstrates his use of different levels of English, whereas his eye for detailed observation is fixed in "A Ballad of Oyo."

Mphahlele's *African Image* (1962) is an attempt to evaluate African literature. Not until 1971 was his first full-length novel, *The Wanderers*, published. Timi Tubane, the chief character, is, like the author, a Black South African exile.

Told through a series of time-shifts, *The Wanderers* begins with the death of Timi's twenty-year-old son Felang, while fighting in Zimbabwe. A flashback takes the reader to South Africa when Timi was a teacher and Felang only eight. The father reviews his life and how he had to flee from South Africa after writing a report about prison conditions. To get information for his report, Timi had traveled with Naledi to the hinterland and had slept in the same room with her. He is prevented from making love to her because they are both involved in a deeper inquiry. Finally she goes to England and Timi receives a letter from her saying that she will make England her home. Timi has no such easy choice, nowhere he can call home.

The Wanderers echoes the tone of the dirge as it recounts Timi's story. Instead of the fierce anger of the short stories, there is now anguish. Timi seems to conclude that his entire life has had little value: he has had a son who is now no more; he once had a lover but was unable to consummate the relationship. Timi's fate as a`wanderer is to be a man who is forever luckless—the imposition of being born in an unhappy corner of the world.

DOMINIC MULAISHO: POLITICS IN THE GROUP

For various reasons Zambia has not produced much literature in English. One explanation is that writers have tended to use indigenous Zambian languages. Not surprisingly another reason might well be the long power struggle between whites and Blacks in Zambia, a struggle raised to the height of epic in Kaunda's *Zambia Shall be Free*. Mulaisho is also interested in political struggle, and in his novel one obtains a glimpse of the inner workings of tribal politics.

The Tongue of the Dumb (1971) is about power conflict in an African village. With a blend of humor and seriousness, the writer describes Lubinda's ambitions to oust the ruling Chief Mpona. His treacherous schemes, however, prove to be futile, and at the end the chief is reinstated and Lubinda conveniently dies.

On the whole the work is successful especially in the glimpses it offers of European authoritarianism. The European—be he cleric or administrator—is made to look foolish in his failure to understand what he sees in Africa. But the focus of the book is political; just as the priests fight over ideologies at the mission, so do Lubinda and Chief Mpona. Mulaisho's use of proverbs, songs, and other oral material help to give the book validity. However, he does not seem to be at all times aware of the strictness of control that a novel imposes; so journeys are made, characters introduced, incidents narrated without contributing to the central effect of the novel. Often it is not clear *what* Lubinda stands for. He certainly is a *person*, articulate and brave, who does not fear opposing the white administration. On the other hand, Chief Mpona, with whom the reader is expected to side, is a kind of absent major character. Perhaps because he is half-god, half-man this is as it should be.

The Tongue of the Dumb is impressive as a novel that describes conflict within the group itself. Few writers have attempted this and managed to maintain Mulaisho's neutrality. This is no pretty picture of a romanticized Africa; the passages dealing with hunger have a pathetic realism about them. At the conclusion one feels that Chief Mpona triumphs because he represents order while Lubinda, who had flirted

239

with the forces of evil, fails because his success would have brought disorder.

In South Africa the writers are concerned with the problems of everyday life, of the Black man dwarfed by the racial circumstances in which he finds himself. They have important messages and have little time to describe village ceremonies. Because they are actively involved in crippling social and economic conditions, many have been forced into exile. But their accounts are not removed from everyday reality in South Africa, for it is a nightmare they experienced firsthand.

Important differences therefore emerge among these writers in English. In West Africa the tendency is to regard the tribe as the microcosm through which these authors record and interpret events of significance. Historically this is easily explained; no large settlements of whites were ever created in West Africa—the presence of the mosquito ensured that the European remained a stranger. But East Africa—Kenya, Tanzania, and Uganda—was "home" for large colonies of English settlers. East African writers reacted to the battle for independence by elevating the forest fighter to his proper place, that of a hero. As yet the struggle in South Africa is still to come and the writers anticipate it. Therefore most African novelists are protagonists; in West Africa for the tribe, in East Africa for the large group of have-nots, in South Africa for the race. And it is as spokesmen of tribe, group, and race that they speak. This is their chief claim as valid exponents of the nature of the Black mind.

Chapter 11

African Poetry in English

Poetry by Africans in English began appearing in the 1940s. The period seemed right because of the intense political activity (to which the poetic expression was geared) that was taking place in West and South Africa. A new type of artist was needed, for no longer was the traditional artist able to voice the aspirations of the nation. At first the writer did not acquire an individual voice; instead he extended the boundaries of tribe to include the nation. Although no longer merely the mouthpiece of the tribe, these poets were nevertheless still committed. They extolled the virtues of their race; they preached Christianity; they resurrected the heroes of the nation; they enjoined brotherhood. Assimilated into the white man's ways, they spurned his motives. They were completely Europeanized themselves, but continuously aspired to be African.

From this and other standpoints they were little different from the négritude poets. Because the English and French colonies were separate, it is unlikely that the two literatures influenced each other, but it is not difficult to see that since English- and French-speaking African societies shared mutual aspirations, they created the poet and the poetry out of an identical situation. However, the English-speaking writers lagged behind; whereas Senghor's anthology of poetry by Black writers in French appeared in 1948, its counterparts in English did not appear until 1957 and 1958.[1] The important difference between the two is that the poetry in English remained confined to public posturings and survives today as merely a curious showpiece. Négritude, whatever may have been its shortcomings, managed to make the public statement and still retain elements of good poetry.

Early Poets: God and Africa

H. I. E. DHLOMO: PROTEST

Not surprisingly the movement was spearheaded from South Africa. H. I. E. Dhlomo, who published his *Valley of a Thousand Hills* in 1941, had half a century of written vernacular verse to draw from and in particular the Zulu verse of B. W. Vilakazi, which had introduced an insistent tone of protest into the rather weak effusions of some of his predecessors. Dhlomo used this valley in Natal Province to signify, in Mphahlele's words, "a symbol of despair and hope for the underdog."[2] The poet sought to reorder Christian creation in terms of his own traditional and historical past; in doing this he attempted to come to grips with himself and to invoke, from what the valley represented, palliatives for his own pain and suffering. As the epilogue says:

> Creator who created sights so fair
> Create again
> But leave out pain . . .

It was not the physical consequences of everyday pain that Dhlomo feared, but the suffering of his race who because of "crippling laws and forms have now become Commercial pantomime." The valley is the means by which he discovers the meaningful past of his race and the significant presence of his self. It is a discovery that he will forcibly make, as the images centered on physical assault suggest:

> vouchsafe me power
> This beauty fierce to seize and rape and make
> My own . . .

Through "force," that is, his identification with the animate and the inanimate in the valley, he comes to the realization that he is himself the god of all and his own person. In him good and evil, past and present, are united, and he becomes one with the valley:

> Thus I am God; and God is I . . . this Self;
> So purity and peace reigned everywhere
> Deep in the Valley of a Thousand Hills
> For purity and peace in me then reigned.

After Father Tempels had demonstrated in *Bantu Philosophy*[3] that the Bantu world is one of forces intimately related to each other, it is

242

not difficult to see how Dhlomo arrived at this conclusion. This is no secondhand romantic theosophizing but a view intimately bound up with his own traditional culture.

In Dhlomo's poem there are elements of the Zulu isi6ongo (praise poem) both in the way he views tribal gods and heroes as well as the Christian deity and in the way the mountain is addressed. But two parts of the poem do not succeed—the philosophizing about universal issues and the lamenting of the decline of his race. He seems more genuine when he is dealing with the meaning of good and evil, autocracy and victimization. When he lists the wrongs that his race has suffered, his rather clumsy symbolism is much too obvious and lacks subtlety. The hills, he tells us, are "mountains of strife"; the rivers "deep streams of blood and sweat"; the trees "the swelling song of woe"; the herds "the broken people of the land." The language is too passionate to be convincing, and some of the comparisons seem flagrantly inept. But the rhythm is never boring, varying between the monologue of a praise poem and the dialogue of a play.

This is the nature of Dhlomo's "public" utterance and indicates how he is related to another South African poet, James Jolobe, who translated his own poems in 1946, and to the West African pioneer poets. They all saw the function of poetry as one of public posturing, the role of the poet as that of converter. All else was subjugated to this; and when one examines the work of these poets, it must be realized from the outset that these were the terms they set themselves. They were not poets with an individual voice, but versifiers who, although liberated from declaiming the attitudes of the tribe, were nevertheless echoes of what the public approved. Until the present there have been few individual voices directed against the tribe; instead the borders of tribe have widened to include the *évolué*, the Christian, the elite. Not unnaturally a tension is expressed repeatedly in their work, a yearning toward the life of the soil (which they equated with innocence), as well as their firm conviction of the need for westernization (which is paradoxically associated with corruption). Either they wrote about race, politics, or God, or they were curiously "poetic" in an effete nineteenth-century way—there are poems on death, love, sunrise, and sunset; and with the Second World War came poems pledging unstinted support to Britain.

R. E. G. ARMATTOE: EUROPEAN MAN

One of the most accomplished of these poets was the Ghanaian R. E. G. Armattoe who died in 1953 and whose best work belongs to the late

243

forties. Ras Khan has shown the contrast between Armattoe's poems which demonstrate a "consuming love for Africa" and those which express "disgust and disenchantment." He attempts to diagnose a tension that was endemic to the poetry and concludes that "this poet has great faith in the Negro race in general and vast visions and plans for it as a race. But when he considers the activities of particular black men in politics and in the running of their country, he is rightly or wrongly so disappointed that he lashes out at this beloved black race with serpentine fury."[4]

Either this is an ingenious avoidance of the issues at stake or an insistence on the poet's role as spokesman for the "right" side. This is perhaps how Armattoe and his contemporaries saw themselves and it arose both from their commitment to the expanded doctrines of tribe and from their desire to express individual attitudes. Most were concerned with what they wrote, few with how they said it.

An aspect of the dualism is present in Armattoe's introduction to his first volume of poems, *Between the Forest and the Sea* (1950),[5] in which he argues that it is the responsibility of the African poet "to know his past and express that past in authentic and unmistakable accents" as well as to write "without a conscious appeal in any racial context." It does not surely matter, nor does it seem relevant to ask, who the real Armattoe was. A poet who uses his voice to echo the public mood must record with objectivity what he hears, whether it is in "Ashanti New Town":

> A never-ending din.
> Day and night the women drawl
> Their never-ending talk.
> And in between there's a brawl
> And town and village fight . . . (p. 42)

or in "The Dance" in his second volume of poems, *Deep Down the Black Man's Mind* (1954),[6] where the voice is no longer a din but a rhythm that emancipates and identifies the dancing women with their Black counterparts in the New World:

> Come swing it, sisters
> To the tune
> O' the Caroline Blues
> Here the loose drums beat.
> Come, come, come!
> Feel your hearts beat
> Doom, doom, doom! (p. 79)

244

No longer is the versifier content with statement; he is now interested in form and in the blend of rhythm and language. Intentionally the language here is "jazzy," the rhythm expands in the first four lines and contracts with the onomatopoeic rendering of the drumbeat.

Six years before the publication of his first volume of poems, Armattoe asserted that "aptitude for civilisation is assumed to be dependent on psycho-somatic co-ordination, and therefore the European is held to be the highest type of man. The assumption of a higher aptitude posits the obvious inference that a difference in race type connotes a difference in aptitude and achievement."[7] In cold scientific language he effectively argued against Black inferiority. The comment is interesting because it pinpoints Armattoe as a most consummate performer. This is not an indictment against his "sincerity" but a testament to his versatility. For example his poem "Our God Is Black" in *Deep Down the Black Man's Mind* is an impassioned plea in the manner of the négritude poets and reminds one most forcibly of Damas:

> Our God is black:
> Shout it from the forests
> From the hills to the woodlands
> Let the woodlands re-echo
> Our God is black. (p. 14)

Race is the dominant issue in his poetry and he uses it, even in his love and nature poems, to emphasize emotional discord. "Letter to Marina," a moving piece of lyricism, nevertheless exhibits certain deficiencies of Armattoe's style. Westernized though he certainly was, he was unable to write a love poem, probably because it did not constitute a form he had encountered in the indigenous literature. When he does attempt love poetry, the setting does not accord with the supposed African landscape:

> I am back, Marina, in my own land
> And I sit on the verandah of my father's house
> Listening to the Angelus
> Watching the distant hills and valleys
> The church steeple and tower and orchards . . . (p. 51)

It was as if he could only simulate the love experience when the landmarks were foreign; the love experience could only be poignantly portrayed when the cultural vacillation was emphasized:

> Should I be
> At home here, at my ease here?
> I am not sure of anything here

> No known values hold, nothing certain
> Save uncertainty, nothing expected
> Save the unexpected. (p. 51)

Here his technique of introducing the abrupt intrusion of antonyms gives both a lyrical grace and a paradoxical consistency to his verse. The antonym could be a single word or it could be the repetition of a whole phrase. However, "The Human Race" partly fails because the phrase repeated does not have enough verbal force to justify the repetition:

> How I hate the human race,
> And its ugly smiling face
> And its silly ambling pace
> How I hate, I hate, that race,
> That ugly human race. (p. 32)

Furthermore the unimaginative single rhyme scheme developed throughout the poem restricts the quality of the prosody; there is no feeling of spaciousness in the lines but rather an uncalled-for shuttling backwards and forwards.

What is most apparent in Armattoe's verse (and here he differs sharply from his contemporaries) is his varied experiences and his charming wit. His poems contain French, German, and Italian phrases (he spoke these languages) as well as allusions to various West African deities (he was an anthropologist). He took more liberties with form than his contemporaries; he was able to capture the rhythm of Negro spirituals as well as the contemplative spirit in his Eliotesque "Life Is Movement" (*Deep Down the Black Man's Mind*):

> Eternal movement is
> What stillness is.
> Eternal stillness
> Is perpetual motion,
> Like M'am Hsi vase or
> Ming earthenware or
> Buddha stillness
> In an ancient temple
> Full of jingling dancers.
> We are the dancers
> This alone is life,
> This is life in rest. (p. 62)

Despite the free form of his poetry, the literary devices which he employed were commonplace and unambitious; "Outside Those Castle Gates"[8] uses symbol in the overt manner of Dhlomo and as part-narrative, part-complaint it describes the way the slaves were sold

246

behind the locked gates of the castle. The castle stands for oppression and the poem progresses to the time when the "smooth oily sons" of the slave dealers live as rulers in the castle. Outside are the "lost dark people" with whom he identifies time and time again in some of his verse. The symbol in the poem enables him to view time in its three dimensions—the past of the slave traders, the present of autocratic rulers, the future when the people will rise up and destroy the castle and put an end to their own physical and mental serfdom.

Armattoe's wit is twofold; it is manifested not only in his asides, which frequently indicate that he is a man of varied interests, but in his mischievousness. For instance, he coyly writes "To an African Politician" who always votes with the government, "A glint in your eyes seems to say / You have been a good boy today."[9] And in his "Forensic Airs" he says to a lawyer

> Pray give me none of your airs
> Any clown in wig and gown
> May disport a bay leaf crown.
> Being black and old, I need none;
> No smart black silk, nor false hairs.[10]

Armattoe, however, is not a happy poet. When his poems were broadcast on the BBC in July 1950 the commentator remarked that "the Negro poet is likely to prove a sad songster because he is a late comer on the world's stage, and economic pressure in a changing world is hardly the motif for a man to be happy about."[11] And in his introduction to *Between the Forest and the Sea*, Armattoe, while admitting that the aim of poetry was universal, felt nevertheless that "all poetry is after all personal." But the more personal his poems, the more they border on the sad and the sentimental; there are many such poems—to his wife and his daughters, to friends, and even "Autobiography," a poem in which he portrays himself as he would like to be remembered. Armattoe has said that it is only "a poor craftsman who is hedged about by traditions and is afraid to experiment." He did experiment. But there is a concern with metrical regularity that accounts for the failure of many poems. Few attain the lyrical and verbal ease of "Letter to Marina"; his "Autobiography" (*Deep Down*), for instance, uses fairly conventional rhymes and prosody to say at best something fairly trite and at worst something that seems rather close to nonsense:

> Proud he lived and thus proudly died
> A stranger to fame and fortune
> Who in far-off lands played a tune
> To stir his wide-world's people pride.

He is so involved here with rhyme scheme and the regularities of metrical conventions that his meaning is almost irrelevant. The less personal poems often echo the tone of the public speech or the despair of a self-righteous prophet. But in both the personal and nonpersonal poems, the simulation of grief, whether it arose out of his concern with death or his dismay with the political situation, is redeemed by his faith in humanity.

Armattoe's poetry is typical of, although better than, a great many of his contemporaries. With Armattoe one begins with the personal to apprehend the universal; at least that is how he himself understood his work. The fact is that Armattoe, the liberated African, intentionally spoke in tribal terms, initiating a dialogue with the inarticulate whom he barely knew. Where he differed from one of his contemporaries (the Nigerian Dennis Osadebay) is that he saw English as the definite medium in which the African has to write and westernization as his inevitable course, whereas Osadebay thought that "we all want to make first class writers, and if that is the case we have to express ourselves in African languages; because however well we write in English, we will only succeed in turning out second-rate writers of English."[12] Nevertheless, Osadebay was a member of the "West African Society" which was founded on July 23, 1947, in London. Other members were Robert Wellesley Cole (the author of *Kossoh Town Boy*), Davidson Nicol (a writer of numerous short stories), and J. H. Nketia (a poet and translator of Akan oral verse into English). All these writers (including Osadebay) mainly used English as the medium for their work, and the function of the society to which they belonged and that of the allied "Academy of African Authors in Lagos" was to encourage African literature in English and to help to secure publication. Of the foundation members only Nketia was later to write in an African vernacular language. But Osadebay's debate over language illustrates another aspect of the dualism which was seen in Armattoe's poetry.

DENNIS OSADEBAY: CONFLICTING ATTITUDES

Unlike Armattoe, Osadebay does not work through the medium of the individual to voice a public statement; he begins instead with the public attitude. In his introduction to *Africa Sings* (1952),[13] he mentions that his concern is a public one: "the theme running through the book is the urge in the heart of the African to be free and the desire that African natives should take their rightful places in the world family of free nations" (p. iv).

Osadebay could not have written in any other way. He was not the

African expatriate that Armattoe had been and he was still very close to his own tribal sources. Though he never wrote in the vernacular (he, however, translated poems from Ibo), his poems are an expression of the widening of the tribal enclave to include the nation. Much of his verse is an invocation to Blacks everywhere and his themes never vary between a call to the youth of Africa, praise of the Black race, and either adoration of the white man's ways or condemnation of his values. The poems of gratitude are more than a little embarrassing to read in this decade: poems suffocated by a plethora of sentiments like "England I love you and I fight for you" (p. 28) or

> Thank you
> Sons and daughters of Britannia,
> You gave me hospitals,
> You gave me schools . . .
> Thank you;
> Yours is the happiness of giving
> The joy of doing good. (p. 4)

The poems expressing pro-African sentiments equally embarrass because the feelings seem too large, or rather the poet does not convince us that the language he is using is equivalent to the sentiments he is voicing. His "Ode to the Palm Tree," "Ode to the Niger," and "Au Revoir to the Lordly Niger" are poems in this genre and at times the sentiments stated are not only unconvincing but trite. In "The Rise of Africa" he makes use of the commonplace slogan that Africa is a sleeping giant, and "Africa Arise" is typical of a great deal of this type of poetry in its effortless deployment of inflammatory language for effect: "Let noble voices echo through and through / And hills be filled with Afric's name" (p. 26).

Although his sentiments appear commonplace, his poetic gifts are evident when he experiments with language and writes in a modified pidgin, or when he attempts to dramatize his issues. His poems about miners, farmers, civil servants, and clerks show them in conflict with their white overlords. In "The African Trader's Complaint" the clerk who becomes a trader dramatizes the desire of Africans everywhere to be free; but freedom can be a vicious circle, as the trader soon realizes: "You must become their clerk / Or buy your goods from them" (p. 20).

Osadebay highlights the conflict not only between Black and white, with its neat, ordered solutions, but between the oppressed and the oppressor. Putting pidgin into the mouth of an Englishman, for example, dramatizes both the white man's disdain for the Black farmer and the peasant's plight:

> Friend Whiteman smiled as I carried bags
> Of kernels, cocoa beans and nuts
> To his stores to get in exchange the pounds;
> He gave me pennies and made me angry
> And surprised.
>
> 'Take'm or leave'm
> Me no fit pay you more than that.' (p. 20)

On the whole Osadebay's poetry is unrewarding from the viewpoint of both language and ideas. Like Armattoe, his love poems, nature poems, and such poems as "Death" and "The End of Man" do no more than state hackneyed truths in conventional language. Osadebay's difficulty was one experienced by many of these poets—how to harness public statement to a private form. When the predicament is personalized, it does succeed; "Young Africa's Plea" and "Black Man Trouble" are both poems of defiance, though this is not what makes them successful poetry. Rather it is Osadebay's personal identification with public issues and his control of language, and, in the case of "Young Africa's Plea," his moving away from blind adherence to the canons of prosody. When Osadebay writes,

> Don't preserve my customs
> As some fine curios
> To suit some white historian's tastes . . .
> Let me play with the whiteman's ways
> Let me work with the black man's ways (p. 11),

the language is quiet and free of the bombast of much of his other poetry. He achieves the opposite effect with his modification of pidgin, as is seen in the following stanza which culminates in a vigorous and vicious thrust:

> I no get gun, I no get bomb
>   I no fit fight no more;
> You bring your cross and make me dumb
> My heart get plenty sore.
>   You tell me close my eyes and pray,
>   Your brudder thief my land away. (p. 17)

With his adaptation of dialect English, Osadebay moves closer to the concept of the artist as an individual in society and further away from his anonymous role as an articulator of tribal norms.

250

Gladys Casely-Hayford: Language and Laughter

In the hands of Gladys Casely-Hayford, the daughter of the first African novelist in English, Krio possesses all the authority of an established language. About 1948 she published *Take Um So*,[14] a small volume of poems, three of which are in Krio and are the most successful. For her the English language was only a medium for making trite observations, as is evident in this stanza from "Rejoice":

> Rejoice and shout with laughter
> Throw all your burdens down,
> Yours is a glorious heritage
> If you are black or brown.

It expresses the familiar yearning also observed in Armattoe. Like him she was educated abroad—in Wales—and her poems in standard English are either patriotic like "Freetown" or racial like "The Serving Girl," published in Langston Hughes's *African Treasury* (p. 187).[15] Like many other poets, she even felt compelled to write on the theme of war; "Wings," for example, is a dramatic monologue about a Black man who wants to fight with the R.A.F. and to die the death of a hero:

> I who am black now face the belching fire
> Where bullets spurt, to quench another's ire.
> If I must die; tis always my desire
> I who am black.

As can be seen, her histrionic language is out of all proportion to the sentiments, a flaw also noticed in the works of Armattoe and Osadebay. Moreover, she adheres to conventional metrical arrangement and the rhymed quatrain. As was true of these other poets, her attitude toward the African was a sentimentalized one; in "The Serving Girl," there were "countless things she served with her eyes." And like them she tended to moralize, although her Krio poem "Take Um So" is relieved of the sententiousness of some of her other efforts. In it she simply says that one ought to accept with Christian tolerance whatever life offers, yet the examples she gives of success and failure and the way in which they are mentioned, coupled with the lively meter, make the poem most successful:

> If God full some ouse wid pickin, en 'E no gree full youn.
> Or 'E gie you; don E take de pickin back;
> Or 'E show you road way tranga, en E put you for
>   climb hill
> En guide some oder person pan broad track—
>   take um so.

(If God has filled some houses with children,
  but not yours.
Or if He gave you and then recalled the children;
Or if He showed you a dangerous road and made you
  climb a steep hill
And guided somebody else on a broad track—
  Don't quarrel—accept it as it is.)

The use of Krio brings about a certain economy of diction and makes the poem pointed and terse. Gladys Casely-Hayford has accomplished here a difficult task, since it is commonly accepted that dialect English is appropriate only for comical situations. She does, however, use it for humor as well, as can be seen in "The Sailor" and "Tunday," a lyrical piece in the form of a song by a woman. They are both amusing. The sailor warns women that he is more cunning than a spider, more dangerous than a leopard: "I cunni' pass spider / I danger pass lepet." "Tunday" humorously describes the perennial problem of in-laws; a woman cooks some food for Tunday and he is about to eat it when his mother-in-law appears.

Her most successful pieces are those in which she combines human compassion and deep poetic insight. For instance, in "Thunderstorm"[16] a meeting between two lovers is enacted in terms of the storm. Rain is equated with the woman's presence, lightning with the man's desire, thunder with the power of their sexual union, and the ensuing calm with contentment. The poem concludes with economic artistry: "Is there peace within like peace without? / Only the darkness knows." The symbolism is never forced and the poet makes the reader look outwards from the experience to something profound and commonplace, which hardly seems worth stating, but which one recognizes with joy.

Gladys Casely-Hayford's most important contribution to West African writing remains her ability to develop Krio as a serious language. She has the shortcomings of her contemporaries and her cultural marginality placed her in the same position as Armattoe. However, her mother's influence on her and her mother's love for things European were more than balanced by her father's interest in and influence on Pan-Africanism.

THOMAS DECKER: LANGUAGE AND LORE

Because Gladys Casely-Hayford had shown that it was possible to write Krio and still be serious, Thomas Decker, a Sierra Leonean, was able to become the chief poet of Krio. The reason for the enormous difference between the flashes of inventiveness in pidgin and the serious concern

252

in Krio is suggested by Jack Berry when he writes, "Pidgin is not the native language of any who use it. A creolised language on the other hand is the only language of a group of persons, originally from different speech-communities. . . . Creole languages, as might be expected, are subject to constant amplification and 'improvement' and their vocabularies can be, and often are extensive."[17]

Decker translated the Bible and Shakespeare, demonstrating that Krio could ably render English verse in translation. Moreover, in his own poetry he refused to use the cheap and easy device of humor, as can be seen in this touching lullaby (unpublished):

Slip gud O, bebi-gial!	Sleep well, my "baby-girl"!
Opin yai lilibit	Open your eyes a little bit,
Ehn luk mi wan minit	Look, just for one minute
Bifo yu slip.	Ere you fall asleep.
A wan foh si da ting	I wish to catch a glimpse
We kin de shain insai	Of what peculiar light
Issai yu fain-fain yai	Within your eyes so bright
Ehn koht mi at.	That stuns me so!
So! shet yu yai nau noh,	Now, you can close your eyes.
A tink se a dohn si	I think my heart did see
We tin a man foh si,	What it desired to see.
Gud nait! Slip gud!	Good night! Sleep well!

The original and the translation are both by Decker and are intimately related to lullabies in the oral tradition. Decker once called Krio a language in which "mothers can rock their babies," and he set out to demonstrate its lyrical qualities in his compositions. Most of his work has not been published, and much that he wrote is available only in translation.[18] But even here a certain amount of re-creation has taken place. For just as the telegraphic precision of Krio is apparent in the lullaby above, so in the translations a new significance is evident. In the Krio Twenty-third Psalm, for instance, the exotic imagery of the Bible is reduced to more local terms; also the sharply focused monosyllabic or disyllabic Krio words emphasize the stylistic precision as illustrated by these opening lines:

Lack say me nar sheep, on God nar de man way day men da sheep.
Are nor go want nattin way are not get.
God make are laydon nar sie way better grass day grow.
E go take me go nar sie way better water day run saffle-saffle.[19]

Literally translated this reads:

Suppose I were a sheep and God, the man who looks
after the sheep.

I would want for nothing which I could not have.
God would let me lie down near an ocean where better
  grass was growing.
He would take me near an
  ocean where better water runs, ever so softly.

The Krio translation is more personal than the King James version. New ideas have been introduced, or rather certain ideas have been expanded—the sheep and the good shepherd, the grass and the water, are made the subject of separate lines and subsequently emphasize the idea of bountifulness. At the same time (and this is most difficult to do) the piety of the original is retained. Further, a new element is added: the tag word "saffle-saffle," though related in meaning to the sentence, is a way of introducing a liturgical element—it is the point where the congregation could respond. Other words like "Amin," "gladdy," "tabby-tabby," and "tay-tay" in the rest of the poem have the same effect. This clearly shows that the African poet is still a member of a group, and although not its medium, he continues to write with the group in mind.

CRISPIN GEORGE: THE POEM AS HYMN

Crispin George was one of Decker's colleagues. His single volume, *Precious Gems Unearthed by an African* (1952), is devoted exclusively to expressing Christian views. Although Christian elements are to be found in the verse of Dhlomo, Armattoe, and Osadebay, Christianity is the dominant issue in the work of Crispin George. Thus to label all these writers "virtuous poets," as Ulli Beier has done,[20] is quite misleading, for whereas most were content merely to deal in general melancholic abstractions, only Crispin George emphasized the canons of the church. Therefore, when poets like Osadebay and Armattoe write about the transitoriness of life, they both use the phraseology of the Christian evangelist, but do not openly put forward God as the solution. Crispin George, on the other hand, does just this:

Alive today and dead tomorrow?
Why do you think of death with sorrow?
Embrace your God with all your heart
And gain perpetual life with Christ. (p. 8)

This is not to say that Osadebay and Armattoe are any more subtle than Crispin George, for they all use the trite language of the faith. Simply, Crispin George saw his function as pastor, they as lay propagandists. Nevertheless, they were all teachers.

Crispin George was little more than a sermonizer in verse: he employed the folktale to lend narrative interest to his poetry and to emphasize the moral slant, and he was not averse to writing a whole allegorical poem in order to accomplish an unintentional anticlimax in the last two lines. In "God is at the Helm," for example, a boy experiences a storm at sea but feels secure because his father is at the helm. Crispin George's conclusion indicates his disarming inclination for stating the obvious: "No earthly storm can scare us, since / God's always at the helm" (p. 24). Another poem, "True Greatness," tells of a tailor who spends his life doing good; again the moral point is so obvious throughout the poem that the conclusion seems to be a mere tautology.

Crispin George's humor, however, redeems a great deal of his didacticism. "The Rivals" is a humorous animal tale in verse, and humor is uppermost in such a poem as "What Is Life without the Women," where the injunction to do good is not delivered in the manner of a wooden-faced *gravitas*. Those poems which lack either the folk interest or the humor tend to be occasions for moral advice, couched in the usual language of revivalist hymns and religious pamphlets. But because Crispin George is not a poet anchored to the unchanging currents of prosody, he is capable of giving more satisfaction in his verse. The opening of "A Timely Advice" is good by any standard; not only is it a description of organ music but the words suggest both the music and the player's response:

> That instant spell brought Heaven's hall of music
> near my reach
> I had a glimpse of what it is to roam in Heaven's
> street.
> In raptured strains my soul proclaimed untutored
> thanks in song . . . (p. 32)

The long lines and the sibilants reinforce the effect of awe and magnificence, but the rest of the poem provides an example of Crispin George's major weakness. He had artistic gifts but no imaginative insight; that is, he could organize meaning but was limited in thought. In the same way that the last two lines of "God Is at the Helm" are an anticlimax, so the rest of this poem is. For it turns out to be no more than an exhortation to drivers to "heed this timely note" and not sound their horns.

Surprisingly there are only a few poems about Africa in Crispin George's collection, but here his manner is much the same as that of the other poets of this period. According to Abioseh Nicol, "the European influence felt by these poets is that of the nineteenth and early twentieth century,"[21] and to a large extent they seem curiously uninfluenced by African norms or culture. Their verse seems more closely related to the Bible and hymnbooks than to fin-de-siècle nature poetry, and is made up of "stock" diction and situations which remind one of newcomers to a language.

ROLAND DEMPSTER: THE DECAY OF THE PRAISE SONG

The Liberian poet Roland Dempster is no newcomer to English, for it has always been the mother tongue of many Monrovians. With Dempster, the poet has become sycophant; his verse is not only stylistically inept, but is overconcerned with the external trappings of prosody and form. The poet, formerly spokesman for the tribe, has become in Dempster the puppet of the autocrat. It would be ridiculous to claim that his form was influenced by the praise song, for the praise song was never studied outpourings of obsequious flunkeyism, but spontaneous effusions of gratitude and love. Dempster published his first poems in 1947; five more volumes appeared between then and 1963.[22]

Most of his work is dedicated to the president of the Republic of Liberia and the theme of the party and the presidency dominates even over that of Liberia and identification with Africa. About his *Anniversary Ode* (1959), a panegyric to President Tubman, the national party chairman was moved to remark, "This is indeed fine; it fully expresses the sentiments of the party. I thank you" (p. ii). Dempster said he wrote the poem in one day, and parts of it readily reveal his haste:

> Twas in this sunkissed November,
> When nature did her work complete
> To hand to us a great redeemer
> To rule Liberia brave and free. (p. 1)

His concern with Africa is slightly absurd because it is so obviously influenced by the party program. As expressed in *To Monravia Old and New* (1958), the past is when

> beasts of every clime
> Infested lived—deer braying; snakes hissing,
> Flung their venomous fangs as for kissing. (p. 8)

The party's health program, on the other hand, has ensured a more promising present with

> The streets paved, the houses with newer view:
> The shooting water has replaced the dangered well
> And now the high or low where'er they dwell
> Today have access to the shooting thing;
> Ah, what joy the light and telephone bring. (p. 8)

If his poetry were not so blatantly servile, it might be unintentionally comical, especially when one considers the remark by a colleague that Dempster used "his active imagination and facile pen."[23]

Africa features quite often in Dempster's poetry but his is still not an individual voice but one tuned to the sounds of the party manifesto. This is not the only disappointing aspect of his poetry; he simply has not acquired a diction of his own, and trite poetic phrases and doggerel abound as can be seen in these lines from *A Song out of Midnight* (1960): "Wake up, dear Africa, wake up your day has dawned! / Redeem the glories, the treasures your ore had pawned!" (p. 36.) Dempster the romanticist is even more absurd: "The Bushman and their arrows / Shooting swift at the sparrows" (p. 38). In a surprising paragraph at the end of *A Song out of Midnight*, he piously adds a kind of footnote to God: "He has led me thus far successfully toward achieving my life's goal and abundantly given me gifts with which to satisfy my highest ambition: to become one of Africa's foremost poets, philosophers and authors. O God! how grateful am I to Thee" (p. 42).

At times, however, the note of an authentic poet unwillingly breaks through his verse. For instance, a short poem entitled "The Tom-Toms Are Beating," although indulging in the most obvious kind of romanticism, is free of his appalling attitudinizing and his rigid adherence to formal meter. A stanza like this, though not entirely successful, is a relief to encounter in his otherwise tedious verse:

> I hear, I hear the tom-toms
> Of Africa, the waking jungles
> Beating far, beckoning unto me
> Of new regions and kingdoms. (p. 13)

He asserted in an article that "the African writer must be brave and sacrificial . . . he must also be cautious not to abuse his liberties."[24] But it is a dictum he followed on few occasions. When he was not being "patriotic," he tended to be sanctimonious, and many of his poems of moral exhortation are too heavily flavored with didacticism to be palatable. He has the moral sententiousness of the poets of Ghana and Nigeria, he has their preoccupations with the theme of Africa and Christianity, but since he never freed himself from sycophancy, he never managed to be any more than an ineffective and slightly disreputable laureate.

MICHAEL DEI-ANANG: "I SING OF AFRICA"

In one poem Dempster touched on the culture conflict in Africa without being altogether convincing. He was unable to see that his "African's Plea: Let Me Be" did not have the texture of tough diction to stand up to intellectual or rhythmical manipulation. His conclusion "God made me / And He made you you / So please *let me be*"[25] reiterated throughout the poem is an exercise in the exaltation of the trite. In contrast the Ghanaian poet Michael Dei-Anang succeeded in dramatizing the conflict by reorienting his diction. As Beier said, "He critically examines the loosely used words 'backward,' 'forward' and 'superstition' and by putting them into a more precise context he is redefining their meaning."[26] The poem Beier is analyzing asks:

> Whither Bound, O Africa?
> Backwards?
> To days of drums
> And festival dances in the shade . . .
> Or forward?
> Forward! to what?
> The slums where man is dumped upon man; . . .
> The factory
> To grind hard hours
> In an inhuman mill
> In one long ceaseless spell?[27]

It is a mood that was taken up by the poets of the fifties and sixties, who reacted completely against the pious poets of the forties. But they could not have written without these models, and certainly in the poem above Dei-Anang has dispensed with standard meter; instead jagged broken lines emphasize the tragedy. The prosaic quality is a relief from the tedium of the poetizing of his contemporaries. From 1946 until 1965 Dei-Anang published five volumes of poetry[28] and established himself as a poet second only to Armattoe.

Africa in its largest continental and historical sense is the theme that primarily preoccupies Dei-Anang. As he said in "A Writer's Outlook," "I sing of Africa because I know her best. I am proud of her beauty, music and folklore, because these come nearest to my heart."[29] Naturally he tends to over-romanticize, to treat Africa as if it were a continent of the mind. Nearly always he emphasizes the past, a past which has at times been misinterpreted. With ironical annoyance he asks in "Africa Speaks":

> Dark Africa?
> I, who raised the regal pyramids,

And held the fortunes
Of conqu'ring Caesars
In my tempting grasp.[30]

Intentionally the language is lofty, the sentiments grand, for all of Dei-Anang's verse expresses the mood of anthems. But he yearns not only for the physical superiority of the past, but for its spiritual benefits when "wild men and wilder beasts / kept close company." Equally he wants to retain "the fertile laws of Faraday."[31] There is no open conflict here, although it is perhaps inherent in what he is saying. Instead his inheritance is reorganized in his poetry; there is no loss, only a need for new convictions, for re-evaluation. Nor is his past the same as Dempster's, for he does not err on either side of dishonesty—he despises neither all that is indigenous nor all that is western. His verse is therefore neither a severe denunciation of the West nor a one-sided appraisal of Africa. In his introduction to *Africa Speaks*, Dei-Anang remarked that "poetry has a rich and fertile soil in Africa because Africans have no inhibitions about their emotions" (p. ix). This may be true but his own poetry is surprisingly free of unrestrained emotional outbursts.

EFUA SUTHERLAND: THE INDIVIDUAL?

Michael Dei-Anang, like two of his Ghanaian contemporaries, still identifies with the group. Interest in the group may have expanded from a tribal preoccupation to a religious or racial one, but the poetry remains a verse of commitment and is still very close to the oral tradition, which had no artistic justification other than the social needs of the community. With the verse of Efua Sutherland one moves a step closer to the beginning of the emancipation of poetry. Mphahlele has called her "the only highly individualistic writer in her country" and added that "the rest of the poets in Ghana express nationalist sentiments and revive old hurts like slavery. . . ." But this is too large a claim to make for her; she like the other poets of her generation remained confined to group issues, although she was not dominated by them. Her poem "Redeemed," which literally is about a snake overcome by the beauty of a woman whom it wants to destroy, could readily be about how "a man wants to bring to her knees a beautiful woman."[32] But nothing else in the scanty publications of Efua Sutherland would suggest that there is anything but the barest of superficial meanings in her work. For instance her three poems printed in Olumbe Bassir's anthology, although free from the themes that preoccupied some of her contemporaries, are nevertheless a publicizing of the individual. "It Happened" is the sentimental story of

259

two lovers of different colors. "An Ashanti Story" makes little pretense at being anything more than an Ananse story in verse. Even apart from its rather rigid quatrains and its archaism, the "moral" at the end does not contribute to the poem's artistic possibilities. It possesses neither the exuberance of a tale nor the freedom of a song; the poet is entirely hamstrung by the tradition. "Little Wild Flowers" is conventional landscape description, although the dispensation with rhyme and the disarrangement of the lines are in keeping with her theme. This emerges clearly in the last stanza which invokes the flowers:

> And when I come again
> After the next night's rain
> Of dew. grant
> A like vision of yourselves
> Your budded yellows
> Of today, that stud the grass
> As the stars the skies . . .
> And take my breath away! (p. 23)

The grim play on words in the final line, added it seems as an afterthought, is a fitting climax. Since descriptive nature poetry does not occur in traditional oral verse, and since Efua Sutherland does not externalize nature as do the other poets of this period, it can be said that the merest glimpse of the individual begins to emerge in her verse.

J. BENIBENGOR BLAY: FIRST AND LAST

With the poetry of J. Benibengor Blay[33] one returns to the verse of typical poets of the forties and fifties; his works reflect their interests and their themes and he was in fact the first among them to publish. His *Immortal Deeds* (1940) clearly began a movement and made no secret of its pedagogical intention. Blay commented that he hoped "it may serve as another Excelsior carrying a message to International Youths, and arousing them to higher deeds of immortality" (p. iv). The volume contains only twenty-four poems and deals, as might be expected, with natural scenery, religion, the theme of Africa, and semi-philosophical speculations about the nature of love and death. Since 1940, Blay has written five volumes of verse, the most recent being *Ghana Sings* (1956). He is the only poet of the forties who continues to write. His verse has not altered a great deal, and his dictum in his preface to *Ghana Sings* that "a good poem should be considered as having the following essentials: Meter, Rhythm and Rhyme" is what he believed when he started composing. All in all this has tended to restrict his development as a poet; some of the laudatory verse in his

260

last book (poems like "Birth of Ghana" and "Welcome, Kwame!") is reminiscent of Dempster, but Blay is more restrained and his tone is in the manner of a praise poem.

Many of the poems are prefaced by newspaper excerpts and in this, as well as in his choice of topic and treatment, Blay reminds one that the poets of his period were very much "pop-poets." Therefore Blay could write equally eloquently on imagined love and a dead mother; of how "a sound / In dreams of love, draws nigh my breasts"[34] or of his "Fearful Testament" to his dead mother:

> Where go'st thou, mother, mother sweet?
> Is it where once in pair we trod?
> Or where in dreams we father met?
> The sacred world!—the veil of God? (p. 6)

Doubtless he wrote this without the slightest embarrassment, since for him poetry was the publicizing of the intimate. The poet's pen was also always at the service of just causes, and when a certain Miss Gwendoline Mary Jones was inspired to give her life "to save twelve baby patients in a fire" (an incident duly reported by the *Daily Mirror* of May 21, 1938) Blay was similarly moved to write:

> Nurse Mary Jones—a very simple name,
> Yet one deserving an undying fame,
> Alone she bravely faced a glorious end,
> From more cruel flames those babies to defend. (p. 5)

A pop-poet had to be a good Christian and Blay's verse is full of Christian sentiments; and the poet had to adopt conventional attitudes toward Africa, the war, indeed toward all the subjects that he was supposed to deal with, and he was expected to write in a certain way. Thus it is pointless to take Blay to task for lack of inventiveness—it was not his business to invent. Beier's remark in an article on "Some Nigerian Poets" is quite surprising when viewed in this context, for he said that these poets wrote at a time when "there were no forerunners, no modes, no tradition."[35] This is quite wrong: tradition was surely always there; it did not suddenly emerge. And their modes and forerunners were the hymns and the standard English literature poems of the school syllabi.

Like Dhlomo, Blay tried his hand at the epic; *King of the Human Frame* describes in twenty cantos how Abdomen becomes king over Head, Hand, and Foot. This is good, lively verse, a little impeded by rhyme but nevertheless carried along by the narrative line, which is not bogged down by any weighty moralizing such as was observed in Crispin

George. According to a note in the preface, an old man told Blay the folktale, but he "reformed" the setting (p. vii). The story is related as a conventional "romance," the chief characters becoming knights who live in medieval castles. This is an example (perhaps an extreme one) of the lengths to which these poets were prepared to go to alter their material, but the whole flavor of the tale is not lost here. What had taken place was not so much distortion as an attempt at blending. What succeeds above all is the narration—the element of surprise is maintained until the end when it is finally revealed that Abdomen wins because Sir John Head, Lord Hand, and Justice Foot proved themselves ungrateful toward their father, who had come to them disguised as a beggar. The use of extended similes in the epic manner and the archaic turns of phrase contribute to the effect of grandeur.

All in all these poets used what was at hand; by following the rigid conventions of meter and rhyme, they attempted to convey standard beliefs on life, death, love, religion, the Second World War, nature, and "Africa." There is no denying that their work is derivative, that it is obsessed with didacticism and evangelical fervor, that their tone is rhetorical. But their influence cannot be disregarded, for at least they made a negative contribution to the development of African poetry in English. They lacked the tough fiber of poetic imagery that one finds in their contemporaries, the French négritude poets, but this had an important effect on African English verse. For whereas the poetry in French was good enough to exert a positive influence, theirs was the point of reaction and departure. Their identification was more with the group and this is why one finds apparently "conflicting" attitudes in their poetry toward religion and the benefits of white imperialism; they had to be all things to all men. They were the last wearers of the mask in African English poetry; the new poetry was to reject the group and the mask that symbolized it, and to attempt to articulate the agonies of the individual. African poets in English could more easily do this since they could readily discard their predecessors; to this day French African poets are bogged down in the morass of négritude.

Contemporary African Poetry in English

Between the verse which has just been considered and more recent African poetry in English there is a decided break. No longer are poets merely content with adopting social attitudes, although they still display an interest in social issues. The viewpoint is now more firmly centered on the individual—the poet is the hero and it is *his* tensions, *his* world, *his* solutions that are emphasized. This alteration in the very locus of the imagination is no accident; the new poets probably know more about modern English literature than about their indigenous oral verse, but they are conscious of this disjunction. In a way their poetry makes a reparation; they invent myth, use available popular beliefs, and borrow ideas and phrases from verse that has been translated from vernacular languages. They are the experimentalists and are not content with the mere deployment of Biblical injunctions but distort them into new unlikely contexts. Associated with political turmoil in modern Africa or with the ritual of a pagan shrine, their poetry startles one into a new awareness.

West Africa

GABRIEL OKARA: A DISORDERED WORLD

One of the oldest of the contemporary writers is Gabriel Okara. He was born in 1921 and so far as chronology is concerned he belongs to the generation of dedicated versifiers. But his mind is closer to the contemporary ethos. Nevertheless, he is the link between the two generations of poets, for some of his dicta sound surprisingly like négritude: "As a writer who believes in the utilisation of African ideas, African philosophy and African folklore and imagery, I am of the opinion the only way to use them effectively is to translate them almost literally from the African language native to the writer into whatever European language he is using as his medium of expression." This coincides with Davidson Nicol's definition of négritude as "an assertion of the good things in Negro culture," and some of Okara's early poetry seems written to this specification. In "Spirit of the Wind,"[36] for instance, the storks returning from northern latitudes demonstrate a freedom that the poet seems to envy. Operating through a manipulation of symbols which emphasize the predicament, the last couplet, however, abruptly pushes the protagonist into the forefront and destroys the symbol because it equates it too exactly with the reality:

> O God of the gods and me,
> shall I not heed
> This prayer-bell call, the noon
> angelus, because my stork is caged
> in Singed Hair and Dark Skin?

Okara was not to compose many more poems in this vein, but this example demonstrates both the positive and the negative qualities of his verse. In "Once upon a Time" Okara reminds one even more forcibly of the earlier generation of poets. There is the same public appeal, the same "darkie" posture castigating the Europeans:

> There was a time indeed
> they used to shake hands with their hearts
> and laugh with their eyes;
> But now they only laugh with their teeth . . .

Also apparent is the veneration of the past, as well as the belief in the "unspoilt native." For instance, the last lines of the poem to his son (typifying innocence) read:

> show me how
> I used to laugh and smile
> once upon a time when I was like you.

Okara, however, was to move away from the obvious to the profound, from social issues to a more personal viewpoint.

Yet his first poems do show an individual concern, although the action (and it is correct to speak of action in an Okara poem, since the situation is intensely dramatized) tends to be converted into weak posturings. At the center of every poem is a protagonist, and the poem charts the history of his attitudes by subtly juxtaposing dissimilar images that help to emphasize his quandary. This occurs in such poems as "Piano and Drums" where the piano represents the European presence, the drums the African past, and "You Laughed and Laughed" where western "idiocy" is equated with cars and ice cubes, and African rationality with

> the fire
> of the eye of the sky, the fire
> of the earth, the fire of the air
> the fire of the seas and the
> rivers fishes animals trees . . .

Again in this poem the protagonist is at the center and reflects both the unity and the disparity of his world.

Okara achieved success not only by using symbols to illustrate certain attitudes, but by reorganizing the trite language of the public poem. "Piano and Drums" introduces technical terms at appropriate points to emphasize the cerebral nature of western culture, and it is a measure of stylistic exactitude that the harsh images associated with the piano culminate in the word "counterpoint" which later on the poet, almost naively, associates with "daggerpoint." Okara also reorganizes language by rendering it lyrical, and it is the ease of a songster that makes him

264

such a satisfying poet. He adopts the techniques of song-writing by repeating whole phrases, each time with a slightly different emphasis, by beginning with dependent clauses, and by making the poem grow into a long main statement which gathers momentum as it develops. "To Paveba" well illustrates his method; here he uses the paradoxical images of fire and ash to describe the powerful past and the quiescent present. The first three stanzas of the poem easily demonstrate this rhythmical technique:

> When young fingers stir
> the fire smouldering in my inside
> the dead weight of years roll
> crashing to the ground
> and the fire begins to flame anew.
>
> The fire begins to flame anew
> devouring the debris of years—
> the dry harmattan-sucked trees,
> the dry tearless faces
> smiling weightless smiles like breath
> that do not touch the ground.
>
> The fire begins to flame anew
> and I laugh and shout to the eye
> of the sky on the back of a fish
> and I stand on the wayside
> smiling the smile of budding trees
> at men and women whose insides
> are filled with ashes who
> tell me, "We once had our flaming fire."

Here fire symbolizes the theme of the new consciousness of the past; the repetition of "the fire begins to flame anew" in each stanza reinforces and expands the meaning and rhythm. It is no accident that the longest stanza of the poem is the third, for here the meaning culminates in a shriek of despair and the paradoxical symbol of ash is subtly introduced. This is developed in the rest of the poem with a pensive, almost corrosive, lyricism until the final stanza, which poignantly links the symbols and reconciles the image: "So let them be. Let them smoulder. / Let them smoulder in the living fire beneath the ashes." This poem is typical of many of Okara's in that the images demonstrate a dramatic progression and the rhythm gathers the poem together in powerful folds only to peter off in contemplative resignation at the end.

In all his poems a point is reached when protagonist and symbol are indistinct, when a powerful upsurge of feeling, essentially pure, is divorced from everything but its own intimate existence. This is exemplified in "The Mystic Drum" when

> trees began to dance,
> the fishes turned men
> the men turned fishes
> and things stopped to grow.

The curve of dramatic progression is similarly charted in "One Night at Victoria Beach" in which Okara records a time when

> dead
> fishermen long dead with bones rolling
> nibbled clean by nibbling fishes . . .

The moment is explained in "Spirit of the Wind" as one of "the instinct's vital call," and it is the fleeting second of profoundest experience when the natural world is disorganized and reordered into a new and revealing whole. It is when, in "The Fisherman's Invocation," the Back (the past) and the Front (the present) unite the protagonist in appropriate sexual imagery:

> I am wrapped
> in song of the Back wrapped
> in steps of the dancing Back
> and I can hear, I can hear the Front
> coming gently coming painfully coming.

These moments reflect the heights of Okara's poetic achievement.

Okara's work indicates a break with the traditional role of art in African society. Nkosi has commented that "there was no recognized or readily ascertainable conflict between the poet and his community in traditional Africa. The poet's ideals and his social goals were not seen to be necessarily separable from and in conflict with those of the rest of the community."[37] But Okara stresses the separation not only from humanity by proclaiming his private territory of anguish, but from nature. This marks him as belonging to a modern consciousness, for the modern African poets all emphasize this break. The separation can also be historical, as depicted in "Stanley Meets Mutesa" by the Malawian poet David Rubadiri:

> The village looks on behind banana groves.
> Children peer behind reed fences.
> Such was the welcome
> No singing women to chant a welcome
> Or drums to greet the white ambassador;
> Only a few silent nods from aged faces

And one rumbling drum roll
To summon Mutesa's court to parley
For the country was not sure.[38]

The Ghanaian poet Kofi Awoonor is less sure of the historical details, but certain of the tragic consequences for himself: "Something has happened to me / The thing's so great that I cannot weep."[39] This isolation of the spirit, the divorce of man from tribe, is the obsessive theme of contemporary African poets.

FRANK PARKES: THE DEFECTIVE VOICE

To refer to the Ghanaian Frank Parkes as a poet of political bewilderment is only to emphasize one aspect of cultural loss. His poetry[40] is positive about nothing, for it has arisen out of a denial of heritage:

I do so want to sing the songs
Of *Homowo* and *Adae*
Of *Aboakyer, Odwira* and *Bakatue* . . . (p. 7)

From this disavowal comes the poetry of disenchantment with nature, with religion, with the traditional past and the corrupt present, with the mechanization of impulse which has corrupted the self. The jagged, disorganized pattern of Parkes's verse stresses the disintegration that has taken place, as do the short, irregular lines that often break off as soon as they begin:

What had Communism to do with death,
The many weak queried

Everything
The few strong replied
Everything
Hungary . . .
Siberin . . .
Nuclear tests . . .

And we took the cue and continued:
Suez . . .
1914 . . .
1939 . . . (p. 33)

It is bitter poetry whose effect is best achieved in the terse, cryptic monosyllables.

At times, however, it is clearly not poetry. The poet in Parkes is shouted down by the pamphleteer in him, and there are many instances where the language is the speechifying tirade of a demagogue. In a way he has inherited this approach from the first generation of poets but it is also the language of a diluted kind of négritude:

> Give me black souls
> Let them be black
> Or chocolate brown
> Or make them the
> Colour of dust . . . (p. 26)

On the other hand Damas, one of the first négritude poets, was indeed writing poetry when he demanded in "Limbé":

> Give me back my black dolls
> that I may play with them
> the simple games, of my instinct
> to rest in the shade of their laws
> to get back my courage . . .[41]

Parkes's attempt, translated in an early number of *Black Orpheus*, is an obvious echo of this;[42] it also echoes Armattoe's "Our God Is Black" both in its rhythm and in its doctrinaire assertiveness. Even when, in the manner of Césaire, Parkes condemns the western world for its reliance on science and the subsequent loss of magic, his manner is crude:

> Too much it seeks
> And in its erudition
> The metal becomes a trumpet
> The trumpet . . . (p. 24)

What has really happened is that the subtle distinction between thought and feeling has vanished. This is not merely a question of the inadequacy of the voice; the entire articulation has become defective.

His poetry is at its best in its quieter moments. At such times he is closest to his Nigerian counterparts, although he is still very much himself, concerned with the political nature of man. His "Modern Nursery Song" can be compared with J. P. Clark's "Streamside Exchange"; each uses as the basis of his poem a familiar West African children's play song in which a child addresses a bird. Both manage to retain the plaintive rhythm of the child's words as well as the apparent simplicity of the dialogue. Although both recount a moment of discovery in the awareness of a child, Clark dramatizes a truth that is reflected in the natural world, whereas Parkes's truth is perverted by the natural world.

At times there are echoes of both Christopher Okigbo and Wole Soyinka in his poetry. Okigbo's poetry attains its maximum effect through the ritualizing of all experience—Christian and pagan—into a

268

revealing whole; Parkes attempts this too in "Blackman's God": "I stay here with the Eucharist / Of *kpekple* and rich palm nut soup" (p. 17). But Parkes's result is much more studied and lacks Okigbo's lyrical ease; indeed sometimes his writing borders on doggerel as in "To My Sister's Ghost":

> As mark of repentance
> I besmear me with blood
> With blood of the goat
> I besmear me with clay
> With clay of the earth
> Gin, as libation
> For you and for mother
> Our mother
> For Janie and me. (p. 15)

The last three lines do not develop the poem but merely distort the ritual by overemphasizing the personal element. Nor do the quotations from Eliot and the Bible in Parkes's poetry help since they only super-impose an artificial calm tone on his own high-pitched sounds. Only once does he himself manage to attain this type of tone—at the end of "Two Deaths, One Grave" where a person similar to Dag Hammar-skjøld is compared with Christ. The Christ figure waits for his own ascension, and the language is suitably pointed and linked to a restrained kind of mysticism:

> And he sat still
> Above the black mushroom clouds
> And awaited the third death. (p. 38)

Some of his poetry takes us in this direction, but this is not necessarily different from the rest of his poems. For instance, in "A Call to Youth for Sanity" he drops the banner-waving at one point to reflect:

> I nurse a beard, as rebel young men do
> And I love to sit and watch its bohemian growth
> Each hair a sonorous protest . . . (p. 57)

His half-mocking self-castigation is very reminiscent of the attitudes that underlie some of Soyinka's early poems like "Telephone Conversation," "The Immigrant," and "The Other Immigrant." But Parkes's heavyhand-edness always brings him back to his demagoguery:

> He died
> Not because he was black
> (Or goateed)
> He died because he stood for right. (p. 54)

269

Always his assertions are delivered in the trite language of the public rostrum. The words in parentheses do not redeem the situation, but seem to have been added as a humorous afterthought.

Parkes's relationship with his Nigerian colleagues establishes his link with modern African poetry in English. His obsession with political pamphleteering makes him no less realistic in a world where the ritual of religious worship and the formality of public occasion seem to be symbiotic. In the manner of a seer he employs two proverbs in his poetry; in one case "the sea never dry," a fairly commonplace Ghanaian proverb, is perverted to mean human suffering cannot cease, and in two cases he actually invents proverbs. The message of "Twentieth Century Epiphany" is built around the opening line that "the Kente [Ghanaian clothing] is the mind of Africa," which illogically at the end comes to mean that the Africans possess spiritual qualities far superior to those of Europeans (pp. 23–25). In "A Thought" the purpose is associated with the chewing of tigernuts—"It's the chewing / (And what we chew) that counts."

Allusion has been made to the way in which African poets chart the passage and moment of their disordered inheritance. Parkes does not dramatize it the way Okara does, but his most successful images arise out of his attempt to state the nature of the disorder. The recurrent images of the hungry child and the absent or unwilling mother symbolize the chaos:

> that sucking babe
> Torn from its mother's breast
> In this dark hour . . . (p. 12)

> The babbling of a wretched child
> Struggling for milk at the breast of savage mother. (p. 20)

> I was a little child
> And my mother sent me out for to play. (p. 104)

But for the protagonist all is not lost. The return to a oneness with the natural world, the escape from European tyranny over matter is the answer; indeed the last poem, "Renaissance," concludes the book on just this note:

> Sea, sea, swallow me whole
> Swallow this towering, far isolation
> Swallow this mindedness that narrows the light . . . (p. 64)

Parkes is describing a time when God, man, and the whole of the natural world were linked together:

Look at me, oh birds and creatures
Look at me, both birds and beasts
We shall not from waters perish
While this web hangs from the sky . . . (p. 45)

The web, in West African mythology, is the means by which human beings can visit the sky-god and the deities can come to earth. In Parkes's poetry it symbolizes the tenuous link that still exists.

One has to admit that Parkes's view of the universe is tragic, springing out of his closeness to what he once imagined to be an unpleasant political situation in Ghana.[43] Finally one is left with a feeling of dissatisfaction; the poetry is nothing more than rather hoarse political rallying in the name of art. Yet the means Parkes used to achieve his purpose are commendable—the symbol of mother and child, the distorted Bible renderings, but not, however, his obsession with the immediate politics of the day. For long after the situation has altered (and already one wonders what justification can there be for reading Parkes except as a chronicler of a period already past), one will only go to the poetry if it possesses elements of permanence that transcend his preoccupation with the transient. But as has been shown there are few of these. His failure is that his emotion is never elevated into form.

CHRISTOPHER OKIGBO: THE VOICE IN RITUAL

Okigbo's work is much more rewarding; all his poetry is in fact one long, elaborate poem. The chief difference between Parkes and Okigbo is that the former is preoccupied with latter-day Ghanaian politics, whereas Okigbo transmutes all experience into ceremony. The only apparent exception to this is his "Lament of the Masks,"[44] a praise poem to Yeats. But the poem is dissimilar only in that it is not concerned with Okigbo's favorite dramatization of a protagonist before a shrine; instead he relies on the indigenous praise poem, using the appropriate vocabulary of a warrior's eulogy to honor Yeats:

you were never at rest
Who, fighting a battle in front,
Mapped out, with dust-of-combat ahead of you,
The next battle field at the rear.
That generations unborn
Might never taste the steel—

These lines have their origin in, and are almost a word-for-word adaptation of, a Yoruba *oriki* (praise song) to a king of Ede:

He slept soundly, unmindful of war.
Fighting a battle in front,

He marked out the next battle field behind him,
So that the young generation might no longer
Have to fight any wars.[45]

In another *oriki* a king is praised because he

converted
A thick jungle into a habitable place
Who made impassable bush
Into a broad trodden path;
Who made a small Rouse
Into a magnificent palace.[46]

In this case Okigbo does not merely adapt; he summarizes and converts the imagery of the original into terms that seem both startling and fresh:

Who converted a jungle into marble palaces
Who watered a dry valley and weeded its banks. (p. xv)

All types of influences are to be found in Okigbo's verse; indeed Wole Soyinka was only stating half a truth when he referred to "the new poets in Nigeria who regroup images of Ezra Pound around the oil bean and the nude spear."[47] For there are also blatant liftings in "Lament of the Masks" and elsewhere from Eliot (a relationship Okigbo has with Parkes) such as "The moon has now gone under the sea / The song has now gone under the shade" (p. xiv), which is a mere variation of Eliot's lines from "East Coker," "The houses are all gone under the sea / The dancers are all gone under the hill." And later in "East Coker" Eliot writes of "The captains, merchant bankers, eminent men of letters, / The generous patrons of art," whom Okigbo in a poem in *Heavensgate* refers to as "fanatics and priests and popes / organising secretaries and / party organisers" (p. 3). The instances can be multiplied, but such imitation does not mean that Okigbo is at worst a derivative poet or at best a welder of two poetic traditions. He is much more complex than this and part of his success derives from his distinctive and private voice.

It is a voice that is not always clear; a hotchpotch of trivia makes it at times inarticulate—a solemn reference to yam tubers is based on a lewd Ibo song about the testicles of a ram—and titles of books like *Radiance of the King* or of films like *Island in the Sun* are numerous in his poetry. Then there are snatches of the Bible as well as a poker-faced pidgin version of Little Bo Peep meant to look as "classical" as possible: "*etru bo pi alo a she e anando we aquandem . . . / ebili malo, ebili com com, ebili te que liquandem.*"[48] Words and allusions to a private mythological world abound—allusions to Enki, to someone called Flannagan who "preached the Pope's message," to Yunice "at the passageway." All this can be terribly misleading and can be stumbling blocks not only for eager non-African postgraduates bent on finding the "Africanness" of the work, but even for Nigerian Ibo speakers like Okigbo himself. For instance the Nigerian Ibo Donatus Nwoga in his University of London doctoral thesis commented on the Little Bo Peep lines: "The italicised passages in the poem look like quotations and could lead to a frantic search through the classics Okigbo has studied. But they are the sounds of his childhood, an irrelevant mixing of bird songs with the Latin endings overheard at the Catholic mass" (pp. 281–82). No doubt a non-Nigerian might have thought of an even more ingenious explanation and certainly in this context one is inclined to think that Beier was wrong when he said that "Okigbo is not simply enjoying a private joke."[49] He *is* enjoying a private joke, although there is another level of apprehension to his poetry.

An early poem not published until after his first two volumes demonstrates a little of his technique—his borrowings and alterations, so that the poetry becomes his. The point of departure in the poem is the same as Parkes's—the poem by Damas in which black dolls represent his loss and innocence. But in Okigbo they become

> BLACK dolls
> Returning from the foam . . .
> DOLLS . . .
> Forms
> Of memory,
> To be worshipped
> Adored
> By innocence:
> Creatures of the mind's eye
> Barren—
> Of memory
> Remembrance of things past.[50]

It is important to note what has happened to Damas's black dolls—they have been deified. This process of transformation is the key to all of Okigbo's verse: how can human beings grow again into gods, how can they regain their pristine state of spiritual innocence and yet retain their own sensuality? To achieve this Okigbo forsakes the commonplace world that obsesses Parkes and chooses instead to re-enact the entire cycle of birth, initiation, and death. Because of the nature of his quest, his images tend to dwell on the disparity between man's ambition and his futile attempts to become God.

Okigbo's verse emphasizes a separateness from the ordinary which represents his search for ultimate wisdom. The five sections of the *Heavensgate* sequence clearly stress this striving—passage, initiation, watermaid, lustra, and newcomer. Before the "passage" begins, there is a prayer to Mother Idoto, a deity invented by Okigbo. "Passage" takes the reader back to the world's beginning and the protagonist's childhood, and introduces conflicting influences—"the bell tower" (p. 10) and "the idols" (p. 11)—and ends with the preparation for, although distrust of, baptism:

> smell of rank olive oil
> on foreheads,
> vision of the hot bath of heaven
> among reedy spaces. (p. 11)

The next section, "Initiation," rescues this vision of chaos "in a symbolic interplay of geometric figures."[51] Here the angle, orthocenter, fourth angle, square, rhombus, and quadrangle all indicate that a certain kind of order has been imposed; they represent the protagonist's various intimations of a complete harmony with himself and his world. "Watermaid" introduces the intercessor: a mixture between a classical muse, the Virgin Mary, and a local priestess. At the end of this section the protagonist finds himself in a state of cosmic aloneness, completely alienated from everything he knows: "The stars have departed, / and I—where am I?" (p. 27.)

"Lustra" suggests with appropriate Christian and African pagan imagery that there is hope which comes through a redeemer who is neither Christian nor pagan:

> Messiah will come again,
> After the argument in heaven;
> Messiah will come again,
> *Lumen mundi* . . .
>
> Fingers of penitence
> bring
> to a palm grove
> vegetable offering
> with five
> fingers of chalk. (p. 32)

But the dramatic quality of the poem is spoiled by the last four pieces called "Newcomer" which are irrelevant verses written to the poet's teacher-friend and to his niece. They do scarcely anything for the continuity of the piece and betray a dangerous side of Okigbo, that is, his poetry at times is so very personal that there seems little room for any universal message. Besides the private jokes, there are also local references like "jam jam jam dum" (p. 17). No one can be expected to know that this refers to a madman named Jadum who went through the markets in the Aguata division in eastern Nigeria lecturing to people by singing; and when one does discover this, it still does not contribute to the poem's effectiveness. The most that can be said is that Okigbo is perhaps interested neither in religion nor in the muse, but rather, as Eldred Jones has written, "in the posture of searching for . . . wisdom."[52] It is a wisdom that lies beyond the world and cannot easily be labeled.

"Silences" is the liturgy of the intending initiates who "camp in a convent in the open" (p. 15). Their trancelike state is to prepare them for the ultimate revelation. As they say, "Silences are melodies / Heard in retrospect" (p. 16). Reliving their own past in the present is their preparation for the future. The poem is appropriately in the form of a dialogue with an introit, a chorus, and a part for the silent sisters. And it is on such occasions that Okigbo shows he is a very conscious craftsman; for if, as David Cox says, "ritual was understood as the representation of events described in myths," then all Okigbo's verse is concerned with the presentation of myth in this most basic sense. This partly accounts for the "absent" reader, the feeling that the poetry is not intended for one's ears. Numerous critics, including Ulli Beier, have pointed this out; "the moment you start to read you feel you have intruded into the sacred enclosure of a secret cult. You have no right to be there." More recently Wole Soyinka has commented that "intruder though the audience must always be in such personal poetry . . . yet the invitation is contained in language and mood,"[53] and Robert Serenuga, interviewing Okigbo in London for the Transcription Centre, again spoke of the readers being like "outsiders eavesdropping on private conversation or intruding into a secret ritual." What enables the outsider to participate is that, in spite of the personal nature of his poetry, Okigbo is bound to no standard creed, he is the apologist for no doctrine, the spokesman for no faith; because he invents and alters, because his poetry is a way of syncretizing all belief, he is able to make his grandest appeal.

The opening lines of *Limits* (unpaginated) explore the unconscious state of nonbeing and narrate the progression toward wisdom. The images describe the unification of flesh and soul, for "I have had my cleansing":

> Into the soul
> The selves extend their branches . . .

And out of the solitude
Voice and soul with selves unite . . .

Thus the protagonist achieves harmony with the natural world, though it is one that can wound; for example, the pain from "the cruelty of the rose" is aesthetically purifying:

When you have finished
and done up my stitches
Wake me near the altar . . .

The second part, "Fragments out of the Deluge," describes the inner ruin that is symptomatic of a revolution of the spirit; from this the cleansing comes about, again appropriately couched in the imagery of a tree: "You might as well see the new branch in ENKI; / And that is no new thing either . . ." The renewal of life clarifies the mystery of the meaning of living. Christ or Buddha or an *abiku*, anyone who has been reborn from the dead, knows the truth about self and matter, a truth that might well elude others:

HE STOOD in the midst of them all
and appeared in true form
He found them drunken, he found none
thirsty among them.

The "messiah" realizes of course that they were "thirsty" and that he had to follow the inevitable process toward martyrdom.

The last section assumes the role of personal quest. It is clear now that it is the protagonist who is aspiring toward the last glory of flesh, to be a living god, and the final triumph over death, to be resurrected. At the end of the poem when "the cancelling out is complete," one can be sure that he has come nearer this concept of godhead.

Although the verse is not as straightforward as it has been made to sound, its basis is the quest for ultimate wisdom. Okigbo has himself helped to obscure the real issues relevant to an appreciation of his poetry by asserting that he does not strive toward meaning in his poetry, in the acceptable sense of the word. He has described himself to me as a "composer of sounds," and has maintained in an interview at the Transcription Centre that

because what we call understanding—talking generally of the relationship between the poetry—reader and the poem itself—passed through a process of analysis, if you like; there is an intellectual effort which one makes before one arrives at what one calls the meaning. Now, I think it is possible to arrive at a response without passing through that process of intellectual analysis, and I think that if the poem can elicit a response in either physical or emotional terms from an audience, the poem has succeeded. I don't *think that I have ever set out to communicate a meaning.* It is enough that I try to communicate experiences which I consider significant.

Yet there is meaning in Okigbo's poetry even though it might be obscured by his anxious desire to pun or to exploit the more obvious devices of language for its tonal rather than its semantic effects. From this viewpoint "Distances" is the most pretentious and the least successful of his poems. Besides the emblematic writing (which not only is out of place here but also does not succeed) there is a tendency to write nonsense; only sometimes is this redeemed by lines of beauty and meaning. "Distances" centers on the ritual of preparation and is couched in the sensuous imagery of a love poem.

Okigbo's two recent poems "Lament of the Drums" and "Dance of the Painted Maidens" are both concerned with redemption and sound, but do not sacrifice sense. His "Lament of the Drums" is the second part of "Silences," and the techinque in both is the same: a basic image, or a basic set, is built up into a hierarchy of images. Here the images emphasize a certain loss: "Where shall we go / The robbers have taken all our members . . ." (p. 16). "Dance of the Painted Maidens," on the other hand, attempts to reintroduce the theme of hope:

> For YOU return to us
> From a forgotten farewell
> From the settled abyss
> Where the twilights cross . . . (p. 64)

As yet the protagonist in Okigbo's poetry has not come to a full understanding of all that life is; it is as if Okigbo feels that his protagonist must endlessly strive toward an elusive something which is afterlife and art and heaven and ideals, and which he can never really grasp. All Okigbo's poems enact the drama of the realization that this quest for fulfillment is necessary. His final "Poems Prophesying War" showed that fulfillment was still not attained.

MICHAEL ECHERUO AND POL NDU: SEARCH

The same ritualistic quest is observed in the poetry of Michael Echeruo and Pol Ndu. Both dramatize the inner predicament of the protagonist, torn between a ritual to which he must conform and the glimmer of an ideal toward which he aspires. Their poetry, unlike Okigbo's, is more concerned with involving the reader in that the protagonist frequently becomes identifiable with the poet, and the observer with the reader. It is tempting to say that these poets derive some of their competence from Okigbo, but it is possible that the similar cultural environment (they are all eastern Nigerians) has fed the roots of their work. An important difference is that Echeruo's verse possesses a certain cryptic and oracular quality that Okigbo's lacks: "Go seek the vices now / Of the world that bore you,"[54] and in Ndu one finds a prosaic identification with the everyday world:

> I may get home again
> this or some other day
> because I know
> my way home.[55]

This marks an important distinction between these poets and Okigbo; whereas their work portrays the real world of man and his everyday experiences, Okigbo's centers on the spiritual nature of existence. But the device of exploiting words for their tonal possibilities is often the same; Echeruo and Ndu, however, are concerned more with immediate meaning, Okigbo more with postponed effect.

OKOGBULE GLORY NWANODI (NOW OKOGBULE WANODI): THE OLD MAN AND LIFE

In Wanodi's poems he often assumes the posture of an old pagan who is against the new standards upheld by the younger generation. He is not the divided man, but one who believes in the values of his old culture even though he realizes that both this and the new way of life are, in the words of Bona Onyejeli, "involved in inevitable collapse." His viewpoint is not, however, without hope, for the end is not death but rather "a new birth springing from death."[56]

"Icheke," in his book of poems of the same name published in 1964,[57] attempts to show the confrontation that has taken place in Africa between

> Aka, that heard the cocks at dawn
> when the old drink the remains of dusk . . .
> he swore,
> refusing to sleep,
> hands on hoe . . . (p. 25)

and the new materialistic, artificial generation in whom has entered an amalgam of cheap cultural influences. With this generation the poet identifies. his protagonist:

> We pulled our English shirts
> peeled off our Italian sandals;

> our American hats we laid on the trunks
> letting our bodies bare to the sun
> While our sausages in a can
> stayed in a French bag
> as the German record player
> whisped [*sic*] a Spanish sentimental. (p. 26)

The itemizing is not successful poetry, but it makes the point; whereas Aka guards the traditional truths, the young are involved in a cheap travesty of culture. The young, however, do not remain apart from the indigenous truth that Aka stands for. In "Icheke" the truth they seek to elude finally dawns on them:

> A tune arose—
> that we have not left our fathers,
> we, that bend and write
> sow and care like others. (p. 26)

Wanodi is suggesting that all types of human activity are justifiable, that nothing can be entirely discarded, and in a final synthesis the leftovers of a hybrid European culture merge with a full African inheritance to introduce a new and significant whole. Peasant and writer are one.

Other poems in *Icheke* (the term means "parrot" and comes to stand for "wise old man" as well as "poet") and elsewhere develop these themes. In particular, "Verses for the Harvest" in *Icheke* treats the idea of the aloneness of the younger generation. Some of the lines distinctly remind one of the Ghanaian poet Kofi Awoonor, who poses a similar predicament. Wanodi pictures his protagonist in the poem "Intimacy" as "lost in a search for something / something that does not exist" (p. 6). Similarly "Echoes of the Gone" carries forward the theme of how the past is buried but cannot die, of how "the man shall grow to god." Because, ultimately, Wanodi's hope is bound up with the stature of man, he is forced to view man as capable of becoming God if he is to visualize any true salvation. His long poem "Verses for the Harvest," part of which was published in *Black Orpheus*,[58] again dramatizes the opposition between Aka and the protagonist. Here the singular "I" is used: the protagonist is very alone and waiting for Aka, but the conclusion is not that of "Icheke." The poet now is humbler and seeks to become part of that old world he has always intrinsically known.

> No father.
> I am yet your harp;
> tune me but gingerly
> and my strings will echo
> songs of my inside.

279

> I am your right hand,
> I will mend your barn
> and girdle my breath
> for after this harvest
> there's the visit
> adults orphans will call
> from windowless houses;
> then will come the test
> of my planting songs. (p. 30)

When Wanodi is not working out these ideas in his poetry, he tends to write lines of the most appalling banality. In the first section of "New Days" in *Icheke*, he describes activity as "bustle, scruffle and ruffles" (p. 10). And some of the more pastoral pieces are his worst efforts; "Enugu to Millike Hill," for example, opens with the meaningless lines:

> Down
> crispstars stare
> criss-cross. (p. 15)

At times, like Okigbo, he seems to be more in love with the sound than the sense of words, and at other times the expression of these illustrative pieces is rather whimsical:

> Me,
> a prisoner of august fancies
> fancies shrubs that grew
> on clay . . . (p. 23)

When Wanodi's poetry lacks a tough undergrowth of thought, it tends to sprout fastidious over-refinements. Lewis Nkosi's comment about Nigerian poets in general is applicable to Wanodi: "In the end, one is likely to remember how something was said rather than what was being said."[59] This is certainly true of Wanodi because he is still trying to express, through a limited control of language, a set of ideas that have become commonplace. At times the vision is refreshing, but more often than not there is a straining for effect, when the words are stretched too tight to carry any meaning.

GEORGE AWOONOR-WILLIAMS (NOW KOFI AWOONOR): TRADITION AND THE POET

Like Wanodi, Kofi Awoonor attempts to describe the plight of the younger generation who have been educated away from the norms of their fathers. But his poetry is a conscious effort to use imagery from the oral vernacular poetry to give added effect to this feeling of loss. At the Freetown Conference in April 1963 Kofi Awoonor suggested that "there is a wealth of material of tremendous degree of coherence, depth and interest in traditional practice possessing its own linguistic strength which will be of immense interest to the student of African Literature."[60] It is this very tradition that he turns to in his poetry and at times some of his verse, like Okigbo's, is almost a line-for-line translation of his own local oral material. His "Songs of Sorrow," which depicts the protagonist's spiritual dichotomy, owes much to a religious song collected by J. H. Kwabena Nketia. In Awoonor's poem, the protagonist's quandary is described, and the vague allusions to "somewhere," "something," and "someone" express his inability to identify the cause of his loss. In the Akan song, the singer bewails the loss of a chief whereas in Awoonor's poem, the loss is not as immediate; the loss of the chief has become the loss of an inheritance:

> Something has happened to me
> The things so great that I cannot weep
> I have no sons to fire the gun when I die
> And no daughters to wail when I close my mouth.[61]

The boys who possess the paraphernalia of European culture in Wanodi's poem have removed themselves from the old man's jurisdiction. Unlike the dramatic course that Wanodi charts, Awoonor's way reveals that the return is not easy. Even the accustomed props depicted in another traditional song are no longer available, "and the tree on which I lean is fallen."[62] When seen against the traditional background, the poetry of Awoonor takes on additional pathos.

His technique of enlarging ideas by repetition is evident in other poems in his *Rediscovery* (1964), and it reinforces the sense of a lost heritage. It is quite wrong for Anne Tibble to suggest that "his wholly African culture spares him the most acute sense of alienation." On the contrary, he bemoans the fragmentary nature of his African culture and, as Eldred Jones has written, "the technique of emphasis through accumulation is particularly suitable to portraying the almost physical weight of loneliness."[63] Often it is stated in bare, pathetic terms:

> I have seen the green cool, sea
> And I plunged into it
> Only to bash my head against the old jetty.[64]

And in "I Have Heard a Bird Cry," published in *Présence Africaine* no. 57, he speaks of how

> The winds of the storm have blown,
> Destroying my hut

Goats came and did a war dance
On the fallen walls of my father's hut. (p. 303)

In the loneliness experienced after the divorce from tribe, even the art of the poem has ceased to matter; "our songs are dead and we sell them dead to the other side." The god of songs is ill and the fetish priest cannot cure him for "I had violated my god." In both form and content Awoonor attempts to remain close to the culture within him which he is always trying to rediscover. He once remarked that if the poet "shifts away from the informing sources of his own experience, he will write nonsense."[65] Awoonor's poetry persists in being firmly concentrated on the quest for a culture which, paradoxically, is in the work itself.

The note of despair sounded in his poetry is sometimes intensified by appropriate biblical references or a direct prayerlike appeal to God. This latter quality, as well as the high-pitched hysteria in some of the poems, is strongly reminiscent of Frank Parkes. But Awoonor, unlike Parkes, is a poet first and a propagandist second. Therefore, although there are lines like "Christ is risen" and "not beyond oh Lord," and although, in one case, there is an intentional misquotation from Eliot—"in our beginnings lies our journey's end"—he is unlike both Parkes and Okigbo. Awoonor has a distant voice; its sad lyricism is a suitable medium for the frozen attitudes of his protagonist, out of whose adversities the art of the poet has emanated.

WOLE SOYINKA: SATIRE AND THE SUPERNATURAL

Wole Soyinka's poetry, some of which is collected in *Idanre* (1967), marks a progression of intellectual growth—from the alienated individual who satirizes society to the protagonist who has attained a new understanding of what his culture means. His verse does not dramatize the separation depicted in the work of Awoonor; it is as if Soyinka had already overcome the struggle and the doubt, and is now able to crystallize the whole experience. However, again the poet is very much at the center, and thus the poem unfolds as a personal drama.

Private experience, not ritual or cultural conflict, is the keynote to Soyinka's poetry. At times he merely organizes these experiences and gives them artistic finish. For instance, the satirical "Telephone Conversation"[66] portrays a young Black man telephoning a white landlady about lodgings. She is made to look a bit absurd when she insists on knowing just how black he is. Soyinka's ability is as evident here as is his concern with minutiae; he describes in detail the telephone box, the

282

street outside, and what the woman looks like when she speaks. All is conveyed in a clipped, staccato style:

> Voice, when it came
> Lipstick coated, long gold-rolled
> Cigarette-holder pipped. Caught I was, foully.
> "HOW DARK?". . . I had not misheard . . ."ARE YOU
> LIGHT OR VERY DARK?" Button B. Button A. . . . (p. 111)

The nervous sentences reveal the tenseness of the situation as well as pinpoint the feel of the action.

Two other poems of his early period, "The Immigrant" and "And the Other Immigrant,"[67] are pictures of a Black worker and a student in Britain. Although the satirical tone of the first mocks in part the prostitute who refuses to give herself to the Black laborer, on the whole it sounds more like the introspective poems that Soyinka was to write later. But the mature touch is lacking, and Soyinka is capable only of sentimentality when he describes the frustrated workman:

> The fingers shift
> From blood
> To feel the folded
> Shrewish savings of his menial post.
> His little brain seeks
> Factual negation of her estimate . . .

"And the Other Immigrant" is more successful, for it takes an acid look at the self-assured Black student in England. The opening lines set the tone:

> My dignity is sewn
> Into the lining of a three-piece suit.
> Stiff, and with the whiteness which
> Out-Europes Europe . . .

The satiric jibe was to vanish from his poetry, while his plays retain an enormous sense of fun. In the poetry the dramatic element, though given a different sound, remained and still emanates directly from the person.

Beier has remarked that in his later poetry Soyinka has shown an interest in "more serious, more difficult subjects, and his language has become far richer in imagery." Olumbe Bassir has pointed out that in "Abiku" Soyinka "makes a conscious effort to sermonise to the international audience the doctrine of 'abiku' (born to die)." But what has really happened is that the poet has become more concerned with an individual view of the world, what Abiola Irele has described as

283

"an almost exclusively personal awareness of things, of events and of peoples."[68]

Soyinka's poem, "Abiku,"[69] reveals one way in which an aspect of the cultural heritage enters into African verse. In the poem, the protagonist is the child who is reborn time and again to the same mother, dying soon after each successive birth: "I am Abiku, calling for the first / And the repeated time" (p. 28). "Abiku" is very different from J. P. Clark's poem of the same name where the personal element is absent. Whereas Clark's poem reads like a footnote in an anthropological textbook, Soyinka's poem is to all *abiku* and comes to represent the inevitability of death when "Abiku moans, shaping / Mounds from yolk" (p. 30). Clark does not experience the *abiku* the way Soyinka does; although his poem is also dramatized in that the *abiku* is addressed by an irate person, too much externalized description spoils the supernatural quality of the experience.

In Soyinka all experience is precious and has the ability to alter the individual. "Death in the Dawn" and "Season" both depict the novel nature of awareness that springs from experience. In "Death in the Dawn" it is a single experience, in "Season" it is the experience of all life; in both, the experience results in a new expectancy. "Death in the Dawn" involves an intensely felt personal encounter. While traveling by car the poet/protagonist first kills a white rooster on the road. Further on he meets "another wraith"—a dead man, clothed in white *agbada*, lying on the side of the road. The counterpointing of the two incidents forcefully reveals the whole problem of permanent significance in a disintegrating world. The poem asks, "Is this mocked grimace / This closed contortion—I?" (p. 11.)

Soyinka is not yet content with the discovery of the individual self. After separating from the tribe and enduring the same anguish that Awoonor witnessed, Soyinka was ready to make his assessment. Thus there is no conflict for its own sake in Soyinka, for his poetry arises from the aftermath of the combat, not from the combat itself as in the verse of Parkes, Okigbo, and Awoonor. Matters, however, have yet to be resolved. "Season" is therefore as much a personal confession as a private manifesto of art; the poem concludes, "We await / The promise of the rust" (p. 45). The poetry, like the poet/hero, occurs at a significant moment of inertia. The action is therefore of an introspective nature, deep and profound. It focuses inward and thus never descends to the histrionic tirades of Parkes or the ritualistic gestures of Okigbo.

This is not to imply that Soyinka's poetry does not feed on traditional sources. He does use traditional material, as was seen in "Abiku" and as is most evident in his recent "Idanre." But the poet is always present, yet within the tradition, directing the experience and giving it meaningful force and lucidity. Though "Idanre" is a praise poem to Ogun, the Yoruba god of iron, it shows Soyinka's identification with the god who represents the harvest, physical birth, and spiritual rebirth. Soyinka intentionally distorts the tradition to render it significant and meaningful for him. The oneness that he achieves with the deity reflects the self-identity toward which Okigbo aspires in his verse and from which Awoonor mourns his own separation.

Soyinka is the most confident of the African poets. To him the gods are not guests, but are domesticated in a shrine that is the poet's own. He is far more sensitive to the causality of an inner hurt that has resulted from his being linked to contrary cultures, and this accounts for the quiet reflective mood of his poetry. After the public-speaking tone of some of his contemporaries, Soyinka's privacy is a fitting corrective.

J. P. Clark: Technical Ability

African poets have expressed their individual freedom partly in their attitude toward form. They have not been concerned with preconceived notions of meter or formal technique, preferring to let their form develop from the experience of the poem. Some, however, have borrowed from oral traditional verse, and Okigbo in his rituals and Awoonor in his dirges had ready-make forms into which to fit their relevant experiences. Clark is the only "versifier" in the sense that what he writes is often not poetry, and his concern with the metrical technicalities of poetry often makes his work, as Denis Williams has remarked, "forced and synthetic."[70]

At times Clark seems to use rhyme only because it is a standard poetic device. This is apparent in "Easter" (wisely omitted from his selections published in England).[71] The whole poem reads:

> So death
> being the harvest of God
> when this breath
> has blown uncertain above the sod,
> what seed, cast out in turmoil
> to sprout, shall in despair
> not beat the air
> who falls on rock swamp or the yielding soil?
>
> In thrall
> mute with the soft pad of sheet
> hung up on the wall,

> I draw in my hook-feet:
> hear the reaper's cry! the rap
> of his crook on the door—
> but the poor
> dupe! opening, shall find bats far gone with my sap. (p. 33)

Words like "sod" and "sap" are inserted for rhythmical effect, and sentences are broken up merely to allow words like "door" and "poor" to rhyme. Nor is the thought particularly original; the first stanza draws its images from the parable about the sower and his seed, and the second stanza with its private symbolism is so personal that it is bewildering. In a conversation with me, Clark revealed that "the soft pad of sheet" refers to a holy picture (he was in the hospital when he wrote the poem) and "hook-feet" means "unusual feet." The only objective image in the second stanza is the one relating to bats; in the mythology of some Nigerian groups (including Clark's own, the Ijaws) bats are thought to be the reincarnation of witches. The point is that the protagonist has cheated death by being removed by supernatural forces.

Clark's purely descriptive poems sometimes succeed even though they are written in a fragmentary fashion. Others utilize folk belief which he attempts to work imaginatively into a significant whole. "Fulani Cattle," "Night Rain," "Agbor Dancer," and the short poem "Ibadan" are his best descriptive poems. Clark gives accurate and personal observations in these poems, but nevertheless his reflections tend to be sententious. So after portraying Fulani cattle "undulating along in agony," the poet asks,

> But will you not first vouchsafe to me,
> As true the long knife must prevail,
> the patience of even your tail?[72]

The end of "Night Rain" is like an anthem; after describing the rain falling, Clark writes that the children can now "settle to sleep of the innocent and free" (p. 11). At the end of "Agbor Dancer," the poet says that he wants to lose himself "in her warm caress / Intervolving earth, sky and flesh." Only in "Ibadan," an intensely visual poem and the most successful of these pieces, is the sentimental attachment lacking. Clark fails in these descriptive poems because, after juxtaposing a number of images, he is not content to leave the final assembling untouched in the reader's mind. The weakness of these poems is that he intrudes either by extracting some general point or by involving himself in an issue that up until then had not been paramount. The end of "Night Rain" is such an example.

286

Poems like "Abiku," "The Imprisonment of Obatala," and "Olokun" directly use local traditional beliefs. In "Abiku" not only does Clark describe the meaning of an *abiku*, the child-born-to-die, but he incorporates literal translations of Yoruba names that are given to *abiku* children: for instance "Malomo," which means "step in and stay," and "Arcad'Ojo," which means "her body is tired," are references to the child and its mother. It is with these words that Clark's "Abiku" ends:

> Then step in, step in and stay
> For her body is tired,
> Tired, her milk going sour
> Where many more mouths gladden the heart. (p. 5)

Though not original this is clever and much more effective than anything attempted in the descriptive poems.

"The Imprisonment of Obatala," "Olumo Rock," and "Olokun," on the other hand, seek to escape from legend and exemplify how African poets intentionally misuse legend. "The Imprisonment of Obatala" is based on a *batik* in which an Austrian artist, Susanne Wenger, represents the legend of the omnipotent Yoruba god Obatala, who, after being tricked, is imprisoned as a vagrant. The poem is less concerned with the legend than with the *batik*, which Clark reproduces in words. "Olumo Rock" and "Olokun" derive from traditional belief but discard this to present the individual; the first, while mentioning a sacred rock in Abeokuta, Nigeria, is actually a vehicle by which the poet works out his unfulfilled relationship with his mother. "Olokun," though indirectly dealing with the deity of the sea, is really about a flirtatious girl. The two themes combine in fine association at the end:

> And as the good maid of the sea,
> Full of rich bounties for men,
> You lift us all beggars, to your breast. (p. 18)

In many of his poems Clark is concerned with doom, the tragedy imposed by history. Some, like "To a Learned Lady" and "The Water Maid," are erotic pieces, while still others, like "Agbor Dancer," "Girl Bathing," and the long poem "Ivbie," are in a négritude vein. A common reservoir of imagery supplies all these poems and a tough rhythm makes them distinctive. The frequent use of sea imagery is most effective, suggesting both cleansing and destruction.

Very different in feeling and content from any other poem is "Ivbie," which is found in Clark's first volume entitled *Poems*. According to Clark, it enacts "the historical life of the Negro race." Its ambitions are not that comprehensive, however, for in actual fact the poem is an attack on the colonizer and the colonial. It is not really a successful work, since it is content with being a mere "cry of agony," which is what the title means.

The first section bemoans the colonial's ignorance of his African past. The poet resorts to exhortation:

> Dig well below wild open steads
> Dig well below dry riverbeds
> The ivory bust
> 　　　　The terra cotta
> In the shadow of all trees
> Lie holy-unravelled dust
> Seek out the shrines of Ifa
> For wood carvings done in blood . . . (p. 45)

The second part describes the coming of the imperialists; perhaps here the style is more convincing, though at times it is obscure. Clark satirizes Mrs. Camp who "followed her man into the wild" and "delivered amid cries in the mission ward / A wisdom-teethed child" (p. 46). The child will of course carry on the traditions of the rulers, and in the next section the smallmindedness of the world the imperialists seek to preserve is hinted at:

> And Austin Herefords go toot
> Tooting in mad rush for loot
> Go hooting. (p. 47)

This time the rhyme is appropriate; the very fact that it is forced and artificial emphasizes the ludicrous picture of the imperialist enriching himself.

The next three sections do not advance the poem; they are of a reflective nature and are supposed to be a warning against the imperialist. The lines vary from absurdities like "Fear him children O fear the stranger / That comes upon you" (p. 51), to sentiments that melodramatically express the poet's personal plight, which colonialism is said to have caused. The protagonist is "a toy twirled on by complexity," and his self-pity descends to a mawkish level when the imperialist is asked to "Leave behind unhaunted / An innocent in sleep of the ages" (p. 51).

Although the poem is too obviously a sermon on anti-colonialism (with Clark merely repeating outdated charges), the two conflicting images of the imperialist riding in a motor-powered vehicle and the protagonist reared on "a cow-dung floor" are startling and correct. They emphasize the disparity between ruler and ruled, a disparity that is difficult to bridge, as Clark insinuates.

Beier maintains that "there is always immediacy, urgency and spontaneity" in Clark's work, but often these qualities give the impression of hastily devised notions, easily executed rhymes, and the use of commonplace ideas from the stock philosophy of the dedicated African versifier. Nevertheless, the way in which Clark can be very close to his subject shows not so much that he is a reflective poet, but one who observes what is near to him and reproduces it accurately. He is very much a poet of the active present, involved in what is near, and to him tradition is only real in a personal and contemporary situation. Because he is so contemporary, so obsessed with "now," his poems that revert to the négritude model seem incongruous. Abiola Irele has said that Clark, Okigbo, and Awoonor are separated from the older generation of dedicated poets concerned with race not only by language, "but by the years in which an acceptance of African values gradually became a matter of course." Similarly, I. Neustadt commented in 1960 that "not so long ago, African writers, especially poets found some of their immediately relevant themes in the rejection or criticism of what were regarded as non-African cultural values and ways of life. As a correlative of these attitudes, the African poet might glorify his own traditional institutions, or an idealized past."[73] Neustadt was referring to the generation of poets who preceded Clark. When Clark writes in their manner, he is simply adopting their attitudes and responses toward issues that had long ceased to be important.

Clark's more recent poems expand his world, but not his technique. Many of these are included in his travel book *America, Their America* (1964) where he attacks much that he finds abominable in the American way of life. Some of them seem to have originated in much the same way as "I Woke to the Touch" which, in Clark's words, owes its genesis to the following experience: "And when sleep came at last, it turned out to be one nightmare featuring my brother and James Meredith all mixed up in one terrible role and struggle for identity and survival, a nightmare short but self-repeating and more live than anything I remember on screen or stage. So that all I did on waking up shaky from bed was put the seal of my hand on the brand new piece that had forged itself in the automatic boiler of my subconscious even while I slept" (pp. 62–63). The result was, not unnaturally, a piece of doggerel. The urgency of composition is apparent, for the poem, reprinted in his second book of poems, *A Reed in the Tide* (1965), never moves away from a private level, and its archaic and slightly histrionic quality is as bad as the hastily constructed similes. Clark writes of how he dreamed of a snake and

> My brother in India, up, stick
> In hand, poised to strike—
> But ah, himself is struck
> By this serpent, so swift,
> So silent, with more reaction
> Than a nuclear charge. (p. 31)

No one can pretend that this is poetry. The rough, uneven language is the result not of forced rhymes, as in the earlier poems, but probably of a hastiness with language and a genuine ignorance of what constitutes a poem.

"Boeing Crossing," "Three Moods from Princeton," "Home from Hiroshima," "Service," "Two Views of Marilyn Monroe," "Times Square," "Cave Call," and "The Leader," all published in *A Reed in the Tide*, speak of America. Clark's closeness to his subject, his active presence, does not operate to his advantage in these poems. One gets the impression of the poet fervently penning lines without allowing his experiences to take root. "Boeing Crossing" describes his flight across the Atlantic; "Three Moods from Princeton" uses natural imagery of tree and snow to convey the poet's revulsion against America; "Cuba Confrontation" and "Home from Hiroshima" are direct attacks on American foreign policy; the remaining poems in the volume deal with various aspects of American life. They all appear to have been written in a hurry. Clark seems to feel that because he is discovering something for the first time then it must be so for all his readers. However, on occasions he is capable of the tender moments of his earlier verse, and in "Times Square" he writes of how

> Two figures,
> Fugitive from light, go kicking
> Their shadows down steps belching up
> The corner . . . (p. 35)

And in "The Leader" he uses the vocabulary of the praise poem:

> Who announced home from abroad
> Wrestled to a standstill his champion
> Cousin the Killer of Cows. (p. 37)

Each poem of Clark's is self-contained. He does not, like Okigbo, make each poem represent a certain stage of an experience. Ezekiel Mphahlele, writing about Clark's "Night Rain," commented quite rightly that "the emotion is compact." But this is not true of all his poetry, and it is the diffuseness that accounts for the sermonizing in the later poetry and the attitudinizing in the earlier pieces. Clark attacked the poetry of the first generation of West African versifiers in his article "Poetry in Africa Today." Though he excluded himself when he wrote of their successors who had a "ready stock of vocabulary, phrases and sentiment,"[74] nevertheless it is this very dependence on an effete tradition that spoils his verse.

LENRIE PETERS:
AFRICAN IMAGINATION IN THE EUROPEAN WORLD

Lenrie Peters came to maturity as a poet while he was living in Europe. His poetry is therefore fed by his European experiences. Although some of his poems could have been written by an English poet, certain qualities of his verse and the selective nature of his experiences identify him as an African poet.

Melvin B. Tolson has remarked that "Peters is good at vignettes,"[75] but this is an understatement. His poems reveal a wide range of interests, and each is complete in itself, as is true of Clark. Unlike Clark, however, Peters allows his poems to live through their own experience— there is no interference by an inquisitive inventor. There is the sound of the sermonizer like Clark or, what's more, like Parkes, but at times it is muffled.

Often there is the slightest hint that Peters is thinking of a racial situation: in the poem beginning "They have stood waiting" people trapped on a hill hope to be rescued. The poem could well exist on this level alone were it not for the stanza which pitilessly states,

> But for those who are waiting
> Who have to wait
> Those who are born to wait
> Time is like the smoke
> Which smarts the eyes
> Brings out the tears . . .[76]

At times the voice of the preacher is more evident:

> We have come home . . .
> Supporting the tortured remnants of the flesh
> The spirit which asks no favour of the world
> But to have dignity. (p. 9)

And in another poem the call is equally as persistent:

> Tell those who came
> To ravage: of a new world

291

Harmony with nature
And strength in goodwill. (p. 5)

Peters is very much the individual found in African poetry. He seeks to preserve the purity of his self, apart from "people, Cannibals, ghosts, women" (p. 25), to attain this sublime goal:

the crystal spring
Where I have found
The purest living thing. (p. 11)

This has led him, rather like Awoonor, to decry his aloneness, as he does in a poem where he equates himself with a man in a parachute "holding an open umbrella / In a windy place" (p. 6). But this is not a separation caused by any fondness for dramatizing the familiar agonies of the man torn by conflicting cultures; it is more universal and is the same as that of the old women

Picking each final step
In which they see
Their death fall
Certain as the leaves. (p. 13)

Peters has a wider range of ideas than any other African poet thus far considered because his exposure to the claims of metropolitan culture awakened his sensibility to new pressures. He suffers from some of the sicknesses of twentieth-century Europe—a too great obsession with "naked breasts," "affectionate thighs / Sweating," and at times a morbid desire to pontificate on the basis of these experiences. So a prostitute in Hyde Park is "prostituted fruit of Eve / Edging the Park trees" (p. 26), and a description of fog introduces "rancid old women [who] / Cough their Haemorrhoids out" (p. 37). His professional interests as a doctor are probably responsible for this ugly image which harms the poem, and these interests most certainly contribute to the grotesque picture of petals "neatly curled / like the foetal head" (p. 22). Nevertheless these images prevent his poetry from becoming overly sweet like his frequent nostalgic glances at an over-romanticized Africa.[77] By injecting a feeling of toughness into the poetry, these images help his verse to retain a distinctly masculine tone.

CHINUA ACHEBE: NOVELIST TURNED POET

Because African oral literature is a combination of the "spoken" and the "sung," not infrequently there is a mixture of "poetry" and "prose" in what is written. Achebe has made use of the oral tradition, with varying degrees of success. After the Biafran War, Achebe, one of the more exciting novelists in Africa, published *Beware Soul Brother and Other Poems* (1971), his first volume of poetry. This appeared in the United States as *Christmas in Biafra*. Its twenty-three poems describe the horrors of war and reveal the author's political commitments. Thus the irony of "he loves me: he loves me not" shows the apathy of the big powers as Africa fights its wars, and in "Vultures" he attacks the fence-sitters: "Hurrah! to them who do nothing / see nothing feel nothing . . ." Obviously, the poetry is harsh. Achebe knew firsthand the tragedies of wartime Biafra and the poetry describes the hunger, the treachery, the privation. But one must conclude that even if one's sympathies lay with Achebe, the poetry is too raw to succeed. Whereas his novels re-enact the historical drama of Europe's meeting with Africa, his poems simply narrate attitudes and feelings. In the final analysis, Achebe has to be seen as a great novelist and a bad poet.

KWESI BREW: MOCK PRAISE POEM

Kwesi Brew's voice is a very traditional one. He shares the beliefs of his people and centers his poetry on them; he acknowledges the stereotype of the good mother and the masquerader's license to attack those detrimental to the group. When he departs from traditional genres (the praise song, masquerade verse), his poetry becomes overly sweet, complete with "tortured men," "white lilies," and "moon-steeped ponds." But a poem such as "The Dirge" shows exquisite control, which results from his use of Fanti proverbs and beliefs as well as his excellent command of language:

> I was talking to a girl at the well
> When they came to tell me
> The sun has fallen
> On the leaves . . .[78]

His "love poetry" is repetitive and boring; clumsy images like that in "The Two Finds" where he "pursued her through the forest / And along the lonely paths of my heart" abound. The much-anthologized poem entitled "The Woods Decay" is equally clumsy and sentimental. But when his observations of nature are not associated with private feelings of love, they do succeed. The best examples of this are "The Dry Season," "Vulture," "Locusts," and especially "The Sea Eats Our Lands."

Often, as in "Through the Forest" and "A Plea for Mercy," Brew comes close to describing the magic that is Africa. Lines such as these convey his meaning:

> Someone called,
> I said I could not walk!
>
> He called again
> And god of my fathers,
> I walked. (p. 54)

As do these from "The Heart's Anchor": "But the peace you promised me stays / In your heart—beyond my reach" (p. 56).

Kwesi Brew seldom deals with politics, though "A Sandal on the Head" is a mock praise poem to Nkrumah. The poem works through allusions to reveal vivid aphorisms and the nature of such customs as touching a deposed chief's head with sandals. All in all, the main strength of Brew's verse lies in his dependence on tradition and what he makes of it. For instance when he uses symbolically the theme of the lost woman, it acquires richer nuances of meaning and he then becomes a traditional poet who speaks for a lost past which he venerates and for a present of which he is uncertain.

ALBERT KAYPER-MENSAH: LIGHT AND DARK

In *The Dark Wanderer* (1970) Kayper-Mensah writes of Africa in the manner of a British expatriate. Cambridge is very present in such poems as "A Second Birthday" and "Purged of Failures." But as can be seen in "The Ghosts"[79] he is a poet of ecstasy and vision. On the surface it recounts a meeting between two ghosts, yet its real purpose is to describe the excesses of a time when Ghana seemed divided. A successful poem, "The Ghosts" has a lyrical smoothness which moves from reality to unreality and back again. Images of light, darkness, and pregnancy suggest that a new world is being born:

> Some of what we left must die
> But love and keep alive the best
> And let the common love
> Make you friends . . .

As a poet of vision he is always conscious of paradox. This is well exemplified in "The Place Is Here" (in manuscript):

> The place of struggle
> And the place of fire
> Share one divinity . . .

294

And in "Our Heirs" (in manuscript):

> But when we look beneath
> The dreamy threat or the binding light,
> We see we move among friends and heirs:
> Trees with seeds to grow
> On our graves . . .

The paradoxes make for a curious visual quality in his verse.

When Kayper-Mensah writes about Africa, especially national feeling, he fails. Parts of "The Ghosts" suffer as a result, as does "Nation Feeling," whose prosaic quality does a disservice to the verse. Phrases like "nation feeling" and "our present struggle for prosperity" as well as the injunction to Ghanaians to be "originals / Not faded carbon copies . . ." are unfortunate, for they belong to the public podium.

Kayper-Mensah's favorite images of day and night, light and dark, life and death indicate the large concerns in his poetry. When he reverts to mere nature descriptions as in "November up the Venusberg" or "Beyond the Senses," the reader is aware of the poems' visual effects, but little else is communicated. Nor do such phrases as "Niggers—Made in Whiteman's Land" communicate much. Kayper-Mensah has witnessed vast changes in the social structure of his country and in poetic styles. One feels that at times he cannot make up his mind what his true role is—attacker or defender of white values. One suspects that this poet, with his excellent ability to evoke the visual, stands somewhere in between.

JOHN OKAI: SEXUAL LOVE

The Ghanaian John Okai received a master's degree in literature from the Gorky Literary Institute in Moscow. After spending six years in Russia, he returned to Ghana for a year, but on being awarded a scholarship by the University of Ghana, he went to the School of Slavonic and East European Studies, University of London, to prepare a dissertation on Dostoevsky. Although his poetry has appeared in journals, *Flowerfall* (1969)[80] is his first published volume. His verse shows evidences of this varied background.

Okai's poetry charts the emergence of the individual voice. Okai is not bound in a traditional straitjacket and his images (at times clumsy) are drawn from both African and European sources. If one considers the five sections of *Flowerfall* to be musical evocations, as the titles suggest, then one would have to conclude that they fail. But if one forgets the attempt to fit African forms into a European mold and regards this as African poetry, then it can be said that some do succeed.

For instance, lines linking "the blood of the ancestors" with "the breath of children / Tomorrow to be born" reveal a plodding repetitive rhythm and an instinctive interest in an African concept of "force":

> Why not leave me to live,
> While yet I breathe,
> Like the others around.

But philosophical concepts alone do not make for successful poetry, and some of Okai's verse is spoiled by his rash insistence on juggling with the superficial aspects of style; he is fond of pun, alliteration, and bad wordplay, e.g., "the widow whose window . . .," "morning" and "mourning," "towers" and "tutters." However, some of these obvious devices do work especially when the sex act and conception are described in emblematic style.

God, the destroyer, and sex, the creator, are always present in Okai's verse. His images frequently unite both:

> God is an artist . . .
> Call forth my river, draw
> Out that river flowing in the
> Roots
>
> Of my being—a river longer
> Than your hair, fuller than
> Your
>
> Breasts, warmer than your
> Flesh . . .

The stanza breaks and the special arrangement of words help to emphasize certain words. The reader is not sure of the relation between "river" and "roots" until "breasts" is thrust suddenly into the sentence.

The physical pleasure of sexual love has been, to a great extent, ignored by many African writers. Okai's images of sexual pleasure associated with those relating to water and his keen landscape observations make him an interesting poet. His sexual imagery conveys a passion for *all* experience. Although he does tax the language, sometimes he does succeed in teasing new meanings out of English. On the whole his poetry is a fine exercise in the balance of sound and vision.

East Africa

JOSEPH BURUGA: DRAMATIC MONOLOGUE

Buruga's book of verse, *The Abandoned Hut* (1969), uses the dramatic monologue to attack the Africanized conception of western values. His work reminds one of the poetry of Okot p'Bitek and Oculi. The long poem which constitutes the volume comes out strongly on the side of tradition. The girl to whom it is addressed falls prey to the lures of western pseudo-sophistication and neglects her traditional role in life. Since the poet is the would-be lover, his verse to her is in the genre of the mock praise poem. The poet/lover compares Basia's present attitudes with her ideal role in traditional society; he also intrudes and gives his own views (at times boring) of the traditional past. Obviously the poem is intended to be like Okot p'Bitek's *Song of Lawino* but it does not quite succeed because it lacks p'Bitek's humor in parts.

Use is made of folk-elements; there are references to folktales and proverbs as well as to the dirges that evoke the orphan (here compared with the lover). But the style is best when the poet openly chides Basia:

> You want us
> To go to houses
> You call Cinema Halls
> Houses which are always dark,
> Dark even during the day . . . (p. 17)

He is even amusing when he describes western dancing (as opposed to African communal dancing) where

> The dancers are all alone
> Dancing silently
> As if they have been visited
> By the spirits . . . (p. 23)

Basia's customs—her shoes, her "legs in bags" (stockings)—and her refusal to live like a traditional wife give the protagonist the opportunity to point out the absurdities of the transition from the African to the western way of life. His wit is best when he describes in apparently simple terms some common object; for example telephones are "the wires that carry / Voices from one place to another" and cars are "the houses / That move on four legs." Careful reading also reveals the use of roundabout allusions—the descriptions of men climbing the path has sexual connotations, and Basia is constantly condemned, frequently by the voice of a bishop, for being promiscuous.

Buruga's way of expressing his love for Basia is very trite. His best

297

devices are satire, injected suddenly into the verse, and his seemingly naive descriptions to make some derogatory remark:

> She complains
> That my visitors
> Do not make Appointments . . . (p. 80)

One does not necessarily sympathize with the protagonist, for this is a slight piece with only occasional touches of irony.

TABAN LO LIYONG: AFRICA AND BLACK AMERICA

Franz Fanon's Uneven Ribs (1971) is a collection of Taban lo Liyong's poetry. Some of the poems are bitter vignettes, sketched with economy and bite, while others show signs of humor. His topic can be anything that his eye and mind happen on—a battered bicycle, a dead father, right and wrong, reminiscences.

His style attempts to use the repetitive devices of oral poetry but he is no mere translator. He admits, "I have strived to say the things that are new / But the things that are new take long to understand" (p. 22). His laughter at times is directed at the poet himself.

> *I say*
> *This has been said before*
>
> So what
> It is new to me. (p. 30)

Indeed this makes him a kind of poet's poet, for as he writes he manufactures his own rules, he tells the reader how he creates and about the subjects that interest him.

In his serious moments he reflects on the experience (his experience) of being Black in a white country. "Uncle Tom's Black Humour" is a skit on the alleged racial prowess of the Black man, in which the dialect switches from straight English to a supposedly "darkie" speech: "Aunt Jemima she done teach young master how to be / man yes sir she done it yes maam he gone done it" (p. 70). In "Telephone Conversation Number Two" he takes up where Soyinka left off in his encounter with a white woman two decades before. But here the white woman is not the magisterial landlady; she is a whore who settles for the cook.

At times, as in "Un Chef's Choice," he is not subtle and the poem does not succeed until he makes this gentle aside:

> 'Tis taboo to talk of African Americans
> Even Black Muslins bypass Africa
> To Arabia they look for salvation . . . (p. 87)

The long poem "The Marriage of Black and White" tries to be both a love poem and a joke on traditional marriages in the style of Okot p'Bitek, but since we never *know* the girl in the poem it remains a one-sided debate.

The last two poems in the volume, "Student's Lament" and "The Dirge Our Moms Are Singing," show occasional flashes of wit but, as Taban lo Liyong has pointed out, the function of the poet is not to be a "jester." Therefore whether his topic is love, sex, religion, racism, politics, or society he is never just a humorist. His line arrangement, punctuation, use of capitals are the outer manifestations of the poetry which he considers to be a science. Taban lo Liyong applies this science very well in both his prose and his poetry.

OKELLO OCULI: THE AFRICAN AS ORPHAN

Oculi's *Orphan* (1968) is a dramatic tale centered on the orphan who symbolizes the child without kin in African folklore and also Africa without knowledge of its heritage. Throughout the poem he sits at the crossing of village paths and is the object of comment by those who pass by—his sister, the village elders, various gossips, members of the village, and distant relatives. Each comment confirms his isolation.

The poem then discusses the absence of kinship through the voice of the uncle:

> The empty silence in the home
> And the dead bones . . .
> All is dying and shallow . . . (p. 20)

A woman who has married into the orphan's clan maintains that he will grow up to be an exploiter of ordinary people. In the interests of "research" he will "capture our shadows / In machines for money," that is, he will take photographs of village people with no regard for their privacy.

Orphan is intended as an attack on western values. The orphan criticizes modern women as typified by his own mother who heeds "the bewitching flames in the west." But several people express hope; a village elder advises the orphan not to "crumble and die on self-pity" but to "rise and face isolation's challenge." This is a way of saying that as a detribalized man he must face the consequences of being sequestered. The orphan's friend also hopes that "the date of outburst and assertion will come."

Oculi's writing has a very visual quality to it and represents a new type of genre, being in part snatches of conversation, proverbs, comments on society, a debate, a type of poem. He has an occasional weakness for the pompous turn of phrase, but he succeeds best when, like Okot p'Bitek, he makes western institutions seem ridiculous by describing them in an apparently naive way. So women who press their hair have "toasted hair" and the camera is something that "capture(s) . . . shadows." Throughout the poem there are strong sensual observations which make use of indirect references very effectively. The orphan adequately serves as a symbol of Africa with lost traditional values.

OKOT P'BITEK: SONG OF THE OUTSIDERS

Okot p'Bitek is one of the most important writers emerging on the East African scene. His work represents almost a complete break with the traditional past, for instead of praising the group, he berates it. This is, however, only apparently so, for Okot p'Bitek is really a traditionalist and whether his poems are for or against westernization, somehow he always manages to show where his true feelings lie. This may be a dramatic fault or it may well be a result of his refusal to adopt any role other than that of a group spokesman.

His first work was the novel *Lak Tar* (1953) written in Lwo, but fame did not come until he published his *Song of Lawino*, a long dramatic poem, in 1967. The poem centers on traditional Lawino and her westernized husband, and this gives the poet an opportunity to compare the European and African ways of life. Through Lawino's eyes, western religion, politics, education, and dress are seen as absurd. She praises the Acoli way of life which is close to her own. In spite of Lawino's abuse, she still respects Ocol, and her song ends with her wish that he become more like his ancestors.

It would be tempting to say that *Song of Ocol* (1969) is her husband's rejoinder but Okot p'Bitek is too much a believer in the traditional way of life to make Ocol's attack convincing. She asserts in her song:

> He abuses all things Acoli
> He says
> The ways of black people
> Are black . . . (p. 200)

And he responds in his song:

> Africa,
> Idle giant
> Basking in the sun . . .

Diseased with a chronic illness,
Choking with black ignorance. (p. 19)

The dichotomy of views continues, but he is not the Ocol of Lawino's lament. She complains that her husband's house is "a dark forest of books," yet he cries out against the charlatans of African culture:

we'll destroy all the anthologies
of African literature
And close down
All the schools
Of African studies. (p. 30)

Despite Ocol's criticism of Africa, he does show compassion for ordinary people, for the beautiful woman with the waterpot. By the end of the poem, Ocol is preparing us for what the poet was to write next—a call for change. *Song of Ocol* is in a way a negative statement of the positive values of the traditional life.

Okot p'Bitek is at his finest in *Song of a Prisoner* (New York, 1971), which originally appeared with "Song of Malaya" in *Two Songs* (Nairobi, 1971). "Song of Malaya," a monologue by a prostitute, is a slight piece reminiscent of his earlier style. The poet uses the work to attack the would-be guardians of contemporary African morality. Lawino was comical when she denounced the insane social attitudes of her husband and his friends. She touched on the political troubles of her country when she asked what was the meaning of freedom if there were two opposing parties. *Song of a Prisoner* takes up this political motif in a grim dramatic contest. The speaker, a member of a minority party in jail for a political offense, must plead "guilty or not guilty," but one never learns what the charges are.

Unlike *Song of Lawino* and *Song of Ocol, Song of a Prisoner* has no humor. The prisoner is beaten, refused a blessing, his wife is raped, and his children cannot go to school or find employment. He is the "inarticulate" man become articulate. Hence all social mores are torn down. No longer are his own mother and father sacred, as they are in most African literature. Both are condemned for not marrying into the right group, and thus

Big chief
Is dancing [with] my wife
And cracking
My sacred rock!

Therefore the prisoner cries out,

> I plead
> Guilty
> To hatred . . .

Song of a Prisoner is a beautifully executed poem. The anger is passionate but never overdone, and the dream refrains, when the prisoner dreams of a minister's car driving through the night or thinks of himself as having ministerial power, are juxtaposed with scenes which remind him of his lack of power:

> Ring up my wife
> And tell her
> I am on *Safari*
> And will not come home
> Tonight,

> Tell her I will be back
> In two or three days . . .
> I am sure
> I will be free
> Next week . . .

Toward the end he exclaims,

> I want to dance
> And forget my smallness,
> Let me dance and forget
> For a small while
> That I am a wretch
> The reject of my Country . . .

Neither *Song of Lawino* nor *Song of Ocol* states the case as bitterly as this poem does. One might say that whereas the first two poems *mask* (and it is a comic mask) the issue of lack of power, *Song of a Prisoner* openly and forcefully reveals its reality. Recurrent images of lost virility have more impact here, for the protagonist is concerned not just with his lack of social grace but with the complete emptiness of all he professes to be. However, a common link through all these poems is Okot p'Bitek's concern beneath his comicality—his concern with the changing impact of the times and his real attempt at rectifying them. This would apply equally for some of his contemporaries and for some of the dynamic poets in South Africa.

South Africa

B. W. Vilakazi had set the precedent for protest verse in South Africa. The contemporary writers all live outside the claustrophobic conditions of racial segregation, but they draw heavily from the very experiences they no longer share. They are not dissimilar to the prose writers, but an important difference lies in the snappy, precise nature of their poetry.

DENNIS BRUTUS: LOVER AND HATER

Brutus has published three volumes of poetry in English—*Sirens, Knuckles, Boots* (1963),[81] *Letters to Martha* (1968), and *Poems from Algiers* (1970). He is president of SANROC, the committee that was instrumental in excluding South Africa from the Olympics. His collected poetry has been published in *A Simple Lust* (1973).

Although Dennis Brutus claims that he is only incidentally a poet, he once commented that "the disgust I feel for the political system [in South Africa] is mirrored in my poetry." The first volume is full of the fear that Brutus knew firsthand—"the siren in the night," "the keening crescendo of faces split by pain." But the agony, though painful, gives birth to a beautiful kind of joy in living: "Somehow we survive / and tenderness, frustrated, does not wither . . . ." This tenderness (and its voice is lyrical) accounts for the poet's lovely landscape descriptions, his nostalgia for home and friends, and the sensuousness of his love for a waiting wife. Wife and land merge in images like the following:

> and sharper than our strain, the passion
> against our land's disfigurement and tension;
> hate gouged out deeper levels for our passion—
>
> a common hate enriched our love and us.

But it is never just "love poetry," for in it there is always the high-pitched passion and fevered emotionality of sincere involvement.

Letters to Martha is concerned primarily with Brutus's experiences when he was imprisoned on Robben Island. The poems are ostensibly "letters" because he was banned from producing anything that could be published. They convey the violence as well as the yearning of the previous volume. In solitude, the poet/protagonist is near the instruments of torture but sees a strange relationship between a bullying warden's "lust for power" and "strange love," from which perhaps "human hunger" is born. The poet/protagonist reflects on religion, on the fate of his companions who die either physically or morally.

Brutus does not pretend that this is any carefully conceived philo-

303

sophical discourse. Rather it is "random pebbles . . . / from the land-scape of my own experience" (p. 10). And the poet touches on every aspect of his experience: the urge for sex, for music, the need to accept the new position of prisoner, the sudden, beautiful meaning of birds and clouds and stars.

Some of the poems do not take on their full significance until the reader becomes aware of the agony that went into their creation. This does not necessarily make them good poetry, but they do demonstrate that Brutus the man and Brutus the poet are one and the same. He is not simply writing; he is involving the reader in human suffering and forcing him to see himself as both accomplice and victim.

The social urges alter in *Poems from Algiers*, in which Brutus treats the question, Who is an African? In the first poem he reveals that he cannot identify—he is "driftwood." But later he finds solidarity with the Nigerian poets Christopher Okigbo and Wole Soyinka. Like them he prays: "Make me strong and brave / make me too the bruised and ready ripened fruit" (p. 11). These poems attempt to adopt various diffident stands and to work through to a conclusion.

Dennis Brutus's work has the quality of honesty. His poetry is decep-tively simple in its use of rhetoric and descriptive terms and its haunting laments. But over all there is a tough texture in the jagged lines that suddenly bursts into beauty and is equally capable of rendering the unseemly. The poet is at the center of the work, its recorder, and attempts to draw conclusions from the experiences he describes. But he does not preach; his work has a rare economy of diction that says just so much and no more.

KEORAPETSE KGOSITSILE: THE BLACK UNIVERSE

After leaving South Africa in 1961, Kgositsile worked for some time with *Spearhead Magazine* in Dar-es-Salaam, Tanzania, before moving to America. His poetry has appeared in *Journal of Black Poetry*, the former *Negro Digest*, and the anthology *Black Fire*. His published vol-umes include *Spirits Unchained* (1969), *For Melba* (1970), and *My Name Is Afrika* (1971).

Kgositsile is one poet who has been almost completely "assimilated" into the Black American struggle for freedom; his style has been modi-fied by such Afro-Americans as LeRoi Jones, Malcolm X, and Rap Brown. His subject matter tends to be the same throughout all his works; the Black proclamation against the Man's (the white man's) persistent desire to downgrade the Blacks. Though African, he is a very

Black American poet, for he is able to give firsthand accounts of the Pan-Africanism his American counterparts describe; a South African martyr, a dead West African poet, a Black American blues singer all merge in his poetry. Thus in *Spirits Unchained* he can castigate "All the butcher criminals who sat in judgement / Over Lumumba, Mandela, Sobukwe, Brother Malcolm . . ." (p. 8), or he can merge in one image the violence inflicted on oppressed Black people from different corners of the earth: "WATTS happening / SHARPEVILLE BURNING" (p. 12).

Kgositsile is an angry, bitter poet, siding with the lot of Black people the world over. But he has other moods. There are evidences of African oral stylistic devices in his poetry, and some poems, like "The Creator" ("let me back in the rhythm of your smile / tropical as tom-tom ecstasy"), are traditional in scope or like "Of Deaths and Lives" echo the dirge.

On the whole what emerges is a very individual voice. Kgositsile is not merely an Afro-American poet or an African poet. He fuses the two roles into one, and the two experiences are one. His work shows that he is never at loggerheads with the Black society he describes. His is the truly universal Black voice.

RAYMOND MAZISI KUNENE: AFRICAN POWER

Kunene composes his work in Zulu and then translates into English. His first collection of verse is entitled *Zulu Poems* (1970). His poetry makes use of Zulu cultural references and historical allusions. As in the oral tradition, he is the speaker for his people. One can therefore easily identify certain genres: the praise song, the dirge, the war song. His verse, especially its fierce, denunciating tone, also indicates that he was influenced somewhat by Vilakazi. "Vengeance" is but one example of his anger:

> How would it be if I came in the night
> And planted the spear in your side
> Avenging the dead;
> Those you have not known. (p. 67)

The note of protest places him in the modern Black South African tradition; the references to the ancestor make him a traditional poet.

Kunene's style is abrupt, aggressive, telegraphic. In a poem entitled "Europe" he describes the conflict between generations in Europe:

> Your children fill us with fear:
> They are like the young of a puff adder
> Who devour the flesh of their parent . . . (p. 76)

In another poem, "Thought on June 26," he mentions the "cultures" that the "great" powers represent to him and his people:

> Was I wrong to ignite the earth
> And dance above the stars
> Watching Europe burn with its civilisation of tire,
> Watching America disintegrate with its gods of steel,
> Watching the persecutors of mankind turn into dust
> Was I wrong? Was I wrong? (p. 41).

Kunene's first volume shows great talent. His "Anthem of Decades," extracted from a longer epic, displays his broad range. Here he is concerned with depicting Zulu concepts of the significance of life and the universe. Through the personification of ideas, Kunene the traditional poet attempts to dramatize the Zulu concept of the force at work in the universe. Kunene's closeness to traditional ideas and beliefs as well as his awareness of the repressive elements in modern life makes him a serious poet within the Zulu tradition of both oral and written poetry.

African poetry in English shows in its early stages a close adherence to the norms of the metropolis. But then writers begin to look more closely at their own culture and to select those parts which seem relevant. In West Africa the poet is closer to his roots and his poetry in English grows from them. East African poets, on the other hand, inherited the legacy of West African poetry in English; they transmuted this in terms of their own legacy—the folly of the African who tries to seem European. Emphases in South Africa are different and racial injustice and complaint tend to dominate, exposed as these writers are to ceaseless catalogues of hatred. In varying degrees they all belong to African culture which helps make their poetry what it is.

Chapter 12

Négritude and Black Writers

Before embarking on an account of the written literatures of Africa in Portuguese and French, we should venture some wary remarks about the nature of the task awaiting us. In the first place so much has been said about a homogeneous literature on the African continent—that is, a Black literature—that geographical definitions have often sufficed, as I demonstrated in my introduction, to establish the reality of a remarkable literary phenomenon. Critics have seemed to shy away from justifying their choice of material, and one could argue that this is unnecessary since the literature can be defined at least by its own attributes.

As has been mentioned before, the literatures in vernacular languages in French and Portuguese territories exhibit a paucity in output and a poverty in achievement. Eradication of traditional values accompanied the aspired development toward *évolué* and *assimilado*. Hence in former French and Portuguese territories assimilationist attitudes and directives caused the emergence of a detribalized literature. In former English-speaking territories this was not the case and we have seen and will see later that the tribal being was left whole; the writer was able to incorporate large segments of his world into the new literature he was developing in an alien language. Briefly then, the literature in French (especially from the communes) and Portuguese had no or little relationship with tribal consciousness, whereas in English to a large extent the wholeness of tribal life was left undisturbed.

However, no African territory was peopled by disinherited spectators

307

as was the New World. The consequences of colonialism in French and Portuguese territories are reflected not only in the attitudes and failings of the colonialist agent but in the willing compliance of the colonized victim who too readily absorbed the lessons of his master. It is therefore no accident that the cultural glance backward, the creative attempt to invent a past (which is really what négritude is), was the product of French West Indian colonials, those notably who found themselves in alien lands that had bred no indigenous culture, raised no gods, fathered no new consciousness.

Négritude as Tract

About négritude a great deal of nonsense has been written and one fears to add to the confusion. In large measure much of what has been stated is contradictory; for instance, Gerald Moore had said of Tchikaya U'Tamsi that since "the materials of his imagination, his whole sensibility, the very music of his life, have all been shaped by Africa [then] to that extent we can certainly speak of his négritude." U'Tamsi has denied that he is in any way a poet of the négritude movement and his poetry would seem to support this conclusion. Léopold Senghor has argued that emotion and feeling are African, that they are at the heart of négritude. To this the Ghanaian philosopher W. E. Abraham has retorted: "When Senghor says that the African is non-intellectual—that reason is Greek and feeling is African, that the African knows things with his nose—that's sheer nonsense! What does he think I have above my nose?" Abraham adds that there is "nothing particularly African about his [Senghor's] poetry" and that he is an "apologist of France speaking to Africa."[1]

The argument has continued: Clive Wake maintains that "the idea of commitment among African poets has been called *négritude*," whereas Senghor, who has come to be regarded as the movement's spokesman, emphasizes the universal significance of négritude, associating it with Arabism, Greek classicism, Marxism, indeed with all humanism. But earlier, in 1962, Senghor himself defined négritude as "the sum total of the cultural values of the Negro world." How does this compare with Thomas Melone's assessment of négritude, for which he says he depends on Senghor, as "a concert where Europe is the conductor and Africa the drummer"? Against this contention Claude Wauthier has argued that there was no participation on equal terms as far as the African was concerned.[2]

Associated with the attack on négritude as a philosophy, woolly as some of it might seem, are the vituperations against négritude as a respectable form of composition. Understandably Africans from former British territories and English-speaking Africans have fiercely condemned négritude as a prescriptive art. Wole Soyinkà is often quoted as having said that he sees no necessity for a tiger proclaiming its tigritude and Lewis Nkosi, a Black South African writer, has added that "one sees in these poems and stories the implications of a literary ideology which may be as crippling to young writers as the high-handed dictates of a cultural commissar in Communist countries." Ezekiel Mphahlele considers it "sheer romanticism, often it is mawkish and strikes a pose." But Janheinz Jahn firmly asserts that "it demonstrated that poetry and literature were not only possible in the African manner and out of an African attitude of mind, but that only such poetry was legitimate," and his more recent *History of Neo-African Literature* indicates that he still holds to this position. He demonstrates that négritude helped to bring about a new approach to "semantics, rhythm and subject-matter."[3]

From this sample of confused minds groping toward a political definition of what is a literary happening, it would be useful to attempt to trace the historical origins of the movement. We have already indicated its cultural necessity, but to suggest that it is a French phenomenon is both misleading and untrue. It will be seen in our study of poets who wrote in English in the thirties and forties (when there was little or no contact between Paris-oriented and London-oriented Africans) that they expressed concern for the predicament of their race and the legacy of a colonial bondage. Where négritude differs is that it was a conscious effort to reach back into a wide array of lost traditional values. On the other hand, English-speaking writers always possessed tribal awareness—a completely different world view from that of white authors.

In June 1932 a journal was produced in Paris by young French West Indians—the most important of whom were Etienne Léro, René Ménil, and Jules Monnerot—who, it can definitely be said, launched what came to be called the négritude movement. Their journal, *Légitime Défense*, had only a single issue but in it the writers did what had never been done before. True one might argue that Negrismo in Cuba during the twenties and the Haitian revolution of Dr. Price-Mars had anticipated this, but it was to the American Langston Hughes and the Jamaican Claude McKay that these writers paid their debt of gratitude for the "African love of life, the African joy of love and the African dream of death." Not only did they celebrate Africa, which we will see extolled as well in the poetry of the pioneers—Léon Damas, Aimé Césaire, and the two Africans, Léopold Sédar Senghor and David Diop—but they castigated the colonial overlord in a manner unlike any of these poets. They were young—between twenty and twenty-three years of age—and can be forgiven if they scorned everything their world had taught them. They attacked the middle classes, the capitalists, the whole concept of Christianity. They stated clearly that they wanted no pity and that they would no longer refuse to "come to terms with the shame around them." Nor were they all self-admirers, for they also rejected the "pretensive personality" of the very middle-class West Indians they were being groomed to be. Their search may be equated with the "Harlem Renaissance" in the United States.

Although this journal had only one issue, it did indicate that the tools of the conquerors—Marxism and surrealism (Léro was himself a poet)—were being turned against them. Associated with the student journal *L'Etudiant Noir* of 1934 were not only Damas, Césaire, and Senghor, who would later become exponents of the literary creed of négritude, but two other Africans, Birago Diop and Ousmane Socé. The New World had exported its phantoms to those on the African continent who recognized ironic parallels.

Senghor spoke of one obvious difference between the approaches of the two journals when he wrote that "we therefore felt different from our fellow students. This accounts for our habit of meeting on Sundays. Before long we were to form an 'Association of Students from Black Africa' and to stretch out our hands to those Caribbean and Malagasy students willing to join us."[4] What he meant was that African awareness was no longer a West Indian monopoly but had become a Black African enterprise. But it must not be forgotten in an assessment of the literature which is its offspring that this attempt at restructuring the African past was done via the New World: the descendants of slaves who did not know their Africa firsthand taught the original African négritude writers about the complex re-entry into the ancestral womb. And if at times the work of some Africans seems public, that is, too generalized to take the tribe into consideration, it is because they, like the West Indians, were imaginatively removed from the source of the experiences they related.

The foundation of the periodical *Présence Africaine* by Alioune Diop in October 1947 and an associated publishing house represents one of the more practical efforts to develop the movement. By 1939, when Césaire published his long poem *Cahier d'un retour au pays natal*, the movement was to be called négritude. The aim of *Présence Africaine* was to "explain the originality of Africa and hasten its appearance in the modern world."[5] But the most important aspect of négritude

310

was not to be found in periodicals and student manifestoes. After the first declarations of the movement came its dynamic application—in Césaire's *Cahier d'un retour au pays natal*, which was first published in the review *Volontés*, in Damas's *Pigments* (1937) and his later poems, and in Senghor's *Chants d'ombre* (1945) and *Hosties noires* (1948). Indeed by 1947 Damas was able to produce an anthology, *Poètes d'expression française*, and Senghor brought out another, *Anthologie de la nouvelle poésie nègre*, a year later. Now we must consider the extent to which these writers had or had not by then created a justifiable form of art.

By way of a postscript it should be mentioned that négritude is at times wrongly confused with Pan-Africanism. The essential difference is that Pan-Africanism (essentially "British") had definite political motives which it set out to achieve. Its second conference, held in Paris in 1919, had fifty-seven delegates, but only nine African countries were represented, "with twelve delegates."[6] Not until the sixth and last conference, held in Manchester in 1945, does one find a solid African interest, represented by Nkrumah, Kenyatta, and Azikiwe. The ready conclusion springs to mind that disinherited slaves were more concerned with the vague concept of Africa than were Africans themselves, secure as they were in tribal enclaves. But there the comparison with négritude ends, for the literature of Pan-Africanism was propagandist literature devoted to a specific cause. By 1945 when the Pan-African Congress declaration of having "the right to express our thoughts and emotions, to adopt and create forms of beauty" was passed, the literary homework had already been done. Indeed négritude, which Senghor first defined as "the spirit of Negro-African civilisation" later became in his words "neither racialism nor vulgar contortions." Perhaps Sartre was right in his assertion that négritude was a "transitory stage as a means and not a final goal." An examination of the literature of the movement should clarify these observations.

Négritude as Art: Poetry

RENÉ MARAN

In 1921 René Maran published a novel, *Batouala*, which was followed by *Djouma* in 1927. Like Césaire, he was from Martinique, but he had lived and worked in Africa. He attempted to divorce writing in French about Africa from the exotic traveler's tales. For example, the hero of *Batouala* remarks that "in the first place they [the French] were not

311

content at suppressing our most cherished customs, but they did not rest until they had imposed theirs on us." The novel describes the breakup and disabuse of tribal life; both Batouala and his father die, for they are both to blame. *Batouala*'s importance is not so much its qualities as a novel but that it acted as a catalyst, for the preface openly attacks French colonialism. According to Roland Lebel, "It attracted attention and curiosity to the indigenous populations and allowed several works of colonial literature, chiefly African novels, to reach more assuredly the public in the motherland." The "works of colonial literature" refer of course to those by French writers who would more imaginatively re-create the African environment for a French audience.

Senghor also notes that "it is only with René Maran that West Indian writers freed themselves from docile imitation of the Metropole and fear of their négritude."[7] He means something quite different; for if one reads "African" for "West Indian," it can be said that the novel in French by African writers recognizes an ancestor in René Maran. For us this is his only significance.

AIMÉ CÉSAIRE

Another West Indian, also from Martinique, was to play a much more important role in the development of French African literature. Aimé Césaire humanized négritude, releasing it from prescriptive codification and establishing it as an informal forum for poets. At first he used the techniques of surrealism which André Breton, its chief exponent, had defined as "everything which by new ways aims at a greater emancipation of the spirit."[8] The revolt of the early student papers was easily enflamed by the dicta of surrealism. Hence especially in Césaire's early poetry this violence is remarkably pictured. It took a personal turn when Césaire became a member of the Communist party. Communist and surrealist—overthrower and confused dreamer—blend in images like the following which describes Toussaint L'Ouverture:

> That which is mine
> is a man alone imprisoned in
> white
> it is a man alone who defies the
> white cries of white death.[9]

Death is no longer "black" as it had been for centuries in the poetic tradition of Europe. Imagery had undergone a change, which Césaire and others were attempting to define. To succeed was no small matter since it meant for them the intentional derangement of a carefully nurtured French sensibility.

Later Césaire was to renounce communism and surrealism—they almost went together—because "we cannot delegate anyone to think for us." But even at the time of writing *Cahier* he was forcefully independent:

> Those who did not invent gunpowder nor compass
> those who never controlled steam nor electricity
> those who explored neither water nor sky
> but who knew in their deepest parts within, the country of suffering
> those who knew of no voyages except when uprooted. (p. 68)

Such is the song of the slave, the expression of his grievances. At the same time Césaire announces his triumph:

> the call to be free at last
> to produce out of its intimate closeness
> the succulence of fruits. (p. 75)

With him négritude became not only a long catalogue of hurt but an inventory of hope, as can be seen in his play entitled *Et les chiens se taisaient* (1956), which is really a long poem dramatizing the colonial conflict. Rebel, traitor, and colonial master are given allegorical roles. On the one hand the rebel endures the torture of a colonial regime (his eyes are stabbed out) and bitterly recalls the "slave raids, chains, jungle paths"; on the other, he sympathizes with "our omniscient, simple-minded conquerors" and feels that all pain in the world, all suffering, is theirs also.

This has always been Césaire's theme within négritude, and in his play about Lumumba, *Une Saison du Congo* (1966), he has the ruler say that revolutions are not made with confetti. One can see the full exposition of this attitude in *La tragédie du roi Christophe* (1963), a play in prose about King Christophe, the liberator-tyrant of contemporary African and West Indian politics. The tragedy can be interpreted as a pessimistic work, though it does express a new hope: people should advance "à grands coups d'années, à grands ahans d'années" (in a long step of years, in big efforts of only a few years). The note is still public, but the tone has meant modulation to the tunings of a private art.

These reflective moments occur more frequently and forcefully in Césaire's poetry than in his plays. After *Cahier*, he published five volumes of poetry and, although he admitted to "mon inspiration négriste . . . mon pan-négrisme,"[10] one finds it difficult to agree with Breton that his language is as violent as "oxygen released from a test-tube."

The tone varies; sometimes it is ironically cajoling as in *Cadastre* (1961) when he says "arrest that guiltless man . . . he / has my blood on his shoulders," or when in the same poem he considers the inability of the self to be complete; in this context through the symbolism of the fallen star "we mourn our fate."

Césaire is much more the poet after the celebrated first volume; his style can be modified to suit his poetic aim. Witness, for instance, the satirical reference to the lynching of Emmet Till in *Ferrements* (1960), written in the form of a presidential report, or the grievance of the dis-inherited in *Les armes miraculeuses* (1946) where mention is made of "the congolese cradle-song that the warders have taken / from me." Unlike his first volume of poems, *Les armes* positively states the virtues of the race. Thus Césaire is able to assert, "I have nothing to fear" and "I am before Adam." Such sentiments are less forcefully expressed in *Cahier* where he writes bitterly of the Black man's acceptance of his inferior lot, which also is the acceptance of the world as it is:

> for me the dance
> the break-yoke dance
> the jailbreak dance
> the it-is-beautiful-and-good-and-lawful-to-be-a-blackman
>   dance . . . (p. 90)

The nostalgic connection with the past establishes at the end of *Cahier* the dignity of being, a theme he was to celebrate again in subsequent poems. For if in the final analysis all organs of opinion are inquisitorial, then the poet must detach himself from them. In doing this Césaire digested material from the past and was able to re-create from a muti-lated environment the presence of the human person within, beneath, and yet above it all. This was the reason for his study in literature of Toussaint L'Ouverture and Henri Christophe. *Une Saison du Congo* likewise seeks to rehabilitate Lumumba and himself: "I speak and I give Africa back to herself."

Léon Damas

Like Maran and Césaire, Léon Damas is from the New World—French Guyana. Like them he inherited a compassion for legacies and the Afri-can artists' problem of assembling the tattered remnants of a disreputa-ble past into a complete present. It did not help that he was the product of a mixed marriage as well as a "cultural mulatto." His early poem "Hoquet" describes the prejudices of the Creole mother:

Quiet
Pray have I told you or not that you must speak French
the French of France
the French of French people
French French . . .[11]

Not only his speech but his entire way of thinking and behaving was
subjected to patterns laid down by the French. In the same poem
Damas writes with bitter sarcasm of the mother's ravings:

> A banjo
> did you say a banjo
> what do you mean by
> a banjo
> did you honestly say
> a banjo
> No, mister-man
>   you ought to know that in this house we allow
> neither ban
> nor jos
> neither gui
> nor tars
> coloured people don't do that kind of thing
> leave it to the niggers. (p. 36)

Damas's early poems struck a note of mockery, muffled laughter, irony.
But in the three volumes following his first, one notices the intensity of
violence that was found in Césaire. In them, however, we see more and
more what becomes less and less apparent in Césaire—a definite rejection of the props of the white world and a turning toward the African
continent which was to become *all* of him.

Damas has defined what for him is négritude and which is imaginatively applied in his poetry. In January 1965 at a talk he gave in New
York, he said about the beginning of the movement: "Whether these
writers came from the Islands, Africa or Madagascar, they had the same
goal; the rehabilitation of the black man, the affirmation of his equality
before the white world, the affirmation of the African personality." But
with the omniscience of hindsight he added that "there exists not one
but many African civilisations; no one contests the image of a multiple
Africa."[12] In fact there is a contradiction here, for the "Africa" of
Maran, Césaire, and Damas (as well as, paradoxically, that of "tribal"
African poets like Senghor and Birago Diop) was actually a rosy reconstruction of the "Africa" of Paris efficiency apartments. It still seems
surprising that the Africans went along with the myth so meticulously
concocted by the West Indians.

315

One finds therefore in Damas's *Pigments* many evidences of an exotic reveling in an Africa of the mind. In the poem "Ils sont venus ce soir" dedicated to Senghor he asks,

> how many of ME ME ME
> all died
> since they came that evening when the
> tom
>   tom
>   rolled from
>   rhythm
>   to
>   rhythm
>   in frenzy (p. 11)

The same flirting with broad African references can be seen in another early poem:

> The days themselves
> have taken the form
> of African masks
> indifferent
> to any profanation . . . (p. 24)

Here the African masks symbolize the escape from the tawdry. These poems also denounce the futility of West Indian/Guyanese upper-crust life as the student journals and manifestoes had done earlier in a more pragmatic manner. But Damas is able to laugh and to make his attack much more powerful than anything written by these doctrinaire reformers. In "Solde," for instance, he even directs the laughter at himself:

> I know I look ridiculous
> when they prattle away
> when they serve you on afternoons
> a little bit of hot water
> with cold cakes (p. 40)

This is the same voice with which he castigated the mother who wanted her son to learn to play the violin rather than the guitar because it was more "proper." It is the laughter of scorn and the biting irony of one who could laugh at himself from within the society to which he always belonged. For he himself admits in the same poem, "I know I look ridiculous / as their accomplice . . ." (p. 40).

Césaire and Damas spoke as accomplices but Maran went further as an apologist. As accomplices they were also rebels, and in "Obsession" Damas writes of rituals he could never know, but which his colleague

316

Senghor could describe at firsthand. Both Césaire and Damas equated their rediscovery of Africa with some pagan fetish that was weird and fanciful: Césaire's "mémoire c'est entourée de sang" (memory is encircled with blood) in *Cahier* and Damas's "un goût de sang me vient" (a taste of blood comes to me). The blood in both cases is associated with the loss of tribe, not the initiation into adulthood which Senghor could write about so confidently. For these West Indian poets, blood is castration not circumcision, sequestration not tribal recognition.

Time and time again in both Damas and Césaire this separation from the tribe, the slave past when humans equaled decimal currency, is bewailed. For Césaire the cry was more directly pathetic and ironical:

> I accept. I accept.
> and the whipped nigger who says: 'Sorry sah'
> and the legalised twenty-nine strokes of the whip
> and the cell as high as four feet
> and the iron collar with spikes . . .[13]

This after all is his inheritance and Césaire does not look back with nostalgia. The past in Césaire's poetry is one long, grim night and when he refers to the glory of Africa, he does so almost with the modesty of the stranger. Damas, on the other hand, recognizes a past within the disturbed environment, for he feels that the efforts of misdirected currents of history were responsible for his dilemma. With anguish therefore he exclaims in "Limbé" that he wishes to be given back the black dolls so that he could play games that would restore his world of instinct. His yesterday is not always the harsh one of Césaire's. Yesterday is

> without complications
> yesterday
> when came the hour of uprooting. (p. 42)

Damas's anger is quieter, more reflective than Césaire's; he can look back on the centuries and forgive. Another interesting point of comparison between Damas and Césaire is that although they share in common the same subject matter, there is a different expression of tone. Whereas Damas laments in "Réalité" that he is almost a negative person because he has accomplished nothing, Césaire ironically celebrates those who do not invent anything. In Damas's poetry little attempt is made to vaunt racial superiority by stating negative virtues. When he does attempt this kind of writing, he does not succeed, as is evident in "Blanche" where he comments, "Alors que tout en moi aspire à n'être que nègre" (Even though all in me aspired to be black) and in the sentimental "S.O.S." where he says, "Soon they will get this idea / to want to gobble up the blackman" (p. 49). Damas stutters because he writes like an outsider witnessing the pain and suffering of another. This is not his real voice and this is perhaps why most of the verse in *Poèmes nègres sur des airs africains* (1948) fails, for despite his fierce assertions, Damas is at his best when, as a participant in the culture, he can nevertheless strongly denounce it. When he goes completely over to the other side and writes semi-songs of mourning or praise, he does not succeed. He is too much the poet and person; the African oral tradition had spokesmen, never individualists.

It is interesting to note that at times Césaire and Damas both adopt approaches contrary to what is expected of them. One finds a startling departure in these lines from Damas's *Black Label* (1956).[14]

> Never will the white man be a black man
> for beauty is black
> and wisdom is black
> for endurance is black
> and so is courage
> for patience is black
> and so is irony
> for charm is black
> and so is magic
> for love is black
> and so is the looseness of limb
> for dance is black
> and so is rhythm
> for art is black
> and so is movement
> for laughter is black
> and so is joy
> for peace is black
> and so is life. (p. 52)

In a different context Césaire, after a studied process of self-denigration, concludes in *Cahier*:

> but the work of mankind has barely begun
> and it remains for him all rigid prohibitions in the corners of his fervour
> and no race possesses the monopoly of beauty, intelligence and strength
> and there is room for all at the meeting-place of conquest. (p. 83)

No longer is Césaire at this point in *Cahier* haranguing the reader; roles have changed and Césaire is reflective, whereas Damas displays the tension of being neither Black nor white which leads him to a kind of imaginative excess. He is not as concerned with his individuality as he is in other poems, but rather he is attempting to take part in some cultural

318

constellation. At least this is the meaning Damas seeks to convey: since he does not exist confidently as a whole person he cannot articulate a firmness of being. Damas forces us to confront a terrifying void and the likelihood of self-abandonment and aloneness in a deserted universe. He looks abjectly to himself for verification and toward Africa for the source of all his contradictions.

LÉOPOLD SÉDAR SENGHOR

As has been suggested so far, négritude like Pan-Africanism was a Caribbean sickness. Only people unfamiliar with the norms of tribal life could have diagnosed in such wide conceptual terms a myth of the heart and boldly prescribed such an imaginative recovery. Senghor was Senegalese; he learned his négritude from *deraciné* West Indians, but to it he brought something new—the novelty of the initiated. He alone knew; they could only hazard guesses. Therefore it was in the language of Césaire and Damas that Senghor wrote that "those who colonised us justified our political and economic independence by the theory of *tabula rasa*. We had, they assessed, invented nothing, written nothing. We had neither carved, painted nor sung." Senghor adds that it was impossible to return to what he considered the sources of négritude and that the time of the Songhai Empire and of Chaka had passed. "We were students in Paris and students of the twentieth century," and this conflict is present in Senghor's verse from the very start. His evocations of Africa are in the Césairean manner, though at times perhaps they echo Damas. Later he would arrive at Claude Wauthier's conclusion that négritude could only be understood "in relationship with other people." At first, however, Senghor bluntly admitted that it was to some extent racism. Sartre commented that "because it is the tension between a nostalgic past into which the Black no more completely enters, and a future where it will give way to new values, Négritude fashions itself in tragic beauty and finds expression only in poetry." Earlier in the same essay, which prefaced Senghor's 1948 anthology, Sartre had contended that "we have one hemisphere with three concentric circles. At the periphery stretches the land of exile, colourless Europe. Next comes the dazzling circle of the Indies and of childhood, which dance the round in circling Africa. And then Africa, the last circle, navel of the world, pole of all black poetry . . . Africa beyond reach, imaginary continent." The Pan-Africanist C. L. R. James was to assert at the time that Sartre's "explanation of what he conceives *négritude* to mean is a disaster." But it must be realized that Sartre was mainly describing all the poets

319

represented in Senghor's anthology, only six of whom were Africans. The majority of poets were West Indians who, according to an American writer, "for the most part are more intense in their reaction to the estrangement of the African in the West than the poets of the continent itself are."[15] And, as has been seen, I have not attempted to argue against this contention.

Because of her failure to place négritude in a historical perspective, Lilyan Lagneau disagrees with Sartre. She maintains that Senghor had to make no great effort to retrieve his sources because "elles sont toutes proches et ont nourri sa jeunesse" (they were all near him and had been part of his youth). The imaginary continent was rightly, as she argues, "inventé par les Antillais au sein de leur exil" (invented by the West Indians on account of their exile). Senghor did, however, publish his first two volumes as a Black man in exile, a man who was formless and faceless and who pretended he had to invent a past. Indeed two recent compilers and translators of some of his poems in English believe that although "Senghor feels that his poetry is closer to folk poetry . . . [his] poetry is not folk poetry."[16] The folk-poet takes his sources for granted; Senghor at times seem to flirt with the folk past.

What, then, is his poetry? Most of it is accompanied by an appropriate traditional instrument which sets the rhythm. He makes use of place names from his childhood—Cayor, Futa, Dyilor, Joal—as well as heroes of his tribe—Dyogoy, Sitor, Kumba, Siga. And to all this the belafong, kora, kalam, gorong, kama are supposed to be fitting complements. Senghor had some obvious advantages over his contemporaries because of his nearness to the object of recall and, perhaps more important, to the ancestor-image that frequently dominates his poetry as it does so much African literature. Nevertheless, the poetry is written in a European language, and one has to inquire how right W. E. Abraham was when he dismissed Senghor's poetry as "French verse interlarded with African allusions." This statement could be modified to include French verse written by other Black "Frenchmen" who made use of certain local Senegalese allusions.

His "Nuit de sine" from *Poèmes* (1964)[17] portrays the African woman who in the poem archetypically symbolizes the omnipresence of death. Lines such as the following do not distinguish the poem as "Black" or "African."

> It is the time of the stars and the night which dreams
> Lying back on this hill of clouds, dressed in a gown of milk

Houseroofs are gleaming gently. What are they saying with such
confidence to the stars?
Within, the hearth is put out amidst intimate bitter and
sweet scents. (pp. 14–15)

This could have been written by any European poet. The "s" sounds in
the French convey the silence and privacy that the poet wishes to intensify, and it possesses none of the harshness of Césaire or the irony of
Damas. Perhaps here the tiger does proclaim its tigritude. Were it not
for other parts of the poem, however, this would be but a slight piece.
The poem builds itself up through spirals of silence until at the apex
an unnamed woman and man emerge. References to palm trees, dark
blood, forests, children on their mothers' backs, the ancients of Elissa,
the smoky hut identify an African (Senegalese) locality. But the high
point of the poem is achieved when Senghor switches from the formless
to the formed, ditching the descriptive element that has no place in the
traditional love for humanizing the abstract.

Woman, light the lamp of clear oil and let the children, like their
parents, talk about their ancestors.
Listen to the voice of the Ancestors of Elissa. Like us exiled
They did not wish to die, to lose their seminal flow in dust.
Let me listen too in the smoky hut for the phantom visit of
propitious souls
My head glistens on your breast like a kuskus ball smoking out
of the fire
Let me breathe the smell of our Dead Ones, let me recall and
repeat their living accents, let me learn
To live before I go down, deeper than the diver, into the deep
darkness of sleep. (pp. 14–15)

Here is expressed the theme of exile; the themes of Damas and Césaire
are apparent, but uppermost is the eternal presence of the ancestors,
who, together with the protagonist and the children, form links in the
chain of humanity. This part of the poem succeeds best; in it we see
the African writer who exists with a past that is never past. The comparison of the dead and the exiled living is a forced one and indeed
does not make sense logically within the poem or within the framework
of the culture recalled by the poet. To say that the ancestors did not
wish to die just as Senghor and his student-friends did not wish to be
exiled from their cultures is wrong. The importance of the ancestors is
in their immortality, in the fact that they did die but continue to live.
Puny comparisons with the predicament of Paris students humiliate the
ancestor-archetype.

Clearly the most noteworthy point to emerge here is that within a French poem Senghor introduces a note that no European or West Indian poet could have struck. Though he was westernized and had been taught of the eternal permanence of matter, his African instincts, in addition, continuously assured him of the indestructible spirit of man. What Senghor is therefore attempting is for him the obvious—the invoking of the ancestor and the presence of the Vital Force in everything, about which Fr. Placide Tempels and Alexis Kagamé have also written.

More obviously but no less powerfully, Birago Diop dramatizes the ancestor-theme in his poem "Souffles."[18]

> Those who are dead have never really gone away
> They are at the Woman's breast
> They are in the Child's weeping
> And in the firebrand bursting into life
> The Dead are not under the Ground. (p. 64)

Earlier in the same poem Birago Diop asserts, "Les Morts ne sont pas morts" (the dead are not dead). It is no accident that in the lines just quoted archetypal mother and child provide a similar link with the apparent dead, as is true as well in Senghor's poetry. Birago Diop returns to this theme in "Viatique," another successful poem in *Leurres at Lueurs* (1960), where one learns of the "ancêtres qui furent des hommes" (the ancestors who were men). It was a subject that Senghor found lacking in Césaire, as he says in his "Lettre à un poète," dedicated to Césaire, "Have you forgotten your nobility, which is to celebrate / The Ancestors, the Princes and the Gods . . ." (p. 12). Senghor failed to realize that Césaire did not have either ancestors, princes, or gods. All Césaire could do was bemoan their loss. But it was with this voice that Senghor and Diop were able—despite their identification—to divorce themselves from Caribbean writers and to announce their place in the cosmos of African reality. Sartre admired this quality in Diop's poetry "because it speaks directly from the tribal story-tellers and in the same oral tradition." Though Sartre's contention is not entirely true, it is certain that the bulk of Diop's work is an attempt, in Senghor's phrase, to return to the sources. Diop's contribution will be assessed more fully when we come to consider his prose.

The ancestor-theme in Senghor as well as in other African writers often gives way to the emergence of the stereotype. "Femme noire," which characterizes the eternal woman, is just this. Written in the form of a praise song, it is nevertheless a startling departure, for traditional

praise songs never extolled the beauty of women. But like the praise
singer the poet assumes the role of custodian of the culture.

> I sing your beauty which passes and fix your form in eternity
> Before a jealous Fate reduces you to ashes to nourish the roots
>   of life. (pp. 16–17)

Through the object of praise Senghor comes nearer to an understanding
of himself. The manner in which the woman experiences her world is
meant to show her familiarity with it. We find therefore that the poem
is a very sensuous one; the sight of the sun and shadow in the first
stanza, the sound of the East wind, the tom-tom, and the lover in the
second bring us closer to the *felt* nature of the experience.

The Black woman in Senghor's poetry is a synthesis of mother and
lover. In this way she is equated with the land, with harvest and
drought; she is both giver and receiver. Therefore she best appeals to
Senghor's poetic demands. As a mere consumer of French culture, must
he be driven to the despair of Césaire and Damas, or could the African
presence give his poetry more vitality and a source of positive values?

Some parts in *Chants pour Naëtt* (1949) provide an answer to this
question. The solution was not the total rejection of the white world
and acceptance of the African world, but the blending of both. This is
what Mbella Sonne Dipoko referred to as the point at which "cultural
negotiations are about to open . . . a meeting-place, a compromise,
was agreed upon." In the same context, Senghor wrote that the hero of
Peter Abrahams's *Wreath for Udomo* is "a tissue of contradictions [for
he] tyrannically loves his black Africa, and he loves a white woman."[19]
It was to Césaire's "rendez-vous de la conquête" that Senghor had
come in this verse in *Poèmes*:

> And we have delighted, my love, in an African presence
> Furniture from Guinea and Congo, heavy and polished, dark and light.
> Masks primitive and pure on walls distant yet so near.
> Tabourets of honour for the hereditary hosts, the princes from the
>   High-Country.
> Wild perfumes from the thick tresses of silence
> Cushions of darkness and leisure like the source of quiet wells.
> Eternal words; faraway the alternating chant as in cloths from Sudan.
> And then the friendly light of your kindness will soften the obsession
>   of this presence in
> Black, white and red oh red like the soil of Africa. (p. 74)

Here the poet frankly admits that the past was an invented one for the
négritude poets. Senghor differed from them in that, though he began

with their conclusions, he escaped their bitterness and turned toward the familiar. At the center was always man, the poet-hero himself.

Senghor's method and manner continue in subsequent volumes. The local Africa is used to describe the general, the symbolic, woman. Less of his vituperation is present in *Nocturnes* (1961). He has come a long way from his *Hosties noires* (1948), which is essentially made up of war poems exploring the love-hate relationship with France. He recognizes his "frères noirs" (Black brothers) but adds "ne dites pas que je n'aime pas la France" (do not say I do not love France). Damas described "cousin Hitler" in one poem but Senghor, as both soldier and prisoner of war, could acknowledge France while still retaining an element of "la voix de l'Afrique planant audessus de la rage des canons longs" (the voice of Africa sounding near the rage of long cannons). By the time of *Nocturnes* the reconciliation between the spiritual longing for Africa and the physical need for Europe was complete. Senghor is no longer capable of writing purely love poems like those in *Chants pour Naëtt* or poems solely concerned with the backward glance to Africa. In *Nocturnes* he reaches the poetic equivalent of what in his essays he calls humanism and he further develops the idea expressed in "Chaka" (*Ethiopiques*, 1956) that poetry must now be sacrificed in the same way that Chaka had to sacrifice Nolivé. The "Elégies" in *Nocturnes* conclude the poetic quest for pacification. The world is one and man and child are indivisible. Chaka's words could well be Senghor's:

> Here I am re-joined with the earth. How shiny in the
> Kingdom of childhood
> And it is the end of my passion. (p. 118)

The poetry had completed a circle, coming back to the childhood of a movement, a race, a person for verification. Senghor's conclusion is probably again Chaka's—"Mais je ne suis pas le poème, mais je ne suis pas le tam-tam / Je ne suis pas le rythme . . ." (But I am not the poem, nor am I the drum / I am not the rhythm . . .). Senghor has liberated the Black poet from his dilemma, the imaginative writer has become more than the agent for executing a people's art. Such a writer can no longer dictate to his audience and the debate has ended. There remains, however, the next task, which offers a wide spectrum of possibilities. Senghor not only is exposing the African writer to the dialogue of the whole world but is also asking him to be a witness to private areas of experience. This could not have been accomplished at an earlier stage, and thus we will now consider another poet, David Diop, and examine what négritude meant to him.

DAVID DIOP

Senghor successfully transformed négritude from a series of public gestures to a lonely confrontation with the self. David Diop lived during the time when négritude was in its infancy and he died at an early age. His *Coups de pilon* (1956)[20] expresses the anger of Césaire, for he was born in France and only visited Africa. He therefore has more in common with the West Indians and less in common with Senghor and Birago Diop.

Something of the nature of David Diop's predicament is seen in "Le Rénegat." He castigates the Black man in the poem for dressing himself in, and behaving in, the manner of the white man. He has gold spectacles, wears silk lapels, and his teeth shine when people pay him hypocritical compliments. The conclusion of the poem is a line of anguish for both the poet and the object of scorn: "Je me sens seul si seul ici!" (I feel lonely here, so lonely!). In "Afrique" Diop confesses that his knowledge of Africa is secondhand:

> Africa my Africa
> Africa of brave warriors in ancient savannahs
> Africa about which my grandmother sings
> On the banks of her distant river
> I've never known you . . . (p. 21)

He could not draw from the ancestral theme as Senghor had done. In him reposed no storehouse of tribal myth. Like the West Indians he had to be absolutely inventive. Therefore his evocation of the mother, of the Black woman, is different from Senghor's, making the poem at best a fair example of moderately good French verse.

> Where behind closed shutters
> Words elude me and I am left with emptiness
> Then mother I think of you . . . (p. 7)

These lines from "À ma mère" seem to suggest that for Diop the mother-image is a substitute for poetic inarticulation, whereas for Senghor the mother/lover/woman *is*; she exists independently and represents an archetypal symbol embodied in all time. Here the poet is referring to his own mother, and what he borrowed from other African writers of the négritude (and later) manner was only the stereotypical characteristics of the mother. She is kind, full of love, patient, understanding, but nothing in the poem convinces us that she is "O mère mienne et qui est celle de tous" (O mother of mine who is the mother of all). Her failure to take on these very ancestral qualities is one of the points of departure between Diop's poetry and that of the tribal African.

Like most West Indian poetry (and noticeably unlike Senghor's and Birago Diop's) his verse is explosive and declamatory. He openly addresses his fellow Blacks as "comrades," and though his poetry is intended for a public conversion he openly bemoans the "suffering of the world," "the memory of my blood," and like Damas and Césaire the slave past. Like them he is unsuccessful when merely cataloguing grievances. Some of the poems are saved by a sudden inventive flash in the last line; in a particular poem Diop lists the familiar grievances of a colonial (except that he was not one), but at the end he comments that after the white man had killed his father, seduced his mother, and tortured his brother, he addressed him with "Boy: a chair, a napkin, a drink." Were it not for this last line, the poem would represent little more than an inventory of ill-treatment.

David Diop is similar to Damas and Césaire in that every poem is a complaint, every exercise an attempt at high-pitched lamentation. But there is a difference: he offers no hope in his poems. They are all morbid pieces. Perhaps one can say that there is a note of joy, sadly reconstructed though it is, as the poet painfully reconnects himself to the imaginary, ancestral past. This contrast emerges best in a certain poem in *Coups de pilon*. Diop depicts the model Africa of the imagination, where women are beautiful, children happy, crocodiles in no way dangerous, and the ever-present moon watches over as people dance. Obviously an insipid portrait of Africa, but the poet jolts us into acknowledging the predicament of the present when in the second stanza he abruptly refers to slavery, which ultimately destroyed the peace and simple joys of old Africa. (For no reason tom-toms are mentioned in the last line of the poem.)

Were it not for Diop's good intentions, the poem might almost be offensive, but we sense that the account of this prematurely aged *gravitas* is one of love, of the desire to make the past and the present the same, of the wish to share in the equality of all. Not surprisingly we find not only images of blood and chains, but references to racial repression, which for him is all repression—a point at which Senghor was to arrive later on. Thus he writes in "Vagues" of the slave, the docker of Suez, and the "coolie" of Hanoi.

In poems of social protest David Diop is not so much concerned with form as with matter, and therefore one wishes he had lived longer so that he might have written more. In "Rama Kam" he seems to experiment with the repetition of sounds, some of which are successful in French:

> Quand tu passes
> La plus belle est jalouse . . .
> Quand tu danses
> Le tam-tam Rama Kam . . .
> Et quand tu aimes
> Quand tu aimes Rama Kam . . .
>
> When you pass
> All the most beautiful girls are jealous . . .
> When you dance
> The tom-tom Rama Kam . . .
> And when you love
> When you love Rama Kam . . . (p. 25)

The three stages in the rhythmical development of the poem turn the poem back upon itself with "quand" and then hurl it forward in a rush of violence. This is aided by the repetition of "Rama Kam" and the explosive symbols of song, desire, rhythm, dance, victory, tornado. To David Diop Africa was the explosive present which would challenge the world with its vigor, its rhythms, its perfections. For him all Black literature had to proclaim this. As he said when reviewing an African novel in 1953, "Around us in Africa so many events need our attention. We do not think it too much to ask our novelists to be the active witnesses of these happenings." This is certainly what David Diop tried to do in his poetry.

Later Poets of the Négritude Movement

Those who advocate that négritude is the sole medium through which the African should convey his feelings have been accustomed to include most French writing in this category. This is of course when they chose the all-inclusive definition that négritude equals Black and that anything a Black writes must express his négritude. This to my mind is confusing the poet with his poetry and using an inquisitorial organ of opinion to prescribe the field of culture and response—a very hazardous undertaking. Certain poets and novelists, however, definitely fit into this category, and these we will now attempt to assess.

ANTOINE-ROGER BOLAMBA

Senghor prefaced Bolamba's *Esanzo: Chants pour mon pays* (1955) by saying that his themes were the "great themes of *négritude*," whereas

327

David Diop rightly asked whether it was "prudence which causes Bolamba to keep away from dangerous themes." David Diop goes on to make an interesting point: Bolamba must have been aware of the great themes of négritude, for he could hardly have seen only what he describes. According to Diop, the verse is little more than simple nature poetry. For Senghor, on the other hand, the very mixture of moon and sun, dance and death, the crocodile and the serpent, dream and desire means that "there is no interruption of continuity between the cowrie and the altar." It has been years since the publication of "Légitme Défense," but the polemics still continue.

What makes Bolamba's verse the poetry of négritude is not immediately clear. He is capable of writing simple love poetry that utilizes local words describing the wonder and the power of the lovers' feelings. As can be seen in the following lines, it is poetry that comes over well in translation:

> This early morning with its little trot of cheerfulness
> Its dance of flowers
> Its waltz of cyclones
> Its *ngomo*
> Its *nkole*
> Its *bisanzo*
> Its *ngombi*
> Its *totola*
> Its *bendundu*
> Its *basanga*
> Which make madness bloom
> In the spirit.
> The river is in commotion,
> Ngoho the river.[21]

Such lyricism mixed with local words does not in any way constitute négritude. In vain one looks in Bolamba's poems for Damas's irony, Césaire's and David Diop's explosive anger, Senghor's intellectual working out of an emotional state of being. Yet this is Bolamba. Some poems like "Mongo Poem" are bilingual, written in both a local language and French. There is again nothing particularly striking about this piece as a négritude creation. However, in "Chant du soir," the black night, the tom-toms, the clapping of hands, the totem all contribute to the protest underlying the poem. Senghor has noted that one of Bolamba's devices was the itemizing of names, from which the imagery was frequently derived. In "Chant du soir" the poet is seemingly describing the evening but the drum-call makes us realize that he is actually depicting his people's objections to an unstated wrong. Despite

328

all obstacles the protagonist still has the will to live, and in the last stanza the mention of a "handful of dreams" blends with images of the drum and seems to suggest the triumph of the human spirit. After the agitation of the spirit comes the peace of the earlier poem we examined.

Négritude poets have frequently felt the need to claim that they wrote in special rhythms, what Jahn supports them in calling the language of the drums. But only in Bolamba is this intense rhythm apparent to me. He blends two voices, a lyrical tenderness in his use of French with his manhandling of the French language, to produce a paradoxical strength. Fond of paradox he speaks for what he calls "women weeping without a voice,"[22] the inarticulate.

One does not find here verse as good as that of the other poets we have considered. Bolamba is too fond of cataloguing, of using local words (thrown in with his French), which sometimes not only are a stumbling block to the reader but interfere with both rhythm and meaning. His slim volume of forty-two pages only marks him as a minor African poet who utilized some of the techniques of the négritude poets. Though not always successful, he does manage to maintain the true rhythm of the drums.

JACQUES RABÉMANJARA

To say that Rabémanjara is from Madagascar immediately establishes his separate identity, which would scarcely be important were it not for the fact that he was at the center of the freedom struggle in his country, was put in prison in 1947, and exiled to France. Hence, his poetry as well as his plays (which are really poems with him as the hero) reflects revolutionary fervor. If one detects here a certain egocentricity, it can be explained by his identifying with Madagascar. For instance he composed *Antsa* (1948)[23] while in prison and therefore it conveys the longing for release, the plight; written out of the necessity of a pathetic situation, it expresses through natural landscape and the pain of patriotism a personal and yet national catastrophe.

At this distance in time one would thus be wrong to feel detached from the ardent enthusiasm that embellishes the poem. For him Madagascar is an "island with syllables of flame" (p. 9), and in erotic imagery he relates the pain of separation from his country. He says he longs to bite the "virgin red flesh" of his island and he describes himself as "the most ardent of your lovers" (p. 11). The poem does not possess the sugary lyricism of Bolamba; it is instead almost the technical application of négritude. Time and again the poet-hero (frequently reminiscent of

329

Senghor) returns to himself in order to pinpoint the predicament of his people.

As the poem progresses, it becomes more and more violent in the manner of Césaire until the image of the mother (the island) appears who sacrifices her own son (the prisoner, Rabémanjara). The mother is Senghor's woman; she represents what the poet had earlier called "a shiver of liberty" (p. 57), and through her the island is delivered. By the end of the poem, Madagascar is free.

Rabémanjara's "play," *Les boutriers de l'aurore* (1957),[24] fails for the same reason that *Antsa* succeeds. *Antsa* is a long monologue; on the other hand, a play must presuppose intermediaries in the form of characters and an audience to whom it is addressed. Because Rabémanjara's play is comparable to a long poem, it will be discussed here. Although it contains long speeches and obvious allegories, if it is considered (as it was in all probability conceived) as protracted verse, one sees that it has certain evocative flashes which recall *Antsa*. For instance, the woman who directs the rowers is equated with hope. The ancestor-theme, apparent in *Antsa*, is more powerfully developed here. Princess Ananda has not remained true to the gods and the Seer movingly delivers a praise poem to her in reverse:

> She was the ark of the new hope
> The ancestral mother of the wayward branch
> Now the Spring is poisoned
> And all her promise poisoned
> And the whole future poisoned . . . (p. 154)

The disillusionment is finalized—what Dipoko referred to as the third stage of négritude had come about: those who had bemoaned their colonial lot had been given power only to misuse it. Rabémanjara, however, does not bequeath a legacy without hope. The child, the symbol of innocence, "disarms the gods" (p. 229) and triumphs. At the end of the play the child goes searching for the gods, thereby vindicating religion, which has the power to revitalize and shape anew.

Lamba, a book of poems published in 1956,[25] could almost have been written by someone else. It has none of the exhortation of *Antsa*, none of the biblical language of *Les boutriers de l'aurore*. The language is tough, difficult, unpleasant, almost like his theme: "Hail beginning of my giddiness!" (p. 17) and "I have had enough, yes I have enough until I am sick of enough" (p. 25). In *Lamba* one hears echoes of Damas, who also had experienced expulsion. And whereas the prison poems in *Antsa* were patriotic and bore no ironical intent, *Lamba* depicts a different mood—now that the poet has been repulsed.

But I'm fed up with it, fed up within me
With the tinkling of cosmetics on the Philistine cheeks
Fed up with waste as wings of the nostrils
Fed up with the technical virginity of the umbilicus and mask
    and falseness . . . (p. 25)

Everything has become distorted (masks are equated with falseness) and Rabémanjara cannot draw strength from the earth, for the earth crushes. *Lamba* is interesting poetry because it counterpoints the images of négritude. In this volume, some of Césaire blends with some of Damas to produce a complete negation of what Rabémanjara had earlier called "the honey of the clear seasons." Landscape images in *Lamba* are reduced to the bitterness of the poetic mood. This is the stage of négritude or rather the stage of the experience of French African writers that Oyono and Beti were later to delineate in laughter, but before they could do this a great deal more had to be written in prose.

Minor Négritude Poets

Présence Africaine exerted such an influence, at once pernicious and fruitful, on poets writing in French that it is doubtful if the seers of négritude have completely exhausted what are by now stock themes. As late as 1960 when a special number of *Présence Africaine*[26] was published, poets were still proclaiming "l'essai aplati de la Négritude à la face du monde" (the attempt to flatten négritude in the face of the world; p. 70) or that "la négritude est le mystère des Siècles" (négritude is the mystery of the centuries; p. 82).

New names appear, but the same themes reappear. Bouna Boukary Dioura from Mali treats patriotic and ancestral themes:

Hymn to my country
Hymn of my green rock
Wake up every morning.
As to you, my ancestor
As to you victims and martyrs . . . (p. 84)

What concerns Patrice Kayo of Cameroon are the dictates of the class struggle as laid down in a now irrelevant négritude manifesto. "Moi le paysan" exclaims somewhat artificaly:

A Mist hides your face in vain from me
and like a drowning man clutching the cliffs
to you I want to cling
O salted day of calmness and brotherhood
day of the wiping-out of classes. (p. 23)

331

The expression of old-fashioned grievances continues, as can be seen in these lines from Francesco N'Dintsouna:

> The whip flew
> The whip whistled
> The whip cracked on their black backs . . . (p. 27)

Thankfully few poets who create in French today speak in this vein; later we shall examine some who wrote before and after the négritude movement and find that they are very different. Other less well-known poets also do not adhere to the overworked themes, but instead insist that all is not right and that comfortable backward glances at imperial wrong do not annul the present. Pierre Bamboté (from the Central African Republic) pulls no punches when he writes in "Vous voyez" about "les crimes pour lesquels on pend nos frères" (the crimes for which we hang our brothers) or about thieves becoming richer so much quicker than do honest men. This is the bitter side of the present reality. One finds too that some can still take a swipe at France and yet write poetry. Jean-Louis Dongmo's protagonist, hearing that an enormous elephant has been slain in a distant land, wishes to go to France to obtain his part of the prize. This type of approach is more similar to the writing that will be discussed below. Perhaps it is true to say that were it not for these satirical writers négritude by now would have reached a dead end.

This satire is poignantly portrayed in "A mon mari," a mock praise poem by the novelist Yambo Ouologuem:

> You used to call yourself Bimbircokak
> And everything was all right like this
> But you became Victor-Emile-Louis-Henri-Joseph
> And bought a dinner-set
>
> I was your wife
> Now you call me the little woman
> We used to eat together
> You separated us around a table
>
> Calabash and ladle
> Gourd and cus-cus
> Disappeared from your meals
> Which your paternal orders dictated to me
>
> You made it clear we are now modern
>
> Hot hot hot is the sun
> As always in the tropics
> But your tie never leaves
> Your neck which looks as if it is about to be strangled . . . (p. 95)

At the end the wife complains that, though he may be underdeveloped, she is undernourished with the new menu he has introduced.

Senghor had stressed that négritude could not be static but must change with new situations. This is what some of these younger poets are doing. In a mock prayer, Emmanuel Boundzéki Dongala confesses that he forgot "the hour of catechism" because he was distracted by a beautiful woman. One realizes, however, that the "sinner" is not at all repentant. Such poetic utterances have emerged from what Wole Soyinka rightly refers to as the "philosophical straitjacket" of négritude and they demonstrate that modern poets in French, who are poets first and foremost, may utilize the past but at the same time move toward the exploration of the present and the self. Roger Assouan puts it well when he describes in "Solitude" how he feels after having seen his own eyes in the mirror:

> With them you left me alone
> I wanted to get away
> A shadow passed under my window
> and I came across myself
> in the narrow corridor of the past. (p. 60)

Négritude in Prose

Although the négritude poets were responsible for the literary creations of what originated as a manifesto, the course of development, not entirely dissimilar, can be charted in prose. When Africans decided to write novels it was to René Maran that they turned rather than to Bakary Diallo whose *Force-Bonté* (1926) appeared only five years after *Batouala*. The obvious reason for rejecting Diallo's novel was that in a simple way it sought to depict the glories of France and its two "cardinal virtues," strength and righteousness. Négritude meant a nostalgic glance back to the African past and, as a corollary to this, a denunciation of all that was wrong with French colonial endeavor. Therefore writers found a natural springboard in Maran's *Batouala*.

OUSMANE SOCÉ

Ousmane Socé published his two novels in 1935 and 1937 and his *Contes et légendes d'Afrique noire* appeared in 1948. Although these stories stress the dignity and originality of the African past, Socé's poetry demonstrates the dualism that was to appear later in the works of many Africans. Nevertheless, for Socé there is no disparity between a genuine love and nostalgia for Paris and the memory of slavery.

The tension expressed in his poetry is also found in his first novel, *Karim*, which depicts the conflict between two worlds as represented by the Europeanized city of Dakar and the Islamic town of Guet N'dar (St. Louis). Karim, a well-dressed, educated, white-collar Wolof worker, falls in love with Marième in St. Louis and attempts to court her with all the extravagance of his ancestors. When a rival also begins to court Marième, she and her mother insist on the traditional *diamelé* (spending-match). Already Karim is in debt so he goes to Dakar to earn enough money to compete with his rival.

In Dakar he meets the new Black elite who use toothbrushes (instead of the usual chewing stick), read books, and dress in European fashion. At first Karim resists these influences, but inevitably he begins to change—he dresses differently, learns European dances, attends the cinema, idles in cafés. Once urbanized, Karim, like other Africans, did not wish to return to his traditions, but when he is in the hospital with malaria, he thinks back on St. Louis and starts to reread the Koran. Thus he returns home, finds Marième free, and his rival in jail for debt. They marry in traditional style.

Throughout Karim is confused about which values are right. Socé has him try both, and his decision to return to his own traditions is seen as the end of his adolescence. Only then does he really deserve Marième. Socé is at home in the ambiguities of Karim's world—extravagance is wrong in Dakar but noble in St. Louis; Karim runs wild in Dakar while Marième remains a virgin until he comes back. The book clearly establishes its polarity, but one frequently wishes that Socé had been able to conceal his own prejudices. His personal comments spoil the telling somewhat, since he is not content to let the action spell out the message he intends.

Mirages de Paris (1937)[27] extends the culture conflict theme, though not *within* the African situation; instead, it attempts to document the négritude movement. White here is seen as opposed to Black; a little boy wipes his hands after shaking Fara's own. Fara, the hero, is perhaps the first Black student depicted in French African prose who is exposed to the culture conflict about which later authors were to write. However, Fara is *not* Karim; he settles for *évolué* status and marries a white girl, despite her father's disapproval. Socé seems to be saying that the gulf between Karim and Marième was far greater than that between Fara and Jacqueline. In a way he is right, for Karim had never been prepared for the European world whereas Fara had.

BIRAGO DIOP

Diop's tales have been collected in three volumes, *Les contes d'Amadou Koumba* (Paris, 1947), *Les nouveaux contes d'Amadou Koumba* (Paris, 1958), with an introduction by Senghor, and *Contes et lavanes* (Paris, 1963). Diop tells us in the first volume that the stories satisfied a need within him during his stay in Paris. The same can also be said of Senghor's work, though Diop's stories force the European reader to participate in a reality that is African and to endure it. At the end the reader realizes that he has sensed something not completely different from his own world. For the telling in many of the tales revolves around universal themes—gluttony is depicted in "Le prètexte," covetousness in "Le tam-tam du lion," convention in "L'os." Nor are the tales simply content with amusing or instructing. Frequently they highlight the plight of the farmer in rural communities with which Diop was so familiar.

As was noted in our discussion of the indigenous artist, all tales were known by the audience. What was important was the manner of presentation and the parallels that could be drawn with contemporary events. Diop set himself an even more difficult task. Because he was writing in French for a foreign audience, he had to rearrange the reader's senses to preserve the original. The reader was made to *hear* with his *eyes*; he was to take part from within his privacy; he was to be transformed from his everyday world of fact into Diop's world, which the western audience would no doubt dub as "fancy." Therefore, although Diop credits his achievement to his *griot*, Amadou Koumba, there is a great deal of craftsmanship at work.

He writes in "Crepuscule," a poem describing a tropical night, about a seeming absence of everything—an "invisible hand," an eye "that wants to see," and light that suggests the grim darkness of death. It is possible to see this as the setting for a story and indeed this type of observation does occur in the *contes*. Little must be disturbed; even a "rival lamp" could spoil the telling. Diop therefore stuck to the original in several important ways. The landscape is bare and against the sparse background the hyena and the lion intermingle with the Prince of the Great River, Samba-de-la-nuit and No-one-can-harm-me. Men and animals share a common world and eke out precarious, sometimes comic, existences in it. In addition to the interaction between men and other beings, Diop uses the sudden switch to song as any good storyteller does in West Africa. He also utilizes repetitive devices, which are not irritable to the reader, as they are to the listener-participator, and he keeps the introduction that jolts listener and reader alike into the story. And through all his tales run a moral, implicitly or explicitly stated.

The five sections of *Leurres et lueurs* (1960) mark a progression from the "leurres" or "bait" of French verse and servile imitation to the "lueurs" or "glimmering lights" of traditional African themes. No longer is it necessary for him to be obsessed with French meter and verse; now his verse can be "African." The *contes* begin with this self-understanding. It is wrong to regard them simply as "animal stories," since they emphasize the important aspects of human concourse—good breeding, the family, prayer, obligations of husbands and wives, and proper etiquette. In other words, the *contes*, told by Amadou Koumba, center on a society of African men and women. Birago Diop generalizes in the manner of the négritude writers, which means he is respectful of tradition. This is illustrated in "Le boli," a story in *Les nouveaux contes*. After his father's death, Tiéni loses all respect for tradition and mocks it. As a result he cannot take his father's place as a blacksmith nor can he be a man. Finally he is saved by the very traditions he despises.

Any writer creating for a French reading public had to consciously refashion part of his narration. In folktales there are no long descriptive passages such as one finds in Diop, nor is there any attempt to delineate character. Diop had to sketch in such details for his alien audience; however, at the same time he makes occasional use of indigenous words, not simply for exotic effect, but to bring the reader nearer to the experience. All his tales end with a return to a recognizable world in which his foreign audience can encounter something of themselves.

BERNARD DADIÉ

While Dadié was at Ponty in 1937, his play *Assémien Déhyle, roi du Sanwi* was produced at the Théâtre des Champs-Elysées in Paris. His poems which appeared in *Afrique debout* (1950) and *La ronde des jours* (1956)[28] show his concern with race and politics. His verse as well as his African tales, collected in *Légendes africaines* (1954) and *Le pagne noir* (1955), contrasts strangely with *Climbié* (1956), *Un nègre à Paris* (1959), and *Patron de New York* (1964).

As in his poems, the author is at the center in these three works, but there is a difference. *Climbié* describes how the "European crushed the Black colonial, with all the superiority of his citizenship." *Un nègre à Paris* (written in the form of a letter) satirizes the French way of life, and *Patron de New York* also makes use of a wider environment. Not only has he progressed from writing boyhood accounts to looking at wider horizons with an African eye, but he even identifies with "nos ancêtres les Gaulois." In general his work is in a curious limbo which is neither pro-African nor pro-European because he is himself too much an *évolué*.

Dadié's most recent work is the play *Les voix dans le vent* (1970). Nahoubou, frustrated and humiliated by the new leaders of his country, dreams of taking over the government and establishing peace. But when he does have his chance, he turns out to be just as corrupt as those he had replaced; he wages war against his neighbors and exploits his countrymen. At the end he is a lonely man, having been overthrown and then stripped of his power by the masses.

Climbié[29] is a short, semi-autobiographical novel in which Dadié speaks for "all the young people of Bassam." Many incidents are vividly described—the death of the police commissioner from yellow fever and the visit of a conjuror—which obviously stem from personal memories. He recalls his school days at William Ponty and the strong nationalistic rivalry among the boys. And he comments that "relations between the Europeans and Africans seemed more cordial [in Dakar] more human than in the Ivory Coast where the Europeans crushed the black colonial with all the advantages of his [French] citizenship" (p. 12).

Dadié was a devoted citizen of the Ivory Coast and after the folk play, he produced praise poems in the oral manner, such as this one to Houphouet-Boigny, later the prime minister:

> You are King of the factories
> You are King of the fields
> You are the people
> You are the master . . .[30]

The lines show Dadié's political commitment, but his commitment is not without hope. His optimism is fully revealed in a poem he wrote for the Dakar Festival of Negro Arts in 1960; his aim was "To replace man on his pedestal / To give him back again intrinsic values . . ." The child's voice reflects that hope is possible in the world.

The period between the publication of his two books of poetry (1950–56) shows a movement away from totally political concerns to racial onés. He does not glorify Africa, as he does in his early verse, nor does he express himself as an enemy of France. The early poetry (and indeed his own experiences) suggests this as a possible direction. Instead, however, Dadié has opted for a softer line. Though he has been in the forefront as an opposer of French "colonial" education, at the same time he is able to praise France and castigate the *évolués* for having forgotten the ways of their ancestors. And because Dadié recognizes this duality he can write of France:

> But it has given me, for example, Vercengetorix fighting
> savagely with Caesar over Gaul,
> It has shown me VOLTAIRE, BALZAC, HUGO, PERI, DANIELLE[31]

The poetry has come full circle: first rejection, then Black identification (later on universal), then acceptance of France.

Dadié has always been true to his particular moment of perception. *Climbié* is a painstakingly constructed pedagogical novel; it exposes the weaknesses of the French educational system, its insistence on competency in French, its harsh examinations that lead invariably to a position at the lower rung of the ladder. Only after the war does Climbié, the hero, muster the courage to tell others of such trickery. For this he is imprisoned. But the novel takes one to the future; the lion will lie down with the lamb—Africa and France will be at peace.

Un nègre à Paris (1959) takes a dispassionate look on France; it is as a "Frenchman" that Dadié praises the Paris that sleeps by day and wakes at night, describes the cruelty of kings who force ordinary men to suffer, and stresses the need for the French revolution which "proved to an astonished world that kings were mortal." Of course he does not "yes" Paris to death; he gently satirizes the Parisians' love of flowers, their lack of family life, and the statues of saints that adorn their churches. He also makes some harsh but true points—about the French lack of respect for age, the women who use so much make-up because "they refuse to die," and the men's feeling that "one white woman's worth two black women." And he is always the African; about Notre Dame he writes, "Our God does not need a house," and about the perversion of Christianity he explains, "Out of a God of Peace, people have made a God of Holy War." The strange love-hate relationship that dominates the book reveals that Dadié is not bitter; he is only attempting to see Paris through the eyes of a Frenchman of a different background. Written in the form of a letter, the book can scarcely be called a novel, though it provides interesting insights into Dadié the man.

Chapter 13

African Literature
in Portuguese

That African literature in Portuguese has received so little attention
seems surprising, for it is a formidable body of work of a varied
and a most appealing originality. Most of the writing comes from
Angola, Cape Verde, and Mozambique, but São Tomé and Guinea are
equally well represented. One need not be an advocate of Gilberto
Freyre's *luso-tropicalismo*[1] or the homogeneity of Portuguese culture in
the tropics to agree that certain common themes and attitudes emerge
from the writing, not least among them being sentiments that are
distinctly anti-Portuguese.

Although the Portuguese were last in the field of collecting folklore,
the actual writing of creative literature had an early beginning. In 1926
the Angolan H. Raposo published a novel, *Ana e Kalunga, os filhos do
mar* (Ana and Kalunga, the Sons of the Sea), and in 1934 the first
novel from Mozambique was written by Amália Proença Norte entitled
Em Portugal e África (In Portugal and Africa). That same year Fausto
Duarte published his novel *Auá* in Guinea. But the man who can be
regarded as the father of Portuguese prose in Africa is Oscar Ribas,
who began publishing as early as 1927. The pioneer in poetry is
undoubtedly Costa Alegre of São Tomé whose *Versos* was published
in 1916, though it must have been written years before, for he died
in 1890.

This impressive literary record is not surprising, for of the European
languages Portuguese has been spoken and, one is tempted to add,

339

written the longest in sub-Saharan Africa. Certainly it was spoken in the sixteenth and seventeenth centuries in places like the Congo and Benin in Nigeria. Pieter Lessing maintains that the Portuguese had been in northern Angola since 1482. In addition there are other references to the relationship between Africana and Portuguese; Columbus himself said in the journal of his first voyage that "on many occasions the men of Guinea have been brought to learn the language of Portugal."[2] Certainly the Congolese King Afonso I wrote to John III of Portugal during the sixteenth century, as is evident in this extract from one such letter from Afonso to John.

We already had written Your Highness that the virtuous priest Br. Álvaro, intending to put an end to our life, conspired on a holiday with seven or eight white men to fire their rifles all at once while we were hearing mass, so that they would kill our person for a celebration of the feast in front of that true Saviour of the world whom it pleased to save us from such great danger so miraculously that the bullet went through the hem of our garment and hit our Chief of Police who stood next to our person and from there went on and killed a man and wounded two others.[3]

But there is no continuous prose tradition from the sixteenth century. The only link has been the writing in Portuguese about Africa which varies from travel accounts to creative literature, literature written by settlers, and to a limited extent folk literature. There is no vernacular literature and little drama.

The Politics of Prose

Mario de Andrade contends that African literature in Portuguese received an impetus with the foundation of the *Vamos descobrir Angola* movement in 1948. Various prose writers attempted to express the ideals of this movement and among them he singles out Óscar Ribas who "in his work of implementing, in the novel and by the story, clearly outlined folkloric aspects of Angolese life."[4] Óscar Ribas, a mulatto, sincerely felt the need to discover his African past. His work is symptomatic of a great deal of African literature in Portuguese in that it is tethered to nationalistic feeling and endeavor.

To say this is not to minimize it; the artist can be a fervent spokesman for a cause and yet be good. The "message" could even be a limitation that he might choose to impose on himself. But it obviously did not restrict Ribas. For example, in the short piece "The Angola" Ribas effectively describes a farewell scene, using poetic generalities to make the departure an occasion of universal sadness:

Like glow-worms in the fastness of night doubt stabbed the fog of sadness. Alas, who knows whether they will come back? How many mothers will be bereft of their sons, how many wives without their husbands? How much joy, how much sorrow, will the separation bring? Will they be happy in those lands of fever? Will they find work there, riches and dignity? God would surely help them in their desires?

Another siren is heard. The air weeps; love weeps within the heart. Handkerchiefs flutter anxiously still, waving "Farewell!" into the deep distance.

In this last farewell, the boat shivers mournfully. The melancholy deepens and grows cold. That sadness, alas, suggests the last throes of death.[5]

The poetic insight Ribas brings to the short story marks him as primarily a writer of short stories. The story "A Praga," published in his last work, *Ecos de minha terra* (Echoes of My Land, 1951) was awarded the Margaret Wrong Prize in 1952.

Leonard Sainville has referred to a certain aspect of Ribas's technique as "the analysis of situation and character,"[6] and this certainly emerges in "Festa de núpcias" (Wedding Feast) from *Uanga—Feitiço* (1951).[7] Centered on a couple in an Angolan village, it describes how Joanna the thwarted lover consults a sorcerer and resorts to slander in order to win back the affection of her former lover Joachim. Although he is telling a story, Ribas unobtrusively slips in information about the marriage customs of his people, the Kimbundu. During the latter part of his life, he made a study of traditional religion and the oral literature of his tribe and he plans to write what will probably be his best work— a historical novel set in Angola. He had obviously not as yet been able to bridge the final gap between generations, which would have made him part of what was really his grandparents' heritage, and thus some of his descriptions are those of an outsider, albeit a sympathetic and humble one. For instance the picture of Joanna and the sorcerer in consultation does not ring true:

The scorcerer made a little hole in the ground with a knife. He scratched a stone in order to polish it and made two strokes on it in the form of a cross; then he put the stone in a hole. Then he counted to nine and the egg was already encased in this mixture of clay. Then he put it upright in the hole and he exclaimed in a solemn tone of voice, "Mr Joachim sit down here. Give up the other woman and come back to this one for this is now your home. Do you hear me?" (pp. 61–65)

Joanna is equally seen in this exotic and over-romanticized light. She is said to have "evocative hunches which are characteristic of the women of her race" and "big white eyes nailed into her olive-coloured face." But the story introduces a note that Ribas will probably explore more and more in his later writing—the note of protest. It is protest made even uneasier because it is blended with exoticism.

Both are best seen in a short story by Manuel Lopes of Cape Verde. There is the poetry, the hunger, the insatiable yearning:

The rainy season only starts some time in July or August, but for me the sky begins to take on a meaning that I had not known it to have before. The loveliest, purest of clouds, those wanderers of the airy spaces, which used to make me dream of adventures on the seven seas, have lost their old magic. It is not easy to reconcile their airiness and dazzling whiteness with the idea of evil. But it is true; they are the most tragic and best hated phantoms that haunt these islands. Their white veils offer no protection, they do not mitigate the thirst and misery of man, they do not even offer any hope whatever. They are sterile and useless. Now they linger high up there, coquettishly, ironical and indifferent, now they pass by flightily, carried by the breeze, like those immaculate princesses who hurry on, when having to pass through the streets where ragged children live . . .[8]

This theme of protest is explored time and again in African poetry of Portuguese expression, but in the prose it is never obtrusive, for it is always conveyed in conjunction with incident, thereby adding a certain toughness to the writing.

Castro Soromenho often succeeds in doing just this. Although he is a white Portuguese who settled and lived in Angola for many years, no consideration of Portuguese literature in Africa can exclude him since he has managed to break away from the exotic to paint a realistic picture of Angola. According to Roger Bastide, "Though he is a white man, Castro Soromenho is an African writer, . . . in the first place because he has lived in Angola . . . Africa has penetrated into his flesh, has grafted itself in his body and the complaint of the Black as well as his music has become the very rhythm of his blood."[9] His novels show this development from exoticism to social realism. For instance, *Homens sem caminho* (Men without a Way; 1942) is the story of a young man who tries to rouse his tribe to defend themselves against another tribe. The later *Calenga* (1945) is a love story. Both attempt to depict an Africa without the whites and suffer from a kind of missionary endeavor, not only to do good but to seem to be doing it. With *Terra morta* (Dead Land; 1949) Soromenho left the romantic novel behind and broke new ground in *neo-realismo*. Influenced by Brazilian *modernismo*, especially the work of Jorge Amado and José Lins do Rêgo, he no longer was interested merely in the literary nature of art but in its social possibilities as well.

Terra Morta is set in an old Angolan trading station, Camaxilo, which comes to stand for colonial values and colonial society; all strands and sections of it are represented—the white settlers and their Black mistresses, the white administrators who feel they are a cut above the settlers, the indigenous Black people, the population of mulattoes, and the "civilized" Negroes (the *assimilados*) who look down on the other Africans.

Silva, the slightly corrupt, hard-hearted administrator, and Américo, the revolutionary who grew up on a Brazilian plantation and knows that integration is possible even in the Angolan *sertão* (bush), are the central figures. The utter frustration of the colonized and the colonizers is seen in the character of Américo. At the end of the novel he has to leave the dying Camaxilo, for the futility of his privileged existence has become a burden to him: "At other times lying low on his couch, he would let the hours of the dusk, the slow and bitter hours, pass in front of him. His thoughts were lost. He was incapable of formulating an idea, even an agreeable memory. He was full of indifference for everything and for all." Though no crusader, Américo is the reflective conscience of the book, its moral and social pivot, lending the novel an extra dimension of imagination. If Soromenho is "the only novelist of Portuguese black Africa who does not limit himself to the examination of simple structures of society,"[10] then it is characters such as Américo who deepen the meaning and significance of his work. There is no apparent dividing line separating good and evil in Soromenho's writing after *Terra Morta*.

For instance *Viragem* (The Swerve; 1957) is an even more bitter presentation of the immorality of colonialism. At the end Américo's character-equivalent is not allowed to escape; he dies. Consequently what a reviewer has said about the style of *Viragem* applies equally well to *Terra Morta*; "purposely dull and lustreless, [it] seems to contribute to the impression of despondency and distress that grips us."[11]

The exoticism from which Ribas and Soromenho managed to rid themselves is very much present in the work of other white Portuguese writers on Africa. One such writer is Rodrigues Júnior, who has received approval for being a writer of "human sympathy."[12] But the following extract from *Muende* (1960) indicates that his efforts are over-romanticized:

Pedro da Maia saw her big, round black eyes, moist with emotion, fixed on his with such tenderness that he was deeply moved. He remembered Francisco Diogo. In Nyassa, Francisco Diogo had spoken to him of the tenderness of the Negro woman, of her devotion, of all the devotion he owed to his Motase, who was his only support during those evil days of life in the backlands, and who was only interested in steadying him during his isolation and solitude.

343

So many whites who had lived in Africa like Francisco Diogo had not had his courage to confess it without a feeling of shame. Pedro da Maia thought that he now approved of Francisco Diogo's life with the girl Motase.[13]

Rodrigues Júnior lives in Mozambique, as does Luís Bernardo Honwana, a more recent Black writer. But he has none of Honwana's ability to penetrate into the personalities and lives of the people about whom he writes. As has been shown with Soromenho, this has nothing to do with color; it has everything to do with sincerity in its narrowest and truest possible sense—in its tryst with reality.

Indeed realism is what one finds in Honwana's world. His short "Inventory of Furniture and Effects" is simply the description of the various rooms of a house in which a large family live and of the conditions they experience. There is the same detachment of Ribas, the same protest of Soromenho, although more muted. As Honwana writes:

> Between the door that opens onto the bathroom and the one that leads into this room there is a bookcase with five shelves, all full of books. It is covered with a cloth matching the sitting-room curtains. The curtains in Mama's room are made of the same cloth. Only in this room the curtains are different. They're made from a thick, yellowish material. Tina says the cloth is ugly, but when Papa was imprisoned she took down two curtains and made them up into a skirt that didn't look like any other skirt I'd ever seen. I think it was ugly.[14]

Honwana's style is very matter of fact, but the protest is nevertheless uppermost. His uninvolved detachment is not uncommon in African poetry in Portuguese. Fernando Mourão partly explains this lack of involvement when he remarks, "Herein lies the principal characteristic that expresses itself in Portuguese, it being the fruit of a social class in full evolution and not of a caste. The dynamic of social evolution is being mirrored in the new literature."[15] Honwana expresses the new social consciousness in stories describing overcrowded houses full of children who all eat noisily and an old woman who represents some kind of hope for an evolution out of chaos. His best portrait of such a woman is in his short story "The Old Woman." The hero has been beaten in a bar and reluctantly goes home to his squabbling children. When they go to bed, he can finally talk; he tells the old woman little, but they understand one another.

> I only stopped looking when the old woman talked in a way that made me realise that she had long been meditating on how to say something she eventually did not say. She only said, "My son."
> Her fingers were rough, but her dark velvet embrace was soft and warm, and exuded the soft pure fragrance of the good years of my faith.[16]

There are times, however, when she refuses to "understand." In "Papa, the Snake and I,"[17] the boy watches a snake kill Mr. Castro's dog. Later Mr. Castro calls and threatens his father; the boy and his father understand the act—it is their vindication for the continuous usurpation of a legion of Mr. Castros. But the mother's considerations are more practical—she accepts her servility and therein lies her capacity for martyrdom, her triumph in suffering, and her aloneness. In "The Hands of the Blacks," the boy hears many stories about the possible reasons why the palms of Black men are white, but the old mother's is the truest, the saddest, the most resigned:

"God made Blacks because they had to be. They had to be, my son. He thought they really had to be. . . . Afterwards he regretted having made them because the other men laughed at them and took them off to their homes and put them to serve like slaves or not much better. But because he couldn't make them all be white, for those who were used to seeing them black would complain, He made it so that the palms of their hands would be exactly like the palms of the hands of other men. And do you know why that was? Of course you don't know, and it's not surprising, because many, many people don't know. Well, listen: it was to show that what men do is only the work of men . . . That what men do is done by hands that are the same— hands of people who, if they had any sense, would know that before everything else they are men. He must have been thinking of this when he made the hands of the Blacks the same as the hands of those men who thank God they are not Black."

After telling me all this, my mother kissed my hands. As I ran off the yard to play ball, I thought that I had never seen a person cry so much when nobody had hit them.[18]

Commitment in Poetry

Unfortunately this type of subtlety is not found in Portuguese poetry by Africans. Moore and Beier even contend that the poetry is "little more than a sheer cry of agony and loss."[19] But it is more than this and certainly one finds the poetry repeating to some extent the pattern of the prose. Costa Alegre, for instance, tends to romanticize the Black woman, as in his "A negra" (The Black Woman):

Friendly black woman, mimosa tender, beautiful coal
Which produces the diamond.
Daughter of the sun, star-burnt
Through the heat of the Highest,

Put your open beautiful face
On my chest
Sleep girl, deserted dove,
I wake for you.[20]

As has been mentioned, Alegre's poetry was published in 1916 and must have stimulated other writing. But Mario de Andrade, who helped edit an anthology in 1953, said that it was the poetry of the Angolan Viriato da Cruz which "inaugurated the modern nationalist current." Da Cruz's verse is revolutionary in flavor, and although one might agree with the sentiments this does not necessarily make it good poetry. For instance, his poem "Kola Nut" depends heavily for effect on the symbol of the kola-nut seller whom no one wants to patronize. It verges on the ridiculous when the poet says that because the demands of the new civilization include coffee for breakfast no one will buy her kola-nuts. If by this the poet hopes to criticize the new civilization and point out the virtues of the old, it must be instantly affirmed that he has failed. Not so, however, with "So Santo" (Mr. Santo), which also makes use of dialogue. Mr. Santo has fallen on evil days but still the people greet him— all except the old grandmother, who sees his downfall as revenge by N'gombo, the god of truth. The old grandmother, like Honwana's old woman, is the embodiment of Africa in woman. It is this that links da Cruz with Langston Hughes and Nicolas Guillen, with what he calls "voz de todas as vozes" (voice of all voices). Thus in "Mama Negra" (Black Mother)[21] he writes with truth and feeling:

> Your existence mother, living drama of a race
> Drama of flesh and blood
> Written by life with the pen of centuries
>
> Through your voice
>
> Came voices of plantations
> U.S.A., Brazil, Cuba . . .

Alfredo Margarido has argued that the satirical tendency in da Cruz's poetry frequently hides the provocative aspect of his work,[22] but this same "provocative" aspect is uppermost in the verse of other poets. As will be noted, the theme of Africa—abstract, impersonal Africa—and its link with the New World repeatedly emerges in the poetry. Though Costa Alegre did not establish this from the beginning, he did emphasize the alienation of the poet. As Almada Negreiros was to write about Alegre after his death:

> As a poet he loved suffering
> And he loved without being loved
> For there is no woman in the world to stand the caresses
>   of a black man; the burning desires
> Of a being who is only an outcast, a condemned man. (p. 62)

What Andrade had commented on years later in his second anthology, Alegre had in fact already done: "Daily every intellectual sees himself obliged through the rapid and exciting course of events of our century to take a stand on—events of human, social or political importance."[23] Alegre had taken his stand firmly on the side of the liberals, at that time the radicals. At this distance from him, our own age can regard him as a man of courage and a poet of worth.

Naturally the temper of the poetry varied from one area to another. The poetry of Cape Verde, for instance, expresses the longing for release from the arid earth, for the liberating journey over the sea, and the frustration resulting from the compulsion to stay. As Barbosa concludes in his "Poema do mar":

> The demand at every hour
> To go away is brought to us by the sea.
> The despairing hope for the long journey
> And yet to be always forced to stay.[24]

This same love-hate relationship, the mixture of yearning and nostalgia, is present in Azevedo's poem "Terra longe" (Distant Land)[25] which describes the desire of those who want to migrate and the injunction to remain at home. This internal conflict is the universal one of the lost individual at odds within himself. As Ovídio Martins puts it in "Poema salgado" (Salty Poem):

> For I am born at a point of the beach
> therefore I bear within me
> all seas of the world.[26]

This universal *Weltschmerz* relates the poetry of Cape Verde to the rest of Portuguese Africa and to the entire continent. It emerges out of the poet's immediate need to write about emigration to the roça plantations of São Tomé and Île de Principe; some of the poets were themselves migrants and their poems gave rise to the *cancioneiro* or a collection of songs of sadness, as this type of poetry is called. It is in this way that the poetry expresses an "extreme sensitivity and pronounced melancholy which is wavering between anguish and fear."[27]

The yearning and hopes of the poets of Cape Verde are not passive; latent in them are the seeds of identification with Africa. Only a few poets in Cape Verde express this but in São Tomé and Île de Principe a type of protest poetry against the poor conditions of the workers and against the white Portuguese administrator has developed. Such protest can take various forms and attention has already been paid to the way in which Alegre glorified the Black woman. But whereas Alegre accepted the quality of being Black, Francisco José Tenreiro used it as a rallying cry. Tenreiro's verse has obviously been influenced by négritude, for one of his best known poems, "Ilha de nome santo" (Island with the Name of a Saint; 1943), concerns itself with the social stratification in São Tomé. But Tenreiro is no die-hard champion of Black racialism. Himself a mulatto, he claims that he is "a European with a darker skin."[28] His poetry is therefore not totally committed to the Black cause as is Damas's, for he feels that the true salvation of the Black man lies in his acceptance of the values of the white world. This, however, does not prevent him from attacking the evils of colonial society, which he does with a delicate blend of satire and wit in his bitter "Romance de Seu Silva Costa":

> Silva Costa
> Came to the island
> Threadbare trousers
> Two pence worth of illusion
> And decided to return.
>
> Silva Costa
> Came to the island
> Alcohol-trade
> Trade with human beings
> Real estate business
>
> Ui!
> Silva Costa
> A great white man
> No threadbare trousers
> Empty of illusions—full of money![29]

A younger poet, Alda do Espírito Santo, is fiercer in her denunciations. Her poetry has the hot histrionic flavor of some of David Diop's verse, as is seen in these lines describing the 1953 uprising and its violent suppression by the Portuguese:

> The blood of those fallen
> In the forest of death
> The innocent blood
> That soaks the earth
> In a shuddering silence
> Will fertilise the earth
> And claim justice
>
> The flame of humanity
> Sings the hope
> For a world without barriers

Where freedom becomes the banner
Of all human beings.[30]

The hymnlike, overflowing patriotism spoils the poem but beneath it lie a sincere desire for freedom and a summons to revolution.

Perhaps the truest poetry of revolt, of the search for origins, of the rejection of European values—a poetry, in other words, strongly influenced by négritude—is to be found in Angola. It is true that Angolan literature is still in the making but one need not agree with a correspondent to a Lisbon review who wrote in 1960, "But what of the Angolan literature one hears so much about? Angolan literature, meaning a literature expressing a peculiar social and cultural reality within the area of Portuguese expansion, is limited till now to a few propositions—not works, because significant works are non-existent." This is indeed a false assertion. There are over fourteen Angolan writers who have published approximately twenty-seven works. Even if one were to exclude from consideration Soromenho who was born in Mozambique, one still finds a sizable body of significant prose by Oscar Ribas and poetry by Thomas Viriato da Cruz and Agostino Neto. These writers are all fully committed to the négritude cause. To say this is not to belittle them, for they are engaged in a quest for identification. Fernando Mourão has correctly identified the dualism of culture that brings this about: "If we find a yearning to rediscover *négritude* through the fixation of characteristically African cultural elements, we note nevertheless that the authors are unable to escape their European education, and thus their works, while recited in Africa, become more easily accessible to the European reader." But side by side with this must be placed Andrade's contention that the Black poets "successfully, to a greater or lesser extent, used the single theme—the darkness of colonial oppression. This results in the political, revolutionary, *engagement* of this poetry which hurts the sensibility of so many Western aesthetes. Who could deny that this poetry confined to reach only African minorities must eventually make room for another one—one with the rhythms of a 'new language of the future'?"[31]

The earliest Angolan poet was Joaquim Dias Cordeiro da Matta who wrote in the nineteenth century. He attempted to create an Angolan idiom in his poetry but it was not until the *Vamos Descobrir Angola* (Let Us Discover Angola) movement was formed in Luanda in 1948 that poetry received an impetus. This was aided by reviews like "Nensagem" (The Message) which was founded in 1951 and centered on the "Movimento dos Novos Intelectuais de Angola" (Movement of the Young Intellectuals of Angola). Although both the movements and the reviews were suppressed, the right atmosphere had been created for literary activity. As Andrade puts it, "Negro and white poets born in the colony exalted the consciousness linked to the soil; they sought an equilibrium of the language; they enriched the 'dominant' language; they erected a new tower to the popular idiom and gave their message a social content. A literature of *national* and *social* emancipation began to develop."[32]

Chief among the articulators of the new social order was Agostino Neto, whose poetry was a fierce protest. In "Adeus à hora da partida" (Farewell before the Hour of Departure) he returns to the familiar themes of the Cape Verde poets, but with an outspoken hostility toward the lot of the Black man:

> Forced to burn away our lives in the coffee-fields
> Black people without knowledge
> Who are to respect the white man
> And to fear the rich man[33]

The identification with Angolan peasant society, or what Andrade calls "the desire to assume the condition of the native," is often subtly revealed. In "Kinaxixi," the poet concludes in lines of moving simplicity:

> After the sun had set
> light would be turned on and I
> would wander off
> thinking that our life after all is simple
> too simple
> for anyone who is tired and still has to walk.[34]

Most of Neto's poems are carefully reasoned efforts; they are not just outpourings of an unrestrained emotionalism. For instance "Criar" (Create) describes man's will to survive in spite of obstacles. Neto is equally capable of writing in the négritude vein, and "Fogo e ritmo" (Fire and Rhythm)[35] is the familiar poem about the rhythm of Black movement. He also can express the passive and futile longing of some of the other poets who have been considered:

> And over my songs
> My dreams
> My eyes
> My cries
> Over my lonely world
> There is the still-standing time
>
> And still my life
> Is ready for life
> And yet my longing.[36]

350

But always Neto's reasoning bolsters the attitudes and transmutes the grandiloquent public statements into murmurings of a refined sensibility. Angolan poets make conscious use of African words in their verse. Antonio Jacinto has written a poem called "Monangamba," which is the Kimbundu word for the son of a slave. Geraldo Bessa Victor speaks in "Kalundu"[37] of a woman who possesses a spirit which enables her to dance the *batuque*. In another poem this African dance is actually described, and the onomatopoeic sound of African musical instruments placed side by side with Portuguese ones is used for evocative effect:

> Marimbas, Ngomas, Tom-toms
> Bells, Kissanges, Chingufos
> Wild batuque and madness
> Soaked in palm-wine.[38]

Andrade has gone a step further, experimenting with traditional songs. "Muimbu ua Sabalu" (Son of Sabalu) is a variation of a folk song about a family which breaks up because the youngest son has to be sent to São Tomé to work. In "Poema,"[39] Oliveira uses lines from a popular song to emphasize the plight of people who are forced to work away from home: "A rotten banana has no luck / fru-ta-ta, fru-ta-ta, fru-ta-ta." The poem ends on a note of frustration; the plight of those away from home is as whimsical as gossip:

> Human beings
> Human beings
> Stories of human beings.

Portuguese Guinea has contributed little to the literature but, as might be expected, some attempt has been made to "Africanize" the poetry. The chief Guinean poet is Terêncio Silva; his "Meia-noite" (Midnight)[40] is a simple descriptive poem which makes use of such words as *tabanca* (village), *djumbaçao* (meeting place), and *messinho* (a good fetish that protects) to achieve its effect. But the effect is a forced one; there is no subtlety, but only a fanciful display, which merely spoils what might have been a good poem.

In Mozambique the political climate is entirely different. As Pieter Lessing has remarked, "A peculiar difference between Angola and Mozambique is that while there is definite 'public opinion' in the former, I found nowhere in Mozambique anything resembling a collective opinion. It is possible because a Mozambique nationalism has not yet developed in the same sense as an Angolan nationalism has emerged." What one finds in the absence of any strong national pride are an identification with a larger-than-life "Africa" and references to social malpractices, especially that of sending men to work in the South African gold mines. One of the older poets, Rui de Noronha, uses biblical terminology in "Surge e ambula" (Get Up and Walk) to contrast unfavorably the dearth he feels exists in Africa with the progress of Europe. As he says tauntingly of Africa, "You sleep and the world turns Oh land of mystery / You sleep . . ."[41] The self-criticism is a new note in this poetry, and the rejection of Mozambique is the acceptance of Africa in its largest and most incomprehensible sense—the Africa of the imagination.

Other poems demonstrate attempts to experiment with language. "My Problem with the Swamps" by Valente Malangatana makes use of standard Portuguese, pidgin Portuguese, creole, and some English, in speaking of the rivalry among prostitutes as they battle for foreigners:

> so many foreigners
> so much cheating: this one's mine, come here, come
> the mulatto girl so fine . . .[42]

The verse also describes the girls' efforts to talk in English—"eh, no sphiki ingiligi"—which culminates in a corrupt policeman's attempt to communicate with an arrested whore:

> my house pretty one just there by swamps
> on road painted blue
> I not go back there, many people I not like.

"The Swamps" is a red-light district in Mozambique and Malangatana devotes several poems to describing its moral turpitude and degradation. In another poem, crisp language makes the point:

> The girl goes with him [a seaman] to the docks
> the guard won't let her in
> but never mind . . .
> he: bye bye, lovely, I'll see you next night
> the taxi takes the lovely back
> the taxi-driver: you not want me?

Malangatana sides with the downtrodden—the poor miner who must go to South Africa, the prostitute, the night-soil worker, and the Chope, a group employed as street-sweepers. The poet writes:

> I am sad
> when they speak ill of the Chope
> the Chope is an inventer
> he is full of promise

José Cravirinha's poetry expresses concern about his country through a pathetic individual questioning. The protagonist in "Apenas" (Just), for example, seeks happiness in the midst of the despair, for "we don't know if we shall come back." "A semente está comigo" (The Seed in Me) is a song celebrating the oneness of all mankind, and "3 dimensões" (Three Dimensions) takes a light look at mechanization. His style, crisp and precise, is exemplified in the first part of the poem which describes how "o deus da máquina . . . tem na mão o segredo das bielas" (the god of machines . . . holds in his hands the secrets of the pistons) and culminates in this wry comment:

> And on the branch line . . .
> —feet pressed against the steel of the coaches—
> bursting his lungs
> god of the trolley.[43]

In "A semente está comigo," Cravirinha uses repetition—"sangue dos sangue de todos os sangues" (blood from the blood of all blood)—to convey something of a liturgical effect which climaxes in "perdoa, irmão" (forgive brother). In the final analysis all men are one.

Noemia de Sousa, the other African woman writing in Portuguese, expresses the imaginative concept of Africa very frequently in her poetry. As she says:

> for I am no more than a shell of flesh
> in which the revolt of Africa congealed
> its cry swollen with hope.[44]

Or again in "Apolo" (Call), she bemoans her separation from the peasant life of her "sister of the bush." She too can be harshly critical and like Rui de Noronha she explores the theme of the men forced to work in the South African gold mines.[45] In "Magaiça" she describes the immigrant upon his arrival in South Africa, his eyes "big with admiration," his heart "narrowed down with fear." His return to Mozambique is satirized, for he is "a strange being in ridiculous clothing." His illusions have become a means to lustful living:

> Youth and health
> And the lost illusions
> Which will shine like stars on the bosom of a lady
> In the nights of some city.[46]

This is the most bitter denunciation; he has squandered his ideals in the pursuit of a physical something that does not matter very much all. The blame is not placed on the society that produced him, but squarely on the man himself. Valente Malangatana, a younger poet, states this more explicitly in "The Miner Who Survived":

> I am the survivor of the millions
> dead for want of pure air;
> they were not accustomed
> to air conditioning,
> and then the mine caved in.
>
> they died, died without farewell
> under that mine of gold
> under that cavern
> where there are no chickens cheeping
> where there are only men[47]

The conclusion of the poem recollects the inevitable history of the colonized and the wickedness to which he has been exposed. Only the brute in him can hope to live on:

> and as we had no beads
> we died, died, died
> and I awoke, I am a survivor.
> I lifted my hands without weeping
> asking for help
> and because they were my friends
> they allowed me to survive[48]

Such poetry leads us to conclude with Margarido that "it is certain that the melancholy and despair with which the poetry of Mozambique is tinged is due to the influence of the English language. Spirits and blues have marked the whole poetry of the country." Most of the poets have in fact experimented with American Negro spirituals and blues— among them José Craveirinha, Noemia de Sousa, and Marcellino dos Santos (who writes under the pen name of Kulungano). Moreover, what one finds is an identification with the Black American. For example, Kulungano mentions Paul Robeson in his poem "Onde estou" (Where I Am), and in "A um menino do meu país" (To a Child of My Country) Emmet Till (the young American boy who was lynched) is described as running barefoot like a Mozambique child.[49] This helps to link the poetry of Mozambique to that of São Tomé and Angola (but not to Cape Verde), for they all actively express frustration and revolution, frequently with reference to lynchings in America, discrimination in the American South, and the misery of Harlem, to the music of the spirituals and the blues, and to Paul Robeson, Louis Armstrong, Marion Anderson, and the poetry of Langston Hughes.

In the final analysis the literature of Portuguese Africa is no negative shriek of despair. It is a positive statement of grievances out of which the writers expect a new hope will emerge. The note of *stirb und werde*, expressed in "Terra mãe" (Mother Earth) by Kulungano, is typical of the faith of African writers in Portuguese:

> Also a young corn
> Broken in its flight
>
> Falls to earth, eternal mother
> And the cornfield grows[50]

It is the statement of an imaginative belief that defies every convention of society in order to express an absolute and irrevocable truth—that man is capable of overcoming the obstacles within him to become spiritually triumphant. From the dismemberment of social values they seek to create a whole man; their commitment is the form and purpose of their art.

Chapter 14

Contemporary African Prose and Poetry in French

The Perfect Past

The perfect past sought to glorify not only African civilization, but the French empire. The first African novel in French, *Force-Bonté* (1926) by Bakary Diallo, merely sang of the splendors of France, its strength and its righteousness. Twelve years later Paul Hazoumé was to write *Doguicimi* (1938),[1] a book centering on tribal customs and kinship loyalty—a theme very different from Diallo's. The novel is ostensibly about the conflict between "enlightenment" and "conservatism" (represented by the main character King Guézo). He is depicted as a man of strength and Hazoumé uses Prince Toffa's long speech early in the work to express anti-white sentiments. But neither Doguicimi (who is either in jail or in tears for the greater part of the book) nor Prince Toffa, each a symbol of enlightenment, is really a live person. It is significant that Prince Toffa is killed at the end. And one finds it difficult to sympathize with Doguicimi who is an apologist for the French, feeling that they are the more fit to rule.

This wealth of information, though interesting, burdens the novel and makes for extremely slow reading. So much, for instance, is said about the king's servants and wives, their morning bath, their cleaning duties, and the king's ritual observance of tradition that the reader seeks in vain to find some link between this and the rest of the book. But there is none; the details are given only to honor the fact that "the day which was rising should be the happiest for Dahomey and its idol." However, although this opening scene is irrelevant in the context of the novel, it remains a powerful praise poem to the king and the people described in the book.

J. Severio Naigisiki has published a two-volume semi-autobiographical novel, *Mes transes à trente ans*,[2] which is a longer version of his earlier *Escapade ruandaise* (1949). Written in the form of a diary, it describes both realistically and para-mystically the life of a man in Rwanda. Although the book does not have any obvious political intentions, Naigisiki manages to convey something of the mood of life in Africa by exposing the problems of daily existence, its hardships and rewards. At times, however, the heavy language and the pompous style spoil the flow of the narrative.

Diallo, Hazoumé, and Naigisiki assert, in varying degrees, the glories of the past. In some instances this is the past that the French brought with them and of which Africans are the natural inheritors. In other instances the past is marred by ingroup conflict between Africans and Africans or Africans and Europeans. In the work of Seydou Badian, however, the traditional world is harmonious.

Badian's *Sous L'orage* takes place in an unnamed town on the banks of the Niger and in a village nearby and contrasts modern and traditional life. Kany, the daughter of Benfa and Jené, is in love with Samou, but her father wants her to marry an old merchant. Although she wishes to heed the traditional ways of her father, she refuses because of her modern education. Ultimately Kany sees that she is being fooled into marrying the merchant and she curses all traditions. So does Samou, but he gradually is made to realize that a few young people cannot alter the authority of tradition; a wise adviser predicts, however, that matters will change. With this question mark, the novel ends.

Badian utilizes the African traditional past to reveal his notion that the artist is a myth-maker and then he uses his story to pinpoint common misunderstandings. These tensions spring from the conflict between tradition and westernization, and Badian inevitably sides with tradition.

Djibril Tamsir Niane's vision is less limited than Badian's but nevertheless he is an advocate of tradition. Whereas in Badian's novel the young are forced to respect the old, in Niane's work the old, the traditional, are given special significance for the young. Niane is a historian and *Soundjata* (1960), which relies on oral sources, is a detailed documentary account of a West African king's *relevance*. His novel, like those so far considered in this section, attempts to enlarge the possibilities of myth by beginning with a well-known hero and giving him the stature of a god. This is not of course foreign to oral literature; *Soundjata* therefore revives the myth.

The story of Soundjata relates how he overcomes all opposition to become king and to establish a reign of peace; it is an affirmation of the presence of legend. Niane uses praise phrases, the apparently fantastic, and myths (the date is 1230) to revitalize the tale. Little is said, however, about the "historical" Soundjata and how he transformed the small kingdom of Kangaba into the great Mali Empire.

The past is therefore true and real, for the *griot* in the novel says so. Soundjata's magic cane, his adroitness as a hunter indicate his affinity to the truths of the traditional world. Often these truths are also apparent in the natural world, and two poets, Joseph Bognini and Yondo Epanya, stress this point in their poetry. Their style harks back to the négritude writers previously considered, but both lament the mockery which the present makes of the perfect past.

Bognini writes with a distinctive African sensibility, using landscape to convey a sense of pride and longing because, as he says, "we have ended our happy days" and to speculate on the nature of life. His verse is full of sounds and scents with sad refrains that pinpoint some particular consideration: "Destiny promised us the moon / It does not respond to us any more."[3] Bognini is unique as an African poet in that he is concerned with the natural world. But he does not allow this to weaken his style nor does he indulge in effete warblings on the glories of nature. Always, nature is related to man and man is forever yearning for a past which can never be regained.

After studying in Douala and Paris, Epanya Yondo wrote *Kamerun! Kamerun!* (1960),[4] the volume for which he is best known. His verse, published in a local language and translated into French, utilizes the folk poetry of Cameroon, and through the use of symbol celebrates the independence of all Africa. Repetition in the volume helps to convey the folk-rhythm of his own oral poetry. For instance, "nous nous retroverons" is built up through successive stanzas until in the final line the last word "demain" is added, suggesting that the return to the African past, though not yet realized, will ultimately come about.

Yondo's poetry also strongly resembles the exoticism of the négritude writers, as evidenced in these lines from "Kamerun":

> Yesterday still it is night bathed in moonlight
> A few bursts of laughter crackle and I hear the tom-tom
> When the flesh stretches, giving itself
> To the black knotting hands, knotted life. (p. 12)

Or in these from "Femme":

Woman!
You are that sacred palm-tree
That I have chosen
Among all the plants
Of the flora of my native village. (p. 15)

In short, his poetry, reminiscent of Senghor's, is a quaint yoking of the natural world and African pride.

Keita Fodeba, Cheick Ndao, Charles Nokan, Joseph Seid, and Martial Sinda are all upholders of the traditional world as well. Whereas Hazoumé had documented a past and Niane had attempted to re-create one, these writers use the immediate present to elevate it to the level of the past. Through references to music, traditional beliefs, and certain sacred relationships within the culture, they endeavor to show that their work is linked very closely with the oral artist's. They are, therefore, not mere entertainers, but serious vindicators of the culture extolling the beauty and dignity of the traditional past.

Like most of the literary artists considered in this section, their writing can be deemed "excessive" in that they do not hesitate to move the reader with flamboyant phrases and exaggerated comparisons. This says nothing about their sincerity but tells one a great deal about the problems that face the upholders of the tradition; how best (and this is indeed the paradox) can they describe the ancient glories of an African culture in a European tongue?

An inherent conflict, therefore, is found in what these authors write and say. Sometimes it is implicit, but often it only becomes explicit when one realizes that, despite the authority of the *griot*, despite the local references, despite the intense concern with traditional form, they are creating in a foreign idiom. As will be seen, the conflict is uppermost in the work of Fily-Dabo Sissoko. The past is still sacred, though scarred by the invasion of the French and their atrocities, but this view is not fully exposed until we meet with such writers as Kane, Laye, and U'Tamsi. Those who stress the perfect African past may be, like the writers now under discussion, upholders of a tradition that goes back to Diallo and Hazoumé or they might fall more conveniently into the category of those who emphasize the sanctity of unity (the village and school) and who symbolize their own loss of culture in the sad portraits of the tragic mulattoes.

Poémes africains (1958) demonstrates Keita Fodeba's technique of blending the oral lore of his people with his own variations on known themes. Also his poetry often utilizes the tale for didactic purposes; for instance *Aube Africaine* (1965) is the story of Haman, a Senegalese rifleman decorated for bravery during the Second World War, who is killed on his return home to Africa. The poem sings Haman's story to the accompaniment of the guitar, cora, and bafalo music; the tom-toms announce his death. Fodeba suggests that this is the reward the colonial master gives to the good colonial. It must be stressed that this is only an imitation of an oral poem; too many overt descriptions of dawn, palm trees, and sky prevent it from being genuine oral literature. However, it does succeed as a piece of excellent propaganda.

Cheick Ndao is also interested in using the folk beliefs of his people and folk forms to create a new mythology. *L'Exil d'Albouri* (1967) is about a *griot* in a Muslim society who believes in the supernatural. At the beginning of the play, the author asserts that "reality borders on fiction" and therefore his play should not be considered as conventional history. With his art wedded to the ideology of his people Ndao is the myth-maker who "will help galvanise the people and help carry them further ahead." This is Ndao's main achievement, for the entire account is set in the nineteenth-century Sudanese kingdom of Djoloff. The present and the past suddenly join together in a moment of pure, artistic splendor.

Charles Nokan's first work, *Le soleil noir point* (1962),[5] is his best. Written like a play, a novel, and a poem, it returns to the oral traditional literature and includes a succession of tableaux that demonstrate the major themes. For instance, tableau 27 focuses on love and describes it in beautiful language: "Sitting at the foot of a cotton tree, her six-year-old son on her lap, Amah waits for Tanou. Knowing that she will see again after so many years her friend creates in her a kind of fear tinged with joy" (p. 37). When Tanou arrives, "they look at each other with tenderness. Their large wet eyes are very beautiful. She falls into his arms. . . . Lying in the grass the child considers them" (p. 37).

In the original French the writer shows an ear for the musical possibilities of the language and gives new meaning to certain stereotypes— mother-love, parent/child relationships. His style is better suited to his second novel, *Violent était le vent* (1967), which is concerned with spiritual uprooting, for Nokan can be extremely poetic when he portrays the social pain that results from the transition.

Though Joseph Seid's *Un enfant du Tchad* (1967) is in part an autobiography, he is best known for his *Au Tchad sous les étoiles* (1962),[6] an improvisation on local folklore from the Kotoko-Kanem area of Tchad. His preface identifies some of the problems encountered by the artist concerned with the oral-visual transition: "These numerous children of Tchad invite you, dear reader, to come and sit among them beneath a blue, star-studded sky and listen to the voice of one of their own people. . . ." For one is *reading* this but one is expected to *listen* to the words, not merely *see* them. Like Birago Diop he not only re-creates a past for his people, but also acquaints Europeans with the reality of this past. At times he is overtly conscious of this second purpose, mentioning that the tales contain "more of the supernatural than the real," but this was *his* quandary, not that of the folk-artist.

Similarly Martial Sinda's poetry makes use of the supernatural and repetitive references. For instance, "Tu marcherais en paix" (You will walk in peace)[7] is repeated throughout one poem and references to an owl, a mole, a knocking at the door are all taken as symbols of death.

> If you hear a soft knocking at your door
> Answer, never, never, never
> Because
> It is Death watching you. (p. 27)

Often his verse takes on a political tone, describing the inability to escape from the memory of slavery. "Clarté de l'aube" is such a poem; it asserts that the "smell of clubs" and "the smell of ropes round [his] neck" stifle the poet's thoughts.

Other poems in his *Premier chant du départ* try to reconstruct the truth of Africa. In "Hymne à L'Afrique" Africa is "le pays des contes déformés" (the country of twisted tales), and in "Tam-Tam" he writes of colonized Africa which nevertheless is still his. Within the vein of négritude poetry, his writing often seems excessive:

> Black princess
> I sing to you a sweet psalm
> Goddess of natural beauty . . . (p. 31)

Sinda's poetry indicates that the négritude of the 1930s is not exhausted. Although one feels that at times his obsession with an exotic Africa cripples his verse, at other times it has the effect of reminding the reader of the poet's love for his land and its people.

Like other Africans who write in French, Sissoko is a traditionalist. In *Les noirs et la culture* (1950), he maintains that "the miracle of adapting Arabic to Fulani phonetics" was accomplished by Black scholars, and although he has not written in Arabic both *Harmakhis* (1955), a volume of poems, and *Sagesse noire* (1955) demonstrate his interest in utilizing traditional sources. But he makes clear in *Sagesse noire* that he is a mere collector and that the *griot* is the real guardian of the wisdom of his people. Sissoko stresses that by resuscitating African lore

361

Africans can preserve their cultural unity from western intrusion. His work was pioneering, and in *Les noirs et la culture* he mentions that Aesop and the two Dumas were all Black. Within this context, it is not surprising that Lilyan Kesteloot considers "the life of the group [Sissoko's] principle subject."[8]

This theme is paramount in his best known work *La savane rouge* (1962),[9] which describes French repression and the Tuareg uprising against the French in the early part of this century. Its style is that of the folktale—part "prose," part "poetry." Entire passages dwell on the horror of French brutality, although it is indicated that the whole of France is not to blame.

The book is amazingly dull at the beginning, detailing the early life of the protagonist at school and the effects of the war. Not until the end of the second part does Sissoko begin to develop his plot. Written in diary fashion, with short, telegraphic sentences, the novel seeks to include everything and reflects the author's various moods, including a bit of humor.

La savane rouge is primarily interesting as a serious chronicle of French education and colonization. Sometimes it reads like a play; at other times like a history book tracing the causes of the uprising, the Tuaregs' skill in battle, their defeat and punishment. The book closes on a lyrical note: "Love expands into a thousand things. It is preserved in the music of the *djimos* in flight, as in the call of the otter in the moonlight, in the *bowé* cooked in the sun and where the grasshopper waits for the awakening of the instinct of great change" (p. 128).

The style allows this, for the end is a tremendous praise song of promise. Sissoko succeeds in involving his readers in a varied experience, exposing them to the different stylistic devices of the *griots* he admires— plain narrative, dry diary entries, personal details, and passages that adequately describe the cruelty of the French and finally hope. "The water lily opens up at dawn, spreads out its alabaster crown on crystalline waves, exposes its hair of golden threads to the sun; until the hour when the partridge cackles at the edge of the wood" (p. 129). This hope, asserts Sissoko, is reflected in the redeeming qualities of an Africa no conqueror can destroy. Through a perfect understanding of this and the god of the Dogons, man can attain "the rhythm of the eternal song."

Village Experience

David Ananou's one novel, *Le fils du fétiche* (1955), shows his preoccupations as a Christian and, at the same time, his interest in traditional village life. The novel relates how the individual is caught up in and affected by historical movements. Sodji is an old man from Ghana who settles in Togo where his son Dansou takes care of him. Dansou is a good son—a farmer, a fisherman, basketmaker, and money-lender. He is also an artist and composes music. His father's death signifies that he will become the leader of the community. But after burying Sodji with suitable ceremonies, he moves back to Ghana and becomes a fisherman. And because progress cannot come about in a country "still in the chain of a thousand superstitions," Dansou gives up the faith of his parents and becomes a Christian.

Dansou is obviously intended as a symbol of the direction in which Ananou feels Africa must go. Therefore even the circumstances surrounding his birth are suspect; was it really the intervention of Dan or the "treatment" of the white doctor that brought an end to Avlessi's apparent barrenness? As a young man he was a traditionalist and even composed the dirges for his father's funeral; yet the author shows his own bias by asserting that the traditional way of life must go, for it is brutal. Hence Dansou becomes "civilized," but the reader remains unconvinced.

Ananou wants to present his Africans in as pious a light as possible; he gives Sodji an opportunity to dispense with polygamy by sending his first two wives away after they have tried to poison him. Ananou suggests that African medicine was useless; thus Avlessi's so-called barrenness is not cured until she goes to a white doctor. The young Dansou teaches his fellow villagers the new ways of the city from roof-building to community fishing. But later, his only psychological victories over his enemies are achieved through magic; this is very difficult to reconcile with what Dansou has represented up to this point. And he has to rely on traditional wisdom to sort out the problems of his life—his sick twins, his debts, his broken marriage. At the ceremony of reconciliation it is necessary "to beg for the intercession of the gods," but soon after Dansou departs for Sekondi where he and his wife are converted to Christianity.

The story displays a lack of balance; the author wishes to describe the movement away from the past (equated with all that was horrible) to the present (equated with Christianity). The main problem is that Ananou does not really *believe* that the past was horrible; hence the confusion of the novel.

This theme—the intrusion of the West—is typical of Francis Bebey's work and emerges best in his *Le fils d'Agatha Moudio*, a study of colonial society in the forties. Set around Douala, the love story depicts the tension between colonized and colonizer. The main plot centers on Agatha Moudio, an African woman who is having an affair with a married French businessman. When she becomes pregnant, she has her child. Her husband, who had been warned about her, accepts his fate stoically—a white child born to a Black father. The child is born of tension and the book asks, To what society will such a child now belong? Both his novel and his short stories indicate Bebey's concern with the problems of the "new" Africa.

R. A. Koffi's *Les dernières paroles de Koime* (1961), a sentimental novel of love, death, and happenstance, also concerns in part the relation between traditional Africa and modern colonization. Koffi's prose style is unexciting and flawed by atrocious solecisms. One part of the book that does stand out is the July 14 celebration in Abidjan when Koiku, the main character, was a schoolboy. The author satirically describes the children assembled in the hot sun awaiting the headmaster's arrival. Later they sing the French National Anthem and military songs. The local chief with his regalia and retinue is also ridiculed. Koffi makes clear that the meeting of colonizer and colonized is a bit absurd. Apart from this episode the book has little to redeem it.

Aké Loba has published two novels, *Koucoumbo l'étudiant noir* (1966)[10] and *Le fils de Kouretcha* (1970). *Koucoumbo*, the better of the two books, has as its main character Koucoumbo, a young man content with life in his African village whose father decides to send him to France. On the journey he meets other students all of whom have great plans for the future. However, only Koucoumbo and his friend Abdou succeed. Abdou is saved by communism; Koucoumbo by M. Gabe (a former French colonialist). The irony is complete.

In many ways the novel documents the hardships of Black students in Paris, who are attempting to reach an ever-elusive goal. In other ways it is a condemnation of the wasteful effort of making people *évolué*. In the secondary school Koucoumbo attends in France, he is much older than all the others. When his father dies, the assiduous scholar who had printed "student in Paris" boldly on his trunks has to work in factories. Misfortune plagues him; he has a nervous breakdown and keeps losing his jobs. Only with Denise, a communist girl friend, does he establish a real human relationship. But she is killed in a railway accident. He winds up as a drummer in a nightclub and it seems as if the purpose of his coming is lost, as it has been for so many others. But Gabe helps him, gives him a job and the opportunity to study law. He returns home as a judge.

Though the "happy" ending is contrived, Loba does not intend to give the impression that Koucoumbo is a good boy. He is lucky that he has triumphed in this hollow way. For the author suggests that the cultural transition can often be too much to bear; sometimes, however, the effect can be comical as when Koucoumbo tries to wear shoes and comments on "this strange mania for imprisoning one's feet." At other times, as during school holidays, he realizes he is alone and has no family. When comparing the Paris of the schoolboy's dream with reality, he reflects, "When he set out all alone to hunt in the bush the invisible presence of millions of animals and insects would accompany him, the spirits of his ancestors would follow in his wake, whispering advice . . . But here nothing but stone choking the empty dusk, here no ancestors, no spirits, no throb, nothing, nothing, nothing . . ." (p. 109). Koucoumbo is an innocent; he wants to become a lawyer because he once saw a lawyer dictate two letters. He badly wishes his hands to lose their roughness because "a man whose hands were losing their roughness must not lose a minute in bringing them into contact with books."

The characterization of Koucoumbo is convincing, but the story is flawed by its episodic structure and the long sections on Koucoumbo's journey. Because Loba uses short sentences, his style is often irritating. He does succeed, however, in showing the folly of false values, for "education" frequently separates the student from his own society, with terrible consequences.

Tragic Mulattoes

The confrontation between victor and victim had enormous consequences, some of which may be seen on a purely personal level—for example, sexual relations between whites and Blacks. Jean Malonga, who had played a leading part in the "Union Française," is such a writer. In 1954 he published both a novelette, Coeur d'Aryenne,[11] and a novel, La légende de M'Pfoumou Ma Mazono, which is based on a folktale. The novelette is the better known work.

As a politician Malonga was interested in the prospects of (French) Africa and France working together; Coeur d'Aryenne, which centers on the love of a Black boy and white girl, is a symbolic representation of this. Its characterizations are crude but understandably so, for the author is more concerned with his message—that interracial love should be condoned. Because he attempts to show the difficulties of whites and Blacks accepting one another and living together in colonial Africa, his use of superlatives to describe his characters can be excused. Morax is loose and evil; his daughter, Solange, and her lover, Mambeké, are innocents who seek the better world. The missionaries are severely criti-

365

cized in the person of Fr. Hux who runs the mission school; when he learns that Mambeké rows Solange to school, he warns Morax that this is not safe. Yet he turns a blind eye to Morax's sexual excesses—his "escapades innocentes"—with his cook's wife, his cook's daughter, or as many as five girls at a time.

Coeur d'Aryenne is therefore *not* about teen-age sex, as some have suggested. It is about the linking of Black and white, African and European, in a personal bond which, for the writer, was certain to have political consequences. To join the two races, Malonga suggests, compromise is necessary; thus Mambeké goes to school and Solange (who commits suicide) yearns to kill the Aryan in her.

There are parts of the novel that deflect from its main purpose; for instance, too much detail is given of Mambeké's school life and how he is considered intelligent and therefore suspected, by the other pupils, of sleeping with the male teachers. A long section is also devoted to a tedious argument between Mambeké and Fr. Hux on the nature of God, which concludes with Mambeké pompously asking, "Tell me why you are the enemy of reason and criticism?" Of course the point that Mambeké (and Malonga) wishes to make is that only a righteous god would regard color as a "righteous accident" (p. 269). And, as has been mentioned, Malonga also exposes Fr. Hux as a hypocrite; he teaches his Black students about the hell that awaits them, and he desecrates the confessional by inviting Morax to hear his cook's confession.

Sentimental in parts, as for instance Mambeké's rescue of Solange and Marie-Rose's death, the novel can at times be absurd. After giving a long speech, Solange's mother dies and then "the children . . . are married in suffering" with their hands on "the mortal spoils of Marie-Rose." This excessive language often ruins parts of the novel.

Nor is the story helped by the author's intrusions. Frequently the language is poor, rising to grandiloquence when Mambeké preaches to Fr. Hux, Solange, or his fellow-pupils. Basically, however, this is a novel of ideas and the author succeeds in expressing his main idea: The child of the union (between Mambeké and Solange) will survive; the "Union Française"—a union of equals—is workable. The "mission civilisatrice" of Hux and Morax must yield to the possibilities of Mambeké, Solange, their child, and the products of Morax's lust. In a strange way the latter, "ces malheureux qui ne sont ni blancs ni noirs" (the unfortunate ones neither white nor Black), are the cultural hybrids of the political bond between Europe and Africa.

Abdoulaye Sadji's *Nini, mulâtresse du Sénégal* (1954)[12] takes up the theme of interracial love from there. In his foreword Sadji comments that he set out to describe "the eternal moral portrait of the mulatto woman"; this he succeeds in doing, although he clearly shows his own prejudices at times.

Educated in a nunnery, Nini was seduced at fifteen by a French corporal. Outwardly, her appearance is that of a white woman but Sadji reveals that she has "a little stubby nose with white open nostrils," "greedy lips," and "a cat-like walk." Although her name means "virgin," she has an album of nude photographs at home. Obviously, the reader is not expected to like Nini, who despises Blacks and looks up to all whites. Sadji does mention points of social interest; even the mulattoes are divided among themselves and the "presque blanches" (almost whites) are highly rated.

The prejudices and the story begin to unfold with Nini's reactions to a love letter she receives from N'Diaye Matar, a Black man. He tells her he is in love with her but she regards this, as she tells Madou, as impertinence. Later she passes the letter around the office where she works and says, "I will make it clear to him that white skins are not for the *bougnols*" (p. 324). Matar's daring act becomes a social matter. The mulattoes want to write a letter of complaint to the governor, but instead they write a warning note to Matar; if he does such a thing again they will go to the police.

More of Nini's character comes through when she plots to marry Martineau, her French lover. Ultimately her schemes fail and Martineau returns to France. Now alone and jobless, Nini tries to obtain a post at the Government House. Nini is accepted with the help of a secret benefactor. When she discovers that the benefactor is Black, she resigns. The irony is increased when Nini's Aunt Hortense reveals that she had received help from a relative on the Black side of the family, adding, "All the power is now in the hands of these people." Her predicament is further compounded when she learns that Martineau is to return to Africa with a wife. Extremely disillusioned, she leaves "the country where she has never known happiness." Aunt Hortense reprimands her for leaving and rejecting Africa.

The end is inconclusive and really tells the reader nothing. Sadji does not succeed in making Nini anything more than a person he despises. Refusing to depend on the novel's action, he constantly intrudes to *tell* the reader how pitiful Nini is. Sadji is also too fond of long, irrelevant descriptions. Because he is a moralizer, he bores the reader, often by dwelling on the obvious.

Sociological in parts, *Nini* is a treatise on mulattoes in Senegal before independence, their refusal to identify with Africans, and their insistence on being with Europeans. Sadji parodies their ambitions and how the "almost whites" (there are three divisions) speak of France as home and the latest Paris fashions. The third class is too poor to be effective.

The novel also criticizes the Europeans. Although Sadji believes in the "civilizing mission" of France, he does indicate that those Frenchmen who become alcoholics contribute nothing to this mission. Martineau is criticized only indirectly, for example, when he takes Nini to the club where there are Europeans and mulattoes, but no Africans. Sadji tells us that another club is reserved for Blacks.

Sadji emerges as a man who closely identifies with Blacks. By denouncing the mulattoes who wish to "turn white bit by bit" and the way they dance the beguine and the rhumba (both accepting and rejecting Africa), he illustrates the cultural confusion of his time.

Nini is in parts a well-constructed book. Sadji's use of dialogue is good and he handles the language competently. His symbolism, especially of Nini looking through the window at the Africans she does not understand at the beginning and end of the novel, sets the mood for the entire book.

A Change of Role

BROKEN HERITAGE

As has been noted, writers frequently beguiled readers with a magnificent defense of a perfect past. In reality the négritude writers had exposed the present as a manner of existence under assault. In some writers elements of this shipwrecked world and its values and attempts to salvage something of the lost heritage are clearly seen. These writers are conscious of the lost nobility of the past and in transporting this to a literary plane they express a colorful reality and truth—at once sad and passionately winsome.

Jean Joseph Rabéarivelo was a melancholy man; he passionately wanted to go to France and when his efforts failed he became a drug addict, committing suicide by drinking poison when he was only thirty-six. Nine volumes of his verse were published, three posthumously. He wrote in Spanish, French, and Malagasy.

Rabéarivelo's work shows his interest in traditional Malagasy lore. For instance, *Vieilles chansons des pays d'Imerina* (1937) is a collection of praise poems in French based on traditional Malagasy love poetry. His first volume, *La coupe de cendres* (1924), is very imitative of

French poetry. Only with *Presque-songes* (1924) and *Traduit de la nuit* (1935) did he establish his claim as an *African* poet.

His poetry is depersonalized, blending cosmic and terrestrial imagery. Concerned with transitions of being, many of the poems describe the imaginative unity of sky and earth—the unification of opposites. Life as seen by Rabéarivelo is suffering and evolves toward little purpose; death is omnipresent.

When people appear in the poems—and this is very infrequent—they seem to represent something elemental, such as a "rude sailor" or "a blind glassmaker." Rabéarivelo dismantles the world we know and then effectuates a cosmic reordering. The cosmos, paradoxically, is then "humanized": the moon in one image is a "cake on which a gnat gnaws"; in another he alludes to a "bird without colour and name." These visual images help to sustain the visual quality of the poetry.

Frustration, despair, catastrophe, death are Rabéarivelo's main themes. The poems are essentially "moods" and the paradoxical imagery conveys the confusion of the moment—"rootless trees," "dumb birds," "unknown birds," "fingerless hands." Repetitive devices and violent images like "dawn marauding in the orchards of the night" and the capsizing of the sun are used to emphasize the horrible mood of despair, hopelessness, and failure.

Often Rabéarivelo takes his art and its inspiration from the natural world, as is seen in the poem "Désert":

> Complete and warming joy of the desert!
> Nowhere is the sky as blue
> than on these hills of sand and fire
> furrowed by powerful and clear winds.
>
> Parched of all greenness as my heart
> of man matured by evil times
> lured by you, o beautiful dreams
> when my sole shelter was apathy!
>
> Here before your barrenness
> your stillness and your thirst and your hunger,
> your landscape seemingly without end.
> like the dread of eternity.
>
> balancing my joy and my emotion
> · I dream of an art as pure as you. [13]

The point is worth emphasizing that this is not just a description of nature but again the balance of opposites, not operating through paradoxical imagery this time but culminating in paradox. Only the *empty* desert is *full* of art—the art of poetry.

Presque-songes continues the observation of the natural world, stressing the theme of opposites already mentioned. A poem called "Cactus" is not mere eulogizing verse; rather it seeks out the apparent lack of beauty in the world and finds it in "hands without fingers," in "lepers bearing flowers." As a result,

> the blood of the earth, the sweat of stone
> and the sperm of wind
> which flow together in these palms
> have dissolved the fingers
> and put flowers of gold in their place.[14]

In the original French the "s" sounds convey a feeling of silence which leads up naturally to the last line quoted above. What *Presque-songes* demonstrates above everything is that the poet is not concerned with self-centered observation (as he is in "Désert"); instead he enters into the world he describes and enhances his theme, that of rebirth, through sexual imagery.

Such poems as "Naissance du jour" and "Autre naissance du jour" in *Presque-songes* speak of natural phenomena without the use of any intermediary. The private agonies of the poet are subjected to the larger cosmic miracle of dawn:

> in their coops pierced by the stars
> and the other spears of darkness
> the cockrels crow to each other . . . (p. 24)

And in another poem, "lovingly [dawn] cuts the prism [of darkness]." Dawn releases birds and all living things. The new day breaks violently, "transpercées par les étoiles" (pierced by the stars), but in all cases the poet is left out. In *Sylves* (1927), one still finds the romantic suffering, the sadness in life, the constant references to death, but here they are always associated with the poet.

As Rabéarivelo continued to write, he moved increasingly away from slavish imitation of French writers. In his first volume, he could put down with a straight face such trite phrases as "my tomb is always my tomb" or express the usual romantic love, "I do not know you, o my dead lovers! / There in my heart another now lives."[15] Even in *Volumes* of 1928 he addresses the "brother of [his] sadness" and as late as 1931 his "Mourir de ne pas vivre" (certainly "un-African" in its concepts) demonstrates his earlier obsession with death. By 1935 when *Traduit de la nuit* was published, his images more vigorously described the inhumanity of mankind and his preoccupation with death was more fearful, less "literary." In a few words he shows his total lack of concern: "The friend who lost everything / Has killed himself."[16]

Here in *Traduit* is the country without a name, the confused, intentionally distorted landscape of "a bird without colour and without name," of cockrels who "sing in dreams / and are fed by the stars," of the mythical spider of African lore which weaves a web between heaven and earth. Here Rabéarivelo is at home, and the backdrop is stark and grim, as in the folktales; the telling is everything. This is the country where paradoxes are reconciled, where "all Religions meet— / and poems too"[17] and where "mon frère errant" is a lime tree. For as the poet says "all seasons have been abolished." It is the final point of reconciliation where all life is canceled out so that only what is truly elemental remains. "Zébu" and "Valiha" from *Presque-songes* had anticipated this; In "Zébu" the bull's life anticipates his death and in "Valiha" the bamboos, "buried living by moonlight," will become "no more than something singing / in the hands of lovers." But in this poem as in many others in *Presque-songes* and *Traduit*, the artist-figure is the savior: "an artist will come / who will shatter their god-like youth."[18] Here man has stumbled upon a freedom of choice, just as in no. 9 of *Presque-songes* the poet had progressed to the meeting place of all poems. This is the high point of mortal and artistic perfection.

As has been said, Rabéarivelo comes closest to his own tradition with *Vieilles chansons des pays d'Imerina*. Many of the songs derive from the traditional *hain-teny*, or love poetry, of Malagasy. The poem is divided into some thirty sections, the poet speaking from "Imerina," a high mountain in the republic. His own voice and the responses of the "parente" (lover) give the poetry the form of a duet, with long passages being reserved for soliloquy and self-comment. The poetry is not the love poetry of his first volume; nor does it possess the disenchanted world of *Traduit* and *Presque-songes*. It is the true reconciliation of the living heart and the adored nature ("I am the most beautiful star in the constellation"). Repetition (in the manner of the folklore) serves to heighten the effect:

—Can I come in? Can I come in?
—Who is there? Who is there?
—It is me, the first born of my father and mother.
—It is the first born of his father and mother . . .[19]

This stylistic device helps each section to progress gracefully. It can be said that Rabéarivelo has not only translated, but has created these songs anew in French.

A journal called *Calepins bleus* that covers the years from 1924 to 1933 remains unpublished. Not "conventional" in any sense, it takes the form of speculative poems that question the meaning of his existence. "Le Bruit humain" is one of its recurring themes—absence, longing, love, unhappiness, speculation about death. Though "prosaic" the journal tells us more than the poems do about the life of this unhappy forerunner and his final hope (expressed in the imagery of the poetry) that the spirit will triumph over the flesh. His own bitter comment serves as an ironic postscript:

> And the books which you write
> rustle with unreal matters—
> unreal since they are too real
> like dreams[20]

Rabéarivelo's despair expressed in his poetry made him deny his poetic creations and finally take his own life. He had hinted in *Traduit* and *Presque-songes* of some great cosmic disaster—eventually it was to engulf the poet himself.

Flavien Ranaivo, who wrote after Rabéarivelo, was likewise influenced by *hain-teny* and seems to have re-created traditional poetry within a French context. Use of local references, words like "cousin" and "parente" for lover, as well as repetitive devices place the poems within the indigenous tradition of Malagasy.

One should emphasize again the difficulties these poets, like the négritude writers, faced as "Black Frenchmen." It is to the credit of most of them that they were able to turn the French language away from itself and toward concerns that mattered to them. This becomes even clearer in the works of Ranaivo and Kagamé.

Most of Ranaivo's poetry is in the form of an address to the loved one. In his "Vieux thème Merina" and "Vulgaire chanson d'amant," the dramatic monologues are spoken by the lover to his loved one. Both poems are from his first slim volume, *L'ombre et le vent* (1947); in the first the poet describes his love for the loved one, in the second he gives her advice on how she should love him:

> Love me like a beautiful dream
> your life at nighttime
> my hope in the day . . .[21]

The translation, out of context of the original *hain-teny*, is obviously lacking, though it indicates some of Ranaivo's preoccupations in his next two volumes—*Mes chansons de toujours* (1955), with an introduction by Senghor, and *Le retour au Bercail* (1962). Another piece in

L'ombre et le vent uses the typical dialogue and situation of the lovers as found in traditional verse. However, the two later volumes refer not only to love between man and woman, but to parental love and to love of the ox (presented in the form of a praise poem). Therefore, all love comes together in these poems. Witness these lines from "Choix":

> she will take a little rice water
> not because she is thirsty
> but only since it is her whim to make you like her.[22]

And these from "Zébu" (Ox):

> His lips move without stopping
> but they are neither swollen nor worn;
> his teeth are two beautiful rows of coral . . .[23]

It is interesting to note that the attributes of beauty given to the woman and to the ox are not dissimilar. Both are loved, and praise phrases apply equally to both. This brings to mind the works of Alexis Kagamé, previously considered with indigenous writers, who translated his poetry into French.

Another aspect of the theme of the African's broken heritage is seen in the writing of Olympe Bhêly-Quenum. For him the meeting of worlds was violent in a very physical sense, whereas for Camera Laye the confrontation brought about a spiritual abrasion.

Bhêly-Quenum's *Un piège sans fin* (1960)[24] is a novel about Ahouna, the son of a former soldier, who leaves his jealous wife, murders another woman, is imprisoned, and ultimately is killed by the family of the woman he has murdered. The plot is despairing, but the work is intended as a parable. Prefaced by quotations from Thomas à Kempis and Baudelaire, the book takes as its theme: "Know and believe firmly that your life is a continual death." Taking its attitude from French existentialism, it portrays the idea that "everything is cruel, inhuman and absurd in life." Ahouna discovers the monster within him. He gives up his beliefs; African gods are "the great lazy ones" since all they desire is sacrifice. Equally he loses all faith in Islam. His marriage to Anatou and her jealousy is the first "trap" he encounters; the prison is another and the "escape" a third. "Human existence," we are told, "is an enormous trap set for man by Allah" (p. 142). Some of the rigid symbolism is spoiled when, after Ahouna's capture, he is taken through the town and the people cry out, "Crucify him."

As a story within a story Ahouna relates his early happy life and later despair to an archaeologist who feeds him and gives him shelter before

373

he is taken away. In prison he meets a Frenchman who does not feel Ahouna's anguish even though he has killed his wife and his mistress. Yet when Ahouna gets out of prison, his plan is to go north and kill his wife. The theme of the despair of life is pursued to the end when a policeman says that it was just as well war had broken out in Europe so that the innate savagery of humans could be directed toward fighting.

One serious technical fault of the novel is that the person to whom the story is told is a type of omniscient author, frequently speaking of Ahouna. Because the philosophical speculations are overdone and much too morbid at times, the reader is not easily convinced of Ahouna's martyrdom. Ahouna, however, is consistent; he willingly gives himself up to his captors outside prison and his actions convince the reader that he is devoted to suffering.

Un piège sans fin is a disturbing novel. There is much violence, particularly in the murder scene and in the prison scenes where a son watches his father kill himself and fall "like a big baboon." The soft pastoral background of the early part of the book is meant to contrast with the harsh urban foreground of the latter part.

Le chant du lac (1965)[25] again centers on peasants, using, as in the previous novel, folklore, symbolism, and allegory to highlight the action. Violence again predominates; a murder is committed followed by the necessary revenge. The murderer is deported to France and serves in the war. Man the monster is compared here with the tyranny and the lack of humanity of the gods of the lake. Bhêly-Quenum portrays the landscape and relates it directly to people. Nature is depicted as ugly; "the sun is selfish today," an elder says. This is a very intricate work poetically interwoven with rich metaphor and symbolic overtones of man's purposelessness:

"I believe that we are continuing to go adrift."
"You are crazy. I am sure a cock was crowing."
"That doesn't mean that the town is near."
"There's always an inhabited land at the end of a cockcrow."
"Of course. But at night the cries of animals carry further than that of men, as Grandma Yaga says, and it is not soon before we get to the town."
"Can we help you by rowing a bit?" interrupted Noussi.
"No, Madam. I'm going slow on purpose. We must be careful about where we are." (p. 125)

The ultimate meaning of life, asserts the author, is to drift directionless toward no known goal.

Bhêly-Quenum has also written an unpublished novelette, *Les brigands*, which relates the story of Akpanakan, a legendary figure in West

Africa. Bhêly-Quenum's work impresses one with its harsh attitude toward life. He is never boring, but at times the morbid tone seems exaggerated. He has much to say but as he comments, "How can one explain these things to people who are in the habit of reasoning on the principle of 'two plus two is four'?" In many ways, he is an African artist committed to the utilization of the African traditional presence, but at the same time aware of the larger implications of this commitment.

L'enfant noir (1953) by Camera Laye[26] is a novel of growing up. The African past, recollected from Paris, is idealized: a young boy, very much at home in the natural world of his African environment, has to leave his village and family to go to school—"a course which led him inexorably to Conakry and Paris." Perhaps *L'enfant noir*'s only flaw is that since it is so close to autobiography, one does not always see it as a successful novel. Nevertheless, it is a beautifully written book, as seen in such passages as those describing the young boy's initiation into manhood, his meeting with Kondén Diara, "the lion that eats up little boys," which ensures his ability to face fear, and his falling in love with Marie. Still another portrays his mother's trepidations as she faces the possibility of losing her son: "He's been away from me so many years already . . . and now they want to take him away to their own land."

Le regard du roi (1954) moves away from the plane of straight realism into the world of symbolism. Clarence, an indigent white man in Africa who has lost all his money at cards, decides in desperation to find the African king and offer him his services. After attempting to see the king, he finally has to depend on a beggar who attempts to intervene for him. But the wily beggar trades him to the king for a wife and a mule. Without realizing it, Clarence is being employed as a stud, for the chief is now old. Lying naked in his hut when the time comes to meet the king, he is afraid to face him. Finally he summons up enough courage and walks naked across the square into the arms of the king.

An exquisitely fashioned work, *Le regard du roi* has been variously interpreted as a search for God, a Kafkaesque search for identification, and a lesson in the wisdom of Africa. But it is none of these. Clarence is white in Black Africa; he journeys from north to south; he meets a beggar, a eunuch, a blacksmith, a fortune-teller. His journey is the mission of every folktale hero who seeks a boon for his tribe. Clarence's tribe is the "white" tribe which can only be redeemed from its guilt by reverently serving the "Black" tribe. Clarence's presumption is that he seeks the boon from the first; only later does he understand that the gift to his kind comes about through suffering and humiliation.

Money cannot buy him the boon and this is why he leaves penniless in the company of a beggar. He has to re-enact the reversal of the roles of his own tribe in its relations with the Blacks. They came to the South coast and pushed their way inward; Clarence moves in the opposite direction. They came as "kings" seeking "servants"; Clarence is a servant seeking an elusive king. They enslaved; Clarence is enslaved. They bastardized; so does Clarence. They came clothed; Clarence has his clothes stolen and can only meet the clothed king naked. Clarence reverses the historical roles of Europe and Africa and is symbolic of both as he attempts to right the wrongs perpetrated by the whites. Only when he succeeds does he win his boon—service with the king, acceptance by the Blacks. Clarence is now a man of the Black tribe and the king is the means through which he loses the props of his own society to become an initiate. The quest is for humility which, the beggar says, "has never been the outstanding quality of your race."

Fatoman (meaning "brother" or "companion"), the "I" character of *Dramouss* (1966), is initiated into another society, that of Paris, and his initiation is even more difficult than Clarence's. During the first few weeks in Paris, he faints from hunger. He tries to mingle with the people, but everything seems strange, for the girls have bobbed hair, wear trousers, and smoke like men. One night an old man sitting next to him in a club begins rubbing his thighs. He does not understand what the old man is doing until it is explained to him; thus he learns about homosexuality. Tenaciously, Fatoman remains in Paris to pursue his education. He rationalizes his existence there by believing "that Paris is not a French city but an international centre in which human beings are grouped solely according to their intellectual affinities."

As Fatoman becomes more involved in French life, he begins to see its many contradictions. For example, when he studies French democracy, he clearly comprehends its fallacies. Despite the existence of the colony where the Black man is the servant and white man is the boss, he rationalizes the theory by saying that at least everybody is allowed to express himself freely. Little by little, he begins to accept the French way of living, but he tries to maintain his Africanness in order to preserve his identity, by wearing his *boubou* even in the winter when it is piercing cold.

But Fatoman has become more French than he realizes and he is very much impressed with the complete freedom that the French have. After living in Paris for six years, Fatoman returns home. He thinks this will reaffirm his identity. But unfortunately he finds that things have changed. His friends are engaged in politics and the mad scramble to obtain automobiles and other western gadgets. He marries Mimie, a childhood sweetheart, and goes to visit his parents. He finds that one thing that has not changed is his father's occupation. One day Fatoman goes into his father's workshop and watches him carve a beautiful female deer. As he views his father's work, he remarks, "In the museum of Paris, I have seen African sculptures but they are very different from yours. Don't you ever make anything like that? The men who created those works were very cunning." At this point, the father suspects that his son values everything the French have proclaimed great just because they have accepted it as such. Without scorn, the father realizes that Fatoman does not understand the history of his own people; therefore he teaches him patiently. He tells him that they were not cunning, but skillful. Their descendants possessed a power of contemplation and insight into creation far greater than Fatoman's. At this point one feels that Fatoman will never receive the guiding spirits from his father, for though he understands, he does not accept what his father tells him— at least not at that moment.

Fatoman and Mimie go to Paris to live, but some years later they return home for a visit. On this particular visit, his father greets them in the courtyard. Immediately they begin to discuss the revolution going on in the country. As they talk, a big hawk plunges to the earth and grabs one of the chickens from the yard. At that moment, the father takes a string of beads from his pocket and shakes them in the direction of the hawk. But by this time, the hawk is high in the sky. The father utters some sacred words. Word by word he lets a pearl in the chaplet pass through his fingers. As the father continues the incantations, the hawk comes back to earth within reach of his hand, and he takes the chick from the hawk's claws. Fatoman is amazed beyond words. The father admits that he often used those words to bring Fatoman home from Paris. Unfortunately, when the father explains the price one must pay to attain this power, it seems that Fatoman will never gain the guiding spirits. For Fatoman, and other African elites like him, must give up everything to establish the spiritual essence of the self.

Dramouss is perhaps Laye's best novel so far. In it he has spoken out, using the poetry and reflections of *L'enfant noir*, the symbolism of *Le regard du roi* to return full circle to the African present. His disenchantment with this present is evident when Fatoman, examining the price he has to pay for spiritual well being, returns to the colonial capital. However, there is hope, Laye suggests, but not just yet. Like Clarence, the people of Fatoman's country have to rid themselves of two obsessions— to be French and to be "chickens." The supernatural can save them, if they are willing to learn. But like Fatoman they are not ready yet and thus *Dramouss* closes with a great question mark.

To Laye the change in roles meant the discovery that there is a curious relationship between victim and victor. The victim seems to recognize the victor, but the very recognition becomes a nightmare of the victim's fears. One need only go back to Rebéarivelo and his uneasy yoking of opposites for verification. The final two writers who will be considered here, Cheikh Kane and Félix Tchicaya U'Tamsi, one a novelist, the other a poet, use various devices to explain the nature of this relationship within the broken heritage.

Kane's *L'aventure ambiguë* (1961)[27] is a novel of ideas. The dialogue is artificially structured to contrast the traditionalists, who advocate that the spiritual oneness of African Islam is the only way of life, with those who assert that the western world with its emphasis on the superficial (the body and the material) is the only viable alternative. Between these two extremes Samba Diallo, the chief character, falls victim.

In a way *L'aventure ambiguë* is part autobiography (Samba is the author's "house-name"), part African folktale (the "anti-hero" sets out on a quest for self-knowledge and understanding), and part existentialism in its grim view of the world. Built into the apparent wholeness of Samba's world, with its sunsets that link him securely to the sky, are evidences of disintegration. Dialogues between Le Chevalier (Samba's father) and M. Lacroix (a Frenchman), between Samba and his father, between Samba and the young Jean Lacroix expose some of the predicaments. Materialism and spiritualism cannot be fused and Jean stands amazed as he watches Samba in prayer.

The novel is neatly balanced in two parts. The first part ends when Samba, having been exposed to some European education at home, goes to France to complete the process of "learning to win without being right." In France in the cafés, alone in his room, he suddenly realizes he shares little of Lucienne's faith in communism or of Adèle's (herself a "cultural mulatto") romanticized view of Africa. But his confusion rocks his own formerly firm faith in himself. Summoned home by his father he arrives too late. At the grave of Le Maître, his former teacher, he can no longer pray and Le Fou, an embodiment of Samba and the predicament of his kind, kills him. At the end the question remains—how can the old values survive?

The plan of this exquisitely contrived novel lies in the debate, which takes place at various points, in Africa, in Europe, between two conflicting ways of life. The result is that Samba becomes a "marginal man," a man who cannot pray, who cannot accept the faith of his father, who

378

therefore must die. Le Fou (as he is ironically named) has also been exposed to Europe but has returned firm in his convictions. He hopes that Samba will take Le Maître's place. Le Fou dresses in clean Moslem clothing topped by dirty western gear; he is the *outer* enigma of what Samba is *within*. He goes mad; Samba dies. As Le Chevalier had said, western education levels down everything to "the pale complexion— deathly pale," and "after the death of God we now witness the death of man." His prophetic words have a grim meaning for his son's death.

Rabéarivelo, Ranaivo, and Kagamé used the oral literature of their people to dramatize the plight of modern African man. Laye used the model of the folktale to describe the confrontation and the ultimate defeat (as he sees it) of the African way of life. Kane lined up his characters for a debate and they constantly sought to prove what was good in the African/Islamic past or in the modern/European present. All these writers and especially Bhêly-Quenum underscored the point they were making with violent images. This type of writing reaches its ultimate achievement in the poetry of U'Tamsi in which one clearly sees evidences of the broken heritage. Although born in the Congo Republic, he has lived most of his adult life in France. The conflict between victim and victor is very present in his poetry, and his obsession with the role of the church, with French education and colonialism, demonstrates his concern for specific aspects of the broken heritage. For this poet, the meeting with the West also signifies "the death of man" as depicted by Kane. His verse seeks to portray the ways in which this has come about.

U'Tamsi says that in his poetry he tries "to face life and not the accident of it," thereby stressing the significance of reality. But he adds, "I give more importance to cultural ideas."[28] Indeed he attempts to break the French cultural link with words and to substitute personal (and sometimes African) associations. The Congo is therefore not just a river but a highway of civilization. Christ is not just a figure of myth, but stands for betrayal (of Blacks), for sacrifice. Thus his poetry seeks to explore stages of consciousness, using such images as absence, death, the body, solitude, blood, sperm, space. His wit, with its emphasis on colonialism, religion, the "cultural mulatto," is a means toward self-knowledge and, ultimately, racial exploration.

Linked to oral poetry, U'Tamsi's verse attempts to create a special type of "spoken poetry" which gives his symbols free rein. The symbols are frequently startling and fierce and convey his defiant attitude to the vicissitudes of life. His symbols are used like repetitive devices in traditional African poetry, but instead of mere repetition U'Tamsi expands

379

his images into a number of parallel meanings. Take for instance his first volume, *Le mauvais sang* (1955),[29] and these lines from the title poem:

> I am the bronze of alloy, of the strong blood which dips when
> the wind of the rising tide blows.
> The destiny of the old divinities crossing through my destiny.
> Is it a reason to dance always against the song? (p. 38)

The history of Black people (a theme U'Tamsi was to return to) is one which brought about a physical, social, and racial change. This is what he means by the "sense of deception" he feels, for he cannot (like the négritude writers) blithely celebrate his blackness. Even this very blackness is denied him and the images throughout *Le mauvais sang* stress his predicament.

Feu de brousse (1957), U'Tamsi's first significant volume, focuses on the theme of self-exploration, though later the poet was to move away from personal considerations. The volume begins by depicting through visual images the plight of man born into a world of disaster. However, there is hope:

> But here the sea skips the reef
> but here the reef makes the sea tremble
> far adrift the seven rivers go
> to discover why the leaves sing
> There remains a river
> and the key to dreams lies in its bosom
> but who will know
> for whom the leaves rustle above the winds with their head bent.[30]

The symbolism, centered on water and leaves, expresses quiescence and violence. The last line poses the enigmatic nature of the inquiry. The dismembered parts of the body ("head," "bosom," and a suggestion of legs) and the lost river all suggest an alienation.

Feu de brousse, like later poems, supports the idea that the Christian church in Africa is a link with colonialism and thus a reason for bringing about the estrangement of African man. Exploitation by the colonizers is also demonstrated in brutal images—"the marching canoers" or "my race / remembers / the taste of bronze drunk hot." Note how "bronze" takes the reader/listener back to the early lines where "bronze" represented racial and cultural assimilation, with a suggestion of debilitation. Now the new image is a roll call for revolution—"Light this fire that washes away my shame." Relating back to the river and couched in appropriate paradox, this suggests the temporary nature of the revolution which moves people away from the brutality of colonization to the new peace of human understanding.

Repetition of words and ideas in *Feu de brousse*—river, sea, rainbow, dream, fire—gives an indication of U'Tamsi's technique. But within U'Tamsi's context, the river/sea is both savior and destroyer, colonialist and accomplice, hope and despair. This pairing of dimensional opposites is the most frequent device in the poetry, serving to link his entire volumes around specific core ideas. Thus the words, images, and symbols coalesce into a cohesive whole.

If *Le mauvais sang* has as its central idea the uncertainty of racial inheritance and *Feu de brousse* moves more positively toward linking person and race in the consequences of history, *À triche-coeur* (1958)[31] takes a dramatic turn in that it concerns the search for what this history means, symbolized here by the quest for a key.

The "key," associated with the "keys to the kingdom," is inverted by U'Tamsi, or rather one begins to see that a key *locks* and also *unlocks*. The entire poem centers on Christ's crucifixion and resurrection, but this is a mere starting point. So rich and varied are U'Tamsi's allusions that this is actually an understatement. For instance, the opening stanzas introduce familiar U'Tamsi themes of disease and deformity to explain the condition of man; the boatman cannot use his arms and the bird emphasizes that it is not leprous. The oral utilization of traditional material reinforces man's (Black man's) plight, for the boatman cannot answer the bird's riddle. Because of the protagonist's confusion, he offers a subverted prayer to the archetypal image of a murdered mother:

> open my mother's breast
> so that I could put my hot head there
> and blessed be the bread taken away from me
> blessed be thirst taken away from me. (p. 25)

In the next section, images of the "bread" are associated with Christ and the last supper. The language is biblical ("le pain que j'ai rompu"— the bread I have broken) and suggests that the protagonist (like the boatman) is isolated from all this.

"L'étrange agonie," the fourth part of the poem, demonstrates best what has been referred to as the inversion of images. Here the Christ-figure (the protagonist) is lame, his "tree" is now his lost genealogy, his "virgin" is an "idiot," and thus he is a man without a land. This lack of heritage is expanded in successive sections until the climax:

> behind each night
> I walk behind a hearse
> but
> what former memories are in my absent heart
> the night carries my mourning. (p. 81)

381

Mourning, one adds, for a lost childhood, a dead mother (on a personal level in the poem), a lost heritage, and a violent present. The conclusion, harking back to the hearse and suggesting crucifixion and ultimate defeat, offers no hope of resurrection. The lightning which earlier had indicated the possibilities of a heritage now makes the protagonist say, "Je n'aperçois [rien] de vivant" (I saw nothing of the living). Since it is only an orphan who is resurrected—a man without kin and an outcast in traditional Africa—the gloomy interpretation of the heritage of colonial Africa is complete.

Epitomé (1962)[32] is a mock praise poem. The "Congo" of the previous volume has witnessed the insurrection of 1960, the murder of Lumumba. The protagonist begins where he left off at the end of *À triche-coeur*, and the orphan and the tree are all present. The first three verses introduce the theme; the poet/protagonist is no longer at the mercy of a destiny he cannot control and he can now believe in the reality of his past. He bemoans his origins because he seems to be without an ancestor; he knows he has an origin but his experiences under colonialism have denied him his past, a past which has been laughed at by many. Because of his colonial experience, even he regards his interest in it as madness. But colonialism and westernization are nothing compared to his own indigenous past.

The protagonist therefore seeks a past which is difficult to find. The image of the head at half-mast and the cock suggest the death of the European way of life. The rising sun, developed from the idea of flame, is the recognition of the African presence. No longer can he be easily fooled; some people can still be fooled for they are asleep and the image of the fortune-teller is that of someone who speaks against the colonialist to Black people who do not fully understand their heritage and its place in the future. These are the people who obey without thinking. The protagonist suffers for such people and for his love of his heritage.

In seeking for his lost heritage, he finds the way to recovery; certain rituals have to be undergone in order to revive the memory of the past. It is a slow process and there is violence and civil war as the Africans attempt to discard the European presence. Out of this suffering, the new African emerges; sexual symbols blend with biblical ones to suggest the new birth. Nakedness emphasizes his new understanding, his purity and simplicity, his return to the origins. Finally, deliverance comes as it can come to anyone. Once the poet lived with the cruelties of colonialism and tried to exclude himself from it. Now he recognizes the betrayal—of all Blacks (references to Emmet Till, to South Africa, and Harlem confirm this). Even the opening lines of the poem, which speak of the three colors of the French flag, focus on the betrayal of Africa by Europe, Black by white, the betrayal which dominates the entire poem.

Epitomé is traditional in the sense that it is a "mock" praise poem with dirge-invocations to the protagonist and to those who seek "neutrality." Irony is the tone as he addresses his countrymen, as he speaks to himself:

> I forget to be black in order to forgive
> I will see no more my blood on their hands;
> the world will repay my clemency
> we were men of night . . . (p. 58)

Betrayal is not described; it is *enacted* in *Epitomé*. Historically, it has always happened; the eruption in the Congo is but another manifestation of it. Even poetry is a betrayal of trust—"I pity those who read me / I address them through their language—here in Europe." Thus, in a moving part of the poem, U'Tamsi uses his own voice when he is questioned by the "echo" of Kinshasa, and as poet he at last *positively* asserts that he wishes to be "a pagan at the pagan renewal of the world." Still he and his kind are the marginal men whom he blames. They are part of the disaster and yet not part of it—"more French than Joan of Arc"—the final condemnation of the "Negro," the *évolué*, the *assimilado*.

In *Le ventre* (1964)[33] there is less emphasis on outside events but, like *Le mauvais sang* and *Feu de brousse*, deep introspective examination of self. However, the poem makes constant references through the image of the "dominant belly" to Lumumba, contrasting his lot with the poet's. The poem develops the theme of the belly as a moral entity— both the womb and the agent of betrayal—identifiable with Lumumba's charisma. Through this motif, the poet expresses his emotions and ideas. He feels that this is the time for truth to be discovered and known: "Too much blood has flown in the prairies / blood is all over." "No" is the best answer to whatever causes blood to flow. Yet, paradoxically perhaps, one must bleed to gain any privileges. This predicament is not single but collective; it is that of millions. Although the burden appears to be different from that of Christ's, it is no less loathsome.

U'Tamsi refers explicitly to the deluge that brought night and confusion (colonialism) and provides images of the cross and flag to denounce Christianity and colonialism as equals. His final reply to the subjugation caused by Christianity and colonialism is a categorical "No." For

383

U'Tamsi, as for Lumumba, there would be no compromise with the person who causes his death.

The poet offers a pathetic tribute to Lumumba for his tenacity and courage in the fight against colonialism. Despite the blows of which his belly was the target, he nevertheless survived, at least momentarily, and said "No" in very clear terms. The passion and the sad irony of this tribute give a very macabre tone to the entire piece. Heroes die lonely in their convictions and hopes. Lumumba was aware of all this. He knew his destiny was to have a short but very turbulent life. "I have only one face. Why should I hide myself . . ."; better to fight against "gusts of wind" rather than give up. Lumumba would have been a coward if he turned away from the fight. Instead he denounced this corruption and opposed the material world to the spiritual. The weakness of the Blacks who put up little resistance to "finance power" and the wicked role of the Catholic church in Congolese politics and all Africa are the poet's objects of complaint and revolt. His disgust is well conveyed by the sounds of the French words used; the "eu" sounds in "fleur," "bleu," "le bleu de chauffe est bleu" convey a melancholy and also a certain absurdity and confusion, as in the association of "blue" the color and "blues" (songs).

In any case the messiah, betrayed by his brothers, has his place in heaven, on the right hand of Okito, his faithful friend in time of trouble. Also, Lumumba will be remembered as one betrayed for as little as three pennies because he never sold out his "belly"—his convictions. The belly stands all alone. The poet chooses to be with the belly, with the melodies of Kinshasa which, however happy they may sound, remind him of blood, the blood that spread all over Kinshasa.

It is important to remember that U'Tamsi is conscious that he looks at this tragic event while in Paris, which means necessarily from a distance. "I was blankly armed." Since he cannot be there physically to provide whatever material help is needed, he can only sympathize and lose himself in those melodies from Kinshasa which obsess his mind. The poet makes some reflections of his own about the tragic event—the violence, the corruption, the horrifying death of Lumumba. Indeed he cannot be quiet; he feels he has to speak out. Suffering, he says, is meaningless if there is no reason why one suffers. For U'Tamsi, the reason for suffering is love for one's brothers, "brothers of Negro obedience."

After the desperate outburst of *Le ventre*, U'Tamsi returns to a less bitter note in *Arc musical* (1970).[34] Here there is hope; the man of mixed culture and race is "bronze" and the hope of the world. Still at present, Europe denies the poet his "magic" as "maker" in traditional

384

society: "It's the bow-harp / we must play in this country" (p. 141). He desires a stronger instrument—the license of his peers in Africa—if he is to effect change. But the "stolen fire" (the poet's knowledge) ought to be restored if he seeks peace. In other words, the truth ought not to be proclaimed too loudly. The effect is not quite as vigorous as in *Le ventre*.

U'Tamsi is a poet of strong conviction. His poetry is not one-sided, but explores intensively the meaning of life, very often for a Black man in a world hostile to his existence. Through rich nuances of language, through symbol and imagery, through pun and displaced syntax, he ardently describes the plight of the Congo, Africa, and all Black men. As has been noted, primary and secondary images dominate each work, but whereas the first poem gives only a half answer to the question of identity, *Epitomé* and *Le ventre* delve into the personal nature of the public manifestations of racial exploitation. U'Tamsi is the greatest African poet, for not only does he side with his people, as spokesman within the African oral tradition, but he also makes alien and alienated respond to his harsh judgments. His poems move away from nice quibbles about himself to the broader concerns of his role in the history of the Black world. In this connection, his close association with the Congo during 1960 was probably a turning point. After Lumumba's death, he came to realize that "the singing violin / has not burnt the wind" and that his own art had to disavow European standards in its attempt to speak for inarticulate millions. This he has certainly managed to do.

A Change of Role

WRITER AS OUTSIDER

There is little tradition of laughter in Africa, for the artist has always been seriously committed to the group. The writers who do laugh are, in large measure, those who have broken out of tribal enclaves. But this does not make them foreign to African literature since in traditional Africa masquerade song had provided a similar outlet.

Mongo Beti's first prose attempt was "Ville cruelle" (published in *Trois écrivains noirs*, 1954).[35] It deals with a theme he was to explore later in his work—the crisis of growth. Though the theme is an important one in African literature, "Ville cruelle" does not succeed as a novel; the story is episodic and the ending sudden and melodramatic. Echoes from the Bible ("get up, take your wife and walk") spoil the narrative flow, for there is no obvious reason for them.

Le pauvre Christ de Bomba (1956) holds more promise. Purporting to be the journal of Denis, a fifteen-year-old altar boy, it describes the shortcomings of the missionary endeavors in Africa. Rev. Father Drumont (whom Denis thinks of as Christ) is soon disillusioned; his own *sixa* where Christian girls are taught to be good mothers is a house of prostitution and syphilis is widespread. Fr. Drumont realizes that despite his hard work his only duty is to leave. When he goes, the mission dies.

This book makes use of gentle irony. Because Denis seems to be the complete innocent, all that happens is very funny. For instance he relates quite straightforwardly how Joseph's genitals were crushed (we are told he had "irregular matrimonial habits"). Zachary the cook is a delightful figure; he forces the children to cook for the priest while he gets drunk. Even the priest (to Denis's surprise) listens to Zachary's interpretation of why people convert to Christianity—not to learn about a god they already have but to hear "the secret of [European] power explained to them."

Denis, like Banda in "Ville cruelle," matures. But a better study of growth is *Mission terminée* (1957) which centers on Medza, the unsuccessful scholar who returns to his village. To his amazement he is held up in honor and esteem and is dispatched to retrieve Niam's runaway wife. In Kala he learns to drink palm-wine and in a very comical scene is seduced by Edima and later is forced to marry her. Despite the adoration he receives from the village people, he knows his own limitations. The fact that he can face up to his father and admit his failure as a scholar and husband is proof that the "village-learning" had helped mature him. The book is beautifully written and in parts the author evokes the lost world of innocence in charming, poetic terms. Comedy and serious purpose blend well to express the viewpoint of the individual who rebels against his society.

Beti's latest novel is *Le roi miraculé* (1958), which returns to the theme of the missionaries. Here Father Le Guen tries to bring about the conversion of the chief of Essazam. The chief resists but when he falls ill Yosifa liberally pours water over him, thereby baptizing him. Now that he is a Christian, he has to give up his wives, but wily as ever he refuses to name the wife who should remain. Later rivalry develops among the various factions of his twenty-four wives. All this is comical, yet Beti does make a serious point. After a civil disturbance breaks out, Le Guen is forced to leave. Church and colonial authority are linked, Beti implies; when the church fails the colonialist, then the missionary is no longer an agent. The novel is a postscript on the sorry nature of colonialism and its accomplices.

On the whole Beti's work is most successful. The novels provide enjoyable reading, though they are not without a message—the maturity of the boy, the group, the people, the hypocrisy of colonial administrators, and the pathetic plight of the missionary who seeks to do well. In all his books, Beti suggests that the Africa of the past will survive since its values are more real than those of church and school.

Ferdinand Oyono's first novel is *Une vie de boy* (1956).[36] Presented in diary form, it describes Toundi Joseph's experiences and highlights the hypocrisy of church and state. Though Toundi is a tragic victim of both, the story is essentially comic in its presentation of Europeans. Toundi becomes a convert because the missionaries give out candy; the local priest pronounces African words so badly that they take on obscene meanings—so the pews are packed. As an altar boy, Toundi tickles white girls under the chin with the paten. Oyono's humorous touch makes the reader see the French "civilizing" mission as essentially comic.

Not only does Oyono laugh at the supposed significance of the church, but the state comes in for a good bashing as well. Moreau, the prison superintendent, honestly feels that Dangau prisons are loved by all Blacks and even those who died there died of pleasure. Toundi writes faithfully (and with deadpan reverence) about whites; the comedy arises out of his seeming objectivity. And the cook is prone to hilarious remarks like the one about whites wearing clothes for everything (after Toundi has discovered Madame's contraceptives)!

Not all is laughter or criticism; Toundi is proud of going to market with Madame and he admires her for what she stands for. Jacques is another European presented in a good light. Toundi reports everything in his diary, and thus the reader is free to respond as he chooses—with laughter or tears—for Oyono can switch the mood very suddenly. Such is his subtlety.

In *Le vieux nègre et la médaille* (1956) the humor is more bitter, directed against the "bon nègre" (good Negro) of the colonial regime. But Oyono, the craftsman, is slow to show his hand. Meka is a cocoa farmer and a Christian. He has given his two sons to fight in the war and his lands to the mission. He is to be compensated and when the day arrives for him to receive his medal, he is forced to wait a long time in the sun. He urgently wishes to relieve himself; his shoes pinch. Finally he receives the medal, is ignored at the ceremony afterwards, and gets drunk. In a comic finale he staggers home, loses his medal, and is arrested. When he is released, his views about Europeans have changed. The style here is different in that the entire story is an ironic commentary on colonialism. But Oyono uses serious images to explain Meka's plight: his standing in a circle, waiting his turn; the rain that washes him of all his delusions. Oyono intentionally builds up a series of episodes that betray Meka's simplicity, but at the same time he is a Christ-figure—he is born into a new world, betrayed, and then crucified. But revelation soon comes; as he stands in the hot sun he yearns for his hut for he realizes the foreignness of the white world. His new awareness is his acceptance of traditional beliefs and his rejection of a servile past. The end offers a firmer statement than the first novel; not defeat but a new knowledge.

Chemin d'Europe (1960) pinpoints the direction Oyono had been seeking. Toundi and Meka, one now realizes, were psychologically mixed up because, born within a colonial world, they never knew themselves; nor could Ari Barnabas, the chief character of this novel, who is obsessed by desire for a French woman. Like Toundi and Meka, all that mattered to Barnabas was France. His education would prepare him to go to France, but he does not complete his schooling because of charges of homosexuality. Fortunately he manages to secure a tutorial post in a French family.

Now his fantasies run riot; he dreams of Madame Gruchet divorcing her husband and going off to France with him. When her husband leaves her for a Black woman (the irony is unmistakable here), she seeks comfort from Barnabas. But he is incapable of satisfying his long-expressed desires. He goes back home to his mother, still burning with desire to go to France. After several attempts to solicit funds prove futile, Barnabas stumbles on a solution; he meets a group of street-corner preachers and is advised by a cynical bystander that if he could confess enough sins, he would be sent abroad to display the powers of the Christian God. The novel ends with Barnabas heading for the altar, mentally calculating the confession that will take him to Europe.

Chemin d'Europe is a grim study of the corrosive effects of colonization on an individual. One laughs at Barnabas's antics, at his grim determination to see France or die. But behind Oyono's laughter is concern—concern that Barnabas's values could be so perverted that he should want the unattractive Madame Gruchet only because she is French; concern too that Barnabas should be prepared to reject his village and his mother in order to try to woo the French administrator. The style here is eminently suited to the novel, making use of grotesque descriptions to convey the comicality of Barnabas's predicament. His solution at the end of the novel is a neat reversal of history: the missionaries *came* to Africa to preach; Barnabas can *leave* Africa only if he is an apostle of the devil. The colonial experience that creates regiments of people like Toundi, Meka, and Barnabas is finally exposed in all its ridiculous folly.

It is evident that both Beti and Oyono not only laugh at the group, but side with the group as well, since they also laugh at the colonial overlord. Their brand of satire is therefore different from western satire because this is a persistent laughter directed at the prejudices of the group itself. Thus the writer is an outsider, but is still concerned with group norms, even though he might not subscribe to them all. Neither Beti nor Oyono really has a definite traditional counterpart, for both assert too much of their own individuality.

When the writer stands completely outside the group, when his laughter is not that of the group, he can truly be termed the "enemy." This is a drastic reversal of roles, but the African artist and the writers who will now be considered have, to a large extent, done this. Not until one encounters the work of Ahmadou Kourouma and Yambo Ouologuem is this abundantly clear. For with Sembène Ousmane the group is fragmented; he stresses that the middle class and the new elite in Africa (the real enemy) have nothing to give. In the writing of Jean Ikellé-Matiba, the new group is depicted as being loyal to a specific colonial master (the Germans). Matip and Boni oppose the leadership of the group (in both cases the elders), but the individual voices of Kourouma and Ouologuem attack the entire group.

Ousmane served in the French army in Italy and Germany. Returning to France after demobilization, he worked as a docker in Marseilles, where he became a trade union leader and began writing his first novel. He has published four novels and two volumes of short stories and is a well-known director, having produced three films.

Le docker noir (1956)[37] is a beautifully written work centered on Diaw, a Black docker who is on trial for murder. Diaw has little education but as a political leader of Marseilles dockers, he helps to organize strikes. He writes a book and entrusts the manuscript to a young white intellectual who promises to try to get it published. When she publishes it under her own name, Diaw goes to Paris and kills her. The judge is convinced that there is some other motive—the Black man attracted by the white skin of the European woman. Even though Diaw recites long passages from the work to prove that it is his, he is condemned.

Although the plot has a melodramatic flavor, Ousmane offers a great variety of political and social attitudes. For instance, one of Diaw's lawyers argues against white superiority, asserting that "learned men

have found and are convinced that there had been an African civilisation which went down the Nile and gave birth to our own" (p. 73).
The rhetorical question is asked, "Where is their [the Europeans']
so-called superiority?" But not only are whites criticized; the assimilated
Africans and West Indians who dress European-style and straighten their
hair come in for attack, as does capitalism for being responsible for
racism. Ousmane speaks of the murder as one of racial revenge, and
Diaw's lawyer maintains that his client is a victim of society. "His freedom was hidden in the act he had committed" (p. 41).

The flashback scenes work well. One witnesses the reaction of Diaw's
mother in Senegal when she hears of his crime; another tells of a fellow-
docker who gets a French girl pregnant and of her death when her
mother tries to procure an abortion. The life of the dockers is realistically portrayed—the hard work, the slums in which they live. Diaw
refers to himself as "un écrivain engagé," but his reciting a whole chapter from his book is an artistic flaw, for it does not prove the point.
Finally it must be noted that Ousmane is so committed to his ideas that
he has little sense of timing; the entire third section is an anticlimax,
made up of a letter from Diaw to his uncle in Senegal, which preaches
to the reader "je suis un nègre." This view is the complete opposite of
the conclusion reached at the end of the first part.

Le docker noir is therefore not wholly successful, though it establishes
Ousmane's claim as a serious writer. *Ô pays mon beau peuple!* (1957)[38]
treats the same theme from a different vantage point: Blacks too can be
racist, as Oumar Faye discovers when he returns home with his white
wife, Isabelle. His family reject him, and he is forced to leave his parents
and live in a tent. Finally he builds his own house. His troubles are further compounded by his difficulties with the white community, Isabelle's
homesickness, plus a near rape—this is too much to take all at once and
Ousmane shows little economy here.

The novel recovers its balance when Oumar Faye takes up farming.
When his fields are besieged by locusts, he organizes his fellow-farmers
and they dig trenches, although the first wish of his people is to resort to
witchcraft. Later he leads a protest against the French who buy farm
produce at too low a price. In trying to break up a monopoly, he
succeeds in beginning a cooperative organization but is murdered.

Parts of the novel are sheer lyricism. Oumar Faye constantly refers
to himself as a Black man and he shows his love for his country in song.
At the end, the people sing to his memory. But there are barren patches
in the work; for instance, the action is suspended to describe the July 14
celebrations when French and Senegalese get together. One is not

entirely convinced of the duplicity of the French or of Oumar Faye's adopted mother in France (suddenly mentioned) who sends him gifts. Throughout all this, Isabelle disappears from the story.

Oumar Faye's tragedy is that he offends the norms of both Blacks and whites, though for different reasons. The Blacks are Muslims and distrust Oumar Faye's new ideas—a separate house, a Christian wife. The whites oppose him because his marriage suggests that their so-called superiority can be challenged. But Oumar Faye's mother becomes reconciled to him and his wife who is pregnant and will have a child for him. The reader is to understand that this child will continue his father's work. Thus Isabelle's words to him on the ship, after he had fought some white men ("You will never win") prove mercifully wrong. But Ousmane warns us that trying to overcome prejudice is too much for one man. Still "the criminal arms which had felled him were misled. His home was not in the tomb. He was in the heart of all the men and women. He was present in the evening near the fire; in the rice-fields; when a child wept, his mother would tell him the story of the young man who spoke to the earth and under the palaver-tree. His memory was honored. Oumar was no more but his beautiful people sang about him always . . ." (pp. 233–34). With this praise song, which raises man from the everyday to the heights of myth, the book ends. Ousmane has created a hero for twentieth-century Africa and has pitted him against the enemy within the tribe itself.

A tireless spokesman for the oppressed, Ousmane devoted his next novel, *Les bouts de bois de Dieu* (1960),[39] to the 1947–48 railway strike on the Dakar-Bambako line for better working conditions. Ousmane relates the privations of the strikers and the daily difficulties they encounter. Though they are murdered, beaten, and cajoled by the white officials, they win through in the end; this is the substance of Ousmane's tale.

The strike signifies the end of an era, when Africa had been just "un potager" (a vegetable garden). But no more, for the people now have courage. They are starving, but still willing to fight for their rights. Ousmane dramatically makes this point when a woman sells herself to help her menfolk. "And the men realised that the time which produced other men, also produced other women."

Ousmane observes a careful time span, October 1947 to March 1948. Equally, there is a rigid control of character, and virtues are the monopoly of no one race. Dejean, the French director of the railway at Thiès, is brutal and forthright and tries to break the workers' resistance. El Hadji Mubigué is a traitor to his own people and even refuses food to his own sister. N'Deye Touti is an educated young African who admires all that is white, but is converted during the course of the strike. Diara, a strike-breaker protected by the police, is arrested and tried by his peers. The characterization is never forced, and the oral tradition is frequently used to express a point; for instance, Bakayoko's mother and her grandchild speak in riddles. "Tell me what washes water?" The boy does not know, for "it is not to youth that knowledge belongs but old age." Later in the novel, after the grandmother's death, the enigma is solved—the spirit washes water.

The book has a cast of thousands and this is, indeed, one of its flaws. A list of characters is given as if the writer anticipated the difficulty but it does not help. One gets confused and people are not easily identified. Perhaps this is intentional, for Ousmane is not narrating the private lives of individuals but their public stands.

In parts, the episodic treatment contributes to the overall effect, for the humanitarianism of the message of the novel is reflected in the roles of the characters. Ramatoulayé, an old woman, kills El Hadji's ram and beats back the police when they come to arrest her. Another episode relates the burning of the *bidonville* (a slum built with petrol containers). Soukaré, a guard at Thiès, makes a halfhearted attempt to join the strikers but he is sent back to his shed where he is eaten by rats. The violence of this scene is vividly described. At the end of the book, his skeleton is found. Other characters are developed in different episodes which together help to give them noble qualities. They grow from being mere individuals to heroes and heroines of stature. The limits of their ideology are the limits of the novel.

Ousmane's account is on the whole realistic, especially his comparison of Bakayoko, "the soul of the strike," and Lahbib, "the brain." Bakayoko demonstrates his utter devotion to the strike; his father has been arrested, his mother is dead, and his daughter is wounded but he would not return to Bamako. Private concerns have become of secondary importance. Bakayoko refuses the decorations which the governor-general wishes to give him and it is with pride that he speaks in Wolof. Close to his own folk tradition, Bakayoko relates a story of a husband killed in the First World War, a son in the Second, and another now in prison. The point is made: France has little to give. And because colonialism is perpetual degradation, Bakayoko's father suffers in prison, Isnard's wife is shot, Penda dies.

Toward the end of the story, the people sing of an ancient hero, Goumba, who fought without hatred and therefore won. It is not difficult to associate the determined mass of people with Goumba. The novel is an authentic report of the strike written by a poet with a great social conscience. The strikers prove at last that Africa could be free. With *Les bouts de bois de Dieu,* Ousmane became a novelist in the realist tradition. He has not departed from this style, and we see aspects of it in his short stories and his films. For instance "La noire de . . ." (The Black Woman of . . .), published in *Voltaïques* (1962), is based on an actual letter printed in a French newspaper revealing the plight of a young girl who goes to France to work for a white family but commits suicide out of frustration. Similarly, the political motif has continued. The first of three projected volumes of *L'harmattan* (1964) called *Référendum* takes as its starting point the 1958 referendum when De Gaulle demanded a "yes" or "no" vote to the question of whether or not the French colonies wished to become part of the "French Commonwealth." Here Ousmane uses a representative country to express his views on colonialism and neo-colonialism. The study is ambitious; he says in his preface he will consider all of the former "French" Africa.

After studying at the Moscow Film School, Ousmane returned to Senegal to continue his work in the cinema. "La noire de . . ." was made into a film. But *Borom sarret* (1963) about a poor cartman was better done in Wolof with French subtitles. A more recent film, *Emitai* (1972), documents Black villagers who defy the French. The film follows the new line of *Les bouts* and *L'harmattan*—the plight of the peasant in modern Senegal and how he is at the end of his tether. The film begins with a prayer and ends with invective.

Two short novels appeared in 1965 under the title *Véhi-Coisane ou blanche genèse suivi du Mandat.* "La Mandat" was made into a film and relates in part the complicated effects of bureaucracy on traditional folk.

Ousmane sides with the everyday lot of his people. No sentimentalist, he chooses as his topics not only moments of glory but times of tragedy. He is a socialist and his works suggest that Africa, like the heroine of "La noire de . . . ," is controlled by forces outside itself. His works document the efforts of individuals who refuse to be seduced by material gain but who seek a better life in the Africa of the present.

Ikellé-Matiba's novel entitled *Cette Afrique-là* (1963)[40] describes German influence on Africans and the effects of the First World War on Africa. It also provides interesting insights into education. Franz Mômha, the main character, obtains a good education in Cameroon under German occupation and is well indoctrinated about the superiority of whites, about the importance of Christianity. After a difficult examination (and suitable floggings), he graduates to the Mittelschule at Lobetal where the indoctrination continues: "There were three powers on earth, Germany, France and England" (p. 78). But as for the French "ils ont vendu le nègre comme une marchandise" (they had sold Blacks like chattels; p. 78) and as for the English "ils sont faux parce que hypocrites et jaloux" (they are dangerous because they are hypocritical and jealous; p. 79). Ikellé-Matiba reports all, with only a trace of irony. Finally he can admit, "J'étais completement détribalisé" (I was completely detribalized).

Ikellé-Matiba claims he has written a document to serve as history, stating in his epilogue that he has been objective. But has he written a novel? One comes away from *Cette Afrique-là* with a feeling that characterization has been subjected to documentation. Nevertheless there are moving moments in the story, and this is perhaps the best defense of a colonial administration written by an African.

Afrique nous t'ignorons (1956) by Benjamin Matip is a semi-autobiographical novel about Samba, a young man who opposes the acquiescence of the elders who tacitly accept colonial rule. Samba sees that the Black farmers are exploited by white traders and he is loud in his denunciations of this practice. Part of the work concerns the excitement in Cameroon caused by the outbreak of the Second World War.

Nazi Boni's *Crepuscule des temps anciens* (1962) is a reconstruction of myth; "Ancestor," the narrator, is an old chief who relates the history of his people three hundred years before the coming of the white man. A time shift takes in the uprising of the Bwawa in 1915. Boni's style of writing constantly alludes to matters external to the action. His descriptions are often pompous—"the town was sunk in heavy sleep"—and the footnotes do not fit the form of the novel. The material is so close to the oral tradition that one suspects a suitable form has not been found to relate it. In the last analysis, the work is simply a rough account of the Bwawa people's legendary past.

Korouma's novel *Les soleils des indépendances* (1968) relates the story of Fama, a chief of Horodougou, who is deposed in favor of Lacina, a man more acceptable to the colonial power. Now he is poor and lives in town, since he cannot reside in Horodougou because "the land is hard and can only be ploughed by sturdy arms and supple backs." Fama is now a parasite and tries to court those in power—the very men he despises as "bastards" and "slaves." Lacina dies and Fama is reinstalled as chief, but eventually he is arrested for anti-government activities. He is sent to a detention camp and later sentenced to twenty years of solitary confinement.

During a time of amnesty he is released and returns to Horodougou where he knows he will die. He is proud to the end, scorning the new elite who guard the borders of his land. Ahmadou Korouma's novel suggests that frequently independence can kill man's traditional dignity. Fama's pride, evident when he opposes the soldier who asks him for his identity card or when he fights within him the strange quirk of fate that made him a nobody, is very praiseworthy. This pride lends purpose and a message to an excellently written novel.

Le devoir de violence (1968) by Yambo Ouologuem is a tale intertwined with legend and history, interlaced with truth and fiction; it is difficult to tell where one ends and the other begins. In Ouologuem's literary fabric one can detect allusions to events in Judaic-Christian lore: the Moses experience and the Christ experience in saving the child to be born. The Nakem Empire under the dynasties of the Saifs rolled onward through the centuries and sank lower with each new act of vileness. The rulers changed often, frequently because of intemperance and debauchery, and perhaps the dynasty sank to its lowest ebb under Saif al-Haram, the wicked one.

The capture of rebel tribes, free men, and defeated warriors is vividly described by such barbaric acts as mass rape, torture, orgies, murder, and cannibalism. Harvests were laid waste and whole populations sold into slavery. The book sees violence as an implicit part of African history.

The main plot centers on the son of Kassoumi, a serf of the Saif. Raymond Spartacus is an excellent student and, after the tragic death of his mother, the Saif sends him to Paris to obtain an education that would enable him to return to Nakem as his puppet against French colonialism.

The war breaks out and Raymond fights for France. Perhaps it tends to crush out the memories of the past, especially the seamy experiences of his student days: his incestuous relation with his sister in a Paris brothel; his homosexual relations with a white man; and his later marriage to Suzanne, a French woman. Later he returns to Africa. He sees his country as he sees himself—struggling for identity. He thinks sadly of the legend of the Saifs, knowing that the source of the Saif's power is sorcery and that he can murder men with the deadly asp. Raymond Spartacus Kassoumi realizes his life will be one of protest as he views the scandalous condition of his country.

Yambo Ouologuem is an angry man and his novel offends because it is a brutal and in part an unwarranted attack on Africa. Africa, the novel says, has had a history of cruelty and the colonialist was a mere pawn in the game. It matters little if what Ouologuem says is true—he is not writing history, but is it convincing? He exaggerates his view of Africa: Were there really so many orgies? So much sensuality? Repression? War? Is the myth of the Saif really convincing—symbolical as the Saif is of oppression whether by African, Arab, Jew, or Gentile? It does not seem to be, for after a while the impact is lost. Too many superlatives spoil the telling; one ends up only with a shriek of despair.

The novel is more convincing when it shifts from apparent myth to obvious reality. Raymond Spartacus is the man of two cultures, the son of slaves. He is the man who will save Africa from the Saifs, for his own personal history (a raped mother, a murdered father) is one that demands this. In his very reality, even though he stands for something outside himself, Raymond Spartacus convinces us. And in this conviction the reader can accept him as a revolutionary. The book does not offer hope at the end—only a large interrogative. It matters little what sources the writer may or may not have used; his own intention is clear.

Because Ouologuem uses such a vast canvas, 1202–1947, his book tends to be episodic and lacks a definite plot. Some of the episodes do contribute to the central meaning but often they are little more than an extravaganza of cannibalism, sexuality, and cruelty. The use of occasional interjections or epigrams gives the novel a traditional aura, but the reader is frequently bewildered by the numerous characters.

Similarly Ewandé's *Vive le président* (1968) is a satire attacking African politicians who behave as badly as former colonial masters. No specific country is mentioned in the book, but each chapter attacks different aspects of government corruption; the new *évolué*, the people themselves who put up with ministers, and a president who courts whites are all satirized.

Ewandé denounces those people who allow a system of waste to flourish. He states tongue in cheek that every president should have a large mansion so that the people can be proud. He adds that a good minister need not have a formal education but should be able to pretend that he does, and he comments, ironically, that he himself wants to be a minister. He takes a swipe too at coups in Africa; all that one needs to do to take over a country is to broadcast and this is done (rather suddenly) at the end.

More a string of satirical jousts than a novel, the book attacks "revolutionaries" and "reformers." He seems afraid of the Chinese presence in Africa and his first act as new president is to cut off all relations with China.

The closest person to the "I" narrator of the book (Ewandé calls it a journal) is a writer who advocates blackness (his alter-ego?). All in all the work primarily expresses the desire to return to traditional values and to give up corrupt western norms. In one chapter, Ewandé mentions that Africans should work as a group and that the individual should be subjugated to the group.

Vive le président would have been more effective if it were not written as a political pamphlet. It is too long and even though there is some kind of climax at the end this does not prevent the book from dragging. It seems that Ewandé still needs to reconcile his intentions as a reformer and his vocation as a storyteller; somewhere between this the failure of the novel lies.

African literature in French demonstrates the possibilities of a European language given a blood transfusion. The works move from slavish imitation of French writing and culture to writings that draw heavily on the African past. One aspect of this, albeit romanticized, is seen in the négritude writers but other aspects are detected in writers of such different kinship as Laye, U'Tamsi, and Ousmane. The past may equally be scoffed at as it is by Oyono and Beti, or outrightly denounced as it is by Ewandé and Ouologuem. But the corpus presents an interesting body of literature, unified not merely by the French language or even by a common set of experiences and privations within the French colonial structure; it represents a whole, along with the literatures in African languages, English, and Portuguese, because it charts a course of concern away from group mores to personal affiliations.

Chapter 15

African Drama
in French and English

European theater assumes that all human relationships are interrela-
tionships and therefore psychological. In unscripted African theater
what was paramount was man's involvement with something extra-
human. The development of African creativity from the anonymous to
the personal effectuated the consolidation of the individual, and in theater it is obviously not only the individual but his relationship with other
individuals that emerges. In other words written drama moved theater
from the shrine and the marketplace to the stage, and the basic assumption was made (and is surely implicit in staged theater) that language
could interpret any psychological relationship. The danger here is that
characterization can become identical with this relationship; the outer
forms of action can take the place of the essential nature of theater and
thus give rise to melodrama.

Early Stagecraft: What Audience?

Ecole William Ponty and H. I. E. Dhlomo are associated with the beginnings of staged African drama in French and English respectively. Ecole
William Ponty was situated in St. Louis, Senegal, although pupils came
from all over French Equatorial Africa, French West Africa, Togoland,
and the Cameroons. In the 1930s an attempt was made to rehabilitate
colonial teaching and the inspector general of education assigned various
vacation projects centered on the students' own lives and customs. This

helped to stimulate a knowledge of ethnology, and the pupils began writing plays which were presented at the end of the academic year. The first play, by some Dahomeyan pupils, was produced at the end of the 1932–33 session. Called *La dernière entrevue de Behanzin et de Bayol*, it set the theme and subject matter for plays written and performed by other groups until 1949.[1]

As Bakary Traoré has shown, the parts of women were at first played by the boys of the school, but from 1939 schoolgirls from nearby Rufisque played the female parts.[2] Ecole William Ponty had additional limitations; the plays were written by schoolboys for a school audience, and though the pupils did much of the necessary research and the actual writing of the drama, it remained a corporate effort to which the French director and the staff of the school contributed. Nevertheless the plays were a useful beginning, demonstrating the possibilities of African drama in French; they indicated that the direction of development would be in the resuscitation of folk forms. That the original intentions of Ecole William Ponty were far from "artistic" cannot be denied; the plays were first and foremost seen as "academic" exercises, but even so, it was a bold step taken at a time when the entire educational emphasis was on the production of the *évolué*. After sixteen years the very educational processes that had encouraged the beginning of drama brought it to an end; the French diploma was introduced into African schools. But this theater's influence did not die. Plays continued to be performed on certain occasions, and there is no way to measure the stimulus they must have exerted; Keita Fodeba, the founder of "Les Ballets Africains," was himself a product of the school.

Because of the school's European directorship, subjects and attitudes were obviously in keeping with European norms. For instance, a close examination of *Sokamé*, one of the two plays performed by the pupils in Paris at the Théâtre des Champs Elysées in 1937, reveals certain devices typical of their entire repertory.[3] The play seems to identify with European values; traditional beliefs are equated with superstition and are inferior to western concepts. But the culture equation in *Sokamé* is not quite so simple; after all Bokonon, the chief priest of Fa, is "un devin" and the weapon he gives to Egblamakou is a magical aid with which the hero is to counter superstition. What the play seems to suggest is that the new generation has to modify values. Instead of depicting an outright clash between Africa and Europe, it describes the conflict of two generations. The younger does not advocate outright revolution but minor change.

Formalized elements of Dahomean life are retained in the play; there

399

are long passages, for instance, devoted to an exchange of greetings, first between the two farmers and later between Egblamakou and Bokonon. Since this freezes the action, one cannot be sure to what extent this device, though realistic and within the ritual of daily routine, could ever become part of the equipment of modern African drama. But the overall plot is the dramatization of the familiar myth of the quarrel between earth and heaven, and the denouement (though invented) describes the triumph of the earth. In the play man brings about the release from drought, whereas in the myth the elements conspire against man, who is a mere intermediary. Consciously or unconsciously the Dahomeyan pupils assert that an individual is able to alter the dictates of the tribe and that this represents his most defiant gesture of will.

Therefore these plays did not merely cater to fashionable European prejudices, although there must have been a temptation to do this, for the school "was a theatre of the salon [and] it addressed itself really to a handful of spectators who represented the privileged people. Its stage was not open enough. In a certain way it was even able to discourage everything that was going on in the vernacular language and which was a little bit apart from the traditional décor of the European theatre."[4] This is a severe indictment and in part it is certainly true. William Ponty was an offshoot of French theater; after all the dramatists were schoolboys working under the supervision of their French teachers. But use was made in *Sokamé*, for instance, of proverbs: Sokamé explains to her lover why her father is unable to help her against the king and asks, "Does the hawk hinder the hen from taking its young ones away?" (p. 634.) The most exciting device which retained a flavor of traditional ritual was the incorporation of songs. They are sung throughout and when at the end the rain begins to fall the king proclaims, "People faithful people sing, life is beautiful" (p. 641). Through the use of proverbs and songs, and by careful description of the ritual associated with the two priests, an attempt was made to place the play in the tradition of unscripted indigenous drama. The praise song to the king is definitely within this tradition:

> Our king has come out
> And the herald sings his praise.
> Walk proudly
> As proudly as you wish
> The land is yours . . . (p. 630)

All these elements, together with the occasional use of vernacular words, give an atmosphere of realism and an air of authority.

A similar search for truth is the subject of H. I. E. Dhlomo's *Girl Who*

Killed to Save (1935), the first African play in English. Like *Sokamé* it has its roots in tradition, and Nongquase was a historical figure, Dhlomo tells us in a note, who "declared that she held converse with the spirits of the old heroes of the tribe, who intimated that they had witnessed with sorrow the ruin of their race through the oppression of the conquerors from overseas." The two plays are similar in other respects; Dhlomo uses songs and a praise poem is recited to Kreli, the paramount chief who agrees with Nongquase that the occasion was auspicious for waging war against the Europeans. There is, however, only a single isolated use of what seemingly is a transposition from the vernacular—the chief, in referring to his own people who dare oppose him, says that his warriors will "eat them up with spear" (p. 17). In response to Nongquase's prophecy, cattle are slaughtered, the ground is left untilled, and the people endure great hardship. It is the selfless service of the commissioner and his wife, her brother Hugh and a missionary, that helps to restore prosperity. The dramatist comes out strongly on the side of "enlightenment" and European church and state.

There is, however, an unstated conflict that can perhaps be deduced from the brief, initial appearance of the heroine and the way in which she is simply referred to in the rest of the play. This is of course bad theater in that her character is not sufficiently developed and the audience is unable to interpret her significance. The only hints are provided by the chance comments of those who speak for and against her. But is it not possible that this was an intentional device? Perhaps Dhlomo could not really trust himself to make a villain of Nongquase, and because he had to write within the conventions of missionary literature, he preferred instead to keep her out of the play. For in spite of the Christian message he does portray her as a heroine; both Hugh and the missionary identify her as the means through which the Xhosa people (however pervertedly) will realize themselves. At the end of the play a dying convert imagines that he sees her surrounded by the people who perished during the famine she had brought about and who hailed her as their deliverance; it is she who finally leads the dying man to God. It is an unsatisfactory resolution but illustrates the nature of the tension. How could the pagan Nongquase be retained as Christian heroine? Although she had fought to liberate her people from the Europeans, she is identified with them and with Christianity. The relationship is forced but almost manages to convince.

Ephemerally there are two significant points in the play that are paradoxically related to each other. One is the love interest; Nongquase is hopelessly in love with Mazwi, who does not believe in her prophecies. The way in which she thinks about him and the manner in which they speak to one another show that Dhlomo was writing outside any common convention and was creating in the theme of idealized love something that had no place in traditional African life. Mazwi says to her, "Come run away with me, now, now. We can easily escape. The guards on the north side are my old pals whom I have bribed. Come escape from yourself—escape from death" (p. 11). He is speaking within a "romantic" convention about which Dhlomo probably had knowledge, but in the context his words are as ridiculous as the parting of the commissioner from his wife:

Brownlee: Thank God I have the noble wife I have.
Mrs. Brownlee: (*Tears in her eyes and running into his open arms*) Oh! Charles!
Brownlee: (*Emotional*) Darling! (*They embrace.*) (*Silence long and profound*). (p. 27)

Perhaps the contemporary reviewer of the play had this scene in mind when he sternly admonished that "it is in the depiction of the Natives themselves that Dhlomo excels and he should bear this in mind in future work."[5]

On the other hand, the reviewer might be objecting because the Europeans come off rather badly in the play. They speculate on the philosophical significance of the famine, each one making a suggestion about its possible implications and each suggestion seeming more outlandish than the other. Dhlomo's best creations are Nongquase, her father, and Chief Kreli. At one point Nongquase's father says with obvious feeling, "I hear the cows lowing in the caves, waiting to come to life. I see, standing out of the caves yonder the horns of thousands of cattle trying to come above ground. By the side of the rivers and along the sea shore I see a cloud of risen warriors armed heavily trying and crying to come and help us against the White man" (p. 14). It is a great call to national unity, Dhlomo's bid at returning to the tribe, the last meeting place of the individual within the security of nation. For Kreli remarks, "Our race cannot suffer because of individuals. Individuals must lose themselves in the race" (p. 17). Dhlomo indicates that although Nongquase is wrong she is not evil; she is the necessary victim of the process of change from tribal acceptance to individual assertion.

This process is also clear in J. B. Danquah's play of the forties, *The Third Woman*, which is based on an Akan myth of how the Highgod created three different types of women. Danquah equates these with three different types of historical development—the traditional, the colonized, and the independent. But he does not depend on just one folkloristic parallel, but introduces Ananse the spider and songs in the manner of the folktale. Ananse is not the hero; he is the "primitive" who "pretends to a conservatism / which, as e'er, is quite re-actionary." Ananse has to be converted to the "world of harmony, concord and peace" which the third woman symbolizes. She is the hope that remains at the end of the play.

In a way *The Third Woman* opposes Africa against Europe, though Danquah views the conflict optimistically; it is easily resolved when the fool, now turned king, is told by Dudente, a traditional priest, that everything of "permanent value . . . inherited from the realistic West" has been lost. However, the priest who advocates science asks about "woman's liberty" and Dudente replies

> That indeed is gained. The contribution
> Of the Western culture has, to woman
> Brought freedom. That freedom must have inspired
> The new creation of the Third Woman . . .

And at the end the king can state, "Glory to God in the highest, glory, / And on earth peace, good will toward all men."

The play suffers from Danquah's heavyhanded attempts to give the tale symbolic import. He is not content merely to tell of a man's search for a good woman but constantly interlards the action with references to the West (Europe?) and the East (Africa?) which muddy the symbolism. The language suffers too, for the playwright consciously creates iambic pentameter lines which are heavy and burdensome. He is also fond of archaisms and biblical language which are often strained in the context of the play. Obviously he intended his work to be regarded as a "classic," for he claimed that he observed the unities of time, place, and action. It is, however, merely an interesting effort in pioneering African drama in English.

Recent Popular Drama by Yorubas: Stage and Shrine

Before moving on to develop some ideas on African theater, it seems worthwhile to mention recent drama by Yorubas. The importance of the individuals who will be briefly discussed is that they were able to link modern stagecraft with traditional theater. Among the first to be considered should be Herbert Ogunde who has composed over thirty operas in Yoruba, four of which have been printed. His "Ogunde Concert Party" has been functioning since 1944.

At first Ogunde wrote operas based on biblical themes for the church, but he broke away from this to deal with more contemporary events. Usually his lyrics and dialogue are improvised on stage but some music has been published.

One of his better known plays is *Yoruba ronu* (Yorubas Must Think) (1964),[6] a satirical account of the strife that plagued Yorubas in the sixties. It was banned in western Nigeria for some time but was produced with great success in other parts of the country.

Ogunde utilizes the commercial repertoire of Yoruba theater, frequently using both western instruments and drums in his plays. Realizing that plays to which people can relate are successful, he continued his attack on the government; in one he shows the trickery at election time and in another he demonstrates the effects of a general strike.

Ife owo (1965) or "Love of Money" by Kolowole Ogunmola is a satire on marriage and wealth. Ogunmola uses mime and singing as well as drumming to convey his message. When he was at the University of Ibadan, the traveling theater took his adaptation of Amos Tutuola's *Palm-Wine Drinkard* around the country with great success. Ogunmola's acting and directing ability come over very well in the play. Another play which similarly utilizes these resources but for more serious purposes is *Agbaraj' agbara* or "The Reign of the Mighty," which was produced in Ibadan in 1962.

Duro Ladipo has published *Three Yoruba Plays* (1964) and *Moremi* in *Three Nigerian Plays* edited by Ulli Beier (1967). His works do not merely tell a story in words; music and especially drums help contribute to the effect. *Oba Koso*, for instance, includes music, dancing, and singing as well as references to traditional Yoruba praise songs. The play concerns a warlike Yoruba king who is unable to control his generals when his people persuade him that they want peace. He therefore feels he has failed his people, and after a period of exile he hangs himself. But his people worship him as a god, for "the king does not hang," that is, he cannot die.

Oba Waja deals with the conflict between Africa and Europe. Tradition demands that when the king dies the commander of the horse must kill himself. Dance and music are introduced as he prepares himself for his death, but his wish is interrupted by the district officer who arrests him. His son, overcome by the disgrace, commits suicide. The people chant:

> White man, bringer of new laws.
> White man, bringer of new times.
> Your work was confounded by Eshu . . .

In *The Wise*, a play so far unpublished but performed throughout Nigeria, Aderoumu is chosen by the oracle to be the new king. Music and chanting express his bewilderment, for he is only a farmer and the *babalola* (priest) promises him, through the chorus, that

> There will be money—yes!
> There will be children—yes!
> There will be peace—yes!

The new king is able to show his wisdom when a wife exchanges her dead baby for another woman's child. He tells both women that they can each have half the child. The mother pleads that the life of the child be spared, and the other insists that the child be divided. At this the chorus chants, "The world hangs by the thin thread of wisdom, / The wise man rules the world . . ."

Duro Ladipo makes use of proverbs and praise phrases to develop his story. When the chorus chants, the audience frequently joins in, and in this Ladipo has made a definite contribution in participatory theater.

So far Obotunde Ijimere's best known work is *Eda* (1965), a Yoruba adaptation of *Everyman*, which was performed by the Duro Ladipo Company in various parts of Europe as well as in Nigeria. His *Woyengi* (based on an Ijaw creation myth) was first played in English by students of the drama department of Ibadan University in 1965. *Born with the Fire on His Head* has been performed and is included in Beier's *Three Nigerian Plays*. Like Ladipo's *Moremi*, it is based on Johnson's *History of the Yorubas*. *Woyengi*, *Everyman*, and *The Imprisonment of Obatala* have been published in *The Imprisonment of Obatala and Other Plays* (1966). Another excellent play is *The Fall of Man* (1966) which is written in pidgin English. Adam, Eve, and God are all seen as Yoruba people.

Ijimere's dramatic pieces re-enact cosmic events. His method is to reveal the plot through song, music, and dance which alternate with the dialogue. For example in *The Imprisonment of Obatala*, Yemanja, Obatala's wife, sings of plentifulness in the land. Previously there had been famine, so when Obatala wishes to visit Shango, god of thunder and lightning, Yemanja protests. Obatala argues with her in proverbs, using even references (modified) to wedding songs; the *babalawo* whom he visits also draws from the stock of oral literature—here folktales and praise songs—to warn him of the falseness of some friends.

Yoruba myth has it that in a fit of drunkenness Obatala created hunchbacks. Thus the priest tells him he must pay for his sins. As Obatala journeys, the prankster god Eshu plays tricks on him and Shango imprisons him for stealing his horse. His imprisonment is that of a mortal

405

man who has to atone for his wrongdoings. The harm Ogun (the god of war) has done to Obatala (the father of laughter) is apparent, for now disharmony is rampant whereas before there was peace.

Ogun, Shango, and Eshu, the symbols of aggression, judgment, and fate, represent facets of human endeavor and failure. The peace at the beginning is no more and will not return until Obatala, or ordinary man, is released. But even when he is freed, there is a sense of strange omens, for Eshu remains almost the last speaker on stage. Man's folly survives.

Similarly *Woyengi* is concerned with large issues—here the apparent quest for progeny, to be the great mother goddess. Again praise songs, riddles, wedding songs, incantations, proverbs, and plain dialogue intermingled with dancing carry forward the action. Once more tradition is sacred; the play ends with the message that things remain much as they are.

Obotunde Ijimere provides entertaining theater, because like few others he has enriched the stage by extending its possibilities. Ogboina in *Woyengi* is left with her "command of the word" and Obatala sees the "fire" in Shango's eyes; the oral artist's purpose is to sing with his nation. This playwright succeeds well in establishing a close alliance with Yoruba lore, making his plays at worst a mosaic of Yoruba oral songs and at best exciting new theater.

Wale Ogunyemi's first play, *Business Headache* (1966), was written while he was working with Theatre Express, a drama group he helped to form in 1965. *The Scheme* has been published in Beier's *Three Nigerian Plays*, and since then Ogunyemi has composed *Be Mighty, Be Mine* (1968) and *Asare Akogun* (1969), both of which deal with the Yoruba pantheon. Fifteen radio and television plays have also been produced. His most recent effort is a Yoruba adaptation of Shakespeare's *Macbeth*, which was performed in 1969. In these latter plays Ogunyemi's treatment tends to be too heavy. He is better in his lighter plays like *The Scheme* and *Business Headache*, which is especially effective because rendered in pidgin.

Olawale Rotimi who has a M.A. in playwriting from Yale, wrote and produced *Kurunmi* and *The Prodigal* for the second Ife Festival of Arts in 1969. These very short pieces were subsequently reprinted in *Nigeria Magazine* (1969). His major work is *The Gods Are Not to Blame* (1971),[7] a Yoruba adaptation of the Oedipus legend. Use is made of mime and choral singing as well as a narrator. It was performed at the Ife Festival of Arts in 1968 and its appeal lies in its complete break from anything in Yoruba traditional theater. For incestuous themes are not usually handled, and nothing on the Yoruba stage equals the force of King Odewale stabbing the queen to death or piercing out his own eyes. Even more interesting is Rotimi's variations on the Oedipus legend; the king is very Yoruba but he is king among an *alien* people. The bitter truth of discovery is given greater effect in the play than in the original legend because it is told by a man of the chief's own clan. Rotimi also changes the reason for the child's not knowing his parents; the gods had ordered his death and the Priest of Ogun had instructed that the order be carried out but Gbonka spared his life.

Use is made of proverbial speaking and of Yoruba daily life and customs. Throughout the play one feels that this is not a mere attempt at rewriting the Oedipus legend in Yoruba terms but a very successful re-creation. *The Gods Are Not to Blame* is the best of Rotimi's plays.

Ogunde, Ladipo, Ijimere, Ogunmeyi, and Rotimi share one attribute in common—the ability to draw from the reservoirs of Yoruba traditional group experience and to give this experience a new and distinct form. In their work the entire realm of Yoruba culture may be seen, and if a comparison may be made between them and any other single group in African literature, then it must be with the writers of Onitsha literature. For the Ibos who produce the prose and the Yorubas who produce the drama have one aim in common—to appeal, directly and forcefully, to a "home" audience.

Recent Staged Drama: Social Reality and the Inner Life

The link between new staged theater and unwritten indigenous drama is a tenuous one. Although some plays feature traditional songs and dances and make use of proverbs and vernacular language idioms in dialogue, African playwrights in general tend to regard the modern stage as a rostrum for public issues. Usually these are centered on a chief protagonist who in his inner attitude toward church, marriage, social beliefs, and traditional culture epitomizes *outer* issues of contemporary African life. Even Wole Soyinka's recent play *Madmen and Specialists* (1971) with its rejection of things *as* they are (the cult of AS) follows this pattern.

In 1956, the Nigerian playwright James Ene Henshaw published *This Is Our Chance*, a collection of three short plays. The title play describes a society that is fettered by an outmoded tradition but nevertheless aspires toward western values. Chief Damba is a supporter of this tradition, for to him "Tradition is sacred. Custom is above all. To question Tradition is sacrilege. If men do not respect Tradition how can our society stand? How can we be proud of our forefathers and pass on our pride to our children?" (p. 19.) Through the course of the play, Damba comes to realize that some of his notions are mistaken. Although his conversion is not entirely convincing, nevertheless it is apparent that Henshaw is implying that Chief Damba's meaning of "tradition," that is adherence to worn-out institutions, is quite wrong. This theme is dealt with to a greater or a lesser extent by many playwrights. Sometimes the conflict can be almost in the nature of an undercurrent—certainly Dauda's ambitions in Sarif Easmon's *Dear Parent and Ogre* seem to provide the issue. In his arrogance he dislikes everyone he considers beneath him, but he is forced by circumstances to make an alliance with a trade union leader, Mahmoud Sawanoh, who is his inferior. However, he comes to feel a strong sense of gratitude toward Sawanoh when he rescues him from drowning. One is therefore convinced of the beginnings of Dauda's change of heart. Eventually, confronted with the threat of a deserting wife (the French woman Françoise), he is forced to give in to his family. But it is all so very civilized.

Françoise: (*breaks down completely and begins to cry.*) There—the—cunning ogre! Words! Words! Words! He only wants to seduce me to stay. I—go away—Dav-veeed—you hear? I go—this very night!

Dauda: Of course you'll do no such thing, *ma cherie*. (*Gently, humbly he puts his arm round her waist and leads her upstage to the settee.*) It sometimes takes a few real shocks in life to bring a man to his senses, dear Françoise. I have had a terrific number of shocks tonight. But none of them was so bad as—when I saw you come in just now, ready to desert me. Françoise, how *could* you? (*Brokenly, he leans over towards her on the settee, pleading with her.*) Even my enemies envy me the influence you have been in my career, and even more, the pure happiness you have brought me and my family within our home. Françoise—how could you even *think* of leaving me *now*?

Françoise: (*still sobbing.*) I—won't believe you, Dav-veed. Jamais! Jamais! Jamais! Words—just words. Words don't matter any more. You've hurt me too much for me to want to stay.

Dauda: Words beget words, and—thank God—they can sometimes unget them. Look, Françoise. (*He leans over to kiss her on the lips as she raises her face to him. He gets up from the settee, moves slightly right and downstage.*) Come here Sekou, and you, Siata. There, my children (*He solemnly joins their hands in his.*), accept the apologies as well as the blessings of one who has seen, while there was still time, that much harm may be done even out of a sincere desire to do good.

Siata: (*throws her arms around his neck.*) Oh, Daddy—bully for you!

Sekou: Oh, Sir—I just can't tell you how happy you made us . . . (pp. 98–99)

As in many other plays, the members of the older generation in Easmon's *Dear Parent and Ogre* have to be convinced of the capacity of the young for leadership; the young do not just make a break—first it is necessary to win over their elders. Here the idea of the stage as rostrum is evident. The playwrights, all young people without exception, are really addressing their fathers and advocating change. That their fathers do alter is due more to the maneuvering of the plot than to the adaptability of the parent.

Many of these plays, perhaps not unsurprisingly, pose the problem of a powerless but articulate younger generation. They are powerless in that they do not have the instruments of authority, although the playwright leaves no doubt in our minds that they have the intellectual equipment to wield them. A favorite device of the authors of Nigerian popular literature is to make the father so obviously illiterate that he is more of a buffoon than an upholder of tradition. To this extent these characters differ from Chief Damba who, in spite of his attitude toward vitamins, nevertheless comes over as someone whose opinions are bound to be respected. But in Ogali's *Veronica My Daughter*[8] it is only a question of bride-price that makes Chief Jombo unwilling to grant his daughter her wish. When he realizes he cannot accept more than thirty pounds whether Veronica marries Michael (whom she prefers) or Chief Bassey (whom he prefers), he finally gives in to Veronica. His reluctant defeat is certainly in character:

> If na so, well make I talk say Veronica my daughter don loss me. If na ten pounds make Mikere pay, but if him talk politician say him no go pay, well make him takam free because Veronica my daughter na loss person for me. (p. 33)
> (If this is really so, well allow me to say that through Veronica my daughter I have lost a great deal of money. Even if it is only ten pounds, let Michael pay, but if he prattles like a politician don't make him pay. He can have her free for I've already lost her.)

Indeed these plays show in personal terms the conflict of cultures inherent in the political situation of the city-dweller. The tension is not as foreign as it has been made to sound in some plays, for it is not only between generations, but between an ancient aristocracy and a new technocracy, between traditionalism and westernization, between the dignity of the old and the sprawling vulgarity of the new. Wole Soyinka, the best playwright of this period, comes out strongly on the side of tradition. In *The Lion and the Jewel* the beautiful Sidi marries the local chief and rejects the schoolmaster despite his fine words; in *The Strong Breed* Emman's obligations to tradition compel him to become a "carrier" at the festival in a strange village, when he had already sought to escape from this duty in his own town; petrol is used to drive away

409

forest-spirits in *A Dance of the Forests*[9] but, as one character says, "you cannot get rid of ancestors with the little toys of children" (p. 41).

Like *Dear Parent and Ogre*, J. Saverio Naigiziki's *L'optimişţe*,[10] published in French in 1954, also dramatizes the conflict of generations as seen in the relationship between father and son and members of hostile tribes. Jules, a Bahutu, wants to marry Monica, a Mututsi, but both fathers disapprove. Monica's parents try to put pressure on Jules's father through his *shebuja* (protector), but once again it is the enlightened young people who represent a rational attitude. In the end the parents have to give in and the marriage is considered in a social context as "l'essor ruandais" (the ascendancy of Ruanda).

According to these playwrights, intertribal marriage can only be justified through national awareness. What the young people are really saying to their fathers is that they actively identify with a nation whereas their fathers passively belong to a tribe. The idea of the group is still there; only the dimensions have altered. Even when the idea of tribe is absent from the conflict, as in Joe de Graft's *Sons and Daughters*, the young characters like those in *This Is Our Chance, Dear Parent and Ogre, Veronica My Daughter*, and *L'optimiste* ally themselves with the forces of progress, and here this means being unconventional. They might not all speak like Bomber Billy in *Veronica My Daughter*, "the young student, who takes the part of Veronica's father against her and who warns her to 'avoid pomposity, proticity, verbosity and rapacity'" (p. 28), but in *Sons and Daughters* Maanan wishes to be an artist, whereas her father is in favor of her becoming a lawyer, and her brother Aaron wants to be a painter, whereas his father prefers him to be an engineer. This suggests that the dramatist intends to present his chief characters as rebels against the established order with its insistence on "safe" vocations. But to make this point the characters do two things: they ally their aspirations with a group and resolve the problem with their father. He agrees to the arrangement, not when he has been proved wrong, but when he is satisfied that dancing does not mean sexual promiscuity, nor art a life of indigence. In a most unsatisfactory ending (from this viewpoint) Aaron's friend manages to sell a painting to an American tourist and this convinces his father of the commercial possibilities of art. Aaron's "to hell with everybody and their talk of money," spoken at the end of the play, suggests that the playwright was possibly dissatisfied with his ending. The placating of the father signified that some of the son's ideals were either wrong or could be distorted.

Opposing values of parents and children mean there is not only a collision of worlds but an intersection of all time. George Lukăcs, commenting on the conflicts of generations on the stage, has added that "the stage has turned into the point of intersection of pairs of worlds, distinct in time; the realm of drama is one where 'past' and 'future,' 'no longer' and 'not yet' come together in a single moment."[11] Because the plays that have been dealt with so far seem overconcerned with identifying the younger generation with the attitudes of a new group, the point made by Lukács has not been very apparent. In oral literature the intermingling of men, gods, and animals represents this intersection in time. Wole Soyinka also manages to incorporate this aspect in his *Dance of the Forests*; his characters are a dead warrior and his wife, Yoruba gods, forest-spirits, and contemporary mortals. The dramatic justification for the assembly is that it is an official "gathering of the tribes." The dead warrior and his wife have been summoned to grace the occasion; they are not, however, what the village council expected since they keep talking about their personal grievances. Because the living are involved in this guilt, they are incapable of judging the dead warrior and his wife. As a reviewer has remarked, "The play's dynamic is the conflict between the desire of the dead for judgment and the desire of the living to avoid it." The gods in the drama are also overcome by this guilt. Thus spirits, gods, and men are not linked by any glorious past but by a mean and contemptible guilt. In the end hope is symbolized in the half-child of the dead woman; it is significant that in the second version of the play's ending, after the battle for the child, Demoke decides to give it to the dead woman. The artist is the instrument for welding the link between past and present. Una Maclean concludes that "Soyinka is suggesting that it is the artist, with his heightened perception of events and his sense of responsibility, who will not only interpret the past to the present but will protect the potentialities of the future."[12]

Whatever other meanings the play evokes, it is certain that in Demoke Soyinka is demonstrating a link in time. One can never really be sure whether *A Dance of the Forests*, which taxes the resources of the stage to the limit, is a work of genius or the magnificent ruins of lofty intentions. Yet Soyinka has succeeded in maintaining at least one device of traditional African theater—the intersection of time and event and the simultaneity of the legendary, the immediate past and the present.

Soyinka has moved the confrontation of generations out of a purely sociological orbit; with him it has assumed religious proportions which he expresses through ritual. The basic style of *A Dance of the Forests* is quite naturally the dirge; dirges are sung, people respond to them, and the dirge-man accompanies action with song. This illustrates one way that traditional indigenous theater can be utilized to bring about a synchronization of time. The quarrel with the past (with parents, gods, or human ancestors) is only a literary rendering of this archetypal experience of time. Soyinka's play is the most ambitious dramatization of this, but other playwrights have attempted to express it by depicting history and legend and by dramatizing tales.

An earlier play, Michael Dei-Anang's *Okomfo Anokye's Golden Stool*,[13] is the story of an Akan priest who appeals to the gods for a golden stool. He provides the link between past and present, gods and man. But Dei-Anang's message, because it is in the manner of the pseudo-nationalist mouthings of writers of this period, is nothing more than an exhortation to tribal unity:

> But, oh great Ashanti,
> Great is your destiny
> And great your power
> If you but knew
> The force of unity;
> With doughty arms and a spirit
> Unrivalled in this land
> You stand yet undistinguished
> By deeds of fame
> Since now confusion reigns
> Within your camp
> And jealousy thwarts
> Your rise to fame!
> But soothe now the gods
> With tympanic notes
> And await the bidding from on high!
> Dance now, dance, chiefs and people,
> And let this new nation be born in merriment. (p. 52)

As a result the play is extremely slow; nothing occurs on any profound level of apprehension and what does happen is of the most obvious nature—it becomes a rallying cry to patriotic feeling.

Dei-Anang's work, however, is not entirely unambitious: his use of dancing and drumming helps to emphasize various stages of the action and provides a commentary on its timeless possibilities. The priest's speech quoted above is followed by the sound of drums and then the priests, chiefs, and elders perform a dance. This is similar to the end of *Sokamé* where the chief also exhorts the people to sing. This singing need not be merely a medium through which the audience can participate, for it can also help to give a play the sanction of tradition—the time depth which has been discussed. Here instead of operating through the interplay of the characters, time more subtly suggests itself in the manifestation of drums and dance.

Tradition also asserts itself in the dramatization of legend and tale. Seydou Badian's *La mort de Chaka* is a re-creation of a Mali legend. A comparable Ghanaian re-creation is J. R. Owusi-Kumi's *Hair-Do Conundrum*;[14] in it Ananse plays a trick on the elders, asking them to guess the meaning of his hairstyle. They agree that if they cannot, they will pay him a hundred pounds, but if they ever do, they will execute him. Ananse prospers until the secret is wrung from his new wife. But he is not executed, for the play cleverly reveals the truth of the three parts of the conundrum, not least among them that wives never keep their husband's secrets. Whereas Badian's play dramatizes a historical legend, Kumi's demonstrates the reworking of a tale. In both cases the traditional material helps to give historical depth and a time perspective to the drama, even though it has been reordered by the imagination of an individual playwright.

The new playwright may convey his attitudes by rejecting the tribe, but nevertheless he appeals to group attitudes that relate to himself and his audience. Certainly from this viewpoint no antagonism can be said to exist between the African dramatist and his audience; he is one with them. The degree to which theater ought to keep pace with opinion or the extent to which it should anticipate it is perhaps a moot point. But the fact that the African audience is in large measure wooed by assurances suggests that the individual playwright is still a descendant of the traditional artist, for he also wants the cooperation of his audience. This explains why the conflict between father and child is stated in such unequivocable terms; the dramatist as propagandist must make his meaning absolutely clear—there must be little room left for controversy. It is no accident that in the plays the politician and the artist are at loggerheads, for the politician desires to maintain the status quo whereas the artist demands a holocaust. In *Dear Parent and Ogre* Dauda is opposed by Sekou, a world-famous musician; in *Sons and Daughters* the father is confronted by his son, a painter, and his daughter, who wants to be a dancer; and in *A Dance of the Forests* the artist is responsible for perpetuating traditional values. There are many other examples but suffice it to say that the artist represents the inner life, the politician the outer. They exist together and what some African dramatists seek to do is to describe the inner in relation to the outer. Hence love, national feeling, alienation are all expressed in terms of political man.

It is on this level that Lewis Nkosi's *Rhythm of Violence* can best be appreciated. Ostensibly it concerns some left-wing students in South Africa who plan to blow up the city hall, but it comes to mean more than this. The situation is translated into human terms that reveal the nature of man's inner crisis. For several reasons the play is most unsatisfactory. There are two Afrikaaner policemen who philosophize about the sunset and the future. The characterization of Tula never really succeeds—at first he seems much too meek for the kind of organization to which he belongs and later too ardent an advocate of his own martyrdom. The students' "liberal" attitudes are too exaggerated and thus do not ring true; the white boy Jimmy has to have a Black girl friend, Gama a white girl friend. When the students are not wrestling or making love with others of suitable opposing shades, they are continually teasing one another about pigmentation, which would suggest that they are not as emancipated as Nkosi would have us believe. One gets a little bored with the long conversation between Tula and Sarie, and there seems no reason why Tula should choose to risk his life for the father of a girl he had only just met. Or if such generous magnanimity does exist in humans, Nkosi has failed to demonstrate its plausibility in his play. But the bomb and the anti-*apartheid* stance are only the outer political symbols of the disintegrated pattern of inner lives. The play is not about *apartheid* but about the collapse of human relationships.

In this play the inner life is love—love for ideals, for humans, for a woman. Tula Zulu most strongly reflects this love in all he does—his attitude toward his brother, his liking for the Afrikaaner girl, his decision to risk his life in pursuit of an ideal he cherishes. Whereas his brother feels "we're giving Jesus a last chance to choose sides in South Africa" (p. 33), and the Afrikaaner policeman comments that "even if there was no future some damn fool would invent a future,"[15] Tula through his love is able to rise above their despair and offer a final gesture of hope. Sarie's epitaph over his charred remains—"he tried to block History" (p. 69)—signifies that he profoundly believed in and desired a future. He failed, however, because he attempted to organize his future —he became a martyr to the inevitability of a history he sought to avoid.

Tula stands out as an individual; he defied the codes of the group which sought to impose sanctions on him. All the heroes of African drama, whether in conflict with the older generation or with one another, aspire toward this same goal—the assertion of self. The politics of the older generation seek to submerge the individual, to impose an anonymity on him which he does not want. Thus, only when the inner conflict is seen in relation to the outer world can it be effectively portrayed. Plays which treat just one or the other world never quite succeed. Jacques Rabémanjara's *Les boutriers de l'Aurore*[16] fails not only because of its repetitive poetic effusions, but because its theme of the triumph of the human spirit over the gods is not buttressed by any rigid fundamentals. The action does not lead the audience to any new significant statements, nor indeed do the characters, for they are simply corpses that Rabémanjara embalms in allegory.

Efua Sutherland's *Edufa*, which attempts to isolate the significance of love from the outer political realities of life, indulges in the same kind of preciosity. Because the "love" predicament is not dramatized in its outer manifestations, the language is unbelievably sentimental and the action painfully affected and slow. It cannot be terribly good theater to watch a dying woman through long scenes mouthing platitudes. A woman's utterances in the prologue typify the thought and language which account for the play's failure:

> I heard tonight, a voice stretched thin
> through the mist, calling
> Heard in that calling the quivers of
> Ampoma's voice. (p. 1)

Foriwa is a better play, for it is stripped of artificiality. Based on her short story "New Life at Kyerefaso," it depicts the lethargy of the village people and elders who use their traditional past and its festivals as a way of escape not renewal. The Queen Mother succeeds in changing this with the help of her daughter Foriwa. Although the Queen Mother and Labaran, a stranger to the town and the author's mouthpiece, are both progressives, they are not opposed to tradition. This is seen when the Queen Mother is sarcastic to the Scholars' Union, which supports her, before she cracks down on the festival of the Asafo, which temporarily opposes her. At one stage after a "scholar" had called the dancers "these illiterates," she retorts, "Linguist, ask the young man who made that statement: if it came to a show of skill, could he dance like that Asafo man if we asked him to?" (p. 47). And, although Labaran criticizes the elders and their rituals, he is the first to advise the two boys Atuo and Brobi that "you need the whole community behind you."

On the whole *Foriwa* is Efua Sutherland's best work intended for adults. She achieves an excellent balance in language, reserving her poetry for Labakan and her more stylized prose for greetings to the Queen Mother and exchanges with her. *Foriwa*, unlike *Edufa*, also flows in a very natural way and is not flawed by artificial climaxes. There is little sentimentality, such as one finds in her poems. Her true forte would seem to be a play that allows her a wide range of possibilities with the language.

Pat Maddy[17] is a playwright who frequently knocks his own society, though he also is an upholder of tradition. In *Gbana-Bendu*, for example, he makes use of popular beliefs and the mores of a society to describe, in ritual form, the dignity of its ceremonies. The Beggar and the Shadow (who also play the parts of drunk people) are outsiders who laugh at the traditional acts of a people they do not understand. Finally they realize that they are the "criminals," having failed to realize that "suffering is the way to truth."

Pat Maddy's plays cannot be read. They are the enactment of the daily lives and rituals of Africans. Therefore music, dance, and song play a large part in his works as do choruses of people who haggle the villain or comment on the action. He frequently uses Krio for satirical effects; he also utilizes long drawn out "o" and "u" sounds to convey authentic West African speech. He can be as contemporary as *Alla Gbah* and *Yon-Kon*, the setting of which is a prison, or as traditional as *Gbana-Bendu*, set in a village. In all his plays he singles out characters who seek to oppose an order that makes little sense to them and more often than not he sides with them (through the chorus). The men outside, according to Pat Maddy, are those who speak for the future of the group; they are "men violating the laws of society." One weakness in the plays is that, in order to make this point, the action is often suspended by the verbosity of the speakers.

When the theme of political strife, which is really the conflict of all human effort, is not utilized, some of the plays possess only a modicum of thought—whether the idea expressed is nationalism or love. It has been suggested that "politics" is only the outward manifestation of an inner tension, and thus plays that deal solely with "politics" are equally unsuccessful. One finds in these works the same failure in language, the same inefficacious posturings. For instance, some Nigerians have written plays inspired by Lumumba's death. In them Lumumba might be "a hero, a martyr, a saint and even a god,"[18] but he is never a person, just as neither Ampoma in *Edufa* nor Princess Ananda in *Les boutriers* is a real person. In drama the internal struggle must individualize them; otherwise they become lost in attitudes that identify them with the uniformity of a group or at worst the tribe. The need to disregard tribe and create individuals is the greatest pitfall of the African writer, and one which he must constantly battle against.

Racial relations supply the dramatist with another theme for his work. For example Joe de Graft's second play, *Through a Film Darkly* (1970), depicts modern Africans in Ghana and their difficulties in coping with interracial situations. The story centers on John who appears to be a sensitive person and a loving husband. Nevertheless, he hates all whites. John's friend, Addo, comes to visit and is soon followed by his lover,

Rebecca. To everyone's surprise, when she enters the house, she runs up to John and begins to kiss him.

It seems that John was Rebecca's first love before he went to school in England. He led her to believe that he would marry her upon his return to Ghana, but he fell in love with an English girl named Mollie. John wrote a letter to Rebecca telling her of his intent to marry Mollie. Though heartbroken, Rebecca felt that since Mollie was white it might be possible that someday John would want her back. During John's affair with Mollie, he stumbled across some of Mollie's notes for a book. She had recorded all the things he had said to her for a sociological study. This became the basis of John's hatred for all whites. After this traumatic experience, John returned to Ghana and married Sewah.

When Rebecca discovers that John has married an African woman, her anger is doubled. She hurls insults at Sewah. John in turn accuses Rebecca of being cheap and abuses her for having waited at a white man's apartment for Addo and him. Rebecca retorts that John made her what she is today when he took her virginity. She eventually regains her composure, apologizes to Sewah for her outburst, and leaves.

After Rebecca's exit, both Addo and Sewah berate John for being insensitive to Rebecca. Sewah is extremely disappointed in John. She has found that he is not the man she has believed him to be. In the last scene, they learn that Rebecca's car has overturned on a bridge. A few minutes later the houseboy runs in to tell everyone that John has committed suicide.

Both of de Graft's plays suffer from his attempt to oversimplify human involvement. In *Sons and Daughters* matters work out because the plot dictates a happy ending; in *Through a Film Darkly*, however, de Graft opts for tragedy. With the exception of Aaron and Maanan, John and Sewah, the characters are clumsily drawn, almost as if they were symbols of a particular human virtue or failing. At times what happens to them would be laughable if one did not know that de Graft is trying his utmost to make a serious point. Surely no audience could be convinced of John's hatred of whites merely because Mollie had used him as a sociological test-case. De Graft's plays succeed only at certain moments, especially when the "characters" talk, for he does have an ear for dialogue. But he is blind to the motivations of the human psyche.

The social realities of contemporary African life can therefore best be described in terms of a personal bewilderment. Where Wole Soyinka's *Kongi's Harvest*[19] fails is that it never creates a single individual to express this. Kongi, the political leader who aspires to the power of the Oba and the significant ritual it involves, is only real when seen against the background of contemporary Africa. His isolation in the mountains, his organizing secretary's lack of ideology, his intellectual advisers, and his strong arm supporters can all represent the trappings that go with the preservation of power in any African state. But this means that in Kongi and the Oba Soyinka has only managed to create types. It is nevertheless entertaining, even at times disconcerting, theater, although its overall effect has no universal impact. The effect is purely local.

For Soyinka's two dramatic sketches, *The New Republican* and *Before the Blackout*,[20] nothing more than local reference was in fact required. They satirize various aspects of Nigerian life—traveling by plane, the unfortunate member of the American Peace Corps who had been too frank in a postcard to her friends at home, rapacious politicians, party thugs, and the new middle class and its comical values. From skits one does not expect a profound theatrical experience. Their maximum effect is to convey a message through snappy dialogues and pointed gestures. In these two works many of the "characters" are recognizable as people, and it is to Soyinka's credit that he avoided the pitfall that lies between outrageous satire and farce.

His radio drama *The Detainee*[21] errs on the other side. The play is in the form of a conversation between Konu, who is in prison for a political crime, and his visitor, Zimole. Konu talks about a number of apparently inconsequential matters in his life—his daily exercise and the rat he has for company. During the conversation Zimole reveals that Konu's wife has left him and his son has been arrested for allegedly attempting to kill the party leader. Zimole promises Konu that his children will not be sent out of the country. They will remain so that they will, in Konu's words, "know what fear is so that they can choose to fight it or live with it." The difficulties are much the same here as in Soyinka's other pieces. Neither of the characters is dramatically convincing because neither has any life apart from the social situation in which he is placed. *The Detainee* simply inhabits the other side of laughter; it has no more substance than *Kongi's Harvest* or the two dramatic sketches.

Similarly, Mariana in *The Scar*[22] by the Ugandan playwright Rebecca Njau is not dramatically persuading. Mariana is placed in a difficult situation in which the moral implications of her action for society are more important than its personal consequences for her. She is presented as a woman who is the leading light in village life, helping in the emancipation of young women. But a pastor arrives to reveal her own past; she has had a child by him and so her work cannot go on. How convincing can this appeal from her to the pastor be, if it is intended only to enlist the sympathies of the audience?

I'm a lantern in this village;
The girls have made me their mother;
The mothers have made me their guide.
I want the girls to jump over the fence I failed to jump
In my youth;
I want them to be like a firm post that cannot be shaken. (p. 27)

Although Mariana is supposed to have freed herself from the strictures of tribe, her dominant "public" personality fails to convince us that she is an individual. The dramatist is struggling through the morass of tribal identification that would make the play *engagé*, and her characters emerge as mere spokesmen for some public message.

Like Efua Sutherland's Ampoma and Rebecca Njan's Mariana, there are a host of heroines in African popular drama whose posterings are not convincing because they are not associated with any inner truth. Numerous plays written by popular Nigerian pamphleteers are devoted to describing the wickedness of women, or how a "good" woman is won by a determined and stouthearted man, or, as in an example already seen, how a determined girl defies her father for love. The love setting is frequently the scene of murder; in Thomas Iguh's *Agnes in the Game of True Love*,[23] for instance, Agnes attempts to defy her parents but they get someone to murder her boy friend, Billy. In other plays the murder results from a struggle over either land or money. These plays are worth mentioning because they are an attempt at popularizing the love story and the "detective story" in drama and in English. They do, however, have their flaws. In form they are only partly "dramatic," in that the authors often arbitrarily switch to a narrative style. What is even more evident is that they possess the same defects found in the other plays considered here. In an effort to reduce the African experience to "love" or "crime" or "politics," there has been distortion, and neither character nor situation bears the slightest resemblance to what is credible.

Two of J. P. Clark's plays, *Song of a Goat* and its sequel *The Masquerade*, are of this nature. Clark isolates two aspects of life—sex and heredity—and gives them a "popular" treatment. The reviewer who commented that "the author of this poetic melodrama [*Song of a Goat*] possibly perceives himself as some sort of Tennessee Williams of the Tropics"[24] was not far wrong in his assessment. In it one character dies by drowning himself, another by hanging; in *The Masquerade* a father shoots his daughter and is in turn killed by her lover. In *Song of a Goat* Zifa sends his wife, Ebiere, to a masseur for a cure for her supposed barrenness. The wife tells the masseur the truth—her husband is himself really impotent—and he advises her that "another should take over the tilling of the fertile soil" (p. 9). Neither Zifa nor Ebiere likes the idea; he feels he would become the laughingstock of the village and she thinks it is incestuous. Meantime the semi-demented Aunt Orukorere prophesies doom, since she has seen a goat captured by a leopard. In the third movement Ebiere seduces her brother-in-law Tonye: "Now, hold me, do hold on and / Fight, for it is a thing not forbidden!" (p. 24). Zifa's child rushes off to his aunt to describe what he had witnessed and her explanation reintroduces the symbol of the goat and the leopard:

> Why, boy, these are no leopard and goat
> Interlocked between life and death, but
> Two dogs at play . . . (p. 25)

Her prophecies come true, for Zifa discovers his wife's infidelity and forces his brother to sacrifice a goat and insert the head into a small pot which breaks. Understanding the significance of this, Tonye attempts to run away and hang himself and the now contrite Zifa drowns himself in the sea.

Several unsatisfactory elements are manifest in this play. First the dramatic effect of Zifa's impotence is spoiled since he already has had a child. There is little stability of character; Ebiere initially rejects the idea of having a child by a member of her husband's family but later she almost forces Tonye to have intercourse with her. The imagery is totally unsuccessful in parts; for example, the masseur painstakingly relates Ebiere's womb to a room and develops various analogies about the inadvisability of keeping a house empty and of barring the doors from her husband. He wonders whether her husband has another "house" elsewhere, and he tells her that her "gates are intact" which presumably signifies her own fecundity. Another set of laborious images compare Ebiere with fertile farmland; her husband has allowed the ground to be taken over by grass and now he must sharpen his "cutlass" to clear the weeds. Zifa refuses to give up his piece of land and the masseur suggests that another person should take over the tilling. These burdensome images result in the painful development of the action in the first movement. The central symbol of the goat struggling to free itself of the leopard does not succeed either. If the drawn-out sexual allusions are due, as Geoffrey Axworthy suggests, "to Ijaw reticence in such matters," then it is equally true that "they are tedious in English on the stage and this is a play written in English."[25]

Clark has said in a talk that his play is based on an Ijaw legend of a chief who becomes impotent. Because he has a good wife who keeps his secret, one day he decides to tell his subjects and afterward he gives his wife to his brother. Clark would have done better had he stuck to the legend; its issues are much clearer. The play leaves one puzzled. Why, for instance, does Orukorere vacillate between seeming dementia and philosophizing? If in fact the community sanctioned the union between Ebiere and Tonye, why is Tonye alarmed at being discovered? Is it good theater to have a goat slaughtered on stage? Can Clark's exaggerated imagery sustain his drama, essentially one of crisis about "individual action in the face of inexorable law"? Achebe asserts that the play maintains "a delicate balance between poetry and action,"[26] but this is not at all apparent. There is a hiatus between the two—the "poetry" contributing to laborious symbolism, the "action" culminating in the most bizarre melodrama. In short, the language merely impedes the action.

Despite the play's flaws, Clark does work within the tradition of the village storyteller. Because the narrative was known to his Nigerian audience, it was Clark's exposition that was of interest to them. It has been suggested that *Song of a Goat* fails to accomplish an interesting pattern of design. This is not, however, the case with *The Masquerade*. It is not really a sequel at all: Tufa is supposed to be the offspring of Tonye and Ebiere (but did Ebiere not have a miscarriage?) and because of this Titi's parents oppose her marriage to him. Titi seemingly is the typical girl of the new literature who defies her parents, but in fact she is the doomed creature of the tales who meets a stranger. Even the rendezvous (the marketplace) of the original tale is retained:

> It seemed he had stopped
> At a stall to pick up some fabric when
> Like others he looked up, and saw the sun
> In the girl or her stepping out of that
> Orb, I don't know which now, and was struck
> To the heart. (p. 5)

The consequences, one knows, are going to be disastrous; Titi's father kills her and Tufa kills the father. The end of the tale has been dramatically altered—before she dies, Titi does not come to the realization of how wrong she was in being so fastidious. Tufa is like Zifa—they both reject the sanctions of the tribe.

Both plays are "love" stories or rather love is the personal experience outside of which the daily activities of the tribe takes place. In Wole Soyinka's *Camwood under the Leaves*[27] love alienates two individuals from the tribe. The situation is artificial and unrealistic; two sixteen-year-olds, Isola and Morounke, escape to a kind of idyllic retreat far away from their prying parents. She is pregnant and he has been accused of seducing and abducting her. His father, after whom the boy has named a snake he wants to shoot, righteously exhorts the villagers to undertake a witch-hunt for the couple. When the boy shoots his father, he is destroying what the snake represents, for since the reptile could not swallow baby tortoises "it would pick them up and dash them to pieces against the rock." The analogue, though effective, merely reinforces the artificial predicament: the baby tortoises are caught when they leave the protection of the mother, just as the couple find themselves trapped when they leave the protection of home and tribe. Soyinka attempts to portray the parents and the villagers as the real culprits, but does not succeed because the young people have broken the tribal contract. However, Soyinka's conclusions are true to form; a traditionalist, he comes out most strongly on the side of established order.

Often man/woman relationships seek to assert themselves through the framework of larger social realities. In Henshaw's play *Medicine for Love*[28] these relationships, though satirized, are the crux of the hero's cultural predicament. Ewia Ekunyah is running for political office and is particularly embarrassed when, as a gesture of goodwill, two chiefs dispatch two wives for him. Auntie Dupeh promises a third, but Ekunyah at first objects. He decides that only magic can see him through the election, and eventually (and perhaps predictably) he loses everything. But "love" saves him: Auntie Dupeh is going to marry Mr. Bonga, one of his former opponents, and as dowry she arranges the return of Ekunyah's houses which he had had to dispose of; she also plans for him to become the chairman of the Committee for Drainage and Sewage. The play is a satire on power, on what Mr. Bonga represents; as he himself says, "Champagne, champagne, from morning till night. Oh, We V.I.P.'s are simply suffering" (p. 98). And Ekunyah learns that he has to buy his popularity, and Joss tells him that once he is elected, "If you sneeze, it will be reported in the newspapers. If you cough it will be broadcast to the world. Gramophone recordings will be made in your name. And you can always get your local people to name streets after you" (p. 64). In the end even Ekunyah is able to marry; the first delegation of wives had got themselves married off and he is now free to wed Auntie Dupeh's choice. Auntie Dupeh's political maneuverings have assuaged the yearnings of the heart.

The Opportunity by the South African Arthur Maimane and *You*[29] by the Kenyan Kuldip Sondhi, both radio plays, effectively combine love with politics to demonstrate how such a union can bring about a disintegration of human worth. In the first play Solomon is promised the post of ambassador; the only impediment is his illiterate wife, Emma. She is unbelievably understanding when divorce is suggested, but their educated daughter sees this as her own inevitable fate if she marries Joe. She argues that Joe in time might also see her in a different light as he moves up in the world. In *You*, Dave is organizing the New Progressive party in East Africa with the help of Jennifer, the wife of an architect. At one point each is left alone and a stranger appears; the architect reveals to him that he once blackmailed a man, Dave admits that he accidentally killed someone, and Jennifer confesses that she has had an abortion. They all decide that the stranger has to be killed before Dave can face his political future in which Jennifer, with whom he is having an affair, profoundly believes. In both plays political aspiration represents the mask that conceals a great deal of inner decay. Wives can be deserted, husbands duped, in the search for a collective good. The playwrights seem to be asking whether the politics of the tribe could ever really justify this perversion of personal values.

Non-members of the specific tribe in a given play, the emancipated woman of questionable morals, the "artist," the Black American woman, are all *individuals* who assert their beliefs over and above the group. They are not outsiders; they merely seek dominion over the tribal sameness that tends to dwarf them. Mapule, in Alfred Hutchison's *Rain Killers*, is such a woman. When she returns to the village, the women complain to their spiritual leader, Mfundisi, who later hangs himself because he attempted to sleep with her, against his strict Christian principles. The women gossip about her:

Ma-Hlope: She's a disgrace. She's spoiling our children. Teaches them bad ways.
Ma-Gwagwa: She has no respect. She's proud. Never greets. I even saw her smoking a cigarette. And she paints her mouth . . .
Ma-Zwane: No, no, Ma-Gwagwa. You're bringing in your own things. We didn't come for that. She has loose morals and is corrupting our children.
Ma-Hlope: We don't want her in our church. (p. 32)

Not only is Mapule unmarried and westernized, but she is a member of a different tribe. She is uncommitted to either side—the conflict in the play between the devout Christian Mfundisi and the diviner Maziya in their bid to end the drought does not interest her. She is too positively herself to take sides on any issue as impersonal as the two manifestations of superstition, although she does say (rather out of character), "It's God's rain" when at last it begins to fall.

Wole Soyinka's Sidi in *The Lion and the Jewel* is similar to Mapule except that she opts for tradition. When the teacher Lakunle and Chief Baroka vie for her affection, at first she will have nothing to do with them. She is a free woman. Yet the kind of "westernization" which

Mapule might have adored is chafed at in Soyinka's play. The pedantic schoolmaster's ideas of what is "civilized" are truly laughable. He promises Sidi that they will eat

> Not with fingers, but with knives
> And forks, and breakable plates
> Like civilised beings. (p. 101)

Finally she agrees to marry Lakunle if he will pay the bride-price. But when she wins a photographic competition in a magazine, she is catapulted far above both him and the chief. It is significant that Sidi dances to celebrate her fame; it is significant that Chief Baroka is prepared to bribe "progress" to stay out of it:

> He loves this life too well
> To bear to part from it. And motor roads
> And railways would do just that, forcing
> Civilisation at his door. (p. 117)

On the other hand Lakunle fondly hopes that when the new civilization enters with its "city ways," its cars, parks for lovers, pin-up photographs, and ballroom dancing, "a motor road will pass this spot." The petrol fumes that drove the forest-spirits out in *A Dance of the Forests* are the same harbinger of "civilization" that would ultimately despoil everything. The Baroka's primitive strength is contrasted with the schoolmaster's weakness, his common sense with the latter's wordiness. He tricks Sidi into visiting him by spreading abroad a false rumor that he is impotent. When he seduces her, her conversion is as voluntary as it is realistic; the audience can share in her choice of values. Afterwards she sneers at Lakunle,

> Did you really think that you, and I . . .
> Why did you think that after him,
> I could endure the touch of another man?
> I who have felt the strength
> The perpetual youthful zest
> Of the panther of the trees? (p. 155)

The sympathies of the audience are entirely with Sidi. All through the play the use of mime, masquerade, and dance is most convincing, anticipating for instance Sidi's seduction scene, emphasizing the virility of the Baroka and the tawdriness of the schoolteacher and the European photographer.

Where Soyinka's Sidi differs from Hutchison's Mapule is that Sidi's zest for life makes her not only an individual but an individualist. Soyinka has advanced the process of individual assertiveness one step further; to Sidi her own personal values are what matter, and, unlike Mapule, she never compromises. Both of these women voluntarily choose to deny their society. But this is not the case of the women in Christina Aidoo's *Dilemma of a Ghost* and Arthur Maimane's *Where the Sun Shines*.[30] Neither Eulalie Yawson, a Black, nor Mandy, a Barbadian, makes this voluntary negation. Both of them are married to West Africans, both find themselves involved in an extended family system which they did not expect when they married their husbands in England, both attempt to reject the tribe (and are rejected in return) but become reconciled in the end. When Stephen says to his wife, Mandy, "You are an African now and you must learn," and Eulalie protests to her husband, "Who married me, you or your goddam people?" it becomes clearer what both women oppose. Unconsciously they are struggling against their husband's instinctive wish to involve them in the business of the tribe; their revolt is against gregariousness. But neither succeeds.

Often it is Christianity that drives the wedge between the tribe and the individual and effectuates the positive assertion of the individual. But usually the Christian hero is cast in a bad light, as is evident in Hutchison's *Rain Killers*, which describes an important confrontation between Christian and pagan leaders:

Mfundisi: Oh, Maziya, you know that's not true.
Maziya: Not true? You are the ones who open us up to the white man. You split the tribe into Believers and Non-believers. Not true! Then what is true?
Mfundisi: That we are leading the people out of darkness into Light. That....
Maziya: Leading the people? Yes, like a mischief-making old cow that leads the herd to the crocodile pool!
Mfundisi: No. We're taking them out of the darkness of the past into a new light.
Maziya: New light! Is it the new light to split the nation? To set brother against brother? No, Mfundisi. You are leading the people into the wilderness.
Mfundisi: And you are holding them back.
Maziya: Yes. Back to their customs and traditions. Back to the ways *Nkulunkulu* showed us from the beginning of time. You want to destroy our roots. (p. 53)

In Obi Egbuna's *Divinity*[31] a catechist mistakenly shoots his son when he decides to fight off the ju-ju that masquerades as "Divinity"; his son, an undergraduate home on vacation, is in fact a member of the secret society. But there can be little individual affirmation if it is linked to social

425

identity. Thus Mfundisi, Maziya, and the catechist do not convince us of their uniqueness since they associate their beliefs with what is outside them. The outer reality has again taken the place of an inner drama of profound experience.

Keyune, in Peter Nasareth's radio play X,[32] does, however, seek to free himself of society's pressures to conform. At school, at the university, later in England Keyune is forced through various processes, none of which he believes in. Religion, education, democracy, and the choice they all involve for the individual impose the same demands that are made by advertisements for detergents. Perhaps this is the inevitable end of true individualism—a recognition of the persuasion of life itself, the need to flirt with it and reject it in an effort to discover the true self.

In Wole Soyinka's *Road* the characters all seek after what the Professor calls "the word"—what Soyinka in a note to the producer means by "the visual suspension of death." The Professor himself is at the center of the play. At the end he makes a last gesture toward individuality, and throughout he prepares himself for a grand ritual sacrifice which will engulf him in revelation. His preparation involves skirting delicately the border line between futile existence and sudden glorious disaster. He contrives "accidents" by removing signposts from the road, he searches among the wrecks of accidents for the elusive relics of life. His priest, Murano the deaf mute, witnesses his immolation and lends the authority of the *egungun* mask to the Professor's final victory. As the Professor himself says when he prepares the audience for his martyrdom with Murano; "And should I not hope, with him, to cheat, to anticipate the final confrontation, learning its nature, baring its sulking face. . ." (p. 90). As he dies the *egungun* masquerader, into which Murano has been transformed, sinks lower and lower to the floor. With Murano, the Professor at last discovers the true meaning of life. They demonstrate that "sacrifice and propitiation of the gods [are] the way of truth."[33]

Soyinka's greatest expressions of this alienation from society are the odd creatures who inhabit the subplots of his plays. The blind Moslem beggar in *The Swamp Dwellers* who leaves the dry north and journeys southward "towards any river, towards any stream," Ifada the idiot boy in *The Strong Breed*,[34] Aroni "the lame-one" and the half-child in *A Dance of the Forests*, and of course Murano in *The Road*. The vision of the abnormal, Soyinka suggests, is the truer one, and Murano is the epitome of these isolated, unfulfilled half-characters, because he demonstrates that they all embody a gesture toward the fulfillment of God-in-man. It is Murano who resurveys new African theater in the rigid dimension of ritual.

This marks the culmination of the groping toward individuality, for it has ceased to matter, it is no longer necessary to upbraid tribe or deride Christianity. Soyinka's Professor and Murano are unlike the four men in J. P. Clark's *Raft*[35] who drift on the Niger journeying toward their death. Though Clark's symbolism is effective, it is unrealistic that the men, confronted by death, should be concerned with the homosexuality of Catholic priests, the misdemeanors of district officers, the labor strikes, and the treachery of politicians. One of the characters, however, is dramatically persuasive, for he is linked to an archetypal experience; Kenigde is an old man who does not need to be reminded by Ogro that "Death that has nothing to do / With God is what has struck" (p. 114).

Clark's latest play, *Ozidi* (1966), is based on an Ijaw saga, originally accompanied by music, dance, and mime and told over a period of seven days. The play begins in the manner of traditional folktale narration with the spectators seated on the floor in a semicircle. The "stage" is not an encumbrance in this play, for it is dispensed with. Instead, the drama is told in a bare setting. Hence there is the need for formality, since the playwright wishes to establish quite early in the play the ritualistic nature of the experience in which the audience is about to participate.

The play does not begin until certain ceremonies are observed; the main storyteller must call for "seven virgin girls" to appear from the sea or else the play cannot take place. He also states that the principal player will not appear in a play that frowns on tradition. Then there is a procession of the volunteer girls from among the spectators, the actors, and the dancers; this is the ultimate in participant theater.

The storyteller's many roles—principal hero, brother of the hero, and father of the hero—emphasize the *group* nature of the play. He assumes a priestlike role, and the girls become "characters" who are directed to play certain parts to the accompaniment of music and singing. Then the storyteller/priest says a prayer during which all music and singing stop; this has a definite religious impact. The storyteller calls on the sea-people, and, after the invocation, actors and dancers perform. Later the actors and dancers separate, and a song leader sings the praise song of the group. Finally all sit down except the storyteller. The ritual, so necessary to African drama, is complete.

This is Clark's best play for in it he seeks to escape from the desire for cheap thrills. Instead he returns to the prototype of the traditional African drama—the myth—and renders it with the sureness and the fidelity of a believer. Yet the myth undergoes a dramatic metamorphosis; Clark skillfully creates a contemporary political play out of the traditional saga. The latter was concerned with ritual rebirth and the need for

427

succession and moral growth; the contemporary play describes the coups of a modern African state—the corrupt politicians who are ousted, the new rich who inherit their place. Clark successfully combines the ritualistic elements, and song, speech, dance, and acting become the vehicles for his message, a message that culminates in an enormous question mark.

One can see significant progression from *Song of a Goat*, which can be dismissed as cheap entertainment, to *Ozidi*. Clark's plays show promise, but the stage is really not a suitable medium for what he envisages. This is particularly a problem in *The Raft*. The play is obviously intended to carry a message, but the message is too overwhelming for the medium. Its failure is basically its essential clumsiness that results from using the western stage. Therefore it is a difficult play to stage. Only part of the stage is used; the entire action is set against the foreground and background of the sea (the bare stage) and the raft which dominates stage center. Furthermore it is bad theater to have the raft disintegrate on the stage; as various pieces become dislodged they are supposed to drift away, which is surely impossible on a stage.

Clark's efforts are at least ambitious theater even if they do not succeed. What is one to make of the bare settings of most of the plays considered?[36] Some belong to an effete drawing-room convention, and, with the exception of Wole Soyinka, few African dramatists have sought to enliven theater by giving to it ritual and realism. Soyinka uses the mask, mime, the pounding of women's pestles, drums, and dance. He employs the "play-within-a-play" technique in *The Swamp-Dwellers* and *The Lion and the Jewel*, and he couches the whole of *The Road* in the terminology and form of ritual. On the other hand, Sarif Easmon's play, because of its overfine drawing-room manner, could have taken place anywhere, as could those by Alfred Hutchinson and Christina Aidoo. They do not attempt to adapt the authentic settings of indigenous drama (settings utilized by the novelists) and to use the open space, for instance, outside the house where life is actually lived. Instead in an effort to cram the experience into the traditional format of the drawing-room stage, African dramatists have done a great deal of harm to their work and the significance of their art. Perhaps a beginning in the emancipation of African drama will be made when the setting shifts from indoors to, say, the marketplace; it would be more realistic and would suggest all manner of possibilities for character and action. To a large extent this is one of the reasons for the success of Soyinka's work in the theater; he has preferred to use open-air settings with large crowd scenes.

In a way this accounts for the difference between Soyinka's *Brother Jero* and Obi Egbuna's *Anthill*. Though both are comic pieces, Soyinka's takes the audience into its confidence; the wily Brother Jero talks to them as naturally as he would speak to an open-air congregation of his believers. Egbuna's play on the other hand is merely delightful drawing-room farce; the duped policeman, the cockney landlady belong to a tradition of farce that is far removed from African literature. When Egbuna throws in for good measure mistaken identity and a convenient marriage at the end, one realizes that this is very different territory from Soyinka's.[37]

Two other plays worth mentioning are Guillaume Oyono-Mbia's *Trois prétendants, un mari* (1964) and his *Jusqu'a nouvel avis* (1970), which was published in English as *Until Further Notice*. Throughout the first very serious events are mixed with so much humor that one's reaction is that of sheer enjoyment. Yet the message is clear: Africa is changing. Oyono-Mbia poignantly describes the old with its taboos, its close family and tribal ties, its superstitions, and its conflict with the new choices, new freedoms, and new perspectives. The theme is a common one but handled here with a delightful freshness.

Jusqu'a nouvel avis explores the same theme, evoking the tension between the traditional outlook of many old-fashioned communities and the more individualistic ways of the modern towns. The dialogue and many of the situations are side-splitting, yet the play has its serious moments. Africa, the playwright informs us, must adapt to modern life, but the African must not forget his beginnings; he must not forsake his family and his tribe.

If one expects that the theater should seek to restore the ordinary truth of life, then the African dramatist has to continue to be concerned with charting the sequestration of individual experience from tribal consciousness. Therefore African dramatists need to be much more violent than they have been, if they want to make the spectator enter their own universe of conviction. In plays man can only best be dramatized by becoming identical with what is inherent in him—by the externalizing of spiritual conflict. The preoccupation with the individual in African theater is as compulsive as it is intrinsic to the experience of all theater, for concerns of a totally public nature cannot possibly be a substitute for intimate analysis. Theatrical experience is above all private and individual; characterization is the medium for a whole range of related audience responses. But violence must take place on the stage—to shock the audience so that it may come to grips with the experience, to attain that moment of fulfillment which is the triumph of true art. This cannot occur until African drama frees itself from the trammels of western stagecraft and restores to the theater the amplitude of indigenous drama. An important play that seems to do this is Cheik Ndao's *L'exil d'Albouri* (1967), which centers on a *griot* in Muslim society who believes in the supernatural. As has been mentioned, at the beginning the playwright asserts that "reality borders on fiction." He adds that his work is not history but a re-creation of myth which "will help galvanise the people and carry them further ahead." This would appear to be the ultimate viewpoint that novelist, poet, and dramatist must express, for it is one that links him securely with his traditional counterpart.

PART IV
CROSSCURRENTS

Chapter 16

"Africa" in Caribbean Literature

An important side to a survey of the Black mind in literature is a consideration of what Caribbean literature has to say about Africa and the Africans. This is not the same as that larger aspect of Caribbean literature which centers on the Black man and the color question. Here the main concern is with the African past in Caribbean literature and its presence in Caribbean life either as a cultural and personal dichotomy or as a unifying influence. The question is, How did Africa come into Caribbean literature and what precisely has the Caribbean environment taught its writers to mean when they write about Africa?

The theme of Africa appears in Caribbean literature as a result of the development of the African theme in Haitian writing, its influence in Cuba and Puerto Rico, and, paradoxically, the interest of Europe in primitivism, especially in the African "primordial." The Haitian interest in Africa was perhaps encouraged by "the nationalist revival which had been precipitated by American occupation"; one of the leading exponents was Carl Brouard. In his poem "Nostalgie" (1927) he combines vigor and gore to create a kind of novel aesthetic. In translation it reads, "Drummer when you resound, my spirit shrieks for Africa. Sometimes I dream of an immense undergrowth, bathed by the moon, where there are naked, sweating, dishevelled women. Sometimes I dream of a dirty hut where I drink blood out of human skulls."[1]

Nicolas Guillen contributed to the Afro-Cuban movement with his *Motivos de son* (1930) and Luis Palés Matos to the Puerto Rican

433

counterpart with his *Tuntún de pasa y griferia* (1937). Nicolas Guillen's well-known poem "Balada de los dos abuelos" (Ballad of the Two Ancestors) illustrates this interest in Africa and the dualism of African and European culture: "The shadows of my two ancestors haunt me, shadows which are only visible to me. A spear with a point of bone, a drum of leather and wood—that's my black ancestor. A ruff around a large neck and bold, grey armour—that's my white ancestor."[2]

This poem imaginatively demonstrates that "it is not always easy to make a division between French or African influences in Haiti."[3] For when this is applied to West Indian literature it means that both European and African influences contribute to theme and manner.

European interest in Africa partly inspired the French Caribbean and Spanish Caribbean interest and therefore, indirectly, the theme of Africa in West Indian writing. But West Indian writers were also directly influenced by the general European interest in Africa and the then current European fashion for Black art. Equal concerns may be seen among the writers of the so-called "Harlem Renaissance."

It should be realized that Africa as a theme entered Caribbean literature in two ways, and thus affected the West Indian writer's concept of the African image. It is equally important to note that there are significant survivals of African culture in Haitian voodoo and among the Maroons of Jamaica, the "Bush Negroes" of Surinam, and the Yorubas of Brazil. These are genuine survivals and they must be differentiated from the popular modern movements that more closely identify with a formerly dormant, only recently emergent Africa. Both the authentic and the modern revivals have, of course, contributed to a greater or lesser extent to the imaginative concept of Africa in the minds of West Indians. Among the modern influences there are, in particular, movements in the West Indies which correspond in feeling to the Black Muslims in the United States, although some, like the Rastafarians in Jamaica, the Jordanites and Coptics in Guyana, and the Shouters and Shango cult in Trinidad, date back to the beginning of the century. They no doubt owe some measure of their recent popular appeal to the fact that there are "many Negroes for whom Africa seemed as remote as the planet Jupiter who now find themselves exhilarated and encouraged by the emergence of black national states in the once 'dark' continent."[4]

Even in the twenties and thirties, West Indian Blacks identified themselves with Liberia and Ethiopia. Calypsos, a unique survival of folk interest, show this; in a Trinidadian one, for instance, the calypsonian says, "Ah want to come back home / Africa" and a Jamaican one calls

Ethiopia "the land of liberty" and Liberia the country where one's "sorrows will all be over."

These popular movements have no direct link with Africa, but they testify to a popular interest in Africa which is part of what West Indian writers describe. Consequently it is worth saying something about these movements so that in the discussion that follows the origins of certain attitudes in the literature will be more readily apparent. For instance, Rev. Frank Mayhew of the Church of the Spiritual Baptists in Jamaica says this about his experience with Shango: "In 1916 I had the first experience about the Shango. One night in my sleep I feel someone sitting on my head and I hear a singing in my ears. . . . And the next morning I ask a woman call Josephine who used to keep Shango dance what the meaning of the singing, and she told me that is what they call a litany, where they sing and call all the saints one after another and she invite me to come to a dance she had . . ."[5] At the meeting he continues, they sang to St. Peter, St. Catherine (Mama Oyo), and St. Michael (Oyo).

This has little to do with the true Yoruba worship of Shango which is not at all connected with Christianity. Shango, the Yorubas believe, "was a strong man, a powerful hunter," who "ascended to heaven and . . . became thereby the creator of lightning and thunder."[6] But even though the West African religion has undergone a strange mutation, certain names are preserved. A ceremony which I recently witnessed in Haiti doubly confirms this.

Perhaps another example will illustrate further the survivals of this African concept in the West Indies. N. E. Cameron has recorded a visit that he paid to the British Guianese Jordanites in 1927 and his conversation with the Lord Elder: "I then told him that I observed his members wearing a certain costume and asked if he insisted on it. He did insist on it and added that it was the costume that our great grandfathers from Africa wore. I asked how he knew that. He told me to ask any soldier who had been to Africa during the War of 1914–1918. I asked how he came by the design. Then he related two dreams—the first of his call to the ministry, the second about the dress."[7] Here again the link with Africa is weak, almost imaginary. But it is in this and the Shango cult that we find the sociological foundations of what Sylvia Wynter has described with great sympathy in the religion of Moses and Obadiah in her novel *Hills of Hebron* (1962).

Then there are the genuine survivals, of which the Maroons of Jamaica are a good example. In a foreword to a West Indian novel about the Maroons, Tom Driberg writes, "Katherine Dunham—a qualified anthropologist as well as a woman of the theatre—eagerly traced back to their African origins many of the cultural patterns of the Maroons." He adds that there are "so many of the human characteristics found in his [the author's] Maroons that go to make up what is beginning to be called the African Personality."[8] Without entering into the very debatable question of what is or what is not the "African Personality," one can at least say that the Maroons do represent an authentic survival, though West Indian writers are divided on whether or not they are primarily and solely an African survival.

Walter Adolphe Roberts in his poem "The Maroon Girl" sees her not as an African but as a cosmopolitan mixture of "vanished Arawak" and "white and black." This is because he wants her to symbolize "Jamaica poised against attack"; in other words what he wants to emphasize is the West Indianness of his Maroon girl. This represents an important thing that has happened to Africa in West Indian literature—it has become localized. In *Black Albino* (1961), Namba Roy stresses the African inheritance. Indeed the novel is concerned with the social upheaval caused in Maroon society when Chief Tomaso has an albino son. Consequently the author establishes quite early that his society is African, that a certain custom was "adopted from the many tribes to which they [the Maroons] once belonged before the coming of slavery" (p. 19). Namba Roy succeeds in showing that the Maroons possess a certain homogeneity of culture that genuinely derives from Africa, even down to the retention of an Akan name for God.[9] His point of view is very different from Roberts's.

In addition to the sociological survivals or renovations there were political incentives, such as the great interest of Blacks in the West Indies and the United States in Pan-Africanism, which helped to arouse West Indian concern for and about Africa and to introduce the idea of Africa into West Indian life and literature. The extent to which West Indians contributed to and inspired the Pan-African ideal is not fully realized. Shepperson argues that the West Indian Edward Blyden was a "pioneer theorist of the African personality" as early as 1850, and he points out that Marcus Garvey, who led the famous "back to Africa" movement in the 1920s, George Padmore, whose interest in Africa began in the 1930s, and H. Sylvester Williams, whose idea it was to hold the first Pan-African Congress in 1900, were all West Indians.[10] It is therefore not unreasonable to claim that "Africa for the Africans" was a West Indian concept which had everything to do with the predicament of the West Indian and little to do with Africa. The American DuBois went along with this.

Indeed one might go even further and assert that négritude, a word invented by the French Caribbean poet Césaire, was the movement from which the Senegalese poet Senghor learned about his Africa. But the political incentive was important not only because it contributed to a certain kind of West Indian attitude toward the whole idea of Africa, but because it produced some imaginative literature. Marcus Garvey, for instance, wrote bad verse but with strong messianic and racialist feelings: "Out of the cold of Europe these white men came / From caves, dens and holes, without any fame."[11] He is the link with the Black world of the twenties.

Other significant influences on the theme of Africa in West Indian literature include folklore and language survivals. A typical example of folklore survival is the West Indian Anancy tales, some of which P. M. Sherlock, Louise Bennett, and Andrew Salkey have collected. Although it is true that none of these tales has ever been worked into a novel, the tar-baby story is nevertheless an example of a tale "carried by the negroes from Africa" which became "the basis of a story which has served to amuse the children and adults of the whole of the English speaking peoples."[12]

Linguistic survivals may be traced back either to vernacular African languages, with words like "foo-foo" (pounded food) occurring in West Indian English, or to the surprising similarity that exists between Krio, West Indian creolese, and West African pidgin. For instance, the West Indian word *pickney* and the West African word *pickin*, both meaning "child," seem to owe something to the Spanish *pequeño*, and it would be interesting, at some later date when more research has been done on the dialects, to compare the modified dialect usage that one finds in the novels of the Nigerian Amos Tutuola and the Trinidadian Samuel Selvon. For even in language usage there is a surprising retention of African forms, and, according to F. G. Cassidy, although "the Jamaican folk has become even more Europeanized, it has tenaciously kept up a strong element of Africanism."[13]

These then are the frail foundations on which the "African" heritage rests in the West Indies and on which West Indians rely for their ideas about Africa. The knowledge is largely secondhand and of the many West Indians who have written about Africa, only a few know Africa at first hand. Two actually lived in Africa: Denis Williams (Guyana) lived in the Sudan for five years (1957–62) and worked in Nigeria until 1967; Neville Dawes, the Nigerian-born Jamaican author of *The Last Enchantment* (1960), lived and taught in Ghana until his return to Jamaica. Several others have visited Africa: the Jamaican dramatist Barrie Rockord has visited both West and East Africa, George Lamming (Barbados) was in West Africa in 1958, Vic Reid of Jamaica was there in 1960, and E. R. Braithwaite (Guyana) visited West Africa in 1961. In addition the poet L. E. Braithwaite (Barbados) worked in Ghana. Does these authors' attitude toward Africa differ significantly from that of the writers who have never been there? Or is the indirect experience of Africa in the West Indies an overriding one? Does personal contact make for a more realistic approach, or does absence from Africa help the West Indian writer to be more sympathetic toward the spiritual and romantic essence of what is truly Africa? Only by examining further what West Indian writers have said about Africa can one come to some understanding of what these questions involve.

The Imaginative Response

"Africa" in West Indian literature consists of a number of half-understood beliefs and values; so much so that, when it is considered all in all, one realizes how relevant are these lines by the Sierra Leonean poet Abioseh Nicol:

> You are not a Country, Africa
> You are a concept,
> Fashioned in our minds, each to each,
> To hide our separate fears
> To dream our separate dreams.[14]

Thus, for the West Indian, whether or not he has known Africa at first hand, it is a mixture of fertile wish and barren memory, what Sartre has called, "Africa beyond reach, imaginary continent."[15]

In no West Indian work is the theme of Africa as an imaginary continent so clearly brought out as in *Africa Sling-Shot* by Cicely Waite-Smith:

Mary: Him a stranger and him come from Africa.
Policemen: Him? Him come from Africa? Him don't never go further than Kingston.
Miss Nath: How can you know that?
Clara: Yes, how you know?
Policeman: We no have the record o' this man? Is the same thing he tell the prison guard—that he is a African and he know obeah and all that sort o' thing, and them make him escape.
Mary (desperate): But how you know him don't never go a Africa?
Policeman: Ask him nuh. Ask him if he ever go a Africa?
Clara (obstinately): No need fe ask him. (*silence*)
Gordie (suddenly running up to fence: to Stranger): Sir! Don't it true you been a Africa?

(The Stranger shrugs him shoulders and says nothing. The villagers are stunned.)

Rattler (sucking his teeth): Him never fool me, you know. I did know him was telling lie all the time.

Clara (savagely): Shut your mouth, Rattler! You never know nothing at all!

Mary (going up to gate: with bitter contempt): Then is true you did fool us, Mr. Witch-doctor o' Africa?

Miss Nath: What a brute though, eeh?

Mary: All you did want was we food and we run, that right? Take him away Corpie!

Several: Yes take him a jail . . . We don't want see him round here again. —You worthless thief! . . . Damn liar! . . .

Policeman: The man fool you up proper, eh? Well, I glad you get sense at last.

Gordie (making one last bid): True, true, Mr. Africa, you don't never leave Jamaica at all?

Stranger: Same like you, me son. I go a Africa in me mind.[16]

The scene takes place in a backyard in a country village and the characters are peasants. They almost will the stranger to be African—a mythical survival of themselves in a unique moment of truth. When he is exposed, he exposes them to the reminder that they are without ethnical reference, that their cultural existence is a phantom one, of the mind.

If the West Indian writer considers Africa an imaginary continent, it means that it can be all countries or one country. The result is a geographical shuffling and reshuffling to suit the whimsies of the imaginative artist. Claude McKay, in his poem "Africa," includes Egyptian achievement as part of the slave heritage:

> New peoples marvel at thy pyramids.
> The years roll on, thy sphinx of riddle eyes
> Watches the mad world with immobile lids.[17]

The same view is expressed in a poem by Harold M. Telemaque; the West Indian's inheritance comprises

> those
> Who lifted into shape
> The huge stones of the pyramid;
> Who formed the Sphinx in the desert
> And bid it
> Look down upon the centuries like yesterday.[18]

But that same heritage also has something to do with those

> Who walked blithely
> On the banks of the Congo

And heard the deep rolling moan
Of the Niger.

At times Africa can be Ethiopia, as the Jamaican Rastafarians believe; this theme is admirably treated in Orlando Patterson's *Children of Sisyphus* (1965). Sylvia Wynter had the Rastafarians in mind when she described the following scene in her novel *Hills of Hebron* (1962):

The van swept out of the market. Through the high barred window in the back, Obadiah saw the bearded man kneeling with his head thrown back, chanting with fervor:
"Ethiopia awaken and hear thy children's cry
Ethiopia now is free, our cry rings o'er the land,
Ethiopia awaken, the morning is at hand!"
. . . One of the men who sat propped against his hand-cart, his cap over his eyes, lifted his cap for a few seconds, laughed raucously, and said: "The poor fool! He don't even know that Mussolini beat the hell out of the Conquering Lion of Judah and not even there the black man is free!"[19]

The theme of Africa, unspecified and without locality, becomes to many writers either the conglomeration or the collision of attitudes. In Andrew Salkey's novel *A Quality of Violence*, two popular West Indian attitudes toward Africa are shown. One of them stands out clearly when Miss Mellie upbraids Mother Johnson's powers: "We not frighten by white fowl talk or Africa or slave power! We don't belong to them things. We is people that you always living-off of. *We is people who live on the land in St Thomas, not Africa*" (my italics).[20] In George Lamming's first novel, written before he visited Africa, the hero expresses a similar view:

I see the purchase of tribes on the silver sailing vessels, some to Jamaica, Antigua, Grenada, some to Barbados and the island of oil and the mountains tops. And then as 'tis now, though the season change, some was trying to live and some trying to die, and some were too tired to worry about either. The families fall to pieces and many a brother never see his sister nor father the son. Now there's been new combinations and those that come after make quite a different collection. *So if you hear some young fool fretting about back to Africa, keep far from the invalid and don't force a passage to where you won't yet belong* (my italics).[21]

V. S. Naipaul goes a step further, claiming that for the West Indian "Africa has been forgotten, films about African tribesmen excite derisive West Indian laughter." After a few years in England and his visit to Africa, Lamming was to adopt a different stance. He replied to Naipaul's criticism by saying that "it is precisely because Africa has not been forgotten that the West Indian embarrassment takes the form of derisive laughter."[22] Often we get the laughter in literature; for example, the Jamaican humorist Louise Bennett asks,

> Back to Africa, Miss Matty?
> Yuh no know wa yuh deh say?
> Yuh haffe come from some weh fus
> Before yuh go back deh.[23]

And Eric Roach in "Ballad of Canga" lightheartedly treats African superstitions:

> He is a old Ashantee man
> Full of wickedness;
> Bring obeah straight from Africa;
> What he curse you don't bless.[24]

But Mother Johnson in Salkey's novel puts forth the other point of view, that Africa is to be taken seriously:

Me and you and the rest-a people in St Thomas all belong to the days that pass by when slavery was with the land. Everybody is a part of slavery days, is a part of the climate-a-Africa and the feelings in the heart is Africa feelings that beating there, far down. . . . We all come from Ashanti people who did powerful plenty, and we have the same bad feelings that them did have. We have the same powerhouse brains that them did have. (p. 151)

Later she expresses her thoughts even more positively: "We haven't changed at all, Africa is still with us. We belong nowhere else" (p. 156). Despite the fact that in the novel Dada Johnson knows nothing of the Ashanti religion,[25] the important point here is that Mother Johnson's attitude is aggressively pro-African, based on a West Indian concept of Africa.

Very often for the West Indian writer Africa can be a means of integrating or disintegrating a person or a society. In Philip Sherlock's poem "Pocomania," the combination of African and Asian elements establishes a new religious association:

> Power of the past returns
> Africa among the trees
> Asia with her mysteries.[26]

Sometimes it is a fusion of the European and African worlds that forms the West Indian social inheritance. A white West Indian writer, Geoffrey Drayton, says in his poem "The Singing Negress" that he can share something of her world:

> A song it was of little sweetness
> But old as slavery

And in the cradle days
My nurse had sung it
Sadly like this—
As though her world were still in chains,
As though when dreams come true
One has forgotten all the joy of dreaming them,
And cannot make fulfillment sweet
With tears of empty waking.[27]

In his semi-autobiographical novel, *Christopher*,[28] his white hero responds sympathetically to the imaginative stimulus of the African world around him:

On moonlight nights the labourers in the plantation villages collected to sing hymns. Their hymns were Christian, but the rhythms to which they sang them were African, simple and repetitive, gaining speed and volume as they gained in length. In the churches the negroes had built for themselves, where untrained negro priests presided, the congregations beat time with tembourines [*sic*]. At nights, in the open air, drums syncopated.

Christopher's body grew taut as he heard the drums begin. . . . The drums beat swiftly and more loudly. He felt his body grow tight and small as their rhythm grew. (p. 28)

George Lamming in his *Season of Adventure*,[29] written after he had been to Africa, describes a ceremony which was "a religious manifestation based on a serpent cult that originated on the slave coast of West Africa" (p. 28). Again, as in *Christopher*, we realize that it is "the music that seemed to preserve the total spirit of this cult" (p. 29), and the whole ceremony is a merging of Christianity and paganism, of Europe and Africa:

About two brief alcoves of candle flame, white pots of clay were crowded on the shelf. Spirits were alive in the two earthen jars where the *Hungnan* had knelt to appease the revolt of the last dead voice. The African goddess, Erzulie, resided in the left alcove. She stared across a cubicle of space at a picture of the Virgin Mary on the other side. The saints of Congo and Senegal were observing them from the far corner of the room. The saints of the Church were in easy alliance with the gods of the tonelle. (p. 43)

Frequently for the West Indian writer the African motif combines effectively with other racial themes to produce, in literature as in society, a racial harmony which the writers use to express their nationalistic feelings; so Telemaque, the same poet who praised the Africa heritage, describes in a moving poem, "In Our Land," the fusion of the races:

In our land
We do not breed

> The taloned king, the eagle,
> In our land,
> The black birds
> And the chickens of our mountains
> Speak our dreams.[30]

The same sentiment is conveyed by George Campbell; love for Africa and for Jamaica can coexist:

> She sings of the African womb
> Everlasting above the tomb
> She sings of her island Jamaica
> She sings of the glory of Africa.[31]

Very often West Indian poets painstakingly construct an image of Africa, only to explode the myth in a burst of conscious anger. For example, Claude McKay exclaims at the end of a poem, "Thou art the harlot, now thy time is done, / Of all the mighty nations of the sun" (p. 40). It is as if the structure of the poem were cynically reconstructing a certain aspect of West Indian society.

Some West Indian writers, in contrast, do concern themselves with glorifying Africa and African culture. Often this involves a rejection of European culture and Christianity; so instead of fusion there is social dislocation. E. M. Roach, for instance, sees the African heritage as one that affords no compromise with other cultures:

> The cock, the totem of his craft, his luck,
> The obeahman infects me to my heart
> Although I wear my Jesus on my breast
> And burn a holy candle for my saint
> I am a shaker and a shouter and a myal man;
> My voodoo passion swings sweet chariots low.[32]

The gods are not companions here, as in Lamming; the African triumphs. Often the supernatural strength of Africa can influence even white people; Annie Palmer in de Lisser's *White Witch of Rosehall* is suspected of being under the powerful spell of Haitian voodoo priests "who are versed in all the old African sorcery, and who do understand how to influence the minds of their dupes."[33] In Derek Walcott it is the personal disorientation that is emphasized. Both cultures are equally strong, but to absorb them both involves a betrayal of one:

> How choose
> Between this Africa and the English tongue I love?
> Betray them both, or give back what they give?
> How can I face such slaughter and be cool?
> How can I turn from Africa and live?[34]

Looking back on the African past often causes a certain amount of romantic attitudinizing, which with good writers is transformed into spiritual analysis as in L. E. Braithwaite's poetry, but with bad writers descends to sentimental affectation, as we shall see later. One way of looking at this past is from the viewpoint of slavery, which sometimes is manifested in what Coulthard calls "attacks levelled against Western civilization's treatment of the Negro in the past."[35] In a poem by Vera Bell, the African slave past is seen as something to be ashamed of:

> Across the years your eyes seek mine
> Compelling me to look
> I see your shackled feet
> Your primitive black face
> I see your humiliation
> And turn away
> Ashamed.[36]

But frequently, as in the conclusion of this poem and in Martin Carter's "Death of a Slave," the slave past can incite revolutionary fervor:

> Slave staggers and falls
> face is on earth
> drum is silent
> silent like night
> hollow like boat
> between the tides of sorrow
>
> in the dark floor
> in the cold dark earth
> time plants the seeds of anger.[37]

A. M. Clarke, however, sees the slave past as a fertile period:

> Your spirits were dancing on African shores
> To wild jungle rhythms
> On beaten earth floors . . .
> So while some curbed your freedom
> With bayonet and gun
> You snatched crumbs of freedom
> From music and song.[38]

Yet it is surprising how little West Indian writing is concerned with slavery, probably for the very practical reason that there are several other racial groups in the West Indies who would not "necessarily wish to be absorbed into an ex-slave society which is by admission lacking in 'culture,' poor, irresponsible, lacking in direction and purpose."[39]

Perhaps it is for this reason that Africa is often mentioned as a place of freedom. In Claude McKay's novel *Home to Harlem*,[40] Jake hears about his African past from a Haitian waiter who tells him

of the old destroyed cultures of West Africa and of their vestiges, of black kings who struggled stoutly for independence of their kingdoms: Prempeh of Ashanti, Behanzin of Dahomey, Ewari of Benin, Cetawayo of Zulu-land, Menelile of Abyssinia.

Had Jake ever heard of the little Republic of Liberia, founded by American Negroes? And Abyssinia, deep-set in the shoulder of Africa, besieged by the hungry wolves of Europe? The only nation that had existed free and independent from the earliest records of history until today! (p. 135)

Here there is no mention of slavery, and the African past becomes an anthology of certain historical moments of glory.

To John Hearne's Marcus Heneky in *Land of the Living*[41] (does he represent Marcus Garvey?) the African past stabilizes a chosen moment of wonder. In his house his visitors are amazed:

Instead of the customary Hanoverian images and meaningless landscapes from an unrelated climate, there was a large photograph of the Ethiopian Emperor, with two green, yellow and red flags above the frame, their sticks crossed, the cloth spread flat, and a loudly coloured relief map of Africa on which Addis Ababa was symbolized by a huge, gilt Star of David. On the third wall, facing this, was a framed text in twelve point Baskerville: *For the hurt of the daughter of my people am I hurt: I am black: astonishment hath taken hold on me.* (my italics; pp. 106–7)

Marcus Heneky is very different from Sylvia Wynter's bearded eccentric. Later Stefan, the hero of Hearne's novel, tries to explain what he thinks Marcus Heneky and his Pure Church of Africa Triumphant stand for: " 'That's what I'm trying to tell you,' I said, 'The triumph of Africa and the black race was only the external part of it. . . . a sort of symptom' " (p. 109). He continues, " 'In Heneky's case the lie was that the black man was faceless. What he had to do was to try to change that, to give the black man the sort of vision of himself that would make him free. And make the whites and the browns free, because they were shackled to the lie too' " (p. 109). The interest in Africa is to some extent therefore a conscious attempt at reordering the consequences of history.

The West Indian who comes to Africa as writer or fictional hero makes a conscious effort to interpret this history in two ways. In comparing the West Indian in Africa with the white American in Europe, Lamming comments that "his relation to that continent is more personal and more problematic. It is more personal because the conditions of his life today, his status as man, are a clear indication of the reasons which led to the departure of his ancestors from that continent. . . . His relation to

Africa is more problematic because he has not, like the [white] American, been introduced to it through history." E. R. Braithwaite in his travel book, *A Kind of Homecoming*, describes his first impressions of Africa, which convey his personal relationship to the country: "So this is Africa, and these trees were here a long, long time. It must take many, many years to make such big trees, and maybe, in the long ago, someone walked here, or slept here and loved here to start or continue the sequence which involved me, produced me. . . ."[42]

The search for identity is most interesting and universal when it is not a racial investigation, but the private quest of a bemused individual in an alienated world. Consequently, according to Lamming, "the Negro writer joins hands . . . not so much with a Negro audience as with every other writer whose work is a form of self-inquiry, a clarification of his relations with other men, and a report of his own, very highly subjective conception of the possible meaning of man's life."[43]

Froad's predicament in *Other Leopards* (1963),[44] a novel by Denis Williams, is that he is not permitted to be morally neutral—"Selling Christians to Arabs, Arabs to Christians: needed time to think out the difference" (p. 64). There is of course no difference, but Froad cannot comprehend this; he is socially maladjusted among stable people. Even the chief, *his own countryman*, has a certainty of purpose that he admits he lacks: "Catherine and her granite hillsides and ruins and legends and history flitted through my mind. Now what the hell does it really feel like? Hughie and his traditions and his burden and his conscientious fanaticism. The Chief and his certainty and his duty and truth and all that. Every man a place! I'm like the bloody scavengers; no shadows" (p. 96). At the end, because the novel is about self and not race, he has to annihilate his physical being to come to terms with himself in the community—a re-enactment of self-crucifixion that jeopardizes body and soul in order to realign man with society.

In *The Leopard*,[45] set in East Africa, Vic Reid seems to make much the same point. Nebu, the African, has killed a white man and is pursued by a leopard. In his company he has a "half-bwana" boy with a lame foot who turns out to be his son by the wife of the murdered white man. Reid came to Africa only after he had written the novel, but it is remarkable for certain things. It would not be illogical to see the half-bwana as a West Indian who has two fathers—the dead European, to whom he wants to cling, and the dying African who loves him but whom he continually abuses. Though the novel can stand up to this interpretation, it is a much less ambitious attempt than, say, Denis Williams's, mainly because much of the dialogue between Nebu and his son is unconvincing and the thought of the novel is inadequate to sustain the prolonged periods of inaction. But it redeems itself when it establishes a truth—one that goes beyond the racial confines that have bogged it down—and it becomes a sincere statement of every man's quest for origin:

"Nebu," the boy said softly. The black looked curiously at him. "You love me very much," the boy said.
The boy's eyes were opened wide, stretched boldly wide so that they were two strangely lit rooms into which the black almost wandered. (p. 170)

Then the boy tells Nebu that he knows he is his father:

"Father," the boy said softly, grinning at him. Through the soles of his feet, he could hear the ocean at Mombassa. The great waves stood straight up in the water, fifty yards out, and tossed their shaggy heads and roared in and shook the beach in their teeth.
The Negro said gently: "Then you know, toto. I would not have hurt the half-bwana by telling him." (p. 171)

When father and son make this ideological truce, the dialogue achieves more than racial comprehension; it attains a new kind of truth which annuls all differences. It is here that we realize that in his search for roots the West Indian writer is "forced to consider the whole problem of significance."[46]

One of these problems—what constitutes freedom?—is faced by Azi, the African in George Lamming's *Emigrants*. Is freedom "an experience of the self in a state of unconditioned awareness"?[47] Azi has been given the accolades of success in the European world but he has to reject these to find himself. Indeed he does not convince us that he is an African at all but rather a West Indian concept of an African. In a wider sense he symbolizes a man at loggerheads with his history. For, like Walcott, Lamming tends to emphasize the cultural disunity, but of course it is visualized in broader and more significant terms. And for Lamming, as for so many other West Indian writers, the African presence nevertheless exists—whether one absorbs it or rejects it, incorporates it into, or estranges it from, one's culture. Few writers would be bold enough to agree with George Campbell that there is

> No more reality from our
> Forbears
> Only this fervid languid
> Severance
> Of limp moonlight
> Mountain bamboo trellis
> Darkness gaol night.[48]

447

However, Lamming must have been aware of the dangers inherent in being overly concerned with Africa and the Black question, when he advocated that the concept of the Black writer should be more universal. There have been several poems written by West Indians in which Africa is a stock theme. Consider this one by Philip Sherlock, for instance:

> Across the sand I saw a black man stride
> To fetch his fishing gear and broken things,
> And silently that splendid body cried
> Its proud descent from ancient chiefs and kings
> Across the sand I saw him naked stride;
> Sand his black body in the sun's white light
> The velvet coolness of dark forests wide,
> The blackness of the jungle's starless night.[49]

This is externalized romaticizing whereas in "Pocomania" I feel the poet has come closer to his subject; indeed his interpretation is from within. But at least Sherlock is not overtly sentimental; his ability as a poet enables him to convey his message with some conviction. Frequently we find Lamming doing the same thing. In *Season of Adventure* there is a powerful evocation that is somewhat spoiled by excessive romanticizing: "The smell of cemeteries rotted his hand. His eyes were the colour of burnt hay. . . . He carried an axe in his right hand, a bracelet of black bones were swinging freely round his wrist when he waved the axe in worship round his head" (pp. 31–32). But the description is not a failure because Lamming's imaginative strength comes to the rescue. The passage concludes, "The gods resided in every tooth of point and blade. Invisible by choice, their absence had made the night more nervous." Often the romanticizing is confined to remarks by characters. We have already seen an example of this in McKay's *Home to Harlem*. In another of McKay's novels, *Banjo*, one of his characters says that he loves to hear African dialects and he even claims that Africans are superior to West Indian and American Blacks.[50]

Perhaps it is apparent by now that West Indians who have never been to Africa, or West Indians who prefer to believe that there is no *country* called Africa, often express a truer concept of Africa, embodied in larger and more significant terms, than do those West Indians who have seen Africa. Two possible exceptions are Césaire and L. E. Braithwaite. To a large extent the realistic shock of Africa being a large not easily comprehended continent, coupled with the West Indian's feeling that he is "lost," tends to obscure the wider concept of man in search of his roots as it heightens the theme of the West Indian in search of his past. In a recent novel by Wilson Harris the theme of the African in West Indian literature is given greater dimensions. Poseidon, in *The Secret Ladder*,[51] is an archetypal figure from myth who embodies the vigor of the aboriginal: "His grandfather had been a runaway African slave who had succeeded in evading capture and had turned into a wild cannibal man in the swamps, devouring melting white concerite flesh wherever he spied the mirage of high banking land; feasting on the quivering meat of sensitive turtle (until he turned to human jelly-fish himself) as well as the soft underbelly of fear-some alligator" (p. 21). Poseidon's links are firm; he is himself completely united with the forces of the natural world: "He was as dry as a gnarled stump . . . his ancient feet webbed with grass and muck— . . . his hands were wreathed in a fisherman's writhing net of cord. . . . The living cords seemed to grow along his arms and body until they turned matted as thick hairy straw upon his chest" (p. 49). This is no externalized romanticizing of the African, nor is it a carbon copy of the typical oft-repeated West Indian attitude toward Africa. Instead Poseidon is universal, he is a reservoir of the original freedom of Man before the Fall, before the perversions of civilization "would turn the tables on him and rob him of the last freedom he possessed" (p. 49). When he dies it is not just because the old must give way to the new, nor is his death only of racial significance, for he dies "on the cruel knuckles of the one who loved him best, the grandson he had begotten in the dreadful apotheosis of history" (p. 118); he dies because historical stature cannot compare with the grandeur of myth, and what one cannot understand one destroys.

Perhaps Harris sees this as the inevitable fate of African influences in the West Indies, a view with which W. E. Abraham would agree: "The West Indies, where the acculturation into Europe has gone very far, will by contrast find very little to pose against the European cultures, now or at independence. The West Indies are Western and might do well to accelerate the process of westernization as the only really practical alternative given to them." On the other hand, Ezekiel Mphahlele does not support this contention. He comments rather bitterly, "I am not asking them [the West Indians] to identify themselves with us; after all it isn't their fault if they were taught some nasty things about us by their colonial masters and pseudo-historians."[52]

It seems that even the Africans cannot agree about the identity of West Indians so it is scarcely surprising that West Indians themselves are divided on the question of whether there is or is not an African presence. But it is from this ambiguity and from the attempt to reconcile the paradoxes that some worthwhile literature has been written which expands the imaginative potentialities of the African mind.

The Black Environment

The writer in a developing country, in his dilemma of sensibility, comes to his material with an environment within. In this way he is to a large extent not a creator of the environment, but brings to the environment some of all that he has inherited. For instance, New World cultures have a child-parent relationship with Old World cultures, and therefore Europeans in America tend to ally themselves with European culture just as Black people tend to identify with African culture. It follows from this that it is extremely difficult for the subject culture to surpass the parent host culture, and therefore there occurs a bewildering example, for instance, on the part of the writer when he attempts to use his imagination, given these limitations.

Perhaps an example of the kind of writer that I am thinking of, in America, would be James Baldwin, who seeks to leap over the direct relationship to his own particular brand of Old World culture (that is the African culture) and who instead associates with European norms. Because the writer is concerned with operating in this kind of enclave, made up as it is of New World cultures, he is to a large extent inhibited. And because of this inhibition, people in the United States frequently fail to possess a unique identification which is properly theirs, and thus deny themselves a certain kind of artistic autonomy which is also properly theirs. This point is well exemplified by the plight of Richard Wright in Africa who said, "I was black, they were black, but my color did not help me."

450

There is no collective myth or general wisdom indigenous to the present inhabitants of the New World. These lands were peopled, but the people who inhabited them bear little resemblance to those who inhabit them now. And therefore all gods have been imported; all conceptual thinking, ideas, technology, the entire view of life come from other lands. As a result, there is a certain irreverence, so that the inhabitants do not identify with, or empathize with, the past and the land. That closeness with soil which is part of the traditional Old World understanding in both Europe and Africa is lacking in the New World.

What then can one understand by the past? What does the writer understand by the past? In traditional African society, the past was in large measure geared to occasion. That is, it functioned because certain demands were made of it; therefore, at funerals, dirges were sung; at weddings, wedding songs were sung. Even the most cursory glance through Frazer's *Golden Bough* reveals much the same about the European past. In other words, there was no such thing as a purely aesthetic literature in the European or the African past; all literature conformed to the demands of occasion. Because of the traditional societies' compassion for legacy, a great body of literature is rooted in undisturbed aristocratic values. And in Africa these tend to be tribal ones.

In the New World, the very ground is saturated wth tragedy to the extent that its inhabitants brought tragedy with them when they came. Therefore the literature charts, to some degree, the course, the development of this tragedy. But frequently one comes up against an enormous void. The confrontation with something which cannot be fully apprehended defines the present because in the twentieth century seemingly few creative dimensions can be given to literature, since it lacks a past. There are, of course, "gateway" manifestations in the novel, the poem, the short story. But these are only indicative of a culture. Before a new and full culture and literature can be developed, there must be a completely new architecture of being. Part of this structure must be founded on the concept of the ancestor. Who are these people in the New World? Where do they come from? These problems naturally affect everyone in the New World, because the concept of the in-dwelling ancestor—the ancestor who is in them—is something alien. The inhabitants of the New World are like shapes, in a way, that have been vacated by Old World presences. They are arrested; they have stopped; it is as if we were to take a look at the entire history of the Old World as it manifests itself in them, as it halts for one moment for our attention and perusal. Thus, it seems that there is no charter for destiny; people have little which awaits them, again because they are not sure of a "tribal" past.

The Jamaican novelist Sylvia Wynter expresses this well when she writes, "They [people from the Caribbean] are in every sense a new people, without knowledge of themselves, without a documental history of their past, without legendary heroes, without myths."[1] On the other hand, the Old World tends to be completely different, because it still retains a mythological element; it has a past and, consequently, archetypal patterns from which writers can draw. This sometimes means that writers reproduce items of alarming sameness, from a kind of static mold. Nevertheless the writer does not have to operate in a vicarious vacuum. He can digest the material of recall—all that has gone on for centuries and centuries—and he can re-create the presence of man as he finds him today. When this present is enunciated in New World terms, the writer frequently has to distort the language and mutilate what little he has of this inherited aristocratic value. A ready example is a poem from Surinam (Dutch Guyana) by Eugene Relbum in which the average English reader will find a great deal that is incomprehensible:

Sranan na mi
mi na Sranan
Sranan a no wan noh wawan
Sranan na
mi mati
mi granwan
moksi kon Kronwan
dis na mi bribi
mi skrooe moes kan bigi
lek wan kankantri
foe fiti Sranan glori
mi sjen na Sranansjen
na ini joe bere mi wani mi bongo foe tan
Sranan
Joe wanga mi na wan.

A line-for-line translation is as follows:

Surinam is me
I am Surinam
Surinam is not only a name
Surinam is
my friends
my ancestors
mixed up as one
this is my belief
my shoulders must grow as big
as a kankan tree
to fit Surinam's glory

my shame is Surinam's shame
in my belly I want your dead bones to stay
Surinam
You and I are one.[2]

This is the present in the New World; the writer makes use not of tribal illusion, but of national identification. He can no longer claim to be any one thing or the other, and therefore he takes in a larger circumference, saying in essence, "I am Surinam, and this nationalist identification is part of what is going on within the new world." It is no accident that today in America people address themselves to the saluting of flags, because this is a way back to the ancestral past that is connected only by loose ties. But one might say, "Well, so what? This is only natural. In this part of the world we are cosmopolitan. We are made up of different peoples, and it is very unlikely that we would have a common heritage; therefore it is only normal that we should try to prop up what we see around us." But this assertion is wrong because the African writer experiences the exact same predicament—the breakup of his world, the crumbling of an entire sensibility. What has happened is that the African writer no longer can take sides, as did the oral artist. He no longer finds that he can identify as closely with his tribal group, or with his national group, as the oral artist could. A poem written sometime in the late fifties by the Nigerian Gabriel Okara illustrates some measure of this. In the poem, entitled "Piano and Drums," the piano symbolizes the European way of life, the drums the African way of life, and the poet cannot quite make up his mind which rhythm to follow:

When at break of day at a riverside
I hear jungle drums telegraphing
the mystic rhythm, urgent, raw
like bleeding flesh, speaking of
primal youth and the beginning . . .[3]

If the material of recall is at hand, what exactly does one *do* with it? Perhaps in the New World people have lost the spiritual ability to deal with it at all—thus they inhabit a kind of no-man's-land. This failure can be partly accounted for; no longer can artists, like the African oral artists, acknowledge the capacity for action which is still vested in the object. In other words, no longer can one say that things have a life and a substance of their own. And it is only in the New World's "borrowed" folktales and legends that some of this interaction takes place, like in the account of the Signifying Monkey and Shine's conversation with the whale.

The artist, in both worlds, is in a predicament. Should he be con-

453

cerned with himself, with his own private problems, or should he address himself to an audience? Should he be conscious of a "home" audience as opposed to an "alien" audience? The Nigerian writer Chinua Achebe sees the role of the African artist as that of a teacher. This is in many ways ironical, since in large measure the African writer is creating for an audience in Europe, and former colonialists are now addressing themselves to their erstwhile colonial masters. They are now speaking to them, teaching them, informing them. This is no different, of course, from what is taking place in America, where from the beginning of the century there has been this vast movement of the proletariat, this enormous manifesto of the ordinary man, who desires to enunciate his own thoughts and beliefs. He asserts, "I don't any longer want the bourgeois to tell me how and what to think. I will now speak." And if there is any one outstanding feature in twentieth-century Black literature, it surely must be that this man in the street has begun to write, speak, and express himself as a thinking person, as someone engaged in the phenomenon of true being.

All this of course has something to do with the human person, with his inverse, although perhaps not reluctant, acceptance of the role of the artist as man, rather than as spokesman for the people. The West Indian Edward Braithwaite has published a volume of poems entitled *Rights of Passage*. Among other things it is concerned with the problems of that journey that had to be undertaken by slaves—the rigors of the "middle passage." But far from being verse which, in Ralph Ellison's words, is "trading on one's anguish," it begins with the assumption that here is a man speaking to men; in other words, the new artist has been born.

> To hell
> with Af-
> rica
> to hell
> with Eu-
> rope too,
> just call my blue
> black bloody spade
> a spade and kiss
> my ass, O-
> kay? So
> let's begin.[4]

Begin what? The writer in the New World is engaged in an attempt at articulating a trueness of being—just *as* he is in this strange place, the no-man's-land to which he brought no gods, in which he found no gods, and to which he had to bring his own inventions. He accepts his confusion. What becomes important is the power of the word. Just as the spinner of words, the teller of tales in Africa is a particular type of magician, in that he is able to *transform* a situation, so the artist in the New World is the person who *organizes*, who modifies rhythm so that it is in accordance with the word. Thus we find American writers, both Black and white, taking a great deal of liberty with the English language, which no Englishman would dare to take. They take such liberties because they lack a heritage, because they live in this peculiar no-man's-land, this place that belongs to nobody, and because they are partly cut off from the Old World cultures and are in no way bound by them. The word is stripped of connotations and is used as raw material for a new kind of image making. Out of the confusion emerges a strange type of freedom.

An extraordinary process is therefore taking place and, as a result, the writers in the New World and African writers for whom the "word" is new, are infusing the Old World languages—Portuguese, Spanish, French, English—with a different kind of vigor, a different kind of rhythm, a different set of images. They are of course bringing their own peculiar situation to bear on these languages and they are stretching the languages, doing what a South African writer has rightly called "violence" to these languages. But, what of the audience? Now it has been said that the African writer writes for a "home" audience, that he is concerned with being a teacher, with teaching his own people how to live. But the publishing facts remain, and they reveal that most of the Caribbean and African writers tend to publish in England and that most of the people who buy the books do not live in the Caribbean or in Africa. The majority of books written by "radical" Black Americans are probably bought by "conservative" white Americans. One, therefore, has to ask certain questions: Are paintings made to be looked at? Does one write to have an audience? And, of the writer, Why did you come? Why have you written? Why did you come when you had nothing to give? For if you don't take sides with me, the reader, I am entitled to ask this of you. But Jean-Paul Sartre has written of the Black poets included in Senghor's 1948 anthology, "All these, colonialists, and accomplices who open this book, will know that all these poets are black. Such people that read this will have the sensation of reading as though over another's shoulder, words that were not intended for them. It is to black men that these black poets address themselves. It is for them that they speak of black men."[5] Thus it seems that whether the audience is in America, or in Africa, or in the Caribbean, whether the audience is a book-buying audience or not, whether, in other words, the audience is literate or not should make no difference. What should be of concern is what was in the mind of the writer. For whom was he creating his material? Time and time again one answers this question by saying that the writer was creating the material because he felt it necessary to explain something, and only secondly because he thought it applicable to others who were faced with a similar kind of problem. With this kind of understanding, it becomes almost ludicrous to assert that the Black artist has a responsibility. But he does. He is responsible not only to the art itself, but to the very function which the art is performing—the social role of the artist, the purpose of the traditional artist in the Africa that is the oral Africa, which is past and which exists now. Within this context one sees the quality of an international Blackness.

One sometimes thinks that an audience expects little more from their artists than that they should familiarize themselves with structures. I get the feeling that frequently, as a writer, I am merely expected to reproduce—to acquaint myself with what is around me and then show people that this is how it is. In other words, you have seen it like this, and I will simply hold up the mirror for you. But the writer's role is not necessarily to convey to the audience a certain kind of image of itself. In some ways, the role of the writer should be to distort this image and to give it a different perspective; in other words, to express for the audience what *he* makes of the situation, not what the *audience* makes of the situation. This is another side to the expression "tell it like it is."

New writers in the New World do violence to a language that is essentially a borrowed one. Black writers on the African continent also do this because they have their own terms and, in addition, they have the language of the "mother country." But in regard to the audience, one is entitled to agree at this stage with Achebe that "no man can understand another whose language he does not speak." And by language we do not mean verbal craft but a cultural view. How many Europeans and Americans know African languages? Achebe is asking, in other words, about the ability of the critic to respond fully to a work of art. He is assuming that the work of art will be judged away from the center of creation, and, therefore, he is wondering to what extent the work of art might be misinterpreted as a result of the critic's lack of understanding.

New World artists are not only concerned with the problem of the artist in the New World and the inability of critics to understand fully what the artist is saying; they are also concerned with erecting new kinds of structures. For instance, it is considered conventional within the novel to have a plot develop so that the end is a kind of climax. This is evident in most popular novels and on television. One can see, "almost guess"— even without looking at one's watch or realizing when the commercials take place—that a television play is coming to an end because inevitably good is going to triumph, the hero is going to defeat the villain, the cowboys are going to conquer the Indians. One knows that this must happen and, when it does happen, one realizes that this is the end. This is obviously an artificial element and the new writer in the New World is endeavoring, some in a small way and many in a very large way, to bring about not so much a climax as an illumination, so that the end reflects the beginning by being continuous and following logically from what was said before. The entire process involves the transformation of the bitter, ominous, horrifying material of recall into art. Thus the plot scheme is not simply a neat assembling of characters who function within a set space and a set time, but the antithesis of all this. And at the end one is left with the kinds of questions with which life leaves us. More important than anything else is that the Black writer today is concerned with the function of the individual in the world. Jean Toomer's *Cane* (1923) is the best example of this by a New World Black.

Up until now the Black African writer was concerned, to a large extent, with expressing group attitudes to various problems. He was not motivated by a private psychology, but by a sort of public and social duty. The danger is that this can become institutionalized, but when the writer seeks a new type of individuality, when he rebels against what the audience wants him to do, he is no longer blindfolded by these other urges. And incidentally, these urges may not be easily apprehended, but they are acutely felt. The writer may in some cases come to terms with this idea of social responsibility; on the other hand it may prompt him to say things which, if intended for the mass public, may well be expressed in the crude and oratorical manner of the public spokesman. The individualist writer does not write for the mass audience; he expresses caveats for himself. He asserts, "I am not going over there because the politician will take care of that sort of ground and the churchmen will take care of the other ground—I'm not going over there." Having voiced his opinion, he can now bear witness to the hidden areas of experience within the sensibility, within his own moment of time. This is, of course, what links him to contemporary worker and peasant. Therefore when LeRoi Jones writes in his poem "Black Art" "we want poems like fists," he is attempting to loosen the tight structure that has evolved over the centuries. He is recasting the unemotional climate that has crept into art, the attitude that claims art is for the thinking man, a thinking man's job. Art is only for people who think. Ezra Pound is, of course, a good example of the thinking man—the man who is "educated" and who knows it and who will put it all down in his writing. The poems of the new writers in the New World spill over at the pages when they write, as is evident in this poem by Don L. Lee:

> newnigger
> lost his way
> a whi-te girl gave him direction
> him still lost
> she sd whi-te/he thought bite
> been eating everything in sight
> including himself.
>
> suppose those
> who made
> wars
> had to fight them?
>
> the lone ranger got a new tonto
> he's 'brown' with a Ph.D. in
> psy-chol-o-gy
> & still walks around with
> holes
> in his brain
> losthismind.

This type of writing demands a new kind of criticism, just as a great deal of the new writing must be approached with a new way of thinking.

Because these writers are not indulging themselves, as their predecessors did, they represent the possibility of an orientation toward a new kind of reality, a reality in which one will be able to express something which is not as yet fully apprehended, but is coming into being. This is the translation of mutilated legacies; one admits them as art. It is a deserted world, a world abandoned by God, but nevertheless a universe in which the private person features, in which he can question himself about the whole nature of his being, the whole nature of his purpose. And he does this without any reference whatsoever to the past.

What of the future then? There will come about a grim impact with the alien things of being, so that one will be able to see and perceive the wholeness which was lost a long time ago and which will now disentangle the Black artist from the petty. Because of the fierce conflicts generated in the United States, this could well become the society of the future, but only if the dilemma of the sensibility of the artist—Black and white—can once and forever be resolved.

NOTES

Notes

Chapter 1. The Traditional Artist

1. T. Adeboye Lambo, "The Place of the Arts in the Emotional Life of the African," *AMSAC Newsletter*, 17 (January 1965), 4.

2. Deborah Lifchitz, "La littérature orale ches les Dogon du Soudan Français," *Africa*, 13 (July 1940), 241. J. H. Nketia, *Funeral Dirges of the Akan People* (Achimota: privately published, 1955), p. 3.

3. Alta Jablow, *Yes and No: The Intimate Folklore of Africa* (New York: Horizon Press, 1961), p. 30. H. L. M. Butcher, "Four Edo Fables," *Africa*, 10 (July 1937), 342.

4. W. E. Abraham, *The Mind of Africa* (London: Weidenfeld and Nicolson, 1962), p. 91.

5. Hugh Tracey, *Chopi Musicians* (London: Oxford University Press, 1948), *passim*. John Reed and Clive Wake, eds., *Léopold Sédar Senghor: Selected Poems* (London: Oxford University Press, 1964), p. 96. F. Brigaud, "Les contes du Sénégal," *Notes africaines*, no. 101 (January 1964), 3. André Sauvant, "Le vieux griot," *Jeune Afrique*, no. 9, p. 16.

6. "Taga for Mbaye Dyop," *Senghor*, ed. Reed and Wake, pp. 42–43. A *taga* is a praise poem; the *tama* mentioned in the quotation is a small drum carried by Senegalese *griots*.

7. Lilyan Lagneau, "Les problèmes du critique littéraire," paper submitted to Berliner Festwochen, September 22–27, 1964, p. 7. K. R. S. Iyengar, *The Adventure of Criticism* (London: Asia Publishing House, 1962), p. 47.

8. Bakare Gbadamosi and Ulli Beier, eds., *Yoruba Poetry* (Ibadan: Ministry of Education, 1959), p. 2.

9. E. Bolaji Idowu, *Olódùmarè: God in Yoruba Belief* (London: Longmans, 1962), pp. 137–38. The actual number of *Odu* is unknown. All that is reasonably sure is that there are sixteen principal sections which are subdivided and then further subdivided.

461

10. Wande Abimbola, "The Odu of Ifa," *African Notes* (Institute of African Studies, University of Ibandan), 1 (April 1964), 7.

11. Jan Vansina, *Oral Tradition: A Study in Historical Methodology* (London: Kegan Paul, 1963), p. 5. Cyprian Ekwensi, "Problems of Nigerian Writers," *Nigerian Magazine*, no. 78 (September 1963), 217.

Chapter 2. African Script

1. I. J. Gelb, *A Study of Writing* (Chicago: University of Chicago Press, 1952), p. 67. Lyndon Harries, ed., *Swahili Poetry* (Oxford: Clarendon Press, 1962), p. 1. An article in *Man*, no. 85 (September–October 1943), points out that Toma in French Guinea and Liberia is "distinct from both the Vai and Mende systems" (p. 108). But the argument is based on the isolated fact that Toma is written from left to right, like Vai but unlike Mende.

2. S. W. Köelle, *Narrative of an Expedition into the Vy Country of West Africa and the Discovery of a System of Syllabic Writing Invented by the Natives of the Vy Tribe* (London: Jeys, Hatchards, V. Nisbet and Co., 1849), p. 7. H. M. Stanley, *Through the Dark Continent* (London: Low, Marston, Searle & Rivinton, 1887), p. 259. The Chadwicks add that "it is probable that writing was, first introduced into Uganda by Arab traders" and that "it is certain that outside the court the art of writing was practically unknown." H. Munro Chadwick and N. Kershaw Chadwick, *The Growth of Literature*, 3 (London: Cambridge University Press, 1940), 573–74. F. J. R. Rodd, *People of the Veil* (London: Macmillan, 1926). H. R. Palmer, "The Tuareg of the Sahara," *Journal of the Royal African Society*, 31 (1932), 300.

3. I. M. Lewis, "The Gadabuursi Somali Script," *Bulletin of the School of Oriental and African Studies*, 21 (1958), 134–56.

4. F. E. Forbes, *Despatch Communicating the Discovery of a Native Written Character at Bohmar on the West Coast of Africa Near Liberia* (London: privately printed by Wilham Clowes & Sons, n.d.), p. 3. Köelle, *Narrative of an Expedition into the Vy Country, passim* and p. 19. S. W. Köelle, *Outlines of a Grammar of the Vei Language* (London: Church Missionary House, 1854), p. 235 and *passim*.

5. Köelle, *Outlines of a Grammar*.

6. Momolu Massaquoi, "The Vei People and Their Syllabic Writing," *Journal of the African Society*, 10 (July 1911), 463. E. Norris, "Notes on the Vei Language and Alphabet," in Forbes, *Despatch*, p. 15. H. H. Johnson, *Liberia*, 2 (London: Hutchinson, 1906), 1112.

7. Delafosse, "Les Vai, leur langue et leur systeme d'écriture," *L'anthropologie*, 10 (1899), 129–51, 294–314. F. W. Migeood, "The Syllabic Writing of the Vai People," *Journal of the African Society*, 9 (October 1909), 46–58. A. P. Kup, "An Account of the Tribal Distribution of Sierra Leone," *Man*, 60 (August 1960), 118. P. E. Hair, "An Early Seventeenth Century Vocabulary of Vai," *Man*, 60 (August 1960), 129–39. He was referring to T. Winterbottom, *An Account of the Native Africans in the Vicinity of Sierra Leone*. Johnson, p. 1114. A. Klingenheben, "The Vai Script," *Africa*, 56 (April 1933), 163.

8. L. W. G. Malcolm, "Short Notes on the Syllabic Writing of the Eyap—Central Cameroons," *Journal of the African Society*, 20 (October 1920), 127. For an account of Bamum writing see M. van Gennep, "Une nouvelle écriture nègre: Sa portée théorétique," *Revue des etudes ethnographiques et sociologiques*, 8 (1908), 129–39. A full treatment is found in M. Monring, *Sämtliche Zeichen der vom König Nyoya von Bamum erfundenen Schrift* (Basle, 1907). Göhring has published two informative articles in *Der evangelische Heidenbote*, 80 (1907), 41–42, 83–86. I. Dugast and M. D. W. Jeffreys, *L'écriture Bamum* (Mémoires de l'Institut Francais d'Afrique Noire, Centre du Cameroun, Série Populations, no. 4, 1950), *passim*, 34–62.

9. *Anthropos*, 3 (1908), 838. Gelb, p. 209.

10. R. F. G. Adams, "OB RI KAIM: A New African Script," *Africa*, 17 (January 1947), 24–34. The title of the booklet was *Pogident Giophineus Arien Pogident Gireh Seccuna* (Uyo, Nigeria: edited, printed, and published H. J. P. Ukpaukore, 1953). The church was called Ikpa.

11. J. K. McGregor, "Some Notes on Nsibidi," *Journal of the Royal Anthropological Institute* 39 (1909), 209–19. Elphinstone Daryell, "Further Notes on Nsibidi Signs with Their Meanings from Ikem District, S. Nigeria," *Journal of the Royal Anthropological Institute*, 41 (1911), 523.

Chapter 3. Spoken Art

1. Paul Harvey, ed., *The Oxford Companion to English Literature*, 3rd ed. (Oxford: Clarendon Press, 1960), p. 294. He adds that the term *folklore* was first introduced by W. J. Thomas in *Athenaeum* (1846). Joseph Twadell Shipley, *Dictionary of World Literary Terms* (London: Allen & Unwin, 1955), p. 162.

2. Stith Thompson, *The Folktale* (New York: Dryden Press, 1946), p. 8. *Dictionary of World Literary Terms,* pp. 165, 249. Thompson, p. 8.

3. Maria Leach, *Standard Dictionary of Folklore, Mythology and Legend*, 1 (New York: Funk & Wagnalls, 1942), 18. Melville J. Herskovits, *The Myth of the Negro Past* (New York: Harper, 1941), p. 138. Leo Frobenius, *Der schwarze Decamaron* (Berlin: Vita, Deutsches Verlagshaus, 1910), p. vii.

4. Chadwick and Chadwick, 3, p. 501. Bronislaw Malinowski, *Myth and Primitive Psychology* (London: Kegan Paul, 1926), p. 15. J. H. Kwabena Nketia, "Akan Poetry," *An African Treasury*, ed. Langston Hughes (London: Gollancz, 1960), p. 104. Bernard Dadié, "Folklore and Literature," *Proceedings of the First International Congress of Africanists*, ed. Lalage Bown and Michael Crowder (London: Longmans, 1964), p. 201.

5. Amadou Hampaté Ba, "On animism," *Second Congress of Negro Writers and Artists (Présence africaine)*, nos. 24–25 (February–May 1959), 154.

6. Hans Abrahanson, *The Origin of Death* (Uppsala: Studia Ethnographica Upsaliensia III, 1951), p. 4. Hermann Baumann, *Schöpfung und Urzeit des Menschen im Mythus der afrikanischen Völker* (Berlin: Reiner Steiner, 1936), pp. 270–71. H. A. Stayt, *The Bavenda* (London: Oxford University Press, 1931), p. 362.

7. Alice Werner, *The Natives of British Central Africa* (London: Constable, 1906), p. 201. Leo Frobenius, *Atlantis, Volkmärchen und Volksdichtungen Afrikas*, 11 vols., 10 (Jena: Diederichs, 1921–28), 227.

8. Baumann, p. 1. Emin Pascha, *Sammlung von Reisebriefen* (Leipzig, 1888), p. 469.

9. W. H. Bleek and L. C. Lloyd, *Specimens of Bushman Folklore* (London: George Allen, 1911), p. 45.

10. Elphinstone Dayrell, *Folk Stories from Southern Nigeria* (London: Longmans, 1910). Among the Ga a woman pounding fu-fu with a pestle forces the sky to go further and further away. See C. Fleischer and M. B. Wilkie, "Specimens of Folklore of the Ga People of the Gold Coast," *Africa*, 3 (July 1930), 361n. Among the Ashanti Onyaropon once lived on earth but he was forced into the sky by a woman who used to hit her pestle against him. R. S. Rattray, *Ashanti Proverbs* (Oxford: Clarendon Press, 1916), p. 20.

11. Edwin W. Smith, "Folktales," *Journal of the Royal African Society*, 39 (January 1940), 68–69.

12. P. A. Talbot, *The Peoples of Southern Nigeria*, 3 (London: Humphrey Milford, 1926), 960. Kannenberg, quoted in Baumann, p. 207.

13. John Roscoe, *The Baganda* (London: Macmillan, 1911), p. 318. Baumann, pp. 198, 194–95.

14. Leo Frobenius, *Kulturgeschichte Afrikas* (Zurich: Phaidon, 1933), p. 279. A. Le Herisse, *L'ancien royaume du Dahomey* (Paris, 1911), p. 261. Frobenius, *Atlantis*, 5, p. 72.

15. Alice Werner, *Myths and Legends of the Bantu* (London: Harrap, 1933), considers African myths relating to the fall, the serpent, immortality, and the Tower of Babel. P. A. Talbot, *In the Shadow of the Bush* (London: Heinemann, 1912).

16. Frobenius, *Atlantis*, 9, p. 217.

17. Karasek-Eichhorn, quoted in Baumann, p. 367. *Anthropophyteia*, Hamberger, Pechuel-Losche, quoted in Baumann, p. 369.

18. I. Keller, "Knowledge and Theories of Astronomy on the Part of the Isubu Natives of the Western Slopes of the Cameroon Mountains in German West Africa," *Journal of the African Society*, 3 (October 1903), 61. Leonard J. Beecher, "The Stories of the Kikuyu," *Africa II*, 1 (1938), 80–87.

19. Blaise Cendrars, *L'anthologie nègre*, trans. Margery Bianco, *The African Sage* (New York: Payson & Clarke, 1927), p. 44.

20. Laurens van der Post, "Race Prejudice as Self-Rejection," p. 18, pamphlet. Wole Soyinka, "A Place for West African Literature," BBC broadcast, *Calling West Africa*, February 16, 1956. Castro Soremenho, *A maravilhosa viagem dos exploradores portugueses* (Lisbon, 1956), p. 359, quoted and trans. Gerald M. Moser, "African Literature in the Portuguese Language," p. 288.

21. P. A. Capus, "Contes, chants et proverbes des Basumbwa dans l'Afrique Orientale," *Zeitschrift für afrikanische und oceanische Sprachen,* 3 (1897), 363–64.

22. W. Bodenstein and O. F. Raum, "A Present Day Zulu Philosopher," *Africa*, 30 (April 1960), 170, 169. They add that Laduma Madela possessed a manuscript in Zulu describing the creation of the world and man. Leo Frobenius, *Erythrea* (Berlin and Zurich: Atlantis-Verlag, 1932), pp. 240–41. Robert Graves, *The Greek Myths*, 1 (Harmondsworth: Penguin, 1955), 6.

23. Leach, p. 778.

24. Donald St. John-Parsons, *Legends of Northern Ghana* (London: Longmans, 1958), pp. 1–4.

25. A. W. Cardinall, *Tales Told in Togoland* (London: Oxford University Press, 1931), pp. 100–2. Joseph E. Sidahome, *Stories of the Benin Empire* (London: Oxford University Press, 1931), pp. 100–2.

26. W. H. Laughton, "A Meru Text," *Man*, 64 (January–February 1964), 17–18. The Kikuyu version is almost the same except that a monster, Hitimondo, has to be satisfied before allowing a strong young man to hit him. See "Kikuyu Tales," *African Studies*, 3 (March 1952), 1–3.

27. Roscoe, pp. 460–85. Joseph Campbell, *The Hero with a Thousand Faces* (New York: Pantheon Books, 1949), p. 30.

28. Kathleen Arnott, *African Myths and Legends* (London: Oxford University Press, 1962), pp. 78–84.

29. Jablow, pp. 43–45.

30. *Bantu Studies*, 12 (1938), 279–81.

31. Frobenius, *Kulturgeschichte Afrikas*, pp. 297–306.

32. Henry Callaway, *Nursery Tales Traditions and Histories of the Zulus* (Springvale, Natal: J. A. Blair), p. 331. Arnott, pp. 68–73. For a similar Duala legend, see Wilhelm Lederbogen and M. Huber, "Duala Fables," *Journal of the African Society,* 4 (October 1904), 61–62. For an Acholi (Uganda) tale, see Peter Oryem and M. J. Wright, "Lucoro and Min-kwet: An Acholi Folktale," *Uganda Journal,* 24 (March 1960), 120–22. See also René Basset, *Contes populaires d'Afrique* (Paris, 1903), p. 297.

33. G. Reginald Peel, "The Voice of Africa: Inkosa zana Kararungi," *Africa*, 3 (January 1940), 104–6. Lederbogen and Huber, pp. 63–64.

34. Jack Berry, *Spoken Art in West Africa* (London: Oxford University Press,

1962), p. 7. Adeboye Babalola, "Yoruba Folktales," *West African Review*, 33 (July 1962), 49.

35. R. S. Rattray, *Akan-Ashanti Folktales* (Oxford: Clarendon Press, 1930), pp. 55, 59. See also W. H. Barker and C. Sinclair, eds., *West African Folk Tales* (London: Sheldon Press, 1917), pp. 29–31. F. M. Cronise and H. W. Ward, *Cunnie Rabbit, Mr. Spider and the Other Beef: West African Folk Tales* (London: Swan, Sonnenschein, 1903), introduction, p. 12.

36. Rattray, *Akan*, p. xii. Cardinall. He adds that "the Ashanti or Twi-speakers always insist on the fact that once Anansi was a man" (p. 150).

37. Fleischer and Wilkie, pp. 360–61. Radin and Sweeney, pp. 28–32.

38. Cronise and Ward, p. 40. Peter Abrahams, *Jamaica* (London: Her Majesty's Stationary Office, 1957), p. 132.

39. Arnott, pp. 16–22, and Barker and Sinclair, pp. 69–72, 89–94.

40. Barker and Sinclair, pp. 97–101.

41. "Tales," *Radio-T.V. Times*, 2 (Lagos), 9. For another version see John Parkinson, "Yoruba Folklore," *Journal of the African Society*, 8 (January 1909), 180–81, 177–79. J. C. Cotton, "Calabar Stories," *Journal of the African Society*, 3 (January 1906), 194. Hugh Vernon-Jackson, *More West African Folk Takes*, 2 (London: University of London Press, 1963), 38–40. Kunle Akinsemoyin, *Twilight and the Tortoise* (Lagos: A.U.P., 1963).

42. Babalola, "Yoruba Folk Tales," p. 49.

43. Abayomi Fuja, *Fourteen Hundred Cowries* (London: Oxford University Press, 1962), p. 25. Parkinson, pp. 182–84. Fuja, pp. 40–43. Melville and Frances Herskovits, *Dahomeyan Narrative* (Evanston, Ill.: Northwestern University Press, 1958), pp. 191–93.

44. Henry Cobham, "Animal Stories from Calabar," *Journal of the African Society*, 4 (April 1905), 307–8. Dorothea Bleek, "Bushman Folklore," *Africa*, 2 (July 1929), 302–13.

45. Phyllis Savory, *Matabele Fireside Tales* (London: Bailey Bros. & Swinfen, 1962), pp. 64–68. Edward Steere, *Swahili Tales* (London: S.P.C.K., 1869), pp. 369–75. W. R. E. Clarke, *Folk Tales of Sierra Leone* (London: Macmillan, 1963), pp. 20–23.

46. "A Hare Story in African Folklore," *Journal of the African Society*, 4 (October 1904), 139–41.

47. L. S. Senghor and Abdoulaye Sadji, *La belle histoire de Leuk-le-Lièvre*, ed. J. M. Winch (London: Harrap, 1965), p. 8. Charles Monteil, *Soudain français: Contes sudanais* (Paris, 1905), p. 15. C. M. Doke, "Lamba Folklore," *Bantu Studies*, 1 (October 1922), 139. M. J. Wright, *Fifteen Lango Tales* (London: Longmans, 1958), p. 27. A similar tale of famine and how Rabbit refuses to kill his mother is recorded among the Kaguru of East Africa by Thomas Beidelmann, "Ọtyena and Rabbit: A Kaguru Representation of Matrilineal Relations," *Africa*, 30 (January 1961), 61–74. In the Ugandan version of the tale, Leopard finds out that Hare has not killed his mother and does it. In revenge Hare wraps a stone in fat and puts it in Leopard's mouth. When Leopard dies Hare takes all his cattle.

48. Harold Courlander, *The King's Drum and Other Stories* (London: Hart Davis, 1963), pp. 58–60. Heli Chatelain, *Folk Tales of Angola* (Boston and New York, 1894), p. 27.

49. Doke, "Lamba Folklore," p. 139. G. P. Lestrade, ed., *Some Venda Folk Tales* (Capetown: University of Capetown, 1942), pp. 34–36.

50. A. C. Jordan, "Towards an African Literature, I," *Africa South*, 1 (July–September 1957), 95. M. I. Ogumefun, *Yoruba Legends* (London: Sheldon Press, 1929), no. 29, p. 23. Kolawole Balogun, *The Crowning of the Elephant* (privately printed, n.d.), p. 29. Efua Morgue (now Sutherland), "Some Fanti Folk Tales," BBC broadcast, *Calling West Africa*, January 25, 1950. Lederbogen and Huber, pp. 71–74. Werner, *The Natives of British Central Africa*, p. 240.

51. Phebean Itayemi and P. Gurrey, *Folk Tales and Fables* (Harmondsworth: Penguin, 1953), p. 6.

52. Canon Callaway, *Nursery Tales and Traditions of the Zulus* (London: Trench, Trubner & Co., 1868), p. 16. C. M. Doke, "Lamba Folktales Annotated," *Bantu Studies*, 13 (1939), 82–84.

53. Hugh Vernon-Jackson, *West African Folk Tales*, 1 (London: University of London Press, 1958), 9–14. Lestrade, ed., *Some Venda Folk Tales*, pp. 22–24, 20.

54. Basset, p. xi.

55. A. C. Jordan, "Towards an African Literature, III," *Africa South*, 2 (January–March 1958), 101.

56. C. L. S. Nyembezi, *Zulu Proverbs* (Johannesburg: Witwatersrand University Press, 1963), pp. 5–6. George Herzog and Charles G. Blooah, *Jabo Proverbs from Nigeria* (London: Oxford University Press, 1936).

57. W. E. Abraham disagrees, pointing out in *The Mind of Africa*, p. 94, that the Akans did not consider proverbs among their literary pieces. O. F. Raum, *Chaga Childhood* (London: Oxford University Press, 1940), p. 217.

58. Rattray, *Ashanti Proverbs*, no. 589, p. 152. James Boyd Christensen, "The Role of Proverbs in Fante Culture," *Africa*, 28 (July 1958), 233.

59. Roscoe, p. 488. Fleischer and Wilkie, p. 364.

60. A. C. Hollis, "Taveta Sayings and Proverbs," *Journal of the African Society*, 9 (April 1910), 257.

61. Edward Sapir, "Some Gweabo Proverbs," *Africa II*, 2 (April 1929), 184. Also see T. Cullen Young, "Some Proverbs of the Tumbuka-Nkamanga Peoples of the Northern Province of Nyasaland," *Africa*, 4 (July 1931), 350. Nketia, "Akan Poetry," p. 102.

62. S. W. Köelle, *African Native Literature* (London: Church Missionary House, 1854), p. 1. G. Barra, *1,000 Kikuyu Proverbs* (London: Macmillan, 1960), p. 78. Werner, *The Natives of British Central Africa*, p. 213. Gerhard Lindblom, *Kamba Folklore: Riddles, Proverbs and Songs* (Uppsala: Archives d'Etudes Orientales 20:3, no. 28, 1934), p. 34. T. R. E. Cox, "Lango Proverbs," *Uganda Journal*, 10 (September 1946), 121.

63. Howard S. Olson, "Rimi Proverbs," *Tanganyika Notes and Records*, no. 62 (March 1964), no. 12, p. 74. A. C. Hollis, "Nyika Proverbs," *Journal of the African Society*, 16 (October 1915), 66. M. M. Green, "Sayings of the Okoko Society of the Igbo-Speaking People," *Bulletin of the School of Oriental and African Studies*, 21 (1958), 167. "Proverbs," *ibid.*, no. 461, p. 163. C. M. Doke, "Lamba Literature," *Africa*, 102 (July 1934), 361.

64. Edward Sapir and Charles G. Blooah, "Some Gweabo Proverbs," *Africa*, 2 (April 1929), 183. Cox, p. 122. Barra, Proverb no. 656, p. 75.

65. Köelle, *African Native Literature*, p. 4. Justin Itotia and J. W. C. Dougall, "Kikuyu Proverbs," *Africa*, 1 (October 1938), 489.

66. Nyembezi, *Zulu Proverbs*, pp. 24–32, 14–15. Robert R. Marett, "Introduction to the Proverbs of Africa," *Racial Proverbs*, ed. Selwyn Gurney Champion (New York: Macmillan, 1950), p. xxxv.

67. Berry, p. 11. C. M. Doke, "Bantu Wisdom and Lore," *African Studies*, 16 (1947), 117, says that "though interrogative in intent riddles are never so in form in Bantu." Also see Lindblom, p. 9.

68. Herskovits and Herskovits, *Dahomeyan Narrative*, p. 55. D. W. Arnott, "Proverbial Lore and Word-Play of the Fulani," *Africa*, 18 (October 1957), 380. William R. Bascom, "Literary Style in Yoruba Riddles," *Journal of American Folklore*, 62 (January–March 1949), 4. Berry, pp. 11–12. John Greenaway, *Literature among the Primitives* (Hatboro: Folklore Associates, 1964), p. 67.

69. John Blacking, "The Social Value of Venda Riddles," *African Studies*, 20 (1961), 3. Frederick Johnson, "Kaniramba Folk Tales," *Bantu Studies*, 5 (1931), 355. P. D. Cole-Beuchat, "Notes on Some Folklore Forms in Tsonga and Ronga,"

African Studies, 17 (1958), 189. W. E. Taylor, quoted in A. C. Hollis, "Nyika Enigmas," *Journal of the African Society*, 16 (October 1916).
70. Jordan, "Towards an African Literature, III," pp. 102, 103. Blacking, p. 10. Godfrey Nakene, "Tlokwa Riddles," *African Studies*, 2 (September 1943), 128. Edwin W. Smith and Andrew Murray Dale, *The Ila Speaking Peoples of Northern Rhodesia*, 2 (London: Macmillan, 1920), 333. E. E. Evans-Pritchard, "Three Zande Texts," *Man*, 62 (October 1962), 149. T. O. Beidelmann, "Some Kaguru Riddles," *Man*, 63 (October 1963), 158.
71. Donald C. Simmons, "Efik Riddles," *Nigerian Field*, 21 (October 1956), 21. J. O. Oyelese, "English and Yoruba Riddles," BBC broadcast, *Calling West Africa*, February 14, 1951. Lindblom, p. 12. Ernest Gray, "Some Riddles of the Nyansa People," *Bantu Studies*, 12 (1939), 259. T. Schapera, "Kxatlla Riddles and Their Significance," *Bantu Studies*, 6 (1932), 218. Doke, "Lamba Literature," p. 363.
72. Doke, "Lamba Literature," p. 362.
73. Bascom, pp. 1–16. C. Endelmann, "Rätsel des Sotho," *Zeitschrift für Eingeborene-Sprachen*, 18 (1927–28), 55–74. Blacking, p. 6.

Chapter 4. Sung or Chanted Art

1. Chadwick and Chadwick, 3, p. 576. Shabaan Robert, "Swahili Poetry," *Swahili Poetry*, ed. Harries, is quoted as saying, "Swahili poems and epics are composed to be sung" (p. 281). Frobenius, *Kulturgeschichte Afrikas*, pp. 248–49. Chadwick and Chadwick, p. 501. A. C. Jordan, "Towards an African Literature, II," *Africa South*, 2 (October–December 1957), 98.
2. C. M. Bowra, *Primitive Song* (London: Weidenfeld and Nicolson, 1960), p. 281.
3. J. Torrend, *Specimens of Bantu Folklore from Northern Rhodesia* (London: Kegan Paul, 1921), pp. 24–26.
4. Lestrade, ed., *Some Venda Folk Tales*, p. 13.
5. Miriam Koshland, "Six Chants from the Congo," *Black Orpheus*, no. 2 (January 1958), 19.
6. M. M. Green, "The Unwritten Literature of the Igbo-Speaking People of South Eastern Nigeria," *Bulletin of the School of Oriental and African Studies*, 12 (1947–48), 842.
7. Andrew Macdonald, "Literature in Sierra Leone," BBC broadcast, *Calling West Africa*, February 2, 1949.
8. Dora Earthy, "The Vandan of Sofala," *Africa*, 4 (1931), 229.
9. J. H. Kwabena Nketia, "Akan Poetry," *Black Orpheus*, no. 3 (May 1958), 6.
10. Jordan, "Towards an African Literature, II," p. 101.
11. J. R. Patterson, *Kanuri Songs* (Kaduna, 1925), p. 17.
12. Patterson, p. 27.
13. Gbadamosi and Beier, p. 14.
14. Nketia, "Akan Poetry," pp. 20–21.
15. Apolo Kagwa, *The Customs of the Baganda* (first published in 1917 in Luganda), trans. Ernest B. Kalimbala (New York: Columbia University Press, 1934), p. 141.
16. Chief Olunlade, *Ede: A Short History* (Ibadan: Ministry of Education, 1961), p. 49.
17. H. F. Morris, *The Heroic Recitations of the Bahima of Ankole* (Oxford: Clarendon Press, 1964), p. 14.
18. *Ibid.*, p. 42.
19. Mungo Park, *Travels in the Interior of Africa* (London, 1799), pp. 197–98.
20. F. Laydevant, "Religious or Sacred Plants of Basutoland," *Bantu Studies*, 6 (1932), 69.

21. Lekgothoahe, "Praises of Animals in Northern Sotho," *Bantu Studies*, 12 (1938), 209, 197. E. L. Segoete, *Raphepheng*, quoted and trans. G. H. Franz, "The Literature of Lesotho," *Bantu Studies*, 4 (1930), 155.
22. Harries, pp. 183–84.
23. Morris, p. 14.
24. *Ibid.*, p. 106.
25. D. F. Merwe, "Hurutsche Poems," *Bantu Studies*, 15 (1941), 323.
26. Alexis Kagamé, *Introduction aux grands genres lyriques de l'ancien Rwanda* (Butare: Editions Universitaires du Kwanda, 1964), pp. 196–97.
27. *Ibid.*, p. 45.
28. B. W. Vilakazi, "The Conception and Development of Poetry in Zulu," *Bantu Studies*, 12 (1938), 105. C. L. S. Nyembezi, "The Historical Background of the *Izi6ongo* of the Zulu Military Age," *African Studies*, 7 (June–September 1948), 110–25. Vilakazi, "Poetry in Zulu," p. 105.
29. P. A. W. Cook, "History and *Izi6ongo* of the Swazi Chiefs," *Bantu Studies*, 5 (1931), 187.
30. Translated by Hahn and submitted in typescript by Uys Krige.
31. F. B. Welbourn, "The Idea of a High God in Three East African Societies," paper submitted to a conference on the High God in Africa, University of Ife, Ibadan, December 14–18, 1964, p. 9.
32. Germaine Dieterlen, ed., *Textes sacrés d'Afrique noire* (Paris: Gallimard, 1965), p. 18.
33. R. S. Rattray, *Religion and Art in Ashanti* (London: Oxford University Press, 1927), p. 135.
34. Idowu, pp. 8, 9, 6. Ulli Beier, *A Year of Festivals in One Yoruba Town* (Lagos: Nigeria Magazine Publication, 1959), p. 56.
35. Gbadamosi and Beier, p. 26.
36. *Ibid.*, p. 27.
37. *Ibid.*, p. 26.
38. Nketia, *Funeral Dirges*, p. 131. See also R. F. Storch, "Writing in Ghana," *Universitas*, 2 (March 1957).
39. F. T. Wilson and R. W. Felkin, *Uganda and the Egyptian Sundan*, 2 vols., 1 (London, 1882), 214.
40. Dennis Osadebay, "West African Voices," *African Affairs*, 48 (January 1949), 153.
41. Idowu, p. 200.
42. Enoch Azu, *Adangwe Historical and Proverbial Songs* (Accra: Government Printer, 1929), p. 130.
43. Margaret Mead, "Songs of the Ngoni People," *Bantu Studies*, 11 (1937), 16.
44. Rattray, *Religion and Art*, p. 131.
45. Uys Krige, translation in typescript.
46. Nketia, "Akan Poetry," p. 18.
47. Vilakazi, "Poetry in Zulu," p. 120.
48. Trans. Uys Krige, *African Poetry*, ed. O. R. Dathorne, p. 8.
49. Jordan, "Towards an African Literature, II," p. 99.
50. E. Dora Earthy, "A Chopi Love Song, a Story in Ki-Lenge," *Africa*, 4 (October 1931), 475–76.
51. Gbadamosi and Beier, p. 51.
52. J. L. Döhne, *A Zulu-Kaffir Dictionary* (Capetown: privately printed, 1857), p. ix. The Chadwicks, p. 576, cite Roscoe to show that there was a definite meter but add that Livingstone mentions a Botoka song in which each line consisted of five syllables. See David Livingstone, *Narrative of an Expedition to the Zambesi and Its Tributaries* (London, 1865), p. 236.
53. Gbadamosi and Beier, p. 8.
54. Vilakazi, "Poetry in Zulu," p. 112.

55. Adeboye Babalola, "The Characteristic Features of Outer Forms of Yoruba Ijala Chants," *Odu*, 2 (July 1964), 34.

56. Green, "The Unwritten Literature of the Igbo-Speaking People of South Eastern Nigeria," p. 843. R. P. Bernard Zuure, "Poésies chez les Barundi," *Africa*, 5 (July 1932), 345. Werner, *The Natives of British Central Africa*, p. 220. E. L. Lasebikan, "Yoruba Poetry," *African Affairs*, 48 (April 1949), 154.

57. G. Lestrade, "Traditional Literature," *The Bantu-Speaking Tribes of South Africa*, ed. I. Schepera (London: Kegan Paul, 1937), pp. 302–13. A. M. Jones, "African Rhythm," *Africa*, 24 (January 1954), 26.

58. For a discussion of language in oral poetry see S. Pfeffer, "Prose and Poetry on the Fiel'be," *Africa*, 12 (July 1939), 285–307, and F. Laydevant, "La poésie chez les Basuto," *Africa*, 3 (October 1930), 534.

59. "Literature in Sierra Leone," BBC broadcast, *Calling West Africa*, February 2, 1949.

Chapter 5. African Literature in Latin

1. Quoted in Cedric Dover, "*The Black Knight*," *Phylon*, 15 (1943), 49. See also Norbert Lochner, "Ein gelerhter aus Ghana in Deutschland des 18th," *Überseerundschau*, no. 1 (Hamburg, 1958).

2. J. W. Schulte Nordholt, *Het Volk dat in duisternis wandelt* (Arnhem, 1956), p. 17. See also F. L. Bartels, "Jacobus Eliza Johannes Capitein 1717–1747," *Transactions of the Historical Society of Ghana*, 4 (1959), 3–13.

3. For most of the biographical information I am indebted to Valaurez B. Spratlin, *Juan Latino: Slave and Humanist* (New York: Spinner Press, 1938). But Spratlin is not accurate with regard to Latino's own work, and intentionally mistranslates when he wishes to support a point. Therefore for the Latin I have gone to Latino's original text and done my own translations. Ambrosio de Salazar, *Grammatica francesca y castellana en dialogos* (Rouen, 1615), p. 482, cited by Spratlin. See also Henri Grégoire, *De la littérature des nègres* (Paris, 1808), p. 139. Antonio Marin Ocete, *El negro Juan Latino* (Granada: Libreria Guevara, 1925). Lope de Vega, quoted by Spratlin, p. 16.

4. Page numbers given in the text will hereafter refer to the page on which the passage is found in the work under discussion.

5. Ocete, p. 44.

6. Translated in Spratlin, pp. 70–202.

7. Edward Long, *A History of Jamaica* (London: printed for T. Lowndes, 1774), p. 478.

8. Long gives the biographical note on Williams as well as the example of his poetry and a comment on it (pp. 475–85). I have not been able to trace any other odes.

9. T. H. Green and T. H. Grose, eds., *David Hume: Philosophical Works*, 3 (London: Longmans, 1875), 252n. Long, pp. 480–83. Long translated the ode into his own version and then attempted to show that Williams's verse was derivative and that his classical allusions were wrong. But he did add: "To consider the merits of this specimen impartially we must endeavour to forget in the first place that the writer was a Negroe; for if we regard it as an extraordinary production, merely because it came from a Negroe, we admit at once the inequality of genius which has been before supposed and admire it only as a rare phenomenon" (p. 484). Grégoire, p. 184.

10. My translation. The Latin version is in Long, pp. 479–81. Long translated the first four lines in this way:

> At length revolving fates th' expected year
> Advance, and joy the live-long day shall cheer,

Beneath the fost'ring law's auspicious dawn
New harvests rise to glad the enliven'd lawn.

This had little to do with Williams's original, which reads:

Denique venturum fatis volventibus annum
Cuncta per extensum laeta videnta diem
Excussis adsunt curis, sub imagine clara
Felices populi, terraque lege virens.

Chapter 6. Three Eighteenth-Century African Writers in English

1. Wylie Sypher, *Guinea's Captive Kings: British Anti-Slavery Literature of the Eighteenth Century* (Chapel Hill: University of North Carolina Press, 1942), pp. 2–3.

2. Kenneth Little, *Negroes in Britain: A Study of Racial Relations in English Society* (London: Kegan Paul, 1947), p. 167. Sypher adds that by 1770 there were 14,000 Blacks in England. See Sypher, p. 2. N. V. McCullough, *The Negro in English Literature* (Ilfracombe: Stockwell, 1962), p. 52.

3. Henry Angelo, *Angelo's Pic Nic; or, Table Talk* (London: John Ebers, 1834), p. 61. For a further account see Henry Angelo, *Reminiscences of Henry Angelo* (London: Henry Bolburn, 1828), pp. 447–53. For more details of Francis Barber see James Boswell, *The Life of Samuel Johnson*, 1 (London: Swan, Sonnenschein, 1888 ed.), 145, 388.

4. I omit Phillis Wheatley. She is considered "American," although her *Poems on Various Subjects, Religious and Moral* (London: printed for A. Bell, 1773) had a British readership. Vernon Loggins, *The Negro Author: His Development in America to 1900* (New York: Kennikat Press, 1931), p. 6.

5. Ignatius Sancho, *Letters of the Late Ignatius Sancho, an African*. The third edition (1784) is used in this work. The 1784 edition is in one volume.

6. There is some wrong dating in the letters. A letter to Sterne is dated July 1776 in the third edition of Sancho's *Letters*, but in the fifth edition the date given is July 27, 1766. There are some disparities that cannot be explained; in a letter dated August 28, 1776, he writes that his son "William grows and tries his feet briskly" but a year later, in a letter dated August 14, 1777, "Billy has suffered much in getting his teeth . . . he took resolution at last and walked." Billy was born on October 20, 1775.

In the published letters four of the letters to the press are not numbered but printed. One dated August 29, 1780, to the *General Advertiser* and signed "Africanus" is, however, numbered. There were two other letters to the *General Advertiser* dated February 9, 1774, and March 12, 1780. There was one to the *Morning Post* in 1778 which was printed in Sancho's *Letters* but not published by the newspaper. Also there was one dated May 13, 1778, to the *Public Advertiser* asking for help for a poor actor named de Groote.

7. Quite an argument arose over Sancho's portrait, reproduced in front of his *Letters*. It was painted by Gainsborough and engraved by Bartalozzi. A Mr. Wigan wrote in *Notes and Queries*, June 8, 1889, that "he is certainly a very ordinary looking individual and I should like to hear what there was about him that his lineaments should be handed down, by artists of such eminence." A month later a Mr. John Pickford was even more outspoken. He described the portrait as that of "a hideously ugly black man apparently dressed in livery." *Notes and Queries*, July 13, 1889. Sancho was so well known that he was caricatured in an anonymous play, *Memoirs and Opinions of Mr. Blenfield* (1790).

8. Thomas Jefferson, *Notes on the State of Virginia* (New York, 1782), p. 258.

9. *Monthly Review*, 69, p. 493.

10. Jefferson, p. 257.

11. Little, p. 199. Supporting information on Sancho is to be found in the *Dic-*

tionary of National Biography. He himself mentions his poetry in his letters but I have not been able to trace any published examples of his verse.

12. Compare Equiano's "it would be tedious and uninteresting to relate all the incidents which befell me during this journey" (p. 61).

13. Cugoano refers to *The Historical Account of Guinea,* pp. 96–103; he does not state the author or the extent of his indebtedness.

14. Grégoire praised Cugoano for using the Bible to argue against slavery instead of reason, which would have been more fashionable in his day. See Grégoire, p. 166.

15. *Monthly Review,* 49 (July 1773), 63.

16. Janheinz Jahn, *Die neoafrikanische Literatur,* pp. 32–33.

17. This is probably Nsukka in eastern Nigeria.

18. J. W. Bready, *England before and after Wesley: The Evangelical Revival and Social Reform* (London: Hodder and Stoughton, 1938), p. 229.

Chapter 7. Written Indigenous Literatures

1. These figures have been compiled from various bibliographies and verified in collaboration with Janheinz Jahn. For summaries of historical and geographical facts relating to the continent, see Violaine Junod, *The Handbook of Africa* (New York: New York University Press, 1963), and Colin Legum, *Africa: A Handbook to the Continent* (London: Blond, 1961).

2. A. M. Chirgwin, "Christian Literature in Africa," *Africa,* 5 (July 1932), 327. C. M. Doke also shows in "Lamba Literature" that the first book translated was the Book of Jonah and this was followed by *Pilgrim's Progress.*

3. R. H. W. Shepherd, *Lovedale and Literature for the Bantu* (Lovedale: Lovedale Press, 1945), p. 3. John A. Ramsaran, *New Approaches to African Literature,* p. 9.

4. Davidson Nicol, *Africa: A Subjective View,* pp. 28, 70.

5. See F. H. Hilliard, *A Short History of Education in British West Africa* (London: Nelson, 1957), pp. 1–7. See Roland Oliver and J. O. Fage, *A Short History of Africa* (Harmondsworth: Penguin, 1962), pp. 138–39.

6. L. J. Lewis, *Society, Schools and Progress in Nigeria* (Oxford: Pergamon Press, 1965), p. 25. Nnamdi Azikiwe, "Dare to Defend the Weak," a message to the first annual assembly of AMSAC. Reprinted in *AMSAC Newsletter,* 8 (1966), 2. Isaac B. Thomas, *The Autobiography of Segilola—The Lady with the Delicate Eye Balls* (Lagos: C.M.S. Bookshops, 1930). This has been privately translated by Razak Solaja. All references are to the page numbers of the original Yoruba.

7. Ulli Beier, "Fagunwa: A Yoruba Novelist," *Black Orpheus,* no. 17 (June 1965), 54.

8. For a fuller account see A. Olubummo, "D. O. Fagunwa: A Yoruba Novelist," *Odu,* no. 9 (September 1963), 26–27. Also Wole Soyinka gives a vivid translation of the hunter's contest with Agbako in *Black Orpheus,* no. 15 (August 1964), 5–7. In addition Soyinka has translated one novel as *The Forest of a Thousand Daemons* (London: Nelson, 1968).

9. Quoted in Beier, "Fagunwa," p. 55. Also see another translation by W. H. Whiteley, *A Selection of African Prose,* 2, p. 79.

10. Femi Fagunwa, "Fagunwa [Son] writes about Fagunwa [deceased father]," *Sunday Express* (Lagos), January 10, 1965, p. 7.

11. Adeboye Babalola, "Some Yoruba Poems," BBC broadcast, *Calling West Africa,* August 2, 1950.

12. Broadcast on BBC.

13. "Village Characters: The Trouble Lover," *An Anthology of West African Verse,* ed. Olumbe Bassir (Ibadan: Ibadan University Press, 1957), p. 8. For more poems see Adeboye Babalola, "Yoruba Poetry," *Présence africaine,* 18 (1963), 184–90.

14. "Village Characters: Beauty," *Anthology*, ed. Bassir, p. 3.

15. "Returning Home from Work," broadcast on BBC.

16. Introduction to BBC broadcast.

17. See Yusuf Kamal, *Monumenta cartographica Africae et Aegypti*, 3 (Leiden: privately printed by E. J. Brill, 1926–51), fasc. 3, p. 915. H. R. Palmer, *Sudanese Memoirs* 31 (Lagos: Government Printer, 1928), 104–5. A. D. H. Bivar and M. Hiskett, "The Arabic Literature of Nigeria to 1804: A Provisional Account," *Bulletin of the School of Oriental and African Studies*, 25 (1962).

18. Collected and translated by an informant. Mention is made of Hausa books in Rupert East, "Books for Northern Nigeria," *Oversea Education*, 7 (July 1936), 200–2.

19. Mallam Hassan and Mallam Tukur, "Hausa Poetry," BBC broadcast, *Calling West Africa*, April 6, 1949.

20. These poems have appeared in *Gaskiya* (Zaria, northern Nigeria), which began in 1940 as *Gaskiya ta fi kwaba*. The poems are not outstanding but are mentioned only to demonstrate a trend. Collected and translated by an informant.

21. An account of the Kano Chronicle appears in an article by Richmond Palmer in *Journal of Royal Anthropological Society of Great Britain and Ireland*, 38 (1908), 58. For the translation of the Abuja Chronicle see Alhaji Hassan and Shuaibu Naibi, *A Chronicle of Abuja* (Lagos: African Universities Press, 1962).

22. Mary Smith, trans., *Babo of Karo* (London: Faber, 1954).

23. R. M. East, "A First Essay in Imaginative African Literature," *Africa*, 9 (July 1936), 355.

24. *Ibid.*, p. 356.

25. *Ibid.*

26. Zaria: Literature Bureau, 1940. 2 vols.

27. Zaria: Gaskiya Corporation, 1952.

28. *Iliya, dam-mai-karfi* (Zaria: Gaskiya Corporation, 1951). *Shaihu Umar* (Zaria: Gaskiya Corporation).

29. James Frederik Schon and Samuel Crowther, *Journals of the Rev. James Frederik Schon and Mr. Samuel Crowther* (London: Hatchard; Nisbet: Seeleys, 1842).

30. London: Atlantis Press, 1935; reprinted London: Longmans, 1951.

31. Translated by an informant.

32. London: Longmans, 1952.

33. Third ed. (London: Longmans, 1950).

34. *Akiga's Story* (London: Oxford University Press, 1939). Review in *Africa*, 13 (1940), 89.

35. F. L. Bartels, *The Roots of Ghana Methodism* (London: Cambridge University Press, 1965), pp. 3, 72. See also Henry Swanzy, ed., *Voices of Ghana* (Accra: Ministry of Information and Broadcasting, 1958), p. 11. *Bere Adu!* (Akropong: B. M. Press).

36. London: Sheldon Press, 1932.

37. Ephraim Amu, "Yen aka asase ni" (This Is Our Land), quoted in Swanzy, p. 12.

38. H. E. Addae-Obeng, *Okunini Aggrey* (Aggrey, the Important Person) (Edinburgh: Nelson, 1949).

39. Cape Coast: Methodist Book Depot, 1952.

40. London: Longmans, 1939. The translation used is by M. B. Walton, "Fanti Literature," BBC broadcast, *Calling West Africa*, March 23, 1949.

41. Walton, "Fanti Literature."

42. "Dwen, Kwe, Kan!!!" (Think and Look Ahead!), trans. M. B. Walton.

43. Joseph Ghartey, "Poems in Fanti and English," BBC broadcast, *Calling West Africa*, October 4, 1950, read (and translated?) by Efua Sutherland. Quotations are from this reading.

44. G. Adali-Mortty, "Ewe Poetry," ⊃*kyeame I* (Accra: Ghana Society of Writers, 1960), p. 51.

45. Israel Kofu Hoh, "Dzifo le fie" (The Sky), *Voices of Ghana*, p. 100.

46. "Xexeeame" (The World), *ibid.*, p. 104.

47. "Ozisolefie." *ibid.*, p. 101.

48. Compiled from various bibliographies and verified in collaboration with Jan-heinz Jahn. It should be added that as early as 1624 Jesuit priests translated Mario Jorge's *Doctrina Christa* (Lisbon, 1602). James Barbot wrote in 1688 that "the Jesuits have a college where they daily teach and instruct the Blacks in the Christian faith, in an easy and winning method. There are also schools where youth are brought up and taught Latin and Portuguese." "A Description of Lower Ethiopia," *A Collection of Voyages and Travels*, 5 (London: A. J. Churchill, 1732), 482.

49. For a reference to this and information on Kayonga, see Alexis Kagamé, "Les poétes du Ruanda et la famine," *Jeune Afrique*, no. 9, pp. 5–13.

50. *Umulirimbyi wa nyili-ibiremwa*, 2 vols. (Vol. 1, Astrida, Rwanda, 1952; vol. 2, Kabgayi, Rwanda, 1953). *La divine pastorale*, 2 vols. (Brussels: Editions du Marais, 1952, 1955), p. 19. All quotations are from the French translation. Review in *Zaïre: Revue congolaise* (November 1952), p. 986.

51. A good account of the missionaries in Malawi is found in Frank Debenham, *Nyasaland* (London: Her Majesty's Stationary Office, 1955), pp. 130–44. T. Cullen Young, "The Native Newspaper," *Africa*, 1 (January 1938), 63–72.

52. Information supplied by S. A. Paliani, the author.

53. Trans. T. Cullen Young (London: Lutterworth Press, 1949).

54. See *Nyasaland Journal* (Blantyre, Nyasaland), 14 (July 1961), 13–26.

55. *Zomfula mkazi wacimaso-maso* (London: Heinemann, with Northern Rhodesia and Nyasaland Publications Bureau, 1961). *Cibwana ndi ukwati* (Oxford: Blackwell, with N.R.N.P.B., 1962).

56. Information on books and translations of titles supplied by the former Northern Rhodesia Publications Bureau for Writers from Malawi and Zambi. For publication particulars, see Jahn's bibliography.

57. *Cekesoni aingila ubusoja* (Capetown: Oxford University Press and N.R.-N.P.B., 1950). *Bamusha ulweko* (London: University of London Press and N.R.N.P.B., 1962).

58. M. K. Chifwaila, *Ululumbwi iwa mulanda kukakaata* (A Simple Man Can Help Himself by Working Hard) (London: University of London Press and N.R.N.P.B., 1960). Albert Kacuka, *Ushifwayo umbi* (Another Ushifwayo) (Lusaka: Publications Bureau, n.d.).

59. Trans. M. Guthrie in "The Voice of Africa," *Africa*, 17 (1947), 275–76.

60. East African Literature Bureau, *Annual Report* (1955–56), introduction. John S. Mbiti, "Reclaiming the Vernacular Literature of the Akamba Tribe," *Second Congress of Negro Writers and Artists, Présence africaine*, special issue nos. 24–25 (February–May 1959), 245.

61. See Jahn, *A History of Neo-African Literature*, pp. 70–79.

62. Shaaban Robert, "Lecture on Poetry," *Swahili Poetry*, ed. Harries, p. 281.

63. *Ibid.*, p. 2.

64. Quoted in Alice Werner, "Native Poetry in East Africa," *Africa*, 1 (July 1928), 353.

65. Alice Werner, ed., *The Advice of Mwana Kupona upon Wifely Duty* (Medstead, Hampshire: Azonia Press, 1934), p. 57.

66. W. H. Whiteley, "The Changing Position of Swahili in East Africa," *Africa*, 26 (October 1956), 343. Edward Steere, *Swahili Tales* (London: Sheldon Press, 1929), pp. 452–69. Also see C. G. Buttner, *Anthologie ans der Swaheliliteratur* (Berlin, 1894).

67. London: Nelson, 1954.

68. *Ha munwa gw'ekituuro* (Nairobi: Longmans, 1963). Information and trans-

lation have been supplied by Timothy Bazzarabusa, the author. *Kalyaki na Marunga* (Nairobi: Longmans, 1964).

69. *Obu ndikura tindifa* (Kampala: privately published, 1965).

70. See Y. K. Musia, review in *Uganda Journal,* 14 (1950), 228. *Ekitabo* was translated in 1934 by Ernest Kalibala. See J. T. K. Ggomotoka, "History and Legend of the Rocks of Kakumiro and of Some Other Places in the Sagas of Mubende," *Uganda Journal,* 14 (1950), 85.

71. *Ennyimba ezimu* (Kampala: Eagle Press and East African Literature Bureau, 1953). "Kintu," trans. J. E. Laight, *Africa,* 18 (January 1948), 45–48.

72. See Richard West, *The White Tribes of Africa* (London: Cape, 1965), pp. 62–86, 87–104.

73. Jahn, *Die neoafrikanische Literatur,* pp. 81–129.

74. "The Work of the Shona Orthography Committee," *N.A.D.A.: The Southern Rhodesia Native Affairs Department Annual,* 32 (Salisbury, Rhodesia, 1955), 114–19.

75. Musa Shamuyarira, ed. (London: Longmans, 1959).

76. Quoted in "Modern Mashona Poetry," *Times Educational Supplement,* no. 2517, August 16, 1963, p. 189.

77. Information on Wilson Chivaura and others supplied by the former Southern Rhodesia Literary Bureau. George Fortune, "Shona Literature," paper read before meeting of the Mashonaland Branch of the Library Association of Central Africa; cyclostyled.

78. "Taima, taima," in "Modern Mashona Poetry." Fortune.

79. Fortune.

80. *Feso* (Capetown: Oxford University Press and S.R.L.B., 1956). Information on this and other works in Shona and Ndebele supplied by Southern Rhodesia Library Bureau and Solomon Mutswairo. *Murambiwa Goredema* (Capetown: Oxford University Press and S.R.L.B., 1959). *Nhoroondo dzukuwanana* (Capetown: Oxford University Press and S.R.L.B., 1958).

81. Capetown: Longmans and S.R.L.B., 1958.

82. *Uvusezindala* (Capetown: Longmans and S.R.L.B., 1958). *Qaphela ingane* (Pietermaritzburg: Shuter and Shooter, and S.R.L.B., 1963). *Amandebele ka-Mzilikazi* (Capetown: Longmans, 1956).

83. *A History of Neo-African Literature,* p. 100.

84. Reported by G. H. Franz, "Literature of Lesotho," *Bantu Studies,* 6 (1930), 159. This account has been of great use with regard to information on Sotho literature. *Har'a libatana le linyamat'sane* (Morija: Morija Sesuto Book Depot, 1913). Quoted in Franz, p. 160.

85. *Raphepheng* (Morija: Morija Sesuto Book Depot, 1915). Quoted in Franz, p. 153.

86. Morija: Morija Sesuto Book Depot, 1910.

87. *Ibid.,* 1912.

88. *A History of Neo-African Literature,* p. 102. J. J. Niemandt, *Bibliographie von die Bantoetale in die Unie von Süd-Afrika,* 2 (Pretoria and Johannesburg: Bantoe-Onderwysblad, 1959), *passim. Moeti oa bochabela* (Morija: Morija Sesuto Book Depot, 1907). Eng. trans. H. Ashton (London: S.P.C.K., 1934).

89. *Pitseng* (Morija: Morija Sesuto Book Depot, 1910). *Chaka* (Morija: Morija Sesuto Book Depot, 1925). Eng. trans. Hugh Frederick Dutton (London: Oxford University Press. 1931). See Peter Sulzer, *Chaka der Zulu* (Zurich: Manesse Verlag, 1953), p. 252.

90. For summary of plot of *Pitseng* and comment, see Franz, pp. 171–73.

91. Noni Jabavu, BBC broadcast, *Calling West Africa,* February 16, 1949.

92. Ezekiel Mphahlele, *The African Image* (London: Faber, 1962), pp. 169–74.

93. "A la tombe de Moshesh," Fr. trans. Georges Dieterlen from Bereng, *Litho-*

thokiso tsa Moshoeshoe le tse ding (Morija: Morija Sesuto Book Depot, 1931), in *Africa*, 17 (July 1947), 206.

94. "Boast of Mosopha," from a typescript by Uys Krige.

95. *Bukana ea tsomo tsa pitso ea linonyana le tseko ea Sefofa le Seritsa* (A Book of Narratives about the Meetings of the Birds and the Lawsuit between Sefofa and Seritsa) (Morija: Morija Sesuto Book Depot, 1928).

96. Franz, p. 176.

97. Tšhukudu (Bloemfontein: Nasionale Pers Boekhandel, 1941). For more recent publication, see G. L. Letele, "Some Recent Literary Publications in Languages of the Sotho Group," *African Studies*, 3 (December 1964), 161–71. *Tsiri* (Pretoria: Van Schaik, 1960). *Motangtang* (Pretoria: Van Schaik, 1960). *Moêlêlwa* (Bloemfontein: Nasionale Pers Boekhandel, 1940). *Molato* (Bloemfontein: Nasionale Pers Boekhandel, 1943). *Meokho ea thabo* (Johannesburg: Afrikaanse Pers Boekhandel, 1951). C. R. Moikangoa, *Sebogoli sa ntsoana tsatsi* (Soothsayer of the East) (Maseru Basotoland: Masenod Institute s.a., n.d.). *Lilahloane* (Masenod: Catholic Centre, 1951). James J. Machobane, *Maheng a matšo* (At the Black Caves) (Morija: Morija Sesuto Book Depot, 1946). Information supplied by Morija Sesuto Book Depot. M. L. Maile, *Ramasoabi la Potso* (Ramasoabi and Potso) (Morija: Morija Sesuto Book Depot, 1954). Maile, *Ngoanana ha a botsa telejane* (An Unhappy Young Wife) (Morija: Morija Sesuto Book Depot, 1947). Information about Maile's books was supplied by Morija Sesuto Book Depot.

98. R. H. W. Shepherd, *Bantu Literature and Life* (Lovedale: Lovedale Press, 1955), pp. 30–38, 28–41. See also Shepherd, *Lovedale and Literature for the Bantu*, pp. 11–14.

99. Shepherd gives the original in *Bantu Literature and Life*, p. 20.

100. See Jordan, "Towards an African Literature, II," p. 101. A metrical examination of Ntsikana's hymn is made by Alice Werner, "Some Native Writers in South Africa," *Journal of the African Society*, 30 (January 1931), 35.

101. Trans. John Brownlee in a letter in *Glasgow Missionary Society Report*, 1823, pp. 12–13. Quoted in Shepherd, *Bantu Literature and Life*, p. 21.

102. R. H. W. Shepherd, *Lovedale* (Lovedale: Lovedale Press, 1940), p. 20. An account of Ntsikana's life has been written by John Knox Bokwe and is entitled *Ntsikana, the Story of an African Convert* (Lovedale: Lovedale Press, 1914).

103. Jordan, "Towards an African Literature, II," pp. 113–15. W. B. Rubusana, *Zemk' inkomo magwalandin* (The Cattle Are Being Driven Off Ye Cowards! or Preserve Your Customs) (London: Butler and Tanner, 1906). C. M. Doke, ed., "A Preliminary Investigation into the State of Native Languages of South Africa." The relevant section on Xhosa is compiled by W. G. Bennie in *Bantu Studies*, 7 (1933), 40–46.

104. *U Hambo luka gqoboka* (Lovedale: Lovedale Press, 1909). *Ityala lama wele* (Lovedale: Lovedale Press, 1914). Trans. in *New African*, 2 (January, February, May 1966), 5–8, 42–45. D. D. T. Jabavu, *The Influence of English on Bantu Literature* (Lovedale: Lovedale Press, 1943?), p. 24.

105. Diedrich Westermann, *Afrikaner erzählen ihr Leben* (Essen, 1938), p. 312. Trans. from S. E. K. Mqhayi's autobiography, *U-Mqhayi wase-Ntab'ozuko* (Mqhayi of the Mountain of Prayer) (Lovedale: Lovedale Press, 1939), pp. 312–14.

106. Quoted in Jordan, "Towards an African Literature, II." One of Mqhayi's sacred poems is translated by A. C. Jordan in *Poets in South Africa*, ed. Roy Machib (Capetown: Miller, 1958), p. 72.

107. *U-Zandiwe wakwa-Gcaleka* (Lovedale: Lovedale Press, 1914). *U-Nomalizo okanye izinto zalomhlaba ngamagingigiwu* (Nomalizo or the Uncertainties of Life) (London: S.P.C.K., 1923; 1st ed., Lovedale: Lovedale Press, 1918). Eng. trans. S. J. Wallis (London: Sheldon Press, 1928), p. 64.

108. John Riordan, "The Wrath of the Ancestral Spirits," *African Studies*, 20 (1961), 57. Sinxo, *Isakhono somfazi namanye amabalana* (A Woman's Dexterity and Other Stories) (Johannesburg, 1956).

109. James J. R. Jolobe, *U-Zagula* (Lovedale: Lovedale Press, 1923), foreword.

110. James J. R. Jolobe, *Lovedale Xhosa Rhymes* (Lovedale: Lovedale Press, 1957), p. 27. Trans. informant.

111. *The Sunday School* (Lovedale: Lovedale Press, 1940).

112. James J. R. Jolobe, "To the Fallen," *Poems of an African* (Lovedale: Lovedale Press, 1946), p. 2.

113. *Ibid.*

114. English version in Jahn, *A History of Neo-African Literature*, p. 112.

115. D. D. T. Jabavu, review of *UmYezo, Bantu Studies,* 10 (1937), 53.

116. Henry Masila Ndawo, *U-Nolishwa* (Lovedale: Lovedale Press, 1931). Trans. informant.

117. *Ingqumbo yeminyanya* (Lovedale: Lovedale Press, 1940). Riordan, p. 53.

118. Riordan, p. 59. Mphahlele, *The African Image*, p. 202.

119. Shepherd, *Lovedale and Literature for the Bantu*, p. 90.

120. Jabavu, *The Influence of English on Bantu Literature.* Shepherd, *Lovedale and Literature for the Bantu,* p. 10. See J. J. Niemandt, *Bibliography of the Bantu Languages in the Republic of South Africa: In Zulu* (Pretoria: Government Printer, 1961). For a critical account see also C. L. S. Nyembezi, *A Review of Zulu Literature* (Pietermaritzburg: Shuter and Shooter, 1961).

121. *Isitha esikhulu somuntu emnyama nguya ugo6o iwa khe* (Marianhill: Marianhill Mission Press, 1958?). Daniel Malcolm, "Zulu Literature," *Africa*, 19 (January 1939), 37. Some information on Dhlomo and Vilakazi comes from this article. B. W. Vilakazi, review of R. R. R. Dhlomo's *U Shake, Bantu Studies,* 11 (1937), 66. *Indlela ya6i6i* (Pietermaritzburg: Shuter and Shooter, 1946). Malcolm, p. 37. *UNomalanga kaNdengezi* (Pietermaritzburg: Shuter and Shooter, 1947).

122. *UDiNgiswayo kaJo6e* (London: Sheldon Press). *Noma nini* (Marianhill: Marianhill Mission Press, 1935). Malcolm, pp. 37–38.

123. See Jahn, *A History of Neo-African Literature*, p. 108. *Inkondlo kaZulu* (Zulu Poems) (Johannesburg: Witwatersrand University Press, 1935). J. Dexter Taylor, "Inkondlo kaZulu: An Appreciation," *Bantu Studies*, 9 (1935), 164. *Inkondlo*, pp. 18–21.

124. Trans. Taylor, p. 165.

125. *Amal'ezulu* (Johannesburg: University of Witwatersrand Press, 1945). Eng. trans. M. Malcolm and F. L. Friedman, *Zulu Horizons* (Cape Town: Timmins, 1962).

126. Malcolm and Friedman, p. 24.

Chapter 8. Beginnings in English

1. The author's wife, Adelaide Casely-Hayford, added in her memoirs published in *West African Review* (between 1953 and 1954) that her husband's letter of proposal to her was couched in "a strange, uneven English."

2. *Eighteenpence* (Ilfracombe: Stockwell, 1943).

3. J. B. Danquah, foreword to *Eighteenpence.*

4. Review in *Ibadan*, no. 12 (June 1961), 32. Onuora Nzekwu, in *Nigerian Magazine*, no. 69 (August 1961), 191.

5. William Conton, *The African* (London: Heinemann, 1960), p. 2.

6. Mphahlele, *The African Image*, p. 22.

7. Camara Laye, *The African Child* (ed. used, London: Fontana Books, 1958), p. 84. Elsewhere Laye has added about this book, "Everything I wrote down, every-

thing I remembered was a really true picture." See Gerald Moore, ed., *African Literature and the Universities* (Ibadan: Ibadan University Press, 1965), p. 69.

8. Judith Illsley Gleason, *This Africa: Novels by West Africans in English and French* (Evanston, Ill.: Northwestern University Press, 1965), p. 110.

9. Lalage Bown, review in *West Africa*, no. 2515 (August 14, 1965), 913.

Chapter 9. West African Novelists in English

1. Chinua Achebe in a television interview for National Education Television, New York. Reprinted in *Classic*, 1 (1965), 58. Achebe in *New Statesman*, January 29, 1965, p. 162.

2. Ben Obumselu, review in *Ibadan*, no. 5 (February 1959), 38. G. Adali-Mortty, review in *Black Orpheus*, no. 6 (November 1959), 48.

3. Gerald Moore, "English Words, African Lives," p. 90.

4. "The Old Order in Conflict with the New," *Herald* (University College, Ibadan, May 1952), pp. 6–10. Untitled short story, *Herald* (January 1953), pp. 9–16.

5. Chinua Achebe, "A Look at West African Writing," *Spear* (July 1962), p. 26. Abraham, p. 100. Mphahlele, *The African Image*, p. 22.

6. Wole Soyinka, "From a Common Back Cloth: A Reassessment of the African Literary Image," p. 359.

7. Ben Mkapa, review in *Transition*, 2 (January 1962), 36. Todd Matshikiza, review in *Drum*, no. 145 (May 1963), 30.

8. Adisa Williams, review in *Spear* (May 1964), p. 43. I. N. C. Aniebo, review in *Nigerian Magazine*, no. 81 (June 1964), 150.

9. Caius Anike, review of *A Man of the People*, NBC broadcast, *The Critic*, Lagos, March 1, 1965.

10. "The New Engineer," BBC broadcast, *Calling West Africa*, January 1, 1948. Published in Cullen Young, *African New Writing*, pp. 33–36. "The Vision of Brother Sandrach," BBC broadcast, *Calling West Africa*, February 9, 1949.

11. "The Judgment of Heaven," BBC broadcast, *Calling West Africa*, May 4, 1949. "Fiction Writing in West Africa," first of the two talks, BBC broadcast, *Calling West Africa*, February 24, 1949.

12. Review in *Black Orpheus*, no. 6 (November 1959), 53.

13. Mabel Segun, review in *Sunday Express* (Lagos), January 31, 1965, p. 7.

14. Chinua Achebe, in *New Statesman*, January 29, 1965, p. 162. Ekwensi, "Problems of Nigerian Writers," p. 217.

15. "The Fiction of Cyprian Ekwensi," *Nigerian Magazine*, no. 75 (December 1962), 63.

16. Important critical articles have been published on Onitsha literature by three people: Ulli Beier, "Public Opinion on Lovers," *Black Orpheus*, no. 14 (February 1964), 4–16, is concerned with the production and some literary assessment of the writing; Donatus Nwoga, "Onitsha Market Literature," *Transition*, 4 (1963), 26–33, attempts to evaluate the work in terms of literature; Nancy J. Schmidt, "Nigeria: Fiction for the Average Man," *Africa Report*, 10 (August 1965), 39–41, is a more general account. Recently Harold Collins has published *Onitsha Chap-books* (Athens: Ohio University Press, 1971). Beier, "Public Opinion on Lovers," p. 4. Nwoga, "Onitsha Market Literature," p. 26.

17. Onitsha: privately published for the author, 1956.

18. Okwenwa Olisa, *How Lumumba Suffered and Died* (Onitsha: privately published for the author, 1964?). An article in *Journal of Modern African Studies*, 2 (November 1964), lists four such works by Nigerian writers on Lumumba and about the Congo and considers them as indicative of popular Nigerian attitudes toward that country.

19. Leslie Murby, "West African Writers II," BBC broadcast, *Calling West*

Africa, November 18, 1947. Paul Edwards, letter in *Transition*, 3 (January–February 1964), 9.

20. Cyprian Ekwensi, *Ikolo the Wrestler* (1947). Reprinted as *The Great Elephant Bird* (London: Nelson, 1965), p. 29.

21. "Ritual Murder," *Darkness and Light,* ed. Peggy Rutherfoord, pp. 126–34. "Law of the Grazing Fields," *An African Treasury,* ed. Hughes, pp. 157–61.

22. Cyprian Ekwensi, "Sharro," BBC broadcast, *Calling West Africa,* November 30, 1949.

23. "African Novelists and Social Change," *Phylon*, 26 (Fall 1965), 237.

24. Review in *Nigerian Magazine*, 70 (September 1961), 87.

25. Review in *West Africa*, no. 2312 (September 23, 1961), 1055.

26. Review in *West Africa*, no. 2356 (July 28, 1962), 827.

27. August 10, 1962, p. 571.

28. "The Theme of Alienation and Commitment in Okara's *The Voice*," *Bulletin of Association for African Literature in English*, no. 3 (November 1965), 56.

29. "From a Common Back Cloth," p. 360.

30. Dylan Thomas, review in *Observer*, no. 8405 (July 6, 1952). *British National Bibliography Annual*, 1952 (London: Council of the British National Bibliography, Ltd., 1953), 636.

31. Ulli Beier, "Nigerian Literature," *Nigeria: A Special Independence Issue of Nigeria Magazine* (Lagos: Federal Government of Nigeria Publications, October 1960), p. 213. Christina Aidoo (now Ama Ata Aidoo), letter in *Transition*, 4 (1963), 46.

32. *L'art nègre*, in *Black Orpheus* (Paris: Aux Éditions du Seuil) and in *Présence africaine*, nos. 10–11 (1951), 231. (Originally the preface to *L'anthologie de la nouvelle poésie nègre et malgache de langue française*, ed. Léopold Sédar Senghor.)

33. Idowu, p. 196.

34. *Seven African Writers*, p. 196.

35. Ogumefun, p. 86.

36. J. A. Ramsaran, "African Twilight—Folktale and Myth in Nigerian Literature," *Ibadan*, no. 15 (March 1961), 17, 18.

37. Interview with other Nigerian writers for Transcription Centre, London.

38. *African Heritage*, p. 144.

39. *African/English Literature*, p. 100.

40. Review in *Ibadan*, no. 7 (November 1959), 30.

41. Review in *New Statesman*, January 20, 1965, p. 164.

42. Emmanuel Obiechina, review in *Nigeria Magazine*, no. 84 (March 1965), 62. Francis Hope, review in *Observer*, no. 9037 (September 13, 1964), 25.

43. April 1, 1965, p. 260.

Chapter 10. East, Central, and South African Novelists in English

1. Nairobi: East African Publishing House, 1970.

2. London: Heinemann, 1971.

3. Nairobi: East African Publishing House, 1970.

4. *Ibid.*, 1971.

Chapter 11. African Poetry in English

1. Bassir, ed., *Anthology of West African Verse*, is restricted to poetry by West Africans but includes translations from French. Swanzy, ed., *Voices of Ghana*, is restricted to indigenous Ghanaian writing and English prose and poetry from Ghana.

2. *The African Image*, p. 186.

3. Paris: Présence Africaine, 1959, pp. 68–69.

4. Ras Khan, "The Poetry of Dr. R. E. G. Armattoe," *Présence africaine*, no. 12 (February–March 1957), 31–47. There is also a biographical and bibliographical note: "The Work of Dr. Armattoe," *West African Review*, 20 (March 1949), 239.

5. Londonderry: Lomeshie Research Centre, 1950. The entire volume is cyclostyled and some poems were reproduced in his second volume.

6. The title probably owed something to R. E. Dennet, *At the Back of the Black Man's Mind* (London: Macmillan, 1906), which attempted to set out an African philosophy.

7. R. E. G. Armattoe, "A Racial Survey of the British People," lecture delivered to the Free German Institute of Science and Learning, London, on March 17, 1944, and reprinted in *Londonderry Sentinel*, April 4, 1944.

8. *Between the Forest and the Sea*, pp. 66–67.

9. *Ibid.*, p. 5.

10. Armattoe, *Deep Down the Black Man's Mind*, p. 14.

11. *Calling West Africa*, July 12, 1950.

12. Armattoe, *Deep Down the Black Man's Mind*, introduction, and BBC broadcast, *Calling West Africa*, July 12, 1950. Armattoe expressed similar views in *The Golden Age of West African Civilization* (Londonderry: Lomeshie Research Centre, 1946). Dennis Osadebay, BBC broadcast, *Calling West Africa*, January 12, 1949.

13. Ilfracombe: Stockwell, 1952. It will be seen that a remark by Henry Swanzy was then true that "Nigerian poets do not only reflect personal life. They are concerned above all with politics."

14. Freetown: New Era Press, 1948? not paginated. Also "Nativity," "The Serving Girl," and "The Souls of Black and White" were published in Langston Hughes and Arna Bontemps, eds., *The Poetry of the Negro* (New York: Doubleday, 1949), pp. 384–86.

15. See also *Atlantic Monthly*, which had published some of Gladys Casely-Hayford's poetry.

16. Donald St. John-Parsons, ed., *Our Poets Speak* (London: University of London Press, 1966). I have written a general introduction for this volume.

17. Quoted in "It's No Joke—A Spotlight on Krio," produced by John Akar on Sierra Leone Broadcasting Service, script in typescript.

18. "Crusader for Krio," *West Africa*, no. 2515 (August 14, 1965), 903. See "Three Krio Poems," *Sierra Leone Language Review*, 3 (1964).

19. Recited in program produced by Akar.

20. *Precious Gems Unearthed by an African* (Ilfracombe: Stockwell, 1952). Beier, "Contemporary African Poetry in English," paper submitted to Makerere Conference, 1962.

21. "The Soft Pink Palms," *Présence Africaine: The 1st International Conference of Negro Writers and Artists*, nos. 8–10 (June–November 1956), 116–17.

22. Roland Dempster, *Echoes from the Valley*, with contributions by B. T. Moore and H. Carey Thomas (Cape Mount, Liberia: Douglas Mair Press, 1947). His five volumes are *The Mystic Reformation of Gondolia, Being a Satirical Treatise on Moral Philosophy* (Monrovia: privately published, 1953); *To Monrovia Old and New* (Monrovia: privately published, 1958); *Anniversary Ode to Dr. William V. S. Tubman* (Monrovia: privately published, 1959); *A Song Out of Midnight* (Monrovia: privately published, 1959); *Tubman: Reflections from the Poet's Pen and Other Poems* (Monrovia: privately published, 1963).

23. *To Monrovia Old and New*, p. 5. An introductory remark by H. Carey Thomas.

24. "The Writer, His Work and His Gain," Fr. trans. in *Présence africaine*, no. 31 (1951), 87; Eng. trans. in *ibid.*, 8 (1961), 48.

25. *Ibid.*, p. 87.

26. Ulli Beier, "The Conflict of Cultures in West African Poetry," *Black Orpheus*, no. 1 (September 1957), 20.

27. *Ibid.*

28. *Wayward Lines from Africa* (London: United Society for Christian Literature, 1946); *Cocoa Comes to Mamphong* (Cape Coast: Methodist Book Depot, 1949); *Africa Speaks* (Accra: Guinea Press, 1959); *Ghana Semi-Tones* (Accra: Presbyterian Book Depot, 1962); *Two Faces of Africa* (Accra: Waterville Publishing House, 1965), with his son; *Ghana Glory: Poems on Ghana* (London: Nelson, 1965), with Yaw Warren. For additional comments on Dei-Anang, see Parsons, ed., *Our Poets Speak*, p. 36.

29. Ɔ*kyeame*, 1 (July 1963), 40–43.

30. Michael Dei-Anang, "Africa Speaks," *An Anthology of Commonwealth Verse*, ed. Margaret J. O'Donnell (London & Glasgow: Blackie, 1963), p. 335.

31. "My Africa," *Poems from Black Africa*, ed. Langston Hughes (Bloomington: Indiana University Press, 1963), p. 73.

32. Mphahlele, "African Literature," *The Proceedings of the First International Congress of Africanists* (London: Longmans, 1964), p. 227. "Redeemed," *African Affairs*, 51 (April 1952), 157.

33. The five poetic publications of J. Benibengor Blay are *Immortal Deeds* (Ilfracombe: Stockwell, 1940); *King of the Human Frame* (Ilfracombe: Stockwell, 1944); *Memoirs of the War* (Ilfracombe: Stockwell, 1945); *Thoughts of Youth* (Aboso: Benibengor Book Agency, 1961); *Ghana Sings* (Accra: Waterville Publishing House, 1965). Blay wrongly says in the preface (not paginated) to *Ghana Sings* that it was "the fourth in this collection of Poems."

34. Blay, *Immortal Deeds*, p. 20.

35. *Présence africaine*, nos. 4–5, p. 52.

36. Okara, "African Speech . . . English Words," *Transition*, 3 (1963), 15. Nicolson, *Africa, a Subjective View* (London: Longmans, 1964), p. 76. "Spirit of the Wind," "The Call of the River Nun," and "Were I to Choose" were all first published in *Black Orpheus*, no. 1 (September 1957), 36–38. Okara also published "Piano and Drums" and "You Laughed and Laughed" in *Black Orpheus*, no. 6 (November 1959), 33–34, and a long poem, "The Fisherman's Invocation," in *Black Orpheus*, no. 13 (November 1963), 34–43. In addition, some of these appeared, along with "To Paveba," in *Reflections*, ed. Frances Ademola (Lagos: African Universities Press, 1962), pp. 50–58. "The Snowflakes Sail Gently Down," "The Mystic Drum," "Adhiambo," and "One Night at Victoria Beach" were published in *Modern Poetry from Africa*, ed. Gerald Moore and Ulli Beier (London: Penguin, 1963). Some of these poems, in addition to "Once upon a Time," are to be found in *Poems from Black Africa,* ed. Hughes, pp. 82–89. "The Passing of a Year" and "Music from Songs without Words" appear in *Young Commonwealth Poetry '65*, ed. Peter Brent, pp. 131–33. Okara is an important poet but has not yet published his own collection.

37. Lewis Nkosi, *Home and Exile*, p. 102.

38. John Reed and Clive Wake, eds., *A Book of African Verse*, p. 70.

39. George Awoonor-Williams (now Kofi Awoonor), "Songs of Sorrow," in Moore and Beier, p. 79.

40. *Songs from the Wilderness*. Parkes's poems are also found in *A Book of African Verse*, ed. Reed and Wake, pp. 56–58, and Peter Brent, pp. 76–77.

41. *Pigments* (Paris: Présence Africaine, 1962), p. 42.

42. *Black Orpheus*, no. 2 (January 1958), 24. The translation is by Miriam Koshland and the relevant part reads:

> Give me back my black dolls to play
> the simple games of my instincts

to rest in the shadow of their laws
to recover my courage.

43. The poem "The Deathless Child" was taken out at proof stage and replaced by "Monsters" and "After the Holocaust." "The Deathless Child" was an open attack on Nkrumah:

One of the prophets of this anti-Populism
Parades the street in this garb
Of African Socialism (whatever that means)
And will give peaceful nights to none.
Subversion and Machiavellism
Are his guiding lights.

The publishers then omitted it less for reasons of taste than tact.

44. Christopher Okigbo, "Lament of the Masks," *W. B. Yeats 1865–1965: Centenary Essays*, eds. D. E. S. Maxwell and S. B. Bushrui (Ibadan: Ibadan University Press, 1965), pp. xiii–xx. His others are *Heavensgate* (Ibadan: Mbari, 1962); *Silences, Transition*, 3 (March 1963), 13–16; *Limits* (Ibadan: Mbari, 1964), not paginated; "Distances," *Transition*, 10 (1964), 9–13; "Four Canzones," *Black Orpheus*, no. 11; "Lament of the Flutes," *Poems from Black Africa*, ed. Hughes; "Lament of the Drums" (pt. II of *Silences*), *Black Orpheus*, no. 17 (June 1965), 13–17; "Dance of the Painted Maidens," *Verse and Voice: A Festival of Commonwealth Poetry*; "Path of Thunder: Poems Prophesying War," *Black Orpheus*, 2, no. 1 (1968), 5–11. Some of these have been collected in *Labyrinths*, which includes "Heavensgate," "Limits," "Distances," and "Path of Thunder," published by Heinemann.

45. Chief Olunlade, the Otun Seriki of Ede, *Ede: A Short History* (Ikeja, Nigeria: Sankey Printing Works, Ltd., 1961). "Oriki to Olunloye," p. 42.

46. "Oriki to Olunloye," p. 28.

47. "From a Common Back Cloth," p. 20.

48. *Heavensgate*, p. 9.

49. Review, "Three Mbari Poets," *Black Orpheus*, no. 12, p. 46.

50. "Lament of the Lavender Mist," *Black Orpheus*, no. 11, p. 8.

51. S. O. Anozie, "Okigbo's *Heavensgate*: A Study of Art as Ritual," *Ibadan*, no. 15 (March 1963), 11.

52. "Jungle Drums and Wailing Piano," *African Forum*, 1 (Spring 1966), 102.

53. Cox, *History and Myth* (London: Darton, Longman & Todd, 1961), p. 24. Beier, "Three Mbari Poets," p. 47. Soyinka, "And after the Narcissist," *African Forum*, 1 (Spring 1966), 63.

54. Echeruo, "Talk, Patter and Song," Brent, p. 123.

55. Ndu, "Homesick," *ibid.*, p. 128.

56. Onyejeli, review in *Nigerian Magazine*, no. 84 (March 1965), 63. Theo Vincent, review in *Black Orpheus*, no. 18 (October 1965), 58.

57. Ibadan: Mbari, 1964.

58. Vol. 19 (March 1966).

59. "African Literature, Part II: English-Speaking West Africa," p. 16.

60. "Teaching and Presentation of English Language and Literature."

61. "Songs of Sorrow," Moore and Beier, p. 79.

62. *Ibid.*

63. Tibble, *African/English Literature*, p. 94. Jones, "Jungle Drums and Wailing Piano," p. 105.

64. "The Nim Trees in the Cemetery," *Rediscovery and Other Poems*, p. 8.

65. "We Have Found a New Land," *Rediscovery*, p. 10. "My God of Songs Was Ill," *ibid.*, p. 31. "On Writing Poetry," p. 46.

66. It is interesting to note that this experience is almost repeated word for word

in Ruth Glass, *Newcomers* (London: Centre for Urban Studies and Allen & Unwin, 1960), p. 61. This is an instance of Wole Soyinka taking real-life experience and giving it form. "The less self conscious the African is, and the more innately the individual qualities appear in his writing, the more seriously he will be taken as an artist of exciting dignity." *Makerere Journal*, no. 7, p. 46.

67. "The Immigrant," *Black Orpheus*, no. 5 (May 1959), 10, and *An African Treasury*, ed. Hughes, pp. 194–96. "And the Other Immigrant," *Black Orpheus*, no. 5 (May 1959) 10, and *An African Treasury*, pp. 196–98.

68. Beier, "Some Nigerian Poets," p. 50. Irele, "African Poetry of English Expression," *Présence africaine*, no. 57 (1966), 263.

69. "Abiku" and other poems discussed are in *Idanre*.

70. "The Mbari Publications," *Nigeria Magazine*, no. 75 (December 1962), 71.

71. "Easter" and other poems discussed are in *Poems*, unless stated otherwise.

72. "Falani Cattle," *Modern Poetry from Africa*, p. 90.

73. Beier, "Three Mbari Poets," p. 48. Irele, review in *Présence africaine*, no. 49 (1964), 277. Neustadt, "The Challenge of Social Change," *West African Review*, 31 (June 1960), 51.

74. Mphahlele, "African Literature," p. 227. "Poetry in Africa Today," paper delivered at the Berliner Festwochen, 1964, and reprinted in *Transition*, 4 (1965), 22.

75. Review in *African Forum*, 1 (Winter 1966), 122.

76. *Poems* (Ibadan: Mbari, 1964), p. 28. Other poems discussed are in this work.

77. Eldred Jones feels that in Okara's "Jungle Drums and Wailing Piano" the image of Africa and Europe are superbly wed. He argues that in the poem about a London prostitute "there is nothing self-conscious about Lenrie Peters's use of images from his African experiences in his description of a prostitute. The tropical and classical imagery place a new Eve against the background of the trees of a London park." *African Forum*, 1 (Spring 1966), 103. As I suggested, my own feelings are quite different.

78. *The Shadows of Laughter*, p. 12. All quotations are from this work. His poetry also appears in *Messages*, ed. Awoonor and Adali-Mortty.

79. *African Poetry*, ed. Dathorne, pp. 48–53.

80. London: Cyclostyled, not paginated.

81. Ibadan: Mbari, 1963, not paginated.

Chapter 12. Négritude and Black Writers

1. Gerald Moore, "Surrealism and Négritude in the Poetry of Tchikaya U Tamsi," *Introduction to African Literature*, ed. Ulli Beier, p. 108. W. E. Abraham, in a National Education Television interview.

2. Clive Wake, ed., *An Anthology of African and Malagasy Poetry in French*, p. 5. Léopold Sédar Senghor, "Négritude and Marxism," *Africa in Prose*, ed. O. R. Dathorne and Willfried Feuser, p. 341. All translations in this section are mine unless stated otherwise. See Thomas Melone, *De la négritude dans la littérature negro-africain* (Paris: Présence Africaine, 1962). Claude Wauthier, *The Literature and Thought of Modern Africa*.

3. Lewis Nkosi, in *Transition*, 3 (January–February 1964), 28. Mphahlele, *The African Image*, p. 27. Janheinz Jahn, *Muntu*, p. 29. Jahn, *A History of Neo-African Literature*, p. 244.

4. Senghor, "Négritude and Marxism," pp. 340–41.

5. Alioune Diop, in *Présence africaine*, no. 1 (November–December 1947), 1.

6. W. E. B. DuBois, "Africa and the American Negro Intelligentsia," *Présence africaine*, no. 5 (December 1955–January 1956), 41–42.

7. Roland A. Lebel, *L'Afrique occidentale dans la littérature française* (Paris,

1925), p. 217. Léopold Sédar Senghor et al., *Les plus beaux écrits de l'union française* (Paris, 1947), pp. 256–57.

8. Quoted in Freddy Bulte, "Surrealisme et négritude," *Jeune Afrique*, no. 30 (December 1958), 14.

9. Aimé Césaire, *Cahier d'un retour au pays natal*. Originally published in *Volontes*, no. 20 (August 1939), 23–51. 2nd ed. (Paris: Présence Africaine, 1956), p. 45.

10. Aimé Césaire, "Sur la poésie nationale," *Présence africaine*, no. 4 (October–November 1955), 41.

11. Damas, *Pigments*, p. 35.

12. Léon Damas. Talk in New York reported in *AMSAC Newsletter*, 7 (February 1965), 1, 3.

13. Césaire, *Cahier*, p. 78.

14. Paris: Gallimard, 1956.

15. Léopold Sédar Senghor, Congress speech at "Parti du rassemblement africain" in 1959. Jean-Paul Sartre, "Orphée noir," pp. ix–xliv. Samuel Allen, "Tendencies in African Poetry," *Africa Seen by American Negroes*, p. 176.

16. Lilyan Lagneau (now Kesteloot), "La négritude de Léopold Sédar Senghor," *Présence africaine*, no. 39 (1961), p. 166. Reed and Wake, eds., *Senghor*, introduction.

17. Paris: Éditions du Seuil, 1964.

18. In *Leurres et lueurs* (Paris: Présence Africaine, 1960).

19. Mbella Sonne Dipoko, "Cultural Diplomacy in African Writing," *The Writer in Modern Africa*, ed. Per Wästberg, pp. 64, 68. Léopold Sédar Senghor, *Liberté I: Négritude et humanisme* (Paris: Éditions du Seuil, 1964).

20. Paris: Présence Africaine, 1956.

21. Antoine-Roger Bolamba, *Esanzo: Chants pour mon pays* (Paris: Présence Africaine, 1955), p. 15. This translation appears in *African Poetry*, ed. Dathorne, p. 11.

22. Bolamba, p. 26.

23. Paris: Présence Africaine, 1956.

24. Paris: Présence Africaine, 1957.

25. Paris: Présence Africaine, 1956.

26. The poems by Dioura, Dayo, N'dintsouma, Bamboté, Dongmo, Ouloguem, Dongala, and Assouan all appear in *Nouvelle somme de poesie du monde noir*, *Présence africaine*, no. 57 (1966). All page numbers in the text refer to this publication.

27. Paris: Nouvelles Éditions Latines, 1937.

28. *La ronde des jours* (Paris: Seghers, 1956).

29. Paris: Seghers, 1956.

30. Bernard Dadié, *Afrique debout* (Paris: Seghers, 1950), p. 25.

31. See "Un grand poète africain: Bernard B. Dadié," *Poésie vivante*, no. 14 (September–October 1965), 13.

Chapter 13. African Literature in Portuguese

1. Gilberto Freyre, cited by Mário de Andrade, "Poètes noirs d'expression portuguaise," *Europe*, no. 381 (1961), 4. Andrade argues that Freyre is only partly correct.

2. Peter Lessing, *Only Hyenas Laugh* (London: Michael Joseph, 1964), p. 101. Christopher Columbus, "Journal of the First Voyage of Christopher Columbus 1492–1493," cited in Bourne, *The Northmen, Columbus and Cabot*, p. 145.

3. Quoted in Moser, p. 287. The full letter appears in *Monumenta missionaria africana, Africa ocidental*, ed. A. Brasio, 2 (Lisbon, 1953), 103–6. For an account

of Afonso I's life and reign, see J. Duffy, *Portugal in Africa* (Harmondsworth: Penguin, 1962), pp. 40–43.

4. Mário de Andrade, "Literature and Nationalism in Angola," *Présence africaine*, no. 41 (1963), 121.

5. Oscar Ribas, "The Angola," *Ecos da Minha Terra* (Luanda: Lello & Ca, 1952), in Rutherfoord, p. 92.

6. Leónard Sainville, ed., *Letteratura negra*, 12 (Rome: Editori Riunti, 1961), 108.

7. Luanda: Lello & Ca, 1951.

8. Manuel Lopes, *O galo que cantou na baía, e outros contos cabo-verdeanos* (Lisbon: Orion Distribuidora, 1959), trans. Moser.

9. Roger Bastide, preface to Fr. ed. of *Terra morta* (Rio de Janeiro: Casa de Estundantedo Brasil, 1949), called *Camaxilo* (Paris: Présence Africaine, 1956).

10. Castro Soromenho, *Camaxilo*, p. 216. Alfredo Margarido, "Castro Soromenho: Romancista angolano," *Estudos ultramarinos: Literatura e arte*, no. 3 (Lisbon: Instituto Superior de Estudos Ultramarinos, 1959), 139.

11. M. Ligny, review of *Virage* (Paris: Gallimard, 1962). This is the French version of *Viragem* (Lisbon: Editora Ulisseia, 1957). Review in *Présence africaine*, no. 41 (1963), 173.

12. See "Ficcao: Tres prosadores ultramarinos," *Estudes ultramarinos: Literatura e arte*, no. 3 (1959), 285.

13. Rodrigues Júnior, *Muende* (Lorenço Marques: Edição Africa Editora, 1960), pp. 71–72, trans. Moser.

14. Luis Bernardo Honwana, "Inventory of Furniture and Effects," trans. Dorothy Guedes in *We Killed Mangy Dog & Other Mozambique Stories* (London: Heinemann, 1969), p. 22.

15. Fernando Mourão, *Contistas Angolanos* (Lisbon, 1960), p. xi, trans. Moser.

16. Luis Bernardo Honwana, "The Old Woman," trans. Guedes, p. 31.

17. *Modern African Prose*, ed. Richard Rive, pp. 101–16, and Guedes, pp. 32–48.

18. L. B. Honwana, "The Hands of the Blacks," *Black Orpheus*, no. 17 (June 1965), 12, and Guedes, pp. 51–52.

19. Moore and Beier, p. 22.

20. *Antologia*, ed. Andrade, p. 29.

21. Tenreiro F. Francisco and Mário de Andrade, eds., *Poesia negra de expressão portuguese*. Andrade, "Literature and Nationalism in Angola," p. 120. Viriato da Cruz, "Kola Nut," *Poesia negra*, ed. Mário de Andrade (Munich: Nymphenburger Verlagschandlung, 1962), pp. 83–84. Viriato da Cruz, "Sû santo," *Antologia*, ed. Andrade, p. 78. Viriato da Cruz, "Mama negra," *Antologia*, ed. Andrade, p. 67.

22. Alfredo Margarido, "Incidences socio-economiques sur la poésie noire d'expression portugaise," *Diogène*, no. 37 (January–March 1962), 70.

23. Mário de Andrade, "Cultura negro-africana e assimilação," preface to *Antologia*, p. vii.

24. *Poesia de Cabo Verde*, ed. José Osório de Oliveira (Lisbon, 1944), not paginated.

25. *Ibid.*

26. *Ibid.*

27. Margarido, p. 59.

28. Francisco José Tenreiro, *Ilha de nome santo* (Coimbra: Tip. da Atlântida de Coimbra, 1942). Margarido, p. 65.

29. *Antologia*, ed. Andrade, p. 31.

30. Alda da Espirito Santo, "Onde estao os homens cacades neste vento de lououra" (Where Are the Men Seized by the Wind of Madness), *Antologia*, ed. Andrade, pp. 27–28. For another translation see Moore and Beier, p. 140.

31. See "Five Angolan Poets," *London Magazine*, 2 (October 1962). Mário António Fernandes de Oliveira, letter to *Coloquio*, no. 9 (June 1960), quoted in Moser, p. 304. De Oliveira is himself a poet who lived in Angola. Margaret Amosu, *Creative African Writing* (Ibadan: Institute of African Studies, University of Ibadan, 1964), pp. 3–4. Mourão, p. xi. *Antologia*, ed. Andrade, p. xiv.

32. Margarido, p. 68. Andrade, "Literature and Nationalism in Angola," p. 121.

33. *Antologia*, ed. Andrade, p. 41.

34. Agostinho Neto, "Three Poems by Agostinho Neto," *Black Orpheus*, no. 15 (August 1964), 40.

35. *Antologia*, ed. Andrade, pp. 39–40.

36. Agostinho Neto, "A Spiracao" (Longing), *ibid.*, pp. 43–44.

37. "Monangamba," *Ibid.*, pp. 47–58. This translation appears in *African Poetry*, ed. Dathorne. "Kalundu," *Antologia*, ed. Andrade, pp. 52–54.

38. António Jacinto, "Batuque," *Poesia negra*, ed. Andrade, p. 68.

39. "Muimbu ua Sabalu," *Antologia*, ed. Andrade, pp. 57–58. "Poema," *ibid.*, pp. 61–62.

40. "Meia-Noite" (Midnight), *ibid.*, p. 19.

41. Lessing, p. 146. "Surge et Ambula," *Antologia*, ed. Andrade, p. 94.

42. Valente Malangatana, from manuscript. Trans. author. The following quotations from this poem are all from this manuscript.

43. José Craveirinha, *Chigubo* (Lisbon: Edição da Casa dos Estudantes do Império, 1964). All selections are from this volume.

44. "If You Want to Know Who I Am," *Classic*, 1 (1964), 46.

45. "Apolo," *Antologia*, ed. Andrade, p. 91. See also Moore and Beier, pp. 169–70. Margando, p. 76.

46. "Magaica," *Antologia*, ed. Andrade, pp. 88–89.

47. Malangatana.

48. *Ibid.*

49. Margarido, pp. 78–79. "Onde estou," *Antologia*, ed. Andrade, pp. 74–76. "A um menino do meu pais," *ibid.*, pp. 92–96.

50. "Terra mãe," *Antologia*, ed. Andrade, p. 96.

Chapter 14. Contemporary African Prose and Poetry in French

1. Paris: Larose, 1938.

2. Astrida: Groupe Scolaire, 1955. 2 vols.

3. Joseph Miezan Bognini, *Ce dur appel de l'espoir* (Paris: Présence Africaine, 1960), p. 71.

4. Paris: Présence Africaine, 1960.

5. Paris: Présence Africaine, 1962.

6. Paris: Présence Africaine, 1962.

7. In *Premier chant du départ* (Paris: Seghers, 1955).

8. *Les écrivains noirs de langue française* (Brussels: Université Libre de Bruxelles, 1963), p. 307.

9. Avignon: Presses Universelles, 1962.

10. Paris: Flammarion, 1960.

11. In *Trois écrivains noirs* (Paris: Présence Africaine, 1954).

12. In *ibid.*

13. Jean-Joseph Rabéarivelo, *Volumes* (Tananarive: Imp. de l'Imerina, 1928). Poem reprinted in *An Anthology of African and Malagasy Poetry in French*, ed. Wake, p. 22.

14. Jean-Joseph Rabéarivelo, *Presque-songes* (Tananarive: Henri Vidalie, 1924). Poem reprinted in Wake, pp. 27–28.

15. Jean-Joseph Rabéarivelo, *La coupe de cendres* (Tananarive: Pitot de la

Beaujardière, 1924). Reprinted in P. Valette, *J. J. Rabéarivelo* (Paris: Fernand Nathan, 1967), p. 15.

16. Jean-Joseph Rabéarivelo, *Traduit de la nuit* (Tunis: Éditions de Mirages, 1935). Reprinted in Wake, p. 29. Translations of parts of *Traduit* and *Presquesonges* appear in *24 Poems*, trans. Gerald Moore and Ullis Beier (Ibadan: Mbari, 1962). The latter work is not paginated.

17. Rabéarivelo, *Traduit de la nuit*. Trans. in *24 Poems*, poem no. ix.

18. Rabéarivelo, *Presque-songes*. Reprinted in Wake, p. 43.

19. Jean-Joseph Rabéarivelo, *Vieilles chansons des pays d'Imerina* (Tananarive: Impr. Officiele, 1937). Reprinted in *J. J. Rabéarivelo*, p. 55.

20. Rabéarivelo, *Presque-songes*. Reprinted in Wake, p. 48.

21. Flavien Ranaivo, *L'ombre et le vent* (Tananarive: Impr. Officiele, 1947). Reprinted in Wake, p. 123.

22. Flavien Ranaivo, *Le retour au Bercail* (Tananarive: Impr. Nationale, 1962). Reprinted in Wake, p. 128.

23. *Ibid.* Reprinted in Wake, p. 126.

24. Paris: Stock, 1960.

25. Paris: Présence Africaine, 1965.

26. Camara Laye's books have been translated into English as *The Dark Child*, *The Radiance of the King*, and *A Dream of Africa*.

27. Paris: Julliard. Eng. trans. *Ambiguous Adventure*.

28. Personal interview with author in Tunis, Janaury 14, 1967. A selection of his poems has been translated by Gerald Moore in *Tchicaya U'Tamsi: Selected Poems* (London: Heinemann, 1970).

29. Paris: Caractères, 1955.

30. Félix Tchicaya U'Tamsi, *Feu de brousse* (Paris: Imp. Édition Caractères, 1957). Trans. U'Tamsi in *Brush Fire* (Ibadan: Mbari, 1964), not paginated.

31. Paris: Éditions Hautefeuille, 1958.

32. Tunis: Societé Nationale d'Édition et de Diffusion, 1962.

33. Paris: Présence Africaine, 1964.

34. Paris: Oswald, 1970.

35. Three of Mongo Beti's four works have been translated into English: *Poor Christ of Bomba, Mission Accomplished*, and *King Lazarus*.

36. Two of Ferdinand Dyono's works have been translated into English: *Boy* (New York; Collier, 1970) and *The Old Man and the Medal* (London: Heinemann, 1967).

37. Paris: Nouvelles Éditions Debresse, 1956.

38. Paris: Amiot-Dumont, 1957.

39. Paris: Le Livre Contemporain, 1960. Eng. trans. *God's Bits of Wood*.

40. Paris: Présence Africaine, 1963.

Chapter 15. African Drama in French and English

1. Bakary Traoré, *Le théâtre Négro-Africain et ses fonctions sociales* (Paris: Présence Africaine, 1958), pp. 47–54. This book is extremely useful for information on the Ponty theater. See Jahn's bibliography for information on other plays.

2. Traoré, p. 52.

3. *Sokamé; adaptation d'un conte indigène* was billed as a "pièce tragique en 3 actes et 4 tableaux" and performed by the Dahomeyan pupils. Reprinted in *Présence africaine*, no. 4 (1948), 627–41. Page numbers in the text correspond to this reprint.

4. Tidiane Dali, p. 60.

5. Review in *Bantu Studies*, 11 (1937), 64.

6. Yaba, Nigeria, 1964. Privately printed for the author.

7. In *African Arts/Arts d'Afrique*, African Studies Center, UCLA (Winter 1970), pp. 64–70.

8. Aba, Nigeria: Okeudo & Sons, n.d.

9. *The Lion and the Jewel.*

10. Astrida: Emma Maquet, 1954.

11. "The Sociology of Modern Drama," *Tulane Drama Review*, 9 (September 1965), 148.

12. "Third World Stage," review of Soyinka's *Five Plays, Times Literary Supplement*, April 1, 1965, p. 252. Maclean, "Wole Soyinka: Soyinka's International Drama," *Black Orpheus*, no. 15 (August 1964), 49.

13. London: Stockwell, 1959.

14. *La mort de Chaka* (Paris: Présence Africaine, 1962). Senghor has also written a play on Chaka's death but it is more properly "a dramatic poem for several voices." See Reed and Wake, eds., *Senghor*, pp. 67–77. *The Hair-Do Conundrum*, Ghana Drama Studio production, ms., n.d.

15. Act I, sc. 1. The words of the Afrikaaner policeman echo the sentiments of one of the characters in another (unpublished) South African play, *The Blood Knot* (1961), by Athol Fugard. The play is set in a slum where two brothers eke out a dreary existence. It is Morris who says quite placidly, "A lot of people get by without futures these days."

16. Paris: Présence Africaine, 1957.

17. *Obasai and Other Plays* (London: Heinemann, 1971).

18. Ken Post, "Nigerian Pamphleteers and the Congo," *Journal of Modern African Studies*, 2 (November 1964), 406.

19. First performed at the Federal Palace Hotel, Lagos, AMSAC Annual Assembly, August 12–13, 1965.

20. *The New Republican*, first performed at Arts Theatre, University of Ibadan, 1964. *Before the Blackout*, performed at Arts Theatre, University of Ibadan, March 11, 1965.

21. BBC, *African Theatre*, first broadcast September 5, 1965.

22. In *Transition*, 3 (March 1965), 23–28.

23. Onitsha, Nigeria: All Star Printing Press, n.d.

24. In *Three Plays*. Review in *Ibadan*, no. 14 (October 1962), 28.

25. "1960 Masks at Mbari," *Service*, Lagos, Literary Supplement, 2 (March 10, 1962), 17.

26. Clark's talk was given to the Poetry Group, University of Ibadan, April 14, 1964. Denis Williams, review in *Sunday Express*, Lagos, January 31, 1965, p. 6. Achebe, review in *Sunday Times*, Lagos, January 21, 1962, p. 12.

27. BBC, *African Theatre*, first broadcast March 21, 1965.

28. London, 1964.

29. *The Opportunity*, BBC, *African Theatre*, first broadcast April 18, 1965. *You*, BBC, *African Theatre*, first broadcast May 16, 1965.

30. *Where the Sun Shines*, BBC, *African Theatre*, first broadcast January 23, 1966.

31. BBC, *African Theatre*, first broadcast September 27, 1964. Reprinted in two parts in *New African*, 4, nos. 6–7 (August–September 1965).

32. BBC, *African Theatre*, first broadcast August 8, 1965.

33. Review in *Insight* (Lagos), no. 10, p. 24.

34. In *Five Plays.*

35. In *Three Plays.*

36. In "Vers un théâtre Congolais," *Jeune Afrique 27*, Jacques Collard writes that the setting for *Dans l'autobus* by Albert Mangita was a bus and the story simply centered round people getting off and on. Similarly *Mangengenge* by the same dramatist was set on a riverboat about to come to Leopoldville. The characters represented all classes and types. Each person interpreted in his own way the superstition that says there is a spirit which guards the entrance to the harbor.

37. *Brother Jero*, in *Five Plays*. As in fact does David Rubadiri's *Come to Tea*.

The play has not been published and is "done in ironic English drawing room style" and "describes an African clerical assistant's visit to tea with a British colonial officer and his wife" but "interspersed between the scenes are choral and solo passages in the form of chants and praise poems, dealing with African history, traditional African life, and the relationship between man and nature. The juxtaposition of the two forms makes this play a powerful cry of protest against the white man's rule." See Herbert Shore, "African Drama Today," *AMSAC Newsletter*, 6 (March 1964), 5.

Chapter 16. "Africa" in Caribbean Literature

1. G. R. Coulthard, *Race and Colour in Caribbean Literature* (London: Oxford University Press, 1962), p. 71. For some relevant selections see O. R. Dathorne, ed., *Caribbean Narrative* (London: Heinemann, 1966) and *Caribbean Verse* (London: Heinemann, 1967). "Nostalgie," *La Trouée* (Port-au-Prince, 1927). All translations from French and Spanish are mine.

2. Guillen, *Élégies et chansons Cubaines* (Paris: Seghers, 1959), p. 14.

3. A. Metraux, *Haïti: Poètes noires* (Paris, n.d.), p. 13.

4. C. Eric Lincoln, *The Black Muslims in America* (Boston: Beacon Press, 1961), pp. 9–10.

5. "My Life," *Caribbean Quarterly*, 3 (January 1954), 16.

6. Idowu, pp. 90, 91.

7. *Thoughts on Life and Literature* (Georgetown, privately printed, 1950), p. 138.

8. Namba Roy, *Black Albino* (London: New Literature, 1961).

9. "The Maroon Girl," *A Treasury of Jamaican Poetry*, ed. J. E. Clare McFarlane (London: University of London Press, 1949), p. 143. See *Nigeria*, 71 (December 1961), 379, and J. B. Danquah, *The Akan Doctrine of God* (London: Lutterworth Press, 1944), *passim*.

10. George Shepperson, "Notes on Negro American Influences on the Emergence of African Nationalism," *Journal of African History*, 1 (1960), 299.

11. This is strongly denied in an article by Lilyan Lagneau (now Kesteloot), "La négritude de Léopold Sédar Senghor," p. 166. Garvey, *The Tragedy of White Injustice* (New York: A. J. Garvey, 1927), p. 3.

12. Andrew Salkey, "Anancy," *Black Orpheus*, no. 5, pp. 5–8, and *Black Orpheus*, no. 7, pp. 26–33. Barker and Sinclair, p. 19.

13. For an interesting comparison between Sierra Leonean Krio and West Indian Creolese, see a letter in *Times Literary Supplement*, August 24, 1962, p. 641. F. G. Cassidy, "Language and Folklore," *Caribbean Quarterly*, 3 (January 1954), 4.

14. "The Meaning of Africa," *A Book of African Verse*, ed. Reed and Wake, p. 45.

15. "Orphée noir."

16. Jamaica: Mona, 1958, pp. 19–20.

17. *Selected Poems* (New York: Bookman Associates, 1953), p. 40.

18. "Poem," *Anthology of West Indian Poetry*, special issue of *kyk-over-al*, ed. A. J. Seymour, no. 22 (1957), 84.

19. London: Cape, 1962, p. 271.

20. London: Hutchinson New Authors, 1959, p. 151.

21. *In the Castle of My Skin* (London: Joseph, 1953), p. 211.

22. Review in *New Statesman*, 55 (December 1958), 827. Lamming, *The Pleasures of Exile* (London: Joseph, 1960), p. 224.

23. Louise Bennett, "Back to Africa," *Laugh with Louise* (Kingston, privately printed, 1961), p. 12.

24. *Caribbean Quarterly*, 4 (December 1955), 165.

25. Dada Johnson is parson, magician, and doctor in Salkey's novel. But R. S.

Rattray points out in *Religion and Art in Ashanti*, that "the Ashanti make a distinction between the following: the *okomfo* (priest); the *sumankwafo* or *dunseni* (medicine-man); and the *Bonsam konfo* (witch-doctor)" (p. 39).

26. Seymour, pp. 70–71.
27. *Caribbean Quarterly*, 5 (April 1958), 153.
28. London: Collins, 1959.
29. London: Joseph, 1960.
30. Seymour, p. 81.
31. *First Poems* (Kingston: City Printery, 1945), p. 10.
32. "I Am the Archipelago," Seymour, p. 56.
33. London: Benn, 1929, p. 142.
34. "A Far Cry from Africa," *In a Green Night* (London: Cape, 1962), p. 18.
35. Coulthard, p. 80.
36. "Ancestor on the Auction Block," *Caribbean Quarterly*, 5 (April 1958), 126.
37. Seymour, pp. 11–12.
38. "Native Aliens," mimeographed.
39. L. E. Braithwaite, "Roots," *Bim*, 10 (July–December 1963), 16.
40. New York and London: Harper, 1928.
41. London: Faber, 1961.
42. Lamming, *The Pleasures of Exile*, p. 160. *A Kind of Homecoming* (London: Bodley Head, 1963), p. 63.
43. "The Negro Writer and His World," *Caribbean Quarterly*, 5 (February 1958), 112.
44. London: Hutchinson New Authors, 1963.
45. London: Heinemann, 1958.
46. Lamming, "The Negro Writer and His World," p. 111.
47. London: Joseph, 1954, p. 207.
48. "Black Cat Eyes," *Focus*, 3 (1956), 141.
49. "Jamaica Fisherman," *Focus*, 3 (1956), 109.
50. *Banjo* (New York: Harper, 1929), p. 202.
51. London: Faber, 1963.
52. *The Mind of Africa,* p. 133. *The African Image,* p. 41.

Chapter 17. The Black Environment

1. Sylvia Wynter, "The Strange Presences," *Vogue*, 114 (June 1958), 97.
2. Eugene Rellum, from cyclostyled manuscript. Trans. Robin Dobru.
3. In *African Poetry*, ed. Dathorne, p. 26.
4. *Rights of Passage* (London: Oxford University Press, 1967).
5. "Orphée noir," pp. ix–xliv.

SELECTED BIBLIOGRAPHY

Selected Bibliography

Bibliographies

Abrash, Barbara. *Black African Literature in English since 1952*. New York: Johnson Reprint Corp., 1967.

Allary, Jean. *Littérateurs et poètes noirs; aperçu bibliographique*. In *Documents pour l'action*, 3 (January–February 1963), 38–49.

Amosu, Margaret. *A Preliminary Checklist of Creative African Writing in the European Languages*. Ibadan: Institute of African Studies, University of Ibadan, 1964. (Special supplement to *African Notes*.)

Baratte, Thérèse. *Bibliographie-auteurs africaines et malgaches de langue française*. Paris: Office de Coopération Radiophonique (OCORA), 1965; rev. ed., 1968.

Bol, Victor, and Jean Allary. *Littérateurs et poètes noirs*. Leopoldville: Bibliothèque de l'Étoile, 1964.

Jahn, Janheinz. *Approaches to African literature*. Ibadan: University Press, 1959.
———. *Die neoafrikanische Literatur. Gesamtbibliographie von den Anfängen bis zur Gegenwart*. Düsseldorf: Diederichs, 1965. Eng. ed. *A bibliography of Neo-African Literature from Africa, America and the Caribbean*. London: André Deutsch; New York, Washington: Praeger, 1965.

———, and Claus Peter Dressler. *Bibliography of Creative African Writing*. Nendeln: Kraus-Thomson, 1971.

Mercier, Roger. *Bibliographie africaine et malgache*. Dakar: L'Université, Faculté des Lettres et Sciences Humaines, 1963. *Extrait de la revue de littérature comparée*, 37 (Paris, 1963).

Porter, Dorothy Burnett. "African and Caribbean Creative Writings: A Bibliographic Survey," *African Forum*, 1 (Spring 1966), 107–11.

Ramsaran, John. *New Approaches to African Literature*. Ibadan: University Press, 1965.

Schöne schriften aus Afrika. Bonn: Deutsche Afrika-Gesellschaft, 1962.

Zell, Hans, and Helene Silver, et al. *A Reader's Guide to African Literature*. London: Heinemann, 1972.

Literary Journals

Abbia. Cameroon cultural review. No. 1. Yaoundé: Éditions CLÉ, February 1963. Bilingual; texts in either French or English. Irregular.

African Forum. A quarterly journal of contemporary affairs. Vol. 1, no. 1. New York: American Society of African Culture, Summer 1965. Publication ceased.

African Literature Today. A journal of explanatory criticism. No. 1. London: Heinemann, 1968. Semiannual.

L'Afrique littéraire et artistique. No. 1. Paris: Société Africaine d'Édition, 1968. Bimonthly.

Afro-Asian Theatre Bulletin. The newsletter of the Afro-Asian Theatre Project (AETA). Vol. 1, no. 1. Lawrence, Kansas, 1965. Semiannual.

Black Orpheus. A journal of African and Afro-American literature. Nos. 1–22. Ibadan, 1957–67. Vol. 2, no. 1. Lagos: Daily Times of Nigeria Ltd., 1968.

Bulletin of the Association for African Literature in English. Nos. 1–4. Freetown: Sierra Leone, 1964–66. Mimeographed.

Busara. Vol. 1, no. 1. Nairobi: East African Publishing House, 1968. Three times a year.

Claridade. No. 1. Cabo Verde, 1936. Until 1960 only nine issues had appeared.

Classic, The. Vol. 1, no. 1. Johannesburg: Classic Trust Fund, 1963. Irregular.

Conch, The. A Biafran journal of literary and cultural analysis. Vol. 1, no. 1. University of Texas, 1969. Semiannual.

Darlite. A magazine of original writing from University College, Dar es Salaam. Vol. 1, no. 1. Dar es Salaam: Department of Literature, University College, 1966. Semiannual; mostly mimeographed. Available on microfilm from Xerox University Microfilms, Ann Arbor, Michigan.

Dombi. Revue congolaise des lettres et des arts; création et critique. Vol. 1, no. 1. Kinshasa: Kalina Dombi, 1970. Bimonthly.

L'Étudiant noir. 10 nos. Paris, 1934–35.

Ghala. East Africa Journal's special issue on creative writing. 1st issue, July 1968 (vol. 5, no. 7, of *East Africa Journal*). Nairobi: East African Publishing House, 1968. Semiannual.

Horn, The. Vol. 1, no. 1–vol. 7, no. 1. Ibadan: English honors students, Department of English, University of Ibadan, 1958–64. Publication ceased.

Jewel of Africa, The. A literary and cultural magazine from Zambia. Vol. 1, no. 1. Lusaka: Mphala Creative Society, 1968. Irregular.

Journal of Commonwealth Literature. Nos. 1–8. London: Heinemann and the University of Leeds, 1965–69. Semiannual from no. 2, December 1966. No. 9. London: Oxford University Press, 1970.

Journal of the New African Literature. A biannual international publication. (From no. 2 called *Journal of the New African Literature and the Arts.*) Nos. 1–4. Stanford, Calif.: Joseph O. O. Okpaku, 1966–68. Publication ceased.

Muse, The. Literary magazine of the University of Nigeria. No. 1. Nsukka: English Association, University of Nigeria, 1963. Annual.

New African, The. The radical monthly. Vol. 1, no. 1–vol. 3, no. 5. Cape Town, 1962–64. Vol. 4, no. 1. London: Gransight Holdings Ltd. (vol. 7, no. 2— *The New African*), 1965. At first ten to twelve times per year, then ceased.

New Writing from Zambia. No. 1. Lusaka: New Writers Group, 1964. Semiannual; nos. 1–2 of 1964 cyclostyled.

Nexus. Prose, poetry, and criticism. Vol. 1, no. 1–vol. 2, no. 1. Nairobi: English Department, University College, 1967–68. Continued as *Busara*, 1968–.

Ɔkyeame. Vol. 1, no. 1. Accra: Ghana Society of Writers. Vol. 2, no. 2. The Writers' Workshop, 1961. Irregular.

Ozila. Forum littéraire camerounais—Cameroon literary workshop. No. 1. Yaoundé: Jean-Pierre Togolo/Max F. Dippold, 1970. Mimeographed; monthly.

Penpoint. No. 1. Kampala: English Department, Makerere University College, 1958. Semiannual.

Présence africaine. Revue culturelle du monde noir. Nos. 1–14. Paris: Présence Africaine, 1947–53. Nouvelle série bimestrielle, nos. 1–35, 1955–61. Nouvelle série trimestrielle, nos. 36–60, 1961–66. Nouvelle série bilingue, nos. 61 – –, 1967 – –.

Research in African Literatures. Vol. 1, no. 1. African and Afro-American Research Institute, University of Texas, 1970. Semiannual.

Transition. Nos. 1–37. Kampala, Uganda: Transition Ltd., 1961–68. Quarterly and bimonthly. Nos. 38 – –. Ghana.

Zuka. A journal of East African creative writing. No. 1 – –. Nairobi: Oxford University Press, 1967 – –. One or two issues a year.

General Critical Works

Achebe, Chinua. "The Role of the Writer in a New Nation." *Nigeria Magazine*, no. 81 (June 1964), 157–60.

––––––. "English and the African Writer." *Transition*, 4, no. 18 (1965), 27–30.

––––––. "The Novelist as Teacher." In *Commonwealth Literature*, pp. 201–5. Reprinted in *New Statesman*, January 29, 1965, pp. 161–62.

––––––. "The Black Writer's Burden." *Présence africaine*, Eng. ed., 31 (1966), 135–40.

Actes du colloque sur la littérature africaine d'expression française. Dakar, March 26–29, 1963. Dakar: L'Université, 1965.

Allen, Samuel Washington. "Tendencies in African Poetry." In *Africa Seen by American Negroes*, pp. 175–98. Paris: Présence Africaine, 1958.

Andrade, Mário de. "Poètes noirs d'expression portugaise." *Europe*, 39, no. 381. (January 1961), 3–10.

Awoonor-Williams, George. "Fresh Vistas for African Literature." *African Review*, 1, no. 1 (May 1965), 35, 38.

Beier, Ulli, ed. *Introduction to African Literature.* An anthology of critical writing from *Black Orpheus*. London: Longmans; Evanston, Ill.: Northwestern University Press, 1967.

Bilon, Max. "Le poète africain, chantre de son peuple." *Présence africaine*, no. 54 (1965), 137–41.

––––––. "The African Poet as Bard of His People." *Présence africaine*, Eng. ed., 26 (1965), 141–45.

Bodurin, A. "What Is African Literature?" *African Statesman*, 1, no. 1 (January–March 1966), 33–42.

Cartey, Wilfred. *Whispers from a Continent.* New York: Random House, 1969.

Catrice, Paul. "L'Afrique noire au miroir de ses écrivains." *Rhythmes du monde*, 8, no. 2 (1960), 101–7.

Chukwukere, B. I. "The Problem of Language in African Creative Writing." *African Literature Today*, no. 3 (1969), 15–26.

Clark, John Pepper. "Poetry in Africa Today." *Transition*, 4, no. 18 (1965), 20–26.

Colloque: Fonction et signification de l'art nègre dans la vie du peuple et pour le peuple (March 30–April 8). Festival Mondial des Arts Nègres. Dakar, April 1–24. Paris: Présence Africaine, 1967.

Commonwealth Literature: Unity and Diversity in a Common Culture. Extracts from the proceedings of a conference held at Bodington Hall, Leeds, September 9–12, 1964, under the auspices of the University of Leeds. Ed. John Press. London: Heinemann, 1965.

Cook, Mercer, and Stephen E. Henderson. *The Militant Black Writer in Africa and the United States.* Madison, Milwaukee, and London: University of Wisconsin Press, 1969.

Culturel panafricain: Premier festival. A symposium in Algiers, July 21–August 1, 1969. Algiers: Société Nationale d'Édition et de Diffusion, 1969.

Dathorne, Oscar Ronald. "The African Novel—Document to Experiment." *Bulletin of the Association for African Literature in English,* no. 3 (1965), 18–39.

———. "African Writers of the Eighteenth Century." *London Magazine,* 5, no. 6 (September 1965), 51–58.

———. "African Literature: Writers, Publishers and Their Public." *Books—The Journal of the National Book League,* no. 361 (September–October 1965), 159–66.

———. "Document and Imagination." *New African,* 5, no. 3 (April 1966), 57–59. (On African novelists.)

Dipoko, Mbella Sonne. "Cultural Diplomacy in African Writing." *Africa Today,* 15, no. 4 (August–September 1968), 8–11.

Éliet, Édouard. *Panorama de la littérature négro-africaine (1921–1962).* Paris: Présence Africaine, 1965.

Figueiredo, Antonio de. "The Children of Rape." *New African,* 4, no. 9 (November 1965), 203–7. (On African writers in Portuguese.)

Gérard, Albert S. "The Neo-African Novel." *Africa Report,* 9, no. 7 (July 1964), 3–5.

———. "Le missionarisme dans le roman africain." *Revue générale belge* (August 1964), pp. 43–59.

———. "African Literature." In *The New International Year-Book.* New York, 1966.

Green, Robert. "Under the Mango Tree: Criticism of African Literature." *Journal of the New African Literature and the Arts,* no. 3 (Spring 1967), 25–30.

Grégoire, Henri. *De la littérature des nègres.* Paris: Makadan, 1808.

Grunebaum, G. E. von. *French African Literature: Some Cultural Implications.* The Hague: Mouton, 1964.

Ilboudo, Gilbert. "Modern Literature in French-Speaking Africa." *Ibadan,* no. 19 (June 1964), 28–31.

Jahn, Janheinz. *Approaches to African Literature.* Non-English writings by Janheinz Jahn and English writings in West Africa by John Ramsaran, with reading lists. Ibadan: University Press, 1959.

———. *Muntu. An Outline of Neo-African Culture.* Trans. Marjorie Grene. London: Faber, 1961. Also *Muntu. The New African Culture.* Trans. Marjorie Grene. New York: Grove Press, 1961.

———. "African Literature." *Présence africaine,* Eng. ed., 20 (1963), 47–57.

———. *A History of Neo-African Literature. Writing in Two Continents.* Trans. Oliver Coburn and Ursula Lehrburger. London: Faber, 1968. Also, *Neo-African Literature. A History of Black Writing.* Trans. Oliver Coburn and Ursula Lehrburger. New York: Grove Press, 1969.

Jetha, Abdul. "A Consideration of Modern African Poetry in English." *Nexus,* 1, no. 2 (August 1967), 29–35.

Jones, Quartey (Kwatei Asoasa Brempong). "The Problems of Language in the Development of the African Theatre." *Ɔkyeame,* 4, no. 1.

Jordan, Archibald Campbell. "Towards an African Literature." *Africa South,* 1, no. 4 (July–September 1957), 90–98.

Kane, Mohamadou. "Naissance du roman africain francophone." *African Arts/Arts d'Afrique,* 2, no. 2 (Winter 1969), 54–58.

Killam, Douglas. "Recent African Fiction." *Bulletin of the Association for African Literature in English,* no. 2 (March 1965), 1–10.

Kunene, Daniel P. "Deculturation—The African Writer's Response." *Africa Today,* 15, no. 4 (August–September 1968), 19–24.

Lagneau-Kesteloot, Lilyan. "Problems of the Literary Critic in Africa." Trans. Kamala-Veloso. *Abbia,* no. 8 (February–March 1965), 29–44.

Leshoai, Bob. "Theatre and the Common Man in Africa." *Transition*, 4, no. 19 (1965), 44–47.

Lienhardt, Peter. "Tribesmen and Cosmopolitans. On African Literature." *Encounter*, 25, no. 5 (November 1965), 54–57.

McLeod, A. L., ed. *The Commonwealth Pen*. Ithaca, N.Y.: Cornell University Press, 1961.

Mahood, M. M. "Le théâtre dans les jeunes etats africains." *Présence africaine*, no. 60 (1966), 16–33.

Mazrui, Ali Al'Amin. "Meaning versus Imagery in African Poetry." *Présence africaine*, no. 66 (1968), 48–57.

———. "Some Socio-political Functions of English Literature in Africa." In Joshua A. Fishman, Charles A. Fergusion, and Jyotirindra das Gupta, eds., *Language problems of developing nations*, pp. 183–98. New York: John Wiley & Sons, 1968.

Mazrui, Molly. "Religion in African Fiction: A Consideration." *East Africa Journal* (January 1968), pp. 32–36.

Melone, Thomas. "La critique littéraire et les problèmes du language." *Présence africaine*, no. 73 (1970), 3–19.

———. "New Voices of African Poetry in French." *African Forum*, 1, no. 4 (Spring 1966), 65–74.

Mercier, Roger. *Les écrivains négro-africains d'expression française*. Paris: "Tendances," 1965.

Mezu, Sebastian Okechukwu. "The Origins of African Poetry." *Journal of the New African Literature and the Arts*, no. 2 (Fall 1966), 16–23.

Modisane, Bloke. "Literary Scramble for Africa." (Writers' conference at Makerere.) *West Africa*, no. 2352 (June 30, 1962), 716.

Moore, Gerald. "African writing Seen from Salisbury." *Présence africaine*, Eng. ed., 3 (1960), 87–94.

———. *Seven African Writers*. London: Oxford University Press, 1962. Reprinted with corrections and extended bibliography, 1966.

———. "African Literature, French and English." In collaboration with Donald Stuart. *Makerere Journal*, no. 8 (1963), 29–34.

———. "English Words, African Lives." *Présence africaine*. Eng. ed., 26 (1965), 90–101.

———. "The Arts in the New Africa." *Nigeria Magazine*, no. 92 (March 1967), 92–97.

———. *The Chosen Tongue. English Writing in the Tropical World*. London and Harlow: Longmans, 1969.

———, ed. *African Literature and the Universities*. Ibadan: Ibadan University Press, 1965.

Moser, Gerald M. "African Literature in the Portuguese Language." *Journal of General Education*, 13, no. 4 (January 1962), 270–304.

———. *Essays in Portuguese-African Literature*. University Park: Pennsylvania State University, 1969. (The Pennsylvania State University Studies, no. 26.)

Mphahlele, Ezekiel. "Writers in Search of Themes." *West African Review*, 32, no. 416 (August 1962), 40–41.

———. *The African Image*. London: Faber, 1962, 1964.

———. "Conference of African Writers." *Nigeria Magazine*, no. 76 (March 1963), 74–76.

———. "The Language of African Literature." *Harvard Educational Review*, 34, no. 2 (Spring 1964), 298–306.

———. "African Literature for Beginners." *Africa Today*, 14, no. 1 (January 1967), 25–31.

———. "Literature and Propaganda." *Jewel of Africa*, 1, no. 4 (1968), 19–23.

————. "Realism and Romanticism in African Literature." *Africa Today*, 15, no. 4 (August–September 1968), 4.

————. "Writers and Commitment." *Black Orpheus*, 2, no. 3 (1969), 34–39.

Munro, Donald, and Cosmo Pieteise. *Protest & Conflict in African Literature*. London, Ibadan, Nairobi: Heinemann, 1969.

Nicol, Davidson. "Our Writers." In Davidson Nicol, *Africa: A Subjective View*, pp. 65–88. London: Longmans; Legon, Accra: Ghana Universities Press, 1964.

————. "Modern African Writing." *Présence africaine*, no. 62 (1967), 13–14.

Nkosi, Lewis. "African Fiction." Pt. I: "South Africa"; Pt. II: "English-Speaking West Africa." *Africa Report*, 7, nos. 9, 11 (October, December 1962), 3–6, 15–17.

————. "Some Conversations with African Writers." *Africa Report*, 9, no. 7 (July 1964), 7–21.

————. "African Writers of Today." (Interviews conducted by Lewis Nkosi.) *Classic*, 1, no. 4 (1965), 55–78.

————. "Black Power or Souls of Black Writers." In Lewis Nkosi, *Home and Exile*, pp. 91–107. London: Longmans, 1965.

————. "Toward a New African Theatre." In *Home and Exile*, pp. 108–14.

————. "Relating Literature and Life." (Interview by Nkosi with David Rubadiri and Joseph E. Kariuki.) *Negro Digest*, 15, no. 9 (July 1966), 39–46.

————. "Where Does African Literature Go from Here?" *Africa Report*, 11, no. 9 (December 1966), 7–11.

Obiechina, E. N. "Cultural Nationalism in Modern African Creative Literature." *African Literature Today*, 1, no. 1 (1968), 24–35.

Obumselu, Ben. "The Background of Modern African Literature." *Ibadan*, no. 22 (June 1966), 46–59.

Okpaku, Joseph Ohiomogben O. "The Philosophy of the New African Literature." *Journal of the New African Literature and the Arts*, no. 1 (Spring 1966), 1–2.

————. "The Western Africanist versus the African Intellectual: An Examination of the Present State of African Humanities." *Journal of the New African Literature and the Arts*, no. 2 (Fall 1966), 1–4.

————. "Culture and Criticism: African Critical Standards for African Literature and the Arts." *Journal of the New African Literature and the Arts*, no. 3 (Spring 1967), 1–7. Also "African Cultural Standards." *Darlite*, 2, no. 1 (August 1967), 28–35.

Oliveira, Mário António Fernandes de. "African Writers in Portuguese." *African Arts/Arts d'Afrique*, 3, no. 2 (Winter 1970), 80–84.

Povey, John. "The Quality of African Writing Today." *Literary Review*, 11, no. 4 (Summer 1968), 403–21.

Press, John, ed. *Commonwealth Literature*. London: Heinemann, 1965.

Ramsaran, John Ansuman, *New Approaches to African Literature*. Ibadan: Ibadan University Press, 1965; 2nd ed., rev., 1970.

Redding, Jay Saunders. "Modern African Literature." *CLA Journal*, 7, no. 3 (March 1964), 191–201.

Reed, John. "Between Two Worlds: Some Notes on the Presentation by African Novelists of the Individual in Modern African Society." *Makerere Journal*, no. 7 (1963), 1–14.

Rubadiri, David. "Why African Literature?" *Transition*, 4, no. 15 (1964), 39–42.

Soyinka, Wole. "From a Common Back Cloth: A Reassessment of the African Literary Image." *American Scholar*, 32, no. 3 (Summer 1963), 387–96.

————. "The Writer in an African State." *Transition*, no. 31 (1967), 11–13.

Theroux, Paul. "Voices out of the Skull. A Study of Six African Poets." *Black Orpheus*, no. 20 (August 1966), 41–58.

Tibble, Anne. *African/English Literature. A Short Survey and Anthology of Prose and Poetry up to 1965.* London: Owen; New York: October House, 1965. Reprinted, 1969.

Timothy, Bankole. "British Publishers and African Publishing." *West Africa,* no. 2610 (June 10, 1967), 761.

Tucker, Martin. *Africa in Modern Literature. A Survey of Contemporary Writing in English.* New York: Frederick Ungar, 1967.

Wake, Clive H. "African Literary Criticism." *Comparative Literature Studies,* 1, no. 3 (1964), 197–205.

Wali, Obiajunwa. "The Dead End of African Literature?" *Transition,* 3, no. 10 (1963), 13–15.

———. "The Individual and the Novel in Africa." *Transition,* 4, no. 18 (1965), 31–33. See also *Transition,* no. 20, for a reply by Austin J. Shelton and its rejoinder by Wali.

Wästberg, Per., ed. *The Writer in Modern Africa.* Contributors: George Awoonor-Williams, Olympe Bhêly-Quénum, Dennis Brutus, and many others. Uppsala: The Scandinavian Institute of African Studies, 1968. New York: Africana Publishing Corp., 1969.

Wauthier, Claude. *The Literature and Thought of Modern Africa. A Survey.* London: Pall Mall Press, 1966.

Anthologies

Andrade, Mário de. *Antologia de poesia negra de expressão portugesa.* Paris: Oswald, 1958.

———. *Poesia negra. Schwarze Dichter portugiesischer Sprache.* Trans. Irma Bouvier. Munich: Nymphenburger Verlagshandlung, 1962.

Auteurs africains. Leopoldville: Ministère de l'Éducation Nationale; Paris: Hachette, 1964.

Beier, Ulli, ed. *Black Orpheus. An Anthology of African and Afro-American Prose.* London: Longmans; Ikeja: Longmans of Nigeria, 1964. Also *Black Orpheus. An Anthology of New African and Afro-American Stories.* New York: McGraw-Hill, 1965.

———. *Political Spider. An Anthology of Stories from Black Orpheus.* London, Ibadan, Nairobi: Heinemann, 1969.

Brent, Peter, ed. *Young Commonwealth Poets '65.* London: Heinemann in association with Cardiff Commonwealth Arts Festival, 1965.

Brownlee, P., and Brian Waldron Rose. *Commonwealth Short Stories.* (An anthology for schools.) London, New York: Nelson, 1965.

Castellaneta, Carlo, ed. *Poesia d'Africa.* Florence: Sansoni, 1969.

Caverhill, Nicholas, ed. *Recueil de textes africains.* (An anthology of modern African writing in French.) London: Hutchinson, 1967.

Cook, David, ed. *Origin East Africa.* London: Heinemann, 1965.

Curtin, Philip DeArmond, ed. *Africa Remembered. Narratives by West Africans from the Era of the Slave Trade.* Madison, Milwaukee, and London: University of Wisconsin Press, 1967.

Damas, Léon-Gontran, ed. *Poètes d'expression française, 1900–1956.* Paris: Éditions du Seuil, 1947.

Dathorne, Oscar Ronald, ed. *African Poetry for Schools and Colleges.* London: Macmillan, 1969.

———, and Willfried Feuser, eds. *Africa in Prose.* Harmondsworth: Penguin, 1969.

Denny, Neville, ed. *Pan African Short Stories.* London: Nelson, 1965, 1967.

Drachler, Jacob, ed. *African Heritage.* New York: Crowell-Collier, 1963. New York: Collier Books; London: Collier-Macmillan, 1964. 2nd printing, 1969.

Edwards, Paul, ed. *Through African Eyes*. 2 vols. Cambridge: Cambridge University Press, 1966.
———. *Modern African Narrative*. London: Nelson, 1966.
Harries, Lyndon, ed. *Swahili Poetry*. Oxford: Clarendon Press, 1962.
Hollo, Anselm, ed. *Negro Verse*. London: Vista Books, 1964.
Hughes, Langston, ed. *An African Treasury*. New York: Crown Publishers, 1960. London: Gollancz; New York: Pyramid Books, 1961.
———. *Poems from Black Africa*. Bloomington: Indiana University Press, 1963. Bloomington and London: Indiana University Press, 1966.
Ikiddeh, Ime, ed., *Drum Beats*. Leeds: E. J. Arnold & Son, 1968.
Jahn, Janheinz, ed. *Schwarzer Orpheus*. Munich: Carl Hanser Verlag, 1954.
Justin, André, ed. *Anthologie africaine des écrivains d'expression française*. Paris: Institute Pédagogique Africain, 1962.
Kesteloot, Lilyan, ed. *Anthologie négro-africaine*. Verviers: Gérard, 1967.
Koomey, Ellis Ayitey, and Ezekiel Mphahlele, eds. *Modern African Stories*. London: Faber, 1964, 1966.
Krog, E. W., ed. *African Literature in Rhodesia*. Gwelo: Mambo Press and Rhodesia Literary Bureau, 1966.
Letteratura negra. 2 vols. Rome: Editori Riuniti, 1961. 1. *La poesia,* ed. Mário de Andrade. 2. *La prosa,* ed. Leonard Sainville.
Litto, Fredric M., ed. *Plays from Black Africa*. New York: Hill and Wang, 1968.
Lomax, Alan, and Raoul Abdul, eds. *3000 [Three Thousand] Years of Black Poetry*. New York: Dodd, Mead, 1970.
Mercier, Roger, ed. *La poésie des noirs*. Lyon: Institut Pédagogique National.
Modern African Poetry. Nairobi: Chemchemi Cultural Centre, 1964.
Moore, Gerald, and Ulli Beier, eds. *Modern Poetry from Africa*. Harmondsworth: Penguin, 1963.
Mphahlele, Ezekiel, ed. *African Writing Today*. Harmondsworth: Penguin, 1967.
Neves, João Alves das, ed. *Poetas e contistas africanos de expressão portuguêsa*. São Paulo: Editôra Brasiliense, 1963.
Nouvelle somme de poesie du monde noir. *Présence africaine,* no. 57 (1966).
Perham, Margery, ed. *Ten Africans*. London: Faber, 1936; 2nd ed., 1963.
Pieterse, Cosmo, ed. *Ten One-Act Plays*. London, Ibadan, Nairobi: Heinemann, 1968.
Reed, John, and Clive Wake, eds. *A Book of African Verse*. London: Heinemann, 1964, 1969.
Reygnault, Christiane, ed. *Trésor africain et malgache*. Paris: Seghers, 1962.
Ridout, Ronald, and Eldred Durosimi Jones, eds. *Adjustments. An Anthology of African and Western Writing*. London: Edward Arnold, 1966.
Rive, Richard, ed. *Modern African Prose*. London, Ibadan: Heinemann, 1964.
Rutherfoord, Peggy, ed. *Darkness and Light. An Anthology of African Writing*. London: Faith Press; Johannesburg: Drum Publications, 1958. Also *African Voices. An Anthology of Native African Writing*. New York: Vanguard Press, 1960.
Senghor, Léopold Sédar, ed. *Anthologie de la nouvelle poésie nègre et malgache de langue française*. Intr. Jean-Paul Sartre. Paris: Presses Universitaires de France, 1948; 2nd ed., 1969.
Sergeant, Howard, ed. *Commonwealth Poems of Today*. London: Murray, 1967.
———. *New Voices of the Commonwealth*. London: Evans Brothers, 1968.
———. *Poetry from Africa*. Oxford: Pergamon Press, 1968.
Shelton, Austin J., ed. *The African Assertion*. New York: Odyssey Press, 1968.
Ten African Short Stories. Nairobi: Chemchemi Cultural Centre, 1964.
Tenreiro, Francisco, and Mário de Andrade, eds. *Poesia negra de expressão portuguesa*. Lisbon: Livraria Escolar Editora, 1953.
Verse and Voice. Poems and ballads of the Commonwealth at the Royal Court

Theatre. September 20–25, Empire into Commonwealth. September 26–October 2, Commonwealth Poetry Today. A festival promoted by the Poetry Book Society. London: Poetry Book Society, 1965.

Wake, Clive, ed. *An Anthology of African and Malagasy Poetry in French*. London: Oxford University Press, 1965.

Whiteley, Wilfred Howell, ed. *A Selection of African Prose*. 2 vols. Oxford: Clarendon Press, 1964.

Young, T. Cullen, ed. *African New Writing*. London and Redhill: Lutterworth Press, 1947.

Selected Writers in English and English Translation

This is merely a selection of some of the more easily accessible works discussed in this book. I have cited the American publishers where appropriate and, in relevant instances, paperback editions. For a complete listing consult the bibliographies mentioned.

Abrahams, Peter (South Africa). *Mine Boy*. London, 1946. London: Heinemann, 1963. Novel.

———. *Path of Thunder*. New York: Harper, 1948. Novel.

———. *Wild Conquest*. New York: Harper, 1950. Harmondsworth: Penguin, 1966. Novel.

———. *Tell Freedom*. London: Faber; New York: Knopf, 1954. Autobiography.

———. *A Wreath for Udomo*. London: Faber; New York: Knopf, 1956. Novel.

———. *A Night of Their Own*. London: Faber; New York: Knopf, 1965. Novel.

———. *This Island Now*. London: Faber, 1966. New York: Knopf, 1967. Novel.

Abruquah, Joseph (Ghana). *The Catechist*. London: Allen & Unwin, 1965. Biographical novel.

———. *The Torrent*. London and Harlow: Longmans, 1968. Novel.

Abubakar Tafawa Balewa, Alhaji Sir (Nigeria). *Shaihu Umar*. Trans. from Hausa and intr. by Mervyn Hiskett. London and Harlow: Longmans, 1967. Novel.

Achebe, Chinua (Nigeria). *Things Fall Apart*. London: Heinemann, 1958. New York: McDowell, Obolensky, 1959. Novel.

———. *No Longer at Ease*. London: Heinemann, 1960. New York: McDowell, Obolensky, 1961. Novel.

———. *Arrow of God*. London: Heinemann, 1964. New York: John Day, 1967. Novel.

———. *A Man of the People*. London: Heinemann; New York: John Day, 1966. Novel.

Agunwa, Clement (Nigeria). *More Than Once*. London: Longmans, 1967. Novel.

Aidoo, Christina (now Ama Ata Aidoo) (Ghana). *The Dilemma of a Ghost*. Accra: Longmans, 1965. Play.

———. *Anowa*. London: Longmans, 1970. Play.

Albert, Miller O. (Nigeria). *Rosemary and the Taxi Driver*. Onitsha: Chinyelu Printing Press, 1960? Novelette.

Aluko, T. M. (Nigeria). *One Man, One Wife*. Lagos: Nigeria Printing & Publishing Co., 1959. Novel.

———. *One Man, One Matchet*. London: Heinemann, 1964. Novel.

———. *Kinsman and Foreman*. London: Heinemann, 1966. Novel.

———. *Chief the Honourable Minister*. London: Heinemann, 1970. Novel.

Amadi, Elechi (Nigeria). *The Concubine*. London: Heinemann, 1966. Novel.

———. *The Great Ponds*. London: Heinemann, 1969. Novel.

Armah, Ayi Kwei (Ghana). *The Beautyful Ones Are Not Yet Born*. Boston: Houghton Mifflin, 1968. Novel.

———. *Fragments*. Boston: Houghton Mifflin, 1970. Novel.

Armattoe, R. E. G. (Ghana). *Deep Down the Blackman's Mind*. Ilfracombe: Stockwell, 1954. Poetry.

Asalalache, Khadambi (Kenya). *A Calabash of Life*. London: Longmans, 1967. Novel.

Awoonor-Williams, George (now Kofi Awoonor) (Ghana). *Rediscovery and Other Poems*. Ibadan: Mbari, 1964. Poetry.

———. *Night of My Blood*. New York: Doubleday, 1971. Poetry.

Badjan, Seydon (Mali). *The Death of Chaka*. Trans. from French and intr. by Clive Wake. Nairobi: Oxford University Press, 1968. Play.

Beti, Mongo (pen name of Alexandre Biyidi; also used pen name Eza Boto) (Cameroon). *Mission Accomplished*. Trans. from French by Peter Green. New York: Macmillan, 1958. Novel.

———. *King Lazarus*. Trans. from French and intr. by O. R. Dathorne. New York: Collier-Macmillan, 1971. Novel.

Brew, Kwesi (Ghana). *The Shadows of Laughter*. London: Longmans, 1968. Poetry.

Brutus, Dennis (South Africa). *Letters to Martha and Other Poems*. London: Heinemann, 1968. Poetry.

———. *Poems from Algiers*. Austin, Tex.: African and Afro-American Research Institute, 1970. Poetry.

Buruga, Joseph (Uganda). *The Abandoned Hut*. Nairobi: East African Publishing House, 1969. Poetry.

Casely-Hayford, Joseph (Ghana). *Ethiopia Unbound*. London: Reprinted Cass, 1969. Novel and tract.

Clark, John Pepper (Nigeria). *Song of a Goat*. Ibadan: Mbari, 1961. Play.

———. *Poems*. Ibadan: Mbari, 1962. Poetry.

———. *America, Their America*. London: Deutsch, 1964. Narrative and poetry.

———. *Three Plays*. London: Oxford University Press, 1964. Play.

———. *A Reed in the Tide*. London: Longmans, 1965. Poetry.

———. *Ozidi*. London: Oxford University Press, 1966. Play.

———. *Casualties*. London: Longmans, 1970. Poetry.

Cole, Robert Wellesley (Sierra Leone). *Kossoh Town Boy*. Cambridge: Cambridge University Press, 1960. Biography.

Conton, William (Sierra Leone). *The African*. London: Heinemann; Boston: Little Brown, 1960. New York: Signet, New American Library, 1961. Biographical novel.

Cugoano, Ottobah (Ghana). *Thoughts and Sentiments on the Evil and Wicked Traffic of Slavery . . .* London, 1787. Biography and tract.

Danquah, Joseph Boakye (Ghana). *The Third Woman*. London and Redhill: United Society for Christian Literature, 1943. Play.

De Graft, Joe (Ghana). *Sons and Daughters*. London: Oxford University Press, 1964. Play.

———. *Through a Film Darkly*. London: Oxford University Press, 1970. Play.

Dei-Anang, Michael (Ghana). *Africa Speaks*. Accra: Guinea Press, 1959. Poetry.

Dhlomo, H. I. I. (South Africa). *The Girl Who Killed to Save*. Lovedale: Lovedale Press, 1935. Play.

———. *Valley of a Thousand Hills*. Durban: Knox, 1941. Poetry.

Dhlomo, Reginald Rolfus Robert (South Africa). *An African Tragedy*. Lovedale: Lovedale Press, 1928. Novelette.

Diop, Birago (Senegal). *Tales of Amadou Koumba*. Trans. and intr. Dorothy Blair. London: Oxford University Press, 1966. Traditional stories.

Dipoko, Mbella Sonne (Cameroon). *A Few Nights and Days*. London: Longmans, 1966. Novel.

———. *Because of Women*. London: Heinemann, 1969. Novel.

SELECTED BIBLIOGRAPHY

Djoleto, Amu (Ghana). *The Strange Man*. London: Heinemann, 1967. New York: Humanities Press, 1968. Novel.

Duodu, Cameron (Ghana). *The Gab Boys*. London: Deutsch, 1967. Novel.

Easmon, Raymond Sarif (Sierra Leone). *Dear Parent and Ogre*. London: Oxford University Press, 1964. Play.

————. *The New Patriots*. London: Longmans, 1965. Play.

Echeruo, Michael J. C. (Nigeria). *Mortality*. London: Longmans, 1968. Poetry.

Egbuna, Obi (Nigeria). *Wind versus Polygamy*. London: Faber, 1964. Novel.

————. *The Anthill*. London: Oxford University Press, 1965. Play.

Ekwensi, Cyprian (Nigeria). *People of the City*. London: Dakers, 1954. Reprinted Greenwich, Conn.: Fawcett, 1969. Novel.

————. *Jagua Nana*. London: Hutchinson, 1961. Reprinted London: Panther Books, 1968. Novel.

————. *Burning Grass*. London: Heinemann, 1962. Novel.

————. *Beautiful Feathers*. London: Hutchinson, 1963. Novel.

————. *Iska*. London: Hutchinson, 1966. Novel.

Equiano, Olaudah (Nigeria). *The Interesting Narrative of the Life of Olaudah Equiano or Gustavus Vassa, the African, Written by Himself*. London, 1789. New York: Praeger, 1967. Biography and narrative.

Fagunwa, Daniel (Nigeria). *The Forest of a Thousand Daemons*. Trans. from Yoruba by Wole Soyinka. London: Nelson, 1965. Novel.

Fiawoo, F. Kwasi (Ghana). *The Fifth Landing Stage*. Trans. from Ewe. London: United Society for Christian Literature, 1943. Play.

Guma, Enoch S. (South Africa). *Nomalizo*. Trans. from Xhosa by S. J. Wallis. London: Sheldon Press, 1928. Novelette.

Henshaw, James Ene (Nigeria). *This Is Our Chance*. London: University of London Press, 1964. Play.

————. *Dinner for Promotion*. London: University of London Press, 1967. Play.

Honwana, Luis Bernardo (Mozambique). *We Killed Mangy Dog & Other Stories*. Trans. from Portuguese by Dorothy Guedes. London: Heinemann, 1969. Short stories.

Hutchinson, Alfred (South Africa). *The Rain Killers*. London: University of London Press, 1964. Play.

Ijimere, Obotunde (Nigeria). *The Imprisonment of Obatala and Other Plays*. London: Heinemann, 1966. Play.

Ike, Vincent Chukwuemeka (Nigeria). *Toads for Supper*. London: Harvill Press, Collins (Fontana), 1965. Novel.

————. *The Naked Gods*. London: Harvill Press, 1970. Novel.

Jolobe, James (South Africa). *Thuthula*. Trans. from Xhosa by author. London: Stockwell, 1938. Poetry.

Kachingwe, Aubrey (Zambia). *No Easy Task*. London: Heinemann, 1966. Novel.

Kane, Cheikh Hamidou (Senegal). *Ambiguous Adventure*. Trans. from French by Katherine Woods. New York: Walker, 1963. Novel.

Kayira, Legson (Malawi). *The Looming Shadow*. New York: Doubleday, 1967. Novel.

————. *Jingala*. New York: Doubleday, 1969. Novel.

Kayper-Mensah, Albert (Ghana). *The Dark Wanderer*. Tübingen: Horst Erdmann Verlag, 1970. Poetry.

Kgositsile, Keorapetse (South Africa). *Spirits Unchained*. Detroit: Broadside Press, 1969. Poetry.

————. *For Melba*. Chicago: Third World Press, 1970. Poetry.

Konadu, Samuel Asare (Ghana). *A Woman in Her Prime*. London: Heinemann, 1947. Novel.

————. *Ordained by the Oracle*. London: Heinemann, 1969. Novel.

503

Kunene, Mazisi (South Africa). *Zulu Poems*. New York: Africana Publishing Corp., 1970. Poetry.

Ladipo, Duro (Nigeria). *Three Yoruba Plays*. Ibadan: Mbari, 1964. Play.

La Guma, Alex (South Africa). *And a Threefold Cord*. Berlin: Seven Seas Publishers, 1964. Novel.

———. *The Stone Country*. Berlin: Seven Seas Publishers, 1967. Novel.

———. *A Walk in the Night and Other Stories*. London: Heinemann, 1967. Novelette and short stories.

Laye, Camara (Guinea). *The Dark Child*. Trans. from French. New York: Noonday Press, 1954. Biographical Novel.

———. *The Radiance of the King*. Trans. from French by James Kirkup. London: Collins (Fontana), 1965. Novel.

———. *A Dream of Africa*. Trans. from French by James Kirkup. London: Collins, 1968. Novel.

Liyong, Taban lo (Uganda). *Franz Fanon's Uneven Ribs*. London: Heinemann, 1971. Poetry.

Masiye, Andreya (Zambia). *Before Dawn*. Lusaka: National Educational Company of Zambia, Ltd., 1971. Novel.

Mbiti, John (Kenya). *Poems of Nature and Faith*. Nairobi: East African Publishing House, 1969. Poetry.

Mofolo, Thomas (South Africa). *Chaka*. Trans. from S. Sotho by Frederick Dutton. London: Oxford University Press, 1931. Novel.

———. *The Traveller to the East*. Trans. from S. Sotho by H. Ashton. London: Society for Promoting Christian Knowledge, 1934. Novel.

Mphahlele, Ezekiel (South Africa). *The Wanderers*. New York: Macmillan, 1970. Novel.

Mqhayi, Samuel Edward Krune (South Africa). *The Case of the Twins*. Trans. from Xhosa by Collingwood August in *New African*, 5, nos. 1, 2, 3 (January, March, April 1966), 5–7, 41–44, 74–76. Novel.

Mulikita, Fwanyanga Mutale (Zambia). *Shaka Zulu*. Lusaka: Longmans of Zambia, 1957. Play.

Munonye, John (Nigeria). *The Only Son*. London: Heinemann, 1966. Novel.

———. *Obi*. London: Heinemann, 1969. Novel.

———. *Oil Man of Obange*. London: Heinemann, 1971. Novel.

Mutwa, Vusamazulu Credo (South Africa). *My People, My Africa*. New York: John Day, 1969. Biography, folklore, and novel.

Ngugi, James (Kenya). *Weep Not Child*. London: Heinemann, 1964. Evanston, Ill.: Northwestern University Press, 1967. Novel.

———. *The River Between*. London: Heinemann, 1965. Evanston, Ill.: Northwestern University Press, 1967. Novel.

———. *A Grain of Wheat*. London: Heinemann, 1967. Novel.

———. *The Black Hermit*. London: Heinemann, 1968. Play.

Niane, Djibril Tamsir (Mali). *Soundiata. An Epic of Old Mali*. Trans. from French by G. D. Pickett. London: Longmans, 1965. Novel.

Nkosi, Lewis (South Africa). *The Rhythm of Violence*. London: Oxford University Press, 1964. Play.

Nwankwo, Nkem (Nigeria). *Danda*. London: Deutsch, 1964. Novel.

Nwapa, Flora (Nigeria). *Efuru*. London: Heinemann, 1966. Novel.

———. *Idu*. London: Heinemann, 1970. Novel.

Nzekwu, Onuora (Nigeria). *Wand of Noble Wood*. London: Hutchinson, 1961. New York: New American Library (Signet), 1963. Novel.

———. *Blade among the Boys*. London: Hutchinson, 1962; Arrow Books, 1964. Novel.

———. *Highlife for Lizards*. London: Hutchinson, 1966. Novel.

Oculi, Okello (Uganda). *Orphan.* Nairobi: East African Publishing House, 1968. Poetry.

———. *Prostitute.* Nairobi: East African Publishing House, 1968. Novel.

Ogot, Grace (Kenya). *The Promised Land.* Nairobi: East African Publishing House, 1966. Novel.

Okafor-Omali, Dilim (Nigeria). *A Nigerian Villager in Two Worlds.* London: Faber, 1965. Novel.

Okara, Gabriel (Nigeria). *The Voice.* London: Deutsch, 1964; Panther Books, 1969. Novel.

Okigbo, Christopher (Nigeria). *Labyrinths.* London: Heinemann, 1971. Poetry.

Okpewho, Isidore (Nigeria). *The Victims.* London: Longmans, 1970. Novel.

Ouologuem, Yambo (Mali). *Bound to Violence.* Trans. from French by Ralph Manheim. New York: Harcourt Brace Jovanovich, 1971. Novel.

Ousmane, Sembene (Senegal). *God's Bits of Wood.* Trans. Francis Price. New York: Doubleday, 1962. Novel.

Oyono, Ferdinand (Cameroon). *The Old Man and the Medal.* Trans. from French by John Reed. London: Heinemann, 1967. Novel.

———. *Boy.* Trans. from French by John Reed. New York: Collier-Macmillan, 1970. Novel.

Oyônô-Mbia, Guillaume (Cameroon). *Three Suitors One Husband and Until Further Notice.* Trans. from French by author. London: Methuen, 1968. Play.

Palangyo, Peter (Tanzania). *Dying in the Sun.* London: Heinemann, 1968. Novel.

Parkes, Frank Kobina (Ghana). *Songs from the Wilderness.* London: University of London Press, 1965. Poetry.

p'Bitek, Okot (Uganda). *Song of Lawino.* Nairobi: East African Publishing House, 1966. Poetry.

———. *Song of Ocol.* Nairobi: East African Publishing House, 1966. Poetry.

Peters, Lenrie (Gambia). *The Second Round.* London: Heinemann, 1965. Novel.

———. *Satellites.* London: Heinemann, 1967. Poetry.

———. *Katchikali.* London: Heinemann, 1971. Poetry.

Plaatje, Solomon (South Africa). *Mhudi.* Lovedale: Lovedale Press, 1930. Novel.

Rabéarivelo, Jean-Joseph (Malagasy Republic). *24 Poems.* Trans. from French Gerald Moore and Ulli Beier. Ibadan: Mbari, 1962. Poetry.

Rive, Richard (South Africa). *Emergency.* London: Faber, 1964. Novel.

Rubadiri, David (Malawi). *No Bride Price.* Nairobi: East African Publishing House, 1967. Novel.

Sancho, Ignatius (West Africa). *Letters of the Late Ignatius Sancho, an African.* London, 1782. Reprinted London: Dawsons, 1968. Letters.

Selormey, Francis (Ghana). *The Narrow Path.* London: Heinemann; New York: Praeger, 1966. Biographical novel.

Senghor, Léopold Sédar (Senegal). *Selected Poems.* Trans. from French and intr. by John Reed and Clive Wake. London: Oxford University Press; New York: Atheneum, 1964. Poetry.

———. *Prose and Poetry.* Trans. from French and intr. by John Reed and Clive Wake. London: Oxford University Press, 1965. Essays and poetry.

———. *Nocturnes.* Trans. from French and intr. by John Reed and Clive Wake. London: Heinemann, 1969. Poetry.

Seruma, Enriko (Uganda). *The Experience.* Nairobi: East African Publishing House, 1970. Novel.

Serumaga, Robert (Uganda). *Return to the Shadows.* London: Heinemann, 1969. Novel.

Soyinka, Wole (Nigeria). *Five Plays.* London: Oxford University Press, 1964. Play.

———. *The Interpreters.* London: Deutsch, 1965; Panther Books, 1967. Novel.

———. *The Road.* London: Oxford University Press, 1966. Play.

———. *Kongi's Harvest.* London: Oxford University Press, 1967. Play.

————. *Idanre & Other Poems*. London: Methuen, 1967. Poetry.

————. *Madmen and Specialists*. London: Methuen, 1971. Play.

Sutherland, Efua Theodora (Ghana). *Edufa*. London: Longmans, 1967. Play.

————. *Foriwa*. Accra: State Publishing Corp., 1967. Play.

Tutuola, Amos (Nigeria). *The Palm-Wine Drinkard*. London: Faber, 1952. New York: Grove Press, 1953. Novel.

————. *My Life in the Bush of Ghosts*. London: Faber; New York: Grove Press, 1954. Novel.

————. *Simbi and the Satyr of the Dark Jungle*. London: Faber, 1956. Novel.

————. *The Brave African Huntress*. London: Faber, 1958. New York: Grove Press, 1970. Novel.

————. *Feather Woman of the Jungle*. London: Faber, 1962. Novel.

————. *Ajaiyi and His Inherited Poverty*. London: Faber, 1967. Novel.

Ulasi, Adaora Lily (Nigeria). *Many Thing You No Understand*. London: Michael Joseph, 1970. Novel.

U Tam'si, Tchicaya (République Populaire du Congo). *Brush Fire*. Trans. from French by Ulli Beier and Gerald Moore. Ibadan: Mbari, 1964. Poetry.

————. *Selected Poems*. Trans. from French by Gerald Moore. London: Heinemann, 1970. Poetry.

Vilakazi, Benedict Wallet (South Africa). *Zulu Horizons*. Trans. from Zulu by D. Mck Malcolm and Florence Friedman. Cape Town: H. Timmins, 1962. Poetry.

Wachira, Godwin (Kenya). *Ordeal in the Forest*. Nairobi: East African Publishing House, 1968. Novel.

Waciumba, Charity (Kenya). *Daughter of Mumbi*. Nairobi: East African Publishing House, 1969. Semibiography.

INDEX

Index

INDEX

517